MEDIATION

MEDIATION

Practice, Policy, and Ethics

Carrie Menkel-Meadow

A.B. Chettle, Jr. Professor of Law, Dispute Resolution, and Civil Procedure, and Director,
   Georgetown-Hewlett Program on Conflict Resolution and Legal Problem Solving
Georgetown University Law Center

Lela Porter Love

Professor of Law and Director, Kukin Program for Conflict Resolution and the Cardozo
   Mediation Clinic
Benjamin N. Cardozo Law School, Yeshiva University

Andrea Kupfer Schneider

Professor of Law
Marquette University Law School

ASPEN
PUBLISHERS

111 Eighth Avenue, New York, NY 10011
http://lawschool.aspenpublishers.com

© 2006 Aspen Publishers, Inc.
a Wolters Kluwer business
http://lawschool.aspenpublishers.com

Printed in the United States of America.

1 2 3 4 5 6 7 8 9 0

ISBN 0-7355-4445-X

Library of Congress Cataloging-in-Publication Data

Menkel-Meadow, Carrie.
   Mediation : practice, policy, and ethics / Carrie Menkel-Meadow, Lela Porter Love, Andrea Kupfer
Schneider. — 1st ed.
      p. cm.
   ISBN 0-7355-4445-X (alk. paper)
   1. Dispute resolution (Law) — United States — Cases.   2. Mediation — United States — Cases.
I. Love, Lela Porter, 1950-   II. Schneider, Andrea Kupfer.   III. Title.

KF9084.A7M4566 2006
347.73'9 — dc22

2005032198

About Aspen Publishers

Aspen Publishers, headquartered in New York City, is a leading information provider for attorneys, business professionals, and law students. Written by preeminent authorities, our products consist of analytical and practical information covering both U.S. and international topics. We publish in the full range of formats, including updated manuals, books, periodicals, CDs, and online products.

Our proprietary content is complemented by 2,500 legal databases, containing over 11 million documents, available through our Loislaw division. Aspen Publishers also offers a wide range of topical legal and business databases linked to Loislaw's primary material. Our mission is to provide accurate, timely, and authoritative content in easily accessible formats, supported by unmatched customer care.

To order any Aspen Publishers title, go to *http://lawschool.aspenpublishers.com* or call 1-800-638-8437.

To reinstate your manual update service, call 1-800-638-8437.

For more information on Loislaw products, go to *www.loislaw.com* or call 1-800-364-2512.

For Customer Care issues, e-mail *CustomerCare@aspenpublishers.com*; call 1-800-234-1660; or fax 1-800-901-9075.

Aspen Publishers
a Wolters Kluwer business

For our students — the next generation of lawyers and mediators, who will be better prepared to seek more innovative processes and more creative solutions to legal and human problems.

And for those pioneers — parties, mediators, and lawyers — who have used mediation to craft a better future for families, workplaces, communities, and nations.

Summary of Contents

Contents

Preface

A belief that there is a different and often better sensibility for solving human and social problems inspires this book. We have witnessed, as have many of the authors represented in the text, mediation used to achieve consensual resolution of seemingly intractable problems in ways that are responsive to the relationships and the needs and interests of the parties. We believe that mediation, when properly used, can achieve justice for the parties — a justice distinct from what a court or legislature could provide. For some in our field, this is called self-determination or empowerment; for others, a form of individualized democracy in decision making.

Mediation, or facilitated negotiation, has reached an important point of its development within modern legal institutions and legal education. Where once the adversary model of argument, adjudication, and case analysis comprised the full program of legal processes presented in law schools, a modern evolution from the days of the Legal Process school of the 1950s, through the clinical education movement of the 1960s and 1970s, to the newest legal "movement" of appropriate (or alternative) dispute resolution has expanded the repertoires of modern law students and lawyers. Where once we studied only appellate cases and conceptual analysis of doctrines, we now study the processes of client counseling and interviewing, negotiation, mediation, advocacy, representation, neutraling, facilitation, legislation, policy development, and dispute system design. Not only have the number of processes been expanded, but we now teach with more experiential models, having learned from John Dewey's pragmatic education theories and the "theories-in-use" of Donald Schön and others, that we learn best about ideas and theories of dispute processing when we are in role and are analyzing what does and can happen.

This book is part of our larger project, *Dispute Resolution: Beyond the Adversarial Model* (Menkel-Meadow, Love, Schneider & Sternlight, 2005), designed to bring the study of "process pluralism" to the modern law student and lawyer, and contains both more and less than the larger text. This volume is explicitly devoted to the study, teaching, and performance of all the roles implicated in the mediation process.

We provide full treatment of a variety of different models of mediation currently being theorized and practiced, encouraging the reader to see the differences and to assess which kinds of mediative processes might be appropriate in different contexts. We also examine, in depth, the different roles in mediation processes — party, representative, and neutral.

Like our larger text, this book is committed to the idea that one must learn about legal and problem-solving processes on various levels at the same time: theory, skills and practices, ethics, policy, and critique. The reader of this book will likely encounter here one of the richest treatments of the field currently available, one incorporating explorations of mediation model variations, legal issues, examples and transcripts of actual mediations, challenging questions of policy and practice to think about, and discussion of some of the leading controversies in the field (such as whether mediation inappropriately "privatizes" public justice).

We begin with the general theory and jurisprudence of conflict resolution, now a multidisciplinary field. We move from foundational principles to the skills needed for mediation, providing both theoretical descriptions and examples of the variety of mediation models currently in use, from facilitative to evaluative to transformative to community-enhancing. We then provide materials and instruction for lawyers or representatives inside the mediation, urging the modern lawyer to think of him/herself as a creative problem solver and not necessarily as an advocate whose job is to maximize gain for one's own client at the expense or harm of the other party. We then provide material and instruction on the skills necessary for the mediator as third-party facilitator of party communications and negotiations, presenting a wide array of foundational skills and interventions.

After focusing on the theory, practice, and skill sides of mediation we look at a variety of legal, policy, and ethical issues, including the roles of law and justice in mediation, the tensions in the role of the "neutral," duties or obligations to both the parties in a mediation, and to those who might be affected by any mediation's outcome, legal liability and malpractice, confidentiality, legal immunity, diversity, good-faith participation obligations and requirements, and the ethics of mediation — for mediators, parties, and their representatives.

Like our larger project, this book treats mediation as part of a larger family of dispute resolution and transaction-planning processes. We explore the uses of mediation in a wide variety of contexts (lawsuits, contracts, community disputes, public policy formation, and international relations). We also explore how mediation has been combined with other processes to create a host of modern hybrid forms for use in legal disputes and decision-making situations. We look at how mediation is used, with great subtlety and complexity, in disputes involving multiple parties and multifaceted issues. We then provide material to help the modern lawyer counsel a client in designing, choosing, planning for, and drafting clauses and rules for these new processes. We ask the reader to think about how mediational processes might be utilized in a wide variety of situations to affect the consciousness and sensibility of guiding how people approach each other when in trouble or pain or when they, more happily, want to build something new. Indeed, we hope that this book will be used to inspire the creation of new mediational processes and applications. We conclude the book with some hard thinking about and critiques of mediation. What is the role of private and consensual justice in a world that needs the clarity of a rule of law? How is power exercised in mediation outside of formal structures and institutions? Has mediation been co-opted by its increasing use in the formal justice system? How can we evaluate the promises made by mediation proponents or detractors? Can we use mediation to achieve peace and justice?

The authors of this book are committed to the idea that we can learn to get along with one another in this increasingly diverse world if we approach one another with deep respect and care and some ideas about reciprocity, active listening, and problem solving. We are also rigorous realists — if mediation is to offer a better mode of dispute resolution and problem solving, we must also examine how it actually operates and whether, in fact, it delivers on its promises to create peace and justice.

The accompanying *Teacher's Manual* to this book provides a comprehensive set of exercises, role-plays, and discussion questions for teachers (and students) to explore the material here in great experiential depth. This casebook should also be able to "stand alone" (as we have been conceptualizing it) as a comprehensive and sophisticated description of the field. Two of the present authors were there at the modern "birthing" of this field, and we are proud to be joined by one of the leading scholars of negotiation, foundational to all mediation. All of us participated fully in writing this book, and we hope you will use it in the spirit that moved us: the goal of helping to educate and raise a new generation of lawyers and other professionals as adept at problem solving as they are at advocacy. And, yes, we think this book can be used by both lawyer and non-lawyer mediators and parties.

Footnotes by the authors of this book, in both the excerpts and our text, are marked using symbols. The order of the footnote symbols, if more than one symbol appears on a page, is * † ‡. The original footnote numbering in the excerpts has been retained.

* * *

A few thanks before we get started. . . . We begin with some intellectual thanks to Lon Fuller, who inspired much of our deepest thinking about the purposes of process in general and of mediation in particular. We next thank Jean Sternlight, our coauthor on the larger project, who could not participate in this one (due to her other book on mediation) but who remains with us in spirit.

All of us thank various mentors and colleagues in this work. From Carrie, special thanks to Jack Himmelstein, Howard Gadlin, Howard Lesnick, Larry Susskind, and Gary Friedman, who were there at the beginning, taught me to mediate, and remain my continuing guides; to Carol Liebman and Margaret Shaw for shared mediative colleagueship and guidance (as we constituted a first generation of "women mediators"); to Susan Gillig for being the best co-teacher and co-traveler one could have in this journey of pedagogical innovation. To Howard Bellman and Frank Sander for organizing the "Senior Mediators Group," which has been a touchstone of inspiration for the last ten years. From Lela, special thanks to Josh Stulberg, Jim Coben, Kitty Atkins, Jim Alfini, and Hal Abramson for teaching me so much about mediation and life and helping make many exciting dreams come true. And most of all, to the parties in many mediations who, with courage and persistence, have made all the work worthwhile. From Andrea, special thanks to

Janine Geske, Jay Grenig, Chris Honeyman, and Moira Kelly, for all of their work in mediation and mediation advocacy.

Carrie profoundly thanks her able support team: research assistant extraordinaire David Mattingly; administrative assistants Corrie Mathiowetz and Carolyn Howard; research assistants Veronica Teresa Lerma, James Bond, and Jaimie Kent; the faculty production team at Georgetown, Sylvia Johnson, Toni Patterson, and Ronnie E. Rease, Jr. (I promise I will stop killing trees soon!); and Hewlett Fellows, Peter Reilly, and Sara Thacker, who taught with these materials and have been my teaching family the last few years.

Lela thanks her great support team: Roger Deitz, Malte Pendergast-Fischer, Becca Benghiat, Justin Braun, Chris Fugarino, Tracey Pastan, and Daniel Zinn, for their painstaking work on the manuscript; Kaaron Saphir, for dealing with computer glitches and other nightmares; and Harold Abramson, James Kornbluh, Michael Lang, Ray Patterson, Frank Scardilli, Joseph Stulberg, Peggy Sweeney, and Dan Weitz, who have been central and critical pillars of the Cardozo mediation family.

Andrea thanks her fabulous assistant, Carrie Kratochvil, who mediates both the large and small crises in the law school while getting everything done; and her great research assistants, Anna Coyer and Stacey Meyer.

All of us feel enormously grateful to our home institutions, which gave us support in so many different ways: thanks to Deans Judith Areen and Alex Aleinikoff and Associate Dean Vicki Jackson at Georgetown University Law Center (and to the donors of the A.B. Chettle, Jr., Chair in Dispute Resolution and Civil Procedure); and to Carol O'Neil for academic and pedagogical support and interest way beyond the call of duty. Thanks also to Dean David Rudenstein and former Dean Monroe Price at Cardozo School of Law; and thanks to Dean Joseph Kearney and Associate Dean Peter Rofes at Marquette University Law School.

We are also appreciative of the various "pushes" and "pulls" of the Aspen team — Melody Davies, Jay Boggis, Laurel Ibey, Susan Boulanger, Elsie Starbecker (who guided the first volume with care and beauty), Elizabeth Ricklefs, Richard Mixter, and others behind the pages.

We thank the many reviewers of this text, some known to us (Jennifer Gerarda Brown, Ellen Deason, Carol Liebman, Michael Moffitt) and other undisclosed helpers. We hope we have met your needs and answered your concerns.

We thank our families, to whom the larger ADR book was dedicated: Robert Meadow; Peter Popov and Nicole Love Popov; and Rodd, Joshua, Noah, and Zachary Schneider — for their patience, support, and, on very rare occasions, some opportunity to practice our conflict resolution and mediation skills!

And most, we thank our students, who we hope will use these materials to create a better world — one with peace, sensitive and rigorous problem solving, and justice.

Let us know what you think.

Carrie Menkel-Meadow
Lela Porter Love
Andrea Kupfer Schneider

December 2005

Acknowledgments

The authors wish to express thanks to the following authors, periodicals, and publishers for their permission to reproduce materials from their publications:

Abel, Richard. Reprinted from THE POLITICS OF INFORMAL JUSTICE: THE AMERICAN EXPERIENCE. Copyright © 1982. "The Contradictions of Informal Justice," 270-272. Reprinted by permission of Elsevier.

Abramson, Harold I., Mediation Representation: Advocating in a Creative Problem-Solving Process, 1-4. Copyright © 2004 by National Institute for Trial Advocacy (NITA). Reprinted with permission.

Alfini, James J., Trashing, Bashing, and Hashing It Out. 19 FLORIDA STATE UNIVERSITY LAW REVIEW 47, 66-71, 73 (1991). Reprinted with permission of FLORIDA STATE UNIVERSITY LAW REVIEW.

American Bar Association, ABA Annotated Model Rules of Professional Conduct, Preamble, Rules 1.0, 1.2, 1.4, 2.4, 3.3, 4.1, 4.4, 5.6, 8.3, 8.4 from the ABA ANNOTATED MODEL RULES OF PROFESSIONAL CONDUCT (2004). Reprinted with permission of the American Bar Association. Copies of ABA Model Rules of Professional Conduct, 2004 are available from Service Center, American Bar Association, 321 North Clark Street, Chicago, IL 60610, 1-800-285-2221.

Anderson, Mary B., Do No Harm: How Aid Can Support Peace — or War, 23-29, 31. Copyright © 1999 by Lynn Rienner Publishers. Reprinted with permission.

Arnold, Tom, 20 COMMON ERRORS IN MEDIATION ADVOCACY, ALTER-NATIVES 67-71 (May 1995). Reprinted with permission of the author.

Axelrod, Robert, THE EVOLUTION OF COOPERATION. Copyright © 1984 by Robert Axelrod. Reprinted by permission of Basic Books, a member of Perseus Books, L.L.C.

Ayres, Ian, Further Evidence of Discrimination in New Car Negotiations and Estimates of Its Cause, 94 MICH. L. REV. 109 (1995). Reprinted with permission of the Michigan Law Review.

Bazerman, Max H., and Roy Lewicki, eds, Achieving Integrative Agreements, in NEGOTIATION IN ORGANIZATIONS 24-37. Copyright © 1983 by Sage Publications, Inc. Reprinted with Permission of Sage Publications, Inc.

Bazerman, Max H., and Margaret A. Neale. Reprinted with the permission of The Free Press, a Division of Simon & Schuster Adult Publishing Group, from NEGOTIATING

RATIONALLY, by Max H. Bazerman and Margaret A. Neale. Copyright © 1992 by Max H. Bazerman and Margaret A. Neale. All rights reserved.

Begley, Sharon, The Stereotype Trap, NEWSWEEK, at 66-68 (Newsweek, Inc., November 6, 2000). Reprinted with permission from the publisher.

Bercovitch, Jacob, The Structure and Diversity of Mediation in International Relations, in MEDIATION IN INTERNATIONAL RELATIONS: MULTIPLE APPROACHES TO CONFLICT MANAGEMENT 4, 7-10, 12-14 (1996). Reprinted with permission of the author and Palgrave Macmillan.

Binder, David, Paul Bergman, Susan Price, and Paul K. Tremblay. Excerpts reprinted from LAWYERS AS COUNSELORS: A CLIENT-CENTERED APPROACH, 3d ed. Copyright © 2004. Reprinted with permission of Thomson West.

Breger, Marshall, Should an Attorney Be Required to Advise a Client of ADR Options, 13 GEORGETOWN JOURNAL OF LEGAL ETHICS 427, 429-430, 433-441, 449-451, 452, 454, 456-458, 460-461 (2000). Reprinted with permission of Georgetown Journal of Legal Ethics. Copyright © 2000.

Brown, Jennifer Gerarda, Creativity and Problem-Solving, 87 MARQUETTE LAW REVIEW 697, 697-705 (2004). Copyright © 2004. Reprinted with permission.

Bush, Robert A. Baruch, Mediation and Adjudication, Dispute Resolution and Ideology: An Imaginary Conversation, 3 JOURNAL OF CONTEMPORARY LEGAL ISSUES 1, 1-6, 12 (1990). Reprinted with permission of the publisher.

Bush, Robert A. Baruch, and Joseph P. Folger, THE PROMISE OF MEDIATION: THE TRANSFORMATIVE APPROACH TO CONFLICT THROUGH EMPOWERMENT AND RECOGNITION. Copyright © 1994 Jossey-Bass, Inc. Reprinted with permission of Jossey-Bass, a subsidiary of John Wiley & Sons, Inc.

Center for Public Resources, The ABC's of ADR: A Dispute Resolution Glossary, 13 (11) ALTERNATIVES TO THE HIGH COST OF LITIGATION 1. Copyright © 1995. Reprinted with permission from the CPR International Institute for Conflict Prevention and Resolution.

Coben, James R., Mediation's Dirty Little Secret: Straight Talk About Mediator Manipulation and Deception, 2 JOURNAL OF ALTERNATIVE DISPUTE RESOLUTION IN EMPLOYMENT 4, 4-6 (2000). Reprinted with permission from the publisher.

Coben, James, and Peter Thompson, Disputing Irony: A Systematic Look at Litigation About Mediation, 11 HARVARD NEGOTIATION LAW REVIEW (2006). Reprinted with permission of the publisher.

Coleman, Peter T., and Morton Deutsch, THE HANDBOOK OF CONFLICT RESOLUTION: THEORY AND PRACTICE. Copyright © 2000 by Jossey-Bass, Inc. Reprinted with permission of Jossey-Bass, a subsidiary of John Wiley & Sons, Inc.

Craver, Charles B., and David W. Barnes, Gender, Risk Taking, and Negotiation Performance, 5 MICHIGAN JOURNAL OF GENDER AND LAW 299, 320-321, 346-347 (1999). Reprinted with permission.

Curran, Daniel, James K. Sebenius, and Michael Watkins, Case Analysis: Two Paths to Peace: Contrasting George Mitchell in Northern Ireland with Richard Holbrooke in Bosnia-Herzegovina, in NEGOTIATION JOURNAL 513-531 (2004). Reprinted with permission from the publisher.

Delgado, Richard, Chris Dunn, Pamela Brown, Helena Lee, and David Hubbert, Fairness and Formality: Minimizing the Risk of Prejudice in Alternative Dispute Resolution, WISCONSIN LAW REVIEW. Copyright © 1985 by The Board of Regents of the University of Wisconsin System. Reprinted by permission of the WISCONSIN LAW REVIEW.

Fisher, Roger et al., BEYOND MACHIAVELLI: TOOLS FOR COPING WITH CONFLICT. Reprinted by permission of the publisher from BEYOND MACHIAVELLI:

TOOLS FOR COPING WITH CONFLICT, by Roger Fisher, Elizabeth Kopelman, and Andrea Schneider, 14-15, 32-35, 123-132, Cambridge, Mass.: Harvard University Press. Copyright © 1994 by the President and Fellows of Harvard College.

Fisher, Roger, William Ury, and Bruce Patton. From GETTING TO YES, 2d ed., by Roger Fisher, William Ury, and Bruce Patton. Copyright © 1981, 1991 by Roger Fisher and William Ury. Reprinted by permission of Houghton Mifflin Company. All rights reserved.

Fiss, Owen M., Against Settlement. Copyright © 1984 by THE YALE LAW JOURNAL. Reprinted by permission of The Yale Law Journal Company and William S. Hein Company from THE YALE LAW JOURNAL, Vol. 93, 1073-1090.

Folger, Joseph P., and Robert A. Baruch Bush, Transformative Mediation and Third-Party Intervention: Ten Hallmarks of a Transformative Approach to Practice, 13 MEDIATION QUARTERLY 263, 264-267 (Jossey-Bass,1996). Reprinted with permission from the publisher.

Follett, Mary Parker, Constructive Conflict, in MARY PARKER FOLLETT — PROPHET OF MANAGEMENT: A CELEBRATION OF WRITINGS FROM THE 1920S, 67-69, 75, 77, 79, 82, 84-86 (1995). Harvard Business School Publishing. Reprinted with permission.

Freshman, Clark, Privatizing Same-Sex 'Marriage' Through Alternative Dispute Resolution: Community-Enhancing Versus Community-Enabling Mediation, 44 UCLA LAW REVIEW 1687, 1692-1697 (1997). Copyright © 1997 by Clark Freshman, Professor of Law. Reprinted with permission.

Friedman, Gary, and Jack Himmelstein, The Loop of Understanding, The Center for Mediation in Law, available at *http://www.mediationinlaw.org/contact.html* (2005). Reprinted with permission.

Friedman, Gary, and Jack Himmelstein, The Understanding-Based Model of Mediation, The Center for Mediation in Law, available at *http://www.mediationinlaw.org/contact.html* (2005). Reprinted with permission.

Fuller, Lon L., Collective Bargaining and the Arbitrator, 3 WISCONSIN LAW REVIEW 3-4 (1963). Copyright © 1963 by The Board of Regents of the University of Wisconsin System. Reprinted by permission of the Wisconsin Law Review.

Fuller, Lon L., Reprinted with permission. Chapter 2, 8, 29-30, and 32-22, from COLLECTIVE BARGAINING AND THE ARBITRATOR'S ROLE (Proceedings of the 15th Annual Meeting National Academy of Arbitrators, by Lon L. Fuller). Copyright © 1962 by The Bureau of National Affairs, Inc., Washington, D.C. 20037. For copies of BNA Books publications call toll free 1-800-960-1220 or visit *http://www.bnabooks.com.*

Fuller, Lon L., Mediation — Its Forms and Functions, 44 SOUTHERN CALIFORNIA LAW REVIEW 305-339 (1971). Reprinted with the permission of the Southern California Law Review.

Galton, Eric, Mediation: A Texas Practice Guide, TEXAS LAWYER PRESS 31-39, 42-46, 50-51 (1993). Reprinted with permission.

Galton, Eric, Mediation of Medical Negligence Claims, CAPITAL UNIVERSITY LAW REVIEW 321, 324-325 (2000). Reprinted with permission.

Galton, Eric, A Meeting of Strangers, Ripple from Peace Lake: Essays for Mediators and Peacemakers, available at *http://www.trafford.com.* Reprinted with permission from the author.

Gifford, Donald G., A Context-Based Theory of Strategy Selection in Legal Negotiation. Originally published in 46 OHIO STATE LAW JOURNAL 41, 52-54 (1985). Reprinted with permission.

Gobodo-Madikizela, Pumla. Excerpt from A HUMAN BEING DIED THAT NIGHT: A SOUTH AFRICAN STORY OF FORGIVENESS, by Pumla Gobodo-Madikizela. Copyright © 2003 by Pumla Gobodo-Madikizela. Reprinted by permission of Houghton Mifflin Company. All rights reserved.

Greatbatch, David, and Robert Dingwall, Selective Facilitation: Some Preliminary Observations on a Strategy Used by Divorce Mediators, 23 LAW AND SOCIETY

REVIEW 613-618, 621-623, 626-629, 635-637, 639 (1989). Reprinted with permission from the publisher.

Grillo, Trina, THE MEDIATION ALTERNATIVE: PROCESS DANGERS FOR WOMEN. Reprinted by permission of The Yale Law Journal Company and William S. Hein Company from THE YALE LAW JOURNAL, Vol. 100, 1545-1610.

Gunning, Isabelle R., Diversity Issues in Mediation: Controlling Negative Cultural Myths. Reprinted with permission of the author and the JOURNAL OF DISPUTE RESOLUTION, University of Missouri-Columbia, Center for the Study of Dispute Resolution, 206 Hulston Hall, Columbia, MO 65211.

Harter, Philip J., Negotiating Regulations: A Cure for Malaise, 71 GEORGETOWN LAW JOURNAL 1, 28-31, 33-34, 42, 82-86, 112-113 (1982). Reprinted with permission from the publisher.

Hofstadter, Douglas R., METAMAGICAL THEMAS: QUESTING FOR THE ESSENCE OF MIND AND PATTERN. Copyright © 1985 by Basic Books, Inc. Reprinted by permission of Basic Books, a member of Perseus Books, L.L.C.

Hyman, Jonathan M., and Lela P. Love, If Portia Were a Mediator: An Inquiry into Justice in Mediation, 9 CLINICAL LAW REVIEW 157, 158-174 (2002). Reprinted with permission from the publisher.

International Institute for Conflict Prevention and Resolution, CPR MEDIATION PROCEDURE. Reprinted with permission from CPR Institute, 575 Lexington Ave., New York, NY 10022. The CPR Institute is a non-profit initiative of 500 general counsel of major corporations, leading law firms, and prominent legal academics whose mission is to install alternative dispute resolution (ADR) into the mainstream of legal practice.

Kahneman, Daniel, and Amos Tversky, Conflict Resolution: A Cognitive Perspective. From BARRIERS TO CONFLICT RESOLUTION, edited by Kenneth J. Arrow et al. Copyright © 1995 by The Stanford Center on Conflict & Negotiation. Used by permission of W.W. Norton & Company, Inc.

Kakalik, James S. et al., AN EVALUATION OF MEDIATION AND EARLY NEUTRAL EVALUATION UNDER THE CIVIL JUSTICE REFORM ACT, Santa Monica, CA: RAND Corporation, 1996. Reprinted with permission.

Kichaven, Jeff, Apology in Mediation: Sorry to Say, It's Much Overrated. Copyright © 2003 by International Risk Management Institute, Inc. Reproduced with permission of the publisher, International Risk Management Institute, Inc., Dallas, Texas, from *IRMI.COM.* Further reproduction prohibited. Visit *http://www.IRMI.com* for free practical and reliable risk and insurance information.

Korobkin, Russell, A Positive Theory of Legal Negotiation, 88 GEORGETOWN LAW JOURNAL 1789, 1791-1794, 1799, 1816-1817 (2000). Reprinted with permission.

Korobkin, Russell, and Chris Guthrie, Psychological Barriers to Litigation Settlement: An Experimental Approach, 93 MICHIGAN LAW REVIEW 107, 144-146 (1994). Copyright © 1994 by The Michigan Law Review Association. Reprinted with permission.

Kovach, Kimberlee K., Good Faith in Mediation—Requested, Recommended, or Required? A New Ethic, 38 SOUTH TEXAS LAW REVIEW 575, 622-623 (1997). Reprinted with permission from the publisher.

LaFree, Gary, and Christine Rack, The Effects of Participants' Ethnicity and Gender on Monetary Outcomes in Mediated and Adjudicated Civil Cases, 30 LAW AND SOCIETY REVIEW. 767, 768-772, 788-793. Copyright © 1996 by Blackwell Publishing. Reprinted with permission.

Lande, John, Using Dispute System Design Methods to Promote Good-Faith Participation in Court-Connected Mediation Programs. Originally published in 50 UCLA LAW REVIEW (2002). Excerpt reprinted with permission of the author.

Lax, David A., and James K. Sebenius. Reprinted with the permission of The Free Press, a Division of Simon & Schuster Adult Publishing Group, from THE MANAGER AS NEGOTIATOR: BARGAINING FOR COOPERATION AND COMPETITIVE GAIN, by David A. Lax and James K. Sebenius. Copyright © 1986 by David A. Lax and James K. Sebenius. All rights reserved.

Lederach, John Paul, Cultivating Peace: A Practioner's View of Deadly Conflict and Negotiation, in CONTEMPORARY PEACEMAKING: CONFLICT, VIOLENCE AND PEACE PROCESSES (John Darby and Roger MacGinty eds., 2003). Reprinted with permission of Palgrave Macmillan.

Lehman, Warren, The Pursuit of a Client's Interest, 77 MICHIGAN LAW REVIEW, 1078-1079, 1088-1089, 1091-1093. Copyright © 1979 by The Michigan Law Review Association. Reprinted with permission.

Levin, Murray S., The Propriety of Evaluative Mediation: Concerns About the Nature and Quality of an Evaluative Opinion, 16 OHIO STATE JOURNAL ON DISPUTE RESOLUTION 267, 270-271 (2001). Reprinted with permission from the publisher.

Levitt, Matthew A., Kilometer 101: Oasis or Mirage? An Analysis of Third-Party Self-Interest in International Mediation, 15 MEDIATION QUARTERLY 2, 155-161 (1997). Reprinted with permission from John Wiley & Sons, Inc.

Levy, J.S., and R.C. Prather, FLY ON THE WALL. Copyright © 1999 by Thomson West. Reprinted from TEXAS PRACTICE GUIDE: ALTERNATIVE DISPUTE RESOLU-TION, by Jerome Levy (Attorney-Mediator, Dallas) and Robert Prather, Sr. (Jordan, Dunlap, Prather & Harris in Dallas), with permission of West, a Thomson business.

Liebman, Carol, Mediation as Parallel Seminars: Lessons from the Student Takeover of Columbia University's Hamilton Hall, 16 NEGOTIATION JOURNAL 157-182 (Program on Negotiation at Harvard Law School and Blackwell Publishing, 2000). Reprinted with permission from the publisher.

Love, Lela P., Images of Justice, 1 PEPPERDINE DISPUTE RESOLUTION LAW JOURNAL 29, 29-32 (2000). Copyright © 2000 by the Pepperdine University School of Law. Reprinted with permission.

Love, Lela P. Adapted from Love, Lela, Training Mediators to Listen: Deconstructing Dialogue and Constructing Understanding, Agendas, and Agreements, 38 FAMILY AND CONCILIATION COURTS REVIEW 27-40 (2000). Copyright © 2000 by Sage Publications, Inc. Reprinted with permission of Sage Publications, Inc.

Love, Lela, Glen Cove: Mediation Achieves What Litigation Cannot, 20 CONSENSUS 1, 1-2 (1993). MIT-Harvard Public Disputes Program, 1993. Reprinted with permission of the publisher.

Love, Lela, and Kimberlee K. Kovach, ADR: An Eclectic Array of Processes, Rather than One Eclectic Process. Reprinted with permission of the author and the JOURNAL OF DISPUTE RESOLUTION, University of Missouri-Columbia, Center for the Study of Dispute Resolution, 206 Hulston Hall, Columbia, MO 65211.

Love, Lela, and Joseph Stulberg, Partnerships and Facilitation: Mediators Develop New Skills for Complex Cases, by Lela Love and Joseph Stulberg, published in DISPUTE RESOLUTION, Volume 9, No. 3, Spring 2003. Copyright © 2003 by the American Bar Association. Reprinted with permission.

Love, Lela, and Joseph Stulberg, Targets and Techniques to Generate Movement, in TRAINING MATERIALS. Copyright © 2004. Reprinted with permission of the authors.

Love, Lela, and Joseph Stulberg, Understanding Dispute Resolution Processes, MICHIGAN MEDIATOR SKILL-BUILDING MANUAL. Copyright © 1997 by Michigan Supreme Court. Reprinted with permission of the Michigan Supreme Court.

Love, Lela, and Joseph Stulberg, Practice Guidelines for Co-Mediation: Making Certain That 'Two Heads Are Better than One,' 13 MEDIATION QUARTERLY 179 (1996). Reprinted with permission of John Wiley & Sons, Inc.

Luban, David, Settlements and the Erosion of the Public Realm, 83 GEORGETOWN LAW JOURNAL 2619, 2621-2626, 2642-2646, 2648-2649, 2662 (1995). Reprinted with permission from the publisher.

Meltsner, Michael, and Philip G. Schrag, Negotiation, PUBLIC INTEREST ADVO-CACY: MATERIALS FOR CLINICAL LEGAL EDUCATION (Little, Brown, and Co., 1974): 232-238. Reprinted with permission.

Menkel-Meadow, Carrie, Aha? Is Creativity Possible in Legal Problem Solving and Teachable in Legal Education?, 6 HARVARD NEGOTIATION LAW REVIEW 97, 106, 122-123, 125, 127-128, 131, 133, 135-136 (2001). Reprinted with permission from the publisher.

Menkel-Meadow, Carrie, Conflict Theory, in ENCYCLOPEDIA OF COMMUNITY: FROM THE VILLAGE TO THE VIRTUAL WORLD, Vol. 1, 323-326, by Karen Christensen and David Levinson eds. Copyright © 2003 by Sage Publications, Inc. Reprinted with permission.

Menkel-Meadow, Carrie, Ethics, Morality and Professional Responsibility in Negotiation, DISPUTE RESOLUTION ETHICS: A COMPREHENSIVE GUIDE, by Phyllis Bernard and Bryant Garth, 131-139. Copyright © 2002 by the American Bar Association. Reprinted by permission.

Menkel-Meadow, Carrie, For and Against Settlement: Uses and Abuses of the Mandatory Settlement Conference. Originally published in 33 UCLA LAW REVIEW 485 (1985). Reprinted with permission of the author.

Menkel-Meadow, Carrie, Introduction: From Legal Disputes to Conflict Resolution and Human Problem Solving, in DISPUTE PROCESSING AND CONFLICT RESOLU-TION. Copyright © 2000 by Ashgate Publishing Limited. Reprinted with permission.

Menkel-Meadow, Carrie, Introduction, MEDIATION: THEORY, POLICY AND PRACTICE, xiii-xviii, xxix. Copyright © 2000 by Ashgate Publishing Limited. Reprinted with permission.

Menkel-Meadow, Carrie, Practicing 'In the Interests of Justice' in the Twenty-First Century: Pursuing Peace As Justice, 70 FORDHAM LAW REVIEW 1761, 1764-1765, 1767-1770, 1773-1774 (2002). Copyright © 2002. Reprinted with permission.

Menkel-Meadow, Carrie, Public Access to Private Settlements: Conflicting Legal Policies, 11 Alternatives to the High Cost of Litigation, Vol. 85, No. 6. Copyright © 1993 by CPR Institute for Dispute Resolution. Reprinted with permission of John Wiley & Sons, Inc.

Menkel-Meadow, Carrie, Professional Responsibility for Third-Party Neutrals, 11 Alter-natives to the Higher Costs of Litigation 129-131 (1993). Reprinted with permission from the publisher.

Menkel-Meadow, Carrie, Remembrance of Things Past? The Relationship of Past to Future in Pursuing Justice in Mediation, 5 CARDOZO JOURNAL OF CONFLICT RESOLU-TION 97. Copyright © 2004 byYeshiva University, Cardozo School of Law. Reprinted with permission.

Menkel-Meadow, Carrie, The Lawyer's Role(s) in Deliberative Democracy, 5 NEVADA LAW JOURNAL, 347, 352-353, 357 (William S. Boyd School of Law, University of Nevada, Las Vegas, 2005). Reprinted with permission.

Menkel-Meadow, Carrie, The Trouble with the Adversarial System in a Postmodern, Multicultural World, 38 WILLIAM AND MARY LAW REVIEW 5, 6-10 (1996). Copyright © 2000 by the WILLIAM AND MARY LAW REVIEW. Reprinted with permission.

Menkel-Meadow, Carrie, Toward Another View of Legal Negotiation: The Structure of Problem Solving. Originally published in 31 UCLA LAW REVIEW 754 (1984). Reprinted with permission of the author.

Menkel-Meadow, Carrie, What's Fair in Negotiation? What Is Ethics in Negotiation?, in WHAT'S FAIR: ETHICS FOR NEGOTIATORS xiii-xvi. Copyright © 2004 by Jossey-Bass, Inc. Reprinted with permission of John Wiley & Sons, Inc.

Milner, Neal, From the Trenches and the Towers: Illusions and Delusions About Conflict Management — In Africa and Elsewhere, 27 LAW AND SOCIAL INQUIRY 621-622, 624-626 (2002). Reprinted with the permission of the University of Chicago and the author.

Mnookin, Robert H., Strategic Barriers to Dispute Resolution: A Comparison of Bilateral and Multilateral Negotiations, 159 JOURNAL OF INSTITUTIONAL AND THEORETICAL ECONOMICS 199-200, 201, 219 (2003). Reprinted with permission.

Mnookin, Robert H., When Not to Negotiate: A Negotiation Imperialist Reflects on Appropriate Limits, 74 UNIVERSITY OF COLORADO LAW REVIEW 1077, 1078, 1081-1083, 1085, 1088-1090, 1095-1096, 1106-1107 (2003). Reprinted with permission of the UNIVERSITY OF COLORADO LAW REVIEW and the author.

Mnookin, Robert H., Why Negotiations Fail: An Exploration of Barriers to Conflict Resolution, 8 OHIO STATE JOURNAL ON DISPUTE RESOLUTION 235, 239-242 (1993). Reprinted with permission.

Mnookin, Robert H., and Lewis Kornhauser, Bargaining in the Shadow of the Law: The Case of Divorce. Reprinted with permission of The Yale Law Journal Company and William S. Hein Company from THE YALE LAW JOURNAL, Vol. 88, 950-997.

Mnookin, Robert H., Scott R. Peppet, and Andrew S. Tulumello, BEYOND WINNING. Reprinted by permission of the publisher from BEYOND WINNING: NEGOTIATING TO CREATE VALUE IN DEALS AND DISPUTES, by Robert H. Mnookin, Scott Peppet, and Andrew S. Tulumello, 27-28, 40, 42-43, Cambridge, Mass.: The Belknap Press of Harvard University Press. Copyright © 2000 by the President and Fellows of Harvard College.

Moffitt, Michael, Ten Ways to Get Sued: A Guide for Mediators, 8 HARVARD NEGOTIATION LAW REVIEW 81, 96, 111, 113-114, 116-117, 120, 122, 125 (2003). Reprinted with permission.

Moore, Christopher W., THE MEDIATION PROCESS: PRACTICAL STRATEGIES FOR RESOLVING CONFLICT. Copyright © 1986 by Jossey-Bass, Inc. Reprinted with permission of Jossey-Bass, a subsidiary of John Wiley & Sons, Inc.

Nader, Laura, and Elisabetta Grande. Excerpts from Current Illusions and Delusions About Conflict Management — in Africa and Elsewhere, 27 LAW AND SOCIAL INQUIRY 27, 573, 574, 578-582, 589, 591, 631-636 (2002). Reprinted with the permission of the University of Chicago and the authors.

Nadler, Janice, Electronically Mediated Dispute Resolution and E-Commerce, 17 NEGOTIATION JOURNAL 333-347 (2001). Reprinted with permission from the publisher.

National Conference of Commissioners on Uniform State Laws, Uniform Mediation Act, Sections 1-13. Copyright © 2001 by the National Conference of Commissioners on Uniform State Laws (NCCUSL). Reprinted with permission.

Nelken, Melissa, Negotiation and Psychoanalysis: If I'd Wanted to Learn About Feelings, I Wouldn't Have Gone to Law School, 46 JOURNAL OF LEGAL EDUCATION 420, 426 (1996). Reprinted with permission.

Peppet, Scott R., Contract Formation in Imperfect Markets: Should We Use Mediators in Deals? 19 OHIO STATE JOURNAL OF DISPUTE RESOLUTION 283, 298-301 (2004). Reprinted with permission.

Price, Marty, Personalizing Crime: Mediation Produces Restorative Justice for Victims and Offenders, 7 (1) DISPUTE RESOLUTION MAGAZINE 8-11 (2000). Copyright © 2000 by the American Bar Association. Reprinted by permission.

Pruitt, Dean, Achieving Integrative Agreements, in NEGOTIATION IN ORGANIZA-TIONS 36-41 (1983). Reprinted with permission.

Putnam, Robert D., Peter B. Evans, and Harold K. Jacobson, eds., Diplomacy and Domestic Politics: The Logic of Two-Level Games, in DOUBLE-EDGED DIPLOMACY: INTERNATIONAL BARGAINING AND DOMESTIC POLITICS, 436-442, 459-460. Copyright © 1993 by University of California Press. Reprinted with permission.

Raiffa, Howard. Reprinted with permission of the publisher from THE ART AND SCIENCE OF NEGOTIATION: HOW TO RESOLVE CONFLICTS AND GET THE BEST OF OUT BARGAINING by Howard Raiffa, Cambridge, Mass.: The Belknap Press of Harvard University Press. Copyright © 1982 by the President and Fellows of Harvard College.

Riskin, Leonard L., Mediator Orientations, Strategies and Techniques, 12 ALTERNATIVES 111, 111-114 (1994). Reprinted with permission of John Wiley & Sons, Inc.

Riskin, Leonard L., Mediation and Lawyers, 43 OHIO STATE LAW JOURNAL 29, 43-46 (1982). Reprinted with permission.

Ross, Lee, Reactive Devaluation in Negotiation and Conflict Resolution, in BARRIERS TO CONFLICT RESOLUTION (1995). Reprinted with permission from the publisher.

Rubin, Jeffrey, and Frank E.A. Sander, Culture, Negotiation, and the Eye of the Beholder, 7 NEGOTIATION JOURNAL 249, 251-253. (Program on Negotiation at Harvard Law School and Blackwell Publishing, 1991). Reprinted with permission from the publisher.

Sander, Frank E.A., and Michael L. Prigoff, At Issue: Professional Responsibility: Should There Be a Duty to Advise of ADR Options? 76 AMERICAN BAR ASSOCIATION JOURNAL 50. Copyright © 1990 by the American Bar Association. Reprinted by permission.

Sander, Frank E.A., Varieties of Dispute Processing, in FEDERAL RULES DECISIONS 79, 111-118, 120, 124-132. (West Group, 1976). Reprinted with permission.

Sander, Frank E.A., and Stephen B. Goldberg, Fitting the Forum to the Fuss: A User-Friendly Guide to Selecting an ADR Procedure, 10 NEGOTIATION JOURNAL 49 (1994). Reprinted with permission from the publisher.

Scanlon, Kathleen M., CPR Institute for Dispute Resolution Drafter's Deskbook for Dispute Resolution Clauses. Reprinted with permission of the author and CPR International Institute for Conflict Prevention and Resolution.

Scardilli, Frank J., Sisters of the Precious Blood v. Bristol-Myers Co.: A Shareholder-Management Dispute, 362-367, in Leonard Riskin and James Westbrook, DISPUTE RESOLUTION AND LAWYERS 2d ed. Copyright © 1997 by Thomson West. Reprinted with permission of Thomson West.

Schneider, Andrea Kupfer, Building a Pedagogy of Problem-Solving: Learning to Choose Among ADR Processes, 5 HARVARD NEGOTIATION LAW REVIEW 113 (2000). Reprinted with permission from the publisher.

Schneider, Andrea Kupfer, Excerpts from Shattering Negotiation Myths: Empirical Evidence on the Effectiveness of Negotiation Style, 7 HARVARD NEGOTIATION LAW REVIEW 143, 171-175, 181, 183-184 (2002). Reprinted with permission from the publisher.

Sebenius, James K., Sequencing to Build Coalitions: With Whom Should I Talk First? in WISE CHOICES: DECISIONS, GAMES, AND NEGOTIATIONS. Copyright © 1996 Harvard Business School Publishing. Reprinted with permission.

Senger, Jeffrey M., Decision Analysis in Negotiation, 87 MARQUETTE LAW REVIEW 723-725 (2004). Copyright © 2004. Reprinted with permission.

Shell, G. Richard, Bargaining with the Devil Without Losing Your Soul, The First Foundation: Your Bargaining Style, and other excerpts from BARGAINING FOR

ADVANTAGE, by G. Richard Shell. Copyright © 1999 by G. Richard Shell. Used by permission of Viking Penguin, a division of Penguin Group (USA), Inc.

Sibley, Susan S., and Sally Merry, Mediator Settlement Strategies, 8 LAW AND POLICY QUARTERLY 7, 19-20 (1986). Reprinted with the permission.

Sternlight, Jean R., Lawyers' Representation of Clients in Mediation: Using Economics and Psychology to Structure Advocacy in a Nonadversarial Setting, 14 OHIO STATE LAW JOURNAL 269, 274, 291-292, 295-296, 354-360, 365 (1999). Reprinted with permission.

Stone, Douglas, Bruce M. Patton, and Sheila Heen. Excerpts from DIFFICULT CONVERSATIONS: HOW TO DISCUSS WHAT MATTERS MOST, by Douglas Stone, Bruce M. Patton, and Sheila Heen. Copyright © 1999 by Douglas Stone, Bruce M. Patton, and Sheila Heen. Reprinted by permission of International Creative Management, Inc., and Viking Penguin, a division of Penguin (USA), Inc.

Straus, David, Managing Meetings to Build Consensus in THE CONSENSUS BUILDING HANDBOOK: A COMPREHENSIVE GUIDE TO REACHING AGREEMENT 287, 289-292, 302, 304, 310-311, 313-314, 321-322 (1999). Copyright © 1999 by Sage Publications, Inc. Reprinted by permission of Sage Publications, Inc.

Stulberg, Joseph B., TAKING CHARGE/MANAGING CONFLICT 59 60, 107-109, 121-122. Reprinted in 2001 by The Wooster Book Company. Copyright © 2001 by Joseph B. Stulberg. Reprinted with permission of the author.

Stulberg, Joseph B., The Theory and Practice of Mediation: A Reply to Professor Susskind, 6 VERMONT LAW REVIEW. Copyright © 1981 by Vermont Law School. Reprinted with permission of the VERMONT LAW REVIEW.

Sunstein, Cass R., Deliberative Trouble? Why Groups Go to Extremes. Copyright © 2000 by THE YALE LAW JOURNAL. Reprinted by permission of The Yale Law Journal Company and William S. Hein Company from THE YALE LAW JOURNAL, Vol. 110, 71-119.

Susskind, Lawrence, Environmental Mediation and the Accountability Problem, 6 VERMONT LAW REVIEW. Copyright © 1981 by the VERMONT LAW REVIEW. Reprinted with permission of the VERMONT LAW REVIEW.

Susskind, Lawrence, Sarah McKearnan, and Jennifer Thomas-Larmer, eds., THE CONSENSUS BUILDING HANDBOOK: A COMPREHENSIVE GUIDE TO REACHING AGREEMENT 3, 3-13, 20-35, 55-56. Copyright © 1999 by Sage Publications, Inc. Reprinted by Permission of Sage Publications, Inc.

Susskind, Lawrence, and Liora Zion, Strengthening the Democratic Process in the United States: An Examination of Recent Experiments, 2002 working paper, Consensus Building Institute, Cambridge, Massachusetts. Reprinted with permission.

Thompson, Leigh L., THE MIND AND HEART OF THE NEGOTIATOR 3d ed. Copyright © 2005. Reprinted by permission of Pearson Education, Inc., Upper Saddle River, NJ.

Trantina, Terry L., How to Design ADR Clauses That Satisfy Clients' Needs and Minimize Litigation Risk. Copyright © 2001 by CPR Institute for Dispute Resolution, 366 Madison Avenue, New York, NY 10017-3122; 212-949-6490. Reprinted with permission.

Waldman, Ellen A., Identifying the Role of Social Norms in Mediation: A Multiple Model Approach. Copyright © 1997 by University of California, Hastings College of the Law. Reprinted from HASTINGS LAW JOURNAL, Vol. 48, N. 4, April 1997 (703), by permission.

Watson, Lawrence M., Jr., Effective Advocacy in Mediation: A Planning Guide to Prepare for a Civil Trial Mediation, available at *http://www.uww-adr.com/2002/pdfs/effectiveadvocacy.pdf*. Reprinted with permission of the author.

Welsh, Nancy, The Thinning Vision of Self-Determination in Court-Connected Mediation: The Inevitable Price of Institutionalization, 6 HARVARD NEGOTIATION LAW REVIEW 1, 4-5, 25-27 (2001). Reprinted by permission of the publishers.

Wissler, Roselle L., The Effects of Mandatory Mediation: Empirical Research on the Experience of Small Claims and Common Pleas Courts. 33 WILLIAMETTE L. REV. 565 (1997). Reprinted with permission.

Zartman, William, The Timing of Peace Initiatives. Copyright © John Darby. CONTEMPORARY PEACE MAKING: CONFLICT, VIOLENCE, AND PEACE PROCESSES 19-20, 24, 26 (2003). Reprinted with permission from Palgrave MacMillan.

MEDIATION

PART 1 | FOUNDATIONS OF MEDIATION

Chapter 1   Conflict and Dispute Resolution

The skillful management of conflicts, [is] among the highest of human skills.
    —Stuart Hampshire, *Justice Is Conflict* 35 (2000)

The core mission of the legal profession is the pursuit of justice, through the resolution
of conflict or the orderly and civilized righting of wrongs.
    —Howard Gardner, Mihaly Csiksentmihali, and William Damon,
    Good Work: When Excellence and Ethics Meet 10 (2001)

Conflicts among human beings are as old as life itself. From the time we began to work and socialize with other people, we have had to learn how to resolve conflicts. Using approaches ranging from flight to fight, from negotiation to violence, we have, in some eras, been more successful than in others, in resolving our conflicts effectively and productively. Indeed, our success in dealing with the conflicts inevitable to human interdependence is one measure of our success in achieving an advanced civilization.

This book focuses on the use of mediation to resolve conflict. Mediation should be viewed in the context of a broad array of potential methods to resolve disputes. In this introductory chapter we explore conflict and the progeny of conflict — disputes — and dispute resolution generally, since that provides the context for most mediation. In Chapter 2, we examine negotiation, which provides the foundation upon which mediation — a form of assisted negotiation — operates. The balance of the book is devoted to different facets of mediation, including different models of mediation, skills for mediators and representatives in mediation, and the policy, legal, and ethical issues implicated in the use of this process of conflict resolution.

This book will teach you how to think about mediation from several different vantage points — that of the mediator (teaching you skills, and asking you to think about policy and ethical issues), that of a lawyer representing a party in a mediation (teaching you particular skills in how to be an effective representative and problem solver and not just a traditional advocate), as well as serving as a process advisor and designer. Given the different types of conflicts, disputes, and transactions that lawyers and clients confront, what are the best processes for effectively dealing with the matters presented? Newer uses of mediation are explored toward the end of this book — mediation in complex, multiparty settings, in international settings, in post-conflict settings (after civil or international wars), in transactional, rather than in dispute settings, and in system design (helping parties design processes in advance for the resolution or prevention of conflicts and disputes in a wide variety of settings, including organizations, as well as contracts and ongoing relationships).

We introduce you, in this chapter, to the different kinds of conflicts that exist, what our orientations to conflict do to shape our responses to them, what different kinds of processes are available for conflict "handling" (if not full resolution or management), and how mediation attempts to solve problems, improve relationships, and, at the same time, secure both peace and justice for the parties (as well as others affected by the parties' conflicts).

A. CONFLICTS AND DISPUTE RESOLUTION

The disputes described in most law school casebooks represent the tip of the iceberg of human conflict. Lawyers initiate and defend lawsuits. They also help prevent conflicts from arising and resolve disputes outside of court. Thus it is essential for lawyers to have a broad understanding of the different types of conflicts that exist. It is important to realize that not all conflict is bad or ought to be avoided. Social psychologists and sociologists, such as Morton Deutsch, George Simmel, and Lewis Coser, have reminded us that conflicts can be constructive as well as destructive. Carrie Menkel-Meadow briefly explores different aspects of conflict.

 Carrie Menkel-Meadow, **CONFLICT THEORY**

> **in Encyclopedia of Community: From the Village to the Virtual World**
> **323-326 (Karen Christensen & David Levinson eds., 2003)**

There are many reasons for conflicts to develop, at both the individual and at the group level. Some conflicts are based on belief systems or principles, some are based on personality differences, and others on conflicts about material goods or personal or group status or reputation. Because there are so many different reasons conflicts develop and because much conflict is dangerous and unproductive, the theory of conflict attempts to understand the different sources of conflict, the dynamics of how conflict develops, escalates or declines and how conflict can be managed, reduced or resolved.

At the same time, it must be recognized that conflict can have social utility as well. Many important changes in human society, many for the betterment of human life, have come from hard-fought conflicts that resulted in the change of human institutions, relationships or ideas. The United States Civil War, for example, was a bloody and painful war in which over a million Americans died, but this war eliminated slavery in the United States and ushered in a long period of change in race relations in the United States. . . . Even small interpersonal conflicts (like between a husband and wife or parent and child) can lead to important changes, not only in relationships between the people in conflict, but in larger social movements, such as the women's rights or feminist movement and the children's rights movement. Conflicts with outsiders often clarify and reinforce commitments and norms of one's own group. And internal conflict within the individual can lead to changed views and intellectual and emotional growth. . . .

A conflict can be experienced as a simple disagreement, a feeling of discomfort or opposition, and a perception of difference from others, or a competition or incompatibility with others. Conflicts, then, can be perceptual, emotional or behavioral. When a conflict is actually acted on it becomes a dispute with someone or a group of others. In order for a conflict to fully develop into a dispute we have to experience some sense of wrong to ourselves, someone else to "blame" for that wrong and some way to take action against those we think caused our difficulty — what one set of scholars have called, "naming, blaming and claiming."[1] How the conflict turns into a dispute and how it is labeled ("framing") then may affect how it progresses and how it may either escalate and get worse, leading in extreme cases to war, or how it can be handled, managed or resolved ("reclaiming").

TYPES OF CONFLICTS

Conflict can exist on many different levels, including the intrapersonal, interpersonal, intragroup, intergroup, and international. Conflicts can exist about different subject matters — ideational or beliefs, values, materiel and resources, emotions, roles and responsibilities. Conflicts vary in terms of the social contexts in which they are located (two old friends, family members, neighbors, strangers, consumers and merchants, distant nation-states) and in the time span in which they are located ("one-off" or "one-shot" encounters and conflicts, long -standing or "embedded" conflicts, temporary or "repeated" conflicts in ongoing relationships like families and employment settings). Conflicts vary, even within the same social environment or subject matter by how the disputants treat the conflict, in the strategies, tactics and behaviors they employ (avoidance, self-help, peaceful negotiation, argument, escalation, physical violence, peace seeking, mediation or settlement) and how the strategics chosen interact with each other. And conflicts are often classified by how they affect the parties in the conflict (the consequences of the conflict) and those outside of the conflict (the "externalities" of the conflict, like children in a marital argument or divorce and neighbors of warring states who accept refugees)....

Conflicts often take somewhat predictable turns ranging from precipitating event, response or reaction, development of in-group-out-group loyalties and the development of both offensive and defensive strategies, followed by escalation, impasse or stalemate and then, motivation for resolution, settlement, and solution seeking (or, in highly competitive or violent conflicts, victory or "annihilation" of the other). But while many think of conflicts as necessarily competitive and antagonistic, there really are a wider range of behaviors that occur in most conflict situations, many of them dependent on the situation and social and political environment of the conflict, as well as the sophistication of the parties in using multiple strategies.

Many of those who study conflict see a greater variety of possible conflict modes or strategies in handling conflict that can occur at individual, group, organizational, and even nation-state levels of action. There are those who *compete* (or seek to maximize their own self-interest, even at the expense of others), those who *cooperate*

---

[1] William L.F. Felstiner, Richard Abel & Austin Sarat, The Emergence and Transformation of Disputes: Naming, Blaming and Claiming..., 15 L. & Socy. Rev. 631-654 (1980-81).

(seeking to work with the other side(s) to find some middle or compromise grounds), those who *accommodate* (who may simply give in to the other party), those who *avoid* (by exiting or absenting themselves from the conflict) and those who *collaborate* (by seeking to work for joint and mutual gains for all parties, without unnecessary harm to others or needless compromise or giving in).[2]

What makes conflict processes so complex are the strategic interactions that occur when more than one party must interact to start, maintain, interrupt or resolve the conflict. These different conflict management strategies interact with each other and can produce reactive and unproductive responses, such as when competing leads to more competing and escalation of competitive behavior causes more violence, less information sharing and an inability to seek mutual gain possibilities. This "mirroring" effect, when each party merely returns the behavior that is offered to it, often leads to stalemates or the impossibility of achieving some resolution because the parties cannot even see or hear beyond the one strategy they have chosen.

Thus, much recent empirical work in conflict processes has been to study the conditions under which parties in conflict can alter their behavioral or strategy choices and open themselves up to new ways of communicating or testing the possibilities with other parties. Conflicts have been studied at the level of community relations, ethnic-racial conflicts, economic and resource competition, environmental disputes, lawsuits (both individual and class actions) and international conflicts. Parties in conflict are now asked to explore their underlying interests (apart from their conflict-producing "positions"), to consider the needs and interests of other parties ("role-reversals" and other communication technologies) and to develop strategies of collaborative and creative problem-solving (by expanding and creating resources and alternatives, by trading non-mutually exclusive preferences or goods, by using contingent or "trial" agreements, rather than permanent solutions, by developing processes and rules for respectful co-existence, such as in Truth and Reconciliation Commissions in politically divided nations).

Both modern research and recent history have demonstrated the importance of third party interveners (mediators, conciliators, fact-finders and facilitators) who can effectively manage processes. These third party efforts have been effective at interpersonal (divorce and family), organizational (labor-management), and international (Northern Ireland, Mid-east) levels of conflict in developing both interim "cease-fires" and more permanent resolutions or agreements to end conflicts and to attempt to resolve larger and underlying problems and conflicts.

Notes and Questions

1.1 Look through a case reporter or one of your casebooks, or make a random search on a computer service, and choose three reported cases. What dispute brought the parties to litigation? What underlying conflicts existed between the parties or between other people involved in or affected by the dispute? How would you describe these conflicts using some of the categories used by Menkel-Meadow?

---

[2] K. Thomas, Conflict and Conflict Management, in Handbook of Industrial Organizational Psychology (M.D. Dunnette ed., 1976).

1.2 Read a newspaper or magazine and find a conflict that is reported. How might the disputants (or possibly attorneys) have avoided such a conflict in advance? Do you think that the conflict you identified has positive or negative aspects, or both? What are they?

1.3 Kenneth Thomas' model for describing a party's orientation to conflict focuses on the degree to which a party wants to satisfy his own concerns and the degree to which he wants to satisfy the concerns of others. Would you describe yourself as competitive, collaborative, avoidant, accommodative, or sharing with respect to your response to conflict?

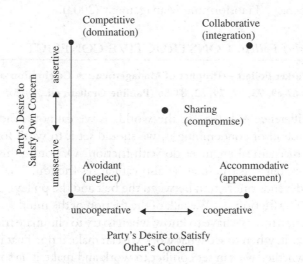

Five Conflict Handling Orientations

1.4 Would (or should) your orientation shift depending on the context (family, school, work)? Consider the "mirroring" effect discussed by Menkel-Meadow. Does (or should) your orientation depend on the other side's approach?

Conflicts will always exist. While we may prevent and avoid some, we will never succeed in eliminating all of them. Nor should that be the goal, given the constructive potential of conflict. The remainder of this section examines how to deal with conflicts that already exist.

In focusing on conflict, it is critically important to examine what it means to "win" in a conflict. Thomas Schelling, a Harvard economist, examines the nature of conflict from a game theoretic perspective. He explains that while a person who approaches conflict strategically always tries to "win" in the sense of doing as well as possible for herself, that does not mean that other disputants need to lose:

> "[W]inning" in a conflict does not have a strictly competitive meaning; it is not winning relative to one's adversary. It means gaining relative to one's own value system; and this may be done by bargaining, by mutual accommodation and by the avoidance of mutually damaging behavior. Thomas C. Schelling, The Strategy of Conflict, 4-5 (1960).

While many people assume that someone must lose when another person wins, the following readings show that this either–or mentality is often fallacious and can be dangerous. The first excerpt is taken from the work of Mary Parker Follett, an important early theorist in the field of conflict resolution. In many ways Follett is the "mother" of the field of dispute resolution. A political scientist by training and an early social worker by practice, she worked in labor-management relations, administrative "science," and business management. She urges that conflict can lead to a creative process that allows constructive solutions to come from the friction created by conflict. For more background on Follett, see Joan C. Tonn, Mary P. Follett: Creating Democracy, Transforming Management (2003).

 Mary Parker Follett, **CONSTRUCTIVE CONFLICT**

in Mary Parker Follett — Prophet of Management: A Celebration of Writings from the 1920's 67-69, 75, 77, 79, 82, 84-86 (Pauline Graham ed., 1995)

As conflict — difference — is here in the world, as we cannot avoid it, we should, I think use it. Instead of condemning it, we should set it to work for us. Why not? What does the mechanical engineer do with friction? Of course, his chief job is to eliminate friction, but it is true that he also capitalizes friction. The transmission of power by belts depends on friction between the belt and the pulley. . . . The music of the violin we get by friction. . . . We talk of the friction of the mind on mind as a good thing. So in business too, we have to know when to try to eliminate friction and when to try to capitalize it, when to see what work we can make it do. That is what I wish to consider here, whether we can set conflict to work and make it *do* something for us.

There are three main ways of dealing with conflict: domination, compromise and integration. Domination, obviously, is a victory of one side over the other. This is the easiest way of dealing with conflict, the easiest for the moment but not usually successful in the long run. . . .

The second way of dealing with conflict, that of compromise, we understand well, for it is the way we settle most of our controversies; each side gives up a little in order to have peace, or, to speak more accurately, in order that the activity which has been interrupted by the conflict can go on. . . .

Yet no one really wants to compromise, because that means a giving up of something. Is there any other method of ending conflict? There is a way now beginning to be recognized at least, and even occasionally followed: when two desires are *integrated*, that means that a solution has been found in which both desires have found a place, that neither side has to sacrifice anything. Let us take some very simple illustration. In the Harvard Library one day, in one of the smaller rooms, someone wanted the window open, I wanted it shut. We opened the window in the next room, where no one was sitting. This was not a compromise because there was no curtailing of desire; we both got what we really wanted. For I did not want a closed room, I simply did not want the north wind to blow directly on me; likewise the other occupant did not want that particular window open, he merely wanted more air in the room. . . .

[T]he revaluing of interests on both sides may lead the interests to fit into each other, so that all find some place in the final solution. . . . If the first step is to uncover the real conflict, the next is to take the demands of both sides and break them up into their constituent parts. . . . On the other hand, one often has to do just the opposite; find the whole demand, the real demand, which is being obscured by miscellaneous minor claims or by ineffective presentation. . . .

Finally, let us consider the chief *obstacles to integration*. It requires a high order of intelligence, keen perception and discrimination, more than that, a brilliant *inventiveness*. . . . Another obstacle to integration is that our way of life has habituated many of us to enjoy domination. Integration seems a tamer affair, it leaves no "thrills" of conquest. . . . Finally, perhaps the greatest of all obstacles to integration is our lack of training for it. In our college debates we try always to beat the other side. . . .

I should like to emphasize our responsibility for integration. . . . One test of business administration should be: is the organization such that both employers and employees, or co-managers, co-directors, are stimulated to a reciprocal activity which will give more than mere adjustment, more than an equilibrium? Our outlook is narrowed, our activity restricted, our chances of business success largely diminished when our thinking is constrained within the limits of what has been called an "either-or" situation. We should never allow ourselves to be bullied by an "either-or." There is always the possibility of something better than either of two given alternatives.

Notes and Questions

1.5 Follett points to domination, compromise, and integration as three main ways of dealing with conflict. These categories are similar to Thomas' orientations of competition, sharing, and collaboration. Follett does not mention Thomas' orientations of avoidance and accommodation. Do you think walking away from conflict (avoidance) or giving in to the other side (accommodation) are effective ways of "dealing" with conflict?

1.6 For the next 24 hours, keep a list of all the conflicts, disputes, or disagreements you are (or could be) involved in. What did you do? Argue, compromise, accommodate, get your way, avoid, "integrate"? How? Why?

In contrast to this aspiration of integration, the following excerpts describe a win-lose attitude that has permeated both our culture in general and our concept of the legal system in particular. Popular writer and professor of linguistics Deborah Tannen critiques the adversarial mindset of our society, arguing that it limits the possibilities of better alternatives and also makes for an uncomfortable civil society. Finally, Carrie Menkel-Meadow outlines some of the problems that arise when the legal system is envisioned in purely binary win-lose terms.

 Deborah Tannen, **THE ARGUMENT CULTURE: MOVING FROM DEBATE TO DIALOGUE**

3-4, 8, 10 (1998)

The argument culture urges us to approach the world — and the people in it — in an adversarial frame of mind. It rests on the assumption that opposition is the best way to get anything done: The best way to discuss an idea is to set up a debate; the best way to cover news is to find spokespeople who express the most extreme, polarized views and present them as "both sides"; the best way to settle disputes is litigation that pits one party against the other; the best way to begin an essay is to attack someone and the best way to show you're really thinking is to criticize. . . .

Our determination to pursue truth by setting up a fight between two sides leads us to believe that every issue has two sides — no more, no less: If both sides are given a forum to confront each other, all the relevant information will emerge and the best case will be made for each side. But opposition does not lead to truth when an issue is not composed of two opposing sides but is a crystal of many sides. Often the truth is in the complex middle, not the oversimplified extremes.

 Carrie Menkel-Meadow, **THE TROUBLE WITH THE ADVERSARY SYSTEM IN A POSTMODERN, MULTICULTURAL WORLD**

38 Wm. & Mary L. Rev. 5, 6-10 (1996)

Binary, oppositional presentations of facts in dispute are not the best way for us to learn the truth; polarized debate distorts the truth, leaves out important information, simplifies complexity, and often obfuscates rather than clarifies. More significantly, some matters — mostly civil, but occasionally even criminal, cases — are not susceptible to a binary (i.e., right/wrong, win/lose) conclusion or solution. The inability to reach a binary resolution of these disputes may result because in some cases we cannot determine the facts with any degree of accuracy. In other cases the law may be conflicting, though legitimate, legal rights giving some entitlements to both, or all, parties. And, in yet another category of cases, human or emotional equities cannot be sharply divided.

Modern life presents us with complex problems, often requiring complex and multifaceted solutions. Courts, with what I have called their "limited remedial imaginations," may not be the best institutional settings for resolving some of the disputes that we continue to put before them.

Even if some form of the adversary system was defensible in particular settings for purposes of adjudication, the "adversary" model employed in the courtroom has bled inappropriately into and infected other aspects of lawyering, including negotiations carried on both "in the shadow of the court" and outside of it in transactional work. . . .

Furthermore, the complexities of both modern life and modern lawsuits have shown us that disputes often have more than two sides in the sense that legal disputes and transactions involve many more than two parties. Procedures and forms like interpleader, joinder, consolidation, and class actions have attempted to allow for more than just plaintiffs' and defendants' voices to be heard, all the while structuring the discourse so that parties must ultimately align themselves on one side of the adversarial line or the other. Multiparty, multiplex lawsuits or disputes may be distorted when only two sides are possible. Consider all of the multiparty and complex policy issues that courts contend with in environmental clean-up and siting, labor disputes in the public sector, consumer actions, antitrust actions, mass torts, school financing and desegregation, and other civil rights issues, to name a few examples.

Finally, scholars have criticized modern adversarialism for the ways it teaches people to act toward each other.

Notes and Questions

1.7 Notes and Questions 1.1 asked you to examine a series of reported cases and consider what underlying conflicts brought the parties to litigation. Now consider the following with respect to these cases:

   a. Who were the "real parties in interest," whether they were named in the reported case or not? Who else might be affected by a judicial resolution or settlement of the matter at issue?

   b. How were the issues framed? In terms of perceived wrongs and rights? Legal entitlements? Were there any instances of cases where not all the wrongs or rights existed on one side?

   c. Consider what solutions, other than those ordered by the court, might have resolved the conflict among all interested parties.

1.8 Is the legal system capable of encouraging "reciprocal activity," as Follett suggests should happen in business management, or is it only an either-or process? Is litigation different from transactional settings?

1.9 Consider a current issue of domestic or international policy. What are the sides of the issue? Are there more complicated issues at stake? How should such issues be decided? Would debate on the issue, whichever one you have chosen, present the best way to get information, make a decision, or resolve a conflict in policy options?

B. PROCESSES FOR HANDLING CONFLICTS AND DISPUTES

With this brief examination of the nature of conflict and approaches to its resolution, we consider the processes available to disputants, lawyers, and others. In other words, as William Felstiner, Richard Abel, and Austin Sarat explain, once a "perceived injurious experience" (PIE) (or a potential conflict) occurs, the next question is what to do about it. The Emergence and Transformation of Disputes: Naming, Blaming and Claiming, 15 L. & Socy. Rev. 631-654 (1980-81). In the background, of course, are social processes and psychological factors that lead us to identify an "experience" as "injurious" or not and that lead us to blame someone other than ourselves. But, taking as given a body of PIEs, one can create a pyramid of possible ways in which disputes are handled. The size and shape of the pyramid differ from culture to culture or legal system to legal system, as no system treats all conflicts the same. Nonetheless, most have developed hierarchical systems for dealing with conflicts and disputes. In the U.S. legal system, for example, despite all the claims that we are so litigious (Marc S. Galanter, Reading the Landscape of Disputes: What We Know and Don't Know (and Think We Know) About Our Allegedly Contentious and Litigious Society, 31 UCLA L. Rev. 4-71 (1983)), most people avoid bringing every conflict to court.

Figure 1-1 shows our current U.S. legal system (which has been changing dramatically in the last few decades). At the top of the pyramid are those important disputes that go all the way to the Supreme Court and culminate in a reported precedent. Note that most of your legal education focuses on reported cases from the top of the pyramid. From a social scientific perspective, this may be a very unrepresentative sample of the actual disputes or conflicts that people have, since the vast percentage of PIEs are resolved outside of courtrooms, whether through the choice not to pursue the claim, settlements, or third-party assisted processes such as mediation or arbitration. Indeed scholars have recently documented a phenomenon known as "The Vanishing Trial" (see Marc Galanter, The Vanishing Trial: An Examination of Trials and Related Matters in Federal and State Courts, 1 J. Empirical Legal Studies 459 (2004); Carrie Menkel-Meadow, Is the Adversary System Really Dead? Dilemmas of Legal Ethics as Legal Institutions and Roles Evolve, in 57 Current Legal Problems (Jane Holder, Colm O'Cinneide & Michael Freeman, eds.) 85 (2004). One commentator has called this whole field the practice and study of legal "informalism." Richard Abel, The Politics of Informal Justice (1982).

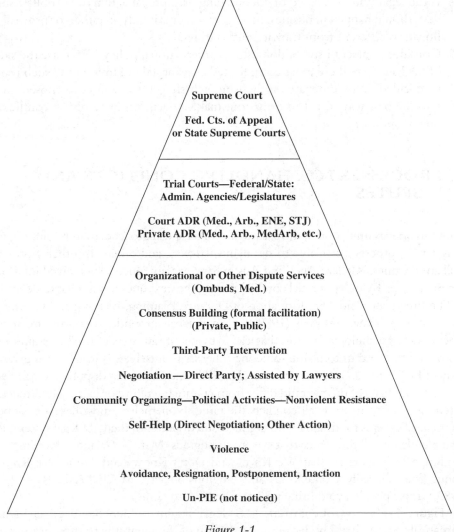

Figure 1-1
U.S. Legal System

Notes and Questions

1.10 Find a reputable data source (such as the Annual Reports of the U.S. Administrative Office of the Courts, *http://www.uscourts.gov*, and its state equivalents) and map the increases and decreases of cases and categories of cases that have been "handled" in each of the conflict processes in the pyramid. Which parts of the pyramid are getting "thicker" or "thinner" over time? How might the pyramid differ from culture to culture? What processes are readily available in your community?

1.11 What are the "rules" or "definitions" that allow a dispute to enter a particular level of the pyramid? To go from a PIE to a formal lawsuit, for example, one must be able to state a cause of action in legal terms and within the requisite time period (statute of limitations) and in the right court (personal and subject matter jurisdiction). To resolve a dispute through two-party negotiation, the other party must be willing to engage. To get a third party involved (as a mediator, arbitrator, or judge), must one have consent of the other party? Some forms of conflict resolution are voluntary (dependent on all the disputants being willing to engage with each other), and others are less voluntary or even compulsory (service of court process on unwilling litigants, conditions precedent for appeals, or "tiered" dispute resolution).

The pyramid of dispute resolution is not a "given" in any society, but rather the result of choices made by policy makers and individuals in that society. Policy makers decide which dispute resolution mechanisms should be made available for which kinds of disputes, and choose whether and how to fund or subsidize particular dispute resolution tools. Disputants and their attorneys then make choices about how to approach a particular dispute, given the options provided in the society. Critical factors influencing such a choice include the parties and their relationship; the nature of the issues; the need for support and guidance, and perhaps for a legal precedent; the cost of the process; and what is at stake.

Once a problem has been analyzed for these (and possibly other) factors, only then can one consider what process might best effectuate the needs and interests of the parties to achieve their goals. (Of course, this becomes quite complicated when the parties don't agree on what their goals are or if they seek different things from the conflict before them.)

But the analysis does not stop there. The choice of a process itself shapes the outcomes. For example, the choice of an adjudicative process (litigation or binding arbitration) results in a definitive, usually win-lose, ruling and requires adversarial presentations. The behaviors necessitated by such a process (presentation of evidence, witnesses, and arguments) reinforce the competitive nature of the situation. Adversarial behaviors produce more conflict, making the likelihood greater that the parties will produce a "competitive" or "zero" or "negative-sum" result. Similarly, if the parties choose negotiation but use adversarial and competitive techniques (such as debate, argument, persuasion, and, more extremely, lying, deception, threat, and intimidation), rather than a problem-solving approach, they may wind up either in a total loss or a stalemate (or at best, a coerced "compromise" or accommodation). Choosing a more "cooperative process" (explained in Chapter 2) can result in more joint gain, but it also presents the risks of being taken advantage of. When one party openly reveals information, for example, the other party may use this information against him. Thus behaviors and processes cannot be chosen for themselves; they must be related to the analysis of what the problem looks like and what goals and outcomes are possible. You can also see that choices about process or behavior are "strategic" in the sense that they are necessarily affected by what the other parties do.

The three major third-party processes — mediation, arbitration, and litigation — provide a framework for understanding formal responses to disputes. The following excerpt describes these processes, noting their advantages and disadvantages and which cases are most suitable for each process. Note that the definitions below describe the traditional, classic variant of each process — there are hybrids and adaptations that would make elements of the description inaccurate, as you will see later in this chapter and Chapter 10.

 Lela P. Love & Joseph B. Stulberg, **UNDERSTANDING DISPUTE RESOLUTION PROCESSES**

in Michigan Mediator Skill-Building Manual, Michigan Supreme Court (revised 1997)

I. DEFINITIONS:

A. **Mediation**: A private, voluntary dispute resolution process in which a third party neutral, invited by all parties, assists the disputants in: identifying issues of mutual concern, developing options for resolving those issues, and finding resolutions acceptable to all parties.

B. **Arbitration**: A private, voluntary dispute resolution process where the parties to a dispute agree in writing to submit the dispute for binding resolution to a third party neutral, chosen pursuant to the agreement of the parties.

C. **Litigation**: An involuntary, formal, public process for dispute resolution, where a government-appointed or elected judge and/or jury determines facts and decrees an outcome to legal causes of action based on adversarial presentations by each party.

II. ADVANTAGES, DISADVANTAGES AND CASE CHARACTERISTICS

A. Mediation:

Advantages:

1. Mediation is the least intrusive form of third party involvement in a dispute. Parties retain control over vital decisions affecting their lives.

2. Outcomes are tailored to the needs and interests of the parties, and represent the parties' own preferences.

3. Since parties create the resolution and since mediators have a duty to ensure "durable" agreements, there is greater satisfaction with the outcome and a higher level of compliance than with judicial decrees.

4. Process addresses all negotiating issues raised by the parties and is not limited to legal causes of action.

5. "Empowers" parties in that disputants understand the process and control the outcome.

6. Improves parties' capacity to resolve future disputes. Helps disputants learn to work together.

7. Process is confidential. Parties can keep their affairs private.

8. Process may be faster and cheaper than litigation.

Disadvantages:

1. Process does not create precedents, and hence it is not "efficient" in that the same types of disputes are resolved again and again. (This criticism ignores the fact that mediation focuses on <u>future</u> arrangements between the parties, and, since each party's needs and interests will vary, "precedents" are of little value.)

2. Process does not create/refine and/or enforce societal norms for behavior.

3. Process may advantage a more skillful or "powerful" party.

4. Since mediation is voluntary, it is difficult to get another party to mediate. Suggesting mediation may indicate weakness.

5. Process does not guarantee an end to the dispute. Mediation may result in no resolution.

Suitable Case Characteristics:

- Disputes among persons with an ongoing relationship.
- Disputes raising issues not easily catagorizable into legal causes of action.
- Disputes where integrative/"win-win" solutions seem particularly appropriate.
- Disputes in which an enhanced level of understanding and a history of successful negotiation will facilitate future dealings.
- Disputes with many issues, suggesting the potential for beneficial trade-offs.

B.   Arbitration:

Advantages:

1. Parties control process (in their agreement to arbitrate) and select a mutually satisfactory neutral.

2. Neutral has special expertise or "wisdom" appropriate for the subject matter of the dispute (where parties select neutral on this basis).

3. Process is confidential. Parties can keep their affairs private.

4. Arbitration can be faster and less expensive than litigation if the parties so tailor the process.

5. Parties are assured a final, binding resolution.

Disadvantages:

1. No formal precedents are created. The process does not help define/refine societal norms.

2. A "bad" decision cannot be appealed (except on very narrow grounds). (The free market is a check on the quality of arbitrators; those who render poor decisions will not be chosen in the future.)

3. Outcomes are "win/lose." There is no possibility of integrative solutions.

4. Adversarial nature of process inhibits parties' ability to understand one another or create beneficial future arrangements.

5. Process can only address those issues that parties agreed could be addressed and which the arbitrator was given the power to resolve by the parties.

Suitable Case Characteristics:
- Disputes where publicity would disadvantage parties.
- Disputes where "expert" or "commercial man" or particularly trusted third party would render a more acceptable decision.
- Disputes where parties do not want to create a precedent.
- Disputes where parties want a fast, binding decision by a third party.
- Disputes where there is limited potential for an integrative resolution.

C. Litigation:

Advantages:

1. Process creates precedents, which help define/refine social norms. Thus, it is "efficient," as the same issues/cases need not be decided again and again.

2. The process is involuntary, allowing a mechanism for forcing another party to resolve a dispute.

3. Unsatisfactory decisions can be appealed.

4. The public nature of the process is an advantage where the dispute involves an issue impacting important societal concerns.

5. Adversarial process is an advantage for party seeking to "punish" his/her adversary and not wanting to further communications or relationship.

Disadvantages:

1. Adversarial process inhibits parties' ability to understand or cooperate with one another and may foreclose mutually advantageous future relationships.

2. Disputants are dependent on the discretion of a judge they cannot choose.

3. The skill of the parties' advocates is of crucial importance. This disadvantages parties unable to pay for or unsophisticated in finding skilled advocates.

4. The process is expensive and time-consuming.

5. Litigation only resolves issues that can be translated into legal causes of action. The parties' real concerns may be neglected.

6. Process is "win/lose," sometimes "lose-lose" (where costs and attorneys' fees swallow what is won). It does not allow for creative, integrative solutions.

7. It is difficult for parties to understand the process ("disempowering"), which may result in lower compliance with judgments or dissatisfaction with the process.

Suitable Case Characteristics:
- Disputes where there is a need for a precedent.
- Disputes where there is an important social issue at stake where a public forum is most appropriate.
- Disputes where the extreme adversarialness of the parties precludes a voluntary process.

Notes and Questions

1.12 Write down particular kinds of conflicts that you think belong exclusively in one form of conflict resolution or another (negotiation, mediation, arbitration, litigation, legislation, voting, or lottery).

1.13 What kind of dispute process do you think would be appropriate for each of the following conflicts?

    a. Disagreement between the president and U.S. Congress over the federal budget;

    b. A grade dispute between you and your professor;

    c. A car accident between strangers involving only property damage;

    d. A parent–child dispute about going to school;

    e. A dispute between a high-tech employee and her former employer when she is fired and takes the company source code with her, claiming she developed it and it is hers;

    f. Whether and how much the federal government should pay victims of terrorism against the United States.

1.14 What is the basis of legitimacy for different conflict processes? Consent? Rule of law? Authority? Respect for "wise elders" or "neutral third parties"?

1.15 Can you think of a time when a conflict you were involved in was resolved in a way that seemed deeply unfair in process, even if not wrong in outcome? What aspects of this situation made you conclude it was handled unfairly? What might have been done differently? See discussion of the field of "procedural justice" in Nancy Welsh, Remembering the Role of Justice in Resolution: Insights from Procedural and Social Justice Theories, 54 J. Legal Educ. 49 (2004).

1.16 Who should decide on the structure of a dispute resolution process—the parties (the "dispute resolution" aspect of conflict resolution) or the larger society (the "social control or precedent-setting function" of conflict resolution)? See Carrie Menkel-Meadow, Whose Dispute Is It Anyway? A Philosophical and Democratic Defense of Settlement (in Some Cases), 83 Geo. L.J. 2663-2696 (1995).

In thinking about dispute resolution processes you may find it useful to consider where each process falls on a variety of continua including the following:

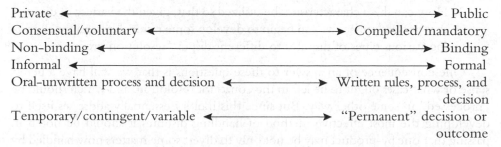

Private ⟵⟶ Public
Consensual/voluntary ⟵⟶ Compelled/mandatory
Non-binding ⟵⟶ Binding
Informal ⟵⟶ Formal
Oral-unwritten process and decision ⟵⟶ Written rules, process, and decision
Temporary/contingent/variable ⟵⟶ "Permanent" decision or outcome

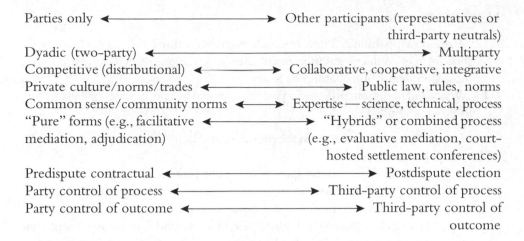

Parties only ⟷ Other participants (representatives or third-party neutrals)

Dyadic (two-party) ⟷ Multiparty

Competitive (distributional) ⟷ Collaborative, cooperative, integrative

Private culture/norms/trades ⟷ Public law, rules, norms

Common sense/community norms ⟷ Expertise — science, technical, process

"Pure" forms (e.g., facilitative mediation, adjudication) ⟷ "Hybrids" or combined process (e.g., evaluative mediation, court-hosted settlement conferences)

Predispute contractual ⟷ Postdispute election

Party control of process ⟷ Third-party control of process

Party control of outcome ⟷ Third-party control of outcome

In an influential speech at the 1976 Pound Conference on the Causes of Popular Dissatisfaction with the Administration of Justice, Frank Sander reflected on the range of available process alternatives. Sanders introduced the idea that courts might be a place where multiple processes are offered to disputants with a procedure for matching the case to the most optimal process, known now as "The Multi-Door Courthouse." The Pound Conference and Sander's ideas ushered in an era of expanding process options in the legal arena. As you read this excerpt, refer back to the continua above describing processes to note how various factors affect Sander's analysis.

 Frank E.A. Sander, **VARIETIES OF DISPUTE PROCESSING**

70 F.R.D. 79, 112-118, 120, 124-126, 130-132 (1976)

By and large we lawyers and law teachers have been far too single-minded when it comes to dispute resolution. Of course, . . . good lawyers have always tried to prevent disputes from coming about, but when that was not possible, we have tended to assume that the courts are the natural and obvious dispute resolvers. In point of fact there is a rich variety of different processes, which, I would submit, singly or in combination, may provide far more "effective" conflict resolution.

Let me turn now to the two questions with which I wish to concern myself:

1. What are the significant characteristics of various alternative dispute resolution mechanisms (such as adjudication by courts, arbitration, mediation, negotiation, and various blends of these and other devices)?

2. How can these characteristics be utilized so that, given the variety of disputes that presently arise, we can begin to develop some rational criteria for allocating various types of disputes to different dispute resolution processes?

One consequence of an answer to these questions is that we will have a better sense of what cases ought to be left in the courts for resolution, and which should be "processed" in some other way. But since this inquiry essentially addresses itself to developing the most effective method of handling disputes it should be noted in passing that one by-product may be not only to divert some matters now handled by the courts into other processes but also that it will make available those processes for grievances that are presently not being aired at all. We know very little about why some individuals complain and others do not, or about the social and psychological costs of remaining silent. It is important to realize, however, that by establishing new dispute resolution mechanisms, or improving existing ones, we may be encouraging the ventilation of grievances that are now being suppressed. Whether that will be good (in terms of supplying a constructive outlet for suppressed anger and frustration) or whether it will simply waste scarce societal resources (by validating grievances that might otherwise have remained dormant) we do not know. The important thing to note is that there is a clear trade-off: the price of an improved scheme of dispute processing may well be a vast increase in the number of disputes being processed.

THE RANGE OF AVAILABLE ALTERNATIVES

There seems to be little doubt that we are increasingly making greater and greater demands on the courts to resolve disputes that used to be handled by other institutions of society. Much as the police have been looked to to "solve" racial, school and neighborly disputes, so, too, the courts have been expected to fill the void created by the decline of church and family. Not only has there been a waning of traditional dispute resolution mechanisms, but with the complexity of modern society, many new potential sources of controversy have emerged as a result of the immense growth of government at all levels, and the rising expectations that have been created.

Quite obviously, the courts cannot continue to respond effectively to these accelerating demands. It becomes essential therefore to examine other alternatives.

The chart reproduced [in the figure below] attempts to depict a spectrum of some of the available processes arranged on a scale of decreasing external involvement.

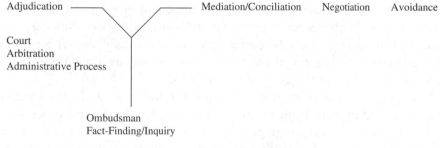

Figure 1-2
Process Flow Chart

At the extreme left is adjudication, the one process that so instinctively comes to the legal mind that I suspect if we asked a random group of law students how a particular dispute might be resolved, they would invariably say "file a complaint in the appropriate court." Professor Lon Fuller, one of the few scholars who has devoted attention to an analysis of the adjudicatory process, has defined adjudication as "a social process of decision which assures to the affected party a particular form of participation, that of presenting proofs and arguments for a decision in his favor." Although he places primary emphasis on process, I would like for present purposes to stress a number of other aspects — the use of a third party with coercive power, the usually "win or lose" nature of the decision, and the tendency of the decision to focus narrowly on the underlying relationship between the parties. Although mediation or conciliation also involves the use of a third party facilitation (and is distinguished in that regard from pure negotiation), a mediator or conciliator usually has no coercive power and the process in which he engages also differs from adjudication in the other two respects mentioned. Professor Fuller puts this point well when he refers to the "central quality of mediation, namely, its capacity to reorient the parties toward each other, not by imposing rules on them, but by helping them to achieve a new and shared perception of their relationship, a perception that will redirect their attitudes and disposition toward one another."

Of course quite a variety of procedures fit under the label of adjudication. Aside from the familiar judicial model, there is arbitration, and the administrative process. Even within any one of these, there are significant variations. Obviously there are substantial differences between the Small Claims Court and the Supreme Court. Within arbitration, too, although the version used in labor relations is generally very similar to a judicial proceeding in that there is a written opinion and an attempt to rationalize the result by reference to general principles, in some forms of commercial arbitration the judgment resembles a Solomonic pronouncement and written opinions are often not utilized. Another significant variant is whether the parties have any choice in selecting the adjudicator, as they typically do in arbitration. Usually a decision rendered by a person in whose selection the parties have played some part will, all things being equal, be less subject to later criticism by the parties.

There are important distinctions, too, concerning the way in which the case came to arbitration. There may be a statute (as in New York and Pennsylvania) requiring certain types of cases to be initially submitted to arbitration (so-called compulsory arbitration). More commonly arbitration is stipulated as the exclusive dispute resolution mechanism in a contract entered into by the parties (as is true of the typical collective bargaining agreement and some modern medical care agreements). In this situation the substantive legal rules are usually also set forth in the parties' agreement, thus giving the parties control not only over the process and the adjudicator but also over the governing principles.

As is noted on the chart, if we focus on the indicated distinctions between adjudication and mediation, there are a number of familiar hybrid processes. An inquiry, for example, in many respects resembles the typical adjudication, but the inquiring officer (or fact finder as he is sometimes called) normally has no coercive power; indeed, according to Professor Fuller's definition, many inquiries would not be adjudication at all since the parties have no right to any agreed-upon form of presentation and participation.

But a fact finding proceeding may be a potent tool for inducing settlement. Particularly if the fact finder commands the respect of the parties, his independent appraisal of their respective positions will often be difficult to reject. This is especially true of the Ombudsman who normally derives his power solely from the force of his position. These considerations have particular applicability where there is a disparity of bargaining power between the disputants (e.g., citizen and government, consumer and manufacturer, student and university). Although there may often be a reluctance in these situations to give a third person power to render a binding decision, the weaker party may often accomplish the same result through the use of a skilled fact finder.

There are of course a number of other dispute resolution mechanisms which one might consider. Most of these (e.g., voting, coin tossing, self-help) are not of central concern here because of their limited utility or acceptability. But one other mechanism deserves brief mention. Professor William Felstiner recently pointed out that in a "technologically complex rich society" avoidance becomes an increasingly common form of handling controversy. He describes avoidance as "withdrawal from or contraction of the dispute-producing relationship" (e.g., a child leaving home, a tenant moving to another apartment, or a businessman terminating a commercial relationship). He contends that such conduct is far more tolerable in modern society than in a "technologically simple poor society" because in the former setting the disputing individuals are far less interdependent. But, as was pointed out in a cogent response by Professors Danzig and Lowy, there are heavy personal and societal costs for such a method of handling conflicts, and this strongly argues for the development of some effective alternative mechanism. Moreover, even if we disregarded altogether the disputes that are presently being handled by avoidance — clearly an undesirable approach for the reasons indicated — we must still come to grips with the rising number of cases that do presently come to court and see whether more effective ways of resolving some of these disputes can be developed. . . .

CRITERIA

Let us now look at some criteria that may help us to determine how particular types of disputes might best be resolved.

1.   Nature of Dispute

Lon Fuller has written at some length about "polycentric" problems that are not well suited to an adjudicatory approach since they are not amenable to an all-or-nothing solution. He cites the example of a testator who leaves a collection of paintings in equal parts to two museums. Obviously here a negotiated or mediated solution that seeks to accommodate the desires of the two museums is far better than any externally imposed solution. Similar considerations may apply to other allocational tasks where no clear guidelines are provided.

At the other extreme is a highly repetitive and routinized task involving application of established principles to a large number of individual cases. Here adjudication may be appropriate, but in a form more efficient than litigation (e.g., an administrative agency). Particularly once the courts have established the basic principles in such areas, a speedier and less cumbersome procedure than litigation should be utilized.

2.   Relationship Between Disputants

A different situation is presented when disputes arise between individuals who are in a long-term relationship than is the case with respect to an isolated dispute. In the former situation, there is more potential for having the parties, at least initially, seek to work out their own solution, for such a solution is likely to be far more acceptable (and hence durable). Thus negotiation, or if necessary, mediation, appears to be a preferable approach in the first instance. Another advantage of such an approach is that it facilitates a probing of conflicts in the underlying relationship, rather than simply dealing with each surface symptom as an isolated event.

3. Amount in Dispute

Although, generally speaking, we have acted to date in a fairly hit-or-miss fashion in determining what problems should be resolved by a particular dispute resolution mechanism, amount in controversy has been an item consistently looked to to determine the amount of process that is "due." The Small Claims Court movement has taken as its premise that small cases are simple cases and that therefore a pared-down judicial procedure was what was called for. Next to the juvenile court, there has probably been no legal institution that was more ballyhooed as a great legal innovation. Yet the evidence now seems overwhelming that the Small Claims Court has failed its original purpose; that the individuals for whom it was designed have turned out to be its victims. Small wonder when one considers the lack of rational connection between amount in controversy and appropriate process. Quite obviously a small case may be complex, just as a large case may be simple. The need, according to a persuasive recent study, is for a preliminary investigative-conciliational stage (which could well be administered by a lay individual or paraprofessional) with ultimate recourse to the court. This individual could readily screen out those cases which need not take a court's time (e.g., where there is no dispute about liability but the defendant has no funds), and preserve the adjudicatory process for those cases where the issues have been properly joined and there is a genuine dispute of fact or law. Obviously such a screening mechanism is not limited in its utility to the Small Claims Court.

4. Cost

There is a dearth of reliable data comparing the costs of different dispute resolution processes. Undoubtedly this is due in part to the difficulty of determining what are the appropriate ingredients of such a computation. It may be relatively easy to determine the costs of an ad hoc arbitration (though even there one must deal with such intangibles as the costs connected with the selection of the arbitrator(s)). But determining the comparable cost of a court proceeding would appear to pose very difficult issues of cost accounting. Even more difficult to calculate are the intangible "costs" of inadequate (in the sense of incomplete and unsatisfactory) dispute resolution. Still, until better data become available one can probably proceed safely on the assumption that costs rise as procedural formalities increase.

The lack of adequate cost data is particularly unfortunate with respect to essentially comparable processes, such as litigation and arbitration. Assuming for the moment that arbitration would produce results as acceptable as litigation — a premise that is even more difficult to verify — would cost considerations justify the transfer (at least in the first instance) of entire categories of civil litigation to arbitration, as has been done in some jurisdictions for cases involving less than a set amount of money? One difficulty in this connection is that we have always considered access to the courts as an essential right of citizenship for which no significant charge should be imposed, while the parties generally bear the cost of arbitration. Thus although I believe, on the basis of my own arbitration experience, that process is, by and large, as effective as and cheaper than litigation, lawyers tend not to make extensive use of it (outside of special areas such as labor and commercial law), in part because it is always cheaper for the clients to have society rather than the litigants pay the judges. Perhaps if arbitration is to be made compulsory in certain types of cases because we believe it to be more efficient, then it should follow that society should assume the costs, unless that would defeat the goal of using costs to discourage appeals. . . .

5. Speed

The deficiency of sophisticated data concerning the costs of different dispute resolution processes also extends to the factor of speed. Although it is generally assumed — rightly, I believe — that arbitration is speedier than litigation, I am not aware of any studies that have reached such a conclusion on the basis of a controlled experiment that seeks to take account of such factors as the possibly differing complexity of the two classes of cases, the greater diversity of "judges" in the arbitration group, and the possibly greater cooperation of the litigants in the arbitration setting. . . .

What I am thus advocating is a flexible and diverse panoply of dispute resolution processes, with particular types of cases being assigned to differing processes (or combinations of processes), according to some of the criteria previously mentioned. Conceivably such allocation might be accomplished for a particular class of cases at the outset by the legislature; that in effect is what was done by the Massachusetts legislature for malpractice cases. Alternatively one might envision by the year 2000 not simply a court house but a Dispute Resolution Center, where the grievant would first be channeled through a screening clerk who would then direct him to the process (or sequence of processes) most appropriate to his type of case. The room directory in the lobby of such a Center might look as follows:

Screening Clerk	Room 1
Mediation	Room 2
Arbitration	Room 3
Fact Finding	Room 4
Malpractice Screening Panel	Room 5
Superior Court	Room 6
Ombudsman	Room 7

Of one thing we can be certain: once such an eclectic method of dispute resolution is accepted there will be ample opportunity for everyone to play a part. Thus a court might decide of its own to refer a certain type of problem to a more suitable tribunal. Or a legislature might, in framing certain substantive rights, build in an appropriate dispute resolution process. Institutions such as prisons, schools, or mental hospitals also could get into the act by establishing indigenous dispute resolution processes. Here the grievance mechanism contained in the typical collective bargaining agreement stands as an enduring example of a successful model. Finally, once these patterns begin to take hold, the law schools, too, should shift from their preoccupation with the judicial process and begin to expose students to the broad range of dispute resolution processes.

Notes and Questions

1.17 What Sander calls "indigenous" dispute resolution (for dispute resolution within organizations) has now become quite institutionalized in the form of organizational ombuds, organizational grievance mechanisms, and other variations on this theme, now labeled "internal dispute resolution" ("IDR") by some commentators. See Lauren Edelman, Howard Erlanger & John Lande, Internal Dispute Resolution: The Transformation of Civil Rights in the Workplace, 27 L. & Socy. Rev. 497-534 (1993). Different organizations create different ways of dealing with both internal and external grievances and complaints. See, e.g., Calvin Morrill, The Executive Way: Conflict Management in Corporations (1995), and Craig McEwen, Managing Corporate Disputing: Overcoming Barriers to the Effective Use of Mediation for Reducing the Cost and Time of Litigation, 14 Ohio St. J. on Disp. Resol. 1-27 (1998). What kind of dispute mechanisms exist within your law school to deal with complaints, conflicts, and grievances? What kind of dispute mechanism would you like to see for the following?

    a. Grade complaints
    b. Honor code violations
    c. Sexual or other forms of harassment
    d. Conflicts with other students
    e. Other forms of conflicts or disputes

Must internal dispute resolution track the requirements of formal and legal due process? What other kinds of values, procedures, and outcomes might be appropriate within an organization?

1.18 Consider complaints you have had with major corporations, such as computer manufacturers, airlines, online vendors, or government agencies. How have your disputes been handled? Can you discern differences in corporate or organizational conflict resolution cultures? What might be some of the animating values that lead organizations to design their conflict resolution procedures in a particular way?

Now that you have had exposure to the basic processes of dispute resolution and to an analysis of how diverse processes can be utilized in our legal system, it is important to realize that there is no limit on the creative adaptation of processes to fit particular needs of parties. By way of example, the following excerpt illustrates many variants of the arbitration process, which is often an alternative, complement, or even a supplement to mediation. Similarly, as you study mediation in the chapters that follow, you will discover a multitude of different approaches to mediation and hybrid mediation processes. An awareness of a rich array of process options will make you, as an attorney, a thoughtful consumer of and advisor about particular processes. Once in mediation, mediators and attorneys often search for procedural resolution when substantive resolutions become impossible. Again, process sophistication is important.

CENTER FOR PUBLIC RESOURCES, THE ABC'S OF ADR: A DISPUTE RESOLUTION GLOSSARY

13 Alternatives to High Cost Litig. 147, 147-148, 150 (1995)

- *Arbitration* The most traditional form of private dispute resolution. It can be "administered" (managed) by a variety of private organizations, or "non-administered" and managed solely by the parties. It can be entered into by agreement at the time of the dispute, or prescribed in pre-dispute clauses contained in the parties' underlying business agreement. Arbitration can take any of the following forms:

- *Binding Arbitration* A private adversarial process in which the disputing parties choose a neutral person or a panel of three neutrals to hear their dispute and to render a final and binding decision or award. The process is less formal than litigation; the parties can craft their own procedures and determine if any formal rules of evidence will apply. Unless there has been fraud or some other defect in the arbitration procedure, binding arbitration awards typically are enforceable by courts and not subject to appellate review.

- *Non-binding Arbitration* This process works the same way as binding arbitration except that the neutral's decision is advisory only. The parties may agree in advance to use the advisory decision as a tool in resolving their dispute through negotiation or other means.

- *"Baseball" or "Final-Offer" Arbitration* In this process, used increasingly in commercial disputes, each party submits a proposed monetary award to the arbitrator. At the conclusion of the hearing, the arbitrator chooses one award without modification. This approach imposes limits on the arbitrator's discretion and gives each party an incentive to offer a reasonable proposal, in the hope that it will be accepted by the decision-maker. . . .

- *"Bounded" or "High-Low" Arbitration* The parties agree privately without informing the arbitrator that the arbitrator's final award will be adjusted to a bounded range. Example: P wants $200,000. D is willing to pay $70,000. Their high-low agreement would provide that if the award is below $70,000, D will pay at least $70,000; if the award exceeds $200,000, the payment will be reduced to $200,000. If the award is within the range, the parties are bound by the figure in the award. . . .

- *Med-Arb* A short-hand reference to the procedure mediation-arbitration. In med-arb, the parties agree to mediate with the understanding that any issues not settled through the mediation will be resolved by arbitration using the same [neutral] . . . to act both as mediator and arbitrator. However, that choice may have a chilling effect on full participation in the mediation portion. A party may not believe that the arbitrator will be able to discount unfavorable information learned in mediation when making the arbitration decision. . . .

- *Court-Annexed Arbitration* An adjudicatory dispute resolution process in which one or more arbitrators issue a non-binding judgment on the merits, after an expedited, adversarial hearing. The arbitrator's decision addresses only the disputed legal issues and applies legal standards. Either party may reject the non-binding ruling and proceed to trial.

Court-annexed arbitration is used mainly in small- and moderate-sized tort and contract cases, when litigation costs are often disproportionate to the amounts at stake. . . . Once the premier court ADR process, it has lost popularity in recent years. Most court ADR development focuses on mediation.

The array of processes provides both the backdrop for and the alternatives to mediation, which become particularly relevant if mediation fails to produce a resolution. It is important to emphasize that no list of dispute resolution processes is ever complete. Creative disputants and their attorneys will think of new processes and variations of existing processes. In fact, where mediators cannot help parties resolve a dispute, they will often assist in designing a procedural resolution. At the same time, it is also important to remember that parties may not have a choice about what process is best for them. Courts or legislatures may increasingly require them to use a particular form of dispute resolution. Legislatures and courts may also proscribe the use of certain dispute resolution procedures in particular contexts, such as in constitutional or civil rights cases.

Different approaches raise jurisprudential, policy, and practical issues. The final section of this introduction turns to some fundamental questions regarding the relationship of alternative processes, like mediation, to a formal system of justice.

C. ANIMATING VALUES FOR CONFLICT AND DISPUTE RESOLUTION: JUSTICE AND PEACE

Process diversity generates questions about the underlying justice rationale of different approaches. Although more flexible processes and more tailored solutions can seem to be more "fair" or "just" to particular disputants, litigation offers society the opportunity to frame precedents from public cases, to build and strengthen public law, and thereby to serve broader justice needs. Each process serves different and important goals. Are dispute processes intended for parties in conflict or for the larger society?

The final excerpts examine the justice rationale of different approaches.

 Jonathan M. Hyman & Lela P. Love, **IF PORTIA WERE A MEDIATOR: AN INQUIRY INTO JUSTICE IN MEDIATION**

9 Clin. L. Rev. 157, 158-174 (2002)

The practice of mediation is deeply attuned to issues of justice. To one unfamiliar with mediation, it might seem that mediation marks a flight from justice, a move to crude compromise or the abandonment of rights for the sake of making peace or saving time or money. On the contrary, mediation brings to the fore the perennial questions of justice: Has there been a wrong (or several wrongs) and what is the fair correction that provides a just measure for the kind and degree of harm done? What is a fair and just distribution of the resources available? How can stability and community be restored in light of the wrong? What should a mediator do to try to assure that the process itself remains just? Mediators, like judges and arbitrators, must attend to these issues.

However, justice in mediation is different from justice in adjudication. Unlike a judge, jury or arbitrator, a mediator does not have the responsibility to determine an appropriate remedy or a just distribution. That is for the parties themselves to do. The mediator must attend to the process, help the parties recognize the legitimacy of different perspectives on justice, and work towards a resolution that comports with the parties' considered views of a fair and acceptable outcome....

Using mediation rather than adjudication to resolve disputes carries important implications for justice. How can an agreed-upon solution, crafted by disputing parties rather than by duly appointed arbiters, judges or juries, comport with ideals of justice? Critics claim that mediation and settlement sacrifice a just result, a result in keeping with articulated and accepted societal norms, for mere efficiency or expedience. Such critiques neglect the multi-faceted nature of justice. This article examines how a justice rationale undergirds the consensual resolution of disputes, while another justice rationale undergirds adjudication. Justice-seeking is a central component of all dispute resolution processes, and one that mediators, like judges and arbitrators, must attend to. Rather than abandoning justice, the unique attributes of mediation enable mediators to help those who ultimately have the most intimate understanding of the complexities of their situation achieve a resolution they find "just."

Justice in adjudicative systems comes from above, from the application by a judge, jury or arbitrator of properly created standards or rules to "facts" as determined by the adjudicator. Justice inheres in two aspects of that system — in the standards or rules that are applied, and in the process that is used to apply them. Mediation has parallel, but very different, aspects. The rules, standards, principles and beliefs that guide the resolution of the dispute in mediation are those held by the parties. The guiding norms in mediation may be legal, moral, religious or practical. In mediation, parties are free to use whatever standards they wish, not limited to standards that have been adopted by the legislature or articulated by the courts. Consequently, justice in mediation comes from below, from the parties. Similarly, the process of mediation has different guiding principles than adjudication. Parties may address any issue they wish, not limited to legal causes of action; they may bring in any information they wish, not limited by rules of evidence and procedure to probative evidence, relevant to legal causes of action and meeting evidentiary requirements for authenticity and accuracy. On the other hand, norms of "fair process" guide mediators and adjudicators alike. Both must act in an unbiased and impartial manner and be perceived as neutral. Both must give all participants a level playing field with an equal opportunity to be heard and equal attention and amenities in proceeding through the process....

I. WHAT WE MEAN WHEN WE TALK ABOUT JUSTICE

Because explicit concepts of justice are not a prominent part of the literature or practice of mediation, we would like to sketch out, as a preliminary matter, the kinds of concepts of justice we will bring to our analysis. . . . We start by distinguishing the adjudicative approach to justice and highlighting certain issues that are beyond the scope of this analysis. Lawyers tend to view justice as the application of law through the legal system. Substantive rules of law, judicial discretion, and the procedures for adjudicating disputes all strive to comport with ideals of fairness and justice. How well they succeed is the subject of constant debate and legislative and judicial reform, but justice and fairness provide one standard by which rules, practice and procedure are measured.

The application of a rule of law and the form of justice adjudication provides is not irrelevant to the justice-from-below of mediation. To a significant degree, the public law provides the norms that guide private dispute resolution. Parties often settle disputes by keeping in mind and balancing the entitlements the litigation system promises. Furthermore, some scholars suggest that mediation becomes unjust if the issues it considers and the results it achieves stray too far from the issues and results that would obtain in the adjudicatory system, particularly where parties get diverted to mediation after coming to the courts for a judgment. If mediation too cavalierly ignores the public norms and results that we would expect from the adjudicatory system questions of injustice may arise: Were the parties ignorant of their rights? Did the courts (to which the case was brought) fail to protect important entitlements? Was one of the parties bullied by the other? Did mediator bias and dominant culture norms unfairly disadvantage a party?

Additionally, an analysis of justice as it inheres in particular mediations does not answer the different set of justice issues posed by whether public institutions should require or mandate mediation as part of the public justice system. Should courts require litigants first to use mediation to try to resolve their disputes? If they do, are they robbing the judicial system of its charge to produce just results in a public forum where the outcome can be scrutinized and where the decision will ultimately become a public precedent? Do mediation programs reduce the overall time and resources spent by litigating parties, and if they do, are these efficiencies worth whatever other costs they impose, such as a reduced opportunity for a full discovery and airing of legally relevant facts? Is the societal benefit provided by mediation sufficient to support the complex rules of confidentiality and privilege in mediation that have been developing? Where mediation is incorporated into a larger system of justice, these questions must be answered. However, they can only be answered if it is clear that mediation, like adjudication, rests on a compelling justice rationale. Acknowledging that those important questions must ultimately be answered, this article focuses instead on exploring the justice rationale in mediation itself—a necessary first step in answering questions about designing a coherent justice system.

The justice that pertains in mediation is the justice the parties themselves experience, articulate and embody in their resolution of the dispute. For individuals, public legal norms are but one factor in a constellation of norms and expectations creating a sense of correct conduct, fair procedure and a just outcome. For our discussion, the parties' own views of justice, not the views of judges and lawyers, become the key measure of justice in mediation.

Among the dilemmas of a discussion of justice in mediation is the assumption, not always warranted, that parties settle matters when the proposed settlement comports with their notions of justice. In reality, a party's sense of justice can be but one of several reasons for which she decides to accept or not accept a proposed resolution. The decision-making process entails weighing various reasons and factors against each other to reach a decision to settle. For example, a party may settle a matter because the costs of litigating have become too high, or she feels it is time to move on with her life, or she simply no longer cares about the outcome, or she wants the dispute to end. Justice, in certain instances, may have little to do with the decision to settle a dispute! Notwithstanding this insight, most people do not voluntarily sign agreements which they experience as "unjust." The phenomena of parties persistently and vigorously fighting when relatively little is at stake from a financial perspective and the costs of disputing are disproportionately high argues that justice-seeking is a central preoccupation for many, perhaps most, parties in the disputing universe.

While justice in mediation relies on each party's own private sense of justice, conversations about justice differ from a discussion of competing private tastes or personal preferences. There is a difference, for instance, between wanting money from another party because it is justly deserved, and wanting money because it is pleasurable or satisfying to have more money. A sense of justice is in part a social phenomenon built on family and community beliefs and norms. A discussion in a mediation of what is fair or just, or what is deserved, articulates these norms more explicitly and fully than simply making competing claims for resources or demands for desired actions. When parties bring justice norms to a mediation and make them part of the discussion, they are educating each other, building justice norms in their family, workplace, business or community in a manner parallel to (however different from) the public declaration of precedents and norms that litigation achieves.

The differing sources of justice in mediation and adjudication have important consequences for assessing the role of justice in a mediation. Mediators, as human beings, are part of the same social and moral world as the parties. When parties seek to satisfy their sense of fairness and justice, as well as their psychological and material needs, the mediator can understand the claim to justice with the same kind of empathetic response that she brings to each party's feelings and interests. As with other forms of empathetic response, a mediator need not agree with a party's views about what is more fair or more just, but should be able to articulate the meaning of justice as the party sees it, and help the party think through his ideas in ways that might lead to a resolution. This means that explicit talk about fairness and justice can, and often does, form an appropriate part of a mediation session.

But of what would such talk consist? When parties talk about fairness and justice, without the overlay of the elaborate system of adjudicatory justice, they will most likely find themselves talking about the well-known Aristotelian categories of reparative justice, distributive justice, and procedural justice. They may also find themselves talking about restoration, retribution, revenge and relationships. Each is discussed below: reparative justice, including a discussion of restorative justice; retribution and revenge (which can be forms of reparative justice); distributive justice; relationships; and procedural justice.

A.   Reparative Justice

Parties in mediation may use claims of justice to seek repair of what they see as a wrongful deprivation or harm imposed on them by the other. They need not limit their claims of injustice to acts that may have violated the law. A party who has taken more than is "fair" from the complaining party might have arguably committed an injustice that needs to be corrected, even if the law does not prohibit the taking. Treating someone disrespectfully, taking or diminishing their dignity, for example, might become part of a claim that an injustice was done even though there may be no cognizable "cause of action" for such a wrong. Of course, there can be — and usually is — sharp disagreement between parties over whether a particular action should be characterized as an injustice. Such disagreements are similar to the often-contested question of how much responsibility each party bears for the harm that occurred. A discussion about such disagreements is a form of articulating justice in mediation.

Just as mediation permits the parties to air a wide range of grievances, and permits them to characterize the grievances as injustices if they see them that way, it also permits a wide range of possible repairs for the claimed injustice. Remedies developed in mediation are not limited to adjudicative remedies, such as the payment of money, criminal punishment, or injunctive orders. They can be constructed to deal directly with what the parties see as the injustices that gave rise to the dispute. Examples might include elimination of disparaging comments in a personnel file, correction of the physical condition that caused harm, or a change in certain practices. Sincere apologies, for instance, can serve as a valid remedy to achieve justice in mediation — an outcome not available when a third party adjudicator is imposing a resolution. The recognition and remorse that underlie apology can arise through the dialogue made possible by mediation and the richer understanding of the situation such dialogue can generate.

The practice of "restorative justice" in the criminal law arena is one example of how the justice concept of repairing a wrong can extend beyond punishment or payment of money. Restorative justice brings together criminal offenders (often juveniles) and their victims in an effort to mediate between them. It provides an opportunity for a victim to tell the offender how he or she has been hurt and harmed, for the offender to understand the impact of his or her action, and for both victim and offender to construct an acceptable plan to redress the wrong. Mediation in this context often results in some plan of action for the offender to take, to try to ameliorate the harm and restore the offender to the community. This kind of action is in addition to, or sometimes in lieu of, the formal imposition of sanctions by the adjudicatory system.

B.   Retribution and Revenge

What if a party to a mediation seeks revenge for the wrong claimed to have been done? The notion of "an eye for an eye" is an ancient form of balancing that some experience as both just and "reparative." Frequently, mediated discussions result in the parties' recognition that the wrong they experienced may be counter-balanced by a wrong they sponsored. Or, the proverbial "eye" they wish to extract can be given in a more meaningful (and less costly) way than blinding the other side. In other words, mediated discussions of justice can be responsive to desires for revenge even though revenge, as it is normally conceived, is not usually the product of mediation. Rather, the desire for revenge is transformed either by recognition of the larger context of the dispute and the "opponent," by remorse and apology, or by meaningful reparations. In contrast, lawsuits are often brought to teach the other side a lesson (i.e., get revenge). Occasionally, they do that. More often, both sides are taught lessons about the uncertainty of any given outcome, the enormous costs of litigation and the indignities of being at the mercy of strangers in a public forum.

C. Distributive Justice

We tend to think of distributive justice in terms of legislative debates or negotiations for structuring transactions: What is a just way to distribute society's resources among different groups or classes of people? How should employers and employees, owners and players, divorcing spouses, or business partners, equitably divide resources? Distributive justice plays an important role in mediations.

It is common to analyze a proposed settlement by predicting the value of the alternative to agreement. Where litigation is the alternative to settlement, this means assessing the likelihood of prevailing at trial times the expected trial outcome minus the costs of pursuing litigation. By considering the nature and likelihood of particular trial outcomes, parties can vicariously incorporate in their settlement analysis justice concepts that are embodied in adjudicatory law, although such reasoning measures only anticipated justice, not imposed justice — that is, the shadow of the law, rather than the law itself. When the settlement distribution is looked on as a problem of distribution, however, rather than as a compromise of adjudicatory claims, additional justice concepts come into play. The well-known concepts by which we can measure the justice of distributions are equality, equity, and need.

"Splitting the difference" between settlement demands, a common last step in a negotiated distribution, is a claim to equality, and has a powerful attraction to people's sense of fairness and common sense justice. Similarly, siblings, employees, or victims who must share resources in a common fund may be guided by understandable principles of equal treatment.

Equity, as distinct from equality, can support distributions other than an even split. A victim's feelings or a perpetrator's ability to pay can be more important for determining a just distribution than simply splitting the difference or precisely measuring actual losses. The concept of Pareto efficiency also carries implications for justice. That concept asks us to consider, for any given or proposed distribution of resources, whether there is another possible distribution that would make at least one party better off without making any other party worse off. A Pareto improved distribution would, at a minimum, be more efficient, and — since each party gets more (or closer to their notion of their "just deserts") in a Pareto superior outcome — it will probably be experienced as more just. Even without the logical rigor of the economic concept of Pareto efficiency, such distributions will likely comport with notions of fairness that one "should" relinquish things of low personal value if those things reap enormous benefit for others.

The relative needs of the parties also play into questions of distributive justice. Such considerations make it acceptable for disparate treatment such as the rich being taxed at a higher rate than the poor. The precept from each according to his ability, to each according to his need can fuel claims of justice and lead to responsive settlement terms and sometimes acts of generosity which restore families and communities.

When discussions about fault and blame are not fruitful, mediators may wish to direct the mediation session away from reparative claims and focus on distributional issues instead. Shifting the focus from what happened and who is to blame to the future can ultimately address justice issues. This is true because the ultimate distribution plan needs to balance out how a proposed agreement might divide the available current and foreseeable resources, or might equitably meet the needs of each party, or how the parties might increase the efficiency of their exchange by each trading away things that cost them less in exchange for things they value more. The agreed upon distribution should not violate the parties' senses of equity, equality and need if it is to be acceptable to them. One used to thinking of justice in terms of adjudication might object to such a redirection as turning away from justice concerns and towards satisfying only personal needs and preferences. On the contrary, in determining an equitable distribution, parties are frequently balancing up — or repairing — past harms in a way that will be most productive for them. To some extent, questions of distributional justice are most important in an interest-based, needs-oriented approach to mediation, and questions of reparative justice play a more prominent role in a mediation context where parties (or their "mediator") focus on evaluating the merits of law-based claims. In a larger sense, however, in the work of crafting acceptable outcomes, the two concepts become inextricably intertwined.

D.   Relationships

Mediation can involve efforts to restore or improve a damaged or hurtful relationship between the disputing parties, to re-establish a sense of harmony, or to effect a return to the status quo in a family, business, or community. This can have an instrumental value. If the parties have an ongoing relationship, doing business with each other, living near each other, co-parenting, or being members of common economic or social groups, improving their relationship can reduce disputes in the future and make their interaction more economically or personally rewarding. Improved relationships can be valuable in themselves, can ripple out and affect a community, and can represent a public good that is a component of a justice system.

How are improved relationships an aspect of justice? Would a mediation produce more justice if it strengthened the relationship between the parties? In traditional Navajo systems, for example, concepts of justice are related to healing and to restoring a person to good relations with both her surroundings and herself. Navajo justice concepts focus on helping parties re-integrate with the group with the goal of nourishing ongoing relationships with family, neighbors and community. Similarly, in China, history and tradition place a high value on social order and harmony and the stability of the group as a whole.

Additionally, good relationships are sometimes a precondition for negotiating reparative or distributive justice; that is, the correction of wrongs and a more just allocation of goods can be accomplished more smoothly and thoughtfully if done in the context of good relationships. Mediation is the only third party dispute resolution process that is or can be targeted to improving relationships.

E.   Procedural Justice

While mediation lacks the formality and elaborate procedural rules of litigation, it nonetheless provides a rich opportunity to implement procedural justice. From a disputant's perspective, the perception of fairness is linked to having a meaningful opportunity to tell one's story, to feeling that the mediator considers the story, and to being treated with dignity and in an even-handed manner. Adherence to principles of procedural justice influence the parties' perceptions about the fairness of the process, as well as their perceptions of substantive justice and their willingness to comply with the outcome of the dispute resolution process. The philosopher David Miller argues that a system of justice should be characterized by four critical attributes:

- Equality (treating the participants equally);
- Accuracy (in consideration of whatever information is deemed relevant);
- Publicity (making the rules and procedures apparent to the participants); and
- Dignity (treating the participants in a dignified way, and not requiring undignified actions from them).

To some extent, ethical standards and practice norms for mediators embody these aspects of procedural justice in mediation. First, mediators should remain impartial and without bias between the parties. Second, resolution through mediation should only occur as a result of the knowing, voluntary decisions of the parties. In fact, many accounts of injustice in mediation include stories about mediators who violate such ethical and practice norms in situations where mediation has been mandated.

Mediation (at least the facilitative variety) is most emphatically a forum in which the parties can be heard. Parties' statements and interactions in mediation are not constrained in the way they are in more formal adjudicative forums.

Some evidence suggests that parties tend to regard a more cooperative, problem-solving approach to negotiating conflicts as more just, and as leading to substantive resolutions that are more just, than a negotiating process that is more adversarial and contentious. Good mediation often builds just such a problem-solving framework for the parties. It can thus provide justice of a form and degree not available in adjudication.

We close this chapter with an excerpt by Carrie Menkel-Meadow that focuses on the potential role of individual attorneys in working towards greater peace and justice in our society. Before you read this excerpt, you might spend some time thinking about your own aspirations, goals, and expectations about what legal and conflict resolution processes should accomplish in the world, and about what you personally can contribute. What are your hopes and "higher aspirations"? What are your more "realistic expectations"? How would the larger legal system have to be changed to accommodate your aspirations, or is it possible to accomplish your goals within current institutional frameworks?

Carrie Menkel-Meadow, PRACTICING "IN THE INTERESTS OF JUSTICE" IN THE TWENTY-FIRST CENTURY: PURSUING PEACE AS JUSTICE

70 Fordham L. Rev. 1761, 1764-1765, 1767-1770, 1773-1774 (2002)

In a recent address, . . . former President Clinton, upon accepting the Second Annual Cardozo International Advocate for Peace Award, said, "Throughout human history, tragically, we have seen more advances in tools for waging war than in the art of making peace." That comment, while certainly true of human behavior in general, is applicable to legal behavior as well. We have developed more and more sophisticated forms of legal warfare (discovery and the paper wars of attrition, and, my personal favorite, the recent ad of the Los Angeles Intercontinental Hotel for a "litigation war room" available for lawyers planning strategy, taking depositions and developing their "battle plans," all in facilities with completely up-to-date technology and "close to the battlefield" — the courthouse).[14] Fortunately, I think we have also seen some advances in developing some tools for "making peace" with the proliferation of mediation, prob᠁ ᠁᠁-solving and interest-based negotiation, negotiated rule-making and a variety of consensus building processes, as well as problem-solving courts in a variety of substantive areas. These new tools are intended, in my view, to seek peace and justice simultaneously through the use of a variety of different forms of dialogue, policy-making, rule development, dispute settlement and conflict management. As I now tell my colleagues in a variety of substantive areas, if we cannot make enough peace and quiet to have a reasonable dialogue with each other (see by contrast the continuing violence in the troubled spots of the world) we will not be able to seek justice, let alone substantive solutions to any of our problems. Peace, of at least some minimal sort, is a prerequisite to the search for justice. And to the extent that peace-seeking tools are part of what I would call "process consciousness," lawyers should be — but are not yet, by disposition or training — at the forefront of practicing justice by considering and shaping processes that are more likely to lead to peaceful and better outcomes. . . .

"PEACE WORK" AND PROBLEM-SOLVING WITH CLIENTS

. . . The work of the lawyer as a conflict resolver is to explore not only legal, but also other needs and interests of the parties (including economic, social, psychological, political, religious, moral and ethical concerns). Utilizing theories, not only of law, but of human behavior (sociology, psychology and economics), lawyers as conflict professionals look for situations where these diverse needs and interests do not compete with each other (the assumption of the legal system that "money is proxy" for all other, often non-economic, interests) but complement each other (the "Homans principle").[37] Complementary needs permit "efficient trades" (Pareto-optimal in economic parlance) or "log-rolling" (in the language of political scientists) — positive-sum, rather than zero-sum, results. Thus, at the level of substantive

---

[14] Intercontinental Hotel Advertisement in National Law Journal, Natl. L. J., Apr. 10, 2000, at A-8.

[37] George Caspar Homans, Social Behavior: Its Elementary Forms (rev. ed. 1974).

problem-solving, lawyers seeking to achieve both maximum gain for individual clients and joint gain for all involved in a particular situation, must employ different kinds of cognitive processes and different technologies and techniques in order to fashion good and lasting solutions to disputes and conflicts. At the relational level, where legal disputes and conflicts either begin with or accumulate a large emotional "residue" of resentment, anger and a sense of injustice (and, therefore, demand for both compensation and retribution), skilled lawyers as peace-makers must develop different kinds of communication skills than the traditional forms of argument, debate and adversarial claiming.

Lawyers interested in pursuing "resolution of human problems" as a dimension of justice (beyond the winning of a legal case) can perform such roles in different ways. Not all pursuers of justice in individual cases are mediators. Serving as the "representative" (restoring one of the lawyer's more conventional roles) in a mediation, a lawyer may still serve a client who needs assistance in stating a claim or articulating a need or interest, but will also have to develop a different mind-set of approaching the other side and seeking creative (perhaps beyond precedent and boilerplate) solutions to problems. For the jurisprudentially sensitive lawyer-conflict resolver, the question of justice in a mediative setting may be framed by asking the parties to reflect on what is "fair" to them. In the words of my friend and mediator-collaborator, Gary Friedman, "law may be relevant, but not determinative" of what is fair to each party. . . . The general law may not serve "justice" in an individual case and so, as long as not otherwise unlawful, individual or party-tailored solutions to legal disputes or problems may depart from particular legal formulations. Legal or "legislated justice" may not always be the same as personal or social justice between parties. Consider as examples: mutually agreed to departures from court-suggested spousal and child support guidelines, departures from sentencing guidelines, liquidated damages clauses in contracts and all future-oriented solutions to disrupted past dealings in both business and personal relationships. Lawyers seeking this kind of "individual" justice between parties (where no important public issue demands transparency or where the parties prefer a highly individualized and flexible, future-oriented solution to their problem) seek both a better quality solution and a more lasting "peace" between the parties than a "command" order of court is likely to accomplish. . . .

Lawyers, . . . may be particularly well suited to participating in these new processes. Lawyers have "process consciousness." Aware of procedural rules and concerned about "voice" and procedural fairness, with proper training (facilitation is quite different from argumentation), lawyers may make ideal process leaders of these new processes and institutions. To the extent that efforts at collaboration and community and democratic decision making still implicate legal requirements (siting disputes require zoning and environmental approvals from formal legal authorities), lawyers are well suited to spot the legal issues and provide for their appropriate coordination with less formal processes. To the extent that these new processes are experiments in constitution-making (as some legal scholars have named them) or simply more direct democratic enterprises than local and national and international government is accustomed to, law-trained individuals may be particularly well suited to serving in these processes, whether as "neutral-facilitators" or advocates or party representatives.

These new roles put lawyers in perhaps unfamiliar ways of functioning as they pursue justice. Focused not just on "winning" the case, but on meeting the needs of multiple sets of parties and affected third parties, and on looking for substantive solutions that will require marshaling new resources, drafting new regulations, creating new institutions (including public and private partnerships in some cases) and implementing and enforcing plans, lawyers will have to learn new skills and develop new conceptual frameworks. It will not be easy to do all of this, particularly in light of robust conventional frames and conceptual models through which we process the world, and because our system is more than several centuries old. But, if I can take anything useful out of the recent events [referring to 9/11] . . . , it is clear we are living in a new world with new problems that will require new forms of processes and solutions if we are to achieve a peaceful and just world. If necessity is the mother of invention, we are certainly in need of the birth of some new ideas for pursuing justice, both at home and in the larger world we now all inhabit. Conventional approaches to pursuing "justice" like our "conventional" approaches of military solutions to international problems may destroy the very "res" we are fighting about (producing a "negative sum" game in negotiation parlance). Just as military solutions to "war" may not bring us peace, an exclusive focus on "legal" needs and interests may not bring us justice. This is true, whether we like it or not.

Notes and Questions

1.19 How would you define "justice"? How do different processes achieve (or fail to achieve) your conception of justice?

1.20 Must all disputes be handled publicly to create rules and norms for the rest of the polity? How can private dispute resolution create reasoned norms for the polity? For the parties? Must justice always be public?

1.21 Who should decide if a particular dispute should be public or private? The parties? The lawyers? Judges? Legislatures? Community or other interest groups? Society?

1.22 Are efficiency and "quality solutions" or "participatory process" always compatible? In other words, do some justifications for appropriate dispute resolution potentially conflict with each other?

1.23 Is justice more likely to be achieved through confrontation or reasoned deliberation? What does it mean to say "if we cannot make enough peace and quiet to have a reasonable dialogue with each other . . . we will not be able to seek justice, let alone substantive solutions to any of our problems"?

Chapter 2 | Negotiation: The Foundation for Mediation

When one door closes another door opens; but we so often look so long and so regretfully upon the closed door, that we do not see the ones which open for us.
— Alexander Graham Bell

A pessimist sees the difficulty in every opportunity; an optimist sees the opportunity in every difficulty.

— Winston Churchill

This chapter examines the process of negotiation, which is the foundational process for mediation. As two or more parties seek to resolve matters between them, they often attempt to negotiate directly (or with lawyer representatives) with each other. When those direct efforts fail, parties may engage the help of a third party — the mediator — who "facilitates" negotiation and manages the process. In order to participate in a mediation, whether as a mediator or as a party or lawyer-representative in a mediation, it is essential you know about the models, frameworks, skill sets, and ethics issues implicated in negotiation processes. For more information about the negotiation process, consult the companion volumes to this book, Negotiation: Processes for Problem Solving (Menkel-Meadow, Schneider & Love, 2005) or Dispute Resolution: Beyond the Adversarial Model (Menkel-Meadow, Love, Schneider & Sternlight, 2005).

Chapter 1 described a variety of conflict responses — avoidance, accommodation, sharing, competition, and collaboration. This chapter will examine how those responses intersect with the most prevalent approaches to negotiation — distributional or positional (or competitive) bargaining and integrative or problem-solving (or collaborative) bargaining. Whether you are examining mediation from the perspective of a party or an attorney or a mediator, focusing first on these different approaches to negotiation helps organize thinking about such issues as what kind of problem, dispute, or transaction is involved (what is at stake); who the parties are (what relationships are at stake); and whether what the parties are negotiating about must be divided (scarce resources) or whether it can be shared and "expanded" to create more resources for all parties. Note that, conceptually, what is at stake and who is doing the negotiation influences the approach chosen, even if negotiators have particular default negotiation or conflict resolution styles or behavioral repertoires.

Many visualize negotiation as something akin to arm wrestling — after a struggle one person will win and the other lose. This view comports with the competitive or distributive orientation described first below. Another view of negotiation, however, envisions a problem-solving process in which parties are brought together because of their dispute, and are challenged to generate as optimal a resolution as possible. Mediators can be helpful to negotiators who adopt either approach, though many mediators will try to shift parties toward problem solving.

If you think of negotiation as involving just two parties, consider that the process often involves an array of parties, more than just a plaintiff and defendant, together with an array of representatives. Internal conflicts among members of one side and conflicts between clients and counsel can add to the complexity. The flexibility of negotiation is one of its strengths. While it is true that many negotiations occur across large tables in conference rooms, many others occur in the hallways, on the phone, in the car, on the courthouse steps, and at other everyday locations. Roger Fisher, coauthor of the best-selling book *Getting to YES* and a well-known negotiation professor, says a negotiation occurs every time that a person tries to influence someone else to do something. So, as you read about negotiation, think about negotiations in which you have been involved — with a parent, sibling, spouse, roommate, friend, neighbor, boss, or child — and how you think about these negotiations. How do they start? How do they proceed? What makes one successful and another the quintessential example of "if I had to do it again . . ."?

Section A examines distributive or positional approaches to negotiation because that is the model most lawyers and law students begin with, assuming one party will "win" or that both parties are trying to maximize their individual gains from the encounter. Section B looks at integrative or problem-solving approaches to negotiation, in which the parties recognize that good negotiations can provide for joint gains, expanded resources, and potentially new ideas for resolving differences between the parties when both desired goals and behaviors are employed differently. Section C explores the effectiveness of negotiators who choose particular styles and tactics to advance their goals. Since mediators coach negotiators to be more effective, this analysis is important for both mediators and negotiators. Finally, in Section D, barriers to effective negotiation and optimal outcomes are examined. Since mediators help break impasses caused by barriers to negotiation, this topic leads to the chapters on mediation.

It is helpful to conceptualize negotiation choices as follows:

Goal →	**Orientation** →	**Behavior** →	**Outcome(s)**[*]
Maximize Gain →	Adversarial →	Competitive →	Impasse, Stalemate; Win/ Lose; Compromise, Split the Difference
Joint Gain →	Problem-Solving →	Collaborative →	Solved Problems; Expanded Resources; New Relationships

---

[*] Derived from Carrie Menkel-Meadow, Toward Another View of Legal Negotiation: The Structure of Problem Solving, 31 UCLA L. Rev. 754, 760 (1984).

A. DISTRIBUTIONAL, ADVERSARIAL, OR POSITIONAL BARGAINING

Distributive bargaining, probably the most popular conception of the negotiation process (at least among those who have not studied negotiation), is also called competitive, adversarial, "zero-sum," or "win-lose." Participants view the process as dividing fixed and limited resources. Where one party gains, the other loses. An analogy is often drawn to a pie — where one person gets a larger piece of pie, another will invariably get less. By contrast, in the context of integrative bargaining, negotiators attempt to "expand the pie" — devising ways to generate more pies, or bigger pies, or even soufflés, rather than allocating a fixed quantity. With respect to positional bargaining, parties can be "soft" and give in to each other's positions, they can cooperate by making reciprocal concessions until a point between positions is reached, or they can be "hard," competitive and adversarial. In this latter approach, negotiators use extreme positions, threats, arguments, and tricks to capture as much as they can for themselves, often withholding or distorting information to mislead their adversary.

The first two excerpts introduce distributive bargaining. Howard Raiffa discusses competitive bargaining and highlights one of its dangers — impasse. Russell Korobkin describes a model for conceptualizing distributive bargaining that he labels zone definition and surplus allocation.

 Howard Raiffa, **THE ART AND SCIENCE OF NEGOTIATION**

33-34 (1982)

In . . . distributive [bargaining] . . . one single issue, such as money, is under contention and the parties have almost strictly opposing interests on that issue: the more you get, the less the other party gets, and — with some exceptions and provisos — you want as much as you can get. Of course, if you are too greedy or if your adversary is too greedy, or if you both are too greedy, you will both fail to come to an agreement that would mean profits for both of you (that is why I speak of "almost" strictly opposing interests). Benjamin Franklin aptly summed it up: "Trades would not take place unless it were advantageous to the parties concerned. Of course, it is better to strike as good a bargain as one's bargaining position permits. The worst outcome is when, by overreaching greed, no bargain is struck, and a trade that could have been advantageous to both parties does not come off at all."

 Russell Korobkin, **A POSITIVE THEORY OF LEGAL NEGOTIATION**

88 Geo. L. J. 1789, 1791-1794, 1799, 1816-1817, 1821, 1825, 1829 (2000)

This article presents a new dichotomy that creates a clear theoretical structure for viewing the legal negotiation process. This "zone definition/surplus allocation" dichotomy provides a complete description of the negotiation process: *every* action taken by negotiators in preparation for negotiations or at the bargaining table fits into one of these categories.

First, negotiators attempt to define the bargaining zone — the distance between the reservation points (or "walkaway" points) of the two parties — in the manner most advantageous to their respective clients. I call this activity "zone definition." . . .

Second, negotiators attempt to convince their opponent to agree to a single "deal point" within the bargaining zone. I call this activity "surplus allocation." Surplus allocation effectively divides the cooperative surplus that the parties create by reaching an agreement. For both parties, transacting at any point within the bargaining zone is more desirable than not reaching agreement, but each knows that the same is true for the other. Once the bargaining zone is established, there is no economically obvious way for the parties to select a deal point. As a result, surplus allocation usually requires that negotiators appeal to community norms of either procedural or substantive fairness. . . .

I. ZONE DEFINITION

In any negotiation, the maximum amount that a buyer will pay for a good, service, or other legal entitlement is called his "reservation point" or, if the deal being negotiated is a monetary transaction, his "reservation price" (RP). The minimum amount that a seller would accept for that item is her RP. If the buyer's RP is higher than the seller's, the distance between the two points is called the "bargaining zone."

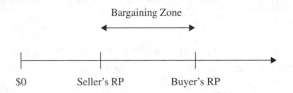

Figure 1
Reservation Points That Create a Bargaining Zone

For example, suppose Esau, looking to get into business for himself, is willing to pay up to $200,000 for Jacob's catering business, while Jacob, interested in retiring, is willing to sell the business for any amount over $150,000. This difference between Esau's and Jacob's RPs creates a $50,000 bargaining zone. At any price between $150,000 and $200,000, both parties are better off agreeing to the sale of the business than they are reaching no agreement and going their separate ways.

The same structure used to describe a transactional negotiation can be used to describe a dispute resolution negotiation. Suppose that Goliath has filed suit against David for battery. David is willing to pay up to $90,000 to settle the case out of court — essentially, to buy Goliath's legal right to bring suit — while Goliath will "sell" his right for any amount over $60,000. These RPs create a $30,000 bargaining zone between $60,000 and $90,000. Any settlement in this range would leave both parties better off than they would be without a settlement.

In contrast, if the seller's RP is higher than the buyer's RP, there is no bargaining zone. In this circumstance, there is no sale price that would make both parties better off than they would be by not reaching a negotiated agreement. Put another way, the parties would be better off not reaching a negotiated agreement. If Jacob will not part with his business for less than $150,000 and Esau will not pay more than $100,000 for it, there is no bargaining zone. If David will pay up to $50,000 to settle Goliath's claim, but Goliath will not accept any amount less than $60,000, again there is no bargaining zone. An agreement in either case would leave at least one party, and possibly both parties, worse off than if they were to decide not to make a deal.

Knowledge of the parameters of the bargaining zone, which is created by the two parties' reservation points, is the most critical information for the negotiator to possess. Those parameters tell the negotiator both whether any agreement is possible and, if so, identify the range of possible deal points. At the same time, the negotiator has an interest in adjusting the parameters of the bargaining zone to his advantage. A buyer not only wants to know his and the seller's RPs, he wishes to make both lower, or at least make both *appear* lower to the seller. . . .

Esau wants to know his and Jacob's RPs, but he also would like to shift both numbers, and therefore the bargaining range, lower. Assuming Esau knows his RP is $200,000 and learns Jacob's is $150,000, Esau knows that an agreement is possible for some amount greater than the latter figure and less than the former. If he could reduce Jacob's RP to $120,000 and his own to $170,000, however, the bargaining zone would remain the same size, but its changed parameters would suggest that Esau would be likely to buy the business for a lower price. Esau could achieve the same advantage if Jacob *believes* the parties' RPs are $120,000 and $170,000 respectively, even if the RPs objectively are $150,000 and $200,000. . . .

Efforts at persuasion in negotiation are best understood as attempts to satisfy one or both of two goals: (1) to shift the bargaining zone to the advantage of the negotiator, either by convincing the opponent that his RP is worse than he believed before beginning negotiations or that the negotiator's RP is better than previously believed; and (2) to establish an objective — and therefore "fair" — method of agreeing on a sale price that falls within the bargaining zone. . . .

II. SURPLUS ALLOCATION

Through zone definition, negotiators establish a bounded set of possible negotiated outcomes, or "deal points." If the bargaining zone consists of only a single point, it is the only possible deal point. Unless the parties mistakenly believe that there is no bargaining zone at all, they should reach a deal at precisely that point. But in many, and perhaps most, cases in which a bargaining zone exists, the zone will include a range of potential deal points. In this situation, agreement at each possible deal point is superior for both parties to not reaching an agreement, or, put in economic terms, every deal point is Pareto* superior to no deal. The problem is that, in this situation, no potential deal point is obviously superior to any other. If Esau is willing to pay $200,000 for Jacob's business, and Jacob is willing to accept $150,000, a sale clearly should take place, but it is unclear whether the price should be $150,000, $200,000, or any amount in between.

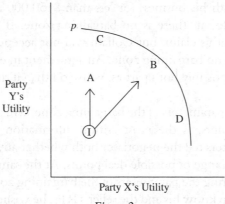

Figure 2
Pareto Frontier

How do negotiators solve this dilemma and agree on a single deal point? This part argues that bargainers usually rely on socially constructed norms of reaching agreement that are based implicitly on notions of fair dealing. Failure to agree on how to fairly allocate the cooperative surplus can, perversely, cause negotiators to fail to consummate a deal even when both would be better off striking a deal than pursuing their BATNAs.† . . .

Many common negotiating tactics are best understood as attempts to establish a procedure that the other party will view as "fair" for agreeing on a deal point within the bargaining zone. In employing such tactics, the negotiator may have either of two motives. He might believe that the procedure is equitable to both parties, and the resulting deal point will thus create a mutually beneficial transaction in which neither side gets the better of the other. Alternatively, he might attempt to establish a procedure that will lead to an agreement that benefits him or his client substantially more than it benefits the other negotiator. Whether the negotiator's motives are communitarian or individualistic, however, the procedures must have the appearance of equity in order to win acceptance. . . .

---

* The Pareto frontier refers to economic maximization as [depicted in the figure above]. For example, assume that X and Y agree on initial solution I. By moving to solution A, X's utility is the same and Y's is increased. A is *Pareto superior* to I since it is better for one party without being worse for the other. If X and Y were able to agree on B, this solution would increase both X and Y's utility — both parties would be better off. On the other hand, C and D are other solutions along the Pareto curve where X or Y would have to give up something in order for the other to gain. The lesson is that either solutions A or B are better for the parties and that it makes sense for parties to push for Pareto optimal solutions.
† BATNA stands for the best alternative to a negotiated agreement. This concept, coined in *Getting to YES*, by Fisher, Ury and Patton, is based on the idea that you should reach agreement only if your agreement is better than your alternatives, including your best alternative.

Singling out a deal point requires the parties to agree on what is fair. In many negotiations, agreement is achieved by the parties acting consistently with procedural norms of bargaining behavior such as reciprocity, splitting the difference, and the selection of prominent focal points. The deal point that emerges from a procedurally fair process is accepted by the parties as itself fair, assuming it lies within the bargaining zone. In other negotiations, the parties instead negotiate over what specific deal point would be most substantively fair....

As is true of any criteria that claims substantive fairness, claims of morality or merit are only as valuable as the similarities in the negotiators' social constructions of fairness. When negotiators share a set of social values, substantive fairness claims are most likely to lead to agreement on a deal point....

Notes and Questions

2.1 If the task of an attorney is to maximize the benefit for her client, how does distributive bargaining achieve such maximization? What roles do you see for the mediator in distributive bargaining?

2.2 Robert Condlin writes that negotiation actually consists of three tasks: assessment — weighing the other side; exchange — the process of offer, concession, and agreement; and persuasion — convincing the other side to view you and your side favorably. Robert Condlin, Cases on Both Sides: Patterns of Argument in Legal Dispute Negotiation, 44 Md. L. Rev. 65 (1985). Gerald Williams posits that there are four stages in a negotiation: orientation and positioning; argumentation and concessions; emergence and crisis; and agreement or final breakdown. Gerald R. Williams, Legal Negotiation and Settlement (1983). How are these frameworks in (or out of) synch with Korobkin's view?

2.3 Frank Sander and Jeffrey Rubin point out differences between negotiations where parties are entering into a relationship (deal-making negotiation) and negotiations where parties are considering whether to remain in or how to leave the relationship (dispute settlement negotiation). Deal making looks forward and is interest-based and problem-solving; dispute settlement looks backward and is rights-based and adversarial. Frank E.A. Sander & Jeffrey Rubin, The Janus Quality of Negotiation: Deal Making and Dispute Settlement, 4 Neg. J. 109 (1988). Mediators are more prevalent in the dispute settlement context. What distinctions can you see between deal making and dispute settlement? Michael Moffitt criticizes this dichotomy in Disputes as Opportunities to Create Value in Michael L. Moffitt & Robert C. Bordone, The Handbook of Dispute Resolution (2005).

2.4 In a recent article, Gerald Williams presents a different set of stages that negotiators go through in resolving conflict. These stages are applicable more explicitly to dispute settlement than deal making. Williams suggests that negotiations resolving a conflict between two parties are often more effective than adjudication because parties can experience genuine reconciliation by having a change of heart that fully resolves any feelings about the current conflict and prevents future conflicts with the same parties or regarding the same issues. Williams proposes a five-step model of the stages that clients are likely to go through on their road to resolving a conflict during negotiation:

1. *Denial*—resistance to admit being the party at fault in the conflict.
2. *Acceptance*—Acceptance that the party him- or herself is part of the problem.
3. *Sacrifice*—To solve the conflict, the parties each must make a sacrifice.
4. *Leap of faith*—A party offers a willingness to make a sacrifice to move toward a resolution. A leap of faith is inherently risky, and often the most powerful leap of faith is a sincere apology.
5. *Renewal of healing from conflict*—If denial, acceptance, sacrifice, and leap of faith all occur, then the parties are ready to take more leaps of faith and move toward agreement. Renewal occurs to the extent that the parties do not simply resolve the conflict but are better off than they were before the conflict.

Gerald Williams, Negotiation as a Healing Process, 1996 J. Disp. Resol. 1, 33 (1996). Think back to a recent significant conflict. How do these psychological stages relate to your experience? Do you agree that negotiation can heal? How can you as a lawyer help your client move through the healing stages? How do these stages comport with Korobkin's map of negotiation or with Williams' five stages described above?

There are a variety of approaches, strategies, and tactics that negotiators adopt within the context of distributive or positional bargaining. Below, three such approaches are examined: accommodative, cooperative, and competitive.

1. Accommodating Approaches to Positional Bargaining

One approach to a negotiation when there are limited resources to divide is to be more concerned with the other sides' needs and happiness. Kenneth Thomas, in Chapter 1, described this orientation as "accommodative." Roger Fisher, William Ury, and Bruce Patton, in the excerpt below, call this approach "soft bargaining." While this approach is completely different from the adversarial approach, it shares the assumption that a distributive negotiation exists. The soft approach is used when the relationship is *so* important that accommodating your counterpart is more important than your own interests; for example, a groom might let the bride choose the wedding date regardless of his own preference.

 Roger Fisher, William Ury & Bruce Patton, GETTING TO YES

8-9 (2d ed. 1991)

The soft negotiating game emphasizes the importance of building and maintaining a relationship. Within families and among friends much negotiation takes place in this way. The process tends to be efficient, at least to the extent of producing results quickly. As each party competes with the other in being more generous and more forthcoming, an agreement becomes highly likely. But it may not be a wise one. The results may not be as tragic as in the O. Henry story about an impoverished couple in which the loving wife sells her hair in order to buy a handsome chain for her husband's watch, and the unknowing husband sells his watch in order to buy beautiful combs for his wife's hair. However, any negotiation primarily concerned with the relationship runs the risk of producing a sloppy agreement.

More seriously, pursuing a soft and friendly form of positional bargaining makes you vulnerable to someone who plays a hard game of positional bargaining. In positional bargaining, a hard game dominates a soft one. If the hard bargainer insists on concessions and makes threats while the soft bargainer yields in order to avoid confrontation and insists on agreement, the negotiating game is biased in favor of the hard player. The process will produce an agreement, although it may not be a wise one. It will certainly be more favorable to the hard positional bargainer than to the soft one. If your response to sustained, hard positional bargaining is soft positional bargaining, you will probably lose your shirt.

Notes and Questions

2.5 Many historians use British Prime Minister Neville Chamberlain's 1938 appeasement of Hitler as a worst-case example of the possible consequences of soft bargaining. To avoid war, Chamberlain agreed not to defend Czechoslovakia against a German invasion if Hitler agreed to end his territorial ambitions at that point. Although Chamberlain kept his promise, Hitler did not. Can you think of other positive or negative examples of soft bargaining?

2.6 When would soft bargaining make sense? What goals might soft bargaining further?

2. Cooperative Approaches to Positional Bargaining

Another approach to positional bargaining is to engage in a predictable "dance" where each side makes concessions until a mid-point between positions is reached. This familiar cooperative approach is described by Donald Gifford in the excerpt which follows.

 Donald G. Gifford, **A CONTEXT-BASED THEORY OF STRATEGY SELECTION IN LEGAL NEGOTIATION**

46 Ohio St. L.J. 41, 52-54 (1985)

A view of human nature different than that upon which the competitive strategy is premised, with its emphasis on undermining the confidence of opposing counsel, underlies most collaborative interaction. In everyday events, even when they are deciding how to divide a limited resource between them, two negotiators often seek to reach an agreement which is fair and equitable to both parties and seek to build an interpersonal relationship based on trust. This approach to negotiation can be designated the cooperative strategy. The cooperative negotiator initiates granting concessions in order to create both a moral obligation to reciprocate and a relationship built on trust that is conducive to achieving a fair agreement.

The cooperative negotiator does not view making concessions as a necessity resulting from a weak bargaining position or a loss of confidence in the value of her case. Rather, she values concessions as an affirmative negotiating technique designed to capitalize on the opponent's desire to reach a fair and just agreement and to maintain an accommodative working relationship. Proponents of the cooperative strategy believe that negotiators are motivated not only by individualistic or competitive desires to maximize their own utilities, but also by collectivistic desires to reach a fair solution. Cooperative negotiators assert that the competitive strategy often leads to resentment between the parties and a breakdown of negotiations.

According to Professor Otomar Bartos, an originator of the cooperative strategy, the negotiator should begin negotiations not with a maximalist position, but rather with a more moderate opening bid that is both favorable to him and barely acceptable to the opponent. Once two such opening bids are on the table, the negotiators should determine the midpoint between the two opening bids and regard it as a fair and equitable outcome. External facts, such as how large a responsive concession the negotiator expects from the opponent, whether she is representing a tough constituency that would view large concessions unfavorably, and whether she is under a tight time deadline and wants to expedite the process by making a large concession, affect the size of the negotiator's first concession. According to Professor Bartos, the negotiator should then expect the opponent to reciprocate with a concession of similar size so that the midpoint between the parties' positions remains the same as it was after the realistic opening bids were made. The concessions by the parties are fair, according to Bartos, as long as the parties do not need to revise their initial expectations about the substance of the agreement.

The term *cooperative strategy* embraces a larger variety of negotiation tactics than Bartos' detailed model. Cooperative strategies include any strategies that aim to develop trust between the parties and that focus on the expectation that the opponent will match concessions ungrudgingly. Endemic to all cooperative strategies is the question of how the negotiator should respond if the opponent does not match her concessions and does not reciprocate her goodwill. The major weakness of the cooperative approach is its vulnerability to exploitation by the competitive negotiator. The cooperative negotiator is severely disadvantaged if her opponent fails to reciprocate her concessions. Cooperative negotiation theorists suggest a variety of responses when concessions are not matched. Professor Bartos recommends that the negotiator "stop making further concessions until the opponent catches up."[100]

Because of its vulnerability to exploitation, the cooperative theory may not initially appear to be a viable alternative to the competitive strategy. As mentioned

---

[100] Otomar Bartos, Simple Model of Negotiation: A Sociological Point of View, in The Negotiation Process: Theories & Applications 23 (I. Zartman ed., 1978).

previously, in tightly controlled experiments with simulated negotiations, the competitive strategy generally produces better results. However, in actual practice, the competitive approach results in more impasses and greater distrust between the parties. Furthermore, most people tend to be cooperative in orientation and trusting of others. Professor Williams found that sixty-five percent of the attorneys he surveyed used a cooperative approach.[102] This, of course, means that in a majority of cases the cooperative negotiator will not be exploited by her opponent, because the opponent also uses a cooperative approach. Most cooperative negotiators probably would not feel comfortable using the competitive negotiators' aggressive tactics, which are designed to undermine the opponent and his case. Nor would they relish living and working in the mistrustful milieu which may result from the use of the competitive strategy.

Notes and Questions

2.7 Compare Gifford's description of cooperative behavior with the description of soft bargaining in *Getting to YES*. What are the similarities? What are the differences?

2.8 Gifford describes an offer-counteroffer negotiation ritual — the negotiation dance. If you foresee such a ritual, where should you start the dance? What is the argument for starting with a moderate opening bid (as a cooperative negotiator might do), rather than an extreme offer that a competitive bargainer would likely make?

3. Competitive Approaches to Positional Bargaining

Unlike an accommodative or a cooperative bargainer, a competitive bargainer has little concern for the welfare of his adversary or a continuing or future relationship. He seeks to "win" the negotiation. Such a bargainer would be likely to: conceal information; make an extreme opening offer; make few and small concessions; and use threats and arguments. The excerpt that follows, describing tactics that flow from a competitive, adversarial orientation, is taken from a handbook for public interest lawyers authored by Michael Meltsner and Philip Schrag. As you read the following, consider what assumptions the authors make about the tactics they suggest.

 Michael Meltsner & Philip G. Schrag, **NEGOTIATION**

Public Interest Advocacy: Materials for Clinical Legal Education
232-238 (1974)

This section catalogs a number of successful negotiating tactics. Of course, not every tactic described is appropriate for every negotiation; the use of each depends on the

---

[102] Gerald R. Williams, Legal Negotiation and Settlement 53 (1983).

particular case and especially upon the perceived relative strengths of the parties during the bargaining process. In general, a party who appears to himself and to his adversary to be strongly desirous of negotiations is less able to use the more powerful tactics set forth. Of course, even the attorney who must negotiate from a position of perceived weakness should be familiar with the tactics that may be used against him, so that he may defend himself as best he can. . . .

A. PREPARATORY TACTICS

1. Arrange to negotiate on your own turf. Whenever possible, insist that the meeting be held in your office, or in another setting where you will feel more comfortable than your adversary; and where he will be at a psychological disadvantage because he has had to come to you. . . .

Neighborhood poverty lawyers who negotiate with attorneys for banks, realty corporations, and other large firms have added a new twist to the "home base" tactic by attempting to maneuver their adversaries into entering the ghetto, sometimes for the first time in their lives. Their fears for their physical safety and their shock at viewing local housing conditions may reduce their bargaining effectiveness. . . .

2. Balance or slightly outnumber the other side. Attempt to ascertain or to estimate the number of persons the other side is bringing to the meeting, and do your best to ensure that your side is represented by the same number of persons, or by exactly one more person. In a bargaining session where two negotiate against one or three against two, the side with fewer representatives is usually at a disadvantage: it will tire more readily, and the other side will be better able to control the flow of discussion. . . . On the other hand, an adversary who feels cornered because he is substantially out-numbered may feel too insecure to bargain seriously. Be prepared therefore to justify the presence of additional representatives on the ground that they have technical expertise necessary to successful completion of the settlement.

3. Time the negotiations to advantage. When one side wants to get the discussion over with quickly, it usually loses. . . . Some public interest lawyers make it a point to schedule negotiations with government attorneys at 4:00 P.M., on the assumption that civil service lawyers expect to go home at 5:00 and will bargain much more quickly and carelessly at that hour than they would in the morning. Similarly, a lawyer who is not used to working on weekends will probably negotiate more poorly on a Saturday or Sunday than during the week.

4. Know the facts thoroughly. An unprepared lawyer is usually at a severe disad-vantage (unless he is deliberately unprepared so that the negotiations will be delayed). He will constantly have to apologize for his ignorance and his apologies often create a subtle pressure to concede points as to which his adversary is better informed. In addition, an unprepared lawyer may feel inner pressure to compromise because he does not wish to reveal his ignorance by participation in an extended discussion.

5. Lock yourself in. This is a risky but powerful prenegotiation tactic and should be used only with the greatest care. In cases that have attracted public attention, an attorney can increase his bargaining power by announcing publicly a position from which he will not retreat so that his adversary knows that he will lose face if he does in fact retreat. . . .

6. Designate one of your demands a "precondition." If the other side wants to talk (for example, if it requested the negotiations), a lawyer can often improve the chances of favorable outcome by calling one of his demands a "precondition" to negotiations. . . .

B. INITIAL TACTICS

7. When it is in your interest, make the other side tender the first offer. The party making the first offer suffers the disadvantage of conceding that it really wants to settle. Furthermore, it may make an offer that actually concedes more than the other side thought it could get at the end of the negotiating process. Of course, the attorney who receives such a surprising offer will declare his shock that so little is being tendered, and will demand much more. One surprisingly successful technique for evoking the first offer is to remain silent. Few people can tolerate more than a few seconds of silence during a negotiation; most feel compelled to say something to break the ice. Or you might simply say to your adversary, "Why don't you start by giving us an idea of your position." There are situations, however, where by making the first offer a party advantageously sets the bounds for the entire discussion. The negotiations may never leave the questions raised initially; other questions, which may be the weakest from your point of view, will fall into place as part of a general wrap up of the deal.

8. Make your first demand very high. Outrageously unreasonable demands become more justifiable after substantial discussion. And even if an initially high demand is rejected, it makes a subsequent demand that is almost as high appear to be a more reasonable compromise. . . .

Nevertheless, some demands are too outrageous to make. They will encourage your adversary to believe that you are not seriously interested in bargaining despite your protestation to the contrary.

9. Place your major demands at the beginning of the agenda. There seems to be a "honeymoon" period, in which negotiators make compromises more freely, at the outset of a negotiation, and another such period at the very conclusion. By forcing your adversary to deal at the outset, when he wants most to compromise, with the items of greatest interest to you, or at the end, when he has invested many hours or weeks of time in negotiating and wants a return on his investment, you can improve your client's position.

10. Make the other side make the first compromise. There is a psychological advantage in benefiting from the first concession. Studies indicate that losers generally make the first concessions in negotiating a dispute.

C. TACTICS GENERALLY

11. Use two negotiators who play different roles. The famous "Mutt and Jeff" technique, in which police use one friendly and one nasty interrogator to extract a statement from a reluctant defendant, works very well in negotiation. Two lawyers for the same side feign an internal dispute concerning their position; one takes the hard line, offering almost no compromise, while the other appears to desire to make small concessions, and occasionally he prevails. . . .

12. Invoke law or justice. To a surprising extent, lawyers are impressed with the citation of authority and laymen tend to be overwhelmed by a reference to a case or statute. If your adversary seems to react to it, quote or advert to legal authority as often as possible, particularly if you can assert that the position you urge is legally compelled, or that the one he desires is legally prohibited, or at least troublesome. . . . If the law is not on your side, avoid using it. Instead, invoke more general principles of justice, or whatever other kind of authority (for example, public pressure) seems to support your position.

13. Be tough — especially against a patsy. Unfortunately, when one party is conciliatory and the other cantankerous, the imbalance usually favors the competitive player in the short run. . . .

14. Appear irrational when it seems helpful. This is a dangerous but often successful tactic. An adversary who is himself an expert negotiator can be thrown off base considerably by a lawyer who doesn't seem to play the same game; for example, one who seems to behave irrationally. Premier Nikita Khrushchev significantly increased the deterrent power of the relatively small Soviet nuclear force by banging his shoe on the table at the United Nations in 1960; he gave the impression of being somewhat imbalanced — a man who might unleash nuclear weapons upon even a slight provocation.

15. Raise some of your demands as the negotiations progress. The conventional model of negotiation contemplates both sides lowering their demands until a compromise is finally reached. But the highly successful negotiator backtracks; he raises one of his demands for every two concessions he makes and occasionally reopens for further discussion topics that everyone thought had been settled and laid aside. . . .

16. Claim that you do not have authority to compromise. You can make a topic non-negotiable by persuading your adversary that you do not have, and cannot obtain, the authority to go beyond a certain point. The freshman negotiator sometimes makes the mistake of trying to impress the other side with his authority; the expert modestly explains that he has very little authority, and that his client's adamant. . . .

17. Clear the agreement with your client before signing it. Before you reach final agreement, you will want to consult with your client. Checking with the client is not only an obligation that you owe to him, it is an important bargaining tactic. It enables you to delay the proceedings while you check, and it gives you a chance to consider any errors you might have made before you sign.

D. POST-NEGOTIATION TACTICS

18. Make your adversary feel good. Never gloat over the terms of a settlement. Not only is such behavior boorish, but it may provoke an adversary to reopen negotiations or to adopt a different and stronger negotiating posture the next time you deal with him. If you can do so with candor, feel free to tell opposing counsel what a hard bargain he drove and what a good job he did for his client. If you meet an adversary and his client together, tell the client what a good job his lawyer did for him. This may please the client, but it certainly will please the lawyer and perhaps make him look forward to doing business with you again. . . .

19. After agreement has been reached, have your client reject it and raise his demands. This is the most ethically dubious of the tactics listed here, but there will be occasions where a lawyer will have to defend against it or even to employ it. After laboring for hours, days, or weeks to work out a settlement, a negotiator is likely to be dismayed by the prospect of the agreement falling through. As a result, his adversary may be able to obtain last-minute concessions. Of course, such a strategy can boomerang. It may so anger an adversary that he simply refuses to bargain, even though bargaining is still in his interest, or he may fight fire with fire by increasing his own demands.

20. Reduce the agreement to writing yourself and except in special circumstances do it promptly. Unless the terms of settlement are reduced to writing a lawyer can never be certain that he has an agreement. Counsel may be laboring under a mistaken impression that they have settled when in fact they have not resolved all of the questions that divided them. Reduction of terms to writing is an effective means of discovering whether there is actual agreement. Not only is the written instrument evidence of the agreement, but the formulation of its terms will tend to govern the conduct of the parties in the future. Quite often the terms that have been agreed upon will be subject to differing interpretations, some of which favor your side, some of which favor your adversary's side. You should, therefore, volunteer to undertake the labor of drafting the agreement. By doing so, you can choose language which reflects your interpretation of the terms agreed upon. . . . If an adversary writes the first draft, you should be prepared to go over it line by line and to rewrite every word, if necessary.

Notes and Questions

2.9 Are there some tactics of Meltsner and Schrag that seem to be good advice regardless of which approach to negotiation you choose? Which of the tactics are the most risky?

2.10 Meltsner and Schrag are writing for a certain kind of lawyer (public interest). How might this affect their advice?

2.11 In *Beyond Winning*, the authors list the top ten tactics their readers and clients have reported to them:

1. Extreme claims followed by small, slow concessions;
2. Commitment tactics ["I already promised my partner that I would not go higher than $25,000"];
3. Take-it-or-leave-it offers;
4. Inviting unreciprocated offers;
5. Flinch [upping the price until the other side physically flinches];
6. Personal insults and feather ruffling;
7. Bluffing, puffing, and lying;
8. Threats and warnings;
9. Belittling the other party's alternatives;
10. Good cop, bad cop.

Robert H. Mnookin, Scott R. Peppet & Andrew S. Tulumello, Beyond Winning: Negotiating to Create Value in Deals and Disputes, 24-25 (2000).

What similarities and differences do you see among the tactics listed by these authors and in the Mettsner and Schrag excerpt? Which tactics would you most fear facing? How could you respond to them?

2.12 One study of negotiators found that adversarial negotiators have become nastier and more negative since the late 1970s. Furthermore, these adversarial negotiators are viewed by their peers as far less effective (25 percent were viewed as effective in 1976; 9 percent were viewed as effective in 1999). Andrea Kupfer Schneider, Shattering Negotiation Myths: Empirical Evidence on the Effectiveness of Negotiation Style, 7 Harv. Neg of L. Rev. 143 (2002). If being adversarial runs a high risk of being ineffective, why do you think negotiators choose this style?

2.13 Note Meltsner and Schrag's vocabulary: "adversary" and "negotiate against" and "lose." These words signal an adversarial competition. If one were thinking in terms of cooperative or collaborative negotiation, the vocabulary might shift to "partner" for the other negotiating party. In an engaging analysis of language used to describe negotiation and its importance, Jonathan Cohen urges the use of "counterpart" to capture both the competitive and collaborative aspects of negotiation (counter = against; and part = partner). Jonathan R. Cohen, Adversaries? Partners? How About Counterparts? On Metaphors in the Practice and Teaching of Negotiation and Dispute Resolution, 20 Conflict Resol. Q. 433 (2003). How would you describe the other party in a negotiation? What insight does this provide to your own negotiation approach?

2.14 As suggested in Notes and Questions 2.12, there are risks associated with adversarial bargaining:

> What is astounding about the conventional literature on tactics and strategies is the assumption of universal applicability. Strategic exhortations are offered without reference to how negotiations might vary in different contexts or under different circumstances, such as under the influence of various clients' desires. Negotiators are admonished to never make the first offer and to always draft the final agreement as if there were a few simple rules negotiators should obey in order always to maximize individual gain. . . .
>
> The recommended strategies may not work even on their own terms. Many commentators have offered a number of competitive strategies designed to force the other side to capitulate. The difficulty with all of these strategic exhortations is the assumption that the other side can be bullied, manipulated or deceived. It is true, for example, that some will wilt under pressure, but others are likely to respond in kind. Moreover, even those who wilt at the negotiation table may be resentful later and exercise their power either by failing to follow through on the agreement or by seeking revenge the next time the parties meet.
>
> Many of these strategic exhortations may work against the negotiator, even in an adversarial negotiation. For example, if, as Meltsner & Schrag suggest, the negotiator chooses his own office for greater comfort in negotiating, the other side may be less comfortable and less amenable to open discussions. In addition, choosing one's own office for comfort minimizes the chances of learning about the other party by not negotiating on their "turf" or by keeping the other party from its sources of information, such as office files. On a more mundane level,

the choice of one's own office for comfort may actually increase discomfort by encouraging interruptions from co-workers and telephone calls. Thus, these strategic exhortations, designed to put the other party at a disadvantage, may not even be effective on their own terms. The literature is replete with advice to overpower and take advantage of the other side. But as one of the popular guides to negotiation has so wisely stated, "a tactic perceived is no tactic." If two competitive negotiators read the same literature it is difficult to see how these strategies will be employed to maximize individual gain. Who will win when both sides know all the same tricks?

Carrie Menkel-Meadow, Toward Another View of Legal Negotiation: The Structure of Problem Solving, 31 UCLA L. Rev. 754, 776, 778-780 (1984). Do you think the potential benefits of competitive bargaining outweigh the risks? If so, under what circumstances?

B. INTEGRATIVE, INTEREST-BASED, OR PROBLEM-SOLVING NEGOTIATION

Many beginning negotiators assume that the three approaches presented in the previous section — accommodating, cooperative, and competitive positional bargaining — are the primary choices of strategy in a negotiation. However, these strategies focus only on distributive aspects of negotiation — dividing the pie — rather than on other activities that can expand the pie. In the next excerpt Carrie Menkel-Meadow introduces problem-solving negotiation. Negotiators may "expand the pie" and create value by adopting an interest or needs-based frame of reference, but at some point they may still have to distribute a fixed amount — often the last issue on the table. Consequently, both perspectives are useful.

 Carrie Menkel-Meadow, **TOWARD ANOTHER VIEW OF LEGAL NEGOTIATION: THE STRUCTURE OF PROBLEM SOLVING**

31 UCLA L. Rev. 754, 795-801 (1984)

Parties to a negotiation typically have underlying needs or objectives — what they hope to achieve, accomplish, and/or be compensated for as a result of the dispute or transaction. Although litigants typically ask for relief in the form of damages, this relief is actually a proxy for more basic needs or objectives. By attempting to uncover those underlying needs, the problem-solving model presents opportunities for discovering greater numbers of and better quality solutions. It offers the possibility of meeting a greater variety of needs both directly and by trading off different needs, rather than forcing a zero-sum battle over a single item.

The principle underlying such an approach is that unearthing a greater number of the actual needs of the parties will create more possible solutions because not all needs will be mutually exclusive. As a corollary, because not all individuals value the same things in the same way, the exploitation of differential or complementary needs will produce a wider variety of solutions which more closely meet the parties' needs.

A few examples may illustrate these points. In personal injury actions courts usually award monetary damages. Plaintiffs, however, commonly want this money for specific purposes. For instance, an individual who has been injured in a car accident may desire compensation for any or all of the following items: past and future medical expenses, rehabilitation and compensation for the cost of rehabilitation, replacement of damaged property such as a car and the costs of such replacement, lost income, compensation for lost time, pain and suffering, the loss of companionship with one's family, friends and fellow employees and employer, lost opportunities to engage in activities which may no longer be possible, such as backpacking or playing basketball with one's children, vindication or acknowledgment of fault by the responsible party, and retribution or punishment of the person who was at fault. In short, the injured person seeks to be returned to the same physical, psychological, social and economic state she was in before the accident occurred. Because this may be impossible, the plaintiff needs money in order to buy back as many of these things as possible.

Some of the parties' needs may not be compensable, directly or indirectly. For example, some injuries may be impossible to fully rehabilitate. A physical disability, a scar, or damage to a personal or business reputation may never be fully eradicated. Thus, the underlying needs produced by these injuries may not be susceptible to full and/or monetary satisfaction. The need to be regarded as totally normal or completely honorable can probably never be met, but the party in a negotiation will be motivated by the desire to satisfy as fully as possible these underlying human needs. Some parties may have a need to get "as much X as possible," such as in demands for money for pain and suffering. This demand simply may represent the best proxy available for satisfying the unsatisfiable desire to be made truly whole — that is to be put back in the position of no accident at all. It also may represent a desire to save for a rainy day or to maximize power, fame or love.

It is also important to recognize that *both* parties have such needs. For example, in the personal injury case above, the defendant may have the same need for vindication or retribution if he believes he was not responsible for the accident. In addition, the defendant may need to be compensated for his damaged car and injured body. He will also have needs with respect to how much, when and how he may be able to pay the monetary damages because of other uses for the money. . . .

To the extent that negotiators focus exclusively on "winning" the greatest amount of money, they focus on only one form of need. The only flexibility in tailoring an agreement may lie in the choice of ways to structure monetary solutions, including one shot payments, installments, and structured settlements. By looking, however, at what the parties desire money for, there may be a variety of solutions that will satisfy the parties more fully and directly. For example, when an injured plaintiff needs physical rehabilitation, if the defendant can provide the plaintiff directly with rehabilitation services, the defendant may save money and the plaintiff may gain the needed rehabilitation at lower cost. In addition, if the defendant can provide the plaintiff with a job that provides physical rehabilitation, the plaintiff may not only receive income which could be used to purchase more rehabilitation, but be further rehabilitated in the form of the psychological self-worth which accompanies such employment. Admittedly, none of these solutions may fully satisfy the injured plaintiff, but some or all may be equally beneficial to the plaintiff, and the latter two may be preferable to the defendant because they are less costly.

Understanding that the other party's needs are not necessarily as assumed may present an opportunity for arriving at creative solutions. Traditionally, lawyers approaching negotiations from the adversarial model view the other side as an enemy to be defeated. By examining the underlying needs of the other side, the lawyer may instead see opportunities for solutions that would not have existed before based upon the recognition of different, but not conflicting, preferences.

An example from the psychological literature illustrates this point.[167] Suppose that a husband and wife have two weeks in which to take their vacation. The husband prefers the mountains and the wife prefers the seaside. If vacation time is limited and thus a scarce resource, the couple may engage in adversarial negotiation about where they should go. The simple compromise situation, if they engage in distributive bargaining, would be to split the two weeks of vacation time spending one week in the mountains and one week at the ocean. This solution is not likely to be satisfying, however, because of the lost time and money in moving from place to place and in getting used to a new hotel room and locale. In addition to being happy only half of the time, each party to the negotiation has incurred transaction costs associated with this solution. Other "compromise" solutions might include alternating preferences on a year to year basis, taking separate vacations, or taking a longer vacation at a loss of pay. Assuming that husband and wife want to vacation together, all of these solutions may leave something to be desired by at least one of the parties.

By examining their underlying preferences, however, the parties might find additional solutions that could make both happy at less cost. Perhaps the husband prefers the mountains because he likes to hike and engage in stream fishing. Perhaps the wife enjoys swimming, sunbathing and seafood. By exploring these underlying preferences the couple might find vacation spots that permit all of these activities: a mountain resort on a large lake, or a seaside resort at the foot of mountains. By examining their underlying needs the parties can see solutions that satisfy many more of their preferences, and the "sum of the utilities" to the couple as a whole is greater than what they would have achieved by compromising.

In addition, by exploring whether they attach different values to their preferences they may be able to arrive at other solutions by trading items. The wife in our example might be willing to give up ocean fresh seafood if she can have fresh stream or lake trout, and so, with very little cost to her, the couple can choose another waterspot where the hikes might be better for the husband. By examining the weight or value given to certain preferences the parties may realize that some desires are easily attainable because they are not of equal importance to the other side. Thus, one party can increase its utilities without reducing the other's. This differs from a zero-sum conception of negotiation because of the recognition that preferences may be totally different and are, therefore, neither scarce nor in competition with each other. In addition, if a preference is not used to "force" a concession from the other party

---

[167] Pruitt & Lewis, The Psychology of Interactive Bargaining in Negotiations: Social-Psychological Perspectives 169-170 (D. Druckman ed., 1977).

(which as the example shows is not necessary), there are none of the forced reciprocal concessions of adversarial negotiation.

The exploitation of complementary interests occurs frequently in the legal context. For example, in a child custody case the lawyers may learn that both parties desire to have the children some of the time and neither of the parties wishes to have the children all of the time. It will be easy, therefore, to arrange for a joint custody agreement that satisfies the needs of both parties. Similarly, in a commercial matter, the defendant may want to make payment over time and the plaintiff, for tax purposes or to increase interest income, may desire deferred income.

Notes and Questions

2.15 Menkel-Meadow argues that problem solving is more likely to meet a client's needs than competition and compromise. What would Korobkin's response be? Are these models of negotiation necessarily in conflict? Could some portions of a negotiation be problem solving and others be competitive?

2.16 Elsewhere in her article, Menkel-Meadow gives a simple example of an integrative resolution. Two children are disputing over a piece of chocolate cake. A distributive approach would result in dividing the cake, perhaps giving each child 50 percent. However, where one child likes icing and the other, cake, each child could get 100 percent of what they want most by dividing the portions into icing and cake. Another example of an integrative outcome is given by Mary Parker Follett, who is introduced in Chapter 1:

> A Dairymen's Co-operative League almost went to pieces last year on the question of precedence in unloading cans at a creamery platform. The men who came down the hill (the creamery was on a down grade) thought they should have precedence; the men who came up the hill thought they should unload first. The thinking of both sides in the controversy was thus confined within the walls of these two possibilities, and this prevented their even trying to find a way of settling the dispute which would avoid these alternatives. The solution was obviously to change the position of the platforms so that both up-hillers and down-hillers could unload at the same time. But this solution was not found until they had asked the advice of a more or less professional integrator. When, however, it was pointed out to them, they were quite ready to accept it. Integration involves invention, and the clever thing is to recognize this and not to let one's thinking stay within the boundaries of two alternatives which are mutually exclusive.

Mary Parker Follett, Constructive Conflict, in Mary Parker Follett — Prophet of Management 69-70 (Pauline Graham ed., 1995). Can you think of examples where, like Follet's example of the Dairymen's League, conflict led to a better idea? In business? In your own life?

2.17 To the four stages in the negotiation process described by Gerald Williams (see Notes and Questions 2.2), Carrie Menkel-Meadow and David Binder add several pre- and post-negotiation steps, including planning for the negotiation, planning with the client on goals and possible solutions, and learning from the negotiation after it is completed. Carrie Menkel-Meadow & David Binder, ABA Lawyering Skills Institute, The Stages and Phases of Negotiation (1983). Is the articulation of a pre- and post-negotiation stage more in keeping with a problem-solving orientation?

2.18 Philip Gulliver writes about the negotiation process as cyclical and developmental:

> In negotiation there are two distinct though interconnected processes going on simultaneously: a repetitive, cyclical one and a developmental one. A simple analogy is a moving automobile. There is a cyclical turning of the wheels (linked to the cyclical action of valves, pistons, etc., in the motor) that enables the vehicle to move, and there is the actual movement of the vehicle from one place to another. . . . In negotiation, somewhat similarly, there is a cyclical process comprising the repetitive exchange of information between the parties, its assessment, and the resulting adjustments of expectations and preferences; there is also a developmental process involved in the movement from the initiation of the dispute to its conclusion — some outcome — and its implementation. . . .

Philip H. Gulliver, Disputes and Negotiations: A Cross-Cultural Perspective 82 (1979). This can help us visualize a process as one that is not always directly linear but may require several moves (or cycles) to move forward. Is this cyclical vision of negotiation more helpful (or realistic) than a linear approach?

2.19 If the linear, competitive, distributive approach is limited in the way Menkel-Meadow suggests, why do you suppose it is used so often in resolving legal disputes?

The next excerpt from the worldwide bestseller on principled or interest-based negotiation (quoted earlier in the section on accommodative positional bargaining) argues against positional approaches and summarizes some of the strategies involved in integrative or principled ones.

 Roger Fisher, William Ury & Bruce Patton, GETTING TO YES

4-6, 9-14 (2d ed. 1991)

Any method of negotiation may be fairly judged by three criteria: It should produce a wise agreement if agreement is possible. It should be efficient. And it should improve or at least not damage the relationship between the parties. (A wise agreement can be defined as one that meets the legitimate interests of each side to the extent possible, resolves conflicting interests fairly, is durable, and takes community interests into account.) . . .

Taking positions, as the customer and storekeeper do, serves some useful purposes in a negotiation. It tells the other side what you want; it provides an anchor in an uncertain and pressured situation; and it can eventually produce the terms of an acceptable agreement. But those purposes can be served in other ways. And positional bargaining fails to meet the basic criteria of producing a wise agreement, efficiently and amicably.

ARGUING OVER POSITIONS PRODUCES UNWISE AGREEMENTS

When negotiators bargain over positions, they tend to lock themselves into those positions. The more you clarify your position and defend it against attack, the more committed you become to it. The more you try to convince the other side of the impossibility of changing your opening position, the more difficult it becomes to do so. Your ego becomes identified with your position. You now have a new interest in "saving face" — in reconciling future action with past positions — making it less and less likely that any agreement will wisely reconcile the parties' original interests. . . .

ARGUING OVER POSITIONS IS INEFFICIENT . . .

Bargaining over positions creates incentives that stall settlement. In positional bargaining you try to improve the chance that any settlement reached is favorable to you by starting with an extreme position, by stubbornly holding to it, by deceiving the other party as to your true views, and by making small concessions only as necessary to keep the negotiation going. The same is true for the other side. Each of those factors tends to interfere with reaching a settlement promptly. . . .

ARGUING OVER POSITIONS ENDANGERS AN ONGOING RELATIONSHIP

Positional bargaining becomes a contest of will. . . . Anger and resentment often result as one side sees itself bending to the rigid will of the other while its own legitimate concerns go unaddressed. Positional bargaining thus strains and sometimes shatters the relationship between the parties. . . .

THERE IS AN ALTERNATIVE . . .

The answer to the question of whether to use soft positional bargaining or hard is "neither." Change the game. At the Harvard Negotiation Project we have been developing an alternative to positional bargaining: a method of negotiation explicitly designed to produce wise outcomes efficiently and amicably. This method, called *principled negotiation* or *negotiation on the merits*, can be boiled down to four basic points.

These four points define a straightforward method of negotiation that can be used under almost any circumstance. Each point deals with a basic element of negotiation, and suggests what you should do about it.

People:	Separate the people from the problem.
Interests:	Focus on interests, not positions.
Options:	Generate a variety of possibilities before deciding what to do.
Criteria:	Insist that the result be based on some objective standard.

PROBLEM		SOLUTION
Positional Bargaining: Which Game Should You Play?		Change the Game — Negotiate on the Merits

SOFT	HARD	PRINCIPLED
Participants are friends.	Participants are adversaries.	Participants are problem-solvers.
The goal is agreement.	The goal is victory.	The goal is a wise outcome reached efficiently and amicably.
Make concessions to cultivate the relationship.	Demand concessions as a condition of the relationship.	*Separate the people from the problem.*
Be soft on the people and the problem.	Be hard on the problem and the people.	Be soft on the people, hard on the problem.
Trust others.	Distrust others.	Proceed independent of trust.
Change your position easily.	Dig in to your position.	*Focus on interests, not positions.*
Make offers.	Make threats.	Explore interests.
Disclose your bottom line.	Mislead as to your bottom line.	Avoid having a bottom line.
Accept one-sided losses to reach agreement.	Demand one-sided gains as the price of agreement.	*Invent options for mutual gain.*
Search for the single answer: the one *they* will accept.	Search for the single answer: the one *you* will accept.	Develop multiple options to choose from; decide later.
Insist on agreement.	Insist on your position.	*Insist on using objective criteria.*
Try to avoid a contest of will.	Try to win a contest of will.	Try to reach a result based on standards independent of will.
Yield to pressure.	Apply pressure.	Reason and be open to reason; yield to principle, not pressure.

[E]motions typically become entangled with the objective merits of the problem. Taking positions just makes this worse because people's egos become identified with their positions. Hence, before working on the substantive problem, the "people problem" should be disentangled from it and dealt with separately. Figuratively if not literally, the participants should come to see themselves as working side by side, attacking the problem, not each other. Hence the first proposition: *Separate the people from the problem.*

The second point is designed to overcome the drawback of focusing on people's stated positions when the object of a negotiation is to satisfy their underlying interests. A negotiating position often obscures what you really want. Compromising between positions is not likely to produce an agreement which will effectively take care of the human needs that led people to adopt those positions. The second basic element of the method is: *Focus on interests, not positions.*

The third point responds to the difficulty of designing optimal solutions while under pressure. Trying to decide in the presence of an adversary narrows your vision.

Having a lot at stake inhibits creativity. So does searching for the one right solution. You can offset these constraints by setting aside a designated time within which to think up a wide range of possible solutions that advance shared interests and creatively reconcile differing interests. Hence the third basic point: Before trying to reach agreement, *invent options for mutual gain.* . . .

[S]ome fair standard such as market value, expert opinion, custom, or law [should] determine the outcome. By discussing such criteria rather than what the parties are willing or unwilling to do, neither party need give in to the other; both can defer to a fair solution. Hence the fourth basic point: *Insist on using objective criteria.* . . .

To sum up, in contrast to positional bargaining, the principled negotiation method of focusing on basic interests, mutually satisfying options, and fair standards typically results in a *wise agreement.* The method permits you to reach a gradual consensus on a joint decision *efficiently* without all the transactional costs of digging into positions only to have to dig yourself out of them. And separating the people from the problem allows you to deal directly and emphatically with the other negotiator as a human being, thus making possible an *amicable* agreement.

Notes and Questions

2.20 Do you agree that principled bargaining is more effective than soft bargaining against hard bargaining? Why or why not?

2.21 Think of the last argument you had. What did the other side ask for? What was the interest behind their position? What were your interests? What positions did you take?

The most common shorthand expression for integrative negotiating is "value creation" or "expanding the pie." David Lax and James Sebenius discuss different types of values negotiators can create.

 David A. Lax & James K. Sebenius, **THE MANAGER AS NEGOTIATOR: BARGAINING FOR COOPERATION AND COMPETITIVE GAIN**

89-90 (1986)

Negotiators can create two distinct kinds of value. . . .

The first kind — what we will call "private value" — includes profits to be split, land to be parceled out, goods to be allocated, and, generally, results of negotiation that one party can consume, use, or enjoy while excluding others from the benefits. Those who mainly think of negotiation as the process of working out mutually beneficial exchanges have traditionally focused on private value. . . .

Yet negotiators can also create "common value," which is exceedingly important but often neglected in thinking about the process. Common value can be shared by all parties simultaneously; no one can be excluded unless all are. . . . For example, suppose that two graphic designers are each committed to a different logo. They bargain for days over which one they will jointly recommend to top management.

But suppose they discover a new logo that both prefer to their original choices. Their agreement to recommend it is good for both at the same time....

The parties must explore — imperfectly — the arrangements they may jointly be able to create. In practice many gains go unrealized. Inferior agreements are made. Impasse results and conflict escalates when cooperative action might have been far better for all. Understanding where private and common value really come from should make jointly creating it more likely. This chapter focuses on three primary sources: (1) the key role of *differences* among the participants in creating private (and common) value [e.g., when one person values X highly and the other does not]; (2) the often-misunderstood role of *shared interests* in creating common value [e.g., when both parties want the venture to succeed or want to avoid a strike]; and (3) how *economies of scale* can create both kinds of value without requiring differences or shared interests [e.g., when merging companies can save on overhead].

Notes and Questions

2.22 The classic example of value creation is the story of two siblings fighting over an orange. They agree to split it in half. One throws out the peel and eats her half of the orange. The other uses her half of the peel in a recipe and throws out the rest of the orange. How could these siblings have better resolved this dispute?

2.23 On the other hand, what arguments could you make that the resolution between the siblings (splitting the orange in half) is a good one?

C. EFFECTIVENESS AND NEGOTIATOR STYLE

The following conclusions are based on a study that asked lawyers how they perceived the other side's negotiation strategy during their most recent negotiation. Over 700 lawyers (of 2,500) returned a questionnaire that asked lawyers to rate their counterparts using 89 adjectives, 60 negotiation techniques, and 14 goals. The attorneys also rated their counterparts for effectiveness. The attorneys were grouped in two, three, and four styles based on statistical analysis. The first excerpt examines adversarial negotiators and finds a distinct difference between perceived ethical and unethical adversarial negotiators. The second excerpt divides problem-solving negotiators into two categories — true problem solvers and cautious problem solvers — and then compares these groups in terms of effectiveness with adversarial negotiators.

 Andrea Kupfer Schneider, **SHATTERING NEGOTIATION MYTHS: EMPIRICAL EVIDENCE ON THE EFFECTIVENESS OF NEGOTIATION STYLE**

7 Harv. Negot. L. Rev. 143, 181-184 (2002)

The more revealing result from [dividing lawyers into four groups] concerns the further division of lawyers in adversarial behavior. The unethical adversarial [is] deceptive, loud, and foolish. On the other hand, the new cluster labeled ethical adversarial has some important differences from ... the ... unethical adversarial group. ... Though many of the adjectives do overlap, the rankings of adjectives are ordered differently. The top five adjectives in the ethical group are confident, assertive, arrogant, headstrong, and experienced. Furthermore, unlike the [unethical adversarial], the ethical group is *not* described as manipulative, conniving, deceptive, evasive, complaining, rude, angry, intolerant, sarcastic, greedy or stern. The ethical adjectives therefore are not particularly negative nor do they suggest the table-banging style of negotiation.

Top 20 Adjectives for Adversarials

	ETHICAL ADVERSARIAL	UNETHICAL ADVERSARIAL
1	Confident	Irritating
2	Assertive	Stubborn
3	Arrogant	Headstrong
4	Headstrong	Argumentative
5	Experienced	Quarrelsome
6	Demanding	Arrogant
7	Egotistical	Egotistical
8	Ambitious	Manipulative
9	Stubborn	Assertive
10	Argumentative	Demanding
11	Tough	Complaining
12	Irritating	Hostile
13	Forceful	Suspicious
14	Firm	Conniving
15	Quarrelsome	Greedy
16	Masculine	Rude
17	Dominant	Angry
18	Ethical	Confident
19	Deliberate	Ambitious
20	Hostile	Deceptive

A review of the bipolar pairs [polar opposite negotiation techniques] further shows the difference between the two adversarial groups. Attorneys falling in the unethical adversarial group had numerous adjectives and behaviors ascribed to them that were not ascribed to attorneys in the ethical adversarial group. First, attorneys in the unethical adversarial group were unpleasant: discourteous, unfriendly, and tactless. Second, they were untrustworthy: insincere, devious, dishonest and distrustful. Third, these attorneys were uninterested in the client or lawyer on the other side: no understanding of the opposing client, unconcerned how opposing counsel would look, no consideration of opposing counsel's needs, infliction of needless harm. Fourth, these attorneys were inflexible in their view of the case and their strategies: narrow view of case, rigid, took one position, narrow range of strategies, focused on a single solution, fixed concept of negotiation. Fifth, they used manipulative tactics: attacked, used take-it-or-leave-it, inaccurate case estimate, advanced unwarranted claims. Finally, their general view of the negotiation process was competitive: unco-operative, unreasonable, viewed negotiation as win-lose, obstructed the negotiation. The ethical adversarials, as compared to the unethical adversarials, had a broader view of the case, a different negotiation style, and were more pleasant. . . .

The effectiveness rating of the unethical adversarial cluster compared to the effectiveness rating of the ethical adversarial cluster completes the story. Seventy-five percent of the unethical adversarial group is considered ineffective. Only two attorneys out of the seventy-seven attorneys in this group, 2.5%, were considered effective. In comparison, the ethical adversarial bargainer is more likely to be average if not effective. Forty percent of ethical adversarials were ineffective, 44% were average and 16% were effective. These are still clearly lower ratios for effective and average behavior than the [true] problem-solving negotiator and even the cautious problem-solving negotiator. On the other hand, they are notably better than the unethical adversarial bargainer is.

Effectiveness in Four Clusters

Effectiveness × Clusters	Ineffective	Average	Effective	Totals by Cluster
Problem-solving (PS)	1% of PS	27% of PS	72% of PS	PS = 238
Cautious Problem-solving (CPS)	12% of CPS	65% of CPS	23.5% of CPS	CPS − 170
Ethical Adversarial (EA)	40% of EA	44% of EA	16% of EA	EA = 133
Unethical Adversarial (UA)	75% of UA	22% of UA	3% of UA	UA = 77
Totals by Effectiveness	Total = 134	Total = 250	Total = 234	Total = 618

Notes and Questions

2.24 The study indicates it is most ineffective to be both adversarial and unethical, and it is also dangerous to be simply adversarial (compared to other approaches). How do these results mesh with your experience? With images from television and movies? With the culture in your law school?

2.25 What are the key perceived behavioral differences between these two types of adversarial negotiators?

2.26 How closely does the description of adversarial lawyer behavior mirror the advice that Meltsner and Schrag give? Are Meltsner and Schrag advocating for ethical or unethical adversarial bargaining? Explain your answer.

The next excerpt, also from Schneider's empirical study, explores the differences between the "true" problem-solving negotiators — those who truly engage in the behavior described in the previous excerpts on integrative bargaining — and "cautious" problem solvers — those who don't fully use the range of problem-solving behavior. Whether one is a true or a cautious problem solver impacts their effectiveness rating, so the distinction is important.

 Andrea Kupfer Schneider, **SHATTERING NEGOTIATION MYTHS: EMPIRICAL EVIDENCE ON THE EFFECTIVENESS OF NEGOTIATION STYLE**

7 Harv. Negot. L. Rev. 143, 171-175 (2002)

[L]awyers were divided . . . more evenly among the three clusters with approximately 36% in the true problem-solving group, 36% in the cautious problem-solving group, and 28% in the adversarial group. . . .

The most interesting result in this analysis is the middle category. Clearly this middle group is comprised of "good" lawyers in that all of the adjectives are positive. . . . [A]ll nine are included in the true problem-solving group. In comparison, however, the true problem-solving group had forty-nine highly rated adjectives. Consequently, I have labeled the middle group "cautious problem-solvers" to high-light the fact that most of these traits are problem-solving, yet this group seems hesitant to utilize all of the problem-solving attributes. By "cautious," I do not mean to suggest that these negotiators are themselves cautious, but rather they are cautious about adopting a completely problem-solving approach to the negotiation. . . .

The bipolar descriptions reveal more about the differences among these three types of negotiators. . . .

The true problem-solving negotiator understands the case well (reasonable, prepared, accurate representation of client's position, did own factual investigation) and wanted to work with the other side (friendly, tactful, cooperative, facilitated the negotiation, viewed the negotiation process as one with mutual benefits, understood my client's interests). This negotiator was flexible (movable position, did not use take it or leave it) and did not engage in manipulative tactics (did not make unwarranted claims, did not use threats, avoided needless harm to my client). The true problem-solving negotiator believed in the good faith exchange of information (cooperative, forthright, trustful, sincere, shared information, probed). . . .

The cautious problem-solving group, as in the adjectives ratings, did not stand out in most of the characteristics and is only rated more than slightly characteristic in eight descriptions. These eight are all positive and also appear on the problem-solving list, but the cautious problem-solving category lacks twenty-two descriptions that true problem-solvers display. As described above, these absent characteristics describe negotiation qualities that add depth and breadth to a negotiator's skills. . . .

The study of effectiveness can demonstrate the impact of these differences in the rating-scale.

First, approximately 25% of the negotiators in the new cautious problem-solving group are effective, whereas 75% of the true problem-solvers are described as effective. The missing negotiation elements between the groups must cause this difference. Adjectives found in true problem-solving but not in cautious problem-solving highlight empathy (communicative, accommodating, perceptive, helpful), option creation (adaptable, flexible), personality (agreeable, poised), and preparation (fair-minded, realistic, astute about the law). These skills make the difference between average skills and truly effective skills. Contrary to popular belief, behaviors described by these adjectives are not risky at all. The traditional fear of problem-solving is that problem-solvers will be taken advantage of by more adversarial bargainers, yet only 1% of true problem-solving negotiators were considered ineffective.

Top 20 Adjectives for Three Clusters

	TRUE PROBLEM-SOLVING	CAUTIOUS PROBLEM-SOLVING	ADVERSARIAL
1	Ethical	Ethical	Irritating
2	Personable	Experienced	Headstrong
3	Experienced	Confident	Stubborn
4	Trustworthy	Personable	Arrogant
5	Rational	Self-controlled	Egotistical
6	Agreeable	Rational	Argumentative
7	Fair-minded	Sociable	Assertive
8	Communicative	Dignified	Demanding
9	Realistic	Trustworthy	Quarrelsome
10	Accommodating		Confident
11	Perceptive		Ambitious
12	Sociable		Manipulative
13	Adaptable		Experienced
14	Confident		Hostile
15	Dignified		Forceful
16	Self-controlled		Tough
17	Helpful		Suspicious
18	Astute about the law		Firm
19	Poised		Complaining
20	Flexible		Rude

Notes and Questions

2.27 What are the primary differences between true and cautious problem solvers? Which of these differences do you think is the most important in terms of effectiveness?

2.28 Does this study adequately counter the common fear that being cooperative or problem-solving will disadvantage a negotiator who faces an adversarial, competitive bargainer? Fisher, Ury, and Patton advise negotiators to be "soft on the people, hard on the problem." Can that be done comfortably? Can it be done safely — that is, without fear of "losing" to the adversarial negotiator?

D. BARRIERS TO NEGOTIATION

This last section of the chapter examines barriers to negotiation that arise regardless of the approach one adopts. The first part describes the Prisoner's Dilemma, a classic scenario from game theory, exploring the difficulties of simultaneous strategic interaction that is often applied to the negotiation context. The second part examines structural, social, cognitive, and psychological barriers to obtaining good outcomes — "good" meaning "pareto superior" and "wise" as Fisher, Ury, and Patton describe. As you read these excerpts, think about what mediators can do to correct for or get around each of these barriers. One of the great advantages of using a third party (mediator) in negotiation is the ability of that third party to see these barriers from the outside, while the participants are too wrapped up in their own assumptions, behaviors, and omissions to perceive accurately what they are doing and what effects they are having.

1. The Prisoner's and Negotiator's Dilemma

 Douglas R. Hofstadter, METAMAGICAL THEMAS: QUESTING FOR THE ESSENCE OF MIND AND PATTERN

716 (1985)

In case you're wondering why it is called "Prisoner's Dilemma," here's the reason. Imagine that you and an accomplice (someone you have no feelings for one way or the other) committed a crime, and now you've both been apprehended and thrown in jail, and are fearfully awaiting trials. You are being held in separate cells with no way to communicate. The prosecutor offers each of you the following deal (and informs you both that the identical deal is being offered to each of you — and that you both know *that* as well!): "We have a lot of circumstantial evidence on you both. So if you both claim innocence, we will convict you anyway and you'll both get two years in jail. But if you will help us out by admitting your guilt and making it easier for us to convict your accomplice — oh, pardon me, your *alleged* accomplice — why, then, we'll let you out free. And don't worry about revenge — your accomplice will be in for five years! How about it?" Warily you ask, "But what if we *both* say we're guilty?" "Ah, well, my friend — I'm afraid you'll both get four-year sentences, then."

Now you're in a pickle! Clearly, you don't want to claim innocence if your partner has sung, for then you're in for five long years. Better you should both have sung — then you'll only get four. On the other hand, if your partner claims innocence, then the best possible thing for you to do is sing, since then you're out scot-free! So at first sight, it seems obvious what you should do: Sing! But what is obvious to you is equally obvious to your opposite number, so now it looks like you both ought to sing, which means — Sing Sing for four years! At least that's what *logic* tells you to do. Funny, since if both of you had just been *illogical* and maintained innocence, you'd both be in for only half as long! Ah, logic does it again.

Notes and Questions

2.29 If one of the prisoners was your client, how would you advise him or her? If both of the prisoners were your clients (forgetting for a moment about the conflict of interest), how would you advise them? Does your advice differ? Why or why not?

2.30 The prisoner's dilemma is a highly stylized interaction. Yet some legal scholars have analogized this situation to discovery prior to trial. See Ronald J. Gilson & Robert H. Mnookin, Disputing Through Agents: Cooperation and Conflict Between Lawyers in Litigation, 94 Colum. L. Rev. 509 (1994). Each side has the choice whether to cooperate in discovery (to turn over requested documents easily, to schedule depositions conveniently, to answer interrogatories fully), or to be more adversarial (to fight document requests, to make depositions a true inconvenience, to evade answering interrogatories). If both sides cooperate, discovery moves forward quickly and relatively inexpensively. If both sides are adversarial, discovery is delayed and is far more costly as the parties file additional motions. If one side is cooperative while the other is adversarial, then the cooperative side ends up spending more money and getting less information. The adversarial side saves money and gets the information it needs. How would you decide what to do? What if the opposing side has a reputation for fairness? What if the opposing side has a reputation for hard bargaining? What if you deal with the opposing side regularly?

What if the prisoners in the Prisoner's Dilemma are going to find themselves in the same situation next week? Does it matter who the prisoners are in relation to each other? Does the idea of repeat interactions change behavior? The next excerpt explains a computer tournament run on that assumption and the lessons that can be drawn from the winning entry.

Robert Axelrod, THE EVOLUTION OF COOPERATION

7-9, 30-31, 40, 54, 110-114, 118-122 (1984)

Under what conditions will cooperation emerge in a world of egoists without central authority? This question has intrigued people for a long time. And for good reason. We all know that people are not angels, and that they tend to look after themselves and their own first. Yet we also know that cooperation does occur and that our civilization is based upon it. But, in situations where each individual has an incentive to be selfish, how can cooperation ever develop? . . .

A good example of the fundamental problem of cooperation is the case where two industrial nations have erected trade barriers to each other's exports. Because of the mutual advantages of free trade, both countries would be better off if these barriers were eliminated. But if either country were to unilaterally eliminate its barriers, it would find itself facing terms of trade that hurt its own economy. In fact, whatever one country does, the other country is better off retaining its own trade barriers. Therefore, the problem is that each country has an incentive to retain trade barriers, leading to a worse outcome than would have been possible had both countries cooperated with each other.

This basic problem occurs when the pursuit of self-interest by each leads to a poor outcome for all. To make headway in understanding the vast array of specific situations which have this property, a way is needed to represent what is common to these situations without becoming bogged down in the details unique to each. Fortunately, there is such a representation available: the famous *Prisoner's Dilemma* game.

In the Prisoner's Dilemma game, there are two players. Each has two choices, namely cooperate or defect. Each must make the choice without knowing what the other will do. No matter what the other does, defection yields a higher payoff than cooperation. The dilemma is that if both defect, both do worse than if both had cooperated. . . .

What should you do in such a game [since] . . . it is better to defect if you think the other player will cooperate, *and* it is better to defect if you think the other player will defect. So no matter what the other player does, it pays for you to defect.

So far, so good. But the same logic holds for the other player too. Therefore, the other player should defect no matter what you are expected to do. So you should both defect. . . . But then you [are both worse off than if you had cooperated]. . . . Individual rationality leads to a worse outcome for both than is possible. Hence the dilemma. . . .

Wanting to find out what would happen [in an iterated game], I invited professional game theorists to send in entries to . . . a computer tournament [based on a monetized version of the Prisoner's Dilemma]. . . .

TIT FOR TAT . . . won the tournament. This was the simplest of all submitted programs and it turned out to be the best! TIT FOR TAT, of course, starts with a cooperative choice, and thereafter does what the other player did on the previous move. . . .

The analysis of the tournament results indicate[s] that there is a lot to be learned about coping in an environment of mutual power. Even expert strategists from political science, sociology, economics, psychology, and mathematics made the systematic errors of being too competitive for their own good, not being forgiving enough, and being too pessimistic about the responsiveness of the other side. . . .

TIT FOR TAT won the tournament because it did well in its interactions with a wide variety of other strategies. On average, it did better than any other rule with the other strategies in the tournament. Yet TIT FOR TAT never once scored better in a game than the other player! In fact, it can't. It lets the other player defect first, and it never defects more times than the other player has defected. Therefore, TIT FOR TAT achieves either the same score as the other player, or a little less. TIT FOR TAT won the tournament, not by beating the other player, but by eliciting behavior from the other player which allowed both to do well. TIT FOR TAT was so consistent at eliciting mutually rewarding outcomes that it attained a higher overall score than any other strategy. . . .

The purpose of this chapter is to translate these findings into advice for a player.

The advice takes the form of four simple suggestions for how to do well in a durable iterated Prisoner's Dilemma: . . .

1.   DON'T BE ENVIOUS . . .

People tend to resort to the standard of comparison that they have available — and this standard is often the success of the other player relative to their own success. This standard leads to envy. And envy leads to attempts to rectify any advantage the other player has attained. In this form of Prisoner's Dilemma, rectification of the other's advantage can only be done by defection. But defection leads to more defection and to mutual punishment. So envy is self-destructive. . . .

2.   DON'T BE THE FIRST TO DEFECT

Both the tournament and the theoretical results show that it pays to cooperate as long as the other player is cooperating. . . . The single best predictor of how well a rule performed was whether or not it was nice, which is to say, whether or not it would ever be the first to defect. In the first round, each of the top eight rules were nice, and not one of the bottom seven were nice. In the second round, all but one of the top fifteen rules were nice (and that one ranked eighth). Of the bottom fifteen rules, all but one were not nice. . . .

3.   RECIPROCATE BOTH COOPERATION AND DEFECTION

The extraordinary success of TIT FOR TAT leads to some simple, but powerful advice: practice reciprocity. After cooperating on the first move, TIT FOR TAT simply reciprocates whatever the other player did on the previous move. . . .

In responding to a defection from the other player, TIT FOR TAT represents a balance between punishing and being forgiving. TIT FOR TAT always defects exactly once after each defection by the other. . . . What is clear is that extracting more than one defection for each defection of the other side risks escalation. On the other hand, extracting less than one-for-one risks exploitation. . . .

4. DON'T BE TOO CLEVER

The tournament results show that in a Prisoner's Dilemma situation it is easy to be *too* clever. The very sophisticated rules did not do better than the simple ones. In fact, the so-called maximizing rules often did poorly because they got into a rut of mutual defection. A common problem with these rules is that they used complex methods of making inferences about the other player — and these inferences were wrong. . . .

In deciding whether to carry an umbrella, we do not have to worry that the clouds will take our behavior into account. We can do a calculation about the chance of rain based on past experience. Likewise in a zero-sum game, such as chess, we can safely use the assumption that the other player will pick the most dangerous move that can be found, and we can act accordingly. Therefore it pays for us to be as sophisticated and as complex in our analysis as we can.

Non-zero-sum games, such as the Prisoner's Dilemma, are not like this. Unlike the clouds, the other player can respond to your own choices. And unlike the chess opponent, the other player in a Prisoner's Dilemma should not be regarded as someone who is out to defeat you. The other player will be watching your behavior for signs of whether you will reciprocate cooperation or not, and therefore your own behavior is likely to be echoed back to you.

Rules that try to maximize their own score while treating the other player as a fixed part of the environment ignore this aspect of the interaction, no matter how clever they are in calculating under their limiting assumptions. Therefore, it does not pay to be clever in modeling the other player if you leave out the reverberating process in which the other player is adapting to you, you are adapting to the other, and then the other player is adapting to your adaptation and so on. . . .

In other words, too much complexity can appear to be total chaos. If you are using a strategy which appears random, then you also appear unresponsive to the other player. If you are unresponsive, then the other player has no incentive to cooperate with you. So being so complex as to be incomprehensible is very dangerous. . . .

What accounts for TIT FOR TAT's robust success is its combination of being nice, retaliatory, forgiving, and clear. Its niceness prevents it from getting into unnecessary trouble. Its retaliation discourages the other side from persisting whenever defection is tried. Its forgiveness helps restore mutual cooperation. And its clarity makes it intelligible to the other player, thereby eliciting long-term cooperation.

Notes and Questions

2.31 How would you compare Axelrod's advice to the negotiation approaches discussed in this chapter?

2.32 Cognitive researchers recently have found a biological reason explaining cooperation:

> Hard as it may be to believe in these days of infectious greed and sabers unsheathed, scientists have discovered that the small, brave act of cooperating with another person . . . makes the brain light up with quiet joy. Studying neural activity in young women who were playing a classic laboratory game called the Prisoner's Dilemma . . . researchers found that when the women chose mutualism over "me-ism," the mental circuitry normally associated with reward-seeking behavior swelled to life. And the longer the women engaged in a cooperative strategy, the more strongly flowed the blood to the pathways of pleasure.

Natalie Angier, Why We're So Nice: We're Wired to Cooperate, N.Y. Times, July 23, 2002, at 1.

The researchers had actually expected that the subjects would feel more emotion when one person cooperated and the other defected. In fact, the subjects were most responsive when patterns of cooperation occurred. Although the experiment was performed only on women, the researchers predicted that these findings would be the same for both genders. The researchers thought that this push to cooperate might explain why humans behave better than other species (assuming you think that). What do you think? If you have participated in a Prisoner's Dilemma game, how did you feel?

The next two excerpts discuss the similarity between the Prisoner's Dilemma and a routine dilemma faced by negotiators. The Negotiator's Dilemma — the tension between collaborating and competing — is a principal rationale for engaging a mediator to manage the negotiation process. A mediator would make it more likely (theoretically) that the gains possible from collaborating are not lost due to the strategies inherent in competition.

 ### David A. Lax & James K. Sebenius, THE MANAGER AS NEGOTIATOR: BARGAINING FOR COOPERATION AND COMPETITIVE GAIN

30, 33, 38-40 (1986)

Negotiators and analysts tend to fall into two groups that are guided by warring conceptions of the bargaining process. In the left-hand corner are the "value creators" and in the right-hand corner are the "value claimers." . . . Both of these images of negotiation are incomplete and inadequate. Value creating and value claiming are linked parts of negotiation. Both processes are present. No matter how much creative problem-solving enlarges the pie, it must still be divided; value that has been created must be claimed. And, if the pie is not enlarged, there will be less to divide; there is more value to be claimed if one has helped create it first. An essential tension in negotiation exists between cooperative moves to create value and competitive moves to claim it. . . .

Consider two negotiators (Ward and Stone) each of whom can choose between two negotiating styles: creating value (being open, sharing information about preferences and beliefs, not being misleading about minimum requirements, and so forth) and claiming value (being cagey and misleading about preferences, beliefs, and minimum requirements; making commitments and threats, and so forth). Each has the same two options for any tactical choice. If both choose to create value, they each receive a good outcome, which we will call GOOD for each. If Ward chooses to create value and Stone chooses to claim value, then Stone does even better than if he had chosen to create value — rank this outcome GREAT for Stone — but Ward does much worse — rank this outcome TERRIBLE for him. Similarly, if Stone is the creative one and Ward is the claimer, then Ward does well — rank this outcome for him as GREAT — while Stone's outcome is TERRIBLE. If both claim, they fail to find joint gains and come up with a mediocre outcome, which we call MEDIOCRE for both. . . . In each box, Ward's payoff is in the lower left corner and Stone's is in the upper right. Thus, when Ward claims and Stone creates, Ward's outcome is GREAT while Stone's is TERRIBLE. [See the following figure] . . .

	Stone's Choice	
	Create	Claim
Create	GOOD GOOD	GREAT TERRIBLE
Claim	TERRIBLE GREAT	MEDIOCRE MEDIOCRE

Figure 2-1
Negotiator's Dilemma
The lower left entry in each cell is Ward's outcome; the second entry is Stone's.

Now, if Ward were going to create, Stone would prefer the GREAT outcome obtained by claiming to the GOOD outcome he could have obtained by creating; so, Stone should claim. If, on the other hand, Ward were going to claim, Stone would prefer the MEDIOCRE outcome from claiming to the TERRIBLE outcome he would receive from creating. In fact, no matter what Ward does, it seems that Stone would be better off trying to claim value!

Similarly, Ward should also prefer to claim. By symmetric reasoning, if Stone chooses to create, Ward prefers the GREAT outcome he gets by claiming to the GOOD outcome he gets from creating. If Stone claims, Ward prefers the MEDIOCRE outcome he gets from claiming to the TERRIBLE outcome he gets from creating.

Both negotiators choose to claim. They land in the lower-right-hand box and receive MEDIOCRE outcomes. They leave joint gains on the table, since both would prefer the GOOD outcomes they could have received had they both chosen to create value and ended up in the upper-left-hand box.

This is the crux of the Negotiator's Dilemma. Individually rational decisions to emphasize claiming tactics by being cagey and misleading lead to a mutually undesirable outcome. As described, this situation has the structure of the famous "Prisoner's

Dilemma." In such situations, the motivation to protect oneself and employ tactics for claiming value is compelling.

 Robert H. Mnookin, Scott R. Peppet & Andrew S. Tulumello,
BEYOND WINNING

27, 40, 42–43 (2000)

We have now arrived at the core of the problem. How can you create value while minimizing the risks of exploitation in the distributive aspects of negotiation?

The challenge of problem-solving negotiation is to acknowledge and manage this tension. Keep in mind that this tension *cannot be resolved*. It can only be managed. The goal is to design processes for negotiation that allow value creation to occur, when possible, while minimizing the risks of exploitation. . . .

No matter how good you are at brainstorming and no matter how carefully you search out value-creating trades, at some point the pie has to be sliced.

What happens to interest-based, collaborative problem-solving when you turn to distributive issues? Some negotiators act as if problem-solving has to be tossed overboard when the going gets tough. We could not disagree more. In our experience, it's when distributive issues are at the forefront that problem-solving skills are most desperately needed. [The] goal at this point is to treat distributive issues as a shared problem. Both sides know that distributive issues exist. She knows that, other things being equal, she'd like to earn more and [he] would like to pay less. There's no getting around it. At the same time, however, she doesn't want to behave in a way that would damage her relationship. . . .

Sometimes, of course, you won't be able to find a solution that satisfies both sides. No matter how hard you try, you will continue to disagree about salary, the amount to be paid in a bonus, or some aspect of a dispute settlement. Norms may have helped move you closer together, but there's still a big gap between the two sides. What should you do?

Think about process. How can you design a process that would fairly resolve this impasse? In a dispute settlement, you might be able to hire a mediator to address the distributive issues that are still open. Is there anyone both sides trust enough to decide the issue? Could you put five possible agreements into a hat and pick one at random?

Procedural solutions can often rescue a distributive negotiation that has reached an impasse. They need not involve complicated alternative dispute resolution procedures that cost money and time. Instead, you can often come up with simple process solutions that will resolve a distributive deadlock and allow you to move forward. . . .

The problem-solving approach . . . will not make distributive issues go away or this first tension of negotiation disappear. But it does outline an approach that will help you find value-creating opportunities when they exist and resolve distributive issues efficiently and as a shared problem.

Notes and Questions

2.33 What are the reasons people choose not to treat each interaction like the Prisoner's Dilemma? Philosopher and moral theorist David Gauthier argues that people can make a rational choice (in addition to a moral one) to become "constrained maximizers," that is, someone who sacrifices short-term self-interest for a longer-term commitment to keep agreements. Gauthier reasons as follows: "A straightforward maximizer, who is disposed to make maximizing choices [i.e., defect in the prisoner's dilemma], must expect to be excluded from cooperative arrangements which he would find advantageous. A constrained maximizer may expect to be included in such arrangements. She benefits from her disposition, not in the choices she makes, but in her opportunities to choose." David Gauthier, Morals by Agreement 183 (1986). What do you think about this argument? Do people cooperate because it is the moral thing to do or the rational thing to do? Is it both? Is it neither?

2.34 The Negotiator's Dilemma suggests one reason why there might be a demand for mediation. The creation of an environment where negotiators can safely explore collaboration (without fear of the other side's defection) has the potential to generate significant payoffs. For a discussion of how this same dynamic might create a demand for cooperative lawyers, see Ronald J. Gilson & Robert H. Mnookin, Disputing Through Agents: Cooperation and Conflict Between Lawyers in Litigation, 94 Colum. L. Rev. 509 (1995).

2. Structural and Psychological Barriers to Negotiation

a. Informational Barrier

The Prisoner's and Negotiator's Dilemma often leads to a key structural barrier to a negotiated settlement: lack of information. When negotiators will not share information (a rational choice from a competitive bargaining viewpoint) it becomes virtually impossible to construct integrative solutions and, in fact, impasse results despite the fact that there is a positive zone of agreement. Robert Mnookin describes this barrier.

 Robert Mnookin, **WHY NEGOTIATIONS FAIL: AN EXPLORATION OF BARRIERS TO THE RESOLUTION OF CONFLICT**

8 Ohio St. J. on Disp. Resol. 235, 239-242 (1993)

[One] barrier to the negotiated resolution of conflict is inherent in a central characteristic of negotiation. Negotiation can be metaphorically compared to making a pie and then dividing it up. The process of conflict resolution effects both the size of the pie, and who gets what size slice. . . .

Because bargaining typically entails both efficiency issues (that is, how big the pie can be made) and distributive issues (that is, who gets what size slice), negotiation involves an inherent tension — one that David Lax and James Sebenius have dubbed the "negotiator's dilemma." In order to create value, it is critically important that options be created in light of both parties' underlying interests and preferences. This suggests the importance of openness and disclosure, so that a variety of options can be analyzed and compared from the perspectives of all concerned. However, when it comes to the distributive aspects of bargaining, full disclosure — particularly if unreciprocated by the other side — can often lead to outcomes in which the more open party receives a comparatively smaller slice. To put it another way, unreciprocated approaches to creating value leave their maker vulnerable to claiming tactics. On the other hand, focusing on the distributive aspects of bargaining can often lead to unnecessary deadlocks and, more fundamentally, a failure to discover options or alternatives that make both sides better off. A simple example can expose the dilemma. The first involves what game theorists call "information asymmetry." This simply means each side to a negotiation characteristically knows some relevant facts that the other side does not know.

Suppose I have ten apples and no oranges, and Nancy Rogers has ten oranges and no apples. (Assume apples and oranges are otherwise unavailable to either of us.) I love oranges and hate apples. Nancy likes them both equally well. I suggest to Nancy that we might both be made better off through a trade. If I disclose to Nancy that I love oranges and don't eat apples, and Nancy wishes to engage in strategic bargaining, she might simply suggest that her preferences are the same as mine, although, in truth, she likes both. She might propose that I give her nine apples (which she says have little value to her) in exchange for one of her very valuable oranges. Because it is often very difficult for one party to know the underlying preferences of the other party, parties in a negotiation may puff, bluff, or lie about their underlying interests and preferences. Indeed, in many negotiations, it may never be possible to know whether the other side has honestly disclosed its interests and preferences. I have to be open to create value, but my openness may work to my disadvantage with respect to the distributive aspect of the negotiation.

Even when both parties know all the relevant information, and the potential gains may result from a negotiated deal, strategic bargaining over how to divide the pie can still lead to deadlock (with no deal at all) or protracted and expensive bargaining, thus shrinking the pie. For example, suppose Nancy has a house for sale for which she has a reservation price of $245,000. I am willing to pay up to $295,000 for the house. Any deal within a bargaining range from $245,000 to $295,000 would make both of us better off than no sale at all. Suppose we each know the other's reservation price. Will there be a deal? Not necessarily. If we disagree about how the $50,000 "surplus" should be divided (each wanting all or most of it), our negotiation may end in a deadlock. . . .

Strategic behavior — which may be rational for a self-interested party concerned with maximizing the size of his or her own slice — can often lead to inefficient outcomes. Those subjected to claiming tactics often respond in kind, and the net result typically is to push up the cost of the dispute resolution process. . . . Parties may be tempted to engage in a strategic behavior, hoping to get more. Often all they do is shrink the size of the pie. Those experienced in the civil litigation process see this all the time. One or both sides often attempt to use pre-trial discovery as leverage to force the other side into agreeing to a more favorable settlement. Often the net result, however, is simply that both sides spend unnecessary money on the dispute resolution process.

Notes and Questions

2.35 How is the problem with strategic barriers linked to the Prisoner's Dilemma and Negotiator's Dilemma?

2.36 How can mediators and attorney representatives overcome these barriers?

b. Irrational Escalation of Commitment

The next excerpt is from Bazerman and Neale's list of common negotiation mistakes. One mistake, the irrational escalation of commitment, occurs when negotiators can't back down—even though it makes rational sense—because they perceive it as "losing" the negotiation.

 Max H. Bazerman & Margaret A. Neale, **NEGOTIATING RATIONALLY**

9-11 (1992)

THE IRRATIONAL ESCALATION OF COMMITMENT

People often behave in ways inconsistent with their own self-interests. One common mistake is to irrationally stay committed to an initial course of action. . . . The desire to "win" at any cost preempts developing a rational negotiation strategy. . . .

Maxwell House and Folgers have battled for over ten years to dominate the U.S. coffee market. In addition to using costly incentives, both companies spent $100 million on coffee advertising in 1990 alone, roughly four times what they spent only three years earlier. This escalation has depressed prices to a level that hurts the entire industry, and neither Maxwell House nor Folgers has significantly improved its market share.

Competition of this type is common. The story of the coffee wars is also the story of the cola wars (Pepsi/Coke) and the camera wars (Polaroid/Kodak). Each side views its goal as beating the other firm as opposed to making the industry more profitable. While the information often exists to pursue a rational end to the conflict, each side sticks with its initial course of action, and catastrophe follows. . . . American coffee makers continue to lose millions of dollars in opportunity costs. Even when conflict is not leading to the desired outcome, decision makers are often obsessed by the small probability that escalating the conflict one step further could lead to victory.

We define *irrational escalation* as continuing a previously selected course of action beyond what rational analysis would recommend. Misdirected persistence can lead to wasting a great deal of time, energy, and money. Directed persistence can lead to commensurate payoffs. Rational analysis enables you to distinguish the two.

You must recognize that the time and money already invested are "sunk costs." They *cannot* be recovered and should *not* be considered when selecting future courses of action. Your reference point for action should be the present. Consider your alternative by evaluating only the *future* costs and benefits associated with each.

This is a hard concept to absorb. Once committed to a course of action, executives often allocate resources in ways that justify their previous choices, whether or not they now appear valid.

c. Justice Seeking

There are a variety of other barriers to negotiation. The first barrier, examined below, is that parties are less willing to compromise when they feel they have been treated unfairly or disrespectfully. Mediation addresses this barrier by allowing parties the opportunity to explain their conduct to each other and to apologize (where appropriate).

 Russell Korobkin & Chris Guthrie, **PSYCHOLOGICAL BARRIERS TO LITIGATION SETTLEMENT: AN EXPERIMENTAL APPROACH**

93 Mich. L. Rev. 107, 144-146 (1994)

We provided subjects with a simple landlord-tenant dispute. Subjects were told that they signed a six-month lease to live in an off-campus apartment beginning September 1. After two months the heater broke down. Although they immediately notified the landlord and requested repair, the landlord failed to fix the heater. As a result, according to the scenario, the subjects spent four winter months in a cold apartment attempting to keep warm with a space heater before moving out at the end of the lease period. Throughout this time period, the subjects had continued to pay $1,000 per month in rent. After moving out, they learned from a student legal service lawyer that "there was a good chance" of recovering a portion of the $4,000 in rent paid over that four-month period of time. The lawyer gave neither a specific prediction of the likelihood of success nor any estimate of the exact magnitude of a judgment. Subjects learned that, with the assistance of their attorney, they had filed an action in small claims court against the landlord. Prior to the court date, the landlord offered to settle the case out of court for $900.

The variable tested in this scenario was the landlord's reason for failing to repair the heater in spite of the tenant's prompt request that he do so. Group *A* subjects learned that they had made a number of calls to the landlord, to no avail. "The landlord promised to fix your heater, but he never did. A week later, you called him again. Again, he promised to fix it, but he never did. Over the next several weeks, you called him a half-dozen times, but he did not return your calls." Group *B* participants received a different explanation: After the second call to the landlord, "[y]ou learned that he had left the country unexpectedly due to a family emergency and that he was expected to be gone for several months." Both Group *A* and Group *B* subjects chose one of the five usual answer choices to indicate their likelihood of accepting the $900 settlement offer.

The given explanation had a significant impact on how likely subjects were to accept the settlement offer and forgo their day in court. Knowing that the landlord did not fix the heater because he was out of the country due to a family emergency, most Group *B* (Family Emergency) subjects were willing to accept the landlord's offer and let the matter rest. . . . Group *A* subjects (Broken Promise), in contrast, were more likely to reject the $900 offer and risk a less favorable decision in small claims court than to accept the offer. . . . The difference between the two groups is highly significant. Fifty-nine percent of the Family Emergency subjects said they would "definitely" or "probably" accept the settlement offer, while only 35% of the Broken Promise subjects provided those same responses. Thirty percent of the Broken Promise subjects said they would "definitely reject" the $900 settlement offer in favor of small claims court, while only 9% of the Family Emergency subjects would "definitely reject" the offer.

Notes and Questions

2.37 Should you or your client care about how the other side treats you in a dispute?

2.38 Think back to the Prisoner's Dilemma. The theory of equity explains why we "punish" the other side when they defect, even if that does not make economic sense. How can attorneys help their clients avoid this situation? What would you suggest?

2.39 Another often-told story shows how children can be wiser than adults in important respects:

> In my first year Contracts class, I wished to review various doctrines we had recently studied. I put the following:
>
> In a long-term installment contract, Seller promises Buyer to deliver widgets at the rate of 1,000 a month. The first two deliveries are perfect. However, in the third month Seller delivers only 990 widgets. Buyer becomes so incensed that he rejects delivery and refuses to pay for the widgets already delivered.
>
> After stating the problem, I asked, "If you were Seller, what would you say?" What I was looking for was a discussion of the various common law theories which would force the buyer to pay for the widgets delivered and those which would throw Buyer into breach for canceling the remaining deliveries. In short, I wanted the class to come up with the legal doctrines which would allow Seller to crush Buyer.
>
> After asking the question, I looked around the room for a volunteer. As is so often the case with first year students, I found there were [none]. There was, however, one eager face, that of an eight-year-old son of one of my students. It seems that he was suffering through Contracts due to his mother's sin of failing to find a sitter. Suddenly, he raised his hand. Such behavior, even from an eight-year-old, must be rewarded.
>
> "OK," I said, "What would you say if you were the seller?"
>
> "I'd say, 'I'm sorry.'"

Kenny Hegland, *Why Teach Trial Advocacy? An Essay on Never Ask Why,* in Humanistic Educ. L. 69 (J. Himmelstein & H. Lesnick eds., 1982).

Would you as the attorney suggest that your client apologize if he or she were involved in a car accident? Why or why not? What if your client was a doctor who made a medical error? Would it matter if the patient knew?

2.40 Professor Jonathan Cohen writes about the Veteran Affairs Hospital in Lexington, Kentucky, which adopted a new policy in 1987 requiring all staff to inform patients about any errors:

> From the financial viewpoint, the new approach of assuming responsibility, including apology, passed the Hippocratic test: it appears to have done the hospital no financial harm and may have done some financial good. Recall that in 1985 and 1986 the hospital paid two malpractice verdicts that together totaled $1.5 million. From 1990 through 1996, the hospital paid an average of only $190,113 per year in malpractice claims, with an average (mean) payment of $15,622 per claim. This placed the Lexington VA in the lowest quartile of thirty-six comparable VA hospitals for malpractice payments and in the bottom sixth in terms of average liability payment per claim. . . .
>
> Many lawyers see only the obvious economic risks to apology but overlook the possible economic benefits. Stepping back for a moment from the example of the Lexington VA, two reasons apology can be economically beneficial to the apologizer are as follows. First, in some cases injured parties may refrain from suing if they receive an apology. . . . Second, an apology can greatly facilitate the settlement process and thereby reduce settlement costs. An apology often cannot substitute for compensation for the injury but can be a way of avoiding compounding insult upon the injury-insult that can prevent settlement. . . . As VA hospital lawyer Ginny Hamm described, "The attorneys around here in Lexington used to think we were crazy [when we initiated our new policy]." As one who studies the possible benefits and risks of apology, I can attest that many attorneys and legal academics greet the idea that apology can financially benefit the apologizer with much skepticism. The Lexington VA's experience helps refute the skeptic's view that apology necessarily entails financial suicide. Rather, it indicates the opposite: apology can be to the apologizer's financial benefit.

Jonathan R. Cohen, Apology and Organizations: Exploring an Example from Medical Practice, 27 Fordham Urb. L.J. 1447 (2000).

2.41 For an interesting empirical examination of the value of apologies in the legal context, see Jennifer K. Robbennolt, Apologies and Legal Settlement: An Empirical Examination, 102 Mich. L. Rev. 460 (2003). Robbennolt suggests "that an apology may favorably impact the prospects for settlement but that attention must be paid to both the nature of the apologetic expression and the circumstances of the individual case."

d. Loss Aversion and Status Quo Barriers

Another barrier to rational behavior in negotiation is the phenomenon of loss aversion — the status quo barrier. This barrier refers to the mistakes or assumptions that negotiators make because they like the status quo. They like the items they have in their possession and fear losing them. Economics professor Daniel Kahneman and psychology professor Amos Tversky discuss a phenomenon called the "endowment effect," which occurs when negotiators value what they own more than what they do not. This effect also brings in the element of risk. What are we willing to risk to avoid losing something we have? In 2002, Kahneman won the Nobel Prize in economics for his work on the endowment effect.

 Daniel Kahneman & Amos Tversky, **CONFLICT RESOLUTION: A COGNITIVE PERSPECTIVE**

in Barriers to Conflict Resolution 54-55 (Kenneth Arrow et al. eds., 1995)

Loss aversion refers to the observation that losses generally loom larger than the corresponding gains. . . . In decisions under risk, loss aversion entails a reluctance to accept even-chance gambles, unless the payoffs are very favorable. For example, many people will accept such a gamble only if the gain is at least twice as large as the loss. . . .

The following classroom demonstration illustrates the principle of loss aversion. An attractive object (e.g., a decorated mug) is distributed to one third of the students. The students who have been given mugs are *sellers*—perhaps better described as owners. They are informed that there will be an opportunity to exchange the mug for a predetermined amount of money. The subjects state what their choice will be for different amounts, and thereby indicate the minimal amount for which they are willing to give up their mug. Another one-third of the students are *choosers*. They are told that they will have a choice between a mug like the one in the hands of their neighbor and an amount of cash; they indicate their choices for different amounts. The remaining students are *buyers:* they indicate whether they would pay each of the different amounts to acquire a mug. In a representative experiment, the median price set by sellers was $7.12, the median cash equivalent set by the choosers was $3.12, and the median buyer was willing to pay $2.88 for the mug.

The difference between the valuations of owners and choosers occurs in spite of the fact that both groups face the same choice: go home with a mug or with a prespecified sum of money. Subjectively, however, the choosers and owners are in different states: the former evaluate the mug as a gain, the latter as something to be given up. Because of loss aversion, more cash is required to persuade the owners to give up the mug than to match the attractiveness of the mug to the choosers. . . . The experimental studies of the discrepant valuation of owners, choosers, and buyers demonstrate that loss aversion can be induced instantaneously; it does not depend on a progressive attachment to objects in one's possession.

Notes and Questions

2.42 Why are negotiators willing to risk more to avoid a loss? Put another way, why do you think people value what they have in their possession more than those things they do not have? What implications for negotiation does this phenomenon have?

2.43 What can the lawyer do to help the client deal with these tendencies (or the lawyer's own tendencies)? Can you frame an offer as a gain rather than a loss? Can you foresee how a mediator might be helpful in framing proposals as potential gains rather than losses?

2.44 Russell Korobkin and Chris Guthrie conducted an experiment in which a hypothetical car accident causes damages of $28,000. The other (negligent) driver's insurance company offers $21,000 to settle. In one set of facts, however, the driver is driving a $14,000 car with $14,000 of medical bills. In the other set of facts, the driver is driving a $24,000 car with $4,000 of medical bills. In both cases, the driver's health insurance already covers the medical expenses (although a jury would not be informed of that fact). The owners of the $14,000 car are more likely to accept the settlement than the owners of the $24,000 car. Russell Korobkin & Chris Guthrie, Psychological Barriers to Litigation Settlement: An Experimental Approach, 93 Mich. L. Rev. 107 (1994). Why do you think this is so? How is a $21,000 settlement perceived as a loss or a gain?

e. Anchoring, Optimistic Overconfidence, and the Winner's Curse

Business school professors Max Bazerman and Margaret Neale identify three mistakes negotiators make: anchoring, overconfidence, and the winner's curse. Anchoring occurs when negotiators rely too heavily on the information at hand. Optimistic overconfidence traps negotiators when they have more faith than they should in the accuracy of their position, their evaluation of the other side, or other events occurring in the negotiation. Often overconfidence stems from an inability to review information objectively. The winner's curse occurs when negotiators get what they want or get it too soon — and then regret it.

 Max H. Bazerman & Margaret A. Neale, NEGOTIATING RATIONALLY

26-28, 49, 54, 62-63 (1992)

ANCHORING

With the cooperation of a real estate agent who had just put a house on the market, we asked a number of real estate brokers to evaluate the house. We also asked a separate group of brokers what information they used in valuing a piece of residential real estate and to give us an estimate of how accurately agents could appraise its value. This second group said that any deviation from the appraisal value of more than 5 percent would be highly unusual and easy to recognize.

To give each agent all the information they needed about the house, we created a ten-page packet of information. . . . We divided up the packets into four groups and changed two pieces of information in each. After having the property independently valued by appraisers, we took their average value and set the listing price 12 percent higher than the appraised value, 4 percent higher, 4 percent lower, or 12 percent lower. We changed the price per square foot so that it correctly reflected the listing price.

When the agents came to evaluate the house (in the normal course of their jobs), we gave them one of the four packets and asked them to estimate (1) the appraised value of the house, (2) an appropriate listing price for the house, (3) a reasonable price to pay for the house, and (4) the lowest offer they would accept if they were the seller. We also asked them to identify from a list the relevant considerations that had gone into their evaluation and briefly describe the process they used to arrive at the four figures.

When we analyzed the data from these real estate agents, we came up with some very interesting results. . . . The listing price had a major impact on their valuation process; they were more likely to have high estimates on all four prices when the listing price was high than when it was low.

> ### HOW HOT IS IT?
>
> It is important to note that anchors do not even need to be reasonable in order for the effect to be felt. In a study on anchoring, researchers asked participants whether the average temperature in San Francisco was more or less than 558 degrees. They were then asked what they think the actual average temperature is. Those participants who were given the outrageously high number guessed that the temperature was higher than those participants who were given a reasonable number.
>
> Scott Plous, The Psychology of Judgment and Decision Making 146 (1993).

When we tried to figure out what information they thought they were using, another interesting pattern emerged. Although it is clear that listing price had played a role in the agents' evaluations of the house, only 19 percent of the agents mentioned listing price as a factor they considered and only 8 percent indicated that listing price was one of their top three considerations. Interestingly, almost three-quarters of the agents reported using a computational strategy to assess the value of the real estate. To determine the value of the property, 72 percent of the agents indicated that they took the average price per square foot of comparable houses that had recently sold, multiplied that number by the number of square feet in our property and then adjusted for the condition of the house. If they had, indeed, used such a strategy, then we couldn't have observed any anchoring effect of the listing price; it would have been irrelevant. Nevertheless, the anchoring effect is not only present, it is pronounced.

Research has shown that final agreements in any negotiation are more strongly influenced by initial offers than by the subsequent concessionary behavior of an opponent, particularly when issues under consideration are of uncertain or ambiguous value. Responding to an initial offer with suggested adjustments gives that anchor some measure of credibility. Thus, if an initial offer is too extreme, you need to re-anchor the process. Threatening to walk away from the table is better than agreeing to an unacceptable starting point. . . .

OPTIMISTIC OVERCONFIDENCE

As we pointed out, when people hold certain beliefs or expectations, they tend to ignore information that contradicts them. Consider the following problem we've given to our classes.

Here is a three-number sequence: 2-4-6. Your task is to discover the numeric rule that produced these numbers. To determine the rule, you can generate other sets of three numbers so that we will acknowledge as either conforming or not conforming to the actual rule. You can stop producing sets of three numbers when you think you've discovered the rule. How would you go about this task?

In our classes, the first response is usually to propose sets of numbers such as 4-6-8 and 10-12-14, using an "ascending even numbers" rule. While our rule would also produce these two sets of numbers, their proposed rule is not ours. Then class members often propose numbers such as 5-10-15 and 100-200-300, the rule being "the difference between the first two numbers equals the difference between the last two numbers." Again, the class has come up with the wrong rule.

The actual rule we used is "any three ascending numbers"—a solution that required the accumulation of *disconfirming*, rather than confirming, evidence. To discover how the true rule differs from your hypothesized rule, you must try sequences that do *not* conform to your rule. Trying the sequences 1-2-3, 10-15-20, 122-126-130, and so forth will only lead you into the confirmation trap. Finding the correct rule often requires a willingness to disprove your initial beliefs or hypotheses.

Managers don't often seek to disprove an initial belief. Charles Lord, Lee Ross, and Mark Lepper selected participants for a study based upon their support for or opposition to capital punishment. The subjects were presented with two (purportedly) authentic empirical studies. One supported their position; the other opposed their position. While they read these two studies, the participants were asked several times to evaluate their quality. Both the proponents and opponents of capital punishment rated the study that supported their beliefs as more convincing and better-conducted than one that opposed their beliefs. Further, the net effect of reading these two studies was to polarize further each group's beliefs. It seems that people are more likely to take at face value information they agree with and scrutinize more carefully information they don't.

Managers tend to enter negotiations with one strategy for reaching agreement. They assume success and develop their strategy accordingly. A very different view, and one we believe is more useful, is to realize that your initial strategy may not work and seek to disconfirm it by searching for new information. If you are not open to disconfirming information, you will have a harder time adapting when confronted by unexpected circumstances in a negotiation. . . .

THE WINNER'S CURSE

The famous comedian Groucho Marx said that he didn't want to be a member of any club that would have him as a member. Why? A club's acceptance of his application told him something about its standards—if they were so low as to accept him, he didn't want to join! Most people don't have Groucho's insight, and often make offers in negotiating without realizing the implications of having those offers accepted. Consider the following story:

You are in a foreign country and meet a merchant who is selling a very attractive gem. You've purchased a few gems in your life, but are far from an expert. After some discussion, you make what you're fairly sure is a low offer. The merchant quickly accepts, and the gem is yours. How do you feel?

Most people would feel uneasy. This is known as the "winner's curse." Yet, why would you voluntarily make an offer that you would not want accepted?. . . .

There are ways to avoid the winner's curse. Sellers of high quality or reliable goods (new or used) and services can take steps to reassure buyers about their quality. . . .

Obviously, an ongoing relationship between parties can also solve or reduce the winner's curse, since a seller may not want to harm the relationship by taking advantage of a buyer. . . .

Government intervention can also help solve the winner's curse. Some state and local governments have created "lemon laws" in the used-car market to protect buyers and promote trade.

People don't fully realize the true importance of getting accurate information when making transactions. There's great value in a mechanic's unbiased evaluation of a used car, a professional inspector's assessment of a house, or an independent jeweler's assessment of a coveted gem. To protect yourself, you need to develop, borrow, or buy professional expertise to make up for any information you don't have. Many people don't like paying for something (an appraisal) that will probably confirm what they already thought was true. They see this as money for nothing. They would be acting more rationally if they looked at independent appraisals as insurance against buying a lemon, whether it's a car, an overpriced house, or a piece of glass disguising itself as a ruby.

Notes and Questions

2.45 If parties can get anchored by information, should you make the first offer in a negotiation? What are the risks? What are the benefits? Should mediators advantage/disadvantage a particular side by inviting it to make the first offer?

2.46 How does the concept of setting aspirations tie in with the concept of anchoring? Can you also anchor yourself?

2.47 How can you protect yourself from the anchoring phenomenon? How can lawyers assist their clients in this?

2.48 This excerpt discusses both our overconfidence in our information and our overconfidence in our negotiation strategy. How can a negotiator deal with each of these problems?

Researchers argue that a valuable strategy to avoid information barriers "may be to frame questions in a way that encourages disconfirming answers." Professor Scott Plous uses the story of a top analyst at Kidder Peabody who asked questions *the opposite* of what he actually believed. "If Freedman thinks the disposable diaper business is becoming less price competitive, for example, he will ask executives a question that implies the opposite, such as, 'Is it true that price competition is getting tougher in disposable diapers?' This kind of question makes him more likely than competing analysts to get the real story." Scott Plous, The Psychology of Judgment and Decision Making 239-240 (1993). How can you translate this advice into lawyering?

f. Reactive Devaluation

This last excerpt focuses on reactive devaluation, which occurs when we automatically discount an offer made by the other side *because it is an offer made by the other side.*

 Lee Ross, REACTIVE DEVALUATION IN NEGOTIATION AND CONFLICT RESOLUTION

in Barriers to Conflict Resolution 28-29, 33-35 (Kenneth Arrow et al. eds., 1995)

One need only pick up the morning newspaper . . . to see that negotiations frequently fail and deadlocks persist even in conflicts where preservation of the status quo clearly seems to be against the best interest of the relevant parties. To some extent, the problem can be traced to barriers — strategic, psychological, or situational — that make it difficult to formulate, and/or get on the table, a proposal that both parties, given their different interests and views and their conflicting strategic goals, deem preferable, at least temporarily, to perpetuation of the status quo. But even when such a "mutually-acceptable-in-principle" proposal *can* be formulated, there may be an additional barrier to be overcome, one that arises, at least in large part, from the dynamics of the negotiation process. This barrier has been termed *reactive devaluation*. It refers to the fact that the very offer of a particular proposal or concession — especially if the offer comes from an *adversary* — may diminish its apparent value or attractiveness in the eyes of the recipient. . . .

Initial evidence for the reactive devaluation barrier was provided in a 1986 sidewalk survey of opinions regarding possible arms reduction by the U.S. and the U.S.S.R. Respondents were asked to evaluate the terms of a simple but sweeping nuclear disarmament proposal — one calling for immediate 50 percent reduction of long-range strategic weapons, to be followed over the next decade and a half by further reduction in both strategic and short-range tactical weapons until, very early in the next century, all such weapons would have disappeared from the two nations' arsenals. As a matter of history, this proposal had actually been made slightly earlier, with little fanfare or impact, by the Soviet leader Gorbachev. In the Stillinger et al. survey,* however, the proposal's putative source was *manipulated* — that is, depending on experimental condition, it was ascribed by the survey instrument either to the

---

* C. Stillinger, M. Epelbaum, D. Keltner & L. Ross (1990). The "reactive devaluation" barrier to conflict resolution. Unpublished manuscript. Stanford: Stanford University.

Soviet leader, to President Reagan, or to a group of unknown strategy analysts — and only the responses of subjects who claimed to be hearing of the proposal for the first time were included in subsequent analyses.

The results of this survey showed, as predicted, that the proposal's putative authorship determined its attractiveness. When the proposal was attributed to the U.S. leader, 90 percent of respondents thought it either favorable to the U.S. or evenhanded; and when it was attributed to the (presumably neutral) third party, 80 percent thought it either favorable to the U.S. or evenhanded; but when the same proposal was attributed to the Soviet leader, only 44 percent of respondents expressed a similarly positive reaction. . . .

To the extent that adversaries devalue the compromises and concessions put on the table by the other side, they exacerbate an already difficult dilemma: that of forging an agreement that the relevant parties, with their differing views of history and their differing perceptions of entitlement, will perceive to be better than the status quo and not offensive to their sense of equity. Beyond alerting us to this dilemma, the Stillinger et al. studies raise two important, ultimately related, questions. First, what processes or mechanisms might cause the offer of a concession or compromise proposal to decrease its attractiveness in the eyes of the recipient? Second, what steps might be taken, either by the adversaries themselves or by third-party mediators, to overcome this barrier?. . .

One set of underlying processes involves changes in *perception, interpretation, or inference,* either about individual elements in a proposal or about the overall valence of that proposal. To the extent that the other side's initiative seems inconsistent with our understanding of their interests and/or past negotiation behavior, we are apt, perhaps even logically obliged, to scrutinize their offer rather carefully. That is, we are inclined to look for ambiguities, omissions, or "fine print" that might render the terms of that proposal more advantageous to the other side, and perhaps less advantageous to our side, than we had assumed them to be (or would have assumed them to be, had the question been asked) prior to their being offered. The results of such skeptical scrutiny — especially if the terms in question are unclear, complex, or imperfectly specified, and especially if trust vis-à-vis implementation of these terms is called for — are apt to be a revised assessment of what we stand to gain, both in absolute terms and relative to what we believe the other side stands to gain, from acceptance of the relevant proposal.

This process of inference and deduction, as psychologists would be quick to note, could be even simpler and less cognitively demanding. . . . [N]o reinterpretation, in fact no consideration of content at all, need take place for devaluation to occur. One might simply reason if "they" are offering a proposal it must be good for them; and if it is good for them (especially if "they" are adversaries who wish us harm) it must be bad for "us." . . . One can be led to conclude that any proposal offered by the "other side" — especially if that other side has long been perceived as an enemy — *must* be to our side's disadvantage, or else it would not have been offered. Such an inferential process, however, assumes a perfect opposition of interests, or in other words, a true "zero-sum" game, when such is rarely the case in real world negotiations between parties whose needs, goals, and opportunities are inevitably complex and varied.

Notes and Questions

2.49 During the 1980s, South Carolina Congressman Floyd Spence stated, "I have had a philosophy for some time in regard to SALT [Strategic Arms Limitation Treaty], and it goes like this: the Russians will not accept a SALT treaty that is not in their best interest, and it seems to me that if it is in their best interest, it can't be in our best interest." Max H. Bazerman & Margaret A. Neale, Negotiating Rationally 19 (1992). Does Congressman Spence's statement make sense?

2.50 How is reactive devaluation linked to issues discussed in the section on informational barriers?

2.51 Can you think of an instance where, in negotiating with a parent or other authority figure, you automatically dismissed an otherwise "good" offer?

2.52 A phenomenon related to reactive devaluation is an elevated willingness to accept proposals — regardless of their objective or rational value or cost — if the proposal comes from someone loved or admired. Are there some people to whom you say "yes" before hearing even what they propose? Knowing that negotiators can gain power from being liked and trusted, how would that influence your strategy as an attorney negotiator? What should a mediator do if s/he sees a party saying "yes" too easily?

PART II   THE MEDIATION PROCESS

 **Chapter 3** Mediation: Concepts and Models

Summum ius. Summa iniuria. (The strictest following of the law can lead to the greatest injustice.)

—Marcus Tullius Cicero

There is no intractable problem.

—Desmond Tutu

A. INTRODUCTION TO MEDIATION

1. What Is Mediation?

Mediation is a process in which an impartial third party acts as a catalyst to help others constructively address and perhaps resolve a dispute, plan a transaction, or define the contours of a relationship. A mediator facilitates negotiation between the parties to enable better communication, encourage problem solving, and develop an agreement or resolution by consensus among the parties. The process of mediation can best be understood by examining the many roles of the mediator.

A variety of metaphors describe the mediator's roles. The mediator acts as *host* and *chair*: convening the parties for discussions; making arrangements for adequate, safe, and comfortable facilities; attending to special needs of disputants (for example, disabilities or language differences); and ensuring that the agenda is constructive, that any obstacles that develop are addressed, and that agreements are memorialized. The mediator is a *guide, coach*, and *educator*, steering the parties toward effective negotiation behavior and away from destructive, self-defeating maneuvers. The mediator is a *referee*, offering each party an equal place at the bargaining table, allowing each voice to be heard, and encouraging parties to get additional resources or to withdraw from mediation if it is no longer constructive. The mediator is a master *communicator* and *translator*, gleaning insights from conversations rife with extreme positions, threats, and blame to help parties hear one another's interests, issues, proposals, feelings, principles, and values. In one sense, this function of translating is akin to that of an alchemist, turning the danger inherent in conflict into the "gold" of possibility and opportunity for disputants. The mediator serves as an *agent of reality*, urging evaluation and reevaluation of positions and assumptions and encouraging assessment and reassessment of what others are saying. The mediator is a *watchdog*, protecting the process itself and prohibiting parties from using a session merely to obtain an advantage in litigation or to abuse one another.

Mediators intervene in a wide array of disputes — from family and community to commercial and international. Mediation is useful for parties facing an actual dispute, trying to reconcile competing interests, or planning for the possibility of conflict. For example, a mediator can help divorcing couples determine parenting arrangements and asset division or help people who are contemplating marriage negotiate a prenuptial agreement. A mediator can help settle a controversy over liability and damages related to an environmental disaster such as an oil spill or can help a community determine the route for a highway or the site of a garbage facility.

In mediation, the parties retain control over the dispute and its outcome. This central feature of mediation — self-determination by the parties — is a facet of democratic process — that the voice and wisdom of people can shape outcomes responsive to particular situations. In this respect, mediation is fundamentally different from adjudication, where power to determine the outcome is ceded to a judge, jury, or arbiter.

Adjudication and the rule of law can clarify and develop public norms. Adjudication supports the stability and predictability inherent in law and evenhanded application of rules. Litigation — at least when decisions are made and published — gives society precedents that promote order by guiding similarly situated actors. Mediation, on the other hand, enhances communication, fosters collaboration, and encourages problem solving. These goals are also important to achieving individual and community well-being. If, for example, landlords and tenants, minority groups and school boards, or employers and employees can resolve existing controversies through mediation, they not only achieve a resolution tailored to their specific situation but also can bank their success in problem solving to help resolve future disputes.

In comparing these two very different approaches to addressing disputes, it is important to note that they serve different masters and have their own distinct logic and integrity. In adjudication, with ideals embedded in concepts of evolving law and precepts for ordering society, an arbiter determines facts and applies rules to determine rights and liabilities with respect to past acts. In mediation, a structuring of the future is possible: to avoid past pitfalls and to build new opportunities. The spotlight moves from evidence of past conduct and historic facts to parties' interests and finally to possibilities for optimal balancing of those interests. Where, for example, a supplier and a customer have taken a matter to court to determine damages for a shipment that was nonconforming under a contract, those same parties in mediation might adjust their differences by arrangements in future contracts, making allowances for past wrongs.

This chapter explores the foundations of mediation, the historical context for current perspectives, and the place mediation holds in the array of dispute resolution processes. As mediation has developed, different orientations, goals, and strategies have been propounded. A sampling of major approaches and varying descriptions of the mediation process follow and conclude the chapter.

2. The Advantages of Mediation

To understand the rationales for mediation, examine the fictional case of Jarndyce v. Jarndyce, the focal point of Charles Dickens' novel, *Bleak House.* The case involves a will contest that consumes several generations in a family. The family members become so obsessed and absorbed by the legal contest that they lose their way in life and become divided one against the other. The legal issues in the fictional case are so complicated that even the lawyers cannot explain or agree on them. Ultimately, the legal costs consume the estate, and the lawsuit ends with everyone (except the lawyers who retain their fees) a loser.

The story illustrates many of the shortcomings of litigation: prohibitive expense, heart-breaking delay, a lack of party participation and control of the process, unsatisfactory outcomes, and an adversarial orientation that alienates parties from one another. Mediation can address each of these shortcomings.

a. Settlement: Avoiding the Expense, Delay, and Risk of Adjudication

The success and efficiency of mediated resolutions are key reasons that many lawyers advise clients to mediate. Compared to the risky undertaking of adjudication — whether litigation or arbitration — mediation offers

> **Jarndyce v. Jarndyce**
>
> Jarndyce v. Jarndyce . . . has, in the course of time, become so complicated, that no man alive knows what it means. The parties to it understand it least; but it has been observed that no two Chancery lawyers can talk about it for five minutes, without coming to a total disagreement as to all the premises. Innumerable children have been born into the cause; innumerable young people have married into it; innumerable old people have died out of it. Scores of persons have deliriously found themselves made parties in Jarndyce v. Jarndyce, without knowing how or why; whole families have inherited legendary hatreds with the suit. The little plaintiff or defendant, who was promised a new rocking-horse when Jarndyce and Jarndyce should be settled, has grown up, possessed himself of a real horse, and trotted away into the other world. Fair wards of court have faded into mothers and grandmothers; a long procession of Chancellors has come in and gone out; the legion of bills in the suit have been transformed into mere bills of mortality; there are not three Jarndyces left upon the earth perhaps, since old Tom Jarndyce in despair blew his brains out at a coffee-house in Chancery Lane; but Jarndyce and Jarndyce still drags its dreary length before the Court, perennially hopeless.
>
> Charles Dickens, Bleak House.

parties the possibility of acceptable conclusions, ones they have crafted themselves. In litigation, a judge or jury decides the matter, checked only by the appeal process. In binding arbitration, an individual decision maker (or a panel of decision makers), chosen by the parties, renders a final decision. Whenever a party gives another person the power to decide a controversy, the outcome is inherently unpredictable and may produce an unhappy surprise.

Litigation tends to be slow and expensive. Centuries ago William Shakespeare's Hamlet complained about "the law's delay." In Jarndyce v. Jarndyce it is clear that *any settlement*—before the estate was exhausted—would have provided greater benefit to the parties than the failed litigation. While the arbitration process, created by the parties in their

> *Justice delayed is justice denied.*
>
> —attributed to William E. Gladstone

agreement to arbitrate, can be fast, arbitration can also resemble litigation, in which case it too becomes slow and costly. The benefits of speedy closure are financial, practical, and psychological. The parties in Jarndyce v. Jarndyce grew old before the litigation whimpered to an end. Many disputes need prompt address. A patent dispute, for example, must be resolved before the patent expires. An allegation of discrimination in the workplace should be addressed before the employee becomes embittered and affects others in the office or before a similar act of discrimination occurs. Businesses embroiled in conflict are diverted from the pursuit of business goals. A mediation can be scheduled quickly, and sessions, for certain cases, can take as little as a few hours. As Jarndyce v. Jarndyce illustrates, a conflict can drag "its dreary length" leading to despair and loss.

Mediation can temper unrealistic positions, unwarranted assumptions, and demonization of another party. Overconfident views of a case and the dynamics of adversarial behavior can box parties into unproductive assertions and claims. Face-to-face interaction forces each side to hear each other and to take into account the other's perspective. The mediation process offers parties a chance to shift expectations and temper self-serving attitudes, while working to reach an acceptable accord; this, in turn, avoids the risk of an adverse judgment in adjudication.

Finally, settlement benefits the court system. In offering a variety of methods to resolve disputes, courts can serve the various interests of disputing parties and may relieve court dockets as well.

b. Participation and Self-Determination: Giving Parties Voice and Choice

A central value of mediation is self-determination. Self-determination means that parties retain control over both the process and the outcome.

Parties in adjudicative processes must fit their story within the narrow frame of a legal "cause of action" or an allowable arbitral claim, confine themselves to evidence that the decision maker will consider relevant and persuasive, and give control over the outcome to a judge, jury, or arbiter. Because of these constraints, parties often do not feel they have had a chance to be heard. In Jarndyce v. Jarndyce, both parties and lawyers were confused about the legal case, and no one seemed capable of controlling the delay (which exceeded the lives of many of the disputants) or the costs (which exceeded the assets being contested). A fundamental lack of control—or self-determination—can be the price of obtaining a third-party decision. Similarly, remedies in adjudicative processes are those prescribed by the particular forum, rather than remedies tailored by the parties.

Mediators promote party empowerment and self-determination by carving out space and time for each side to tell their stories and be heard in a meaningful way. This feature alone can be important to clients. Mediators also seek party involvement in crafting proposals that are responsive to each side's needs. Participation in finding and power in choosing the solution mean the parties are invested in the outcome, and the resolution is more durable. Apologies and other benefits that will "satisfy the heart" can be both more valuable and less costly than outcomes dictated by third parties.

c. Better Outcomes: Generating Creative Problem Solving

Many proponents of mediation emphasize its ability to engage participants in a forward-looking exercise of developing options and optimal outcomes. Mediators try to get parties out of an adversarial contest and into creating better futures. Custom-tailored outcomes, developed to maximize benefits for all sides, can create more value for parties than standardized remedies provided in adjudicative forums. Agreements can be finely calibrated to balance out equities arising from past (mis)conduct and thus be reparative from a justice perspective. At the same time, the outcome must be better than the litigation (or other) alternatives of each party, since either party can "veto" the agreement. Such "quality" solutions will likely be perceived as fairer by the parties. From a societal perspective, community value flows from maximizing individual benefits and from reducing the disaffection costs of conflict.

Mediation can produce outcomes that litigation or arbitration cannot. For example, in commercial settings, parties can agree to enter into future contracts that take into account past wrongs and offer profit for all, instead of the more conventional monetary damages. Apologies can allow parties to have closure and move on with their lives. Agreements to communicate in a certain way, to write letters of reference, to refrain from contact or conduct can be valuable. Such results are not generally part of the remedies available to an arbitrator or judge.

Additionally, party-crafted agreements that are responsive to the interests parties articulate (as evidenced by the voluntary adoption of the agreement) are more durable than judgments that the "losing" party may find unfair and attempt to avoid through using an appeals process or simply by making it difficult to collect the judgment.

No efforts to find a creative and consensual outcome were made in Jarndyce v. Jarndyce. What might have been possible in that case had mediation been tried is an infinite array of solutions. Unfortunately, as the estate in Jarndyce v. Jarndyce shrinks as a result of the litigation, so does the set of possible, creative outcomes. Common sense suggests that the costs of disputing should not exceed the object of the dispute.

d. Relationship, Community, and Harmony: Building Bridges Between People

Many societies see conflict as a potential threat to the social fabric. These cultures value processes that rebuild connections between parties and bring both individual well-being and community harmony. Navajo peace-making tribunals and mediation in China and Japan are examples. Any process such as mediation that allows parties to recognize each other's perspectives and interests — even when these parties are strangers to each other — has a significant value in a world where strife and conflict threaten to tear families, communities, and nations apart. Society's interest in promoting healing relationships is measured, in part, by the costs of disaffection evident in depression, crime, productivity loss, and, ultimately, war.

The benefit of using mediation radiates beyond a single dispute to the larger system. In the context of a family, school, agency, workplace, or industry, mediation is used not only to resolve specific disputes but also to promote understanding and collaboration, for example, among parents and children, stu-

> **"A Contempt for His Own Kind"**
>
> The receiver in the cause has acquired a goodly sum of money by it, but has acquired too a distrust of his own mother, and a contempt for his own kind.
>
> Charles Dickens, Bleak House.

dents from different ethnic groups, supervisors and employees, or customers and suppliers. As parties listen to each other, stereotypes can be shattered and more responsible, responsive, and profitable citizens, communities, and governments can emerge.

Notes and Questions

3.1 Using Jarndyce v. Jarndyce as a springboard to consider various rationales for mediation, what benefits might mediation offer to parties embroiled in probate disputes?

3.2 Are some types of cases or disputes more likely to produce the beneficial results discussed above? For example, are relationship and community as important in a construction case as they might be in a probate matter? Can you make an argument that all of these advantages are useful targets in most case types?

3.3 Are there some types of cases for which mediation should always be the preferred process? For which mediation should be prohibited? What criteria should be used in making the determination?

3.4 In the context of civil litigation, some commentators believe that disputes are "all about money." Do you agree? Can mediation be effective even when a case appears to be "all about money"?

3. The History of Mediation in the United States

a. Roots

The resolution of conflict by both adversarial contest and peace-making activities has ancient origins. History chronicles parallel movements, as well as tension, between justice as embodied in the imposition of law backed by force and justice inherent in voluntary agreement and reconciliation. Jesus Christ is referred to as a "mediator between God and men" (Tim. 2:5-6). The Talmud reports that "the Temple was destroyed because they judged only in accordance with law" (Babylonian Talmud, Bava Mezia 30b). In the Muslim tradition, the Hadith of Abi al Darda reports that Mohammed said, "Shall I inform you of merit greater than fasting, charity, and prayer? It is in the conciliation of people." Various religious groups have long traditions of mediation, from Jewish rabbinical courts to mediative mechanisms used by Puritan, Quaker, and other religious groups.

Professor David Luban describes an early reported settlement of a case that could have become an adversarial contest among the gods:

> The first trial in Greek literature occurs in the Homeric *Hymn to Hermes*. The infant Hermes, on the night of his birth, steals the cattle of Apollo, who eventually tracks him down. Hermes in the meantime has climbed back into his crib and donned his swaddling clothes. He indignantly denies the deed and swears mighty oaths of innocence: "I will swear the great oath on my father's head. I vow that I myself am not the culprit and that I have seen no one else stealing your cows — whatever these cows are" . . . Apollo takes Hermes before Zeus for judgment. Zeus is more amused than angered at Hermes' prodigious theft; he commands the two gods "to come to an accord and search for the cattle." Hermes shows Apollo where he has hidden them, then he placates Apollo with the gift of a splendid tortoise shell lyre, together with the secret of playing it. The delighted Apollo reciprocates by granting Hermes "a beautiful staff of wealth and prosperity"; and the two gods become eternal allies. This delightful comic poem inaugurates a theme of profound importance. It is noteworthy that Zeus is concerned above all with harmony and friendship among the Olympians, and not with punishment for Hermes' crime or for his violation of a sacred oath. The dispute between Apollo and Hermes is resolved by an amicable settlement and not a judgment.

David Luban, Some Greek Trials: Order and Justice in Homer, Hediod, Aeschylus and Plato, 54 Tenn. L. Rev. 279, 280 (1986). Mediation is not a new approach to dispute resolution! What follows is an examination of some recent developments in the United States.

b. Labor

Formal institutionalization of mediation in the United States first occurred in the labor field. The U.S. Department of Labor created a panel in 1913 to handle labor-management conflicts. In 1947, this panel evolved into the Federal Mediation and Conciliation Service, which is charged with maintaining stability in industries through mediation.

Two types of mediation characterize labor and employment disputes: collective bargaining mediation and the mediation of individual employee grievances. In collective bargaining mediation, where the terms and conditions of employment are negotiated, participants are generally experienced professionals representing large constituencies. Mediators must be knowledgeable about workplace issues and special

bargaining dynamics. Where mediators help to address individual employee grievances — including claims of discrimination — the parties describe the issues that
have affected them personally. The discussion can be therapeutic insofar as parties
feel heard, and indirectly the workplace may be improved by individuals getting
responsive treatment to their concerns and reparations for their injuries.

c. Community

The Civil Rights Act of 1964 created the Community Relations Service (CRS)
of the U.S. Department of Justice to help resolve discrimination disputes through
negotiation and mediation. The CRS has intervened in a variety of controversies,
including disruptions around desegregation orders and marches of the Ku Klux Klan.
Today mediation programs in state and federal agencies still respond to disputes
concerning discrimination.

Neighborhood justice centers (also called community dispute resolution centers), where volunteers mediate community cases or minor disputes, have been
funded by state and federal budgets since the 1960s. Community centers receive
case referrals both from the courts and from agencies and institutions. These centers
typically address disputes between landlords and tenants, neighbors, family members,
persons involved in love triangle or work place situations, and a variety of other
matters. Developed to be responsive to disputes that the litigation system cannot
handle effectively, community mediation centers have thrived on the simple premise
that parties can solve their problems with the help of trained interveners and, in so
doing, achieve better outcomes and alleviate the tensions that conflict brings to
neighborhoods and communities.

d. Family

A major growth area for mediation has been family disputes. The acrimony and
expense surrounding divorce and the breakup of families have had such adverse
impacts on parents, children, extended families, and society generally that courts,
clients, and practitioners have sought a better way than litigation. Many states now
mandate mediation in child custody and visitation cases before litigation is permitted.
Private practitioners, as well as court programs, provide mediation services to
families. Success in divorce mediation has encouraged the development of mediation
programs in other family situations such as probate disputes and mediation between
parents and children in PINS (persons in need of supervision) proceedings.

Family mediators come to the field from a variety of backgrounds, including
psychology, mental health, and social work, as well as law. It is not uncommon for
co-mediation teams to work with divorcing parties. One mediator may be an expert
in psychology and the other in law and financial issues. Such teams are often gender-
balanced as well.

e. Civil Cases

In 1976, many eminent jurists and scholars gathered at the Pound Conference to
address public dissatisfaction with the justice system. As Chapter 1 explores in more

detail, at the Conference, Professor Frank Sander described a different vision of a justice system in which courts "have many doors," some leading to litigation and others leading to alternative processes. Many legal scholars trace the modern U.S. alternative dispute resolution (ADR) movement to this event.

Overloaded judges and a purported "litigation boom" in the late 1970s and 1980s created the need to find ways to reduce court dockets. Insofar as relieving court congestion was the motivating factor for instituting mediation, methods that encouraged party understanding and creative problem solving were replaced, in some instances, by mediation techniques aimed more at case evaluation and settlement. Consequently, the lines defining mediation, case evaluation, and judicial settlement conferences in the context of court-annexed mediation blurred.

By 1988, Florida authorized civil trial court judges to refer almost any civil case to mediation. Other states and some federal courts followed suit, and today mediation is a predictable step in the pre-litigation process in many venues.

f. Cybermediation

Mediation and other ADR processes have moved into the twenty-first century with the development of dispute resolution mechanisms on the Internet. Online dispute resolution involves a whole array of dispute resolution mechanisms offered by different providers. Cyberspace offers speed and the convenience of operating from your home computer. Such efficiencies are particularly appealing to parties residing in different countries. However, in the case of mediation services, the lack of face-to-face communication has been criticized as compromising one of mediation's key hallmarks of promoting better understanding between disputants.

g. Other Arenas

It is hard to find an area where mediation is not used for resolving disputes. Mediation is an important resolution tool today in organizations, in schools, for environmental disputes, in government agencies, in the criminal justice system, in construction disputes, in matters between the police and civilians, for international disputes, and for intellectual property disputes.

In business matters, CPR, the International Institute for Conflict Prevention and Resolution, has obtained commitments from many Fortune 500 companies to use mediation and other ADR processes rather than (or at least before) litigation. Mediation, with its forward-looking aspect, appeals to businesspeople who want to avoid the costs and risks of litigation and have an interest in preserving relationships.

4. Two Perspectives on Mediation

The following two excerpts capture critical features of the essence and origins of mediation. Note how mediation does not lend itself to a simple, mechanical description.

Carrie Menkel-Meadow, **INTRODUCTION**

in Mediation: Theory, Policy and Practice xiii-xviii, xxix (2000)

Mediation is both a legal process and more than a legal process, used for thousands of years by all sorts of communities, families and formal governmental units. . . . [It] has become a sort of aspirational ideology for those who see its promise in promoting more productive ways of expressing and dealing with human conflict. . . . Mediation, in this larger sense, represents a political theory about the role of conflict in society, the importance of equality, participation, self-determination and a form of leaderless leadership in problem-solving and decision-making. Mediation, as a theory, is aspirational and utopian. In its most grandiose forms, mediation theorists and proponents expect mediation, as a process, to achieve the transformation of warring nation-states, differing ethnic groups, diverse communities, and disputatious workplaces, families and individuals and to develop new and creative human solutions to otherwise difficult or intractable problems. For some, it is a process for achieving interpersonal, intrapersonal and intrapsychic knowledge and understanding. . . .

Mediation, as a structured form of conflict resolution, challenges the Anglo-American idea of adversarial dispute resolution, which presumes that two sides must argue their case to a third-party neutral who will make rule-based, often binary, decisions about who is right and wrong. Instead, it offers the possibility of party-crafted solutions to problems, disputes, conflicts, transactions and relationships, which are facilitated by a third party with no authority to decide anything or to impose any rules. Parties to mediation may engage in other legalistic processes, developing party-specific rules or understandings, even legislating or creating constitutions for their relationships in the future, all on a voluntary and consensual, rather than coercive, basis. Thus mediation's authority is derived from the voluntary commitment of the parties and their facilitator, rather than the coercion of rules, a judge or the state (with some modern exceptions . . . as when courts sometimes "mandate" mediation). . . .

For some critics of mediation this raises questions about how justice can be measured or achieved in settings where the law is not the final arbiter. For some, legal standards should be the measure of justice, for others, real justice may lie outside or beside the law. Mediation theory thus replicates classic jurisprudential debates about legal positivism, the morality of law, natural law and whether justice or fairness exist outside of law. Mediation theory adds to the jurisprudential debate by questioning who dispute resolution institutions and justice are supposed to serve — the parties in dispute or the larger society?

The culture created by mediation theorists and practitioners has been called "harmony" culture and criticized when compared to alternative political and jurisprudential theories of individual and group justice. Critics are concerned that, in mediation, important social and legal conflict is muted, significant public matters are privatized, power imbalances skew results and disempower the already subordinated and that the mediation process encourages unjust compromises of principles or rights that require sharp demarcations and enforcement. . . .

. . . Mediation permits, indeed often requires, consideration of underlying interests, causes or values that produce conflict and thus permits the management,

handling or resolution of broader concerns than just those "disputes" which crystal-
lize at the tip of the iceberg. . . .

The forms that mediation takes are themselves subject to debate. While most
definitions of mediation conclude that a third-party *neutral* should facilitate the
negotiation among parties, many mediation processes — historically and with cultural variations — in fact involve a third party who is quite enmeshed in the community as a "wise elder" or, in more recent times, as a substantive expert who may
promise *impartiality* to the parties but who may know quite a bit about the disputants
or the subject matter of the dispute. Mediation's forms, then, are variable across
cultures, times and different political systems. . . . To the extent that mediation privileges certain forms of communication ("talking cures") its use and its forms may be
varied in different settings by culture, nationality, ethnicity, gender, race and
class. . . . As anthropologists and other scholars have discovered, there is no cultural
uniformity to the practice or form of mediation, and different social groupings and
political configurations may re-form or deform the mediation mode to respond to
their particular interests. Some have suggested that mediation, with its focus on
words, communications and interpersonal competence, may be ethnocentrically
based in cultures that privilege such forms of problem-solving. . . .

DEFINITIONS, ORIGINS, IDEOLOGIES AND CONTROVERSIES: WHAT IS MEDIATION?

Because mediation is seen as both an ideology (of peace-seeking, transformative
conflict-resolving human problem-solving) and a practice (of task-oriented, communication enhancing dispute settlement) there are many controversies about its
appropriate definitions, forms and boundaries.

The development of mediation as a process for conflict resolution and dispute
management in modern legal systems has its origins in a number of different sources.
As the work of . . . anthropologists made clear, there were many ways for both individuals and social groups to resolve their controversies, with different forms and
structures to reflect different goals. Where continuing relationships were considered
important, solutions that "healed" the parties and provided opportunities for future-
oriented, contingent and compromise solutions in which no party felt like a loser
were often preferred and were likely to be arrived at in different settings than courts.
A community "moot" or a wise elder, conducting either an open or closed mediation with the parties and interested others present were more effective for such kinds
of disputes, especially if disputes were to be "owned" by local indigenous communities and not by colonial and distant court systems. With the interventions of wise
leaders or the public airing of grievances, the need for individualized revenge or
violent vengeance might be avoided. Legal anthropology, with its study of "foreign"
communities, thus communicated an important message of legal pluralism in disputing for the common law jurisdictions.

The study of the "transformation of disputing" also demonstrated the social
construction of disputes and conflicts and illuminated the dynamic, rather than static,
quality of conflict. Issues leading to conflicts could be narrowed (as when lawyers
turn problems and troubles into causes of action) or broadened (as when social

movement groups create demonstrations and political activity or when single lawsuits become class actions) and disputes could be "rephrased" or "reframed" not only
by the disputants or their representatives (lawyers), but by whatever kind of third-party
neutral (judge, arbitrator, mediator, political official) "heard" the case. Advocates, as
well as legal officials and political officeholders, recognized that different processes
could transform political, legal and social conflicts and affect the outcome. . . .

THE FUTURE HOPE AND PROMISE OF MEDIATION

Theorists and practitioners of mediation claim a central core of functions for
mediation:

1. that it is a consensual process, both in participation and in agreements reached;
2. that it is, at its core, voluntarily engaged in (subject to recent efforts to
   mandate mediation in some contractual or court settings);
3. that it is participatory by the principals engaged in whatever problem or issue
   is presented at the mediation (who may have representatives who appear as
   well);
4. that it is "facilitated" by a third party "outside" the immediate dispute or
   conflict (the "neutrality" principle reframed to reflect some of the recent
   developments in use of expert facilitators);
5. that it seeks to develop solutions to problems or resolutions of conflicts or
   disputes on terms of mutual agreement and fairness to the parties;
6. that it seeks to facilitate mutual understanding and apprehension of the other
   parties' needs, interests and situations.

These core functions are located within an ideology or belief system, held by
most theorists and practitioners of mediation, that such a process will reduce unnecessary conflict or acrimony among and between people in conflict, will lead to
increased learning and knowledge about others and, where possible, will facilitate the
creation of mutually satisfactory solutions to problems or resolutions of conflict that
are better than what the parties might have achieved in other fora.

Notes and Questions

3.5 What, according to Menkel-Meadow, are the aspirational goals of mediation?
3.6 As you consider the story of Zeus' intervention in the dispute between Hermes
   and Apollo, what values were served by the approach Zeus took? What arguments could you make that judgment and punishment of Hermes would be a
   more prudent approach?

The excerpt that follows also analyzes the central values of mediation. Themes
raised here by Fuller — how mediation builds a different relationship among parties
and hence affects the resolution of future controversies — emphasize the potential of
mediation beyond settlement of specific controversies.

Lon L. Fuller, MEDIATION — ITS FORMS AND FUNCTIONS

44 S. Cal. L. Rev. 305, 307-309, 325-327 (1971)

Casual treatments of the subject in the literature of sociology tend to assume that the object of mediation is to make the parties aware of the "social norms" applicable to their relationship and to persuade them to accommodate themselves to the "structure" imposed by these norms. From this point of view the difference between a judge and a mediator is simply that the judge orders the parties to conform themselves to the rules, while the mediator persuades them to do so. But mediation is commonly directed, not toward achieving conformity to norms, but toward the creation of the relevant norms themselves. This is true, for example, in the very common case where the mediator assists the parties in working out the terms of a contract defining their rights and duties toward one another. In such a case there is no pre-existing structure that can guide mediation; it is the mediational process that produces the structure.

It may be suggested that mediation is always, in any event, directed toward bringing about a more harmonious relationship between the parties, whether this be achieved through explicit agreement, through a reciprocal acceptance of the "social norms" relevant to their relationship, or simply because the parties have been helped to a new and more perceptive understanding of one another's problems. The fact that in ordinary usage the terms "mediation" and "conciliation" are largely interchangeable tends to reinforce this view of the matter.

But at this point we encounter the inconvenient fact that mediation can be directed, not toward cementing a relationship, but toward terminating it. In a form of mediation that is coming to be called "marriage therapy" mediative efforts between husband and wife may be undertaken by a psychoanalyst, a psychiatrist, a social worker, a marriage counselor, or even a friendly neighbor. In this situation it will not infrequently turn out that the most effective use of mediation will be in assisting the parties to accept the inevitability of divorce. In a radically different context one of the most dramatically successful uses of mediation I ever witnessed involved a case in which an astute mediator helped the parties rescind a business contract. Two corporations were entrapped by a long-term supply contract that had become burdensome and disadvantageous to both. Canceling it, however, was a complicated matter, requiring a period of "phasing out" and various financial adjustments back and forth. For some time the parties had been chiefly engaged in reciprocal threats of a law suit. On the advice of an attorney for one of the parties, a mediator (whose previous experience had been almost entirely in the field of labor relations) was brought in. Within no time at all a severance of relations was accomplished and the two firms parted company happily.

Thus we find that mediation may be directed toward, and result in, discrepant and even diametrically opposed results. This circumstance argues against our being able to derive any general structure of the mediational process from some identifiable goal shared by all mediational efforts. We may, of course, indulge in observations to the effect that the mere presence of a third person tends to put the parties on their good behavior, that the mediator can direct their verbal exchanges away from recrimination and toward the issues that need to be faced, that by receiving separate and confidential communication from the parties he can gradually bring into the open issues so deep-cutting that the parties themselves had shared a tacit taboo against any discussion of them and that, finally, he can by his management of the interchange demonstrate to the parties that it is possible to discuss divisive issues without either rancor or evasion. . . . [This] analysis . . . has dealt only inferentially and indirectly with what may be said to be the central quality of mediation, namely, its capacity to reorient the parties toward each other, not by imposing rules on them, but by helping them to achieve a new and shared perception of their relationship, a perception that will redirect their attitudes and dispositions toward one another.

This quality of mediation becomes most visible when the proper function of the mediator turns out to be, not that of inducing the parties to accept formal rules for the governance of their future relations, but that of helping them to free themselves from the encumbrance of rules and of accepting, instead, a relationship of mutual respect, trust and understanding that will enable them to meet shared contingencies without the aid of formal prescriptions laid down in advance. Such a mediational effort might well come into play in any of the various forms of mediation between husband and wife associated with "family counseling" and "marriage therapy." In the task of reestablishing the marriage as a going concern the mediator might find it essential to break up formalized conceptions of "duty" and to substitute a more fluid sense of mutual trust and shared responsibility. In effect, instead of working toward achieving a rule-oriented relationship he might devote his efforts, to some degree at least, in exactly the opposite direction.

. . . The negotiation of an elaborate written contract, such as that embodied in a collective bargaining agreement between an employer and a labor union, does indeed present a special set of problems for the mediator. . . . [I]t should be remembered that the primary function of the mediator in the collective bargaining situation is not to propose rules to the parties and to secure their acceptance of them, but to induce the mutual trust and understanding that will enable the parties to work out their own rules. The creation of rules is a process that cannot itself be rule-bound; it must be guided by a sense of shared responsibility and a realization that the adversary aspects of the operation are part of a larger collaborative undertaking. The primary task of the arbitrator [sic] is to induce this attitude of mind and spirit, though to be sure, he does this primarily by helping the parties to perceive the concrete ways in which this shared attitude can redound to their mutual benefit.

It should also be noted that the benefits of a collective bargaining agreement do not lie simply in the aptness of the numbered paragraphs that appear over the parties' signatures, but derive also from the mutual understanding produced by the process of negotiation itself. I once heard an experienced and perceptive lawyer observe, speaking of complex business agreements, "If you negotiate the contract thoroughly, explore carefully the problems that can arise in the course of its administration, work out the proper language to cover the various contingencies that may develop, you can then put the contract in a drawer and forget it." What he meant was that in the exchange that accompanied the negotiation and drafting of the contract the parties would come to understand each other's problems sufficiently so that when difficulties arose they would, as fair and reasonable men, be able to make the appropriate adjustments without referring to the contract itself.

Notes and Questions

3.7 After studying Fuller's excerpt, what are the prime benefits of mediation? Is it more important that the process can settle a given dispute or that it can realign relationships so that parties can resolve disputes themselves?

3.8 In light of the benefits that Fuller articulates, consider some reported case you have studied. In what ways might mediation have served the parties better than litigation?

5. Mediation's Place in the Justice System

Although mediation may be an excellent dispute resolution process for many disputes, it is just one among an array of processes that complement each other and serve different goals. The following two excerpts illuminate how mediation fits into this landscape of major processes comprising the justice system. The first, an idealized, simplified description of litigation, arbitration, and mediation, illustrates how each of these processes has a legitimate claim to justice delivery. The second article delineates various rationales a court might consider when including a mediation component and explores the underlying purposes of litigation and mediation.

 Lela P. Love, **IMAGES OF JUSTICE**

1 Pepp. Disp. Resol. L.J. 29, 29-32 (2000)

... In an effort to capture the vision behind the three major dispute resolution processes, this essay will present an image of a judge, an arbiter and a mediator. ...

LITIGATION

Standing straight and tall in public places, a blindfolded woman holds up scales. Since she is blindfolded, she cannot be swayed by gender, race, wealth, or other influences or advantages that one party might hold. On her scales, disputing parties rest their case: the best they can muster for themselves and the worst they can present about the other side. The matter is weighed on these scales in public view, and the balance resolves the matter.

The scales themselves get more precisely balanced after each weighing, after each case. The weight and moment of precise and particular factors are calibrated, and the blindfolded lady announces how much factors weigh, this time, and for all time.

Should a party suspect that the scales were out of balance or the blindfold had been lifted, he may appeal to higher authorities to test the integrity of the process.

This lady is accessible to all, rich and poor alike. Like the other commanding woman standing at the Golden Door in NYC harbor with a torch of liberty, she says, "Give me your tired, your poor, your huddled masses yearning. . . ." And if one party invokes her aid, the other must answer and counter-weight the scale, or risk an unfavorable verdict. He must also risk the power behind this blindfolded figure — the power of the state to take and give property and liberty.

If Martin Luther King were delivering an *I Have a Dream* speech about the process this blindfolded woman symbolizes it might sound something like this:

> I have a dream that every person can bring a claim to a public place and an intelligent, experienced and impartial third party chosen or appointed by democratic process will assess the facts, apply the law and determine the outcome. The whole world will watch to keep this forum honest.
>
> I have a dream that this forum will be accessible, the procedures straightforward, efficient and understandable, the costs appropriate, and the determination speedy.
>
> I have a dream that judges will help define, clarify, and broadcast our public norms by focusing all their attention on the explication of the law as it intersects with the facts of each case.
>
> I have a dream that every judge is charged with ensuring that his or her corner of the dispute resolution universe offers a fair and clean playing field. No judge will try to coerce settlement by threatening parties with onerous outcomes. Every judge will treat each party with courtesy and respect.

ARBITRATION

Wise, sophisticated, trusted, and honored in his community, the arbitrator is chosen by the parties who can agree that whatever such a person decides is just. The arbitrator does not wear blindfolds because the parties trust his discretion. On the other hand, the arbitrator cannot meet privately with a party, because the parties do not trust each other.

The arbitrator stands, aloof from the parties, arms folded in skepticism, but listening attentively for each clue which will piece together the puzzle of facts he must see clearly.

The gift the arbitrator gives the parties is a prompt decision informed by his expertise in the particular arena. His decision is bound to favor one party over the other, but his quick and precise award will allow the parties to move on with their lives and their businesses.

There is no appeal from this arbitrator because, in choosing him, the parties chose to live with what he decides. Thus, the power of the arbitrator is immense, once conferred by the parties, and is further bolstered by the blindfolded lady who will ensure that his awards are honored.

If a party were delivering an *I Have a Dream* speech about arbitration, it might sound something like this:

> I have a dream that I can create my own forum and choose my own arbiter.
>
> I have a dream that a special and wise expert in the particular arena of the dispute, whom I trust, can hear my dispute, and I can accept his or her judgment and put the matter behind me, win or lose.
>
> I have a dream that my dispute can be resolved in a private place, so that the indignities, dangers, and damages of a public forum do not compound the upset and anger of being in conflict.
>
> I have a dream that arbitrators are charged with ensuring that their corner of the dispute resolution universe offers a fair and clean playing field. No arbitrator will try to coerce settlement by threatening parties with onerous outcomes. Every arbitrator will treat each party with courtesy and respect.

MEDIATION

In this image one sees a figure sitting with the parties, her hands reaching towards each of them as if to support them in telling their tale or to caution them in listening to each other to weigh the matter more carefully. It is also possible that her out-reached hands are pointing to the parties to remind them of their responsibility for dealing thoughtfully with their situation and each other, understanding the opportunities and risks inherent in various choices, and summoning their creativity in addressing the conflict.

The figure is not alone or aloof. Her outstretched arms form a bridge between the parties, so that communication and positive energy can flow again. Her presence is a catalyst setting in motion the potential that the parties hold.

Unlike the blindfolded lady, the mediator sees all that is offered unprotected by formal procedure or rules of evidence. Unlike the arbitrator or the judge, the mediator may meet with the parties together or listen to them privately so that each nuance of meaning and each atom of possibility are captured and offered back, in their most palatable form, for the parties.

The mediator's features are hazy, since the focus and light remains on the disputing parties. Her presence, however, exudes optimism, respect, and confidence in the parties' capacity. She brings an energetic and urgent sense that justice can be done by the parties' own hands.

If a mediator were delivering an *I Have a Dream* speech about mediation, it might sound something like this:

> I have a dream that I can offer a safe and private place for parties in conflict to come and sit together at a table.
>
> I have a dream that I can help disputing parties tell their stories and explain their feelings and values to each other in a manner that might enable one another to understand more clearly and perhaps build or preserve their relationship.
>
> I have a dream that the dispute can be resolved in a private place, so that the indignities, dangers, and damages of a public forum do not compound the upset and anger of being in conflict.
>
> I have a dream that I can assist parties in discovering or constructing outcomes that seem reasonable and optimal to them.

Notes and Questions

3.9 When reality diverges from the ideal, problems can arise. In Jarndyce v. Jarndyce, the reality of the court system diverged in important ways from the ideal. Can you articulate the ways?

3.10 You will see later in the book that debates have arisen when mediation moves away from the ideal described in the excerpt above. For example, as mediators shift toward an arbitrator-like role or where mediation becomes "mandatory," some commentators argue dissonance and difficulties emerge.

In the following excerpt, Robert Baruch Bush explores the underlining rationale for litigation and mediation and examines whether and how mediation should become part of court-sponsored dispute resolution. As his various characters talk about the processes, they assume an idealized version of each.

 ### *Robert A. Baruch Bush*, MEDIATION AND ADJUDICATION, DISPUTE RESOLUTION AND IDEOLOGY: AN IMAGINARY CONVERSATION

3 J. Contemp. Legal Issues 1, 1-6, 12 (1990)

The setting for the conversation is as follows. A judge has been empowered by a state statute to refer cases from his civil docket to mediation. The statute says that he can, in his discretion, refer any and all cases; the decision is his, and the parties cannot refuse mediation without showing good cause. The judge can send all his cases to mediation on a blanket basis, or certain categories of cases, or individual cases on a case by case basis, whichever he decides. This is what the statute empowers him to do, and the Supreme Court has set up rules enabling him and other judges to do it. The problem is that the judge is uncertain how to exercise this new power. He has no clear idea which cases, if any, he should refer to the mediation process.

So, he picks six representative cases from his civil docket: a divorce case with a custody question, a complex commercial litigation, a landlord-tenant case, a discrimination suit, a consumer case, and a personal injury litigation. He sends copies of the case files, with names deleted, to four individuals who are friends or associates: his law clerk, his court administrator, his former law professor, and a practicing mediator who is a friend of his. The judge asks each of them for their advice. Should he send any of these cases to mediation? All of them? None of them? What should he do?

He is a bit startled when he gets back the results of this survey, because he gets four completely different recommendations. From the law professor, he gets the recommendation that he should send no cases to mediation; all the cases should stay in court. The law clerk gives him a more complex recommendation. He says that the discrimination case, the consumer case, and the personal injury case should be kept in court, but the divorce, the landlord-tenant, and the commercial cases should go to mediation. The court administrator says he should send them all to mediation, unless both parties to the dispute object; if both parties object, he shouldn't refer them to mediation, whatever the type of case. Finally, the mediator tells him that he should send all the cases to mediation, whether or not the parties object.

The judge is puzzled by this set of responses. Why the divergence in the recommendations; what's going on here? What is the argument that these people obviously must have among one another in order to give him these very different recommendations? Do they have some kind of factual or technical argument about the feasibility of sorting out cases, and referring some to court and some to mediation? Or do they have some kind of ideological argument over the importance and universality of different dispute resolution goals and processes? Clearly, all his advisors think that his decision shouldn't simply be arbitrary, that whatever he does will have important consequences. But, what are they? What is at stake in the decision that he and other judges have to make as to which, if any, of these disputes to refer to mediation?

Faced with these questions, the judge does what judges are very good at doing. He calls all four advisors and says, "I'd like you to argue this out in front of me. I want to hear what you have to say in the presence of one another. That way you can present the reasons for your recommendations, and I can hear some kind of response from you towards one another."

So, the four advisors come together with the judge in an informal meeting over lunch. The court administrator goes first. "Judge," she begins, "I'll tell you the reason for my recommendation. As far as I'm concerned, the most important goal we have here is saving time and money. That's the main goal that we want to keep in mind in using your powers under this new mediation statute. I suspect that was the legislature's main reason for enacting this law. The courts are heavily backlogged, delay is epidemic, and adding new judges and courtrooms appears fiscally—and politically—impossible. Settlements are the only solution. Settling cases is going to save public and private expense. It's also going to increase public satisfaction with the system. Now, since all cases have some potential to settle," she continues, "and we don't know which ones will and which ones won't, it makes sense to refer them all to mediation, unless we have a clear indication in advance that there's no real settlement possibility. For example, if both parties show a clear desire not to go to mediation, not to negotiate, then in that case it makes no sense to waste the time." She concludes, "That is the reason for my recommendation. Refer to mediation, unless it's clear that there's opposition on both sides to settlement."

The law clerk then is called upon. He says, "Judge, as you know, I disagree, and the reason for my recommendation is the following. In my view, the main goal is not saving time and money, regardless of what the legislature may have had in mind. There are other goals of dispute resolution that are much more important.

"Generally, it seems to me," the law clerk continues, "protecting individual rights and ensuring some kind of substantive fairness to both sides in the resolution of the dispute are the most important goals. And when rights and substantive fairness are most important, adjudication in court is the best tool we have to accomplish those goals. However, there are cases where rights and fairness are not the only or the most important goals. For example, if there is an ongoing relationship between the parties, preserving that relationship may be very important both to the parties and to the public. In that case, mediation would be desirable, because preserving relationships is something that mediation does much better than the adjudication process. Therefore, I think that you can distinguish between cases on the basis of the ongoing relationship factor. When you have such a relationship, refer to mediation; otherwise, keep the case in court. That's the way I've split up the cases you sent us. I'm not sure that it's immediately obvious from the way I've divided them, but that was my criterion, and I think it's the best one for you to use."

Next it is the mediator's turn. "I both agree and disagree with the administrator and the law clerk, your Honor," she explains. "Saving time and money must be considered important, and preserving relationships, in certain cases, is also a very important goal. But both of these are really just part of a more general goal that I consider the most important aim of dispute resolution: that is, to reach the best possible substantive result or solution to the parties' problem. Sometimes the best solution will be one that saves the parties time and money; sometimes it will be one that preserves the relationship. Sometimes it will be one that does neither of these. That will depend on many details of the case.

"But whatever the details, there is plenty of evidence now that, in terms of achieving the best results for the individual case in question, mediation is a process that has tremendous advantages over adjudication. The process is flexible, issues can be framed more effectively and discussed more fully, a greater variety of possible solutions can be considered, and unique, innovative and integrative solutions are possible, even likely. Therefore, mediation ought to be tried first in all cases because the potential to arrive at superior substantive results is always greater in mediation than in adjudication. If mediation doesn't work, if there's no resolution, then the parties can go back to court. But, in the first instance, achieving superior results is the most important goal to strive for in every single case. And mediation is the best vehicle we have for doing this. That's why I recommended referring all your cases to mediation, without exceptions."

Finally the law professor speaks. "Your Honor," he begins, "I'm sorry to have to disagree. But all of your other friends here have missed the point. I say this because they're all talking about goals that don't really pertain to your function, the function of a court. A court is a public institution, and the goal of a court as a public institution is not to save time and money; nor is it to help private parties secure private benefits in individual cases. Your goal as a public institution is to promote important public values. That ought to be your primary concern: the promotion and the securing of important public values through the dispute resolution process. That is what distinguishes your function from that of a mere private arbitrator, and justifies the public support — legal and fiscal — given uniquely to the courts.

"I submit to you, your Honor, that the most important public values at stake in dispute resolution are basically four. There may be others; but I think that these four have widely been recognized as the most important ones. First is the protection of the fundamental civil rights of the parties as individuals. Second is the pursuit of substantive or social justice, as between different classes represented by the parties in the case, and especially as between rich and poor, strong and weak, haves and have-nots. Third is the promotion of what the economists call efficiency — that is, the greatest possible level of aggregate societal welfare — through encouragement of activities that make the best use of our limited societal resources. And fourth is the establishment and articulation of public values that give us a sense of social solidarity in our society as a whole, which is of course a very pluralistic one and therefore requires the cement of shared values. . . .

"Your Honor," the professor continues, "adjudication serves every one of these values. It does so because it operates by using and generating both procedural and substantive rules — using them in the instant case, and generating them for future cases. Indeed the rules themselves are often related to and based upon these values. Substantive rules promote economic welfare by signaling economic actors how to use resources efficiently. Substantive and procedural rules promote social justice by reducing the advantage of the powerful, in the aggregate and in the individual case. Procedural rules protect directly against violations of fundamental civil rights. And substantive rules foster solidarity by giving meaning to shared public values. Therefore, the rule-based, public adjudication process is an excellent — an unparalleled — instrument for accomplishing these values. Mediation, on the other hand, weakens and undermines every single one of these values. Why? Because, simply, it neither uses in the instant case nor generates for the future rules, whether procedural or substantive, based on these values or any other values. Mediation rests solely on the expedient of compromise. Therefore it cannot help but undermine all of these important, rule-dependent values.

"This brings me to the heart of my argument, your Honor," says the professor. "First, we can't sacrifice public values of this stature solely to save time and money. Certainly, we can't do so as a matter of public policy. If, as a matter of necessity, the courts can't handle all cases, that's one thing. But to adopt a public policy saying that values like rights protection and social justice are less important than saving money and judicial economy would be inexcusable. Second, there's no way of neatly dividing up cases on the basis that some involve these public values and others do not. That simply isn't true. All six of the kinds of cases that you submitted to us involve one or more of these public values. Indeed, most of them involve several. The same would be true for any other disputes we might examine." Here the professor went into a lengthy analysis of how this was so, which for the sake of brevity we will not reproduce. "Therefore," he concluded, " 'channeling' of different cases to different processes is undesirable."

"Finally, you cannot, as the mediator suggested, consider the value of better results for the parties in the individual case superior to these *public* values. You cannot do so, your Honor, as a matter of public policy. Why not? Because this would be to put private benefit over public values, over the public good, and as a public servant you cannot legitimately do so. And I'm sure you would not want to. Therefore, even if results are superior in mediation in individual cases, that is no basis for a public policy of mandating cases to mediation. In fact, I would say the same about referrals, incentives, or any other form of public encouragement, of this mediation process. The arguments I've made cut against any kind of public support for mediation. If private parties want to go to a mediator, let that be their decision as a matter of private choice. I'm not sure how I feel about that, but in any event that's not the issue here. As a matter of public policy, we cannot put private benefit over the public good. Therefore, your Honor, I say all of these cases should remain in court, unless perhaps a petition is submitted by both parties to adjourn pending voluntarily initiated settlement discussions or mediation." . . .

Before the judge has a chance to adjourn and consider arguments more thoroughly, however, the mediator asks the judge for one more minute. "Judge," she says, "I have another point to make. The reason I didn't make it before is that it's a little hard to articulate. But I see I will have to try. The truth is that the concern for better results in individual cases is not all that makes mediation important, in my view, even though I admit that most advocates of mediation emphasize this as the primary advantage of mediation. But there's more involved, and it goes far beyond expediency and private benefit. When I say mediation ought to be used in all these cases, my reason is also based on promoting public values, public values which are important to all of the cases you sent us, public values, different from and more important than the ones that the professor mentioned. In other words, like the professor's argument for adjudication, my argument for mediation is also a public values argument, but it is based on a different view of public values than the view he presented.

"Now, my problem is that it is hard to articulate clearly what these different public values are. I think they're evoked or implied by concepts like reconciliation, social harmony, community, interconnection, relationship, and the like. Mediation does produce superior results, as I argued earlier. But it also involves a non-adversarial process that is less traumatic, more humane, and far more capable of healing and reconciliation than adjudication. Those are the kinds of concerns that make me feel that these cases ought to be handled in mediation, not for private benefit reasons and not for expediency reasons, but because of these reconciliatory public values promoted by mediation. . . .

"How can I define this public value? Simply put, it is the value of providing a moral and political education for citizens, in responsibility for themselves and respect for others. In a democracy, your honor, that must be considered a crucial public value and it must be considered a public function. As far as I'm concerned, there's the potential for that kind of direct and experiential education in every single one of these cases that you sent to us; and that potential can only be realized in mediation. It cannot be accomplished in adjudication. . . . In my view, this civic education value is more important than the values that the professor is concerned about. . . . Finally, I just want to clarify an important connection between my argument here and our earlier discussion. On reflection, I've realized that the 'superior results' argument that I mentioned at our first meeting is also based, at least in part, on the public value I'm talking about here. That is, many of us place value on the integrative, 'win/win' solutions that mediation helps produce precisely because such solutions embody in concrete terms the kind of respect for others that is the essence of the civic education value. So the 'superiority' of results we speak of is not only, or primarily, that the results better serve the individual interests of the parties — a private benefit — but that they express each individual's considered choice to respect and accommodate the other to some degree — a democratic public value. In short, both the experience of the mediation process and the kind of results it produces serve the public value of civic education in self-determination and respect for others."

Notes and Questions

3.11 If you were the judge, what would you decide? What would be your rationale for choosing to refer or not refer cases to mediation?

3.12 Returning to the case of Hermes and Apollo, Zeus missed an opportunity to underline and elaborate on the importance of honoring sacred oaths and not stealing. Does what transpired between Hermes and Apollo after Zeus' intervention illustrate the values described by Bush's mediator? As you read the case examples in Chapter 4, see which of Bush's characters — the law clerk, court administrator, law professor, or mediator — becomes more persuasive.

B. APPROACHES TO MEDIATION

Mediation takes various forms, depending on variables such as culture, context, mediator goals and strategies, and party participation and preferences. This section explores different approaches that arguably fall within the family group of mediation. As Chapter 7 will reveal, a lively debate about the proper boundaries of the mediation process itself exists. Where does "mediation" — a process where the neutral is in the middle helping parties to understand and resolve their own conflict with their own solutions — stop? And where does adjudication — processes where the neutral provides the answer to the question raised by the dispute — begin? As you read about various approaches to mediation below, keep those questions in mind. Also consider that the variety and flexibility of mediator approaches are cited as among the strengths of the mediation process.

1. Narrow or Broad Problem Definition, Evaluative or Facilitative

The various mediator orientations described by Len Riskin on his grid in the following excerpt are often-cited descriptors of key mediator orientations.

 Leonard L. Riskin, **MEDIATOR ORIENTATIONS, STRATEGIES AND TECHNIQUES**

12 Alternatives 111, 111-114 (1994)

Almost every conversation about "mediation" suffers from ambiguity. People have disparate visions of what mediation is or should be. Yet we lack a comprehensive system for describing these visions. This causes confusion when people try to choose between mediation and another process or grapple with how to train, evaluate, regulate, or select mediators.

I propose a system for classifying mediator orientations. Such a system can help parties select a mediator and deal with the thorny issue of whether the mediator should have subject-matter expertise. The classification system starts with two principal questions: 1. Does the mediator tend to define problems *narrowly* or *broadly*? 2. Does the mediator think she should *evaluate* — make assessments or predictions or proposals for agreements — or *facilitate* the parties' negotiation without evaluating? The answers reflect the mediator's beliefs about the nature and scope of mediation and her assumptions about the parties' expectations.

PROBLEM DEFINITION

Mediators with a *narrow* focus assume that the parties have come to them for help in solving a technical problem. The parties have defined this problem in advance through the *positions* they have asserted in negotiations or pleadings. Often it involves a question such as, "Who pays how much to whom?" or "Who can use such-and-such property?" As framed, these questions rest on "win-lose" (or "distributive") assumptions. In other words, the participants must divide a limited resource; whatever one gains, the other must lose.

The likely court outcome — along with uncertainty, delay and expense — drives much of the mediation process. Parties, seeking a compromise, will bargain adversarially, emphasizing positions over interests.

A mediator who starts with a *broad* orientation, on the other hand, assumes that the parties can benefit if the mediation goes beyond the narrow issues that normally define legal disputes. Important interests often lie beneath the positions that the participants assert. Accordingly, the mediator should help the participants understand and fulfill those interests — at least if they wish to do so.

THE MEDIATOR'S ROLE

The *evaluative* mediator assumes that the participants want and need the mediator to provide some direction as to the appropriate grounds for settlement — based on law, industry practice or technology. She also assumes that the mediator is qualified to give such direction by virtue of her experience, training and objectivity.

The *facilitative* mediator assumes the parties are intelligent, able to work with their counterparts, and capable of understanding their situations better than either their lawyers or the mediator. So the parties may develop better solutions than any that the mediator might create. For these reasons, the facilitative mediator assumes that his principal mission is to enhance and clarify communications between the parties in order to help them decide what to do.

The facilitative mediator believes it is inappropriate for the mediator to give his opinion, for at least two reasons. First, such opinions might impair the appearance of impartiality and thereby interfere with the mediator's ability to function. Second, the mediator might not know enough — about the details of the case or the relevant law, practices or technology — to give an informed opinion.

Each of the two principal questions — Does the mediator tend toward a narrow or broad focus? and Does the mediator favor an evaluative or facilitative role? — yield responses that fall along a continuum. Thus, a mediator's orientation will be more or less broad and more or less evaluative.

STRATEGIES AND TECHNIQUES OF EACH ORIENTATION

Each *orientation* derives from assumptions or beliefs about the mediator's role and about the appropriate focus of a mediation. A mediator employs *strategies* — plans — to conduct the mediation. And he uses *techniques* — particular moves or behaviors — to effectuate those strategies. Here are selected strategies and techniques that typify each mediation orientation.

The following grid shows the principal techniques associated with each mediator orientation, arranged vertically with the most evaluative at the top and the most facilitative at the bottom. The horizontal axis shows the scope of problems to be addressed, from the narrowest issues to the broadest interests.

EVALUATIVE

NARROW Problem Definition		BROAD Problem Definition
• Urges/pushes parties to accept narrow (position-based) settlement • Develops and proposes narrow (position-based) settlement • Predicts court outcomes • Assesses strengths and weaknesses of legal claims	• Urges/pushes parties to accept broad (interest-based) settlement • Develops and proposes broad (interest-based) settlement • Predicts impact (on interests) of not settling • Probes parties' interests	
Litigation Issues Other Distributive Issues	Business (Substantive) Issues Business Interests Personal Interests Societal Interests	
• Helps parties evaluate proposals • Helps parties develop narrow (position-based) proposals • Asks parties about consequences of not settling • Asks about likely court outcomes • Asks about strengths and weaknesses of legal claims	• Helps parties evaluate proposals • Helps parties develop broad (position-based) proposals • Helps parties develop options • Helps parties understand issues and interests • Focuses discussion on underlying interests (business, personal, societal)	

FACILITATIVE

EVALUATIVE-NARROW

The principal strategy of the evaluative-narrow mediator is to help the parties understand the strengths and weaknesses of their positions and the likely outcome at trial. To accomplish this, the evaluative-narrow mediator typically will first carefully study relevant documents, such as pleadings, depositions, reports and mediation briefs. Then, in the mediation, she employs evaluative techniques. . . . [Representative techniques are described on the grid.]

FACILITATIVE-NARROW

Like the evaluative-narrow, the facilitative-narrow mediator plans to help the participants become "realistic" about their litigation situations. But he employs different techniques. He does not use his own assessments, predictions or proposals. Nor does he apply pressure. Moreover, he probably will not request or study relevant documents, such as pleadings, depositions, reports, or mediation briefs. Instead, because he believes that the burden of decision should rest with the parties, the facilitative-narrow mediator might ask questions — generally in private caucuses — to help the participants understand both sides' legal positions and the consequences of non-settlement. Also in private caucuses, he helps each side assess proposals in light of the alternatives. . . .

EVALUATIVE-BROAD

The evaluative-broad mediator also helps the parties understand their circumstances and options. However, she has a different notion of what this requires. So she emphasizes the parties' interests over their positions and proposes solutions designed to accommodate these interests. In addition, because the evaluative-broad mediator constructs the agreement, she emphasizes her own understanding of the circumstances at least as much as the parties'. . . .

The evaluative-broad mediator also provides predictions, assessments and recommendations. But she emphasizes options that address underlying interests, rather than those that propose only compromise on narrow issues. In the mediation of a contract dispute between two corporations, for instance, while the evaluative [sic facilitative]-narrow mediator might propose a strictly monetary settlement, the evaluative-broad mediator might suggest new ways for the firms to collaborate (perhaps in addition to a monetary settlement).

FACILITATIVE-BROAD

The facilitative-broad mediator seeks to help the parties define, understand and resolve the problems they wish to address. She encourages them to consider underlying interests rather than positions and helps them generate and assess proposals designed to accommodate those interests. . . .

The facilitative-broad mediator does *not* provide assessments, predictions or proposals. However, to help the participants better understand their legal situations, she will likely allow the parties to present and discuss their legal arguments. In addition, she might ask questions . . . and focus discussion on underlying interests.

In a broad mediation, however, legal argument generally occupies a lesser position than it does in a narrow one. And because he emphasizes the participants' role in defining the problems and in developing and evaluating proposals, the facilitative-broad mediator does not need to fully understand the legal posture of the case. Accordingly, he is less likely to request or study litigation documents, technical reports or mediation briefs.

However, the facilitative-broad mediator must be able to quickly grasp the legal and substantive issues and to respond to the dynamics of the situation. He needs to help the parties realistically evaluate proposals to determine whether they address the parties' underlying interests. . . .

SUBJECT-MATTER EXPERTISE

In selecting a mediator, what is the relevance of "subject-matter expertise"? The term could mean substantial understanding of either the law, customary practices, or technology associated with the dispute. In a patent infringement lawsuit, for instance, a mediator with subject-matter expertise could be familiar with the patent law or litigation, practices in the industry, or the relevant technology—or with all three of these areas.

The need for subject-matter expertise typically increases to the extent that the parties seek evaluations—assessments, predictions or proposals—from the mediator. The kind of subject-matter expertise needed depends on the kind of evaluation or direction the parties seek. If they want a prediction about what would happen in court, they need a mediator with a strong background in related litigation. If they want suggestions about how to structure future business relations, perhaps the mediator should understand the relevant industries. If they want to propose new government regulations (as in a regulatory negotiation), they might wish to retain a mediator who understands administrative law and procedure.

In contrast, to the extent that the parties feel capable of understanding their circumstances and developing potential solutions—singly, jointly or with assistance from outside experts—they might prefer a mediator with great skill in the mediation process, even if she lacks subject-matter expertise. In such circumstances, the mediator need only have a rough understanding of the relevant law, customs and technology. In fact, too much subject-matter expertise could incline some mediators toward a more evaluative role, and could thereby interfere with developing creative solutions.

Notes and Questions

3.13 Of the four orientations or quadrants described on the grid, which is most in keeping with the description of mediation in Love's article, Images of Justice? Riskin states elsewhere in the article that "many retired judges, when they mediate, tend toward an evaluative-narrow orientation." It is perhaps predictable that judges would gravitate toward a quadrant that is more aligned with the "image of justice" describing an arbiter.

3.14 Facilitative mediation is also known as "pure" or classic mediation. Most of the training programs for mediators are based on a facilitative-broad approach to mediation. Despite this, there is a proliferation of evaluative mediation in legalized cases, that is, cases that are court-annexed or have attorney representatives. How do you explain this? For one interesting analysis of this question, see Robert A. Baruch Bush, Substituting Mediation for Arbitration: The Growing Market for Evaluative Mediation, and What It Means for the ADR Field, 3 Pepp. Disp. Resol. L.J. 111 (2002). The controversy around "evaluative mediation" is explored further in Chapter 7.

3.15 While the terminology of the original Riskin grid has been widely used and debated, in a more recent article, Riskin replaces the "facilitative-evaluative" dichotomy with "elicitive-directive." Leonard L. Riskin, Decisionmaking in Mediation: The New Old Grid and the New New Grid System, 79 Notre Dame L.Rev. 1 (2003). The new terminology may prove more helpful and less controversial, though Riskin expresses reservations about the static quality of the grid and its oversimplification as an accurate "map" of the mediation process. His "New New Grid" is a far more complex system that maps not only the predispositions, intentions, and influences of the mediator, but also those of parties and their attorneys.

2. Bargaining or Therapy

Scholars from the disciplines of anthropology and sociology, observing community, family, and small claims cases, find two types of mediator styles: bargaining and therapy.

 Susan S. Silbey & Sally E. Merry, **MEDIATOR SETTLEMENT STRATEGIES**

8 L. & Poly. Q. 7, 19-20 (1986)

In the bargaining mode, mediators claim authority as professionals with expertise in process, law, and the court system, which is described as costly, slow and inaccessible. The purpose of mediation is to reach settlement. The bargaining style tends toward more structured process, and toward more overt control of the proceedings. In the bargaining style, mediators use more private caucuses with disputants, direct discussion more, and encourage less direct disputant communication than in the therapeutic style. Moreover, in the bargaining style the mediators tend to write agreements without the parties present, summarizing and synthesizing what they have heard from the parties. The job of the mediator is to look for bottom lines, to narrow the issues, to promote exchanges, and to side-step intractable differences of interest. Typically disputants will be asked directly "What do you want?", ignoring emotional demands and concentrating on demands that can be traded off. Following this bargaining mode, mediators seem to assume that conflict is caused by differences of interest and that the parties can reach settlement by exchanging benefits. When parties resist, the role of the mediator is to become an "agent of reality" and to point to the inadequacy of the alternatives, the difficulty of the present situation and the benefits of a settlement of any kind.

By contrast, the therapeutic style of mediation is a form of communication in which the parties are encouraged to engage in a full expression of their feelings and attitudes. Here, mediators claim authority based on expertise in managing personal relationships and describe the purpose of mediation as an effort to help people reach mutual understanding through collective agreements. Like the bargaining style, the therapeutic mode also takes a negative view of the legal system; but, instead of emphasizing institutional values and inadequacies, the therapeutic style emphasizes emotional concerns, faulting the legal system for worsening personal relationships. In this mode, agreement writing becomes a collective activity, with mediators generally maximizing direct contact between the parties wherever it may lead. Following the therapeutic style, mediators will typically ask, "How did this situation start?", or,

"What was your relationship beforehand?" They rely more heavily upon expanding the discussion, exploring past relations, and going into issues not raised by the immediate situation, complaint, or charge. There is less discussion of legal norms than within the bargaining mode, and statements about alternatives tend to focus upon appropriateness of process rather than particular outcomes. In addition, the therapeutic mode tends to emphasize the mutuality, reciprocity, and self-enforcement of the agreement in contrast to court or program monitoring.

Notes and Questions

3.16 Is Riskin's categorization scheme related to that of Silbey and Merry, or are they focusing on entirely different variables? Is the "therapeutic style" on Riskin's grid at all?

3.17 Silbey and Merry characterize mediation as "a bargaining process conducted in the shadow of the court" and "a communication process which resembles therapy." Can it be both? Each of Riskin's quadrants arguably focus on bargaining. Do you think the professional orientation of the scholars—law versus anthropology and sociology—affects what they see when they examine mediation?

3. Problem-Solving, Understanding-Based or Transformative

The problem-solving approach to mediation, most clearly aligned with what has been called facilitative mediation by Riskin above, seeks to assist parties understand both the issues and each other more fully and to generate options and ultimately solutions or agreements.

The following two excerpts describe two different models that take a facilitative orientation in different directions. First, the Understanding-Based Model incorporates knowledge of law with an emphasis on parties working together to find a resolution ideal for them. The second excerpt describes Transformative Mediation, which aims not at solving the problem or finding a resolution, but rather at changing the parties—making the parties stronger themselves ("empowerment") and also more open to and understanding of each other ("recognition").

 Gary Friedman & Jack Himmelstein, **THE UNDERSTANDING-BASED MODEL OF MEDIATION**

The Center for Mediation in Law (2004)

The overarching goal of this approach to mediation is to resolve conflict through understanding. Deeper understanding by the parties of their own and each other's perspectives, priorities and concerns enables them to work through their conflict together. With an enhanced understanding of the whole situation, the parties are able to shape creative and mutually rewarding solutions that reflect their personal, business and economic interests. To these ends, the mediator meets directly and simultaneously (rather than separately) with both sides and, if the parties desire, with their lawyers present as well.

The Center's model shares much in common with a number of other approaches to mediation. For example, we stress the importance of articulating interests that underlie the parties' conflicting positions and developing solutions that will serve those interests. There is also much that distinguishes this approach.

PARTIES' RESPONSIBILITY AND NON-CAUCUS APPROACH

In the Understanding-Based Model, the emphasis is on the parties' responsibility for the decisions they will make. Many models of mediation assume that the mediator should take a strong role in crafting a solution to the parties' dispute and persuading them to adopt it. In this approach, the assumption is that it is the parties, not the professionals, who have the best understanding of what underlies the dispute and are in the best position to find the solution. It is *their* conflict, and *they* hold the key to reaching a solution that best serves them both.

Meeting together with the parties (and counsel) follows from these assumptions about parties' responsibility. Many other approaches to mediation recommend that the mediator shuttle back and forth between the parties (caucusing), gaining information that he or she holds confidential. Our central problem with caucusing is that the mediator ends up with the fullest picture of the problem and is therefore in the best position to solve it. The mediator, armed with that fuller view, can readily urge or manipulate the parties to the end he or she shapes. The emphasis here, in contrast, is on understanding and voluntariness as the basis for resolving the conflict rather than persuasion or coercion.

We view the mediator's role in the Understanding-Based approach as assisting the parties to gain sufficient understanding of their own and each other's perspective so as to be able to decide together how to resolve their dispute. The parties not only know first hand everything that transpires, they have control over fashioning an outcome that will work for both. And they also participate with the mediator (and counsel) in designing a process by which they can honor what they each value and help them reach a result that reflects what is important to both of them. As mediators, our goal is to support the parties in working through their conflict together — in ways that respect their differing perspectives, needs and interests as well as their common goals.

To work in this way is challenging for both the mediator and the parties. The parties' motivation and willingness to work together is critical to the success of this approach. Mediators often assume that the parties (and their counsel) simply do not want to work together, and therefore keep the parties apart. In our experience, many parties (and counsel) simply accept that they will not work together and that the mediator will be responsible for crafting the solution. But once educated how staying in the same room might be valuable, many are motivated to do so. If the parties (and the mediator) are willing, working together throughout can be as rewarding as it is demanding.

ROLE OF LAW AND LAWYERS

Mediators tend to be divided in how they approach the role of law in mediation. Some rely heavily on what a court would decide if the case were to go to trial, authoritatively suggesting or implying that law should be the controlling standard used to end the conflict. Other mediators, concerned that the parties might simply defer too readily to the law and miss the opportunity to find more creative decisions, try to keep the law out of mediation altogether.

In this model, we welcome lawyers' participation and we include the law. But we do not assume that the parties will or should rely solely or primarily on the law. Rather, the importance the parties give to the law is up to them. Our goals are (1) to educate the parties about the law and possible legal outcomes and (2) to support their freedom to fashion their own creative solutions that may differ from what a court might decide. In this way, the parties learn that they can together reach agreements that respond to both their individual interests and their common goals while also being well informed about their legal rights and the judicial alternatives to a mediated settlement. . . .

———————

Friedman and Himmelstein include creative problem solving, along with enriched understanding, as a goal of mediation. Robert Baruch Bush and Joseph Folger, in their Transformative Mediation model, reject problem solving as a goal of mediation and add party empowerment to that of enhanced understanding between parties.

 ### *Robert A. Baruch Bush & Joseph P. Folger*, THE PROMISE OF MEDIATION

45, 49, 51-53, 65-66 (rev. ed. 2005)

The transformative theory of conflict starts by offering its own answer to the foundational question of what conflict means to the people involved. According to transformative theory, what people find most significant about conflict is not that it frustrates their satisfaction of some right, interest, or pursuit, no matter how important, but that it leads and even forces them to behave toward themselves and others in ways that they find uncomfortable and even repellent. More specifically, it alienates them from their sense of their own strength and their sense of connection to others, thereby disrupting and undermining the interaction between them as human beings. This crisis of deterioration in human interaction is what parties find most affecting, significant — and disturbing — about the experience of conflict. . . .

Conflict, along with whatever else it does, affects people's experience of both self and other. First, conflict generates, for almost anyone it touches, a sense of their own *weakness* and incapacity . . . : a sense of lost control over their situation, accompanied by confusion, doubt, uncertainty, and indecisiveness. The overall sense of weakening is something that occurs as a very natural human response to conflict; almost no one is immune to it, regardless of his or her initial "power position." At the very same time, conflict generates a sense of *self-absorption*: compared with before, each party becomes more focused on self alone — more protective of self and more suspicious, hostile, closed, and impervious to the perspective of the other person. In sum, no matter how strong people are, conflict propels them into relative weakness. No matter how considerate of others people are, conflict propels them into self-absorption and self-centeredness. . . .

Taking the transformative view of what conflict entails and means to parties, one is led to a different assumption, compared with other theories of conflict, about what parties want, need, and expect from a mediator. If what bothers parties most about conflict is the interactional degeneration itself, then what they will most want from an intervenor is help in reversing the downward spiral and restoring constructive interaction. Parties may not express this in so many words when they first come to a mediator. More commonly, they explain that what they want is not just agreement but "closure," to get past their bitter conflict experience and "move on" with their lives. However, it should be clear that in order to help parties achieve closure and move on, the mediator's intervention must directly address the interactional crisis itself. . . .

From the perspective of transformative theory, reversing the downward spiral is the primary value that mediation offers to parties in conflict. That value goes beyond the dimension of helping parties reach agreement on disputed issues. With or without the achievement of agreement, the help parties most want, in all types of conflict, involves helping them end the vicious circle of disempowerment, disconnection, and demonization — alienation from both self and other. Because, without ending or changing that cycle, the parties cannot move beyond the negative interaction that has entrapped them and cannot escape its crippling effects.

This is transformative theory's answer to the question posed previously: What kind of help do people want from a mediator? As transformative theory sees it, with solid support from research on conflict, parties who come to mediators are looking for — and valuing — more than an efficient way to reach agreements on specific issues. They are looking for a way to change and transform their destructive conflict interaction into a more positive one, to the greatest degree possible, so that they can move on with their lives constructively, whether together or apart. . . .

[T]ransformative mediation can best be understood as a process of *conflict transformation* — that is, changing the quality of conflict interaction. In the transformative mediation process, parties can recapture their sense of competence and connection, reverse the negative conflict cycle, reestablish a constructive (or at least neutral) interaction, and move forward on a positive footing, with the mediator's help. . . .

[This] brings us to the definition of mediation itself, and the mediator's role, in the transformative model. Both of these definitions differ markedly from the normal definitions found in training materials and practice literature — in which mediation is usually defined as a process in which a neutral third party helps the parties to reach a mutually acceptable resolution of some or all of the issues is dispute, and the mediator's role is defined as establishing ground rules, defining issues, establishing an agenda, generating options, and ultimately persuading the parties to accept terms of agreement. . . .

By contrast, in the transformative model

- Mediation is defined as a process in which a third party works with parties in conflict to help change the quality of their conflict interaction from negative and destructive to positive and constructive, as they explore and discuss issues and possibilities for resolution.

- The mediator's role is to help the parties make positive interactional shifts (empowerment and recognition shifts) by supporting the exercise of their capacities for strength and responsiveness, through their deliberation, decision making, communication, perspective taking, and other party activities.
- The mediator's primary goals are (1) to support empowerment shifts, by supporting — but never supplanting — each party's deliberation and decision making, at every point in the session where choices arise (regarding either process or outcome) and (2) to support recognition shifts, by encouraging and supporting — but never forcing — each party's freely chosen efforts to achieve new understandings of the other's perspective.

Notes and Questions

3.18 Are the goals of a transformative mediator — empowerment and recognition — at odds with the goals of a problem-solving mediator? Of an understanding-based mediator? To understand a situation or solve a problem, it is helpful to have the parties both strong individually ("empowered") and responsive to each other ("recognition"). Consequently, the purposes, strategies, and techniques of transformative, understanding-based, and facilitative mediators may overlap. For an analysis of transformative mediation's comparative advantage in attaining empowerment and recognition, see Jeffrey R. Seul, How Transformative Is Transformative Mediation? A Constructive-Developmental Assessment, 15 Ohio St. J. on Disp. Resol. 135, 171 (1999).

3.19 Providing a laboratory for a particular mediation model, the U.S. Postal Service, one of the largest employers in the United States, adopted a transformative model for workplace disputes involving allegations of discrimination. The program, which is probably the largest employment mediation program in the world, uses outside mediators who have specialized training in transformative mediation. It provides a forum for supervisors and employees to mediate during their working hours. Noted scholar Lisa Bingham has collected data since the project's inception in 1994. Her findings include high levels of participant satisfaction with both the mediation process (91 percent) and the mediators (96 percent), high levels of satisfaction with the mediation outcome (from 64 percent for complainants to 72 percent for management), a significant drop in the number of formal discrimination complaints at the Postal Service, and evidence of improved communication between employers and supervisors during mediation. See Lisa B. Bingham, Mediation at Work: Transforming Workplace Conflict at the United States Postal Service, IBM Center for the Bus. of Govt. (2003), available at *http://www.businessofgovernment.org/pdfs/ Bingham_Report.pdf*. Perhaps most significantly, these findings suggest there is a positive impact on the workplace itself as a result of the transformative mediation program.

4. Trashing, Bashing, or Hashing

Studying mediator approaches in civil court cases, including personal injury, construction, commercial, contract, and real estate, James Alfini finds three dominant approaches. He labels them "trashing, bashing, and hashing." As you read the accounts of these approaches (particularly "trashing" and "bashing"), note how far they are from transformative, understanding-based, or problem-solving mediation.

 James J. Alfini, TRASHING, BASHING, AND HASHING IT OUT: IS THIS THE END OF "GOOD MEDIATION"?

19 Fla. St. U. L. Rev. 47, 66-71, 73 (1991)

MEDIATOR STYLES AND STRATEGIES

Does circuit court mediation—because it is mandatory and conducted by legal professionals—anticipate a deviation from traditional mediation styles and strategies? Our interviews with the circuit mediators and lawyers revealed three distinct styles. These three approaches to the mediation process are characterized as (1) trashing, (2) bashing, and (3) hashing it out.

I. Trashing

The mediators who employ a trashing methodology spend much of the time "tearing apart" the cases of the parties . . . "to get them to a point where they will put realistic settlement figures on the table."

To facilitate uninhibited trashing of the parties' cases, the overall strategy employed by these mediators discourages direct party communication. Following the mediator's orientation and short (five to ten minutes) opening statements by each party's attorney, the mediator puts the parties in different rooms. . . .

Once the trasher has achieved the goal of getting both sides to put what she believes to be more realistic settlement figures on the table, she will shuttle back and forth trying to forge an agreement. If this is accomplished, the mediator may or may not bring the parties back together to work out the details of the agreement. One trasher explained that, once separated, he never brings the parties back together even at the final agreement stage. . . .

II. Bashing

Unlike the trashers, the mediators who use a bashing technique tend to spend little or no time engaging in the kind of case evaluation that is aimed at getting the parties to put "realistic" settlement figures on the table. Rather, they tend to focus initially on the settlement offers that the parties bring to mediation and spend most of the session bashing away at those initial offers in an attempt to get the parties to agree to a figure somewhere in between. Their mediation sessions thus tend to be shorter than those of the trashers, and they tend to prefer a longer initial joint session, permitting direct communication between the parties. . . .

As soon as the basher has gotten the parties to place settlement offers on the table, as one attorney explained, "there is a mad dash for the middle." One of the retired judges described a case he had mediated that morning:

> [T]he plaintiff wanted $75,000. The defendant told me he would pay $40,000. I went to the plaintiff and said to him, "They're not going to pay $75,000. What will you take?" He said, "I'll take $60,000." I told him I wasn't sure I could get $60,000 and asked if he would take $50,000 if I could get it. He agreed. I then went back to the defendant and told him I couldn't settle for $40,000, but "you might get the plaintiff to take $50,000" and asked if he would pay it. The answer was yes. Neither of them were bidding against themselves. I was the guy who was doing it, and that's the role of the mediator. . . .

III. Hashing It Out

The third circuit mediation style can best be described as one involving a hashing out of a settlement agreement because it places greater reliance on direct communication between the opposing attorneys and their clients. The hashers tend to take a much more flexible approach to the mediation process, varying their styles and using techniques such as caucusing selectively, depending on their assessment of the individual case and the needs and interests of the parties. When asked to describe the mediator's role in one sentence, a hasher responded, "Facilitator, orchestrator, referee, sounding board, scapegoat."

The hasher generally adopts a much less directive posture than the trashers and bashers, preferring that the parties speak directly with one another and hash out an agreement. However, if direct communication appears counterproductive, the hasher acts as a communication link. . . .

Flexibility apparently is the hallmark of the hasher style of mediation. Although hashers prefer to adopt a style that encourages direct party communication to hash out an agreement, they are willing to employ trasher or basher methodologies if they believe it to be appropriate in a particular case.

Notes and Questions

3.20 In ancient China, litigants came in to court on their knees, shamed because they could not work out their own conflict. Should "trashing" and "bashing" — arguably akin to shaming — be a part of our justice system? Why or why not?

3.21 Elsewhere in the article, Alfini suggests that experienced trial lawyers tend to use trashing; retired judges tend to use bashing. Why do you think that is?

3.22 Alfini concludes that the growth of the three approaches for civil cases does not signal the end of "good mediation." What is "good mediation"? If his observations are correct regarding the prevalent styles, do you agree with his conclusion?

5. Norm-Generating, Norm-Educating, or Norm-Advocating

Ellen Waldman asserts that what we call "mediation" is, in fact, three separate and distinct models: norm-generating (where parties generate relevant norms), norm-educating (where parties are educated about norms), and norm-advocating (where the mediator enforces norms while supporting peripheral bargaining). Waldman states that each model is more prevalent in particular arenas. As you read the descriptions of these models, consider whether you think "norm-advocating" mediation should be called mediation at all.

 Ellen A. Waldman, IDENTIFYING THE ROLE OF SOCIAL NORMS IN MEDIATION: A MULTIPLE MODEL APPROACH

48 Hastings L.J. 703, 710, 718-719, 723, 731-734, 741-742, 745-746, 755-756 (1997)

DESCRIPTION OF THE NORM-GENERATING MODEL

At no time . . . does the mediator serve as a constraint on the parties' power of decision-making. He may question whether one party's demands are realistic, given the needs articulated by the other. However, he does not restrain deliberations by referencing concerns extrinsic to the parties. That is to say, in the mediation model I have characterized as "norm-generating," the mediator does not remove identified options from consideration simply because those options conflict with existing social norms. . . . The leitmotif of the norm-generating model, then, is its inattention to social norms. In an effort to spur innovative problem-solving, the model situates party discussion in a normative tabula rasa. The only relevant norms are those the parties identify and agree upon. As Lon Fuller has explained, traditional or norm-generating mediation "is commonly directed, not toward achieving conformity to norms, but toward the creation of the relevant norms themselves." . . .

THE NORM-EDUCATING PROCESS USING MEDIATIVE TECHNIQUES

Contrary to the norm-generating model, where discussion of societal standards is thought to impede autonomy and distract parties from their true needs, this [the norm-educating] model's consideration of social norms is thought to enhance autonomy by enabling parties to make the most informed decisions possible. . . .

This model is most visible in the divorce arena. The mid-eighties divorce mediation literature reveals skirmishes between those who thought that divorce mediation should mirror the generic norm-generating model and those who believed that disputants should be educated about the norms encoded in family law. Today the battle has largely subsided. Most commentators agree that a divorce mediator should have some familiarity with family law issues. Descriptions of ongoing programs reveal that the mediator is active in ensuring that disputant negotiations are informed by relevant legal and social norms, either by educating the parties himself or by ensuring that they are educated by retained counsel.

The norm-educating model, however, is not restricted to the divorce context. Court-referred cases, whose subjects range from bankruptcy, to real property, to wrongful termination, are likely to be "mediated" in the thick shadow of the law. In Florida, a state where court-sponsored mediation has grown exponentially, many mediators employ a "trashing" style, dissecting the flaws and weak points in each disputant's case according to prevailing legal norms. Further, the Florida rules governing court-appointed mediators acknowledge the use mediators make of legal rulings and standards by explicitly allowing mediators to provide legal information to disputants, provided the mediator is qualified to do so. . . .

The norm-educating model of mediation strikes a compromise between those who would bar discussions of law entirely from mediation practice and those who would outlaw mediation because it strays too far from the normative moorings of our adversary system. It stands for the proposition that the parties should be educated about their legal rights. However, if one or both of the parties decides to waive those rights, the mediator does not object. The norm-educating mediator views the parties, not society, as rightful possessor of the dispute. Consequently, the parties may, if they choose, reach a resolution that does not correspond entirely with societal norms. . . .

Although parties under this model may waive their rights and entitlements, such waivers, in the face of complete knowledge, seem less likely to occur and will likely be less dramatic than in the norm-generating mediation model. Moreover, such rights-waivers, if made knowingly, may represent a party's conscious trade-off to obtain an alternate form of satisfaction. In such a situation, the legal right has served as an important bargaining chip, and, to the degree that the legal entitlement has empowered one party to advance claims that she would otherwise be poorly situated to assert, the right has served its purpose; the norm has been effectuated. . . .

THE NORM-ADVOCATING PROCESS USING MEDIATIVE TECHNIQUES

In this process . . . the mediator not only educate[s] the parties about the relevant legal and ethical norms, but also insist[s] on their incorporation into the agreement. In this sense, her role extend[s] beyond that of an educator; she [becomes], to some degree, a safeguarder of social norms and values. She apprise[s] the parties of relevant social norms, not simply to facilitate the parties' informed decision making and provide a beginning framework for discussion; she provide[s] information about legal and ethical norms to secure their implementation. . . . Although the norm-advocating model is less widespread, it is used to resolve a variety of conflicts, including bioethical, environmental, zoning, and, in some instances, discrimination disputes. . . .

The norm-advocating model, then, is applicable in disputes which require application of a normative framework, but present gray areas within that framework for negotiation. It may be argued that a process that limits the options available to the parties to those congruent with pre-existing norms is too constrictive to be called mediation. However, considerable negotiation may take place in the open space which normative guidelines leave uncertain. If the mediator uses mediative techniques to help the parties reach agreement within those regions, that process should be regarded as mediation. To call it something else spawns needless confusion.

Notes and Questions

3.23 If you accept all three variations under the umbrella of "mediation," what implications does that have in terms of ethics codes and qualifications for neutrals? Could non-lawyers mediate a dispute with legal issues in a norm-educating or norm-advocating model?

3.24 Like Leonard Riskin, Waldman argues that additional descriptors are necessary to distinguish different types of mediation. As we will see later, there is a debate as to what should be called "mediation." Does it matter what we call a process if it helps to resolve a dispute?

3.25 The norm-generating model matches "classic" or facilitative mediation. Waldman asserts that social norms are largely irrelevant in norm-generating mediation. Do you agree? Do you find social norms, rules, laws, or principles persuasive in negotiations? See Melvin Eisenberg, Private Ordering Through Negotiation: Dispute Settlement and Rulemaking, 89 Harv. L. Rev. 637 (1976).

6. Private Ordering, Community-Enhancing or Community-Enabling

Clark Freshman organizes mediation approaches in yet another way. Classic or facilitative mediation is described by Freshman as a "private ordering understanding of mediation." To this category he adds "community-enhancing" and "community-enabling" approaches.

 Clark Freshman, PRIVATIZING SAME-SEX "MARRIAGE" THROUGH ALTERNATIVE DISPUTE RESOLUTION: COMMUNITY-ENHANCING VERSUS COMMUNITY-ENABLING MEDIATION

44 UCLA L. Rev. 1687, 1692-1697 (1997)

In a *private-ordering understanding of mediation*, a mediator simply teases out the parties' values and helps them craft a resolution that reflects their values. The implicit notion of such mediators is that parties can (and perhaps should) discover their own values and how they apply to problems; the values of law or other parts of a community are relevant only if a party wants to bring up such values. The implicit notion of the good mediator is one who mirrors the parties' values and helps work those values into an agreement about a particular dispute. The implicit notion of neutrality is that a mediator is neutral when the mediator is passive about raising values. . . .

A *community-enhancing understanding of mediation* regards mediation instead as a means of helping individuals order their activities and resolve their disputes consistent with the values of some relevant community. This is sometimes an explicit understanding of some alternative dispute resolution: a rabbinical court or lay Jewish court works to make disputants resolve their disagreements in accordance with

Jewish law. A recent article similarly proposes ADR by the "Islamic community" as a way to enforce Islamic law in the United States. Such community-enhancing mediation involves two levels. At the more superficial level, community-enhancing mediation means that a particular body of principles, such as Jewish or Islamic law, or some less formal set of community practices, should determine the outcome of a particular dispute. This would mean that how a couple divides property and child care should reflect the norms or practices of the community. In a less obvious way, a second aspect is that the process of mediation reinforces the individuals' sense of connection to a particular community and may make the individuals, at some level of consciousness, think of themselves as members of that community so thoroughly that they themselves order their lives according to the norms of the community without any additional process. A Jewish disputant leaves a Jewish tribunal thinking and identifying himself as a Jew and, when faced with a problem in the future, may think, "As a Jew, what should I do?" or even "I am a Jew so, of course, I have to . . ." The implicit image of both mediators and parties is that individuals are members of communities and/or should be members of communities.

I doubt that either the private ordering or the community-enhancing model of mediation is ideal. . . . The private-ordering understanding may neglect the many ways in which individuals may want to know how various communities they respect might understand their disputes. . . . At the same time, wanting to know how communities may understand disputes is not the same, as the community-enhancing account suggests, as surrendering one's ability to resolve disputes to those in positions of power (at least the power to resolve disputes) within those communities. . . .

I therefore propose a rather different model of mediation designed to tease out the kinds of preferences and values that individuals would express if they were given information about different values and different options and were encouraged to consider seriously these different values and options. I call this, rather infelicitously, *community-enabling mediation*. Such a process enables individuals to make informed choices about the kinds of communities they value and what weight, if any, to give to the norms such individuals may associate with that community. . . . [T]his would mean that a mediator would expose Mary and Susan [a same-sex Jewish couple pursuing a divorce] not just to what other women couples do, but also what other Jewish couples do, as well as what other groups of individuals do. Susan and Mary might choose to mimic the most popular practices of women couples, Jewish couples, or some other couples; they might largely construct their own arrangements. Whatever their choice, it would be relatively informed.

. . . [T]he private-ordering vision, in general, places too little emphasis on the potential importance of different communities; the community-enhancing vision, in general, places too much weight on enhancing one aspect of community when parties might value other communities as well. . . . [C]ommunity-enabling mediation should be designed to allow individuals to make informed decisions about how to organize their lives and intimate relationships by exposing them to competing norms, including competing communities. Unlike community-enhancing mediation, this will not *necessarily* enforce existing community norms, nor strengthen the way individuals think of themselves as committed to the communities that claim them among their members. Instead, this vision of mediation facilitates new relationships and arrangements that may better fit individual needs. In any event, even if individuals choose to follow existing community norms, that choice will be an informed one, consistent with the value placed not merely on community but on community as a product of the informed decisions of individuals. . . .

Notes and Questions

3.26 The central aspects of mediation, outlined by Carrie Menkel-Meadow earlier in this chapter, are that it is (1) consensual, (2) voluntary, (3) participatory, (4) facilitated by a third party outside the dispute, (5) seeking solutions and resolutions acceptable to all parties, and (6) seeking enhanced understanding among parties. Do all the variants described above comport with those core aspects? If your answer is no, would you amend the list or exclude the variant from the mediation family?

3.27 Consider particularly whether evaluative-narrow mediation (Riskin), transformative mediation (Bush and Folger), "trashing" and "bashing" (Alfini), norm-advocating mediation (Waldman), and community-enhancing mediation (Freshman) arguably fall outside at least one of Menkel-Meadow's parameters.

7. Dispute Settlement or Transaction and Relationship Formation

In addition to settling disputes, mediation can facilitate deals and help form new relationships or organizations. Facilitating transactions, sometimes called transactional dispute resolution, is perhaps the newest, most informal and undeveloped use of mediation.

Lawyers can bring creative perspectives to deal formation by employing problem-solving concepts, exploring underlying needs and interests, creating value, encouraging participation, and expanding and allocating resources, skills discussed in Chapter 2. A mediator, however, can enhance all of these lawyer contributions by creating value, preventing waste, and removing strategic barriers to information asymmetries. Mediators also help deal with emotional, cognitive, and other barriers to agreement (recall Section D of Chapter 2) to facilitate Pareto-efficient and satisfying arrangements. Mediators, for example, may be better than attorneys at helping parties overcome self-serving assessments and reactive devaluation — phenomena that attorneys can fall prey to as well. Deal-makers may require assistance in solving problems, allocating risk, deflecting future problems, and keeping the social climate positive. For certain matters, bringing in a mediator to develop the deal offers valuable potential benefits: speed, quality, and sustainable agreements. In the following excerpt, Scott Peppet examines the economic justifications of adding third-party mediators to deal creation. If transactional mediators can facilitate more efficient, durable deals and relationships, it follows that they may have a role as significant as that of dispute resolvers.

Scott R. Peppet, CONTRACT FORMATION IN IMPERFECT MARKETS: SHOULD WE USE MEDIATORS IN DEALS?

38 Ohio St. J. on Disp. Resol. 283, 298-301 (2004)

ECONOMIC JUSTIFICATIONS FOR TRANSACTIONAL MEDIATION

Discovering and Optimizing Gains from Trade

Transactional negotiators theoretically face similar adverse selection problems to those faced by disputing parties. First, the parties may not discover that trade is possible. Just as a litigating defendant may posture and bluff to try to low-ball a plaintiff, a buyer in a transaction may be tempted to try to get a better deal by "looking cheap." In other words, even if a buyer is willing to pay a high price, she may do better by looking as if she will only pay a low one. The opposite is true of sellers. One common example from the transactional context illustrates the problem. Because a high-value buyer does not want to signal his type to the seller, and because a seller is likely to equate having deep pockets with a willingness to spend, a deep-pocketed buyer may seek to hide its identity to prevent giving away too much to the seller. In this case an agent—such as an attorney—can be used to present an anonymous offer, thereby eliminating any signal about reservation price that might be inferred from the buyer's identity. An agent cannot, however, overcome the more basic adverse selection problem caused by the simple fact that making *any* offer sends information about the offeror's previously private reservation price. Information asymmetries may thus lead parties to exaggerate offers and demands in order to get a better deal.

In one experiment, for example, small teams of experienced executives were given detailed information about two simulated companies. They were then assigned to represent one company or the other and asked to evaluate the companies and negotiate a merger. Although agreement was possible, only nine of the twenty-one pairings reached agreement. In addition, the executives disagreed wildly about the relevant valuations—selling prices ranged from $3.3 million to $16.5 million. This suggests that occasionally transacting parties fail to "close the deal" because of strategic posturing.

Second, as in litigation, transacting parties may fail to find Pareto-efficient agreements. In an idealized situation with full information and zero transaction costs, the parties should trade until they find an economically efficient contract. It is notoriously unclear, however, whether contracting parties reach Pareto-efficient agreements in practice. Information asymmetries and strategic posturing may again lead to inefficiencies. Two parties may not discover an efficient agreement if one or the other is reluctant to discuss it (or agreements of its type) for fear that doing so will reveal private information about the party's reservation price.

An executive negotiating her employment agreement, for example, might shy away from discussing certain packages that involve accepting a lower salary in exchange for better benefits or greater stock options, if the executive fears that doing so would send an unwise signal about her worth. Similarly, an experiment in the corporate acquisitions context suggests that even when experienced negotiators reach agreement, they do not necessarily reach Pareto-efficient contracts. Even subjects trained in decision analysis and finance succumbed to the strategic difficulties inherent in bargaining and, because of a failure to share information, sometimes concluded inefficient deals.

As in litigation, a mediator should be able to help. Interestingly, the researcher in this corporate acquisitions experiment re-ran the simulation offering each negotiating pair the service of a trained mediator, but not requiring that they use the mediator. Those executives that made use of the mediator reached more efficient contracts than those that did not. Similarly, Max Bazerman et al. found that a mediator intermediary — as opposed to an agent — can lower impasse rates in transactional bargaining. Although experimental economics regarding the role of mediators and intermediaries is in its infancy, and some research suggests that intermediaries merely add costs and thus preclude agreement in some bargaining, there is at least preliminary evidence that a transactional mediator can add value.

For example, as part of a larger project on fair division procedures, Steven Brams and Alan Taylor note that a mediator should theoretically be able to help merging companies resolve disagreements over "social issues," such as how to name the post-merger corporation, how to resolve status and position questions (e.g., who will be CEO), and where to locate the new company's headquarters. After reviewing a sample of large mergers that collapsed because of disputes over such issues, they concluded that "[t]hese deals highlight the need for effective dispute-resolution techniques in merger negotiations." Their "adjusted winner" procedure is designed to reduce deal failure and optimize the efficiency of trades about these social issues. The parties assign points to the various issues in contention and a mediator referee then uses their assignments to plumb for the most value-creating solutions to their disagreements.

Howard Raiffa also suggests that a mediator might serve as a "contract embellisher" in transactions. He suggests that at the start of bargaining a mediator could privately interview each party about its needs, priorities, and perceptions. The mediator would lock away that information and the parties would be left alone to negotiate a deal. At the conclusion of their negotiation, but prior to closing the deal, the intervenor would return. After examining the terms of the parties' agreement, the intervenor would try to use his private information about the parties' interests to craft a superior deal. He would then show his substitute agreement to each party privately. If both sides agreed that the mediator's suggestion was superior to their own contract, the substitution would be made. There would be no haggling about the terms of the mediator's proposal — it would be a take-it-or-leave-it situation.

It is difficult to know whether Raiffa's intervenor would succeed in practice. Nevertheless, the role is certainly plausible. A skilled mediator might find trades or packages that the parties had overlooked because of carelessness, time pressures, limited skills or experience, or strategic posturing. . . .

Notes and Questions

3.28 Peppet argues elsewhere in his article that "neither most existing [state] regulations nor the new [Uniform Mediation Act] extend sufficiently clear confidentiality protections to transactional mediation to foster mediator intervention in deals. . . . As a result, this regulatory regime may inhibit the development of transactional mediators." This conclusion arises from language in regulations that define mediation — and the scope of confidentiality protections — as a neutral's assistance with *disputes*. To remedy this shortcoming, Peppet proposes that "States should modify their existing statutes or their adoption of the UMA to account for transactional mediators. . . . States could simply replace 'dispute' with 'dispute or other matter' [in definitions of privileged mediation] per Rule 2.4's [Model Rules of Professional Conduct] approach."

3.29 What kinds of transactions lend themselves to "deal mediators" (third-party neutrals who help put together the transaction)? What qualities would you look for in a deal mediator? What differences do you see in the roles of a "deal-facilitating" third party and a "dispute-resolving" third party? Can the same people be mediators in both of these contexts? In the same deal, if, after facilitating its making, it then falls apart? Should lawyers or business people take the lead in mediating deals?

3.30 Is it only a question of professional reference group (business or law), or do particular industries or business cultures vary in their willingness to try problem solving or ADR-like techniques? For example, it is now common practice in large construction contracts to use partnering or alliances in which potential signatories to a large project meet in a "workshop" before the deal is fully consummated. During this workshop, the parties develop relationships (social, as well as business) and build teams using cooperative, rather than adversarial, approaches. The parties may employ special experts such as psychologists, meeting managers, dispute system designers, and even social directors to develop a positive "deal culture." See Frank Carr, with Kim Hurtado, Charles Lancaster, Charles Markert & Paul Tucker, Partnering in Construction: A Practical Guide to Project Success (1999), for a fuller discussion of this process. The workshops are often led by a mediator or expert meeting manager in retreat-like settings to encourage more informal relations across formal professional boundaries. Many workshops conclude with a "Partnering Charter" or "Constitution" for the particular project or deal, a vision statement or a set of procedures to be followed when disputes arise. Evidence suggests partnering is expanding to other industries, such as high technology and joint venture capital deals, or settings involving many suppliers to a particular project. In organizational settings, these workshops resemble strategic planning meetings, but they focus on creating a problem-solving culture for a particular contract, project, or deal. When the process works well, it can lead to future deals.

3.31 Consider what the prenuptial and antenuptial agreement has done to make some marriages possible. See, e.g., Howard Raiffa, Post-Settlement

Settlements, 1 Negot. J. 9-12 (1985), in which the author analyzes how a third-party neutral such as a mediator can be a repository of information that parties might not want to reveal to each other without some assurance that the deal will go through or that the information will not be shared inappropriately, as in sharing trade secrets in merger discussions. Consider also the use of escrow accounts for monetary and documentary deposits while parties contingently perform on parts of contracts.

This chapter displays many different visions of the mediators' role: facilitator and evaluator; negotiator and therapist; problem-solving, understanding-based, and transformative; trashing, bashing, and hashing; norm-generating, norm-educating, and norm-advocating; private ordering, community-enhancing, and community-enabling; and dispute resolving or transactional. As you examine the cases in the next chapter, see which of these descriptors and categories are most useful in understanding different variants of the process.

 **Chapter 4** Descriptions of Mediations

Conflicts are created and sustained by human beings. They can be ended by human beings.

— George J. Mitchell (referring to conflicts in
Northern Ireland and the Middle East)

The following accounts of actual and fictional mediations illustrate the variety of practices and outcomes possible in the mediation of real cases. The first case is an appeal by shareholders against a large corporation, which was ordered into the mediation program of the U.S. Court of Appeals for the Second Circuit. The second case involves a minority group, a town, and litigation that raised constitutional questions. The next two cases involve the settlement of damage claims in a personal injury situation. The final example is a medical negligence case.

These provide only a small window into the universe of cases that benefit from mediation. Nonetheless, you will find here examples of (1) outcomes that are more custom-tailored than litigation can provide and a process that leads parties to a deeper appreciation of the other side's perspective (the *Sisters and Bristol* and *A Meeting of Strangers*); (2) outcomes that address a far broader range of issues than litigation and achieve a higher level of cooperation and community among the parties (the *Glen Cove* case and *A Meeting of Strangers*); (3) an account of distributive bargaining and raw compromise, where settlement saves the parties further disputing costs of litigation (*Fly on the Wall*); and (4) an outcome that provides both the closure and cost savings of a settlement and the personal connection and healing available from direct interaction between parties (the medical malpractice case).

As you read about these situations, imagine how the stories would have come out differently if mediation had not been used.

 Frank J. Scardilli, SISTERS OF THE PRECIOUS BLOOD v. BRISTOL-MYERS CO.: A SHAREHOLDER-MANAGEMENT DISPUTE*

reprinted in Leonard Riskin & James Westbrook, Dispute Resolution and Lawyers 362-367 (2d ed. 1997)

This case was on appeal to the U.S. Court of Appeals for the Second Circuit from a grant of summary judgment in favor of Bristol-Myers Co., defendant-appellee

---
*Presented at a Harvard faculty seminar on April 13, 1982.

(hereinafter "Bristol") and against the Sisters of the Precious Blood, plaintiff-appellant (hereinafter "Sisters"). The latter, who owned 500 shares of Bristol stock, started a lawsuit against Bristol under the proxy solicitation section of the Securities Exchange Act of 1934 alleging that a shareholder resolution they proposed was defeated because Bristol's stated opposition to the resolution in the proxy materials distributed to the shareholders was based on serious misrepresentations of fact.

The Sisters were concerned that the company's sales practices in the third world of its infant baby formula were contributing to serious illness, malnutrition and death of infants because of the unsanitary conditions often prevailing there. Frequently the formula is mixed with contaminated water, there is no refrigeration and its use discourages breastfeeding which is clearly healthier in most instances than is the formula.

The Sisters' proposed resolution requested that management report to the shareholders the full extent of its marketing practices of the infant formula in the third world to alert other shareholders to what they perceived was irresponsible business behavior. Their lawsuit was aimed at getting the company to come up with a corrected proxy solicitation to be submitted to a special meeting of the shareholders to be called specifically for that purpose rather than await the next annual meeting of shareholders.

The court declined to grant the relief sought by the Sisters. . . .

MEDIATION EFFORTS ON APPEAL

The first of four conferences seeking to mediate this dispute was held on July 19, 1977. . . . Apparently because they believed no amicable resolution was possible, counsel who appeared for the parties were very able but had virtually no settlement authority. . . .

As is customary, I first explored the arguments of counsel relative to the strengths and weaknesses of their legal positions on appeal. The parties seemed genuinely far apart in their assessment of the likely outcome in our court. The issue on appeal involved some complexity because of the rather technical requirements for suits under Section 14 of the Securities Exchange Act of 1934. While generally appellees have a distinct advantage, if for no other reason than that only about one out of eight cases is reversed on appeal in our court, the outcome of this particular case was hard to predict. Even if the district court decision were deemed technically correct, this could have disturbing policy implications because the decision appeared to create a license for management to lie with impunity whenever it sought to defeat a proposed shareholder resolution. . . . The SEC was apparently disturbed by this implication and advised me it was seriously considering filing a brief amicus curiae urging our court to reverse the decision below. . . .

Predictably, the parties' respective positions on what might constitute a satisfactory settlement were far apart. The Sisters were adamant on the principle that no settlement terms could be discussed unless Bristol openly admitted that it had lied in its earlier proxy solicitation and that this fact had to be communicated through new proxy solicitations at a special meeting of the shareholders to be convened solely for that purpose. Bristol, of course, insisted it had been truthful all along. It offered, however, to permit the Sisters to make any written statement they wished at the next annual shareholders' meeting, and Bristol would simply state its opposition to the proposal without elaboration. This was unacceptable to the Sisters. Because it was clear I needed parties with more authority and flexibility, I set up a second conference requiring senior counsel to come in with their clients.

The second conference held in the middle of August, 1977, was attended by senior counsel for both sides, the inside General Counsel of Bristol, and a representative of the Advisory Committee of the Interfaith Group for Corporate Responsibility, which was the real moving force behind the Sisters' litigation.

It soon became apparent that there was very deep hostility and profound distrust between the parties. Each was convinced the other was acting in bad faith. The Sisters were outraged by Bristol's insistence that it had not lied. Its distrust of Bristol was total and uncompromising. At this conference, the Sisters, for the first time, insisted that they would have to be reimbursed for their litigation expenses of approximately $15,000 before any settlement could be effected. After checking with top management, counsel for management flatly refused to pay anything at all to the Sisters. . . .

It became clear that the respective parties' self-image was significantly at variance with the image each had of the other.

Bristol regarded itself as by far the most responsible marketer of infant formula in the third world, far more so than its three major American competitors and the giant Swiss company Nestle. It claimed it put out a quality nutritional product that was very useful when mothers either could not or chose not to breast feed their infants; that it did not advertise its infant formulas directly to consumers in the third world; that the company policy already sought to minimize the danger of improper use by its labeling. In short, it was convinced that its business practices were both prudent and responsible. Therefore, they were furious that they had been singled out as "baby killers" by the Sisters who had so testified before a Congressional committee and who had lost few opportunities to criticize them in the media. It was clear they viewed the Sisters as wild-eyed, misguided religious fanatics who were themselves engaging in a distortion of the facts and reckless character assassination.

The Sisters, on the other hand, had spent years accumulating data in affidavits taken throughout the world regarding the enormous peril to infants created by the indiscriminate use of infant formula in the third world. They had witnessed suffering and death and were suffused with the self-righteousness of avenging angels. To them, Bristol was a monster who cared only about profits and not at all about the lives and health of infants. . . .

As negotiations proceeded, it became apparent that no meaningful communication could take place until each of the parties realized that its view of the other was a grossly distorted caricature and counter-productive.

I struck often at the theme that it was dangerous to assume that one with whom you disagree violently is necessarily acting in bad faith. Moreover, I stressed to both that I had become fully and firmly convinced that each of the parties was acting in complete good faith, albeit from a different perspective. I strove to get each to view the matter through the eyes of the other. . . .

It was necessary to convince each that its interests were not nearly as incompatible as they perceived them and that the interest of each would be best served by a cooperative problem-solving attitude rather than a litigious one.

I stressed that neither party's true interest would be served by "winning" the appeal. A "win" by Bristol would not be likely to stop the public attacks in the media which so angered and disturbed them. Likewise, a "win" by the Sisters could mean a remand for an expensive trial with no assurance whatever thereafter that Bristol's marketing practices would be altered in any way.

The point was made forcibly to the Sisters that their insistence that Bristol admit that it had lied was totally unrealistic and that progress was impossible so long as they insisted on humiliating the company's management. They were reminded that their real interest lay in effecting marketing changes in the third world and they could best achieve this in a climate of cooperative good will with management. So long as management perceived them as vindictive it was likely to simply dig in its heels and refuse to budge. I urged that a softening of their attitude would in turn create a more flexible attitude in management.

Bristol in turn was forced to concede that notwithstanding what they viewed as the distasteful stridency of the Sisters there was indeed a real moral issue to be faced and they had a real interest in being perceived as highly ethical, responsible businessmen who were not insensitive to the human tragedy which could result from the improper use of their product in the third world. . . .

After considerable negotiation in four face-to-face conferences supplemented by numerous telephone conferences over a period of nearly six months, in the course of which Bristol voluntarily changed some of its marketing practices, the parties finally agreed to resolve their differences as follows:

1. The Sisters were satisfied that Bristol had already changed some of its marketing practices which the Sisters had regarded as particularly offensive.
2. The Sisters would be given direct access to Bristol's Board of Directors and other representatives of the company at various times for the purpose of maintaining a first-hand continuing dialogue on the problems of marketing infant formula in the third world.
3. Bristol and the Sisters would each prepare a separate written statement of its views not to exceed 1500 words to be presented to the shareholders in the next quarterly report of the Company. This would be preceded by an agreed-upon joint preamble which would recite the background of the litigation, its resolution by the parties and that the Sisters and Bristol planned to continue to exchange views in an atmosphere of mutual respect for each other's good faith.

To insure that the statements would not be inflammatory each side was given the right to veto the statement of the other. Agreeing on the principle, however, was easier than its implementation. Numerous drafts were exchanged and when appropriate I mediated between their respective versions. The final agreement on language was arrived at as a result of a 4½-hour drafting session involving 8 people sitting around a conference table in the court in the afternoon of Christmas Eve of 1977. In a sense of relief and elation, the Chairperson of the Interfaith Group for Corporate Responsibility stated: "It is fitting and perhaps prophetic that we have finally resolved our differences on how best to protect tender infants on this [Christmas] eve. . . . "

Notes and Questions

4.1 Using this example to reflect on the potential advantages and benefits of the mediation processes described in Chapter 3 — settlement, participation and self-determination, better outcomes, relationship, and community — how was the mediation reflective (or not reflective) of those advantages? Is there public benefit from these private parties settling a case?

4.2 What arguable loss results from taking this case out of the litigation stream? How do you think the professor in the imaginary conversation by Baruch Bush in Chapter 3 would react to this mediation? Remember that the professor is concerned about litigation's role in protecting individual rights, promoting social justice for the poor and weak, maximizing aggregate societal welfare, and articulating public norms. The Sisters were seeking social justice for a class of poor and weak parties. Were those parties served well by mediation?

The case that follows, like the case of the Sisters and Bristol, has the potential for broad societal impact on groups of relatively weak and disenfranchised parties. As you read the case, reflect on the benefits of mediation to the parties in the case and in comparable situations.

 Lela P. Love, **GLEN COVE: MEDIATION ACHIEVES WHAT LITIGATION CANNOT**

20 Consensus 1, 1-2 (Oct. 1993)

The city of Glen Cove, Long Island, and Central American refugees who sought day labor at a "shaping point" (a locale in the city where employers go to find day workers) experienced a bitter and protracted controversy with no end in sight — despite nearly two years of litigation — when the parties decided to attempt to work out their differences in mediation. Mediation resolved not only the issues which were being litigated, but also many other issues that, although not causes for legal action, were nonetheless extremely important to the individuals and groups involved in the controversy. I had the privilege of mediating the case and report on its success in order to encourage other communities facing difficult disputes to try the mediation process.

BACKGROUND: TENSIONS BUILD

In 1988 tensions began to build between Glen Cove officials and the Central American immigrants (some of whom were undocumented aliens) who congregated in front of Carmen's Deli to find employment. More than 100 men, many from other towns, would gather on a given day to seek odd jobs from landscapers and other contractors.

Local merchants and neighbors expressed concerns about disorderly and noisy behavior at the shaping point, including cat-calling to women, and littering and urinating in public. City officials were also concerned about traffic safety, since employers would stop on a major road to negotiate with and pick up day workers. There also was a sentiment that it was illegal for those who were undocumented to seek employment.

Salvadoran workers, on the other hand, were interested in their survival, since the day labor was their means of livelihood, and a "shaping point" was essential for finding work. Many who gathered were political refugees from El Salvador, to whom a return home might mean a death sentence. There were those who felt that, since the laborers serviced the lawns and country clubs of the wealthy, the effort to remove them from gathering in public was unfair.

In addition to issues about the shaping point itself, the perception among the Hispanic community that the City — particularly the police — were hostile, created problems for both sides: poor channels of communication to cope with the host of problems; and a lack of resources for Central Americans when they were preyed upon by criminal elements in the community (a pressing problem).

ORDINANCES PROPOSED TO DEAL WITH PROBLEM

Tensions heightened in 1989 when the city, in an effort to curb the size of the gatherings, successfully urged the Immigration and Naturalization Service to round up and detain illegal aliens gathering in front of Carmen's Deli. This was followed by the city's proposing first an ordinance making it illegal for groups of five or more persons to assemble publicly to seek employment and later an ordinance which prohibited any "illegal undocumented alien" from soliciting work in a public or private place. These ordinances engendered a strident debate, although neither was adopted. In 1990, the City Council did adopt an ordinance which prohibited standing on a street or highway and soliciting employment from anyone in a motor vehicle and also prohibited occupants of a stopped or parked motor vehicle from hiring or attempting to hire workers.

The Hispanic community and civil libertarians saw the ordinance(s) as specifically targeted against Hispanics, as well as unconstitutional. Several months after the ordinance was adopted, advocacy groups for Central American refugees filed a three million dollar class action suit against Glen Cove, alleging violation of Hispanic persons' First Amendment right of freedom of speech and 14th Amendment right of equal protection.

WHAT MEDIATION ACHIEVED

Two full days of mediation, spaced a week apart to give the parties time to come up with innovative proposals to address the concerns raised the first day, were sufficient to achieve consensus on an outline of an acceptable accord. This agreement was refined over several months and adopted in late 1992, providing for the dismissal of the lawsuit and the enforcement of the terms of the agreement by the federal court.

The significant achievements of the mediation process in this case were:

- The parties recognized their mutual interest in improving communications with each other.
- Greater accessibility to the city soccer field for the Salvadoran community was arranged.
- The City agreed to help find alternative sites for a shaping point (including possible use of Industrial Development Agency funds) or to support alternatives to meet the Hispanic community's employment needs. The Central American Refugee Center (CARECEN) agreed to educate day laborers who congregate in public places about their responsibilities to the community.
- Relations between the police and the Salvadoran community were addressed by CARECEN's agreement to host community meetings giving the police a platform to educate Salvadorans about community interests and concerns and undertaking such education themselves. The police in turn agreed to: cultural awareness training for all city police officers; appointing a liaison to the Salvadoran community who would attend CARECEN-organized community meetings; training two officers in conversational Spanish; taking ability in Spanish into account in hiring officers; adopting a policy barring officers from inquiring about immigration status under certain circumstances; and instituting a written protocol (in consultation with CARECEN) for the police handling of situations where a party does not speak English.
- The Ordinance was amended to a form acceptable to all parties and designed to promote the City's interest in traffic safety without singling out the Salvadoran Community or infringing upon Constitutional rights.

Perhaps most importantly, the mediation created a respectful dialogue between the parties, which should result in an enhanced ability to confront new problems as they arise. . . . Alan Levine, the Director of the Hofstra Constitutional Law Clinic, which represented CARECEN, was quoted as saying, "If everyone lives up to their obligations under this agreement, it promises to establish the kinds of relationships between a municipal government and a minority population that one would hope for."

Notes and Questions

4.3 Glen Cove has enjoyed improved relations between town officials and the Salvadoran community in part, arguably, as a by-product of the mediation. A shaping point, with toilet facilities provided by the city and a variety of supportive services for day laborers, was ultimately put into place. See Lela P. Love & Cheryl B. McDonald, A Tale of Two Cities: Day Labor and Conflict Resolution for Communities in Crisis, 4(1) Disp. Resol. Mag. 8-10 (Fall 1997). If mediation can set new precedents with respect to community interaction and constructive problem solving, do those results counterbalance the loss of a legal precedent in a case with important constitutional issues? For another example of how mediation can accomplish a great deal, between parties in especially significant conflict with each other, by focusing on concrete issues, see Hephzibah Levine, Mediating the War of Olives and Pines; Consensus-Based Land-Use Planning in a Multi-Cultural Setting, 21 Neg. J. 29 (2005).

4.4 Compare the issues addressed in the litigation and mediation of the Glen Cove case:

LITIGATION	MEDIATION
• the *ordinance*: is it constitutional? • discrete incidents of *alleged police misconduct* at the shaping point	• *communication* between town officials and Salvadorans • *a shaping point* • *police interactions with non-English-speaking individuals and groups* (protocols when language barriers are present, cultural awareness and sensitivity, opportunities for communication) • concerns regarding *public conduct of Salvadorans* ("cat-calling," public urination, blocking entryways) • *use of the city soccer field* • *the ordinance*

Litigation entails an intensive inquiry into facts and evidence pertinent to the causes of action presented and the meaning of the norms and rules as they intersect with those issues. If, for example, the case had been litigated and the court had found the ordinance unconstitutional, the ordinance would be struck down. The town, however, could enact a new ordinance sensitive to the court's prohibition of certain language but not responsive to other issues that the mediation addressed.

Mediation, on the other hand, involved an intensive inquiry into information, interests, values, feelings, rules, and norms pertinent to the ordinance, the shaping point, interactions between the police and non-English-speaking civilians, interactions between the town and Salvadoran residents and workers, civic responsibilities of Salvadorans, and the use of the soccer field. Mediation engages participants in a forward-looking, problem-solving exercise, aimed as much at creating relationships conducive to addressing future problems as at solving the problems at hand.

Looked at this way, aren't both litigation and mediation vital to the public interest? Remember that part of the professor's critique of mediation in the imaginary conversation by Baruch Bush in Chapter 3 was that mediation serves private parties rather than the public good. Is that analysis accurate in light of the Glen Cove case?

The following account of a fictional personal injury mediation is an example of a settlement-oriented process where the mediator uses a joint session only at the beginning for making opening statements and at the end of the mediation for bringing the parties together to display agreements. The rest of the process is conducted in caucuses (separate meetings with each side). As you will see, the focus is on arriving at a mutually acceptable dollar amount rather than on exploring the parties' underlying interests or encouraging creative problem solving, a more cynical account of mediation than in the preceding two examples.

 J.S. Levy & R.C. Prather, **FLY ON THE WALL**

Texas Practice Guide: ADR App. A (2004)

To set the stage for the following, it is necessary to establish a factual predicate. Assume that the dispute arose following an intersectional automobile collision that happened approximately three years earlier. Suit was filed a little more than a year ago shortly before the Statute of Limitations barred any recovery. Most of the discovery and other pre-trial work has been completed. Last month the judge ordered the parties to mediate. . . . [After the mediator's opening remarks, each side gives an opening presentation and then are separated into separate caucus rooms. The Plaintiff and his counsel are in one room and the Insurance Adjuster who represents the insurance company is with his counsel in the other room. Here is a slice of what happens in those rooms.]

SCENE ONE: THE PLAINTIFF'S ROOM

Mediator: The door is closed and everything that is said in this room is confidential. Nothing leaves here unless you expressly authorize it. Let's talk. . . . (turning to the Plaintiff) Did you understand what the Adjuster said during the joint session about the most likely jury range?

Plaintiff: No I didn't. How can someone price such a painful injury the way that you price a used car? I don't believe that it can be quantified by some mechanistic formula. . . .

Mediator: Before proceeding, let me repeat one comment that I made a few minutes ago during the joint session: you listen to your attorney and not me. Your counsel is here to represent your best interests, while I am an advocate for settlement.

Having said that, let me continue by observing that there is a certain fiction in our jury system. To illustrate, the loss of a leg has a jury value today in this county of "X" number of dollars, plus or minus 20%. No sane person would "sell" a leg for that amount, but there is a sufficient statistical track record of jury awards to reflect that amount as being the most likely outcome.

From my perspective as the mediator/negotiator, this figure of "X" dollars, plus or minus 20%, is known as the "range of settlement." It is possible that the plaintiff who lost a leg could have a "home run" jury award in the "run away" amount of double or triple "X" dollars. That happens around ten percent of the time. Keep in mind the fact that, at the same time, it is equally logical that the jury in about ten percent of such cases would only award in the area of half of "X" dollars.

I know my remark sounds callous but that is the real world of jury trial. In virtually every personal injury case that I mediate, this county's jury reports are argued as a negotiating tool. It is irrelevant whether you think the Adjuster is a prince or a cretin. The sole issue is whether you can get the Adjuster to make an offer you can accept.... (turning to the counsel for the Plaintiff) Have there been any settlement talks?

Counsel for the Plaintiff: Prior to suit, I offered to settle for the policy limits of $100,000 and the Adjuster responded with an offer of $8,000. The Adjuster said that if I would drop my offer to a "more realistic amount" — whatever . . . that means — that a higher offer would be forthcoming.

After talking with my client, I moved to $70,000 and the Adjuster then made an offer of $12,000. At that point, I asked the Adjuster to double the $12,000 offer and the response was a comment to the effect that my mother wore a flea collar. Suffice it to say that discussions broke down then so I filed suit. There have been no settlement talks subsequently....

Mediator (to the counsel for the Plaintiff): I know that you have a good reputation as a trial attorney. However, let me ask you to momentarily step out of the role of an advocate and let's talk about the most likely jury award if this case were ever to go to trial.

Counsel for the Plaintiff: Why? Aren't you going to be able to settle this case for me?

Mediator: No, I don't settle anything. It's the parties that cause settlement. I help in the communications. It's y'all who settle a case.

Let me phrase my question a little differently. If you were to try this case a hundred times for a hundred consecutive weeks in that same court with that judge, what would be the probable, objective range of jury award figures? Of course, this case can only be tried once. For purposes of your evaluation, disregard the 10% "Armageddon" scenario on the low end and the 10% "home run" result on the other end of the spectrum, since no case ever settles at mediation in either of those areas.

Counsel for the Plaintiff: The numbers would be between $25,000 on the low end and $35,000 on the high end. However, understand that I have a really good Plaintiff. The jury will like the Plaintiff. For that reason, the jury award will be at the top end of that range, so I don't want you to try later today talking about a settlement in the $25,000 to $30,000 area. Do you understand me! . . .

Mediator: You know that the Adjuster is not going to pay $70,000 on this claim, since if the Adjuster were going to do so, we would not be here today. By your own analysis, the case is worth no more than half that figure. Finally, you can safely assume that the other side thinks the jury value of the case is a figure lower than your projection of $25,000 to $35,000.

Plaintiff (angrily to the counsel for the Plaintiff): Stop for a moment. If my case is worth only $35,000, why did we initially demand $100,000 and then offer to settle at $70,000? I was planning on walking away after all fees, medical bills and expenses with a net of more than $35,000. Something is wrong with this equation! I feel like a chihuahua surrounded by a pack of pit bulls.

Counsel for the Plaintiff (turning to Plaintiff): Perhaps I need to refresh your memory. You and I spoke about the most likely outcome at trial before I reduced our settlement offer from $100,000 to $70,000. . . .

Mediator (turning to counsel for the Plaintiff): Realistically speaking, where would you like the Adjuster to be on the next round of offers? . . .

Plaintiff (to the Mediator): What do you mean "on the next round"?

Mediator (to the Plaintiff): A mediation is not the type of function where someone can leave the engine running and quickly go inside to pick up a check. According to one study done on the topic of mediation, there usually are six to eight sets of offers and counteroffers until the parties either agree to a settlement or agree that an impasse has been reached. In short, today's negotiation is a give and take process, with a certain element of a battle of attrition. . . .

Plaintiff: Then let's go to $65,000. . . .

Mediator: Keeping in mind the Adjuster has the checkbook, it may not be wise to anger him. Look at the issue this way, his previous offer was $12,000, which is $13,000 from the bottom of your own jury range. At the same time, the $65,000 figure that you suggest is $30,000 above the top end of your range. . . .

Counsel for the Plaintiff (to the Mediator): What figure would you propose to take to the Adjuster?

Mediator: I propose nothing, as that is not my role. However, if you want a suggestion, let me throw out the idea that you reduce your demand to $50,000, along with a message that the Adjuster needs to double the $12,000 offer.

Plaintiff (to the Mediator): Tell the Adjuster that I will settle for $60,000.

Counsel for the Plaintiff (to the Mediator): That's our decision.

Mediator: Will do. Thank you. . . .

SCENE TWO: THE ADJUSTER'S ROOM

Mediator: Thank you for being patient. Usually the first meeting with the Plaintiff is the longest. . . . The Plaintiff has now moved to $60,000.

Adjuster: That's double where the Plaintiff should be! Why in the world would the Plaintiff think this is a sasquatch-sized claim?

Mediator: If for purposes of discussion the Plaintiff were to go to $30,000, would you pay that amount?

Adjuster: Hell no! I meant that if the Plaintiff is serious about settling this case, the settlement has to be below $30,000.

Mediator: I'm not wishing to put words in your mouth, but please clarify one thing for me. Am I hearing that this case can settle in the 20's?

Adjuster: Perhaps.

Counsel for the Defendant (turning to the Mediator): Do you think that the Plaintiff would accept a settlement figure between $20,000 and $30,000?

Mediator: I don't know. What I do know is that the Plaintiff has moved from $70,000 to $60,000. That isn't where you wanted the Plaintiff to be but — at the risk of sounding patronizing — the Plaintiff is moving in your direction.

You would have liked the Plaintiff to drop from $70,000 to $30,000, but you and I know that a move of that magnitude is not possible. Matter of fact, if I had walked into this room and told you that the Plaintiff had dropped the demand from $70,000 to $30,000, both of you would have had a coronary on the spot. Am I right or am I right?

Adjuster: You're right. . . .

Counsel for the Defendant: What are you trying to do?

Mediator: In the course of the average mediation, I drop more seeds than Johnny Appleseed did in his entire career. Right now, I'm dropping seeds. At the same time, I believe that a reality check needs to be made.

I have twice asked the question about a settlement value between $20 and $30 thousand and neither of you has told me to get lost. That implicitly says to me that you are willing to entertain the idea.

Obviously the Plaintiff is not going to accept your $12,000 offer. Let's talk about jury ranges if the case were to go to trial. . . .

Counsel for the Defendant: Somewhere between $20,000 and $26,000.

Mediator (turning to the Adjuster): Do you agree?

Adjuster: That's about right. . . .

Mediator (turning to the Adjuster): Perhaps this isn't the Enchanted Forest after all, but — correct me if I am wrong — but when I add to the $23,000 judgment roughly $7,000 in pre-judgment interest and $10,000 in expenses, it totals $40,000. That doesn't even consider reimbursement for the Plaintiff's taxable court costs. If my math is correct, it would appear that the moment that the Plaintiff drops below $40,000, you are ahead of the proverbial curve.

Adjuster: Your math is accurate but your logic is flawed. I am not paying more than $30,000 to settle this case.

Mediator: Fair 'nuf. Now throwing caution to the wind, what are you willing to authorize me to take to the Plaintiff at this point in the discussion?

Adjuster: $16,000.

Mediator: May I ask a question. Would you be willing for me to tell the Plaintiff that you would be willing to discuss a settlement in the range of $20,000 to $29,999 if the Plaintiff would?

Adjuster: No, but on second thought offer $18,000 and tell the Plaintiff that if the Plaintiff's offer is cut in half and dropped from $60,000 to $30,000, we can probably settle this case fairly quickly.

Mediator: I commend your negotiating acuity. I will do just that. Thank you. . . .

[After the mediator talked with each side many more times, a settlement was reached. The negotiation dance went like this: The Plaintiff lowered his demand to $55,000, and the Adjuster responded with $20,000 coupled with a commitment to leave if the next offer was over $40,000. The Plaintiff agreed to drop his demand to $35,000 contingent on the Adjuster raising his offer to $25,000; the Adjuster agreed to raise his offer to $25,000 contingent on the Plaintiff lowering his $35,000 demand; the Plaintiff lowered his demand to $32,500; the Adjuster came back with an offer of $27,500; the Plaintiff responded with $30,000 provided that it be paid within two weeks and that the Adjuster also pay $765 to reimburse Plaintiff for mediation fees and taxable court costs; the Adjuster agreed . . .] . . .

. . . [T]he story . . . depicted a typical mediation, with the usual undercurrents of emotion, humor, greed, manipulation and disappointment. Nothing about the mediation process was romanticized. In short, it was a typical mediation, one in which — due to the different personalities and agendas in the two caucus rooms — the mediator consciously employed somewhat differing styles in handling the negotiations. It worked.

Notes and Questions

4.5 What discrete moves does the mediator make to bring the parties closer together? Can you imagine this same scenario being pursued in a more interest-based, problem-solving manner? Can you imagine this same approach being used in the Glen Cove case? The case of the Sisters and Bristol?

4.6 Some commentators suggest that personal injury cases of this sort are more suited to neutral evaluation (a process where the neutral's primary role is to give a legal opinion or economic assessment) than mediation. What do you think?

4.7 Look back at the categories in Alfini's article in Chapter 3 ("trashing, bashing, and hashing"). Is the mediator a trasher, a basher, or a hasher? How does this mediator rate in terms of problem solving or transformation?

The next case illustrates mediation's potential to have a transformative and healing effect on the parties' lives. As you read this story, note how the attorneys did (or did not) support their clients' efforts to obtain meaningful closure to a life-changing situation. What does the mediator do to promote the outcome that is achieved?

 Eric Galton, **A MEETING OF STRANGERS**

> **Ripples from Peace Lake: Essays for Mediators and Peacemakers, Trafford**
> **Publishing,** *http://www.trafford.com,* **copyright Lakeside Productions**

Christmas was coming to West Texas just like it always did. The harsh, cold winds from the west had already cloaked the unforgiving landscape with an extra layer of dust that Virginia Stevens had to sweep off her front porch at least three times a day. As if Ginny didn't already have more than enough to do this time of year.

Nothing much had changed in Odessa, Ginny thought, as she glanced at the same suspended holiday lights that she remembered from high school and maybe even from before that. What was that anyway? Thirty? Forty years? No point in trying to recall exactly. As her doctor husband Bill would say, "Just a damn long time ago." The old nativity scene sure could use a new coat of paint, Ginny also thought as her Saturn breezed by the Catholic church. And that manger sure looked droopy and nothing like the heavenly home she conjured up in October when she felt Christmas coming hard like a train rolling fast down the track.

Well, West Texas was still pretty much the same. Sure, the inevitable and sometimes convenient Wal-Marts, Applebee's, and even a Target Superstore now dotted the landscape. But, the landscape remained sorry, flat, and yes, hopelessly dusty. The dust was such a problem for those baby doctors' wives from Dallas who Ginny, along with the West Texas Medical Recruiting Committee, tried to convince to settle and raise their families in Odessa instead of those green lawns in Highland Park that seemed to hiss in the summers. For heavens sake, the town fathers had even built a special subdivision to recruit doctors, with man-made lakes and artificial "rolling hills." Actually, they looked more like uneven mounds of dirt; but, they called it "Pill Hill" and at least a few of the Dallas wives seemed to like it.

But, most folks who loved this place were born here, grew up here, raised their kids, and were buried a few miles from the house they grew up in. Sometimes it felt like one of those dumb movies in which someone goes back into the past, but the past is the present, and it all ends up in one big stinking mess that was way too confusing to try to figure out.

When out of town folks conjured up stereotypes of Texas and came to Odessa, visitors were rarely disappointed. West Texas was a large place with an open sky and where big men still walked the land, trying often to lasso oil from terrible holes in desolate country. Ten minutes outside Odessa you could set the car cruise control on 85 and drive for over an hour and not see much of anything. Friday nights were only about high school football. And, yes, when folks got divorced, and yes that happened way too much in Ginny's humble opinion, they'd go to court and fight over the football tickets. To heck with the kids and where they'd live. Ginny's brother John had disgraced the family and become a lawyer. John had spent two full weeks in court in Midland trying to convince twelve good citizens that old man Williams was not in his right mind when he bequeathed the season tickets to his daughter Susie instead of his son Alex.

And John, like all West Texas men, especially the lawyers, could sure tell a story. Ginny no longer could excuse them by describing the stories as tall tales. Ginny now called John's stories whoppers, which grew as large as a triple meat, double cheese Number Three at the Burger King by the time John got finished. John, who had passed not so gently through sixty, was obsessed with the "old days when lawyers were really lawyers." Ginny thought she'd just have a stroke if she heard another story about drinking all night on the long train ride to El Paso and trying your case badly hungover. "And as the fog would lift around eleven," John would say, "I knew I was going to win that damn case." The worst part was that John somehow managed to win most of his cases stinking drunk but that did not prevent Ginny from reminding her brother that in most ways he was as sorry as it gets.

Saturdays were mostly spent at the Odessa Country Club. The men would golf, usually badly but lie about it, and the women would start with tea and charity talk and migrate to gin and tonic and pondering who was having an affair with whom and blame it all on whiskey, the modern destruction of proper society, and three well known bars three miles outside of town.

Sunday was church. Visitors never had to trouble themselves about finding religion here. By last count, 87 churches existed to support the need of 57,523 citizens who had a whole lot of confessing to do and required an awful lot of forgiveness.

Ginny also couldn't figure out why, at sixty-five years of age and, albeit the matriarch of a very large family, she was still responsible for Christmas dinner. Adding up the grandkids, her allegedly grown kids and their spouses and even ex-spouses, and purported family who claimed an invitation by about ten degrees of separation, Ginny was going to feed something near ninety bodies, all of whom came as if they had eaten their last meal on Thanksgiving—which also, by the way, was at her house. But, West Texans don't complain out loud much. They moan a lot to the Lord and maybe whimper a bit to their very best friend. And even in moments of terrible crisis, West Texans never wear their hearts on their sleeves. Life is tough. Life ain't fair. And, you just put on your boots, roll up your sleeves, and do what you have to do.

Just when Ginny was beginning to feel that mythical sense of resolve and developing the usual delusion that she would once again pull off Christmas dinner, she remembered the three bean casserole and the absolutely, positively necessary Campbell's Cream of Mushroom soup. She had been in the H.E.B. for two and a half hours. Well, thirty minutes was a brief conversation with Wanda Stewart about her unfortunate daughter who was trying to become a singer and moved to crazy Austin. And, Ginny had even brought a list. She was almost home, but Ginny pulled into the Odessa Church of Christ parking lot, turned her Saturn around, and headed back to the market. "You can't have Christmas dinner without three bean casserole," Ginny thought. And, as Ginny drove back to the H.E.B., she let her mind roll to what else she had forgotten. Growing older had not been the joyride to grace her mother, may she rest in peace, had promised . . .

* * *

Oddly enough, Sam Kitchens was driving to the same H.E.B. feeling very happy and spry, despite the fact and unbeknownst to him, his mission was much the same as Ginny's.

Sam was getting the "fixins," as he was fond of calling them, for Christmas dinner and he had been planning for it for weeks. The funny part, at least funny to Sam, was that he didn't mind at all that later in his life, after his beloved Christine had passed seven years ago, he had become the master chef for his family. Heck, at 72, Sam no longer was fit to drill in the fields. And, if the truth be known, he did not miss it one bit. Christine, bless her heart, used to smile after he walked in and say, "Sam, you stink worse than a hog on a bad day." But, then, Christine would smile, wash his clothes, send him off to the shower and yell, "But I know how to put lipstick on a pig." He sure missed Christine and still thanked God the cancer took her fast. But, Sam still had a mess of kids, grandkids and former comrades from the oil patch who kept him hopping. Sam did think he would be given a special place in heaven for watching way too many Disney videos with his niece Gloria's kids; but, it was a small price to pay for adoration and, more importantly, for an audience who would listen to him with rapt attention.

Sam wasn't sure exactly how much his cooking had evolved. Sam had always been good at cooking large slabs of red meat to perfection on the grill. But, after Christine died, Sam violated one small promise he made to her and got cable. Sam immediately became a food channel junkie. Sam attributed this current obsession to Emeril, who Sam thought was a "man's man" and even though he talked funny, he sure was enthusiastic about his work. Cooking was much like drilling for oil. Sometimes, if you worked hard enough at it, amazing and wonderful things could come out of the ground or the oven. And, more often than you'd care to admit, you could work all day and end up with a complete, total disaster. Sam actually wrote Emeril to find out what went wrong with that veal dish which, when Sam got through it, resembled beef jerky. But, fortunately, only Sam had been there to eat it and Sam very much liked beef jerky. Never had jerky with a veal-like flavor before.

Christmas dinner really was for Sam's four daughters; Ruby, Crystal, Jade and Jackie, each of whom Sam loved beyond life itself. Sam always wondered whether he was slightly closer to Jackie because she was the youngest or because she was the only child not named after some type of rock. Sam and Christine never figured out where the rock thing came from, but once they started with it you just don't fix things if they ain't broke. But, for reasons that Sam could never understand, Christine had always worshipped Jackie Kennedy and when the last one came along Christine had said, "Let's stop doing rocks. She looks just like Jackie." And so the name stuck.

Sam understood completely, although he never said it out loud, that his daughters supported his cooking addiction and especially Christmas dinner because it "kept him busy." His daughters even ordered exotic kitchen utensils for him off the internet from Williams Sonoma. Half the time, Sam could not figure out what the device was for; but, he religiously hung up each new one in his kitchen. Privately, Sam was hoping for a new sweater from Jade instead of the usual four new utensils.

None of this mattered at this special moment. The heater was working in his little Toyota, he was two minutes away from the H.E.B., and the only question was how was he going to navigate two full shopping carts. Sam saw the light turn green and was thinking about his special oyster dressing for the turkey. Sam was halfway through the intersection with the H.E.B. in sight when everything changed forever . . .

* * *

What else had she forgotten, Ginny thought, as she glanced down at her list on the passenger seat.

As she glanced back up, she saw her light had turned red, but she was already through it. She saw the car just ahead, a small one, a man, a full head of white hair, and then everything moved so fast but in slow motion. A horrible, terrible smash and the sound of crashing metal and breaking glass. Ginny hurtled toward the windshield but her seatbelt held. She thought she saw the man's face before everything went black. She thought she heard sirens and someone asking her questions.

Hours later, Ginny woke up in a hospital bed, her husband and children around her. Bill, her husband and one of the few remaining good family doctors in Odessa, was holding Ginny's hand and jumped up when Ginny's eyes opened.

"You gave us all quite a scare," Bill said. "How are you feeling?"

Ginny tried to manage words but she realized she was almost choking on tears that were seemingly rolling down her throat.

"You don't need to speak, Ginny," Bill said. "You're banged up some, but you are going to be all right."

Ginny summoned whatever strength she had and gently tugged Bill closer to her.

"The man?" she breathed. "The man?"

"He didn't make it, dear. He didn't make it," Bill said.

Ginny heard the words and prayed that this was some terrible dream. Mercifully, Ginny fell back asleep. When she woke again the next morning in the same hospital bed, Ginny realized it was not simply a terrible dream and something deep inside told her the nightmare was just beginning . . .

* * *

Ginny reflected on that terrible December day today; but, it was two years later and she glanced at Bill who was driving her in their Navigator to Austin. Reflecting back was pretty much all Ginny had done both before, during and after physical therapy. The fact that it was December made it probably worse. Ginny had come to almost hate Christmas and felt its cold press around Halloween. Christmas was, as always, speeding down the rails; but, now she was lying on the track like in one of those old movies with no hope of escape. Sure, she had met her share of heroic rescuers. The best psychologists, pastoral counselors, and potent anti-depressants had done their level best to unbind the ropes and save the day. But, the mighty Christmas train had her in its sights and Papa Noel wasn't blowing any whistle.

Objectively, if Ginny had any capacity to be objective, Ginny was a complete and total disaster. She had not been behind the wheel since what everyone now referred to as "the accident" and could barely get in a car, even when dependable Bill was driving. Ginny had dropped thirty pounds because depression, she had been advised, had robbed her of her appetite. Bill kept telling Ginny she looked great, but she had, without exception, refused him any hope of intimacy. She slept poorly, but now refused the pills. Ginny had other new addictions. She didn't need the pills.

The need to reflect back on "the accident" seemed especially important today. They were driving to Austin to attend a mediation to end what was now referred to as "the lawsuit" which resulted from "the accident."

Initially, Ginny felt modest relief that she wasn't going to jail although the largest part of her spirit believed that is where she belonged. Ginny, like everyone back home, didn't like to sugarcoat things. The equation was terribly simple. I didn't pay attention. I ran a red light at an intersection I have crossed a zillion times. I killed a man. I killed a very good, kind, vital man. What else was there to say?

And, today, at this mediation thing, I am going to see his precious daughters whom I have never met and have never spoken to even though we live in the same place, probably less than four miles from each other.

That part of it all was the most baffling to Ginny. After Ginny was in the clear, Ginny wanted to call and visit the family. But, her brother the lawyer and the lawyer her insurance company had hired to represent her in "the lawsuit" told her there could be no contact with the other family. Ginny was reminded there could be criminal charges and even, if not, she would surely be sued. Anything Ginny could say could and would be used against her. Her lawyer brother seemed to almost enjoy reminding her "you never listened to anyone before, but this time you just have to keep your mouth shut."

Ginny thought all that was indecent and it certainly was not very Christian; but, everything about this had become indecent. Ginny had told her insurance lawyer that the company should give the family whatever they want. Her lawyer told Ginny it just didn't work that way but hopefully everything would get settled at mediation. Ginny's lawyer told her that he would do most of the talking at mediation and that the mediator was there to help everyone arrive at "a number" that would settle "the lawsuit."

Talking about "a number" made Ginny sick. Whether mediation was about numbers or about something else, Ginny spent most of her time thinking what could she possibly say to Ruby, Crystal, Jade and Jackie, now collectively referred to as "the plaintiffs." Ginny tried to put herself in their shoes. What would they be thinking? Ginny knew what she would be thinking. Some ditsy doctor's wife wasn't paying attention and killed our father and she should pay for it.

Bill pulled the car into a space next to the mediation center by the lake. Ginny's lawyer was already there along with an insurance company representative. As Ginny was escorted into a private room that was going to be "their room," she peered through the glass and saw four women and a man, their lawyer, Ginny guessed, seated on one side of the conference table. "The daughters," Ginny said out loud as she felt her stomach tighten. . . .

* * *

Jackie glanced up as Ginny walked by. She had been wanting to finally get a look at this woman. Jackie saw Ginny look in and it felt as if every bit of her breath had been sucked out. Jackie had been waiting for this very moment. She needed to see the woman who had killed her beloved father.

Jackie was the involuntary spokesperson and decision-maker for her sisters. Ruby had not wanted to file a lawsuit and had told her sisters "Lawsuits don't raise the dead." Crystal and Jade hadn't felt much different but all had succumbed to Jackie's plea, "We've got to do this for Dad. We've got to make this right." In moments of sadness and reflection, none of this felt exactly right to Jackie. Jeff, their lawyer and a certifiably good guy, had done a full investigation of Virginia Stevens. The report, in a tabbed and indexed binder, told the whole story. No prior traffic accidents. Two speeding tickets in the past twenty years. Amazing by West Texas standards. No drugs or alcohol on the day of the accident. No history of drugs or alcohol. Large history of charitable work, volunteer work in the schools, working at a food shelter, and even a volunteer at the rape crisis center. Regularly attends the other Methodist church. No speeding when the accident occurred. Just missed the red light. Virtually admitted the mistake to the police. The mistake that killed my father.

Jackie had been infuriated that Ginny had never tried to contact the family or even send a card until Jeff told her that her lawyers would advise against it and never allow her to do it. "Well, the law sort of stinks on that one, Jeff," Jackie said. Jeff just winked and shrugged his shoulders. Nice guy, never an unkind word about anyone.

As much time as Jackie had spent thinking about the mediation, she never felt less prepared and more uncertain about what she would do. Jeff had provided a full explanation of what mediation was and what might happen. But, Jeff also said "Mediation is also really different and sometimes weird things happen." Jackie actually liked the different part but found "weird things" to be somewhat unsettling. Jackie remembered saying a prayer on Sunday that things go well today. She didn't really know what "go well" meant. Christmas was coming soon and each Christmas since Dad had passed seemed to weigh ever heavier on her heart. It wasn't something she could put her finger on precisely.

Jackie, and her sisters too, still mourned the fact they did not have a chance to say goodbye to their father. Dad, according to the doctors, had died instantly; "sort of like a bug hitting your windshield when you're driving 90," said one of the obviously compassionate physicians. Crystal often commented "at least Dad didn't suffer" and Jade would remind them "he led a vital, healthy life and he went out strong." Sometimes, Jackie found some consolation in such thoughts; but, the plain truth was that Dad didn't need to die and she wasn't ready for him to die.

The oddest thing, at least by Jackie's way of thinking, is that even though Dad had been laid to rest years ago, she didn't feel as if he was buried. Letters from her lawyer, hearing dates, depositions, and now this mediation thing—all of it felt, when she opened some chatty letter from Jeff, like it was just happening. While Jackie ostensibly was back at work and back to being a mom and better than average wife, Jackie felt like her life was somehow on hold. Jackie had little reason to believe today would make things different; but she really hoped that might be so. Dad used to call Jackie "the hope of our family." Sometimes he used the word "glue." Jackie liked "hope" better; but she understood that for reasons she couldn't fully explain that her father bestowed captain of the family ship status on the youngest. Dad said it had everything to do with her heart.

Jackie was hoping at this moment she could find it. . . .

* * *

The next thing Ginny remembered is that somehow she must have sleepwalked into a large conference room. She was sitting at a table with her husband and lawyer next to her. The daughters were less than three feet across the table from her with their lawyer. She could almost reach out and touch them. She wanted to look at each of them straight in the eye, the West Texas way; but, she could only glance from time to time.

The mediator, dressed a little funny, but apparently caring, made a presentation. The tone was comforting but Ginny did not hear many of his words. Next, the daughters' lawyer spoke very briefly. He seemed kind, almost nice. Ginny wanted to hear the four women speak. The mediator encouraged them to speak; but, they didn't. Ginny's counsel told her their lawyer would tell them not to speak; but, Ginny was disappointed anyway. Even if their words were harsh, cruel or condemning, it would have been better. Ginny had it coming.

Ginny's thoughts were disrupted by hearing her own lawyer's words. Ginny was sure she heard her lawyer say "we're sorry." Ginny thought that must be said but she almost resented her lawyer saying it for her. Then there were details about "the accident." Ginny tuned out her own lawyer until she began to hear him talk about her suffering. "You know," her lawyer said to the four women, "my client has been clinically depressed since the accident, has been on medication, and has virtually become a recluse." Ginny's lawyer added more words and then stated, "You know Ginny has never been behind the wheel of a car since the accident."

Sometimes when the fortunes and fates are right in West Texas, the drill hits a special spot in which the physical force becomes so powerful that it blows away all in its black wake. Something like that welled up in Ginny's soul—an irresistible, unstoppable force of amazing clarity.

"This has nothing to do with me or whether I can drive or how badly I am feeling. How dare anyone talk about me?" Ginny blurted. The room fell silent.

"This is about," said Ginny, looking across the table, straight into the eyes of each of the four women, "what I did to your father."

"God forgive me," Ginny said. "I wasn't paying attention. I have wound and rewound what happened a thousand times. I keep asking myself why? Why was I thinking about Christmas dinner instead of driving? What was so important? Why did I look down? It was just for a half a second. And then the red light. I saw the white hair. I think I saw his face. It was all my fault. I didn't mean it to happen. I didn't want it to happen. I've never hurt anyone before. I've learned what a great and wonderful man he was. I am so very, very sorry. I would gladly trade places with your father if I could. I have caused your family such terrible harm. Not meaning or intending it is no excuse. But, I'm sorry for all the pain . . . and all the unimaginable heartache I have caused you."

Ginny's words seemed to echo off the walls into the church quiet of the room. Sometimes silence is uncomfortable. Sometimes silence is necessary. The room felt like it had moved someplace else. Where it was no one really knew.

Certainty and clarity, sometimes elusive, may find you at the strangest times. Something, something beyond labeling, found Jackie. Jackie looked at the mediator and between her own tears asked, "Are Ginny and I allowed to be alone together?" The mediator answered affirmatively and Jackie got up, went around the table, and softly touched Ginny on the shoulder. Ginny got up and, guided by Jackie, went into a room and shut the door. . . .

Jackie and Ginny were in the room alone for over two hours. With regrets to drama and theatre, the words and feelings exchanged between Jackie and Ginny belong uniquely and solely to them.

There was no Spielberg music when they walked out, arm in arm, and for those who witnessed the moment, it did not feel that way. On this day, Jackie felt Dad was finally at peace. Ginny had expressed sorrow and responsibility and without seeking or requesting it had received forgiveness. Dad's hope, the family's hope, had recognized that two families had become inextricably intertwined because of a terrible moment in time. Dad's hope was that Jackie would always find a way to forgive, to heal, and to restore. Jackie always felt that obligation applied to her own family. But today, for reasons that Jackie felt made no objective sense, her family had grown somewhat larger. Ginny and Bill would have Christmas dinner with Jackie's family this year. And Jackie, with Ginny's help, would cook some of Dad's favorite recipes and use all those utensils that had now found their way into her kitchen. In a way, this was an ending and a beginning. Much healing was left to be done. Not everything was neat and tidy and safe and maybe it would never be completely. But just as the West Texas weather can turn on a dime and change on you, something in that large West Texas way had changed — something that would likely grow in the retelling.

When they came out of the room, all Jackie said was "We're going home."

Ginny looked at Jackie and said, "That's right, we're going home."

So, the two women left and headed west. Christmas was coming and it would be here soon.

Notes and Questions

4.8 Galton does not describe the monetary settlement in the case. What if the plaintiff "sold" her case for a very modest sum of money, since that was not important to her family. Or what if Ginny agreed to pay an inordinately high amount of money because the healing she obtained was so valued? What is the role or impact of an insurance adjuster in this equation? What is the role of money in a mediation like this?

4.9 If you were an attorney representative would you have "allowed" your client to go into the caucus without you and without the mediator? Why or why not?

The final case, described below, illustrates a settlement-oriented approach that allows the parties to have meaningful closure to their conflict. Note how the recognition and personal closure generated by mediation was nearly undermined by the lawyers involved.

 Eric Galton, **MEDIATION OF MEDICAL NEGLIGENCE CLAIMS**

28 Cap. U. L. Rev. 321, 324-325 (2000)

During the joint session, it became apparent that both the physician and the parents had been instructed by counsel not to speak during joint session, despite my repeated attempts to engage the parties. Only the lawyers spoke during the joint session.

The case involved the following general facts. The wife was pregnant with the couple's third child. The couple's first two children were born with no complications. The physician caring for the mother delivered the couple's first two children.

The third pregnancy was unremarkable with appropriate prenatal care. The mother goes into labor and is instructed to go to the hospital. She arrives at 6:00 a.m. Although it is the physician's day off, the physician is called when the fetal monitor strips show some signs of distress. The physician arrives and during the fifteen minutes he is attending to the mother, the strips seem to return to normal. The physician leaves.

Thirty minutes later, the strips begin to show even greater evidence of distress. Attempts to locate the physician are initially futile, although the parents hear a nurse say, "Try the golf course." The physician is located on the golf course fifty minutes later, arrives at the hospital, and orders an emergency C-section. The baby is born, barely alive, and dies twenty minutes later.

Counsel for both sides agree to mediation after paper discovery is exchanged, but before depositions are taken. During the joint session, the lawyers make benign, constructive opening presentations. When engaged by the mediator during the joint session, neither the physician nor the husband and wife elect to speak.

The parties are split into different rooms and the mediator begins to caucus, privately, with each side. Negotiations commence and are productive. Five hours later the matter resolves with a written agreement, signed by all parties and counsel, in which the family is to receive $400,000.

As I walk into the physician's room with copies of the executed memorandum of agreement, I sense that the physician has something on his mind. I ask the physician if he wants an opportunity to meet with the family before he leaves. Immediately, the physician's lawyers state that such a meeting is unnecessary, would be awkward, and is something the physician is not required to do. The physician states (and these are *his* words almost verbatim), "I would like to meet with the family. I need some closure."

I next ask the mother and father whether they wish to meet with the physician. Similarly, the lawyers tell the parents they do not have to meet and that such a meeting would be awkward. The mother declares, "Yes, I would very much like to meet with *my* doctor."

The physician is escorted to the parents' room. As the physician enters the room, he stops just outside the door. The mother is seated ten feet away.

For several minutes, no words are exchanged. No one even moves. Suddenly, the mother gets up, tears begin to flow, and she holds out her arms. The physician goes over to the mother. As they embrace, the physician says, "I'm sorry. I'm so sorry." The mother, patting the physician's back responds, "It's okay, we forgive you." The husband comes over and joins the embrace. The lawyers, standing on the opposite end of the room, appear mystified. The physician, father, and mother sit together and talk for ten minutes.

No doubt, the economic settlement was important and a legitimate goal of the mediation process. But, for the parties, the opportunity for conciliation and closure was at least equally important. In cases where the parties desire such closure, the process must provide such an opportunity. In the case described above, the parties, without such opportunity, would have received neither the full benefits of the process nor what they needed or wanted.

It is equally clear in this, and in other instances, that the needs and goals of the parties in mediation are not necessarily the same as their lawyers. In fact, lawyers, because they often fail to either value or recognize or understand such needs, may even discourage a process that attempts to meet their clients' needs.

Notes and Questions

4.10 Think about the important moments in your life. Can you put a monetary value on those moments? Obviously, there are a host of critically important events — an apology, a handshake, a smile — that cannot be financially valued but have an immense impact. Should lawyers be in tune with the whole range of interests of their clients and capable of furthering interests in respect, recognition, healing, connection, and communication?

4.11 Consider the Riskin Grid in Chapter 3. Do the mediators in these five case studies define the problems narrowly or broadly? Can you tell whether the mediators are evaluative or facilitative? Riskin points out elsewhere in the article that "many effective mediators are versatile and can move from quadrant to quadrant (and within a quadrant), as the dynamics of the situation dictate, to help parties settle disputes." Do you see that phenomenon in any of these cases?

4.12 The lawyers in several of the examples above do not encourage their clients to participate but rather try to protect their clients from contact with the other side. Is this a mistake? Chapter 5 explores issues related to representation in mediation.

 **Chapter 5** | # Representation in Mediation: Skills and Practices

Moderate your desire of victory over your adversary, and be pleased with the one over yourself.

—Benjamin Franklin

Our task now is not to fix the blame for the past, but to fix the course for the future.

—John F. Kennedy

Mahatma Gandhi relates that after he persuaded his victorious client to agree to accept installment payments instead of a lump sum, which the defendant would have been unable to deliver, "*[b]oth were happy over the result, and both rose in the public estimation. My joy was boundless. I had learnt the true practice of the law. I had learnt to find out the better side of human nature and to enter men's hearts. I realized that the true function of a lawyer was to unite parties riven asunder.*"

—Mohandas Gandhi

Now that you have learned about both negotiation and mediation, you should be able to put your learning together to consider what the role of an attorney or representative should be in a mediation. Unlike in conventional competitive negotiations, the attorney representative in mediation should always be thinking about how to solve problems, consider the other side, and invent new options — all while effectively utilizing the assistance of a skilled third-party facilitator. The attorney in a mediation is both negotiating on behalf of his client and, at the same time, coaching or counseling his client to negotiate more effectively and to think deeply about what might be needed to resolve a particular matter. In order to do these things, the representative in a mediation must listen well, create constructive relationships, think about creative solutions to problems, analyze well what is going on — both in the moment, and what would be good for the future — be able to describe persuasively the needs and wants of his client, and be able to utilize analytic tools to assist the client with decision making during mediation. This chapter focuses on the development of these skills. As Roger Fisher says, "[E]ven the tennis professionals at Wimbledon bring their coaches with them." And this chapter should inform both representatives and mediators (who need to "manage" them) about what skills are optimal and what behaviors may thwart progress.

The first excerpt discusses the importance of self-awareness in skill building. The second excerpt, by Leonard Riskin, describes an important attitude shift for the attorney-negotiator in mediation. These two features — self-awareness and a proper "map" or mindset — are the jumping off points for skill building. In Section A, the chapter explores a series of critical negotiation skills applicable to all negotiations (whether in mediation settings or not): preparing for negotiation by setting targets and limits; listening effectively and building constructive relationships; being persuasive in conversations; developing creativity and flexibility; using objective criteria to bolster proposals; and using decision-tree analysis. In Section B, considerations targeted more specifically to the mediation context are examined.

 Melissa Nelken, **NEGOTIATION AND PSYCHOANALYSIS: IF I'D WANTED TO LEARN ABOUT FEELINGS, I WOULDN'T HAVE GONE TO LAW SCHOOL**

46 J. Legal Educ. 420, 426 (1996)

Unlike most of what gets taught in law school, negotiation is not actually a new subject to anyone. Everyone negotiates all the time — with family, friends, co-workers, teachers, anyone with whom there is a conflict or a possibility for joint action. This means that someone who thinks she is learning about negotiation for the first time as a lawyer actually has a lifetime of experience in the subject to draw on — or to stumble over. Identifications with parents and other significant people have a powerful impact on how people negotiate, as they do on every other aspect of their lives; and transference reactions are intensified by the level of conflict and anxiety inherent in a negotiation.

Thinking about how her approach to negotiation as well as her negotiation style have been shaped by past experiences helps a lawyer to organize her present experience in a way that maximizes the possibilities for learning. Since she herself is the one negotiator she can't walk away from, the more she can become aware of what motivates her own behavior in negotiations, the more able she will be to step back in the heat of the moment and to reflect on whether what is happening really serves the interests of her client. Along the way, she will also gain considerable skill in reading what is going on in her opponents. . . .

 Leonard L. Riskin, **MEDIATION AND LAWYERS**

43 Ohio St. L.J. 29, 43-46 (1982)

E.F. Schumacher begins his Guide for the Perplexed with the following story:

> On a visit to Leningrad some years ago, I consulted a map . . . but I could not make it out. From where I stood, I could see several enormous churches, yet there was no trace of them on my map. When finally an interpreter came to help me, he said: "We don't show churches on our maps." Contradicting him, I pointed to one that was very clearly marked. "That is a museum," he said, "not what we call a 'living church.' It is only the 'living churches' we don't show." It then occurred to me that this was not the first time I had been given a map which failed to show many things I could see right in front of my eyes. All through school and university I had

been given maps of life and knowledge on which there was hardly a trace of many of the things that I most cared about and that seemed to me to be of the greatest possible importance to the conduct of my life.[99]

The philosophical map employed by most practicing lawyers and law teachers, and displayed to the law student — which I will call the lawyer's standard philosophical map — differs radically from that which a mediator must use. What appears on this map is determined largely by the power of two assumptions about matters that lawyers handle: (1) that disputants are adversaries — i.e., if one wins, the others must lose — and (2) that disputes may be resolved through application, by a third party, of some general rule of law. These assumptions, plainly, are polar opposites of those which underlie mediation: (1) that all parties can benefit through a creative solution to which each agrees; and (2) that the situation is unique and therefore not to be governed by any general principle except to the extent that the parties accept it.

The two assumptions of the lawyer's philosophical map (adversariness of parties and rule-solubility of dispute), along with the real demands of the adversary system and the expectations of many clients, tend to exclude mediation from most lawyers' repertoires. They also blind lawyers to other kinds of information that are essential for a mediator to see, primarily by riveting the lawyers' attention upon things that they must see in order to carry out their functions. The mediator must, for instance, be aware of the many interconnections between and among disputants and others, and of the qualities of these connections; he must be sensitive to emotional needs of all parties and recognize the importance of yearnings for mutual respect, equality, security, and other such non-material interests as may be present.

On the lawyer's standard philosophical map, however, the client's situation is seen atomistically; many links are not printed. The duty to represent the client zealously within the bounds of the law discourages concern with both the opponents' situation and the overall social effect of a given result.

Moreover, on the lawyer's standard philosophical map, quantities are bright and large while qualities appear dimly or not at all. When one party wins, in this vision, usually the other party loses, and, most often, the victory is reduced to a money judgment. This "reduction" of non-material values — such as honor, respect, dignity, security, and love — to amounts of money, can have one of two effects. In some cases, these values are excluded from the decision makers' considerations, and thus from the consciousness of the lawyers, as irrelevant. In others, they are present but transmuted into something else — a justification for money damages. Much like the church that was allowed to appear on the map of Leningrad only because it was a museum, these interests — which may in fact be the principal motivations for a lawsuit — are recognizable in the legal dispute primarily to the extent that they have monetary value or fit into a clause of a rule governing liability.

The rule orientation also determines what appears on the map. The lawyer's standard world view is based upon a cognitive and rational outlook. Lawyers are trained to put people and events into categories that are legally meaningful, to think in terms of rights and duties established by rules, to focus on acts more than persons.

---

[99] E. Schumacher, A Guide for the Perplexed 1 (1977).

This view requires a strong development of cognitive capabilities, which is often attended by the under-cultivation of emotional faculties. This combination of capacities joins with the practice of either reducing most nonmaterial values to amounts of money or sweeping them under the carpet, to restrict many lawyers' abilities to recognize the value of mediation or to serve as mediators.

The lawyer's standard philosophical map is useful primarily where the assumptions upon which it is based — adversariness and amenability to solution by a general rule imposed by a third party — are valid. But when mediation is appropriate, these assumptions do not fit. The problem is that many lawyers, because of their philosophical maps, tend to suppose that these assumptions are germane in nearly any situation that they confront as lawyers. The map, and the litigation paradigm on which it is based, has a power all out of proportion to its utility. Many lawyers, therefore, tend not to recognize mediation as a viable means of reaching a solution; and worse, they see the kinds of unique solutions that mediation can produce as threatening to the best interests of their clients....

I do not mean to imply that all lawyers see only what is displayed on the lawyer's standard philosophical map. The chart I have drawn exaggerates certain tendencies in the way many lawyers think. Any good lawyer will be alert to a range of non-material values, emotional considerations, and interconnections. Many lawyers have "empathic, conciliatory" personalities that may incline them to work often in a mediative way. And other lawyers, though they may be more competitive, would recognize the value of mediation to their clients. I do submit, however, that most lawyers, most of the time, use this chart to navigate.

Notes and Questions

5.1 What are your main strengths as a negotiator? Where did these come from? What are your main fears and weaknesses as a negotiator? Where did these come from?

5.2 What philosophical "map" do you use in negotiations?

A. CRITICAL NEGOTIATION SKILLS

What does it take to be a good negotiator for a client? This section examines key ingredients that go into the mix.

1. Setting Your Goals and Limits

The first excerpt is from Russell Korobkin. We have read parts of his article in Chapter 2 to understand a theory of distributive bargaining — zone definition and surplus allocation. This excerpt provides advice on how to use your BATNA — best alternative to a negotiated agreement — to ensure you achieve a wise agreement. Your BATNA and reservation price should set the parameters of the bargaining zone. Also recall Korobkin's examples of David as defendant and Goliath as plaintiff as well as Jacob purchasing Esau's business; they are developed further here.

 Russell Korobkin, **A POSITIVE THEORY OF LEGAL NEGOTIATION**

88 Geo. L.J. 1789, 1794-1798 (2000)

[P]ainstaking preparation is critical to success at the bargaining table. . . . [T]horough preparation is a prerequisite for the negotiator to accomplish zone definition as advantageously as possible. . . . "Internal" preparation refers to research that the negotiator does to set and adjust his own RP [Reservation Price]. "External" preparation refers to research that the negotiator does to estimate and manipulate the other party's RP.

INTERNAL PREPARATION

After identifying the various alternatives to reaching a negotiated agreement, the negotiator needs to determine which alternative is most desirable. Fisher and his coauthors coined the appropriate term "BATNA"—"best alternative to a negotiated agreement"—to identify this choice. The identity and quality of a negotiator's BATNA is the primary input into his RP.

If the negotiator's BATNA and the subject of the negotiation are perfectly interchangeable, determining the reservation price is quite simple: the reservation price is merely the value of the BATNA. For example, if Esau's [a purchaser of a catering business] BATNA is buying another catering business for $190,000 that is identical to Jacob's in terms of quality, earnings potential, and all other factors that are important to Esau, then his RP is $190,000. If Jacob [a seller of a catering business] will sell for some amount less than that, Esau will be better off buying Jacob's company than he would pursuing his best alternative. If Jacob demands more than $190,000, Esau is better off buying the alternative company and not reaching an agreement with Jacob.

In most circumstances, however, the subject of a negotiation and the negotiator's BATNA are not perfect substitutes. If Jacob's business is of higher quality, has a higher earnings potential, or is located closer to Esau's home, he would probably be willing to pay a premium for it over what he would pay for the alternative choice. For example, if the alternative business is selling for $190,000, Esau might determine he would be willing to pay up to a $10,000 premium over the alternative for Jacob's business and thus set his RP at $200,000. On the other hand, if Esau's BATNA is more desirable to him than Jacob's business, Esau will discount the value of his BATNA by the amount necessary to make the two alternatives equally desirable values for the money; perhaps he will set his RP at $180,000 in recognition that his BATNA is $10,000 more desirable than Jacob's business, and Jacob's business would be equally desirable only at a $10,000 discount. . . .

The relationship between a party's BATNA and his RP can be generalized in the following way. A party's RP has two components: (1) the market value of his

BATNA; and (2) the difference to *him* between the value of his BATNA and the value of the subject of the negotiation. A seller sets his RP by calculating (1) and either *subtracting* (2) if the subject of the negotiation is more valuable than his BATNA (and therefore he is willing to accept less to reach an agreement) or *adding* (2) if the BATNA is more valuable than the subject of the negotiation (and therefore, he would demand more to reach an agreement and give up his BATNA). A buyer sets his RP by calculating (1) and either *adding* (2) if the subject of the negotiation is more valuable than his BATNA (and therefore he would pay a premium to reach an agreement) or *subtracting* (2) if his BATNA is more valuable than the subject of the negotiation (and therefore he would demand a discount to give up the BATNA). . . .

By investigating an even wider range of alternatives to reaching agreement, and by more thoroughly investigating the value of obvious alternatives, the negotiator can alter his RP in a way that will shift the bargaining zone to his advantage. . . .

EXTERNAL PREPARATION

External preparation allows the negotiator to estimate his opponent's RP . . . [t]o accurately predict Jacob's RP and therefore pinpoint the low end of the bargaining zone. This information will also prepare Esau to attempt to persuade Jacob during the course of negotiations to lower his RP. . . .

It is worth noting that in the litigation context both parties often have the same alternatives and the same BATNA. If plaintiff Goliath determines that his BATNA is going to trial, then defendant David's only alternative — and therefore his BATNA default — is going to trial as well. In this circumstance, internal preparation and external preparations merge. . . .

A NOTE ON BATNA

One of the primary concepts in *Getting to YES*, introduced in Chapter 2, is BATNA — best alternative to a negotiated agreement. The phrase, now used frequently, is a mechanism to ensure that you never make an agreement that you should not make. If the alternative to agreement is preferable, you should walk away from the negotiation.

Using your BATNA to protect yourself from unwise agreements takes several steps. First, you need to brainstorm all of your alternatives to an agreement. This might include going to court in certain situations. Or your alternatives might include making an agreement with another company or buying a different house. Second, you choose your best alternative — the one that leaves you in the best situation. Finally, you translate your BATNA into a reservation price. The reservation price is the point at which you would be better with your BATNA.

For example, assume you are purchasing a home. Your first-choice home is priced at $300,000. Your second choice is priced at $250,000 and you assume that you could probably purchase it for $240,000. How do you decide when buying your second choice makes more sense? You need to value the difference between the homes — what makes your first-choice home your preferred choice. List these out: (1) attached garage; (2) better school district; (3) larger back yard; (4) does not need to be painted before moving in. Next, attach values to each of these items. For some differences between the properties, like the garage and the backyard, you might check with your realtor to get a sense of how others might value particular items. For others, like the school district, you are attaching a tangible number to an intangible item. Ask yourself how much more you would pay for the exact same house in one neighborhood versus the other. For the last item, painting, you can price this with some research of your own.

Assume you've set the following values: (1) attached garage ($10,000); (2) better school district ($15,000); (3) larger backyard ($5,000); and (4) not having to paint ($5,000 — for paint, the painter, and the inconvenience). The first-choice home is worth about $35,000 more to you. Therefore, your reservation price is $240,000 plus $35,000 = $275,000. This means that if you can't negotiate the price on the more expensive house down to $275,000 you would be better off, given your preferences, buying the less expensive home.

Notes and Questions

5.3 What is the difference between a BATNA and a reservation price? Why is this important? In what context might the difference not be useful?

5.4 Why does Korobkin suggest preparing with respect to your counterpart's BATNA and reservation price? How can you do this?

5.5 What if, in the course of the negotiation, you find out that your assumptions about your counterpart's BATNA are mistaken? What if, for example, you thought the people placing a bid on your house also were very interested in another house? How would that affect your negotiation? What if you found out, instead, that they loved your house?

5.6 Some authors believe that BATNA is not useful in all negotiations:

> [T]he notion of commitment to a relationship limits the usefulness of the "best alternative to a negotiated agreement" (BATNA) concept. Inherent in the BATNA idea is the assumption that negotiators will walk away from an agreement if there is a higher-utility alternative outside the relationship. This concept, in my opinion, assumes that either the parties' commitment to the relationship is zero, or that the parties factor the cost of sacrificing the relationship when assessing the utility of offers. Both assumptions seem unrealistic when applied to day-to-day negotiations in the real world.
>
> Imagine, for instance, a dispute between a woman and her husband. He wants her companionship in social and leisure events, but she is too busy with her medical practice. The BATNA concept assumes the husband will seriously consider meeting his social needs outside the marriage when evaluating her counteroffers. Examples involving others with whom one frequently negotiates show similar shortcomings of the BATNA concept — for example, negotiations with one's boss, children, key customers, social organizations, and any other entity to which one has a strong, ongoing relationship.

Leonard Greenhalgh, Relationships in Negotiation, 3 Negot. J. 238 (1987). How does Greenhalgh seem to define BATNA in his example? Do you agree with his argument that BATNA is not a useful concept in this context? Can you think of other BATNAs for the husband? How can BATNAs be used in negotiations where strong relationships exist? Can you think of situations where it might make sense to consider WATNAs (worst alternatives to negotiated agreements)? How does this help assess reservation prices or bottom lines?

Business school professor G. Richard Shell urges setting optimistic goals rather than a bottom line. Shell explains why goals are important and how a negotiator can make achieving those goals more likely.

 G. Richard Shell, BARGAINING FOR ADVANTAGE: NEGOTIATION STRATEGIES FOR REASONABLE PEOPLE

31-34 (1999)

SET AN OPTIMISTIC, JUSTIFIABLE TARGET

When you set goals, think boldly and optimistically about what you would like to see happen. Research has repeatedly shown that people who have higher aspirations in negotiations perform better and get more than people who have modest or "I'll do my best" goals, provided they really believe in their targets.

In one classic study, psychologists Sydney Siegel and Lawrence Fouraker set up a simple buy-sell negotiation experiment. They allowed the negotiators to keep all the profits they achieved but told the subjects they could qualify for a second, "double-their-money" round if they met or exceeded certain specified bargaining goals. In other words, Siegel and Fouraker gave their subjects both concrete *incentives* for hitting a certain specified level of performance and, perhaps unintentionally, a hint that the assigned target levels were realistically attainable (why else would subjects be told about the bonus round?). One set of negotiators was told they would have to hit a modest $2.10 target to qualify for the bonus round. Another set of negotiators was told they would have to hit a much more ambitious target of $6.10. Both sides had the same bottom line: They could not accept any deal that involved a loss. The negotiators with the more ambitious $6.10 goal achieved a mean profit of $6.25, far outperforming the median profit of $3.35 achieved by those with the modest $2.10 goal.

My own research has confirmed Siegel's and Fouraker's findings. In our experiment, unlike the one Siegel and Fouraker conducted, negotiation subjects set their own bargaining goals. And instead of letting everyone keep whatever profits they earned, we gave separate $100 prizes to the buyer and the seller with the best individual outcomes. The result was the same, however. Negotiators who reported higher prenegotiation expectations achieved more than those who entered the negotiation with more modest goals.

Why are we tempted to set modest bargaining goals when we can achieve more by raising our sights? There are several possible reasons. First, many people set modest goals to protect their self-esteem. We are less likely to fail if we set our goals low, so we "wing it," telling ourselves that we are doing fine as long as we beat our bottom line. Modest goals thus help us avoid unpleasant feelings of failure and regret.

Second, we may not have enough information about the negotiation to see the full potential for gain; that is, we may fail to appreciate the true worth of what we are selling, not do the research on applicable standards, or fail to note how eager the buyer is for what we have to offer. This usually means we have failed to prepare well enough.

Third, we may lack desire. If the other person wants money, control, or power more urgently than we do, we are unlikely to set a high goal for ourselves. Why look for conflict and trouble over things we care little about?

Research suggests that the self-esteem factor plays a more important role in low goal setting than many of us would care to admit. We once had a negotiation speaker who said that the problem with many reasonable people is that they confuse "win-win" with what he called a "wimp-win" attitude. The "wimp-win" negotiator focuses only on his or her bottom line; the "win-win" negotiator has ambitious goals.

I see further evidence of this in negotiation classes. As students and executives in negotiation workshops start setting more ambitious goals for themselves and strive to improve, they often report feeling more *dissatisfied and discouraged* regarding their performance — even as their objective results get better and better. For this reason, I suggest raising one's goals incrementally, adding risk and difficulty in small steps over a series of negotiations. That way you can maintain your enthusiasm for negotiation as you learn. Research shows that people who succeed in achieving new goals are more likely to raise their goals the next time. Those who fail, however, tend to become discouraged and lower their targets.

Once you have thought about what an optimistic, challenging goal would look like, spend a few minutes permitting realism to dampen your expectations. *Optimistic goals are effective only if they are feasible; that is, only if you believe in them and they can be justified according to some standard or norm.* . . . [N]egotiation positions must usually be supported by some standard, benchmark, or precedent, or they lose their credibility. No amount of mental goal setting will make your five-year-old car worth more than a brand-new version of the same model. You should also adjust your goal to reflect appropriate relationship concerns.

But do not let your ideas of what is appropriate or realistic take over completely. Simply note the reasons you come up with that explain why your optimistic goal may not be possible and look for the next highest, *defendable* target. Your old car may not be worth the same as a new one, but you should be able to find a used-car guide that reports the "average" price for your model. With that foundation, you can justify asking for a premium over that standard based on the tip-top condition of your vehicle.

One danger with being too realistic with your goals is that you may be making unwarranted assumptions about the values and priorities the other side will bring to the deal. Until you know for sure what *the other side* has for goals and what *the other side* thinks is realistic, you should keep your eyes firmly on your own defendable target.

The other party will tell you if your optimistic deal isn't possible, and you will not offend him or her by asking for your goal so long as you have some justification to support it, you advance your ideas with courtesy, and you show a concern for his or her perspective.

Keep this point in mind as you progress toward higher goals: A certain amount of dissatisfaction is a good thing when you first start thinking seriously about improving how you negotiate. Dissatisfaction is a sign that you are setting your goals at a high enough level to encounter resistance from other parties and to take the risk that they may walk away. Eventually, you will learn to set targets that are challenging without being unduly discouraging.

BE SPECIFIC

The literature on negotiation goal setting counsels us to be as specific as possible. Clarity drives out fuzziness in negotiations as in many other endeavors. With a definite target, you will begin working on a host of psychological levels to get the job done. For example, when you land your new job, don't just set a goal to "negotiate a fair salary." Push yourself to take aim at a specific target — go for a 10 percent raise over what you made at your last job. Your specific goal will start you thinking about other, comparable jobs that pay your target salary, and you will begin to notice a variety of market standards that support a salary of that amount.

Be especially wary of goals such as "I'll do the best I can" or, worst of all, "I'll just go in and see what I can get." What we are really saying when we enter a negotiation with goals such as these is, "I do not want to take a chance on failing in this negotiation." Fear of failure and our natural desire to avoid feelings of disappointment and regret are legitimate psychological self-protection devices. But effective negotiators do not let these feelings get in the way of setting specific goals.

Notes and Questions

5.7 Setting aspirational (and higher) targets may result in better outcomes. Recall the "anchoring" phenomenon discussed in Chapter 2. For the attorney as counselor, coach, and representative, however, what dangers do you see for setting the target high?

5.8 Why does Shell think that focusing on the bottom line can be inhibiting? What do you think?

5.9 What does Shell mean by "justifiable target"? Why should your goal be justifiable? How do you make your goal justifiable (or legitimate)? The skill of identifying and using objective criteria will be examined later in this section.

5.10 Jennifer Brown writes that the role of hope in negotiations may explain why setting a specific aspiration point is important. Under one theory of hope, negotiators negotiate harder before they reach their aspiration level than they do after they reach it. In economic terms, negotiators receive more utility for each dollar in reaching their aspiration point and less utility for each dollar above it. Jennifer Gerarda Brown, The Role of Hope in Negotiation, 44

UCLA L. Rev. 1661 (1997). What do you think about this theory of why setting aspirations is important?

5.11 In empirical experiments investigating aspirations in negotiations, Russell Korobkin finds that setting aspiration levels can affect key "settlement levers" including reservation points, the definition of fairness, increased patience at the bargaining table, and rejection of barely acceptable offers. At the same time, Korobkin writes, high aspiration levels can increase the likelihood of impasse and reduce satisfaction with the outcome. Russell Korobkin, Aspirations and Settlement, 88 Cornell L. Rev. 1 (2002). Why might a lawyer-negotiator in particular set lower aspiration levels? Shell notes above that negotiators may set modest goals to avoid feelings of regret. Is it worth setting high aspiration levels if you (or your client) are more likely to be disappointed?

2. Listening to and Understanding Your Client and the Other Side

Conversation in the United States is a competitive exercise in which the first person to draw breath is considered the listener.

— Nathan Miller

We don't see things as they are, we see things as we are.

— Anais Nin

Listening and understanding are linked skills. Talent in listening and understanding will increase a negotiator's effectiveness in multiple ways. Good listening improves relationships, making it easier to engage others in collaboration and creative problem solving. Demonstrating understanding enhances trust and motivates others to listen to you. Critically important, good listening will provide invaluable information about your client and your bargaining counterpart — information that will help you strategize about how to meet the other side's interests while simultaneously getting the most for your client.

Listening is not as easy as it appears! The first excerpt, from a client counseling text, describes active listening. Communication specialists agree that this sort of listening is the most effective means available to understand, demonstrate understanding, and build rapport with the speaker — whether the speaker is your client or the other side.

 David Binder, Paul Bergman, Susan Price & Paul K. Tremblay, **LAWYERS AS COUNSELORS: A CLIENT-CENTERED APPROACH**

41-43, 48-49, 55-56 (2d ed. 2004)

[L]istening is a crucially important skill. In fact, your ability to engender clients' trust, develop rapport, elicit full descriptions of clients' problems and help clients develop effective solutions may hinge as much on your listening as on your questioning and advice-giving skills. Thus, helping clients find satisfactory solutions to their problems often depends on your effectiveness as a listener.

If you listen carefully what will you hear? Of course, you will hear factual content. But often you will also hear feelings accompanying the content. That is, clients' descriptions of what happened often include the feelings that events aroused at the time they took place. Moreover, clients' acts of recall may trigger still further emotional reactions: "At the time I was somewhat upset, but now just talking about it makes me seethe." Finally, clients' discussions of proposed solutions almost inevitably generate emotional reactions. For example, a client may say, "I'm nervous about leaving the terms of the payout provision so uncertain." Accordingly, when you listen carefully you are likely to hear both content and current and past feelings. . . .

[Far] from being an intuitively simple task, listening is a skill requiring positive action. As with other skills, your ability to listen effectively rests on both awareness and use of specialized techniques. . . .

IDENTIFYING CONTENT AND FEELINGS

"Content" consists of information that affects clients' legal interests and the likely effectiveness of potential solutions. "Feelings" are clients' internal reactions to their problems and possible solutions. When describing their feelings, clients may use words such as happy, amused, excited, sad, angry, anxious, disappointed, frightened, irritated, and confused.

Your legal training and experience undoubtedly means that you need no encouragement . . . to attend to the content of clients' problems and possible solutions. . . . To sharpen your ability to distinguish content from feelings, consider the following examples:

> **Client 1:**
> "My husband and I sat down shortly after we got married and wrote a will together, but I guess I never really thought we'd use it. Then they called to say my husband had had a heart attack at work. He died two days later. When he died, I was overwhelmed. Lately, I've been worrying about our finances. It's hard to think of money at a time like this, but I feel like I should. I can't sleep at night, and I just sit around all day. Other times, when I think about him, I start crying and it seems like it will never stop. On top of all this, his children from his first marriage are saying they are going to contest the will. They've already hired a lawyer. I'm really surprised, I never expected this."

What is the content of the client's situation?
What are the client's past and current feelings? . . .

> **Client 1:**
> Content: Husband died unexpectedly and wife must assume responsibility for family finances. Children from the husband's first marriage plan to contest the will and have already hired a lawyer.
>
> Feelings: Sad, overwhelmed, depressed, worried, surprised. . . .

ACTIVE LISTENING

Active listening is the "most effective talk tool that exists for demonstrating understanding and reducing misunderstanding." It is the process of picking up clients' messages and sending them back in reflective statements that mirror what you have heard.

> **Client:** "When I asked him for the money, he had the nerve to tell me not to be uptight."
>
> **Lawyer:** "Rather than offering to pay you back, he suggested that you were somehow wrong for asking. You were angry."

Your reply is a classic active listening response. It demonstrates that you understand the content of the client's remark. Also, the reply reflects back your understanding of the client's feelings that accompanied the incident. Further, the statement only mirrors the client's statement; it does not in any way "judge" it. And, though your statement reflects the client's feelings, you do not ask the client to explore those feelings in greater detail. Rather, the statement simply indicates your awareness that the client was angry.

As in the example above, active listening does not consist simply of repeating, or "parroting," what clients say. Rather, your reply reflects the *essence* of the content of the client's remark, as well as your perception, based both on the statement and on the client's non-verbal cues that indicate clients' feelings. You distill the information and emotion from the client's statement, and then convey back what you have heard and understood—hence the term "active listening." . . .

While an active listening response may mirror both content and feelings, [we] primarily emphasize techniques for using active listening responses to reflect feelings. [We] do so for two reasons:

1. As a general rule, lawyers probably pay too little attention to clients' feelings. Lawyers are prone to seeing themselves as rational fact-gatherers and decision-makers. . . . This attitude towards the non-importance of feelings in the attorney-client relationship is wrong on at least two grounds. First, empathy is the real mortar of an attorney-client (indeed, *any*) relationship. To be empathic you need to hear, understand and accept clients' feelings, and to find a way to convey this empathic understanding to your clients. Second . . . [p]roblems evoke feelings, and feelings in turn shape problems. Lawyers can neither communicate fully with clients nor help fashion satisfactory solutions if they ignore feelings.

2. . . . We have little formal training in listening for and articulating the human feelings that accompany events and future plans. . . . Therefore, you are likely to need to devote more effort to learning to reflect feelings than to learning to reflect content. . . .

NON-EMPATHIC (JUDGMENTAL) RESPONSES

Consider the following examples of responding to clients' feelings in non-empathic ways:

> **Client:** When the promotion list came out, I was not on it. And I know I had been on the preliminary list. To see such blatant discrimination made me realize it was finally time to do something about it.
>
> **Lawyer:** No. 1: I don't blame you.

No. 2: But I guess after a while you calmed down.

No. 3: You finally acknowledged what you probably knew all along. You as well as many others were victims of discrimination, and would probably continue to be.

Lawyer No. 1 has judged the appropriateness of the reaction. Lawyer No. 2 has treated the feeling as irrelevant and shifted the discussion to another time frame. Lawyer No. 3 has played amateur psychologist, by attempting to analyze the reason for the reaction. None has simply mirrored back the client's likely emotions — "You were really furious," or "You feel wronged and want to take action." . . .

If you are wondering why you should focus on listening to your client in a course on mediation, consider the following. You will be working with your client to prepare for mediation. You will be strategizing with your client during mediation and particularly during caucuses (private meetings). With luck, you will be assisting your client long after the mediation, thanks to the good listening skills you displayed in mediation. At the same time, your ability to understand, display understanding, and build a collaborative relationship with the other side will depend in large measure on these listening skills and will impact the outcome of the negotiations.

Notes and Questions

5.12 Why do you think lawyers are sometimes reluctant to explore their clients' feelings? To acknowledge the feelings of the other side? What are the risks — if any — of active listening?

5.13 Binder, Bergman, Price, and Tremblay give the following example of a client interview. Assume the client says, "After the loan officer told me the loan for the dental equipment had been approved, tears almost came to my eyes. My parents had worked so hard to put me through school, and I wish they could have been there with me." How should you as the lawyer respond to this comment?

The next excerpt, from *Difficult Conversations*, describes the importance and power of effective listening and explores three skills: inquiry, paraphrasing, and acknowledgment.

 Douglas Stone, Bruce Patton & Sheila Heen, **DIFFICULT CONVERSATIONS: HOW TO DISCUSS WHAT MATTERS MOST**

163, 166-167, 169-170, 172-174, 178, 180-183 (1999)

Andrew is visiting his Uncle Doug. While Doug is on the phone, Andrew tugs on his uncle's pant leg, saying, "Uncle Doug, I want to go outside."

"Not now, Andrew, I'm on the phone," says Doug.

Andrew persists: "But Uncle Doug, I want to go outside!"

"Not now Andrew!" comes Doug's response.

"But I want to go out!" Andrew repeats.

After several more rounds, Doug tries a different approach: "Hey, Andrew. You really want to go outside, don't you?"

"Yes," says Andrew. Then without further comment, Andrew walks off and begins playing by himself. Andrew, it turns out, just wanted to know that his uncle understood him. He wanted to know he'd been heard.

Andrew's story demonstrates something that is true for all of us: we have a deep desire to feel heard, and to know that others care enough to listen. . . .

LISTENING TO THEM HELPS THEM LISTEN TO YOU

When the other person is not listening, you may imagine it is because they're stubborn or don't understand what you're trying to say. (If they did, they'd understand why they should listen to it.) So you may try to break through that by repeating, trying new ways to explain yourself, talking more loudly, and so forth.

On the face of it, these would seem to be good strategies. But they're not. Why? Because in the great majority of cases, the reason the other person is not listening to you is not because they are stubborn, but because *they* don't feel heard. In other words, they aren't listening to you for the same reason you aren't listening to them: they think *you* are slow or stubborn. So they repeat themselves, find new ways to say things, talk more loudly, and so forth.

If the block to their listening is that they don't feel heard, then the way to remove that block is by helping them feel heard — by bending over backwards to listen to what they have to say, and perhaps most important, by demonstrating that you understand what they are saying and how they are feeling.

If you don't quite believe this, try it. Find the most stubborn person you know, the person who never seems to take in anything you say, the person who repeats himself or herself in every conversation you ever have — and listen to them. Especially, listen for feelings, like frustration or pride or fear, and acknowledge those feelings. See whether that person doesn't become a better listener after all. . . .

THREE SKILLS: INQUIRY, PARAPHRASING, AND ACKNOWLEDGMENT

Inquire to Learn

The heading says it all: inquire to learn. And only to learn. You can tell whether a question will help the conversation or hurt it by thinking about why you asked it. The only good answer is "To learn."

Anyone who has ever been a kid in a car has uttered the cranky words "Are we there yet?" You know you're not there yet, and your parents know you know, and so they respond in a tone as cranky as yours. What you really meant was "I'm feeling restless" or "I wish we were there" or "This is a long trip for me." Any of these would likely elicit a more productive response from Mom and Dad.

This illustrates an important rule about inquiry: If you don't have a question, don't ask a question. Never dress up an assertion as a question. Doing so creates confusion and resentment, because such questions are inevitably heard as sarcastic and sometimes mean-spirited. . . .

Sharing our feelings and making requests are two things that many of us have difficulty doing directly. They can make us feel vulnerable. Turning what we have to say into an attack — a sarcastic question — can feel safer. But this safety is an illusion, and we lose more than we gain. Saying "I'd like you to pay more attention to me" is more likely to produce a conversation (a satisfying outcome) than "Is it impossible for you to focus on me just once?" . . .

A second error that gets us into trouble is using questions to shoot holes in the other person's argument. . . .

Open-ended questions are questions that give the other person broad latitude in how to answer. . . . To understand where the other person's conclusions came from and enrich your understanding of what they envision going forward, it helps to ask them to be more explicit about their reasoning and their vision. "What leads you to say that?" "Can you give me an example?" "What would that look like?" "How would that work?" "How would we test that hypothesis?" . . .

Paraphrase for Clarity

The second skill a good listener brings to the conversation is paraphrasing. . . .

First, paraphrasing gives you a chance to check your understanding. Difficult conversations are made harder when an important misunderstanding exists, and such misunderstandings are more common than we imagine. Paraphrasing gives the other person the chance to say, "No, that's not quite what I meant. What I really meant was. . . ."

Second, paraphrasing lets the other person know that they've been heard. Usually the reason someone repeats himself or herself in a conversation is because they have no indication that you've actually taken in what they've said. If you notice that the other person is saying the same thing over and over again, take it as a signal that you need to paraphrase more. Once they feel heard, they are significantly more likely to listen to *you*. . . .

Acknowledge Their Feelings

Why is acknowledgment so important? Because attached to each expression of feelings is a set of invisible questions: "Are my feelings okay?" "Do you understand them?" "Do you care about them?" "Do you care about me?" These questions are important, and we have trouble moving on in the conversation until we know the answers. Taking time to acknowledge the other person's feelings says loud and clear that the answer to each question is yes.

An acknowledgment is simply this: any indication that you are struggling to understand the emotional content of what the other person is saying. . . .

While you may not agree with the substance of what the other person is saying, you can still acknowledge the importance of their feeling. . . .

Remind yourself that the task of understanding the other person's world is always harder than it seems. Remind yourself that if you think you already understand how someone else feels or what they are trying to say, it is a delusion. Remember a time when you were *sure* you were right and then discovered one little fact that changed everything. There is always more to learn. Remind yourself of the depth, complexities, contradictions, and nuances that make up the stories of each of our lives.

Notes and Questions

5.14 If wanting to be heard is different from wanting the result, how can you use this insight in a negotiation? Procedural justice literature (described in Chapter 1) discusses the importance that participants in conflict resolution procedures attach to the opportunity to voice their opinions and have those opinions heard.

5.15 In recent years, the FBI and a growing number of other law enforcement agencies have used active listening to successfully resolve volatile confrontations. These positive results have led the FBI to incorporate and emphasize active listening skills in its crisis negotiation training. An FBI special agent and a police researcher wrote:

> Despite the popular notion that listening is a passive behavior, abundant clinical evidence and research suggest that active listening is an effective way to induce behavioral change in others. When listened to by others, individuals tend to listen to themselves more carefully and to evaluate and clarify their own thoughts and feelings. In addition, they tend to become better problem solvers, growing less defensive and oppositional and more accepting of other points of view. Subjects who are met with an empathetic ear also become less fearful of being criticized and grow more inclined to adopt a realistic appraisal of their own position. . . . By applying active listening skills, negotiators demonstrate that they are not a threat to the subject and that their goal is to help rather than harm. When negotiators demonstrate empathy and understanding, they build rapport, which, in turn, enables them to influence the subject's actions by providing nonviolent problem-solving alternatives. In short, by demonstrating support and empathy, negotiators often can talk an expressive subject into surrendering largely by listening.

Gary W. Noesner & Mike Webster, Crisis Intervention: Using Active Listening Skills in Negotiations, FBI L. Enforcement Bull., Aug. 1997, at 13-19. Does this advice surprise you?

5.16 How many people try the familiar tactic of raising their voices when someone does not understand them? What is the person who speaks louder trying to do? What effect is such action likely to have? If the speaker was unclear or speaking in a foreign language the first time, what makes the speaker believe speaking *louder* will actually help?

5.17 The following student's story offers one very persuasive reason to improve listening skills. The student was interviewing for a job with a commercial real estate firm for an in-house counsel position. The student had been a realtor for a number of years prior to coming to law school. Here is what he wrote in his journal:

> [The] Partner went on a ten minute tangent about how first year associates were basically "useless" and a dime a dozen. Given, I was not happy at the time and I did not think my chances of getting the job were too positive, I let him go on and kept my thoughts to myself. Thank God for my improvements in listening — old John would have interrupted and clarified that I was not a recent grad, rather I have six years of real estate experience and am now a law school graduate. . . . However, because I politely let him finish he thanked me and said, "I know you're different. I could tell by the way you actively listened to me." I'm not kidding. I got an offer. . . . Thank you for including listening in your class agenda. It not only saved my marriage, but gave me this amazing job opportunity.

The final excerpt on listening and understanding introduces methods for developing empathy or "walking a mile in someone else's shoes" (often by having to take on their, not your, shoe size!). As you will see in the next chapter on mediator skills, mediators try to get parties to reverse roles as a technique to generate movement. If you can do this thoughtfully as a negotiator — and help your client see the other side's perspective — you will be an asset in a mediation!

 Roger Fisher, Elizabeth Kopelman & Andrea Kupfer Schneider, **BEYOND MACHIAVELLI: TOOLS FOR COPING WITH CONFLICT**

32-34 (1996)

OBSERVE FROM DIFFERENT POINTS OF VIEW

To understand conflict well we want to observe it from . . . three positions. (If there are several parties to a conflict, we will want to understand how each sees it.) One who is skilled at dealing with conflict is likely to be adept at jumping back and forth, observing what is going on from each of these three positions. . . .

Three Positions for Observing a Conflict
First Position (Mine): How I see the problem, from my own perspective.
Second Position (Theirs): How I see the problem when I stand in the shoes of the other party to the dispute.
Third Position ("Fly on the Wall"): How a neutral third party would assess the conflict.
These three distinct points of view illuminate a variety of dimensions of a conflict.

TO GAIN EMPATHY, REVERSE ROLES

Understanding is not simply an intellectual activity. Feeling empathetically how others may feel can be as important as thinking clearly about how others may think.

There is a lot of truth in the old saying that "where you stand depends upon where you sit." Another way of trying to understand the other side's perceptions is literally to sit in a different chair, pretend to be someone on the other side, and try to see the situation from that vantage point.

The chairman of a company held liable for a patent infringement had called in a consultant to advise about the negotiation of a possible settlement on the dollar amount of damages. The case had been in litigation for years. The chairman had been told that if the worst happened, and he should be held liable, he could always settle — but he had little appreciation of how much the other side would expect.

Encouraged by the consultant, the executive agreed to switch seats, moving from his own chair to a chair the consultant had designated as that of the president of the plaintiff company. While the executive initially resisted "playing games," he was eventually persuaded to assume the role of that president and to state the plaintiff's case in the first person as forcefully as he could. Within a few minutes he was playing the role well. Asked how much he might accept in settlement (an amount that, in real life, would be paid out by this executive's own company) he replied (still in his role as the opposing company's president), "Why, I wouldn't take their whole damn company!" Shaken by this experience, and with new insight into what might be required to settle this case, his company raised its settlement offer by one hundred fold. It was rejected, and the judgment was ultimately for even more. An earlier attempt to appreciate the other side's partisan perceptions would no doubt have led him to pursue a wiser strategy from the outset. . . .

Notes and Questions

5.18 What are partisan perceptions? Think about an issue about which you have strong feelings. Outline your point of view in one column of a piece of paper. Outline the other side's point of view as best you can in another column. What are the similarities and differences?

5.19 Research has demonstrated benefits of empathetic understanding that underscore the importance of the skill. Negotiators who can see the other side's perspective can negotiate agreements of higher value than those with lower perspective-taking ability. Perspective taking, when combined with active listening to double-check understanding, will reduce the likelihood that negotiators will jump to mistaken conclusions about their counterpart, which in turn can prevent dysfunctional relationships and impasse. Finally, displays of empathy (understanding the other side) garner practical rewards connected to anger diffusion and trust building. Robert H. Mnookin, Scott R. Peppet & Andrew S. Tulumello, Beyond Winning, 46-49 (2000).

5.20 Wittgenstein's Poker tells the story of a famous argument between philosophers Ludwig Wittgenstein and Karl Popper at a Cambridge University meeting in 1946. According to the version Popper published in his autobiography, Wittgenstein threatened him with a poker when Popper challenged Wittgenstein on a philosophical point. As the authors write in the book, each of the nine surviving audience members remembers the events differently: whether Wittgenstein was merely gesturing or actually threatening with the poker; if, in response to Wittgenstein's demand for a moral rule, Popper's witty response of "Not to threaten visiting lecturers with pokers" actually caused Wittgenstein to walk out or if Popper replied after Wittgenstein had left the room. It is a fascinating collection of stories, all purportedly retelling the same event. David Edmonds & John Eidinow, Wittgenstein's Poker (2001). Before the book came out, there was a long exchange of letters in the Times Literary Supplement. There were so many accounts that nearly every surviving witness must have participated. There were even secondhand accounts of what deceased witnesses, such as Bertrand Russell, had seen.

5.21   Building trust, as you have seen, is related to listening, understanding, and empathy. The Prisoner's Dilemma, described in Chapter 2, displays how mistrust can lead to a downward cycle of defection and lost opportunity or how trust can lead to cooperation and profit. Trust is easier to destroy than to build. For an excellent analysis of trust building, see Roy J. Lewicki & Barbara Benedict Bunker, Trust in Relationships: A Model of Development and Decline, Conflict Cooperation and Justice 133 (Barbara Bunker, Jeffrey Rubin et al. eds., 1995). Leigh Thompson in *The Mind and Heart of the Negotiator* discusses various dimensions of trust: similarities and commonalities between people enhance trust; exposure can build trust; self-disclosure can increase trust. These considerations highlight the importance in negotiation and mediation of preliminary meetings, acts of courtesy and generosity, small talk, seating arrangements, and joint sessions. Note the dissonance and differences in this advice and the advice given to competitive bargainers by Meltsner and Schrag in Chapter 2.

5.22   There are many other variables that affect negotiation performance, and hence mediations and their outcomes. Personality, amiability, and mood are among them. For example, positive mood can make parties more creative and cooperative. Anger can negatively impact performance in negotiation and will result in more competitive bargaining. Suppression of emotion can cause cognitive impairment. Such findings suggest that lawyers must work with both their clients and themselves to monitor the impact of a variety of complex variables. For a review of the literature in this area of psychology, see Clark Freshman, Adele Hayes & Greg Feldman, The Lawyer-Negotiator as Mood Scientist: What We Know and Don't Know About How Mood Relates to Successful Negotiation, J. Disp. Resol. 1 (2002).

3. Talking Persuasively

Before the attorney or client makes a presentation to their counterpart in the negotiation, they must consider how to make the most persuasive case. This is not unlike a trial lawyer's task when preparing to make arguments in front of a jury. What is likely to convince them that you should be accommodated?

One of the ways to make your argument more persuasive is to tell a coherent story about what you want. For example, in addition to your legal arguments, you might also base your argument on good policy, a principle to be upheld, the better consequences of your agreement, or the general custom in that type of business.

Additional methods to bolster your argument include framing and analogy. Negotiators sometimes use metaphors and labeling to make their argument more persuasive. In a negotiation, are we partners or opponents? When trying to motivate U.S. involvement in Kosovo, was this another Vietnam or was Milosevic another Hitler? Similar metaphors were used with the Iraq war in 2003. In another case, were the people who took 700 hostages in a Moscow theater in October 2002 terrorists or Chechen freedom fighters? The label simplifies a complex situation to convince and persuade the recipient. How you view the situation clearly affects what action you think is appropriate. In the negotiation context, the label used should not offend the other side, but rather draw them to your point of view.

Other framing occurs through the use of specifics and detail. You can use statistics or expert authority to provide specific support for your argument.

> **Speaking to Be Heard**
>
> The following is a classic example of what happens when people are talking past one another or when they are not sufficiently clear or forthcoming with critical information. This is one version of a story that is based on a radio transcript released by the Chief of Naval Operations from October 10, 1995:
>
> ***Station 1:*** Please divert your course 15 degrees to the North to avoid a collision.
>
> ***Station 2:*** Recommend you divert YOUR course 15 degrees to the South to avoid a collision.
>
> ***Station 1:*** This is the Captain of a U.S. Navy ship. I say again, divert YOUR course.
>
> ***Station 2:*** No, I say again, you divert *your* course.
>
> ***Station 1:*** This is the aircraft carrier Enterprise, we are a large Warship of the U.S. Navy. Divert your course now!
>
> ***Station 2:*** This is the Puget Sound Lighthouse. It's your call.

Sometimes this experience is personal — if you can tell a story about how your motorcycle helmet saved your life, you might be better able to persuade a legislator to change the law. Many congressional hearings focus on this type of framing. Other times you can tell the story using vivid detail to describe what has happened and bring the listener into the situation. Excellent trial attorneys often use this type of framing with the jury. In fact, in a study comparing the use of pallid information ("The defendant staggered against a serving table, knocking a bowl to the floor") versus vivid information ("The defendant staggered against a serving table, knocking a bowl of guacamole dip to the floor and splattering guacamole on the white shag carpet"), members of the mock jury were more likely to find the latter defendant guilty.[*]

---

[*] R.M. Reyes, W.C. Thompson & G.H. Bower, Judgmental Biases Resulting from Differing Availabilities of Arguments, 39 J. Personality & Soc. Psychol. 2 (1980), cited in Scott Plous, The Psychology of Judgment and Decision Making 127-128 (1993).

Notes and Questions

5.23 Think of a recent case you studied in another law class. Suppose you are arguing that case to a jury or to a negotiation counterpart. What are your top three arguments in each situation? Are these based in law, in policy, on consequences, on factual detail? What makes these arguments persuasive?

5.24 Robert Condlin states that legal arguments tend to be the least persuasive to law students or practicing attorneys. Robert Condlin, Cases on Both Sides: Patterns of Argument in Legal Dispute Negotiation, 44 Md. L. Rev. 65 (1985). Why do you think this might be the case?

In the next excerpt, three negotiation trainers and researchers advise how to convey your points in a way that will enhance the ability of the other side to hear you.

Douglas Stone, Bruce Patton & Sheila Heen,
DIFFICULT CONVERSATIONS: HOW TO DISCUSS WHAT MATTERS MOST

195-200 (1999)

TELLING YOUR STORY WITH CLARITY: THREE GUIDELINES

Obviously, how you express yourself makes a difference. How you say what you want to say will determine, in part, how others respond to you, and how the conversation will go. So when you choose to share something important, you'll want to do so in a way that will maximize the chance that the other person will understand and respond productively. Clarity is the key.

1. Don't Present Your Conclusions as *the* Truth

Some aspects of difficult conversations will continue to be rough even when you communicate with great skill: sharing feelings of vulnerability, delivering bad news, learning something painful about how others see you. But presenting your story as the truth — which creates resentment, defensiveness, and leads to arguments — is a wholly avoidable disaster. . . .

Some words — like "attractive," "ugly," "good," and "bad" — carry judgments that are obvious. But be careful with words like "inappropriate," "should," or "professional." The judgments contained in these words are less obvious, but can still provoke the "Who are you to tell me?!" response. If you want to say something is "inappropriate," preface your judgment with "My view is that . . ." Better still, avoid these words altogether.

2. Share Where Your Conclusions Come From

The first step toward clarity, then, is to share your conclusions and opinions as *your* conclusions and opinions and not as the truth. The second step is to share what's beneath your conclusions — the information you have and how you have interpreted it. . . .

3. Don't Exaggerate with "Always" and "Never": Give Them Room to Change

In the heat of the moment, it's easy to express frustration through a bit of exaggeration: "Why do you *always* criticize my clothes?" "You *never* give one word of appreciation or encouragement. The only time anyone hears anything from you is when there's something wrong!"

"Always" and "never" do a pretty good job of conveying frustration, but they have two serious drawbacks. First, it is seldom strictly accurate that someone criticizes *every* time, or that they haven't at some point said *something* positive. . . .

"Always" and "never" also make it harder — rather than easier — for the other person to consider changing their behavior. In fact, "always" and "never" suggest that change will be difficult or impossible. The implicit message is, "What is wrong with you such that you are driven to criticize my clothes?" or even "You are obviously incapable of acting like a normal person." . . .

The key is to communicate your feelings in a way that invites and encourages the recipient to consider new ways of behaving, rather than suggesting they're a schmuck and it's too bad there's nothing they can do about it. . . .

The secret of powerful expression is recognizing that you are the ultimate authority on you. You are an expert on what you think, how you feel, and why you've come to this place. If you think it or feel it, you are entitled to say it, and no one can legitimately contradict you. You only get in trouble if you try to assert what you are *not* the final authority on — who is right, who intended what, what happened. Speak fully the range of your experience and you will be clear. Speak for yourself and you can speak with power.

Notes and Questions

5.25 Attorneys can quickly turn conversations into unproductive fights by using judgmental legal labels: "What your company did amounts to *fraud*." "Leaving the child alone in the apartment — even for one minute — is *child abuse*." While these allegations would appear in legal complaints and answers, they will unnecessarily infect bargaining. How would you raise concerns around these topics without using such labels?

5.26 Your client works for a large international bank and has been pleased with the company's treatment of women. For example, the bank has generous maternity leave provisions, permits part-time work, and has a number of female executives. Recently, however, she has become worried about a particular situation in her department, which establishes new branches overseas. The bank has been working with a country whose representatives have said that their country's cultural norms will make it difficult for their government and banking officials to work with women in the bank. By coincidence, no women were working on setting up that branch at the time these preferences became known. But things have changed recently. As your client has moved up, this project represents her next logical step. Yet so far, she has not been asked to work on the project, although several of her male colleagues with the same level of experience have been. When she initially raised the issue with her supervisor, she was advised to "give it time, and not rock the boat." She felt surprised, let down, and even somewhat hurt to hear this, but didn't push the matter. On reflection, she has consulted you and wants to talk with her supervisor again and let the supervisor know how strongly she feels about this discriminatory treatment. In considering how to coach your client, give three different ways to frame this conversation. If you were preparing for a mediation session, subsequent to filing an EEO complaint, how would you and your client frame the opening presentation?*

5.27 Based on the above facts, rephrase in a sentence or sequence of sentences the following statements to make them more clear, accurate, and conducive to facilitating dialogue. The phrases may conflict slightly from what appears to be true based on the discussion problem. Part of your task is to bring them back in line with what is true in the discussion problem.

   a. "If I can't work on the project, my career will really be damaged."
   b. "I appreciated that you took the time to talk about this before, but I found our conversation really disturbing."
   c. "It seems to me that the bank is acquiescing to the country too easily. We need to put up more of a fight."
   d. "This bank just doesn't seem to care about its female employees."
   e. "Your attempt to set the matter aside really hurt me."
   f. "Do you think that delaying this is the best way to handle the situation?"

For some good suggestions for reframing, see Deborah Kolb & Judith Williams, Everyday Negotiations (2003) and Linda Babcock & Sara Laschever, Women Don't Ask: Negotiation and the Gender Divide (2003).

4. Developing Creativity and Flexibility

An attorney with a flexible and creative approach is a major asset to progress in negotiation and mediation. Solutions to difficult or intractable problems can be developed by those who think creatively or out of the box of ordinary solutions. This section focuses on the advantages that creative thinking brings to a negotiation and then provides some specific ideas to increase creativity. Think about how both attorney-representatives and mediators can use creativity to resolve problems in mediation. When is it appropriate for the mediator to suggest creative ideas that the parties don't think of themselves?

Carrie Menkel-Meadow first discusses the importance of creativity in successful problem solving and then highlights examples of legal creativity and its potential.

---

* Thanks to Sheila Heen, Doug Stone, and Bruce Patton for Notes and Questions 5.26 and 5.27.

Carrie Menkel-Meadow, AHA? IS CREATIVITY POSSIBLE IN LEGAL PROBLEM SOLVING AND TEACHABLE IN LEGAL EDUCATION?

6 Harv. Negot. L. Rev. 97, 106, 122-123, 127-128, 131, 133 (2001)

Dispute negotiation too often looks for its solutions among legal precedents or outcomes thought likely in the "shadow of the courthouse" (these days most often [a] compromise of some monetary values), and deal negotiations too often seek solutions in the boilerplate language of form contracts for transactions. Ironically, these litigated outcomes and boilerplate clauses were once the creative ideas of some lawyers who developed a new reading of a statute, a novel argument before a common law or Constitutional court, developed a new scheme of risk allocation, or found a new source of capital or drafted a new clause for a deal document.

Solutions to legal problems, then, come from creative lawyers, as well as legal or practice precedent. The challenge for negotiation theorists, practitioners and teachers is to find systematic ways to teach solution devising, short of reading thousands of cases, transactional documents, statutes or other legal documents that will show us not only what already has been done, but also what might be done. Are there ways of learning or thinking about solutions to legal problems that are generic or are there only substantive (domain based) solutions? Here the teachings of other disciplines may be useful. Some researchers focus on the positive solution-seeking side of cognition and creativity; others focus on the negative side of impediments to good or, as they define it, rational decision making or problem-solving. . . .

In this literature, the following techniques are suggested as formal ways of enhancing creativity, solving problems and suggesting new ideas, some as separate individual cognitive processes, and others as structured processes to be used in multi-party settings.

1. Uses of analogy (direct, fanciful) and use of metaphor;
2. Aggregation/disaggregation/re-combination of elements of a problem;
3. Transfer (cross-disciplinary use of concepts, ideas, information, solutions from other fields);
4. Reversal (either extreme polarization or gradual modification of ideas) — which is done both in cognitive and in personal forms (as in role-reversal efforts to understand the point of view of others in the situation);
5. Extension — extending a line of reasoning, principle or solution beyond its original purpose;
6. Challenging assumptions — re-examining givens or problem statements and unpacking clichéd, conventional solutions or stereotypes;
7. Narrative — fully describing facts and problems to elaborate on complexity, and producing alternative endings;
8. Backward/forward thinking — focusing on how we came to a particular situation (reasons why, causes) in order to figure out how we get to desired end-state(s);
9. Design — plan for desired future end-state, structures, means;

10. Random stimulation/brainstorming—separation of idea generation, randomly generated, from judgment and evaluation. . . .
11. Visualization—use of different competencies and modes of thinking and processing information; this includes efforts at altered states (e.g., retreats and meditations);
12. Entry points—explicit reframing of problems and solutions from different perspectives. . . .

Lawyers work with words, so most of our creative acts involve the construction of new language and interpretation of existing language, creating new concepts from whole cloth or from the interstices of statutory, regulatory or contractual gaps. Our words have the force of law behind them, however, so that powerfully creative words in law have been known to create whole new institutions. Examples of new legal and real entities that have been created are corporations, trusts, regulatory agencies, condominiums, unions and tax shelters. In addition, our words have created new legal rights and constructs like leases, sexual harassment, probation—and also have recognized (sometimes from conflicting ideologies) new claims like civil rights, privacy, free speech and emotional distress. . . .

A form of creativity somewhat unique to legal reasoning, though similar to our related linguistic intelligences, is the process of characterization or argumentation in which we use our words to re-categorize facts, claims, arguments and rules, which disturb the linguistic purity desired by those outside of our domain. Consider how patent lawyers successfully assimilated the architecture of software to the vocabulary of a machine in order to obtain patent protection for what were thought to be unpatentable "mental processes, abstract intellectual concepts" or ideas. . . .

Similarly, alterations (in the form of aggregations or disaggregations) of concepts is a common legal trope, particularly in transactional legal work. Using basic property principles which combine space and time (time bounded estates in land), creative lawyers created co-ops, condominiums and time shares. . . .

Law's creativity may be somewhat limited by the bounds of law and legal ethics rules, but there still remains a fair amount of problem space to be manipulated within our adversarial culture. At the same time, the adversarial culture may also constrain and cabin our thinking unnecessarily by structuring it in polarized and oppositional terms. Are transactional lawyers more creative by being less constrained? Corporations and trusts, for example, were created legally to accomplish many different goals, some adversarial (tax delay, minimization or avoidance), but also to permit different power and control arrangements and to bundle and unbundle interests of wealth, time and assets to permit great flexibility of action. . . .

Legal creativity is necessarily limited by its need to work within the law, or at least within the foreseeable boundaries of legal change, but for optimal problem-solving it would seem we should try to push the boundaries of little "c" creativity as much as we can to produce at least a greater number of choices about how best to accomplish legal results.

In the next excerpt, Jennifer Brown explains several different creativity techniques that can be useful in negotiation and elaborates on several of the techniques introduced in the previous excerpt by Menkel-Meadow.

 Jennifer Gerarda Brown, **CREATIVITY AND PROBLEM SOLVING**

87 Marq. L. Rev. 697, 697–705 (2004)

Negotiation experts seem to agree that creative solutions are often the key to reaching value-maximizing outcomes in integrative, interest-based bargaining. Sticking to the problem as it is initially framed and considering only the solutions that most readily present themselves will sometimes yield the optimal result, but more often the situation will require the parties and their representatives to think more expansively. This process of thinking more expansively — thinking "that ventures out from the accustomed way of considering a problem, to find something else that might work" — is often referred to as creativity or creative thinking. . . .

I. BEYOND BRAINSTORMING

Most teachers and trainers of interest-based negotiation will spend some time teaching creative thinking. Following the template set forth in *Getting to YES*, they will encourage their students to "brainstorm." Brainstorming, as most readers of this essay know, is a somewhat formalized process in which participants work together to generate ideas. I say that it is formalized because it proceeds according to two important ground rules: participants agree not to evaluate the ideas while they are brainstorming, and they agree not to take "ownership" of the ideas. They strive to generate options and put them on the table, no matter how wacky or far-fetched they may seem. The "no evaluation" rule encourages participants to suspend their natural urge to criticize, edit, or censor the ideas. Evaluation can come later, but the notion here is that solutions will flow more easily if people are not assessing even as they articulate them. The "no ownership" rule also facilitates innovation because participants are encouraged to feel free to propose an idea or solution without endorsing it — no one can later attribute the idea to the person who proposed it, or try to hold it against that person. People can therefore propose ideas that might actually disadvantage them and benefit their counterparts without conceding that they would actually agree to such proposals in the final analysis. The ground rules for brainstorming constrain the natural inclination to criticize, so that participants are free to imagine, envision, and play with ideas, even though these processes come less easily to them. Why is brainstorming so popular, both in practice and in negotiation training? Perhaps the answer lies not so much in what it activates, but in what it disables. What I mean is that it may be easier to teach people what *not* to do — rather than what to do affirmatively — in order to enhance their creative thinking. We may not know much about how to unleash new sources of creativity for negotiators, but we are pretty sure about some things that impede creative thinking. Theory and practice suggest that creative thinking is difficult when people jump to conclusions, close off discussion, or seize upon an answer prematurely. Indeed, the very heuristics that make decision making possible — those pathways that permit people to make positive and sometimes normative judgments — can also lead people astray. One of the ways they may be led astray is that the heuristic prompts them to decide too quickly what something is or should be. Once judgment has occurred, it is tough to justify the expenditure of additional energy that creative thinking would require. Creativity could be considered the "anti-heuristic"; it keeps multiple pathways of perception and decision-making open, even when people are tempted to choose a single, one-way route to a solution. If we do nothing else, we can attempt to delay this kind of judgment until negotiators have considered multiple options. Brainstorming provides the structure for this kind of delay. . . .

A.   Wordplay

Once an issue or problem is articulated, it is possible to play with the words expressing that problem in order to improve understanding and sometimes to yield new solutions.

1.   *Shifting Emphasis*

To take a fairly simple example, suppose that two neighbors are in a dispute because cigarette butts and other small pieces of trash, deposited by Mr. Smith in his own front yard, are blowing into Mr. Jones's yard, and those that remain in Mr. Smith's yard are detracting from the appearance of the neighborhood (at least as Mr. Jones sees it). Mr. Jones might ask himself (or a mediator at the neighborhood justice center), "How can I get Mr. Smith to stop littering in his yard?" Shifting the emphasis in this sentence brings into focus various aspects of the problem and suggests possible solutions addressing those specific aspects. Consider the different meanings of the following sentences:

"How can *I* get Mr. Smith to stop littering in his yard?"
"How can I get *Mr. Smith* to stop littering in his yard?"
"How can I get Mr. Smith to stop *littering* in his yard?"
"How can I get Mr. Smith to stop littering in *his* yard?"
"How can I get Mr. Smith to stop littering in his *yard*?"

As the focus of the problem shifts, so too different potential solutions might emerge to address the problem as specifically articulated.

2.   *Changing a Word*

Sometimes changing a word in the sentence helps to reformulate the problem in a way that suggests new solutions. In the example above, Mr. Jones might change the phrase "littering in his yard" to something else, such as "neglecting his yard" or "hanging out in his yard." It may be that something besides littering lies at the root of the problem, and a solution will be found, for example, not in stopping the littering, but in more regularized yard work.

3.   *Deleting a Word*

Through word play, parties can delete words or phrases to see whether broadening the statement of the problem more accurately or helpfully captures its essence. Mr. Jones might delete the phrase "Mr. Smith" from his formulation of the problem, and thereby discover that it is not just Mr. Smith's yard, but the entire street, that is looking bad. Focusing on Mr. Smith as the source of the problem may be counter-productive; Mr. Jones might discover that he needs to organize all of the home-owners on his block to battle littering in order to make a difference. Deleting words sometimes spurs creativity by removing an overly restrictive focus on the issue or problem.

4.   *Adding a New Word*

A final form of word play that can spur creative thinking is sometimes called "random word association." Through this process, participants choose a word ran-domly and then think of ways to associate it with the problem. Suppose Mr. Jones and Mr. Smith were given the word "work" and asked how it might relate to their dispute. Here are some possible results:

> *Work (time, effort)*: Mr. Smith will try to work harder to keep his yard looking nice, and he will check Mr. Jones's yard every Saturday to make sure there are no cigarette butts or other pieces of trash in it.
> *Work (being operational or functional)*: What the neighborhood needs is a sense of cohesion; Mr. Jones and Mr. Smith will organize a neighborhood beautifica-tion project to try to instill a sense of community among their neighbors.
> *Work (job)*: Although Mr. Smith's odd working hours sometimes lead him to smoke on his front porch and chat with his friends or family late at night (after Mr. Jones has gone to bed), Mr. Smith will stay in the back of his house after 10 P.M., further from Mr. Jones's bedroom window.

As the different meanings and resulting associations of "work" are explored by the parties, they discover new ways to solve their shared problem. Other seemingly unrelated words might trigger still more associations and more potential solutions. . . .

C.   De Bono's "Six Hats" Technique

Edward de Bono has proposed a technique he calls "Six Thinking Hats," in which six aspects of a problem are assessed independently. As problem solvers symbolically don each of six differently colored hats, they focus on an aspect of the problem associated with each color: red for emotions, white for facts, yellow for positive aspects of the situation, green for future implications, black for critique, and blue for process.[22] As Weinstein and Morton point out, the technique of isolating the black/critique hat may be especially important for lawyers, whose tendency to move quickly into a critical mode may prevent them from seeing other important aspects of a problem. If the black hat is worn at or near the end of the process, the Six Hats technique displays a characteristic shared by brainstorming: it delays critique and judgment until other approaches can be tried. And shutting down judgment may enable creativity, as suggested above. By forcing themselves to address separately the emotional, factual, and process issues at stake in a problem, parties may discover room for creative solutions. Similarly, creative solutions are sometimes found in the terms of a future

---

[22] Edward de Bono, Six Thinking Hats (1999).

relationship between the parties. Wearing the green hat may force participants to come to terms with a future they would rather ignore.

The prospect of changing hats, even (perhaps especially) if it is done symbolically, could make some participants uncomfortable. Negotiators and neutrals should bear in mind that age, sex, ethnicity and other cultural specifics may create dignitary interests for some participants that would be threatened or compromised by some techniques for boosting creative thought. Some people would feel embarrassed or humiliated if they were asked to engage in the theatrics required by some of these exercises. For others, the chance to pretend or play might be just the prod they need to open new avenues of thought. In a spirit of flexibility (surely a necessary condition for creativity), therefore, one should be thinking of ways to modify these techniques to fit other needs of the parties.[26]

D.   Atlas of Approaches

Another technique for stimulating creative ideas about a problem from a variety of perspectives is called the "Atlas of Approaches." Roger Fisher, Elizabeth Kopelman and Andrea Kupfer Schneider propose this approach in Beyond Machiavelli, their book on international negotiation.[27] Using the Atlas of Approaches technique, participants adopt the perspectives of professionals from a variety of fields. By asking themselves, for example, "What would a journalist do?," "What would an economist do?," "How would a psychologist view this?," and so on, negotiators are able to form a more interdisciplinary view of their problem. With this more complete picture of the issues and potential outcomes, they might be able to connect disciplines in ways that give rise to creative solutions. . . .

F.   "WWCD": What Would Croesus[30] Do?

This process requires a participant to take the perspective of an unconstrained actor. What solutions suggest themselves if we assume no limit to available money, time, talent, technology, or effort? In some ways, one could think of the WWCD method as a more specific application of brainstorming. As the proponents of brainstorming are quick to point out, creativity and the free flow of ideas can be impeded by criticism or assessment. WWCD takes off the table any assessment based on constraints — financial, technological, etc. If we assume that we can afford and operationalize any solution we can come up with, what might we discover?

A second phase of this approach requires participants to think about the extent to which their unconstrained solution might be modified to make it workable given the existing constraints. . . .

---

[26] For example, the Six Hats technique could be transformed into a "Six Flip Charts" exercise, still using differently colored paper or markers to signal the different focus of each inquiry.

[27] Roger Fisher et al., Beyond Machiavelli: Tools for Coping with Conflict 67 (1996).

[30] Nalebuff and Ayers explain: "Croesus (rhymes with Jesus) was the supremely rich king of Lydia (modern Turkey), reigning from 560 to 546 B.C. His wealth came from mining gold. . . . His lavish gifts and sacrifices made his name synonymous with wealth. Even today we say 'rich as Croesus.'" Barry Nalebuff & Ian Ayres, Why Not? How to Use Everyday Ingenuity to Solve Problems Big and Small (2003).

H. Flipping or Reversal

With this technique, one asks whether flipping or reversing a given situation will work. As Edward de Bono explains:

> In the reversal method, one takes things as they are and then turns them round, inside out, upside down, back to front. Then one sees what happens... one is not looking for the right answer but for a different arrangement of information which will provoke a different way of looking at the situation.

Chris Honeyman sometimes uses this technique in his work as a neutral when he asks the parties to put forward some really *bad* ideas for resolving the conflict. When people offer ideas in response to a call for "bad" ideas, they may free themselves to offer the ideas they partially or secretly support; again, as in brainstorming, they disclaim ownership of the ideas. It is also possible that the instruction to offer bad ideas stimulates creative thinking because it can seem *funny* to people. Humor is a good stimulant for creativity.

Notes and Questions

5.28 This sort of creativity has been exploited in ads. The following is from an advertisement in *Vanity Fair* magazine:

> Two women apply for jobs. They look exactly alike. On their applications they list the same last name, address and phone number. They were born to the same parents, on the same day, same month, same year. Everything is identical. The receptionist says, "You must be twins." They say "no." How is that possible?

What do you think the answer is?

The reader then turns the page over to find the answer.* The ad then continues: "If the answer wasn't obvious, start thinking differently. Which is exactly the strategy behind the totally new 2003 Ford Expedition. Brilliant solutions are easy to see in hindsight. But, having the foresight to come up with one is something completely different. Smart, innovative ideas require unconventional thinking. You have to think without boundaries...."

This could be an ad for creative thinking in general. Why does Ford think this will help sell more cars? What do you think about the ad?

5.29 Another example of creativity demonstrates a different method of influence. In the 1970s, American physician Bernard Lown visited the Soviet Union and formed lasting relationships with his Soviet counterparts, one such physician being Evgenii Chazov. The Lown-Chazov connection paved the way for the Boston-based Physicians for Social Responsibility to evolve into a transnational network that eventually became the International Physicians for the Prevention of Nuclear War (IPPNW). Comprising some 200,000 members from 80 countries, the IPPNW won the Nobel Peace Prize in 1985. While none of these doctors could have individually persuaded his or her own government to

---

* The women are from a set of triplets.

change its arms policy, this group was very persuasive in helping the United States and the USSR sign arms control agreements. What type of creativity does this demonstrate?

In her earlier excerpt, Carrie Menkel-Meadow outlines 12 different ways to be more creative. This next excerpt from psychology professor Dean Pruitt focuses on how to achieve integrative agreements expanding primarily on Menkel-Meadow's second point: aggregation/disaggregation and recombination.

 ### Dean Pruitt, ACHIEVING INTEGRATIVE AGREEMENTS

in Negotiation in Organizations 36-41 (Max Bazerman & Roy Lewicki eds., 1983)

METHODS FOR ACHIEVING INTEGRATIVE AGREEMENTS

Five methods for achieving integrative agreements will now be described. These are means by which the parties' initially opposing demands can be transformed into alternatives that reconcile their interests. They can be used by one party, both parties working together, or a third party such as a mediator. Each method involves a different way of refocusing the issues under dispute. Hence potentially useful refocusing questions will be provided under each heading. Information that is useful for implementing each method will also be mentioned, and the methods will be listed in order of increasing difficulty of getting this information.

The methods will be illustrated by a running example concerning a husband and wife who are trying to decide where to go on a two-week vacation [also used by Carrie Menkel-Meadow in her article on legal problem solving in Chapter 1]. The husband wants to go to the mountains, his wife to the seashore. They have considered the compromise of spending one week in each location but are hoping for something better. What approach should they take?

Expanding the Pie

Some conflicts hinge on a resource shortage. For example, time, money, space, and automobiles are in short supply but long demand. In such circumstances, integrative agreements can be devised by increasing the available resources. This is called expanding the pie. For example, our married couple might solve their problems by persuading their employers to give them four weeks of vacation so that they can take two in the mountains and two at the seashore. Another example (cited by Follett in 1940) is that of two milk companies vying to be first to unload cans on a platform. The controversy was resolved when somebody thought of widening the platform.

Expanding the pie is a useful formula when the parties reject one another's demands because of opportunity costs; for example, if the husband rejects the seashore because it keeps him away from the mountains and the wife rejects the mountains because they deny her the pleasure of the seashore. But it is by no means a universal remedy. Expanding the pie may yield strikingly poor benefits if there are inherent costs in the other's proposal, e.g., the husband cannot stand the seashore or the wife the mountains. Other methods are better in such cases.

Expanding the pie requires no analysis of the interests underlying the parties' demands. Hence its information requirements are slim. However, this does not mean that a solution by this method is always easy to find. There may be no resource shortage, or the shortage may not be easy to see or to remedy.

Refocusing questions that can be useful in seeking a solution by pie expansion include: How can both parties get what they want? Does the conflict hinge on a resource shortage? How can the critical resource be expanded?

Nonspecific Compensation

In nonspecific compensation, one party gets what he or she wants and the other is repaid in some unrelated coin. Compensation is nonspecific if it does not deal with the precise costs incurred by the other party. For example, the wife in our example might agree to go to the mountains, even though she finds them boring, if her husband promises her a fur coat. Another example would be giving an employee a bonus for going without dinner.

Compensation usually comes from the party whose demands are granted. But it can also originate with a third party or even with the party who is compensated. An example of the latter would be an employee who pampers him- or herself by finding a nice office to work in while going without dinner.

Two kinds of information are useful for devising a solution by nonspecific compensation: (a) information about what is valuable to the other party; for example, knowledge that he or she values love, attention, or money; (b) information about how badly the other party is hurting by making concessions. This is useful for devising adequate compensation for these concessions. If such information is not available, it may be possible to conduct an "auction" for the other party's acquiescence, changing the sort of benefit offered or raising one's offer, in trial-and-error fashion, until an acceptable formula is found.

Refocusing questions that can help locate a means of compensation include: How much is the other party hurting in conceding to me? What does the other party value that I can supply? How valuable is this to the other party?

Logrolling

Logrolling is possible in complex agendas where several issues are under consideration and the parties have differing priorities among these issues. Each party concedes on low priority issues in exchange for concessions on issues of higher priority to itself. Each gets that part of its demands that it finds most important. For example, suppose that in addition to disagreeing about where to go on vacation, the wife in our example wants to go to a first-class hotel while her husband prefers a tourist home. If accommodations are a high priority issue for the wife and location for the husband, they can reach a fairly integrative solution by agreeing to go to a first-class hotel in the mountains. Logrolling can be viewed as a variant of nonspecific compensation in which both parties instead of one are compensated for making concessions desired by the other.

To develop solutions by logrolling, it is useful to have information about the two parties' priorities so that exchangeable concessions can be identified. But it is not necessary to have information about the interests (e.g., the aspirations, values) underlying these priorities. Solutions by logrolling can also be developed by a process of trial and error in which one party moves systematically through a series of possible packages, keeping his or her own outcomes as high as possible, until an alternative is found that is acceptable to the other party.

Refocusing questions that can be useful for developing solutions by logrolling include: Which issues are of higher and lower priority to myself? Which issues are of higher and lower priority to the other party? Are some of my high-priority issues of low priority to the other party and vice versa?

Cost Cutting

In solutions by cost cutting, one party gets what he or she wants and the other's costs are reduced or eliminated. The result is high joint benefit, not because the first party has changed his or her demands but because the second party suffers less. For instance, suppose that the husband in our example dislikes the beach because of the hustle and bustle. He may be quite willing to go there on vacation if his costs are cut by renting a house with a quiet inner courtyard where he can read while his wife goes out among the crowds.

Cost cutting often takes the form of specific compensation in which the party who concedes receives something in return that satisfies the precise values frustrated. For example, the employee who must work through dinner time can be specifically compensated by provision of a meal in a box. Specific compensation differs from nonspecific compensation in dealing with the precise costs incurred rather than providing repayment in an unrelated coin. The costs are actually canceled out rather than overbalanced by benefits experienced in some other realm.

Information about the nature of one of the parties' costs is, of course, helpful for developing solutions by cost cutting. This is a deeper kind of information than knowledge of that party's priorities. It involves knowing something about the interests — the values, aspirations, and standards — underlying that party's overt position.

Refocusing questions for developing solutions by cost cutting include: What costs are posed for the other party by our proposal? How can these costs be mitigated or eliminated?

Bridging

In bridging, neither party achieves its initial demands but a new option is devised that satisfies the most important interests underlying these demands. For example, suppose that the husband in our vacation example is mainly interested in fishing and hunting and the wife in swimming and sunbathing. Their interests might be bridged by finding an inland resort with a lake and a beach that is close to woods and streams. . . .

Bridging typically involves a reformulation of the issue(s) based on an analysis of the underlying interests on both sides. For example, a critical turning point in our vacation example is likely to come when the initial formulation, "Shall we go to the mountains or the seashore?" is replaced by "Where can we find fishing, hunting, swimming, and sunbathing?" . . . This new formulation can be done by either or both parties or by a third party who is trying to help.

People who seek to develop solutions by bridging need information about the nature of the two parties' interests and their priorities among these interests. . . . More often, higher-priority interests are served while lower-priority interests are discarded. For example, the wife who agrees to go to an inland lake may have forgone the lesser value of smelling the sea air and the husband may have forgone his preference for spectacular mountain vistas.

In the initial phase of search for a solution by bridging, the search model can include all of the interests on both sides. But if this does not generate a mutually acceptable alternative, some of the lower-priority interests must be discarded from the model and the search begun anew. The result will not be an ideal solution but, it is hoped, one that is mutually acceptable. Dropping low-priority interests in the development of a solution by bridging is similar to dropping low-priority demands in the search for a solution by logrolling. However, the latter is in the realm of concrete proposals, while the former is in the realm of the interests underlying these proposals.

Refocusing questions that can be useful in seeking a solution by bridging include: What are the two parties' basic interests? What are their priorities among these interests? How can the two sets of high priority interests be reconciled?

Notes and Questions

5.30 Pruitt spends much time outlining the questions to ask for each type of creative solution. Note that these questions need to be asked *both* of your client *and* the other side to be successful. Note also that these questions can productively be asked by either the attorney representative or the mediator.

5.31 Another example of nonspecific compensation is provided by Leigh Thompson: Phil Jones, managing director of Real Time, the London-based interactive design studio, recalls an instance where he used nonspecific compensation in his negotiations. The problem was that his client, a Formula 1 motor-racing team, wanted to launch Internet Web sites but did not have the budget to pay him. However, in Jones's eyes, the client was high profile and had creative, challenging projects that Real Time wanted to get involved with. Formula 1 came up with a nonspecific compensation offer to make the deal go through: tickets to some of the major Formula 1 meetings. It worked. Says Jones: "The tickets are like gold dust . . . and can be used as a pat on the back for staff or as an opportunity to pamper existing clients or woo new ones." Leigh Thompson, The Mind and Heart of the Negotiator 163-164 (3d ed. 2005).

5.32 There once was a law student with chronic medical problems. Unfortunately, she was also uninsured. The good news was that she was a fabulous cook. The first time she saw the doctor she explained her financial situation. She was able to work out with her doctor a payment plan for services over time. Using Pruitt's terminology from the preceding excerpt, what kind of solution is this?

After they negotiated the first time, she delivered a chocolate chip cheesecake to the doctor in appreciation for his understanding. The next time she needed the doctor, the doctor requested payment in cheesecakes! What kind of solution is this?

5.33 Many authors use Mary Parker Follett's example of the library window as the classic integrative solution. You may recall the story from Chapter 1 that one library patron wants fresh air while the other does not want the wind blowing her papers around. The solution is to open the window in the next room. As a modern-day update, in the movie *A Beautiful Mind*, there is a somewhat similar scene in which the students in Professor Nash's class want the window open for fresh air. Professor Nash wants the window closed because the construction crew outside is making too much noise for him to be heard giving his lecture. In the movie, the future Alicia Nash leans out the window and asks the construction crew if they could take a break during class. Both professor and students are happy with the open window on a quiet campus. What type of solution is this?

5.34 Despite the obvious benefits of creative development of new possibilities, there may be some downside to too much creativity. Chris Guthrie writes that the creation of too many options may actually hinder clear decision making based on four phenomena:

> The first phenomenon [*option devaluation*] arises when a choice set grows from one option to two or more options. When a choice set expands from the original option under consideration to more than one option, negotiators tend to devalue the initial option. . . . The second phenomenon [*context dependence*] arises when a choice set consisting of two or more options grows by one. . . . [N]egotiators tend to reconsider their relative ranking of the options already under consideration even when the additional option sheds no new light on those options. Negotiators do *not*, in other words, make context-*in*dependent decisions. . . . The third phenomenon [*partial decision making*] arises when a choice set grows to include a large number of options. . . . [N]egotiators tend to abandon compensatory decision-making strategies that take all options and attributes into account in favor of simplified decision strategies that consider only some of the available information. . . . The fourth and final phenomenon [*decision regret*] arises after the decision has been made . . . [when] negotiators tend to feel greater regret when they have selected one option over another than when they have simply selected the sole available option.
>
> Although the prescriptive literature on negotiation is certainly correct that option generation offers potential benefits to negotiators, the four phenomena identified above . . . suggest that option generation poses potential costs as well. Negotiators who generate multiple options may be induced by the very availability of those options to make decisions that run contrary to their true preferences and that induce negative post-decision emotions.

Chris Guthrie, Panacea or Pandora's Box: The Costs of Options in Negotiation, 88 Iowa L. Rev. 601, 607-608 (2003). What do you think about Professor Guthrie's perspective on option creation? How can lawyers help their clients avoid these pitfalls?

5. Using Objective Criteria

This next excerpt focuses on the importance of objective criteria. There comes a point in any negotiation or mediation when decisions must be made about accepting or rejecting proposed agreement terms. Objective indicia of a choice being rational allows for face saving and generates movement at such critical junctures. In Chapter 2, we read excerpts from *Getting to YES* that outlined the major premises of principled negotiation. One of these is that agreements be based on outside legitimate standards. This excerpt explains this concept further.

   Roger Fisher, William Ury & Bruce Patton, GETTING TO YES

85-88 (1991)

DEVELOPING OBJECTIVE CRITERIA

Carrying on a principled negotiation involves two questions: How do you develop objective criteria, and how do you use them in negotiating?

Whatever method of negotiation you use, you will do better if you prepare in advance. This certainly holds true of principled negotiation. So develop some alternative standards beforehand and think through their application to your case.

Fair Standards

You will usually find more than one objective criterion available as a basis for agreement. Suppose, for example, your car is demolished and you file a claim with an insurance company. In your discussion with the adjuster, you might take into account such measures of the car's value as (1) the original cost of the car less depreciation; (2) what the car could have been sold for; (3) the standard "blue book" value for a car of that year and model; (4) what it would cost to replace the car with a comparable one; and (5) what a court might award as the value of the car. . . .

At a minimum, objective criteria need to be independent of each side's will. Ideally, to assure a wise agreement, objective criteria should be not only independent of will but also both legitimate and practical. In a boundary dispute, for example, you may find it easier to agree on a physically salient feature such as a river than on a line three yards to the east of the riverbank. . . .

Fair Procedures

To produce an outcome independent of will, you can use either fair standards for the substantive question or for example, the age-old way to divide a piece of cake between two children: one cuts and the other chooses. Neither can complain about an unfair division. . . .

As you consider procedural solutions, look at other basic means of settling differences: taking turns, drawing lots, letting someone else decide, and so on.

Frequently, taking turns presents the best way for heirs to divide a large number of heirlooms left to them collectively. Afterwards, they can do some trading if they want. Or they can make the selection tentative so they see how it comes out before committing themselves to accept it. Drawing lots, flipping a coin, and other forms of chance have an inherent fairness. The results may be unequal, but each side had an equal opportunity. . . .

NEGOTIATING WITH OBJECTIVE CRITERIA

Having identified some objective criteria and procedures, how do you go about discussing them with the other side?

There are three basic points to remember:

- Frame each issue as a joint search for objective criteria.
- Reason and be open to reason as to which standards are most appropriate and how they should be applied.
- Never yield to pressure, only to principle.

Notes and Questions

5.35 The use of objective criteria is often given as one of the most powerful tools of principled negotiation. Why do you think this is so?

5.36 How can you use objective criteria against a hard bargainer to avoid being taken advantage of?

5.37 If you are trying to settle a case for medical malpractice, what objective criteria could you look to? How would you find these?

6. Using Decision Tree Analysis

The next excerpt discusses decision analysis as a tool for preparing both your goals and your BATNA in a negotiation and for making decisions at the end of the negotiation or mediation as to whether the offer is adequate. Jeffrey Senger, senior counsel in the Office of Dispute Resolution for the U.S. Department of Justice, examines how decision analysis works.

 Jeffrey M. Senger, **DECISION ANALYSIS IN NEGOTIATION**

87 Marq. L. Rev. 721-725 (2004)

Imagine a United States President facing a decision on whether to attempt a military mission to rescue Americans trapped in a hostile country. In a meeting in the White House Situation Room, top military advisers describe a possible plan. The President asks about the chances of success for the mission. The advisers respond that there are six crucial stages of the plan, and all have to go smoothly in order for the mission to work. They state that the overall chances for the plan are good because each individual stage has an eighty percent chance of success. What should the President do?

A field known as "decision analysis" can help answer this type of question and many others in a wide range of situations. When parties understand what their chances of success are for each of several possible choices, they can make better decisions on how to proceed. The tools of decision analysis are particularly useful for negotiators. People who are negotiating need to be able to evaluate what is likely to happen to them if they accept a deal and what will occur if they do not.

In the rescue example above, it is easy to see how a President might be tempted to authorize the plan. If the chances of success at each stage of a mission are eighty percent, it may seem that the chances of success for the overall mission would be reasonably good. However, decision analysis shows that the mission is much more likely to fail than succeed. The statistical method used to calculate the overall likelihood of success in this situation requires multiplying the chances of success of each individual stage. Thus the President should multiply 0.80 (the chance of succeeding in the first stage) by 0.80 (the chance of the second stage), then multiply this result by 0.80 for the third stage, and so on, all the way through the six stages of the mission. This total, $0.80 \times 0.80 \times 0.80 \times 0.80 \times 0.80 \times 0.80$, (or 0.80 to the sixth power), is 0.28. Thus, the overall chances of success for the mission are only twenty-eight percent, or slightly better than one in four.

I. EXAMPLES OF DECISION ANALYSIS

The mathematical processes used in risk analysis may be explained further with several examples. Imagine going to a local carnival and approaching a midway booth with a giant "Wheel of Chance." The wheel has many spaces on it, half colored blue and half yellow. The carnival operator tells you that if you spin and the wheel lands on a blue space, you will win $20.[3] If it lands on a yellow space, you win nothing. How much would you pay to play this game?

Many people can answer this question intuitively, without having to use a mathematical approach. However, following the math in this example can be helpful to understanding what happens in more complicated situations. Decision analysis principles state that the expected outcome of a situation like this is found by multiplying the probabilities of each possible outcome by the result of that outcome (called the payoff), and then summing these products. In the Wheel of Chance example, the probability of landing on blue is 0.50, and the payoff for landing on blue is $20. Multiplying these numbers yields $10. The probability of landing on yellow is 0.50, the payoff for this is $0, and multiplying these numbers yields $0. Adding these two results, $10 plus $0, gives the expected result of the game: $10.

[The following figure] shows a graphical representation of this situation, which is a simple example of a "decision tree."[4] The trunk of the tree (entitled "Wheel of Chance") breaks off into two branches, representing the two possible outcomes of the game, blue or yellow. This juncture is marked with a circle (called a "chance node"), indicating that the results at this point cannot be controlled. The probabilities

---

[3] Assume for purposes of the example that the carnival operator has not rigged the wheel to give an unfair result.

[4] Technically, this figure would be called a "chance tree" or an "event tree," as a decision tree would include another branch to indicate the option not to play the game at all.

of each outcome (0.50) are written below each branch. Each branch ends in a triangle (called a "terminal node"), indicating that the game is over at that point, with payoffs of $20 for blue and $0 for yellow. A computer can be used to "roll back" the tree, which gives the expected value of the tree at the chance node. The box next to the chance node in the figure shows the expected value of $10.

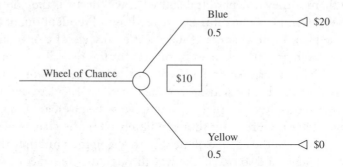

It is worth noting that $10 is not a possible outcome from playing a single game (which yields either $20 or $0). Instead, it is a mathematical construct providing a sense of what the game is worth, in a theoretical sense, to someone who plays it. One way of explaining this is that the expected value represents the average payoff for someone who played the game many times.

Notes and Questions

5.38   What is the minimum you would advise your client to accept as a settlement if, having taken all factors into account, you think you have a 60 percent chance of winning $150,000 and a 40 percent chance of losing (and obtaining nothing)? (Ignore any adjustment for time value of money or costs of disputing.)

5.39   What is the minimum you would advise your client to accept if you think you have a 10 percent chance of winning $1 million in punitive and actual damages, and a 50 percent chance of winning $150,000 in actual damages, and a 40 percent chance of losing (obtaining nothing)? (Ignore any adjustment for time value of money or costs of disputing.) See also Gregory Todd Jones & Douglas H. Yarn, Evaluative Dispute Resolution Under Uncertainty: An Empirical Look at Bayes' Theorem and the Expected Value of Perfect Information, 2003 Journal of Dispute Res. 427 (2003) for another approach to thinking about evaluating information in mediations or negotiations under conditions of imperfect knowledge.

B. REPRESENTATIONAL SKILLS IN MEDIATION

If lawyers are not leaders in marshaling cooperation and designing mechanisms that allow it to flourish, they will not be at the center of the most creative social experiments of our time.

—Derek Bok, former president of Harvard University

The sections above examine negotiation skills generally. Now place yourself in the context of an attorney representing a client in mediation. What else do you need to know to perform effectively?

Larry Watson, a former litigator and seasoned mediator of civil trial cases, highlights how attorneys should treat mediation differently from litigation. His advice provides practical guidance for attorneys representing clients in mediations.

 Lawrence M. Watson, Jr., EFFECTIVE ADVOCACY IN MEDIATION: A PLANNING GUIDE TO PREPARE FOR A CIVIL TRIAL MEDIATION

originally published at *http://www.uww-adr.com/2002/pdfs/ effectiveadvocacy.pdf*

... With the expansion of mediation as the leading ADR process, it is clear that the civil trial counsel's role must thus also expand to include proficiency in reaching acceptable mediated settlements for their clients. The growth of ADR is redefining the role of the American trial lawyer. . . .

STEP ONE: PREPARING THE CLIENT FOR THE MEDIATION EXPERIENCE

It is critically important to have the clients understand that the outcome of the mediation process contemplates "win-win," not "win-lose." Mediation is a process that seeks to *reconcile* disputes. Mediation is not a process that seeks to *adjudicate* disputes. The outcome of reconciliation is an *agreement* with the other side. The outcome of adjudication is a *judgment* against the other side. There are big differences between the two. . . .

Clients should therefore understand that the mediation program does not dwell on who may be proven right or wrong in court — it is a factor, but not a controlling factor. To be successful at mediation, the client must understand the focus must ultimately come to mutually satisfying the interests of all parties to the dispute. Simply stated, the process involves compromise — giving as well as getting. . . .

Bear in mind, one salient difference between resolving disputes through adjudication and resolving disputes through reconciliation is the range of settlement options available to the parties. With the exception of some limited equitable relief that might [be] available in some cases, the judicial resolution of a dispute will be restricted to money judgments. An important benefit offered to parties agreeing to reconcile their differences is the broad range of settlement options that can be deployed. Thinking through and developing contingent plans to utilize these options in advance, doing feasibility research on settlement alternatives before the mediation starts, can dramatically increase the potential for a successful outcome.

While overall objectives and various settlement scenarios should thus be generally discussed in advance, the purpose is to chart a path for preparation and agree in advance as to the ultimate interests that should be addressed. The client's focus should be to offset dollar amounts necessary to settle, and on what is really needed to advance legitimate interests. . . .

STEP TWO: DEFINING THE OVERALL GOALS OF MEDIATION

The first step of any journey is to decide where you want to go. In a civil trial mediation, that step is taken by simply sitting down with the client and mutually agreeing, in concept, on a range of acceptable outcomes to the mediation process. As noted above, every effort should be made to avoid "bottom line" dollar amount absolutes. To the contrary the client should be impressed and thinking about the wide range of objectives which could become available through a well-structured and prepared mediation session. . . .

STEP THREE: DECIDING WHEN, WHERE, WHO AND HOW WE WILL MEDIATE THIS CASE

Although a bit dated, an attitude still exists among many trial lawyers (and litigation clients) that being the first one to suggest mediation — or any settlement process — is a sign of weakness to be avoided. A "macho mind set" about the case would suggest that even discussing reconciliation signals a lack of confidence in the merits of one's position, and involves an immediate loss of face. There are a number of ways to get past this problem.

In jurisdictions where mediation is mandatory, the problem can be avoided by simply noting that going to mediation is an inevitable circumstance and both sides would be better off attempting to take the initiative to control the process. The argument that both parties are better served by deciding on a mutually agreeable mediator, picking a time and location of their choosing, and defining the format for the process themselves rather than allowing the judge or a court administrator to do it for them is compelling. . . .

Another approach is to attribute the idea to the economics. Once a litigation plan is roughly sketched, it is natural for both sides to note the costs involved in legal fees and expenses.

A.   Selection of the Mediator . . .

In preparing the initial list, or in making the final selection from the list, it is wise to take the time to complete some level of research on each mediator under consideration. Ask the mediators under consideration to submit resumes and, more importantly, the names of other counsel with whom they have worked in the past. Contact those lawyers and ask about the proposed mediator's style, energy, creativity and success rate. Network with other lawyers in your own firm or in the field to see if they have had any experience with the proposed mediator as well. Prepare a short report on each and include the client in the final determination. In particularly significant cases where the proposed mediators are unknown, arrange for a short interview session to meet with the proposed mediators in advance. Again, including the client in those sessions will go a long way to help determine the best person for the job.

The overall goal in selecting the mediator should be to find an individual who can truly serve as a neutral, who demonstrates a capacity to work hard, and who will command the respect of both sides.

B. Location, Duration and Timing

The choice of location for a mediation session should be driven solely by the physical requirements necessary to stage the event. Appropriate considerations would thus include reasonable travel accessibility, ample room for attendees in joint and caucus sessions, adequate secured storage space for files and materials, overnight lodging opportunities and some separation from other distractions. Choice of location should never be allowed to become a positional issue involving a "home court" advantage of one party or another.

The duration and timing for a mediation is, perhaps, more important than the location. Sufficient time should be allotted for a mediation to allow for adequate presentations by all parties followed by ample time to privately caucus and develop alternative resolution options. Obviously, the number of parties, complexity of issues, and dollar amounts involved will play into defining an appropriate time to reserve for the mediation. The decision-making temperament of the parties — the amount of time the individuals involved in the dispute will need to make up their minds — is also an important factor in scheduling mediations. Creating situations in which the parties are rushed to judgment, or forced to endure exhausting marathon sessions into the late hours of the night can compromise the validity of the agreement reached. Scheduling or conducting a mediation in a manner that adversely affects the parties' self determination is tantamount to abusing the process. "Mediation remorse" should be carefully avoided. . . .

PREPARATION FOR MEDIATION

The presentation of the client's case in the opening phase of a mediation is a task that must meet two, often conflicting, needs.

First, the client must feel his or her story has been told. Any anger, frustration, and discontent stemming from the events leading to the dispute must be relieved before focused attention can be given to reconciliation considerations. To one extent or another, therefore, the client must be given the chance to vent. In all occasions, the client must feel that the merits of . . . his or her position in the debate have been fairly presented and understood.

Secondly (and often in contradiction of satisfying the client's "venting" needs) there is a need for the opening presentations to clearly and effectively communicate the "other side of the story" to the opposition. Many clients to a dispute might be quite pleased with a lawyer that relieves built up feelings and relates their positions in ominous, scolding, or even threatening terms. An overly aggressive tone or demeanor to an opening presentation in a mediation, however, can serve to "turn off" the opposition and the critical task of expanding their understanding of the dispute is not achieved. . . .

One acceptable method of satisfying both needs is to simply allow the client an opportunity to participate in the opening presentations to satisfy whatever venting needs exist. In that event, counsel would prepare and execute an opening presentation geared toward communicating the reality of the dispute to the opposition in a tone and manner best suited to complete that task. The client could then add the emotive element to the presentation while satisfying his or her need to vent.

Accordingly, the best overall theme and tone of opening presentation in mediation would probably be a matter of fact description of the case to be presented at trial — firmly and unequivocally stated. It should clearly set forth the principal contentions underlying the position asserted, and the facts, principal documents, and expert opinions that support those contentions. There should be minimal argument — let the facts do the arguing. . . .

SOMETHING OTHER THAN MONEY — PREPARING SETTLEMENT OPTIONS

. . . In commercial cases, a systematic search for settlement options other than money should be conducted before the mediation commences. . . . If there is any way to convert a business dispute to a business opportunity, careful consideration should be given to that option in advance. The objective of any advance consideration of "other than money" settlement options is to make sure that they are potentially doable — that there are no legal, contractual, political or physical barriers to including such terms to the final agreement. The ultimate decision whether or not to include these terms in a final arrangement can be made later. The settlement negotiations themselves should be entered with an "anything is possible" frame of mind. . . .

Notes and Questions

5.40 Note that Watson views "venting" as necessary to help clients move to constructing settlement terms. Robert Baruch Bush and Joseph Folger, proponents of transformative mediation, see self-expression as central to empowerment and recognition. In Chapter 6, Lela Love urges mediators to extract constructive components (interests, issues, proposals, feelings, values, principles, BATNAs) from party exchanges. Gary Friedman and Jack Himmelstein underscore the importance of understanding parties. Contrast this advice with the practice of many attorneys representing clients in mediation who advise their client not to speak at all. Do you think that is wise? Why would an attorney want to silence the client and be the sole spokesperson?

5.41 One of the difficulties of other-than-money settlements can be the impact on fees. If the lawyer's fee is based on a percentage of the settlement, then lawyers have an incentive to maximize settlement dollars. An apology, for example, provides no tangible benefit to a lawyer who is paid on a contingency fee. How might lawyers deal with this potential conflict of interest?

Assuming an attorney develops a mental chart that includes perspectives relevant to both mediative and adjudicatory approaches, as Len Riskin suggests, and has strategies specific to the mediation process, as Larry Watson proposes, how can an attorney maximize benefits for her clients in mediation?

Harold Abramson provides attorneys with a formula for representing clients in mediation. This formula calls on attorneys to adopt a problem-solving mode as they operate in a mediation context and to make use of the mediator to advance their client's interests.

Harold I. Abramson, **MEDIATION REPRESENTATION: ADVOCATING IN A CREATIVE PROBLEM-SOLVING PROCESS**

1-4 (2004)

The mediation process is indisputably different from other dispute resolution processes. Therefore, the strategies and techniques that have proven so effective in settlement conferences, arbitrations, and judicial trials do not work optimally in mediation. You need a different representation approach, one tailored to realize the full benefits of this burgeoning and increasingly preferred forum for resolving disputes. Instead of advocating as a zealous adversary, you should advocate as a zealous problem-solver. . . .

[Mediation] offers you access to a neutral third party, a mediator, who is likely to be trained in facilitating problem-solving negotiations. The mediator's sole purpose is to assist the disputing clients and their attorneys in resolving the dispute. . . . The mediator knows how to structure a process that can provide your client and the other side an opportunity to fashion enduring and, when at all feasible, inventive solutions. The mediator knows how to involve clients constructively and to use various dispute resolution techniques at propitious moments in the mediation session.

The familiar adversarial strategy of presenting the strongest partisan arguments and aggressively attacking the other side's case may be effective in court where each side is trying to convince a judge to make a favorable decision. But, in mediation, there is no third-party decision-maker, only a third-party facilitator. The third party is not even the primary audience. The primary audience is the other side, who is surely not neutral and can often be quite hostile. In this different representational setting, the adversarial approach is less effective if not self-defeating. . . .

[Following a problem-solving] representation approach . . . you do more than just try to settle the dispute. You creatively search for solutions that go beyond the traditional ones based on rights, obligations, and precedent. Rather than settling for win-lose outcomes, you search for solutions that can benefit both sides. To creatively problem-solve in mediation, you develop a collaborative relationship with the other side and the mediator, and participate throughout the mediation process in a way that is likely to result in solutions that are enduring as well as inventive. Solutions are likely to be enduring because both sides work together to fashion

> **The Mediation Representation Formula**
>
> The problem-solving approach can be encapsulated in a succinct mediation representation formula:
>
> In mediation, you should negotiate using a *creative problem-solving approach* to achieve the two goals of meeting your client's *interests* and overcoming any *impediments* to settlement. Your negotiation strategy should take specific advantage of the *presence of a mediator* at each of the six *key junctures* in the mediation process. [The six key junctures identified by Abramson are: selecting a mediator, preparing pre-mediation submissions, participating in a pre-mediation conference, presenting opening statements, participating in joint sessions, and participating in caucuses.]
>
> Abramson, Mediation Representation 7 (2004).

nuanced solutions that each side fully understands, can live with, and knows how to implement. Solutions are likely to be inventive because you advocate your client's interests instead of legal positions; use suitable techniques for overcoming impediments; search expansively for multiple options; and evaluate and package options imaginatively to meet the various interests of all parties. And solutions are likely to be found because you advocated as a creative problem-solver.

In this pitch for a problem-solving approach, I do not blindly claim that it is the only one that results in settlements. Attorneys frequently cite success stories when they use unvarnished adversarial tactics or a hybrid of adversarial and problem-solving strategies. The hybrid supporters claim that the best approach is a flexible one, a philosophy that surely is advisable in life as well as in legal negotiations. But, flexibility should not be confused with inconsistency. Shifting between adversarial and problem-solving tactics during the course of mediation can undercut the problem-solving approach. A consistent adherence to problem-solving will more likely produce the best results for clients.

Notes and Questions

5.42 Does Abramson's approach depend on the willingness of the other side to engage in problem solving? Can an attorney be committed in the mediation forum to problem solving regardless of the posture of the other side?

5.43 The advice from Larry Watson and Harold Abramson is that attorneys should have a constructive, collaborative approach in mediation. What pressures and considerations might argue for a competitive, adversarial orientation? For some advice about how to use or even "manipulate" a mediator, see Dwight Golann, How to Borrow a Mediator's Powers, 30 Litigation 41 (Spring, 2004). Consider the adversarial tactics suggested by Meltsner and Schrag in Chapter 2. Can you imagine how some of these tactics could be adapted for use in mediation? What can a mediator do, if anything, about their use?

In the next excerpt, Jean Sternlight suggests a case-by-case approach to attorney strategy for representation in mediation, particularly sensitive to barriers to negotiation (barriers were discussed at the end of Chapter 2). Sternlight's nuanced approach in this excerpt provides examples of the problem-solving orientation that Abramson calls for above.

 Jean R. Sternlight, **LAWYERS' REPRESENTATION OF CLIENTS IN MEDIATION: USING ECONOMICS AND PSYCHOLOGY TO STRUCTURE ADVOCACY IN A NONADVERSARIAL SETTING**

14 Ohio St. J. on Disp. Resol. 269, 274, 291-292, 295-296, 354-360, 365 (1999)

. . . While no single lawyer's role in mediation is always proper, lawyers need to be particularly vigilant in guarding against their own tendencies to behave in mediation exactly as they would in litigation. Instead, to serve their clients' interests, and in light of the conflicts of interest and perception between lawyers and their own clients, attorneys should often encourage their clients to play an active role in the mediation, allow the discussion to focus on emotional as well as legal concerns, and work toward mutually beneficial rather than win-or-lose solutions. Those lawyers who, seeking to advocate strongly on behalf of their clients, take steps to dominate the mediation, focus exclusively on legal issues, and minimize their clients' direct participation, will often ill serve their clients' true needs and interests. Such overly zealous advocates are frequently poor advocates. . . .

If advocacy is defined broadly as supporting or pleading the cause of another, there is no inconsistency between advocacy and mediation. Permitting an attorney to act as an advocate for her client simply allows that attorney to speak and make arguments on her client's behalf and to help her client achieve her goals. . . . Nor is it clear why "adversarial" behavior, at least broadly defined, is necessarily inconsistent with mediation. To the extent that acting adversarially means advocating only on behalf of one's own client and not on behalf of any other party or on behalf of the process or system, the conduct is easy to reconcile with mediation. The problem-solving that works well in mediation does not require sacrifice of one's self-interest, but rather allows parties to search for solutions that are mutually beneficial.

Yet, while attorneys may appropriately advocate for their clients in mediation, it is certainly true that those attorneys who attempt to employ traditional "zealous" litigation tools when representing their clients in mediation may frequently (but not always) fail either to fulfill their clients' wishes or to serve their clients' interests. Those who would hoard information, rely solely on legal rather than emotional arguments, or refuse to let their clients speak freely will often have little success in mediation. This is not because attorneys ought not to advocate for their clients, but rather because attorneys ought not to advocate poorly on behalf of their clients. . . .

PROPOSED GUIDELINES FOR DETERMINING THE RESPECTIVE ROLES OF LAWYER AND CLIENT

While a lawyer should consult with her client in determining how best to divide mediation responsibilities, the lawyer should still play a key role in helping the client to make this decision. As the lawyer does in other contexts, she should facilitate the client's choice by helping to lay out the advantages and disadvantages of various options. . . . To aid attorneys in this endeavor, . . . attorneys [should] ask themselves the following two interrelated questions to help determine how to divide mediation responsibilities: (1) who is this particular client and (2) what barriers seem to be preventing the case from settling.

1.   Who Is This Client?

Attorneys should not assume that all clients are the same, but rather should focus on the potential differences between clients. Nor should they assume that all clients involved in a particular kind of lawsuit — e.g., personal injury, commercial, or employment termination — have the same concerns. They should instead try to determine not only the clients' goals and interests but also the clients' capabilities and even to some degree the clients' psychological makeup. They should recognize that clients and their attorneys often have very different incentives and psychologies.

a. Is This a Client Who Would Benefit from Playing an Active Role in the Mediation?

An attorney preparing to represent a client in a mediation should consider not only how the client's participation is likely to affect the value of the case, but also what benefits the mediation might potentially provide to the client. In doing so, attorneys will find it useful to think in terms of the possible economic and psychological barriers to negotiation and also to consider the many potential conflicts of interest between attorneys and their clients.

Although attorneys often think about cases primarily in terms of likelihood of success on the merits and consequential dollar value, either in court or in a settlement, they should recognize that clients' interests are not necessarily so narrow. Sometimes the client's interests are such that she would benefit from playing an active role in the mediation, even assuming for the sake of argument that such participation might lower the dollar value of the case. For example, the client may have nonmonetary interests or psychological needs such that she seeks an opportunity to voice her concerns or sense of injury to the opposing attorney. Or, the client may feel a strong need to apologize to the opposing party. Alternatively, the client may seek to preserve her relationship with the opposing party. In these and many other situations, it may be beneficial for the client to be provided with extensive opportunities to speak and listen in the mediation, even when such behavior might not be desirable from a purely financial perspective.

b. Is This a Client Who Requires Protection by the Attorney?

The attorney should also attempt to determine whether, in the particular context of the mediation, the client would best be served by having the lawyer play a dominant role. Attorneys can potentially protect clients in a mediation both by speaking on their behalf and also, in terms of perception, by effectively standing between the client and the opposing party or attorney.

The attorney should ask herself whether this particular client would benefit by having the attorney speak for her. Is the client inarticulate? Shy? Prone to anger quickly in a context when such anger would be detrimental to the client's interests or wishes? Alternatively, is the client incapable of providing the analysis that is required? Is she likely to say things she later regrets or that jeopardize her case? Some clients may have some of these characteristics. Certainly, they are not shared by all clients.

As well, the attorney should ask herself whether the client would benefit by having the attorney protect her from the opposing party. Although, ideally, mediation should be an opportunity for clients to communicate directly with one another, sometimes such direct communication by clients or their attorneys may be undesirable. At one extreme, if the client has been subjected to domestic abuse by the opposing party, it may be not only emotionally distressing but also coercive and even unsafe for the victim to converse directly with her abuser. A victim of sexual harassment may similarly be unable to bargain as an equal with her harasser. Even in personal injury or commercial disputes, certain clients may be subject to browbeating or coercion by the opposing party or attorney. Where a client's attorney fears that direct confrontations would have such an impact, she should at least recommend setting up the mediation so as to minimize such problems. For example, the attorney might request that the parties break into caucus immediately, or the attorney might attempt to interrupt the opposing party's presentation or to prevent certain presentations from being made.

In answering these questions, the attorney should be sure to approach them separately. A client who is not good at speaking up for herself might well be perfectly capable of hearing directly from the opposing party or vice versa.

2.   What Are the Barriers to Negotiation?

Once having considered who the client is, an attorney can best analyze how to divide mediation responsibilities with her client by attempting to determine what, if any, barriers are preventing the case from settling in a way that would serve the client's interests. If a case goes to mediation, it is because the parties and their attorneys have not yet reached a mutually acceptable agreement. Why have they not? What has stopped them from predicting how a court would resolve the dispute and reaching the same solution on their own? Or, what has prevented them from reaching an even better solution than the one the court might impose? By focusing on the dispute in this fashion, clients and their attorneys will begin to see how they ought to divide their responsibilities so as to best overcome the barriers to a negotiated agreement. The following discussion organizes potential barriers to settlement in terms of which participant is the primary obstacle to settlement. To clarify the discussion, it uses the following nomenclature: the primary client is labeled "A," her lawyer "AL," her opponent "B," and her opponent's lawyer "BL." [Sternlight proceeds to examine barriers created by each type of participant and appropriate attorney responses. The analysis with respect to barriers created by the opposing party follows.]

i.   B Has Unrealistic Expectations Based on Lack of Information.   If B is blocking a fair settlement because she has unrealistically high expectations regarding her likelihood of success at trial, AL and A should attempt to convince B that B's expectations are overblown. Each may have a role to play, depending on the nature of the misinformation. For example, sometimes a party may refuse to settle because she believes the opposing party will be a terrible witness who will therefore lose big at trial. In this situation, it may be desirable to allow that supposedly terrible witness, A, to play a very active role in the mediation to disprove B's false belief. Alternatively, if B thinks she has a sure winner in terms of the law, it may be important to have AL make a lengthy legal presentation to convince B that she is being overly optimistic. Usually AL will be better suited than A to convince B that her case is problematic in terms of the law.

ii.   B Is Engaging in Strategic Behavior.   If B is blocking a settlement by engaging in strategic behavior, such as hoarding information or bluffing, then A and AL must attempt to convince B to engage in a more problem-solving approach that will allow for the possibility of creative and mutual gains. Roger Fisher, William Ury, and

Bruce Patton, in *Getting to YES*, have offered a series of practical suggestions on how one may convince her opponent to move from competitive to problem-solving negotiation. The gist of their advice is to attempt to move the discussion to the merits and to look behind mere positions to the underlying ideas. Either A or AL may be the person who is better situated to attempt to earn B's trust and convince B to change her orientation. Thus, A and AL should jointly consider which of them, or perhaps both, are most likely to be successful in such a venture and divide their responsibilities accordingly.

If, however, it appears impossible to convince B to approach the negotiation with a positive, problem-solving attitude, it may be necessary for AL to encourage her own client not to share too much information or case strategy. Where one party insists on behaving competitively and the other is attempting to cooperate, the cooperating party may be disadvantaged.

> *iii.   B Has Unmet Nonmonetary Goals.*   If B is blocking a fair settlement because she has nonmonetary goals that are not being met, A and AL should consider whether it is desirable and possible for them to attempt to meet these goals. For example, B may be greatly injured because A chose to sue her, and an apology or explanation might go a long way toward healing the rift. In this event, if A is willing to apologize, it is important that she and her attorney divide responsibilities so she can do so. Alternatively, it may be that B feels the need to really tell A off, face-to-face. If A and AL decide that this would not be too damaging to A, they should again divide responsibilities to provide B with this opportunity. Perhaps A and B were business partners, and perhaps B would like to renew or continue the relationship. If such a result has possible appeal to A, and assuming A would be more capable of working out such an arrangement than her attorney, it is critical that A be provided with the opportunity to play a very active role in the mediation....

[Sternlight goes on to examine how an attorney (AL) can constructively respond to barriers created by the opposing attorney (BL), her own client (A), and also to barriers that the attorney may be creating herself. She concludes:] Anyone who says they have a simple answer to the question of how lawyers and clients should divide their responsibilities in a mediation must be wrong. Either their answer is not simple or their answer is not right. The answer is complicated because the division of responsibilities should vary substantially depending upon who the client is, who the lawyer is, and what factors appear to be blocking a reasonable and fair settlement of the dispute....

Notes and Questions

5.44   In Chapter 2, you studied barriers to achieving good negotiation outcomes. Here you see how attorney advocates might use the mediation process itself to overcome barriers raised by the opposing client. How might an attorney use mediation to overcome unrealistic expectations of her own client? To encourage her client to engage in problem solving? To meet her client's non-monetary needs? How can an attorney ensure that she herself is not constructing a barrier to settlement? For example, Notes and Questions 5.41 discusses potential attorney-client conflicts·that can be created by the fee arrangement. Consider an attorney who has never argued before the Supreme Court, and a settlement will preclude that chance. How should such conflicts be resolved? For an analysis of the tensions between attorneys and clients, see Robert H. Mnookin, Scott R. Peppet & Andrew S. Tulumello, Beyond Winning at 75-76, 83-87, 90 (2000).

CALL THE LAW

How can lawyers assist their clients in maximizing the potential in the mediation process? The following is a list of contributions attorneys can make when called into mediation sessions.

✔ *Courtesy, cooperation and candor.* The attorney should have a respectful tone and be attentive to the other party as the intended recipient of communication, avoiding threats, insults and personal attacks.

✔ *Articulate client's interests, issues and proposals.* Acknowledge interests, perspectives and feelings of the other party. Admit obvious mistakes and apparent weaknesses. Address other side (rather than exclusively addressing mediator).

✔ *Listen to own client and reframe for other side when helpful.* Listen to the other side and reframe for client when helpful.

✔ *Level with client regarding BATNA, particularly the litigation alternative.* Do the math! How much will litigation really cost (in time, money and stress)? Use decision tree analysis.

✔ *Tell a compelling, moving story, using simple, clear language.* The client is the best speaker if the client is capable of speaking well. The attorney should encourage and support the client in speaking. Use visual aids (videos, charts) to make the client's story understandable and moving.

✔ *Highlight common interests.* Most parties share an interest in getting on with their lives, saving the costs of litigation, resolving the matter in a satisfactory way, and feeling respected.

✔ *Elicit and offer proposals responsive to interests of both parties.* Be creative and willing to move "outside the box."

✔ *Link objective criteria to support proposals.*

✔ *Articulate the strengths of your litigation case.* Acknowledge and analyze how vulnerabilities of each side impact the case.

✔ *Win-win result.* Use the goal of a "win-win" result to satisfy your client's interests, while encouraging the other side to move toward your client.

Lela P. Love, Training Materials (2004).

5.45 In the box above, Lela Love describes the attitudes and tasks of an effective attorney representative in mediation. As you examine these goals and behavioral targets, consider whether they are in accord with Harold Abramson's call for attorneys to employ a problem-solving (rather than adversarial) approach in mediation — an approach where the client stays in a central position in the process with the attorney serving in a critical support role. Based on Sternlight's excerpt and your own analysis, are there any recommendations that you might ignore in certain cases?

You now have advice about what you should do as an attorney in mediation; the following excerpt highlights things you should *not* do. Note how many of the errors that Arnold describes come from an attorney's mistaking mediation for an adjudicatory process.

 Tom Arnold, **20 COMMON ERRORS IN MEDIATION ADVOCACY**

13 Alternatives to High Cost Litig. 69, 69-71 (1995)

Trial lawyers who are unaccustomed to being mediation advocates often miss important arguments. Here are . . . common errors, and ways to correct them.

WRONG CLIENT IN THE ROOM

CEOs settle more cases than vice presidents, house counsel or other agents. Why? For one thing, they don't need to worry about criticism back at the office. Any lesser agent, even with explicit "authority," typically must please a constituency which was not a participant in the give and take of the mediation. That makes it hard to settle cases.

   A client's personality also can be a factor. A "Rambo," who is aggressive, critical, unforgiving, or self-righteous doesn't tend to be conciliatory. The best peace-makers show creativity, and tolerance for the mistakes of others. Of course, it also helps to know the subject. . . .

WRONG MEDIATOR IN THE ROOM

Some mediators are generous about lending their conference rooms but bring nothing to the table. Some of them determine their view of the case and urge the parties to accept that view without exploring likely win-win alternatives.

   The best mediators can work within a range of styles . . . on a continuum, from being totally facilitative, to offering an evaluation of the case. Ideally, mediators should fit the mediation style to the case and the parties before them, often moving from style to style as a mediation progresses. . . . It may not always be possible to know and evaluate a mediator and fit the choice of mediator to your case. But the wrong mediator may fail to get a settlement another mediator might have finessed.

OMITTING CLIENT PREPARATION

Lawyers should educate their clients about the process. Clients need to know the answers to the types of questions the mediator is likely to ask. At the same time, they need to understand that the other party (rather than the mediator) should be the focus of each side's presentation.

In addition, lawyers should interview clients about the client's and the adversary's "best alternative to negotiated agreement," and "worst alternative to negotiated agreement." . . . A party should accept any offer better than his perceived BATNA and reject any offer seen as worse than his perceived WATNA. So the BATNAs and WATNAs are critical frames of reference for accepting offers and for determining what offers to propose to the other parties. A weak or false understanding of either party's BATNA or WATNA obstructs settlements and begets bad settlements. Other topics to cover with the client: the difference between their interests and their legal positions; the variety of options that might settle the case; the strengths and weaknesses of their case; objective independent standards of evaluation; the importance of apology and empathy.

NOT LETTING A CLIENT OPEN FOR HERSELF

At least as often as not, letting the properly coached client do most, or even all, of the opening and tell the story in her own words works much better than lengthy openings by the lawyer.

ADDRESSING THE MEDIATOR INSTEAD OF THE OTHER SIDE

Most lawyers open the mediation with a statement directed at the mediator, comparable to opening statements to a judge or jury. Highly adversarial in tone, it overlooks the interests of the other side that gave rise to the dispute.

Why is this strategy a mistake? The "judge or jury" you should be trying to persuade in a mediation is not the mediator, but the adversary. If you want to make the other party sympathetic to your cause, don't hurt him. . . .

MAKING THE LAWYER THE CENTER OF THE PROCESS

Unless the client is highly unappealing or inarticulate, the client should be the center of the process. The company representative for the other side may not have attended depositions, so is unaware of the impact your client could have on a judge or jury if the mediation fails. People pay more attention to appealing plaintiffs, so show them off.

Prepare the client to speak and be spoken to by the mediator and the adversary. He should be able to explain why he feels the way he does, why he is or is not responsible, and why any damages he caused are great or only peanuts. But he should also extend empathy to the other party.

FAILURE TO USE ADVOCACY TOOLS EFFECTIVELY

You'll want to prepare your materials for maximum persuasive impact. Exhibits, charts, and copies of relevant cases or contracts with key phrases highlighted can be valuable visual aids. A 90-second video showing key witnesses in depositions making important admissions, followed by a readable size copy of an important document with some relevant language underlined, can pack a punch.

TIMING MISTAKES

Get and give critical discovery, but don't spend exorbitant time or sums in discovery and trial prep before seeking mediation.

Mediation can identify what's truly necessary discovery and avoid unnecessary discovery. One of my own war stories: With a mediation under way and both parties relying on their perception of the views of a certain vice president, I leaned over, picked up the phone, called the vice president, introduced myself as the mediator, and asked whether he could give us a deposition the following morning. "No," said he, "I've got a Board meeting at 10:00." "How about 7:30 A.M., with a one-hour limit?" I asked. "It really is pretty important that this decision not be delayed." The parties took the deposition and settled the case before the 10:00 board meeting.

FAILURE TO LISTEN TO THE OTHER SIDE

Many lawyers and clients seem incapable of giving open-minded attention to what the other side is saying. That could cost a settlement.

FAILURE TO IDENTIFY PERCEPTIONS AND MOTIVATIONS

Seek first to understand, only then to be understood. . . .

HURTING, HUMILIATING, THREATENING, OR COMMANDING

Don't poison the well from which you must drink to get a settlement. That means you don't hurt, humiliate or ridicule the other folks. Avoid pejoratives like "malingerer," "fraud," "cheat," "crook," or "liar." You can be strong on what your evidence will be and still be a decent human being.

All settlements are based upon trust to some degree. If you anger the other side, they won't trust you. This inhibits settlement.

The same can be said for threats, like a threat to get the other lawyer's license revoked for pursuing such a frivolous cause, or for his grossly inaccurate pleadings.

Ultimatums destroy the process, and destroy credibility. Yes, there is a time in mediation to walk out — whether or not you plan to return. But a series of ultimatums, or even one ultimatum, most often is very counterproductive.

FAILURE TO TRULY CLOSE

Unless parties have strong reasons to "sleep on" their agreement, to further evaluate the deal, or to check on possibly forgotten details, it is better to get some sort of enforceable contract written and signed before the parties separate. Too often, when left to think overnight and draft tomorrow, the parties think of new ideas that delay or prevent closing.

LACK OF PATIENCE AND PERSEVERANCE

The mediation "dance" takes time. Good mediation advocates have patience and perseverance.

MISUNDERSTANDING CONFLICT

A dispute is a problem to be solved together, not a combat to be won. To prepare for mediation, rehearse answers to the following questions, which the mediator is likely to ask:

- How do you feel about this dispute? Or about the other party?
- What do you really want in the resolution of this dispute?
- What are your expectations from a trial? Are they realistic?
- What are the weaknesses in your case?
- What law or fact in your case would you like to change?
- What scares you most?
- What would it feel like to be in your adversary's shoes?
- What specific evidence do you have to support each element of your case?
- What will the jury charge and interrogatories probably be?
- What is the probability of a verdict your way on liability?
- What is the range of damages you think a jury would return in his case if it found liability?
- What are the likely settlement structures, from among the following possibilities: terms, dollars, injunction, services, performance, product, recision, apology, costs, attorney fees, releases?
- What constituency pressures burden the other party? Which ones burden you?

As you just read, Tom Arnold encourages an approach that avoids hurting or humiliating the other side. There is considerable evidence that apologies can be very valuable, in dollar terms, to disputing parties (recall the barrier to negotiation in Chapter 2 of "justice seeking"). If this is true, it follows that attorneys may best serve their clients by encouraging civility, acknowledgment, and perhaps apology in mediation, where appropriate. What follows is the advice of a seasoned mediator, professor, and mediation trainer regarding civility, thoughtfulness, and apologies in mediation.

 Jeff Kichaven, **APOLOGY IN MEDIATION**

International Risk Management Institute (2003)

... [M]ediation provides an oasis in the litigation desert where [the] heart's hunger [for feeling important and appreciated] may yet be sated. There are hundreds of things you can do at a mediation to make others feel important and appreciated. Arrive on time. Bring the right people. Dress respectfully. Listen attentively. Apologize. But don't apologize in the conventional way.

Apologize in a way that admits no liability or fault. Self-flagellation is not required. Any sentence that begins with "I'm sorry" and continues with some recognition of the other side's human condition will do. It will be more than adequate to make the other side feel important and appreciated.

In a medical malpractice case, it might start out as, "I'm sorry the operation had a bad outcome."

In an employment case, "I'm sorry you have not yet found another job."

In any case, "I'm sorry this has reached the point where you felt it necessary to sue me. I did not intend you any suffering." What defendant, after all, is not sorry that he or she has been sued? Do we really intend that others suffer? This kind of apology is sincere, it acknowledges the plaintiff as a human being, it places everyone on a small tuft of common ground, and it sets the stage for tremendous progress in the conversation.

Where the opportunity for such an apology is missed, a mediation can end in disaster. Where the opportunity is seized, success is still not guaranteed, but the chances of a successful resolution are greatly increased. An example of each type of case, from my own experience, makes the lesson clear.

First, the nightmare.

A community bank offers free safe deposit boxes to depositors. An elderly couple takes advantage of the offer. Eventually, the husband dies and the widow, in her 80s, and her daughter, in her 50s, come in to sign new signature cards. The bank takes the new signature cards and does not file them, but rather loses them. At year end, the bank considers the box abandoned, drills it with appropriate witnesses, records its contents as "empty," and life goes on.

Until the widow pays the bank a visit, that is. She is shocked to learn that her safe deposit box is no longer there, and feels that she is not treated appropriately by the bank personnel to whom she complains. Her distress grows so great that she consults a lawyer and a lawsuit is filed.

At the mediation, plaintiff's counsel begins an initial joint session by explaining that the widow does not exactly remember the last time she and her husband visited the deposit box, or just what was in it. The lawyer recounts that the widow thinks there may have been some envelopes there, sealed of course, but perhaps with cash, perhaps with a lock of their children's baby hair, perhaps with a love letter from the husband, to be read after he died. How tragic, the lawyer concludes, that the poor widow will have to go to her grave never knowing what was left behind in that precious safe deposit box.

I paused and counted to ten. Defense counsel was a highly-placed partner in a major law firm. I turned to her and said, "You know, I'm glad you're here in mediation. Because your law firm runs a business, I run a business, your client runs a business. We all have clients, or customers, and we all want to keep our clients happy. Here you have a customer who had been with your client's bank for over 20 years. Now she's a former customer. Nobody wants to have an unhappy customer. Here in mediation, you have a chance to do something you could never do in court. I know you don't believe your client has done anything wrong, and I'd never ask you to acknowledge any such thing. But here you have the unique opportunity to look across the table at this nice woman, and respecting the fact that you don't think your client did anything wrong, you can still tell her how sorry you are that she got so upset that she took the extraordinary steps of hiring a lawyer and filing a lawsuit against you."

Litigator X straightened up in her chair, looked down at her notes, and responded to what I thought was a big fat softball pitch thusly: "I will do no such thing! I am here to explain why all appropriate banking regulations were followed, why my client did nothing wrong, why we are extremely likely to obtain summary judgment in this case and why we think it has at best nuisance value for settlement purposes."

A nuisance! Talk about the antithesis of making someone feel important! Or that their patronage over 20 years was the least bit appreciated! This was the worst mediation advocacy I had ever seen, and the result was predictable. By day's end, the president of the bank had seen fit to offer $30,000 in settlement, an amount in excess of the anticipated future defense fees. But the case did not settle. No matter what the number had been, it could not have been high enough to make up for the manifest disrespect Litigator X had shown the widow and her daughter hours before.

Now the dream. As if to prove how rarely an appropriate apology is used effectively, this anecdote comes from a simulated mediation rather than a real one.

In 2001, we presented the mediation of Palsgraf v. Long Island Railroad as a CLE program for the ABA's Tort Trial and Insurance Practice Section at the Association's Annual Meeting in Chicago. Robin Westerfield of Walnut Creek, California's Bowles & Verna played the role of trial counsel for the LIRR.

As we were walking on stage into the mythical mediation room, before we were even seated, Westerfield turned to Rene Ellis of Duke Law School, who played Mrs. Palsgraf, and said: "Mrs. Palsgraf, before we actually begin the mediation, I just want to let you know how sorry we are that the explosion occurred and how sorry we are that you were caught in the middle of it. We pride ourselves on keeping our passengers safe, and we're sorry that you were hurt while you were standing on the platform of one of our stations."

Did that ever put magic in the air! No admission of liability or fault. Not for any consideration, because Westerfield characterized his apology as taking place "before we actually begin the mediation." A recognition of the facts that Mrs. P. was important as a customer, that her patronage was appreciated, and that she had in fact suffered as a result of all this. Not surprisingly, at the end of our little play, Westerfield and his opposing counsel, Honolulu's Richard Turbin, got the case settled.

A myth? Maybe. But the players were deeply "in role" that day, and really put me through my paces in the role of mediator. It worked for us, and it may well work for you. A well-constructed apology in a mediation, or any other negotiation, is something for which you will never have to say you're sorry.

Notes and Questions

5.46 As discussed in Chapter 2, one study concludes that a full apology that accepts responsibility will have a more favorable impact on willingness to settle than a partial, "safe" apology that expresses sympathy. Jennifer K. Robbennolt, Apologies and Legal Settlement: An Empirical Examination, 102 Mich. L. Rev. 201 (2003). A full apology, however, may be risky if the case does not settle. Nonetheless, given the data, attorneys should hesitate to discourage full apologies that may be both helpful and healing.

5.47 The traditional notion of trial attorneys fighting for their client is different in many important respects from the practice advice in this section on effective representation in mediation. Analyze your own stereotypes about attorney advocacy. Do they include the civility that Kichaven suggests? The openness to problem solving that Abramson advises? The nuanced approaches that Sternlight describes?

The next chapter turns to skills of a mediator. You will find considerable overlap between the skills of good attorney representatives and mediators. If attorneys displayed all the skills described in this chapter, there would be less need for mediators!

# Chapter 6 Mediator Skills and Practices

Leaders must . . . create an attitude of success, the belief that problems can be solved, that things can be better. Not in a foolish or unrealistic way, but in a way that creates hope and confidence.

—George Mitchell

The significant problems we face cannot be solved at the same level of thinking we were at when we created them.

—Albert Einstein

The very first requirement in a hospital is that it should do the sick no harm.

—Florence Nightingale

A mediation is successful if it accomplishes any of the following goals: giving disputing parties an enhanced understanding of their dispute and of each other's perspective, enabling parties to develop options responsive to issues raised by the dispute, and bringing closure to the dispute on terms that are mutually agreeable. Conversely, the mediation process should not make negotiations more difficult, nor should it generate an outcome worse than outcomes available elsewhere. In other words, at a minimal level, the process should do no harm. This chapter explores skills necessary to achieve success and avoid failure in mediation.

Both the mediator and the attorney representatives for each party share the goal of helping disputants achieve their goals and meet their needs. This chapter examines how mediators (and attorney representatives and parties) work to reach good outcomes through effective practices. As this chapter's sections reveal, there are several, not one, models for effective mediation, utilizing a range of particular approaches and skills — all of which are constantly improved with appropriate training, mentoring, and reflective practice. This chapter teaches how mediators work, not just for mediators, but for parties and party representatives who have to understand what mediators will do to help them constructively address their issues.

A. TRAITS, TASKS, AND QUALIFICATIONS OF THE MEDIATOR

1. Mediator Traits

> The ancient Masters were profound and subtle.
> Their wisdom was unfathomable.
> There is no way to describe it;
> all we can describe is their appearance.
> They were careful
> as someone crossing an iced-over stream.
> Alert as a warrior in enemy territory.
> Courteous as a guest.
> Fluid as melting ice.
> Shapable as a block of wood.
> Receptive as a valley.
> Clear as a glass of water.
> Do you have the patience to wait
> till your mud settles and the water is clear?
> Can you remain unmoving
> till the right action arises by itself?
> — *Tao te Ching* 15 (Steven Mitchell trans., 1991)

Persons with a variety of different personality types can be effective mediators. There are nonetheless certain traits that are particularly useful. The *Tao* describes Masters who lead in subtle ways so people believe they have achieved results on their own. "Invisible leadership" that supports parties in determining an appropriate outcome is one vision of the mediation process. Intelligence, care, courtesy, flexibility, receptivity, transparency, patience, and strength are hallmarks of this vision.

Other often-cited attributes of a good mediator include the ability to: stay in the middle — that is, be impartial and nonjudgmental, be a good listener, and take charge or recede into the background when

---

"An Endless Supply of Patience"

[T]here must be an endless supply of patience and perseverance. Sometimes the mountains seem so high and rivers so wide that it is hard to continue the journey.... Seeking an end to conflict is not for the timid or the tentative....

We had 700 days of failure and 1 day of success.

George J. Mitchell (describing negotiations in Northern Ireland).

---

the parties are engaging in constructive conversation. Mediators must have the energy, the optimism, and the dogged perseverance to press on when others lose hope. Confidence, decisiveness, creativity, reliability, nondefensiveness, a sense of humor, and empathy are also important traits. Some mediators are naturally more blessed with these traits than others. However, nurture and support, training and mentoring, and self-reflection can go a long way in developing these qualities.

2. Mediator Tasks

Working with the traits mentioned above, what tasks do mediators perform? One overview of mediator tasks is the following:

Organization

- Serving as host to provide comfort and safety
- Serving as chair to structure the process effectively

Communication

- Enabling parties to express themselves clearly
- Encouraging parties to listen
- Clarifying, summarizing, translating, and reframing to maximize understanding
- Capturing and recording understandings and agreements

Education

- Ensuring understanding of the mediation process
- Modeling and coaching effective negotiation behaviors and attitudes
- Encouraging parties to obtain necessary or helpful information or resources

Negotiation

- Eliciting common interests
- Framing negotiable issues
- Helping parties develop options
- Conveying offers and counteroffers
- Clarifying agreement terms

Protection

- Preventing misuse of process
- Accepting responsibility for missteps and impasse

Section B will explore the knowledge, strategies, and skills that these tasks entail.

3. Qualifications for Mediators

How does society measure capacity to mediate? To practice law, for example, you must pass a bar exam. Other professions have similar licensing requirements.

Courts and other institutions have tried to determine how to measure competence and qualify persons for mediation service. The typical formula for placement on a panel of mediators includes requisites in terms of: the number of hours of training (from 4 hours for civil cases in some jurisdictions to 40 hours in others);

experience observing and co-mediating cases under supervision (from 3 cases in some jurisdictions to 125 hours for some credentialing associations); and continuing education requirements. Some court-annexed panels also rely on educational degree requirements, mandating a college degree or, in some cases, a law (or other graduate) degree, or, in a few cases, having been a practicing member of the bar in a particular state for a number of years. There is little data to indicate which of these approaches (training-based, experience-based, or degree-based) assures competence. Perhaps the most promising approach involves combining training and experience requirements with skills-based evaluation. This last approach, while more difficult to develop and administer, holds more promise for ensuring that mediators are capable of high-quality performance.

No licensing of mediators currently exists, though there are a variety of certification regimes for service on mediation panels with differing training, experience, or degree requirements. In the quest to ensure quality mediation services, a primary challenge is to maintain the current professional and practice diversity in the field and not unnecessarily disqualify competent individuals by setting inappropriate bars and standards.

Another aspect of mediator qualification is culture. Certain cultures have specific requirements and preferences with respect to mediators and the process generally. A North American view of mediator qualifications focuses on neutrality, training, and experience. Other cultures might prefer a "wise elder" who is respected in the community, is not a stranger to the parties, and will lead — rather than follow — the parties to a resolution. A student from Ghana, when asked what key mediator trait would engender confidence and acceptability in his country, answered "old." Every feature of the mediation process — when and where parties meet, how the session is opened, how the seating is arranged, and who attends — is shaped by culture.

Notes and Questions

6.1 The qualifications to obtain a license as a hairdresser in some states require, for example, 1,500 hours of training in Connecticut and either 1,650 hours of course work in an approved school or 2,000 hours of training in an apprenticeship in Alaska. By contrast, mediators qualify to be on panels servicing challenging cases with 25 hours of training (or less) in some locales. Does this seem right to you?

6.2 For further reflections on mediator qualifications, see Ellen Waldman, Credentialing Approaches: The Slow Movement Toward Skills-Based Testing Continues, 8 Disp. Resol. Mag. 13 (2001); Chris Honeyman, On Evaluating Mediators, 6 Negot. J. 23 (1990).

6.3 A variety of approaches, including those mentioned above (training, apprenticeship, continuing education, performance assessment, and educational degrees), have been tried to ensure quality mediation services. Some states require that trainers be certified where the training qualifies mediators for service. Some panels and programs measure mediator skill by the outcomes of mediation sessions or the satisfaction of the parties. Quality initiatives also include the development of ethical codes and grievance processes. Finally, administering an exam is a familiar method of ensuring competence. If you administered a court panel of neutrals, how would you ensure that your mediators were performing well? Over the years, the Association for Conflict Resolution (ACR, previously the Society for Professionals in Dispute Resolution (SPIDR)) and the ABA Section of Dispute Resolution have sponsored several efforts and task forces to consider whether particular credentials, training, and experience should be required or suggested for mediators, but so far there is no national certification regime. Some states, notably Florida, Massachusetts, California, Texas, and Minnesota, have begun programs of formal credentialing in some contexts (such as court mediation programs).

B. MEDIATOR STRATEGIES AND SKILLS FOR STAGES IN THE MEDIATION PROCESS

This section breaks the mediation process into discrete segments and analyzes theory and strategies for each. Keep in mind that mediation scholars and theorists have developed various ways of describing the process — from no stages at all to approaches similar to those described below. Joseph Stulberg uses the mnemonic "BADGER" to describe the stages of the mediation process:

Begin the discussions;
Accumulate information;
Develop the agenda and discussion strategies;
Generate movement;
Escape to separate sessions;
Resolve the dispute.

BADGER signifies that the mediator's role is energetic, proactive, and persistent, while the mediator proceeds through each stage of the process the letters represent. Christopher Moore, a noted writer and trainer, describes a twelve-stage process beginning with pre-session contacts and decisions and culminating in formal settlement. Whatever the approach, there is general consensus that even where one conceptualizes a linear "map" of stages, the reality of mediation is not a linear lock-step process. It is, rather, a more unpredictable process, where a linear map may serve as a useful guide for both the mediator and the attorney representatives, but where there is constant movement forward, backward, and in circles between and among the so-called stages.

1. Beginning

The mediator must consider a variety of issues prior to the start of a mediation session. Among those issues are choosing participants, assessing whether participants have special needs, deciding what procedural issues need to be addressed, and setting the stage.

a. Who Should Participate in the Mediation?

The mediator guides parties in deciding about the best mix of participants. For each case, while the parties ultimately determine who participates, the mediator helps analyze this critical factor. The following chart outlines some potential mediation participants, generalizes about whether they should participate in mediation, and suggests a rationale for inclusion.

PARTICIPANT	INCLUDE?	RATIONALE FOR INCLUSION/EXCLUSION
Party	Yes	The parties are in the best position to examine underlying interests, to develop creative proposals, and to determine whether commitment to a proposal is possible and optimal.
Attorney(s) or other representative	Yes	If a party to the dispute wants a representative — to help articulate the legal case, to be a negotiation coach, to assist in listening, persuading, and developing and analyzing options — then she should be allowed such support. Where attorneys import an adversarial climate, their role may be limited to advising the client about the legal consequences of proposed settlement terms and helping draft a settlement agreement.
Interpreter	Yes, if needed	Since understanding is a central goal of mediation, an interpreter is critical if there are language issues.
Expert	Maybe	An expert may be needed to inform or educate the other side or to expand settlement options. Mutually acceptable experts can also be brought in to provide information where data is lacking.
Witness	Maybe	A witness may be helpful to persuade the other side to consider another perspective. Sometimes a witness will be more persuasive than the party, or the cumulative impact of another voice will be helpful.
Support person	Maybe	A general rule is to "keep it simple" where possible. On the other hand, some parties cannot operate effectively without a support person — for example, a spouse, significant family member, or business partner. It is wise to exclude "extra" persons who have their own agendas and may derail discussions, but it is critical to include support people whose presence is helpful for emotional, data, decisional, or other support.

General guidelines, however, do not answer all questions. For example, situations arise where a party cannot be present and an attorney representative comes as a surrogate negotiator. Unlike litigation, where parties are named in the papers filed with the court, in many situations it is hard to tell who the parties are. For example, a litigated custody dispute typically has as the parties those persons — often the husband and wife — named in the complaint. However, in the mediation of a situation concerning parenting arrangements, the parties may include a much broader array — grandparents, aunts, uncles, and the children themselves.

Although the same people may participate in mediation and adjudication, their role in each process is quite different. In adjudication, parties, attorneys, experts, and witnesses all work for one side or the other to persuade a neutral decision maker. In mediation, on the other hand, all participants increase the common information base and work toward persuading a party to shift his or her perspective and develop proposals responsive to the situation.

Notes and Questions

6.4 Recall a dispute in which you have been involved. If you were to resolve the dispute by mediation, whom would you want to attend? Does it depend on your goals? If the same dispute were brought to court, who would be the parties?

6.5 Now examine a case you have studied in other law school courses — Brown v. Board of Education, for example. Who would be the parties in a mediation of that dispute?

b. What Procedural Issues Must Be Addressed?

In addition to the participant mix, allocating mediation costs, determining information exchange, and deciding the nature of pre-mediation submissions (if any) must be addressed. In the excerpt that follows, Joseph Stulberg discusses the challenges of setting the procedural framework for a mediation.

 Joseph B. Stulberg, **TAKING CHARGE/MANAGING CONFLICT**

59-60 (1987)

Where will people meet? How many will be there? When will they meet? How long will the session last? Will there be food? Who will talk first? Who will sit where? These matters, and others like them, are issues of meeting etiquette. The mediator wants to ensure that meeting arrangements and procedures do not disrupt the substantive discussions. He wants them handled well so that people feel comfortable and there is no awkwardness as they begin to talk with one another.

The mediator begins by taking care of these housekeeping details. Usually he simply announces the rules and makes appropriate arrangements; sometimes, however, these matters become issues of fierce debate among the parties and end up as the first topic for mediated discussion. In any event, no mediator thinks they are trivial. These procedural rules create the framework within which people interact, and one must establish them with care. Like any host, the mediator will receive no compliments for handling them well but will invite interminable haggling and destructive gossip for botching them. . . .

Although these seem straightforward enough, they can be devilishly complicated. If a mediator schedules a meeting for 11:30 A.M., does that mean the meeting will last only until lunch at noon? If only one party has to travel seventy miles to attend a meeting in a city where all of the other parties live and work, should the mediator change the meeting site so that everyone must travel thirty-five miles, or should he alternate meeting sites so as not to favor one group? If one group has only two negotiators, but the other has five negotiating team members and thirty "observers and supporters," should the mediator arrange a meeting site that accommodates eight or thirty-eight persons? The mediator must develop these guidelines with a keen sensitivity to the impact the specific rules will have on the parties' interaction and the way in which the rules might tarnish his own image as neutral.

c. How Is the Stage Set?

Sometimes when I consider what tremendous consequences come from little things . . . I am tempted to think . . . there are no little things.
—Bruce Barton, in Stephen R. Covey, *The Seven Habits of Highly Effective People*
287 (1989)

We shape our buildings: thereafter they shape us.

—Winston Churchill

In determining how to choose and arrange a room for a mediation, key mediation goals must be kept in mind: to enhance communication between the parties, to ensure safety, to maximize comfort, to support mediator neutrality, and to set a stage or create an atmosphere that is conducive to creativity and to inspiration. With those targets in mind, the questions below are a sampling of issues the mediator must address.

Notes and Questions

6.6 Should the mediator sit parties side by side to emphasize that they are facing a common problem and must work together or sit them across the table from each other where direct eye contact is easy and the security of a table between them may provide safety and psychological comfort? Explain your answer. Can you think of other physical configurations?

6.7 The shape of the mediation table, if one is used at all, is a question mediators must address. As a mediator, would you choose a round, triangular, square, rectangular, oval, or some other shaped table? What is the impact of having no table? Would your answer change depending on the type of case?

6.8 In addition to tables and chairs, mediators must consider the artwork, wall color, window configuration, and other features of a room regularly used for mediation. Each of these seemingly insignificant items affects the mood of the parties. Also, accessibility and the proximity of kitchen and bathroom facilities, caucus rooms, photocopy and fax machines, telephones and computers for e-mail and Internet services can be critical. Design an ideal mediation suite.

6.9 Food and beverages are inextricably linked to the success of meetings. In setting the stage for a mediation that may go all day, how might you plan for food? Keep in mind that hunger is related to energy, creativity, irritability, and patience, and consequently the mediator should keep a sharp eye on parties' needs for food and rink. Can you imagine benefits of arranging opportunities for parties to "break bread together"? Can you imagine dangers in doing that?

Israel-PLO Agreement Ceremony

Sometimes getting the atmosphere right is the most important thing. When we signed the Israel-PLO agreement in 1993 on the White House lawn, I had a tough time. First Arafat wanted to bring his gun — he said he didn't go anywhere without his gun. Well I said, "This isn't about guns. If you want to walk away from a televised audience of a billion people because you won't leave your six shooter at the door, I'll be happy to tell them that." So he left his gun.

Then I said to Rabin, "He left his gun. You've got to shake hands with him." He said, "I am signing the agreement, I have to shake his hand?" We are laughing today, but this was a tough thing for him. These guys had fought for decades. How many young Israelis had Rabin put in body bags? He lived and they died. . . . He was considering all that. Finally I said to him, "Yitzhak, you have made all these steps and you have taken all these risks and the whole world will be looking at you. And I have to shake hands with Arafat; so you do too." And he looked at me and he said, "Well I suppose you do not make peace with your friends." And then he smiled at me and said, "but no kissing."

William J. Clinton, Acceptance Speech, International Advocate for Peace Award, Benjamin N. Cardozo School of Law, Mar. 19, 2001.

In addition to these questions, what is appropriate for parties to bring in the room? For example, in mediating police-civilian matters, the mediator or the mediation program must decide whether police officers should bring their firearms, handcuffs, and other indicia of authority into the mediation room. Having their normal paraphernalia may make police officers more comfortable but may simultaneously make civilians less comfortable. Note how former President Clinton struggled with such issues in staging the Israel-PLO agreement ceremony (see box above).

d. How Does the Mediator Open the Session?

Typically, the mediator begins the session by making opening remarks. These remarks have multiple goals: to develop trust and rapport with the parties, to educate the parties about the mediation process and ensure that everyone (mediator and parties) has compatible goals, and to develop guidelines for the process.

What follows is a sample opening statement by a mediator in a community mediation center, which primarily services neighbor, landlord-tenant, and family-related disputes. Keep in mind that the statement might look very different in other contexts, but it would still address the goals set out above.

> Good morning. Welcome to mediation. My name is Kabi Jorgensen, and I have been assigned to assist you.
>
> Please check that I have your names and addresses recorded correctly. Am I pronouncing your names correctly?
>
> I want you both to know that I have never met either of you before, and I know very little about the concerns that brought you here today. I look forward to your explaining this matter to me. I am telling you this because it is my job not to be on either side, but rather remain in the middle, as a neutral. I am not a judge. A judge would decide who was wrong or right with respect to conduct that happened in the past. I am here to help you work out how you want the future to be.
>
> Before you tell me what brought you here, I want to explain the goals of this process and suggest some guidelines for our conversation. My first job is to understand your concerns and to be sure that you understand each other. To do that, it is important that each person has the opportunity to speak without being interrupted. I know you will want to comment about what the other person says and perhaps remember some points that are new to you, so I have given you paper and a pen to make notes. When it is your turn to speak, you will have a full opportunity to explain your concerns and respond. Can you agree not to interrupt each other and not to interrupt me?
>
> After we explore the situation and your goals, I will encourage you to work together to come up with proposals to address the concerns you raised. If you are able to reach an agreement that resolves your concerns, if you wish and at your request, I will write up your commitments to each other.
>
> I will be taking notes as we proceed to help me remember the concerns you raise and the understandings you reach. However, I will destroy my notes at the end of this session. I am telling you this so you will feel comfortable to speak freely here. This session is private and confidential. That means I am under a duty not to reveal what is said in this room to anyone outside this room. There are some exceptions to confidentiality, however. For example, there is an exception for allegations of child abuse. From time to time I do consult with the staff about questions I might have regarding your situation, but the staff here are under the same duty as I am to keep confidential what is said in mediation. The only record of what happened in this session will be the agreement you make to resolve your concerns.
>
> There may come a time when I feel it would be helpful to meet individually with each of you. If that happens, I will explain that process—which is called caucusing—in more detail.
>
> Sessions here generally take two hours. They can also be shorter or longer as you require. I am committed to work with you as long as necessary.
>
> Do you have any questions?
>
> Mr. Chin, since you brought this matter to the attention of the Center, would you please begin and relate what brought you here.

Notes and Questions

6.10 Observe the language in the opening. The mediator refers to *concerns, interests, priorities, proposals, options,* and *agreements.* You do not hear adversarial or potentially abrasive words such as *parties, allegations, claim, position,* or *problem.* Do you think this careful attention to language makes a difference?

6.11 How would you change this opening if attorneys were present? If the mediation was happening in a civil court case rather than a community case? If you were conducting a mediation between fellow law students? Note that every opening statement should include the following: introductions, disclaiming of mediator partiality or bias, explanation of the mediation process and the mediator's role, development of ground rules (including understandings regarding courtesy, note taking, confidentiality, the length of the session, and the use of separate meetings or caucuses), and an opportunity to ask questions.

6.12 Get together with two other classmates. Practice giving an opening statement. In turn, each student in the group should be the mediator and the other students should be parties. Note that even if three people use the same words, the opening may have very different impacts. Give your colleagues feedback on their body language and eye contact (which should not favor either party), whether they created a tone of trust and optimism, and whether they conveyed confidence and competence.

2. Understanding the Conflict and Developing the Information Base

Once the mediator has set the stage and delivered an opening statement, she asks the parties to describe the matter that brought them to mediation. As the mediator listens to the parties and urges them to listen to each other, she is looking for elements of the conflict that will be constructive in developing a better understanding among the parties, that may generate ideas for resolution, and that might become agreed upon commitments.

The first excerpt below, by Gary Friedman and Jack Himmelstein, internationally recognized mediators and trainers, describes a technique for listening called "looping," which is taught in the understanding-based model of mediation introduced in Chapter 3. The essence of looping is a genuine commitment of the mediator to understanding each party and demonstrating that understanding. Consider how looping requires more than the active listening described in Chapter 5.

 Gary Friedman & Jack Himmelstein, **THE LOOP OF UNDERSTANDING**

(2004)

Central to the Understanding-Based approach to mediation is the search for understanding. The "Loop of Understanding," as we have come to call it, gives form and substance to that effort. "*Looping*" is a technique, but it is also much more than a technique. The goal is to *develop understanding* systematically, authentically and compassionately throughout the mediation.

Looping builds on the mediator's intention. Just as successful mediation ultimately must build on the parties' intention to work through their conflict together, looping proceeds from the mediator's intention to understand the parties and to build a ground of understanding between the mediator and the parties.

THE STEPS OF LOOPING

Although the approach is similar to and borrows much from what others have referred to as "active listening," "looping" captures a fuller sense of it for us. We term it the "loop" of understanding because the goal is to complete a loop.

For the mediator, the simple steps are to try within him or herself to understand each party, to try to express that understanding to that party, and to seek and receive confirmation from the party that he/she feels understood. The last step is crucial. When a party confirms that the mediator understands what he or she has been trying to express, that loop is complete. Until then, it is not.

Step 1:	M inquires of	→	P
Step 2:	P responds, asserts	→	M
Step 3:	M demonstrates and confirms understanding	→	P
Step 4:	P responds	→	M
	If yes, loop is complete.		
	If no, go back to Step 1 and ask: "What am I missing?"		

By bringing *looping* to the exchange between him/herself and each of the principal antagonists to the conflict, the mediator has begun to understand each of them. And while they likely do not feel understood by each other, they feel at least somewhat understood by the mediator. He has also begun to clarify the essence of the dispute.

The goal is to understand the speaker *and* to demonstrate that you understand. Already this is much more than many mediators (and others) will do in the effort to listen. Even when we make a sincere effort to understand another, that effort is often evidenced by silent attention, a nod of agreement, or a statement such as: "I understand what you are saying." These are not bad. But when it comes to the goal of resolving conflict through understanding, much more is possible. Stating what you hear the other to have said goes further. It shows that you understand (if you do).

So far we have a partial loop — statement by the loopee and response (restatement) by the looper. The next step begins to close the loop. If done with the intent of fostering understanding, it tests whether the mediator has truly understood. The mediator asks the party whether the response captured the meaning of what he was trying to communicate.

The loopee's response can close the loop. If "yes" — if the speaker confirms that he/she feels understood — this one loop is complete. If the speaker does not feel fully understood by the looper's words (whether because the looper missed something or simply because the speaker has the need to clarify what he/she meant), the loop is not complete. The party can then clarify what he/she meant, the mediator loops back and again seeks confirmation. When the party confirms that the mediator correctly has understood, that loop is complete.

The point is not to convince, nor to contradict, nor to take exception to, nor explain away. The point is to understand.

From the start, we are saying to the parties in word and in deed:

> I am going to do my best to understand each of you. My hope is that if we work together in this way, and it makes sense to you, we can together try to understand what is going on — and from that understanding appreciate what the conflict is about and hopefully enable you to resolve it.

The honest attempt by the mediator to understand each party begins to point to an alternative to the confines of a most basic element that keeps people ensnared in a Conflict Trap. For when people are locked in conflict, they typically tend to want to defend their position, blame the other, try to convince a third party that they are right and the other wrong. The mode is one of defense, persuasion, coercion.

When conflict takes that form, understanding is at a minimum. Misunderstanding prevails. The more the parties to conflict feel blamed or vilified by the other, the more they feel misunderstood. The more that they feel misunderstood, the more they tend to justify, blame and vilify. The cycle is well known and yet, once within its grasp, very powerful. Understanding, from the get-go, can help begin to soften the strictures and be the beginning of pointing the way out.

A caution: our recommendation for looping from the start applies to the mediator looping the parties, not to asking the parties to loop each other. Many mediators, drawn by the desire to increase understanding, will turn to the parties early on and ask: what did you understand the other to say? Our advice, generally, is: NOT YET. People are much more willing and able to understand another when they feel understood themselves. To put it another way, being mired in feelings of being misunderstood is not a good place from which to be asked to understand another. And parties to conflict are often mired in just such feelings. By establishing some understanding at the start (by the mediator of the parties), the mediator can begin to help break the cycle of misunderstanding. The invitation to the parties to loop each other can also prove essential, but it rarely comes at the start.

LOOPING FROM THE INSIDE OUT

As the description we have been giving about *looping* may suggest, it is both a skill and much more than a skill. To understand *looping* and its place in this approach to mediation is to realize that understanding has an inner life. And it is in that inner life that the essential spirit of looping is grounded. The mediator needs to want to loop (and learn to loop) as more than a useful skill. The hard work is to truly want to understand the people before you — to reach inside oneself when each speaker is speaking and make the effort to understand how the other (each of them) really experiences the situation — even (and particularly) when you find it difficult to understand them. That inner desire to understand is key.

Focusing too much on the outer skill, on getting the words right, on learning to rephrase or reframe (which are important skills to learn) can miss the essential point. *That point* is truly *to want to* understand—to connect within oneself to one's own intention to do that. If the inner intent is there, you may at times miss some of the basic steps and still move toward understanding. Like with the "Inner Game of Tennis," this one needs to be played from the inside.

In the next excerpt Lela Love describes another listening skill—reframing. Love urges mediators to translate accusations, put-downs, and threats into interests, issues, proposals, feelings, principles, and so on. These latter elements become "building blocks" for moving forward and helping parties shift their perspectives.

 ### *Lela P. Love,* TRAINING MEDIATORS TO LISTEN: DECONSTRUCTING DIALOGUE AND CONSTRUCTING UNDERSTANDING, AGENDAS, AND AGREEMENTS

adapted from 38 Fam. & Concil. Cts. Rev. 27 (2000)

Much as a miner looks for gold, a mediator listens to the often hostile, accusatory and adversarial dialogue between parties, gleaning the constructive elements—the "heart of gold"—that are being expressed. Amidst the put-downs, insults, and threats that are frequently exchanged by people in conflict, the mediator must extract solid building blocks which will allow disputants to construct different perspectives, clearer understandings and ultimately agreements. The mediator must hear and identify those elements, and also enable the parties to hear each other. This task is difficult because parties in conflict typically experience fear, confusion, anger, hate, frustration, and hopelessness; and the expression of these feelings can be so loud that other elements (to the untrained ear) are drowned out. The mediator must be optimistic that "gold" exists and be able to selectively and thoughtfully frame constructive components at appropriate times in the session.

What are the building blocks of constructive dialogue and how would the mediator translate these building blocks into language that might reorient the parties toward the dispute and toward each other? The "heart of gold" or building blocks of constructive dialogue, hidden in confrontational conversations, are: interests, issues, proposals, feelings, principles, values, rules, visions, stories, and BATNAs. If these can be culled out, brought to light, acknowledged and worked with, a constructive exchange may ensue. A brief discussion of each element follows.

INTERESTS AND NEEDS

Interests are the underlying and inescapable human motivators that press us into action. When interests are frustrated by actions or inactions of others, frequently a conflict ensues. Examples of interests include: survival, security, reputation, financial well-being, respect, career, and health. In many cases, mediators find common

interests among the disputants. In an employment scenario, frequently both a supervisor and an employee share an interest in their respective reputations, careers and
financial security. In a landlord-tenant situation, both disputants often have a common interest in: a safe, clean and serviceable dwelling and responsive and respectful
treatment. Divorcing parents share an interest in the well-being, health and happiness
of their children. A common interest provides a useful foundation upon which to
build. Once framed by the mediator, interests and common interests can seem self-
evident. However, interests do not jump out at the casual listener, as do threats,
accusations and put-downs. Nevertheless, they are there to be found in the dialogue.

ISSUES

Issues are those distinct and negotiable matters or behaviors that are frustrating a
party's interests. Issues are the critical components of the negotiating agenda. Since
mediators are generally charged with helping craft a discussion agenda that is right
"on target" with respect to concerns raised, a mediator's ability to mine the conversation for issues, extract the issues and label them in neutral language is key.

Legal issues or causes of action are distinct from negotiable issues. In a probate
dispute, for example, the litigated issues might be: whether undue influence was
exerted on the testator or whether the testator had testamentary capacity. Negotiable
issues might overlap legal issues, for example: the disposition of the art collection; and
the division of the residuary estate. Negotiable issues can also be much broader than
legal issues, for example: division of photographs, albums and family memorabilia;
the hosting of holiday events; interaction between aunts, uncles, nieces and nephews;
and so on. In a labor-management context, frequent issues that arise include: wages,
benefits, vacations, overtime. In a divorce context, financial and parenting arrangements are frequently key issues. Note that the negotiable issue of "parenting arrangements" would be framed in a litigation context as "custody" and "visitation"—a
framing that invites adversarial positioning rather than creative and collaborative
problem-solving.

One of the unique strengths of mediation compared to litigation or arbitration is
its ability to address the infinitely wide range of concerns that disputing parties have
with each other. Litigation is limited to "issues" which are legal causes of action.
Arbitration is limited to "issues" that are prescribed in the arbitration agreement.
Mediation can address whatever the parties bring to the table, as long as the mediator
is tuned in to capture the issues and incorporate each issue into the agenda. Consider,
for example, the mediation of an estate matter where siblings are disputing over the
disposition of an art collection. One of the siblings raises a concern that her brother
has allowed her 18-year-old son to sleep with his girlfriend in the brother's home.
This is not an actionable issue in court. However, in mediation, the parties can
discuss and resolve the question of "the son's sleeping accommodations in the brother's home," provided they are willing to negotiate about this issue. By framing that
issue in neutral language, the mediator will have provided a necessary, and very
useful, building block toward constructing a better understanding of what is blocking
one party's interest and consequently what needs to be negotiated in order to resolve
the entire conflict.

PROPOSALS

Proposals are offers or suggestions for the resolution of particular issues or of the dispute. Like other elements which require mining, proposals are rarely neatly and attractively packaged by the parties. Disputants frequently embed a proposal in a threat or insult, and mediators must be attuned to extract and display the proposal. A supervisor might say to an employee, for example: "If you didn't have such a nasty attitude, the company might help you. As it is, you're going to walk." From a mediator's perspective, that may be a proposal! The mediator would want to know what specifically the employee might do to display a different attitude and what sort of "help" might ensue.

Opening proposals (often called "positions") tend to be extreme and unworkable, since workable proposals would have led to resolution and avoided the need for a mediator. However, they are nonetheless an important indication of what each party sees as an interest-satisfying outcome.

LEGEND:

Common interests → **Bold**
Issues → Underscore
Proposals which are mutually acceptable → *Italics*

Employer and Employee want to end their employment relationship in an amicable manner.
To that end, they agree:

1. Employment Relationship.
    A. Employee's Employment Status. **Both Employer and Employee would like to facilitate Employee's smooth transition to a new job.**
Consequently, they agree:

> i.   *that Employee shall remain at the company for 3 months with full pay and benefits, retaining her current office, telephone and e-mail privileges, and job title. During that period Employee shall look for other employment and shall have no job-related responsibilities. At the end of that period, Employee shall resign; and*

> ii.   *that Employer shall provide Employee with out placement services at a provider chosen by Employee for one year or until Employee is hired (whichever occurs sooner). . . .*

Lela P. Love, Training Mediators to Listen: Deconstructing Dialogue and Constructing Understanding, Agendas and Agreements, 38 Fam. & Concil. Cts. Rev. 27, 39-40, app. B (2000).

Consequently, a mediator must be encouraged to pay sharp attention to proposals, even though he may not relay or reframe each proposal, as some may be so extreme that they would result in further alienation of the parties.

The relationship of interests, issues and proposals to agreements is the following. Agreements begin with a purpose clause (common interests), they employ headings (the issues in dispute) and they entail understandable and precise arrangements and undertakings between the parties (proposals that are mutually acceptable). Hence the mediator, even as he listens to the opening presentations of the parties, is actually beginning to construct an agreement from the articulated interests, issues and proposals he hears (see box).

FEELINGS

Both recipients of and witnesses to put-downs and insults tend naturally to react with alarm, heightened adrenalin and (especially for the recipient), an attack response. Mediators must hear, and at appropriate points reframe, the feelings that generate such statements: the speaker is angry; the speaker is scared; the speaker is frustrated. It is often the case that all parties to a conflict have similar feelings of anger and frustration. In many cases, a vitriolic insult is the tip of an iceberg of a history of hurt feelings, waiting to be heard and acknowledged. Sometimes the venting and acknowledgment alone can shift the feelings themselves. Mediators should be trained to hear insults and think "this person is/may be upset."

PRINCIPLES, VALUES AND RULES

Parties govern themselves in accordance with certain principles and values they hold dear. A sense of entitlement and need for "justice" and setting things right grows out of parties' understanding of family, industry, community, religious or legal rules and norms. Exposing and clarifying the parties' (and sometimes their attorneys' or other experts') operating principles, values, norms and rules are part of the mediator's task. This is so for several reasons: (1) behavior becomes more understandable when the parties understand the important principles, values and rules governing the other party's behavior; and (2) proposals generally will not work for a party unless they comport with the party's operating norms.

In court-annexed settings or for disputes involving legal claims and lawyers, the law and the parties' perceptions and positions with respect to their legal rights and obligations may play a critical role. If counsel are present in the mediation session, their presentations regarding the legal posture of the case will be a key element in framing the parties' perceptions of legal norms. Such presentations will assist the parties to evaluate and re-evaluate their understanding of the litigation alternative. The mediator should encourage a discussion and analysis of the weaknesses and strengths of elements of each party's case. Risk assessment (or conversely, opportunity analysis) with respect to litigation may provide a key piece to the puzzle of what would provide a meaningful settlement in court-connected cases. It is up to the mediator to encourage the attorneys to make presentations about legal norms, risks and opportunities, which are persuasive in terms of making the other side re-evaluate their litigation option, but are not personally offensive to the other side such that a climate for constructive negotiation is undermined.

In certain arenas, mediators themselves may be asked by the parties to provide legal information and even analysis. Where mediators do provide such services, they must do so in a manner which preserves party self-determination and mediator neutrality and avoids unauthorized practice of law issues (emphatically critical if the mediator is not a lawyer!).

Lawyers, however, can overemphasize the importance of the role of law. Remember that it is usual for legal analysis to result in widely different assessments of likely litigation outcomes. Also, other values and interests come into play for many parties. The power of an apology, for example, and the recognition it entails, is typically underestimated by lawyers. Moral, religious, family or community values can play a more decisive role, in some cases, than legal norms.

VISIONS

A vision in this context is a picture that a party may have of an ideal state. Often the frustration and high tension in a conflict setting is due to the fact that the status quo is so far from where a party would like it to be. Interestingly, "visions" often do not conflict, and sometimes are complementary. For example, in disputes between neighbors parties often say: "I just want peace when I come home"; or "I want my building to feel welcoming"; or "I want to be left alone, not bothered." In an employment situation, parties might say: "I want a friendly workplace"; or "I want co-workers who pull together"; or "I want my employees to care about the business." The mediator can explore these pictures by asking: "Tell me more about how you would like your building to be"; or "Describe how you would like the office to be" (asking both parties, of course). Such an exploration can result in a target status quo that is appealing to both parties. Having some clarity about the ideal makes it easier to dream up intermediate steps to achieve such an ideal.

STORIES

Allowing parties to tell their stories (often a story of a wrong they have experienced) is critical to each party being able to move beyond that experience of wrong and to listen to the other party's story, frequently a quite different story or viewpoint on the same "facts" and invariably expanding the picture or "reality" which informs each individual party's perception of events. Mediators need to understand that they must listen to each party's story and be able to see how that party views events, but — unlike a judge or an arbitrator — they need not judge or determine which version of events constitutes "facts." By preserving for each party an uninterrupted platform for speech, the mediator gives each party voice and respect and encourages a heightened level of understanding.

The story of the death of Charles Drew illustrates that finding factual truth is not necessarily the purpose of story-telling. Charles Drew was a prominent African-American physician and scientist, whose research on the use of blood plasma and whose work in helping to establish the first American Red Cross Blood Bank saved countless lives in World War II. Dr. Drew died after an automobile accident in North Carolina in 1950. There is an often told story that Drew was denied treatment and a blood transfusion at the hospital to which he was taken after the accident because the beds for black people were full, and Drew died as a result. We can listen to that story and learn important lessons about the indignities and tragedies suffered due to segregation policies in the South in the first half of the twentieth century, which may be the "truth" that the speaker is trying to relate. In fact, the story of Charles Drew's death is not historically accurate. Although it is true that many African-Americans were denied critical medical treatment, Dr. Drew received appropriate and energetic care in the small hospital to which he was taken. The legend around Drew, then, is not literally true but reveals a larger truth that the storyteller wants to convey. Such complexities lend themselves to mediation. While an arbitrator or neutral expert must attempt to find "facts," a mediator must give each party the storytelling floor and allow the parties to be shifted by the power of the other's narrative (sometimes assisted by advocates and the translating function of the mediator). The telling of the story may shift the speaker; the hearing of the story may shift the listener; from a mediator's perspective, the parties, as first-hand participants, are in the best position to judge the "truth" around the events related to their conflict.

BATNAS (Best Alternative to a Negotiated Agreement)

A party's BATNA represents their favored or default option if mediation is unsuccessful in resolving the conflict. How the mediator uses BATNAs can be very important. BATNAs are frequently expressed as a threat, for example: "I will pursue this all the way to the Supreme Court"; "I have friends" (sometimes meaning "my friends will injure you"); "we will send in troops"; and "I will tell Mom." Such statements may be expressions of options a party may have, and the mediator will urge the parties to explore and evaluate the realistic costs and opportunities available through each option. Each party's perspective will be informed by the evaluation of the other side. In that manner, the process enables decision-making to take place in an environment providing enriched information. In its least ambitious form, mediation can be seen as an opportunity to "beat the BATNA" of each party through the negotiation process.

When parties make threats — an employee states she will file "a sexual harassment claim," a tenant says she will pay "no rent," the landlord counters he will "evict the tenant," the mediator cannot be paralyzed by such moves. Instead, the mediator must pick up on these BATNAs and assist the parties in considering the reality of such options: How will a protracted dispute impact their emotional well-being? What are the financial and time costs of court processes? Is their analysis of legal or industry norms and procedures fully informed? Have they weighed the other side's perspective on the strengths and weaknesses of various positions? Do they want to extend and compound an adversarial relationship with the other side? Where parties are represented by counsel in the mediation, the lawyers will be called on to make presentations regarding their legal analysis of various BATNAs. Where lawyers are not present, the mediator might urge parties to get advice from lawyers, psychologists, accountants, architects and other experts on whether the party's prediction about their alternative is realistic. For some types of mediation, the mediator may take on (with the parties' request and consent) an additional, evaluative role to assist in reality-testing various options. However, all of these steps and services are predicated on a mediator's hearing what sounds like a raw threat and holding it out (if and when appropriate) as an option for consideration and thoughtful evaluation.

Notes and Questions

6.13 Chapters 2 and 5 explored BATNAs and their role in negotiations as part of an examination of negotiation skills. As you learned in those chapters, highly developed listening skills are also crucial for negotiators. Note how skills and strategies for the mediator are related to those of a talented negotiator.

6.14 Ask a colleague to describe a conflict that is distressing him. As you listen, identify and reframe for the speaker the interests, needs, issues, feelings, proposals, principles, visions, and any BATNA expressed. If these elements are not described, ask questions to elicit them. David Matz, expresses doubt about whether mediators can ever really learn the parties' interests in Ignorance and Interests, 4 Harv. Neg. L. Rev. 59 (1999). He suggests another layer of questioning, trust building, and general human humility about whether we can ever really "know" something about another human being.

3. Constructing a Discussion Agenda

Like any chair of a meeting, the mediator must help the parties build a constructive agenda. The agenda items — the issues — are those matters that require negotiation. After identifying those matters, the next challenge is framing the issues in a neutral manner and inviting discussion by all parties without making any party defensive. For example, if payment of back rent is contested, a mediator who frames the issue as "the delinquent rent owed by the tenant" invites a hostile reaction from the tenant. Identifying the issue simply as "the rent" serves better. The final challenge is to order the agenda in a way most conducive to collaboration, which Joseph Stulberg discusses in the excerpt below.

 Joseph B. Stulberg, THE THEORY AND PRACTICE OF MEDIATION: A REPLY TO PROFESSOR SUSSKIND

6 Vt. L. Rev. 85, 99-103 (1981)

An important consideration for the mediator when trying to structure effective communication is the order in which the parties will discuss the issues. To those unfamiliar with the negotiation-mediation process, this matter might appear to be a trivial house-keeping point. Frequently, however, stalemates and impasses occur not because parties disagree on all matters but because they have failed to structure discussions so that they can distinguish those matters on which they agree from those on which they do not.

... A mediator could adopt one of several approaches in structuring the discussion of issues. He could start by discussing the easy issues first. Everyone can assess matters in terms of degree of importance. If the mediator focuses discussions on those less important matters (i.e. the matters perceived as enhancing the parties' relationship without in any way jeopardizing their substantive interests), then he can help the parties begin to forge some agreements.

Using this approach serves two purposes. First, it begins to develop a pattern of agreement and momentum of progress between the parties. Confidence in the talks grows as agreement is reached on some items, and the parties obtain a limited basis for believing it possible to resolve the more difficult issues. Second, by building a series of small agreements, the mediator has laid a settlement foundation. As the parties reach more difficult issues, the cost of not settling increases since that cost would include relinquishing all agreements which had been reached. That fact alone might give the parties a strong incentive to reconsider any resistance to the remaining matters.

Another approach would involve dividing issues and proposals according to their common subject-matter. The mediator could categorize the proposals [in a labor dispute] into such subjects as vacation, wages, hours of work, and the like and then discuss each party's proposal(s) that falls within that category. The starting point of the discussion would be the category of issues that seems most susceptible to prompt resolution. . . .

[T]he mediator could approach the discussion of the issues and proposals according to existing time constraints. The mediator could suggest that the parties first address those matters requiring prompt attention and defer discussion on the other matters until they could be addressed at a more leisurely pace. . . .

The most effective approach depends on the context of the discussions and the individual parties. What must be underscored is that the approach to the discussion of issues can be deliberate rather than haphazard; it is the mediator's job to ensure that the discussions are intelligently ordered.

Notes and Questions

6.15 Another approach, followed by transformative mediators, is to allow the parties to negotiate the agenda. The mediator might, for example, lay out issues she has heard, check that the list fully represents the topics that must be addressed, and then ask, "What would you like to talk about first?" What are the advantages of the more directive approach that Stulberg suggests? The disadvantages?

6.16 Imagine that you are a mediator faced with parties disputing over the amount of damages a defendant will pay, the timing of the payment, the method of payment, and the type of release that plaintiff will give. In what order would you address these issues? Keep in mind that wherever you start, you can "shelve" an issue and rearrange the discussion agenda to keep the mediation dynamic.

4. Generating Movement: Developing Options and Agreements

Mediator responsibility for "generating movement" and overcoming impasse is frequently portrayed as the use of strategies to find a compromise between two extreme positions that disputants take. For example, if one party demands "$1 million" to compensate for damaged reputation, and the response is "I've done nothing wrong. I'll give you nothing. Everything I said was true!," a "compromise" might be the payment of any amount between $0 and $1 million.

However, the idea of movement—and strategies for achieving movement—is a much richer study than simply techniques to encourage compromise, accommodation, and trade-off. Movement of any sort can engender movement of every sort. Consequently, it is helpful to think of movement from a variety of angles.

Mediators create a safe space where both listening and being heard can encourage softening of extreme positions, lessen demonization of the other party, and abate some of the blame and anger disputing parties often experience. Sometimes, parties need to be understood before they can move on. Any movement toward understanding and "letting go" is potentially impasse-breaking movement. Other times disputants need to confront the cost of being stuck in recriminations, blame, and extreme, unworkable positions before they can move into a collaborative posture to attempt to find mutually acceptable resolutions.

Former President Bill Clinton describes accompanying Nelson Mandela to the prison cell where Mandela slept on the floor for 14 years without heat, toilet, or faucet. Clinton asked whether Mandela was bitter and angry as he walked away from that cell after 27 years of incarceration. Mandela replied that he felt anger rising up, but he said to himself: "Mandela, they had you 27 years. If you are still angry with them when you get out the gate, they will still have you. . . . I wanted to be free, and so I let it go." Mandela thoughtfully weighed the cost of carrying his anger, and he moved beyond it. This internal movement of "letting go" of anger can have powerful consequences, as Mandela's career exemplifies. When negotiating parties relinquish some of their bitterness and animosity, possibilities for resolution emerge.

There are a variety of methods for helping parties generate movement. In Chapter 5, you learned how a decision tree analysis can lead to thoughtful weighing of alternatives. Brainstorming — where parties generate ideas without evaluating the ideas or making any commitments to them — is another useful tool. Generating numerous possibilities (even ridiculous and unworkable options) can lead to creative options, integrative and novel solutions.

The best way to get a good idea is to get a lot of ideas.

— Linus Pauling

Challenged by *Nightline* to redesign the common shopping cart in one week, the company IDEO conceived the following cart [pictured below].

After collecting data to understand the challenge (a more child-friendly, efficient, and safe cart) and observing shoppers in action, the team brainstormed towards a solution:

The classic brainstorming principles were printed on the walls, and we spread giant Post-it sheets with lots of colored markers about and plenty of toys to lighten the mood. We didn't fret if an idea was dull or even goofy, and we encouraged everyone to join the show-and-tell. The wacky concepts cracked everybody up and kept people from editing their own thoughts, like the privacy shade someone sketched (in case you're buying six cases of condoms) or the Velcro Seats with matching Velcro kid diapers to keep unruly toddlers safely stuck in place. . . .

[When] the cart was done . . . and . . . the *Nightline* segment ran, our phones wouldn't stop ringing. I took dozens of calls from executives around the country who'd seen the show. Most of them didn't give a damn about shopping carts. Instead, they wanted to know more about the process we used to bring the cart into being. One CEO told me that he understood, for the first time, what creativity really meant and how it could be managed in a business environment.

Thomas Kelley, The Art of Innovation 10, 13 (2001).

Yet another tool is looking for procedural resolutions when substantive resolutions cannot be found. For example, if disputants agree that Party A should compensate Party B for a piece of antique furniture but cannot agree on the value of the furniture they might agree to accept the valuation of a neutral expert. Tossing a coin to decide an issue is another example of a procedural resolution.

What follows is a short list of techniques to generate movement. They are divided into three categories. The first and second categories highlight strategies that strengthen the individual negotiating parties and enable them to understand each other's perspective. The third category highlights techniques that are targeted toward developing agreements. As you read these, note that many of the ideas for effective mediator strategies parallel approaches for negotiators. In one sense, a mediator is simply supporting and urging parties to be good negotiators.

 Lela P. Love & Joseph B. Stulberg, **TARGETS AND TECHNIQUES TO GENERATE MOVEMENT**

in Training Materials (2004)

POSITIVE PSYCHOLOGICAL STANCE. EMPOWERMENT. STRENGTH.

1. *Compliment productive behavior.* ("Thank you both for coming to mediation." "Thank you for explaining your concerns Ms. A, and thank you for listening patiently Mr. B." "I'd like to commend you both for coming up with a variety of options. Let's try to find one that works for both of you.") Behavior that is commended tends to be repeated! Sincere praise is empowering.

2. *Use a "paradoxical intervention."* Offer the parties a choice. ("It seems as if you keep returning to the question of who was at fault for the project's failure. We can certainly spend our time together exploring that question if you think that discussion would be useful. Or, in the hour we have remaining today, we could examine how you would like to structure future arrangements to address what happened. It's up to you. How would you like to spend the time?") This intervention is "paradoxical" because typically when people are offered the choice as to whether they would like to continue attacking and blaming each other or to move on, they will choose the latter, while, absent the offer, they will continue to attack and blame.

3. *Appeal to principles and ideals.* If disputants both agree that, for example, avoiding unnecessary harm or dividing a family's assets so that children share equally or treating men and women equally are shared principles or ideals, then those common goals can shape various elements of the discussion. The mediator can introduce quotations or images (photographs or paintings) that appeal to the human tendency to collaborate. [The quotation from Abraham Lincoln in the

> *Discourage litigation. Persuade your neighbors to compromise whenever you can. Point out to them how the nominal winner is often a real loser — in fees, expenses, and waste of time. As a peacemaker the lawyer has a superior opportunity of being a good man.*
> — Abraham Lincoln

box is an example of words that might shift lawyer behavior if displayed for the parties and advocates.]

UNDERSTANDING. RECOGNITION. PERSPECTIVE TAKING.

1. *Highlight common interests, common values and common feelings.* ("You both seem to care deeply about the happiness of your child." "If I understand you correctly, you both would like to find a way to end your partnership while preserving the value of the business you have created and also preserving your reputations.") Interests, values and feelings are powerful. When parties discover they share an interest or value or feeling it can become a common motivator and bridge.

2. *Build information base* regarding each party's inter-  ests, assumptions, aspirations, values, priorities, legal ana- lysis and past practices. ("Tell me more about....") Information is frequently the lever that shifts parties in meaningful ways. If you only see a rabbit in the picture (see box) you will be moved (an "ah-ha" moment) when you realize there is also a duck (or vice versa).

3. *Try role reversal.* This technique comprises a variety of methods to challenge a party to see the situation from the point of view of another party or person. A mediator could actually ask the parties to switch seats or to imagine how the other person is feeling or conceive a solution that the other party would find desir- able. ("Putting yourself for a moment in X's chair and considering what he has said here this morning about . . . how would you see this situation?")

BUILDING SETTLEMENTS AND AGREEMENTS.

1. *Explore the costs of no agreement*: quality of life ("What will it be like going home this evening and facing the same situation?") and process costs ("Have you explored the costs — in terms of time, money and stress — of litigation?"). Using decision tree formulas, for example, a mediator can assist parties to develop an analysis of the expected value of a litigated outcome (likely court outcome times % likelihood of that court outcome minus costs of litigation and discounted by the time it will take to get outcome) and to compare that figure to proposals on the table.

2. *Use deadlines to move participants.* ("The building closes at midnight. Up to this point we have achieved x, y, and z. Would you like to bring closure to this in this session? Any ideas?") One reason deadlines may be effective is that loss aversion comes into play. That is, the opportunity to bring closure may be lost forever if movement does not occur.

3. *Seek accommodations to priority proposals of the other side.* ("Ms. A, you have said you need money immediately, and Ms. B you are most concerned about the amount of the payment, is there any amount between $10,000, Ms. B's first offer, and $100,000, requested by Ms. A, that, Ms. A, you would be willing to accept if the money were paid immediately?")

In studying the skills of the problem-solving negotiator in Chapters 2 and 5, creativity was important. A mediator is charged with encouraging and supporting party creativity. Another way to look at generating movement is to examine what supports creativity in conflict. The following excerpt highlights factors that impact the human capacity to be creative. As you read this piece, think about what it tells both mediators who are charged with structuring an environment that supports creativity and lawyers who must assist their clients in the mediation process to be problem solvers.

 Peter T. Coleman & Morton Deutsch, **SOME GUIDELINES FOR DEVELOPING A CREATIVE APPROACH TO CONFLICT**

in The Handbook of Conflict Resolution 355-357, 360-363 (2000)

One of the creative functions of conflict resides in its ability to arouse motivation to solve a problem that might otherwise go unattended. . . . Accepting the necessity for change in the status quo (rather than rigid, defensive adherence to previously existing positions) is most likely, however, when the circumstances arousing new motivation suggest courses of action that pose minimal threat to the social or self-esteem of those who must change.

. . . The circumstances conducive to creatively breaking through impasses are varied, but they have in common that "they provide the individual with an environment in which he does not feel threatened and in which he does not feel under pressure. He is relaxed but alert." . . . Threat induces defensiveness and reduces both tolerance of ambiguity and openness to the new and unfamiliar; excessive tension leads to primitization and stereotyping of thought processes. . . . [T]hreat and excessive tension lead to the closed rather than open mind. To entertain novel ideas that may at first seem wild and implausible, to question initial assumptions of the framework within which the problem or conflict occurs, the individual needs the freedom or courage to express herself without fear of censure. Much research . . . has demonstrated that a competitive, as opposed to cooperative, approach to conflict leads to restricted judgment, reduced complexity, inability to consider alternative perspectives, and less creative problem solving. . . .

Seventeen Camels

There is a story of a man who left seventeen camels to his three sons. He left half the camels to his eldest son, a third to his middle son, and a ninth to his youngest. The three set to dividing up their inheritance but couldn't negotiate a solution because seventeen could not be divided by two or three or nine. The sons finally consulted a wise old woman. After pondering the problem, the woman said, "See what happens if you take my camel." So then the sons had eighteen camels. The eldest son took half — that was nine. The middle son took his third — that was six. And the youngest son took his ninth — that was two. Nine and six and two made seventeen. They had one camel left over. They gave it back to the wise old woman.

William Ury, Getting Past No 137 (1991).

[H]ow is a novel point of view developed and constructed?... [A] novel perspective regarding conflict is to view it as a mutual problem the conflicting parties can work on together, cooperatively, in an attempt to discover mutually satisfactory solutions.... [R]e-framing the conflict so that the conflicting parties see themselves as being in a collaborative rather than oppositional relation with regard to resolving their conflict is crucial to creative resolution. It not only produces an atmosphere conducive to creativity but vastly expands the range of potential solutions as well....

The availability of ideas is also dependent on such social conditions as the opportunity to communicate with and be exposed to other people who may have relevant and unfamiliar ideas (such as experts, impartial outsiders, people facing similar or analogous situations); a social atmosphere that values innovation and originality and encourages exchanging ideas; and a social tradition that fosters the optimistic view that, with effort and time, constructive solutions to problems that initially seem intractable can be discovered or invented....

USE TIME AND SPACE ARRANGEMENTS TO CREATE AN OASIS FOR CREATIVE PROBLEM SOLVING

John Cleese, who first found fame in *Monty Python's Flying Circus* and has been a consultant to many organizations on creativity, coined *time-space oasis* to depict a situation where the most basic conditions are met for functioning creatively.... The condition of time has two dimensions, length and endurance. People must have a sufficient amount of time to open up and see things flexibly and creatively, particularly if working in a conflict situation where they are operating primarily in a critical mode.... Once in a creative mode, disputants need ample time to create, but not so much time that they tire and become discouraged. Cleese recommends ninety minutes as a good amount of time for a working session (thirty minutes to open up and sixty minutes to work constructively).

The other component of time is the need for disputants to persist and endure, even after a marginally acceptable solution presents itself. Research has shown that humans tend to be poor decision makers because they often choose the first acceptable solution to a problem that emerges, even if it is far from being the best that could be developed. Truly creative solutions are usually discovered only after persisting in exploring the problem and its potential solutions. Prolonged and deep engagement with a problem can lead not only to a high level of innovation but also to deep and enduring satisfaction among the disputants with the agreement they produce.

The second dimension of the time-space oasis is having access to a different space. It is often useful for disputants to remove themselves from their customary environments to be able to think afresh. The many demands and distractions of one's usual environment, whether related to the conflict or not, draw one back into habitual or standard ways of seeing a problem and responding to it. A new environment (particularly a confidential one) can allow disputants some degree of freedom to try out new perspectives, behaviors, or ways of working with a problem.

DEVELOP A SERIOUS BUT PLAYFUL ATMOSPHERE

... [P]layfulness is often central to a creative process. Humor, play, and a sense of fun can all contribute to releasing tension and opening up one's view of things, ultimately leading to development of a novel point of view.... But humor, playfulness, and fun are tricky endeavors when working with difficult conflicts. Particularly in escalated conflicts, disputants often approach their problems grimly. Having a conflict resolver introduce humor or play could easily offend or enrage in these situations. If introduced, it must be done with sensitivity and artistry.

FOSTER "OPTIMAL" TENSION

Tension is the primary link between conflict and creativity. Conflict signals dissatisfaction with something or someone.... The tension works to engage the participants, but it also adversely affects their ability to think creatively, even if there is only minimal intergroup competition. Optimal tension ... is a state where there isn't too little tension regarding the problem being faced in a conflict (where the disputants are not sufficiently motivated to deal with the issues and the conflict remains unresolved) or too much tension (which can lead either to conflict avoidance because it is so threatening or to conflict escalation as the tension limits one to an oversimplified black-and-white perception of the issues).

Thus, it becomes critical for conflict resolvers to develop the skills necessary to assess the level of tension in a conflict system, to diagnose what level is optimal for a given system, and to discover levers for increasing tension (such as through using open confrontation or empowering members of low-power groups) or decreasing it (such as through using humor or temporarily separating disputants from one another).

FOSTER CONFIDENCE TO TAKE THE RISK OF BEING OUTLANDISH

Self-confidence is an individual characteristic that can affect a person's ability to take the risk involved in developing a novel point of view. However, a person's confidence level can also be significantly affected by the situation and by those in power (or perceived to be so) in the situation. Conflict specialists who emphasize their expertise and knowledge in a problem-solving session tend to elicit dependence and less confidence from the disputants, with the consequence that fewer novel ideas and recommendations are generated by the parties. A conflict specialist who supports and encourages the ideas of the disputants, highlighting those aspects of their ideas that are particularly useful or innovative, is likely to draw out a flow of ideas that expand the menu of perspectives and alternatives. It is important for facilitators to remember that the open flow of ideas and information is a dynamic responsive to the support (and playfulness) of the facilitator.

HAVE APPROPRIATELY PHASED OPEN (DIVERGENT) AND CLOSED (CONVERGENT) THINKING

This is the yin and yang of the creative problem-solving process. Creativity is most often associated with openness of ideas, a free-flowing of thoughts, images, symbols and so on. Decision making, though, is most often associated with moving toward closure: converging on the alternative or set of alternatives that best address the problem. A creative problem-solving approach to conflict requires both. Disputants must have the capacity and opportunity to open up to understand a problem from various perspectives and to generate many, perhaps novel, ideas or solutions, *as well as* the chance to (eventually) reach closure by taking a good, hard look at those perspectives and ideas and determining if they are any good and if they will work in a particular situation.

The open and closed modes of experience are in opposition to each other, in that it is difficult to remain open to new alternative possibilities while trying to close in on a final decision. It is therefore useful to alternate from one mode to another during the problem-solving process.

Typically, conflict moves people into the closed mode and produces rigid thinking with restricted judgment, reduced complexity, and narrower range of attention. Exactly why this occurs is unclear, but scholars have speculated that it may be due to a number of factors: the conflict triggering a negative affect such as anxiety, a competitive orientation overloading cognitive functioning and leading to preoccupation with formulating strategies and tactics to prevail in the conflict, or simply providing too much cognitive stimulation. If this occurs, conflict resolvers must find the means to reorient disputants, at least temporarily, into an open mode.

Recent research . . . has identified an important qualifier to the causal chain of "conflict equals tension equals impaired cognitive functioning." The research found that people's cognitive functioning does become more rigid and restricted if they either anticipate or engage in competitive conflicts, but not when they expect or engage in cooperative conflict. People in a cooperative experience are better able to combine categories, see commonalities in their positions, and better locate integrative solutions than those in competitive conflicts. . . .

Notes and Questions

6.17 A well-known riddle in mediation circles goes: "How many mediators does it take to hang a picture?" Answer: "None. Mediators don't hang pictures, they reframe them." Coleman and Deutsch recommend reframing to generate creative approaches. Lela Love also urges mediators to reframe. Why is reframing such an important aspect of mediation? By contrast, how do litigators reframe a conflict?

6.18 As mediators, what might we learn from Coleman and Deutsch about the time allotted for a mediation session? An optimal meeting place? The use of deadlines? Appropriate attire for a session? Would devoting a block of time to gathering information — with no proposals allowed — help generate a productive mind-set?

6.19 What implications for fostering creativity are there regarding substantive expertise of the mediator?

6.20 You have examined a variety of mediator strategies and techniques. Do you think it is beneficial for a mediator to explain *why* he is using a particular strategy or technique? For one example of a transparent approach, instead of a mediator's simply asking a party why the party is making a proposal that the lease run for no more than three years, the mediator might say: "I'm hoping you'll change the way you're thinking about your demands. Right now, you seem to be fixed on the idea that there is only one way you can be satisfied in this dispute, and that seems unlikely to me. I think it would be more productive for you and for this process if you (and the rest of us) were better able to understand the things that are motivating you to make these demands. Why is the duration of the lease important to you?" Michael Moffitt, Casting Light on the Black Box of Mediation: Should Mediators Make Their Conduct More Transparent?, 13 Ohio St. J. on Disp. Resol. 1, 13 (1997). What are the potential benefits and dangers of a transparent approach? Moffitt's article gives an excellent analysis of this question.

In the pie chart that follows on the next page, Christopher Moore provides another approach for thinking about generating movement. Inside the circle he shows the impediments that cause impasse in a given dispute. For each type of conflict, outside the circle, he gives a variety of interventions that would be responsive or appropriate to overcome the given impasse.

Christopher W. Moore, **THE MEDIATION PROCESS**

60–61 (1996)

Sphere of Conflict—Causes and Interventions

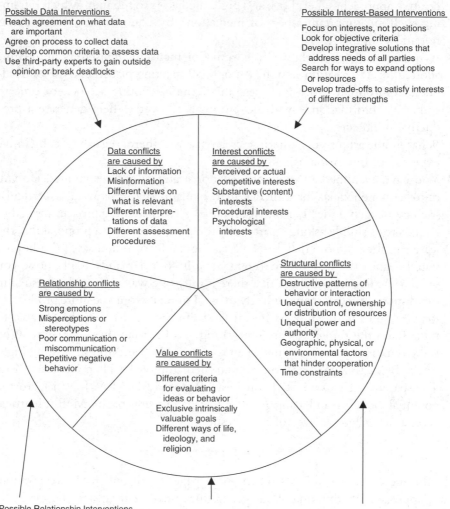

Possible Data Interventions
Reach agreement on what data
   are important
Agree on process to collect data
Develop common criteria to assess data
Use third-party experts to gain outside
   opinion or break deadlocks

Possible Interest-Based Interventions
Focus on interests, not positions
Look for objective criteria
Develop integrative solutions that
   address needs of all parties
Search for ways to expand options
   or resources
Develop trade-offs to satisfy interests
   of different strengths

Data conflicts
are caused by
Lack of information
Misinformation
Different views on
   what is relevant
Different interpre-
   tations of data
Different assessment
   procedures

Interest conflicts
are caused by
Perceived or actual
   competitive interests
Substantive (content)
   interests
Procedural interests
Psychological
   interests

Structural conflicts
are caused by
Destructive patterns of
   behavior or interaction
Unequal control, ownership
   or distribution of resources
Unequal power and
   authority
Geographic, physical, or
   environmental factors
   that hinder cooperation
Time constraints

Relationship conflicts
are caused by

Strong emotions
Misperceptions or
   stereotypes
Poor communication or
   miscommunication
Repetitive negative
   behavior

Value conflicts
are caused by

Different criteria
   for evaluating
   ideas or behavior
Exclusive intrinsically
   valuable goals
Different ways of life,
   ideology, and
   religion

Possible Relationship Interventions
Control expression of emotions
   through procedure, ground rules,
   caucuses, and so forth
Promote expression of emotions
   by legitimizing feelings and
   providing a process
Clarify perceptions and build
   positive perceptions
Improve quality and quantity
   of communication
Block negative repetitive
   behavior by changing structure
Encourage positive problem-
   solving attitudes

Possible Value-Related
Interventions
Avoid defining problem
   in terms of value
Allow parties to agree
   and to disagree
Create spheres of influence
   in which one set of
   values dominates
Search for superordinate
   goal that all parties
   share

Possible Structural Interventions
Clearly define and change roles
Replace destructive behavior patterns
Reallocate ownership or control
   of resources
Establish a fair and mutually acceptable
   decision-making process
Change negotiation process from
   positional to interest-based bargaining
Modify means of influence used by
   parties (less coercion, more persuasion)
Change physical and environmental
   relationships of parties (closeness
   and distance)
Modify external pressures on parties
Change time constraints (more or
   less time)

5. Using the Caucus

Among the strategies to generate movement, perspective taking, and a more creative approach to a dispute is to invite parties to meet separately with the mediator. After the mediator and each side give an opening statement — and at each juncture for the remainder of the mediation — a choice will be made about whether to stay in joint session or move to caucus. A joint session is where all the participants meet together with the mediator. A caucus is where the mediator meets individually with one side or some subset of the entire participant group (for example, one side only, lawyers only, clients only, kids without parents). In a caucus, parties are invited to speak openly with the assurance that the mediator will not share information conveyed unless given permission to do so. Practically speaking, this means that once a caucus is used the mediator must keep track of what he knows *and* how he learned what he knows *and* the constraints regarding use of the information if obtained in a caucus.

Different philosophies guide mediators in determining their preferred approach to using the caucus. Three dominant approaches are followed: caucus selectively, never caucus, always and mostly caucus.

a. *Caucus Selectively*

In the first approach, caucus selectively, most meetings are conducted in joint session unless there is a particular reason to caucus. Mediators following this approach might conduct an entire mediation without ever using a caucus. Such mediators view the caucus as a tool used only for particular applications. Reasons *not* to caucus include the belief that direct communication between parties is superior to using an intermediary and that parties benefit from working out matters themselves. A "selective caucus" mediator might suggest a caucus when, for example, communication becomes so heated or the parties so volatile that constructive progress is threatened, an apparent power imbalance suggests that individual explorations of the underlying dynamic is necessary, or the mediator wants to "reality check" that proposals being considered are doable and optimal.

In the excerpt below, Joseph Stulberg describes the selective caucus approach and some additional purposes for using the caucus.

 Joseph B. Stulberg, **TAKING CHARGE/MANAGING CONFLICT**

107-109, 121-122 (1987)

A mediator chooses to meet separately with the parties — to caucus with them — because he believes that doing so will contribute to the settlement process. The purpose in calling for and conducting any caucus can be stated succinctly: to obtain information and insights that a mediator does not believe he can acquire in joint discussions. Once such information or insights have been secured, the mediator closes the caucus and returns to a joint meeting.

Caucusing is another tool for a mediator. As with any tool, he must know why, when, and how to use it.

There are four primary reasons that guide a mediator's decision to recess a joint meeting in order to conduct separate sessions with the parties. Two are psychological in nature, the other two strategic.

Some persons are willing to share information, insights, or aspirations with a neutral intervener as long as others do not hear what they say. Such behavior is common: a child shares information with one parent about the other parent only on the condition that it remain confidential; students share feelings with deans about a particular professor, but not in that professor's presence; subordinates communicate concerns about their boss to colleagues or resource personnel that they do not reveal to their boss. People's motives for behaving this way are complex, ranging from not wanting to hurt or injure themselves to not wanting to offend the person who is the subject of their remarks. By meeting in a caucus session, a mediator can build on this behavior to shape an agreement. . . .

People also have a psychological need for a safety zone — a penumbra of privacy — during discussions. They need time to consider ideas, evaluate what others have said, or brainstorm possible solutions without feeling pressured into making an immediate response. They need a chance to make tentative commitments — "Well, but if I did that, would he be willing to do this?" — without fear that others will immediately interpret such remarks as definitive concessions. By meeting in a caucus session, a mediator creates this safety zone for each participant.

Strategically, a mediator must chip away at a party's rigidity. Sometimes the only way he can generate flexibility is by firing a series of pointed, stinging questions at the party. But the danger in a mediator's doing that in everyone's presence is twofold: first, he will generate a defensive response that will reinforce the parties' differences; second, he will undercut the parties' perception of his own neutrality. By asking such questions in a caucus format, the mediator can avoid these pitfalls. . . .

Similarly, the mediator probes sharply for weaknesses or loopholes in a party's position in order to convert them into bases for developing settlement terms. But he cannot engage in such an attack on a party's proposal without making that party feel that the mediator has turned against him and is no longer neutral. Conversely, if the other parties witness the mediator engaged in such an attack, they may believe he has now become their advocate, and may begin to take comfort in the belief that they do not need to modify their own position in order to reach a settlement. The mediator escapes both horns of that dilemma by pursuing his analysis in separate meetings. . . .

Caucusing can be very useful. It generates a sense of confidence and intimacy between the party and the mediator. It invites candor and encourages an uninhibited exploration of solutions.

But caucusing has drawbacks as well. It consumes enormous amounts of time. It transfers the responsibility for communication from the parties to the mediator. It blocks the development of creative energy that develops from a lively exchange and interaction among discussants.

So a mediator must use caucusing deliberately and selectively. He must not hesitate to use it when appropriate, but he must realize that he does not need to use it to resolve every dispute. Caucusing is a tool. Just because a person has a hammer, that does not mean he should treat everything else in the world as the head of a nail.

b. Never Caucus

Mediators using a never caucus approach believe that private meetings can taint the mediator's neutrality, can create undue reliance on the mediator, and can cut off the parties' direct communication and undermine the opportunity for collaboration. The Center for Mediation in Law, a prominent group of mediators and scholars using the Understanding-Based model described in Chapter 3, advocate this model. In one of their publications, they describe their "non-caucus" approach:

> The mediator holds all matters confidential as to outsiders, but holds nothing confidential between the parties. If the mediator speaks with either of the parties separately, which we believe is not the preferred way to proceed, that information is available to the other party.... [C]entral to the Center's model is the goal that all parties understand all relevant information rather than the mediator putting him- or herself in the position of being the only one who has the whole picture. The mediator will also not speak with the parties' lawyers unless both parties give permission.

Gary Friedman & Jack Himmelstein, Center for Mediation in Law, Memo No. 2, Elements of Mediator-Parties Contract (2003).

c. Always Caucus

In the always and mostly caucus approach, parties meet jointly at the beginning of the mediation and at the end when a resolution is reached. In the middle, the mediator conducts a series of caucuses. Proceeding in this manner ensures that hostilities between the parties do not escalate the dispute and maximizes mediator control over the flow of information and over the way proposals are developed and presented. The caucus, to the extent parties share information about their bottom line, also maximizes the potential benefit of mediation in preventing impasse where there is a positive zone of agreement. However, the approach also takes power and control away from the parties.

Eric Galton, an experienced mediator and former litigator, describes this approach.

 Eric Galton, MEDIATION: A TEXAS PRACTICE GUIDE

31-39, 42-46, 50-51 (1993)

I will hasten to admit that I rarely hold a collective session immediately after the lawyers' opening statements.... I would much prefer to allow ... venting to occur in separate caucus outside the presence of the other side....

As an experienced trial lawyer, I do not see mediation as ESP, voodoo, or a group therapy session. Anything told to me as a mediator in the privacy of the separate caucus is fine because I only hear it and it won't hurt my feelings. Further, despite the confidentiality of mediation, lawyers may be leery that their clients' candid statements in mediation may be used against them if the case does not resolve. For these reasons, I omit the collective session and move into the separate caucus except in the following situations:

1. When little or no discovery has been done. . . .
2. When the parties have a long-standing business relationship or friendship. . . .
3. It may be appropriate to discuss the procedural posture of the case, what discovery is remaining to get the case ready for trial, the length of the trial, the likelihood of appeal, and the remaining costs. . . .
4. When an acknowledgment of the negotiation posture may be appropriate. . . .
5. When the party has a real interest in "public shaming" as a pre-condition to resolution. . . .
6. When a party needs to express grief. . . .

The separate caucus is the essence of mediation. . . . The mediator will separately caucus with each party several times. In complex cases, I may have nine or ten separate caucuses with each party.

Notes and Questions

6.21 How would particular goals of the mediation process studied in Chapter 3 — settlement, participation, self-determination, better outcomes, better relationships — impact the choice of whether to use a caucus? With which goals is the always caucus model most in synch? The never caucus model?

6.22 Why might it still be useful to meet in a caucus format if the mediator does not offer confidentiality with respect to the other party?

6.23 Stulberg emphasizes that a purpose of the caucus is to *obtain* information. However, in more evaluative models of mediation, might a purpose also be to *provide* information in a more private setting? What kind of information might a mediator provide in a caucus? What are the dangers of giving information in such separate sessions?

6. Drafting Agreements and Closing the Session

Sessions can end: without an agreement, with a written agreement, with a verbal agreement, with a partial agreement regarding substantive issues, with an agreement to return for another session, or with an agreement to use some other procedure to address the dispute. One of the final tasks of a mediator is to help parties capture and memorialize their commitments to each other if they have been able to resolve their dispute. This is an important mediator function for several reasons. First, the mediator must ensure that the parties have a clear — and the same — understanding about the agreement so that a dispute does not arise about its terms. Reviewing the terms of agreement (if it is verbal) or reducing the agreement to a writing (if the parties want a written agreement) can aid that task. Second, helping bring closure with an agreement can be important both psychologically and practically. Psychologically, leaving mediation with an agreement means that the matter is put to rest, that closure is achieved. The internal debate about agreement terms can cease. Practically speaking, the parties can move on with their lives, and the momentum achieved in the session will not be lost by the passage of time and intervening events. If the matter is in litigation, the litigation can end.

Drafting agreements, however, is a task closely connected with the practice of law. Some mediators hesitate to draft agreements or even memoranda of understanding for fear they are engaging in the unauthorized practice of law or may otherwise expose themselves to liability. In business and employment cases where parties have their own attorneys, a mediator may well avoid drafting a detailed and comprehensive agreement, but rather leave that to the parties' attorneys. Many mediators, however, will draft a "bare-bones" memorandum of understanding at the parties' request, capturing essential features of the agreement. Attorney and mediator David Hoffman provides an example. (see box).

In situations where the parties do not have lawyers and ask the mediator to draft an agreement, the mediator can provide a valuable service by capturing agreement terms. In community cases, for example, mediators routinely draft agreements and would be remiss not to offer that service.

The safest posture for the mediator is to view herself as a scribe, capturing the parties' undertakings, using the parties' words, avoiding additional provisions, and advising the parties to get legal advice prior to signing the agreement.

In every case, whether any agreement is achieved, the mediator must end on as positive a

---

Commonwealth of Massachusetts

(Plaintiff) v. (Defendant)

____Superior Court (Docket #)

MEMORANDUM OF UNDERSTANDING

The parties in the above-entitled matter agree to the following settlement terms, which shall be incorporated in a formal settlement agreement.

1. On or before _____, 2003, Defendant shall pay Plaintiff $_____.

2. Contemporaneously with the above-referenced payment, the parties shall execute mutual general releases of all claims against any of the parties, their affiliated entities, officers, employees, agents, and representatives, and a stipulation of dismissal of the above matter with prejudice, without costs, and waiving all rights of appeal.

3. The formal settlement agreement shall contain a confidentiality provision and no-admission-of-liability provision.

4. Regardless of whether a formal settlement agreement is executed, the parties intend the terms of this memorandum of understanding to be legally enforceable.

5. Notwithstanding the confidentiality of the mediation process and the terms of this settlement, the parties agree that this memorandum of understanding may be submitted to any court of competent jurisdiction for purposes of enforcement.

_____   _____
Plaintiff   Defendant

note as possible, commending the parties for their efforts and acknowledging any constructive movement that has been made. The mediator will want both parties to leave the session at the same time, avoiding the appearance of partiality that may be created where one side lingers for a private conversation with the mediator. The mediator will also want to ensure there is an exit strategy so that parties who are still uncomfortable in each other's presence do not find themselves together in a small elevator.

Notes and Questions

6.24 In response to the unauthorized practice of law issue, the ABA Section of Dispute Resolution adopted a resolution on Mediation and the Unauthorized Practice of Law on February 2, 2002 (available at *http://www.abanet.org/dispute/ webpolicy.html*). With respect to agreement drafting, the resolution advises:

GOALS FOR AGREEMENTS

Understandable

✓ Use parties' own words
✓ Use plain English
✓ Use present tense
✓ Use separate, numbered paragraphs
✓ Avoid pronouns and abbreviations
✓ Use headings

Appealing

✓ Use parties' full names, correctly spelled
✓ Begin with aspirational goals and common interests
✓ Put positive commitments and mutual obligations first
✓ Balance the agreement
✓ Use nonjudgmental language
✓ Avoid admissions of wrongdoing
✓ Avoid unauthorized additions or omissions
✓ View agreement as draft until signed

Precise

✓ Have clear and verifiable methods of performance
✓ Be specific regarding payment terms
✓ Nail down the time frame
✓ Avoid valuative terms and vague words

Lela P. Love & Joseph B. Stulberg, Training Materials (2004).

When an agreement is reached in a mediation, the parties often request assistance from the mediator in memorializing their agreement. The preparation of a memorandum of understanding or settlement agreement by a mediator, incorporating the terms of settlement specified by the parties, does not constitute the practice of law. If the mediator drafts an agreement that goes beyond the terms specified by the parties, he or she may be engaged in the practice of law. However, in such a case, a mediator shall not be engaged in the practice of law if (a) all parties are represented by counsel and (b) the mediator discloses that any proposal that he or she makes with respect to the terms of settlement is informational as opposed to the practice of law, and that the parties should not view or rely upon such proposals as advice of counsel, but merely consider them in consultation with their own attorneys.

If you were a divorce mediator without legal training, but with a background
in psychology, would you feel comfortable drafting an agreement in light of
this resolution? If you were an attorney mediator would you feel comfortable
adding boilerplate terms to the parties' agreement?

6.25 There has been considerable and heated debate regarding a mediator drafting
and signing settlement agreements. For an overview of positions taken, see
Harry N. Mazadoorian, To Draft or Not to Draft, Disp. Resol. Mag. (Spring
2004). Do you feel mediators should provide the service of agreement drafting,
whether or not they are lawyers?

C. ANOTHER APPROACH: TRANSFORMATIVE MEDIATION

The model and strategies presented above assume that the mediator is chairing a
negotiation process where negotiable issues are targeted and the parties are accompanied and supported in a problem-solving quest to find resolutions to those issues.
The transformative approach to mediation, introduced in Chapter 3, rejects problem
solving as a goal, seeking instead party empowerment and recognition. Since the
goals of transformative mediation differ, at least in some respects, from other types of
mediation, practitioner skills also vary. The following excerpt describing transformative mediation practice explores some of the differences.

 Joseph P. Folger & Robert A. Baruch Bush, **TRANSFORMATIVE
MEDIATION AND THIRD-PARTY INTERVENTION: TEN
HALLMARKS OF A TRANSFORMATIVE APPROACH TO
PRACTICE**

13 Mediation Q. 263, 264-267 (1996)

At a conceptual level, the transformative approach to third-party practice is based on
certain premises about both the effects and the dynamics of intervention. One major
premise of the approach is that processes like mediation have the potential to generate
transformative effects, and that these effects are highly valuable for the parties and for
society.... Specifically, mediation's potential transformative effects are that it can
strengthen people's capacity to analyze situations and make effective decisions for themselves, and it can strengthen people's capacity to see and consider the perspectives of
others. In short, mediation is a process that enables people in conflict to develop a greater
degree of both self-determination and responsiveness to others, while they explore
solutions to specific issues. However — and this is the second major premise of the
approach — mediation is likely to have these transformative effects only to the extent
that mediators develop a mind set and habits of practice that concentrate on the opportunities that arise during the process for party empowerment and interparty recognition.

A focus on empowerment means that the mediator watches for the points in the
process where parties have opportunities to gain greater clarity about their goals,
resources, options, and preferences, and then the mediator works with these

opportunities to support the parties' own process of making clear and deliberate decisions. A focus on recognition means that the third party watches for those points where each disputant faces the choice of how much consideration to give the perspective, views, or experiences of the other, and then the third party works to support the parties' own decision-making and perspective-taking efforts at these points. It is in this sense that mediation is potentially transformative: It offers individuals the opportunity to strengthen and integrate their capacities for self-determination and responsiveness to others. If these effects are seen as valuable, the transformative approach to practice will make sense at the conceptual level. . . .

HALLMARKS OF TRANSFORMATIVE PRACTICE

When mediators are effectively putting the transformative approach into practice, the . . . patterns or habits of practice discussed below are evident in their work . . . [Two of ten hallmarks follow.]

"The opening statement says it all": Describing the mediator's role and objectives in terms based on empowerment and recognition. Mediators and other third parties following a transformative approach begin their interventions with a clear statement that their objective is to create a context that allows and helps the parties to (1) clarify their own goals, resources, options, and preferences and make clear decisions for themselves about their situation; and (2) consider and better understand the perspective of the other party, *if* they decide they want to do so. . . .

In orienting the parties about what a successful session might achieve, the intervenor frames formal agreement or settlement as one possible outcome of the process. However, instead of adopting a one-dimensional focus on settlement as the only aim of the process, the intervenor, in an opening statement, describes other outcomes . . . can be equally important. He or she emphasizes that the session can be successful if new insights are reached, if choices are clarified, or if new understandings of each other's views are achieved. The parties are encouraged to see any of these as positive outcomes and important accomplishments of the process, as significant as specific terms of agreement or action plans that may be reached. . . .

"It's ultimately the parties' choice": Leaving responsibility for outcomes with the parties. . . . An important hallmark of the transformative approach is that its practitioners consciously reject feelings of responsibility for generating agreements, solving the parties' problem, healing the parties, or bringing about reconciliation between them. Instead, third parties following a transformative framework sensitize themselves to feeling responsible for setting a context for, and supporting, the parties' own efforts at deliberation, decision making, communication, and perspective taking.

Thus, the mediator feels a keen sense of responsibility for recognizing and calling attention to opportunities for empowerment and recognition that might be missed by the parties themselves, and for helping the parties to take advantage of these opportunities as they see fit. In practice, calling attention to these opportunities means inviting the parties to slow down and consider the implications or questions that follow from a statement one of them has made. For example, to frame and help capture an opportunity for empowerment, the mediator may follow up an unclear statement from one party about goals or options by saying, "I'm not sure I understand fully what you've said; can you talk a bit more about that?" The party's ensuing restatement, and perhaps further questions, may produce a greater level of clarity and empowerment. Likewise, to frame and capture an opportunity for recognition, the mediator might call one party's attention to a statement the other has offered to explain their past conduct and then ask the listening party whether the information contained in the statement might alter his or her view of the other disputant or the conflict in general. . . .

Notes and Questions

6.26 It is noteworthy that the transformative mediation program for workplace disputes adopted by the U.S. Postal Service has explicitly rejected *settlement rate* as a measure of program success, but rather looks to *participation rate*. Even though the resolution of the participants' dispute is *not* among the transformative mediator's goals, the case closure rate for the U.S. Postal Service program is nonetheless impressive — between 70 and 80 percent. Case closure means that a resolution is achieved in mediation, a settlement is concluded within 30 days of mediation, or the complainant does not pursue the matter to the formal EEO complaint stage. The participation rate — the percentage of employees offered mediation who agree to participate — exceeds 80 percent. Lisa Bingham, Mediation at Work: Transforming Workplace Conflict at the United States Postal Service, IBM Center for the Bus. of Govt. (2003), available at *http://www.businessofgovernment.org/pdfs/Bingham_Report.pdf.* This data suggests that where mediators target party empowerment and recognition, they may nonetheless achieve settlement.

6.27 Looking back at the opening statement provided earlier in this chapter, does it differ from what a transformative mediator would say? Does the opening statement target goals other than settlement? The "looping" technique, described earlier in this chapter, should result in opportunities for party empowerment and recognition. Can you think of additional overlaps between different mediation models?

D. THE IMPACT OF DIFFERENCES AND DIVERSITY

The parties' experience of the process and the mediator's and representative's theories, strategies, and skills will all be influenced by the cultural context of the dispute. Culture and other differences — gender, age, ethnicity, religion, education, social standing, profession, nationality, and a variety of other factors — will all impact the conduct of negotiation and mediation. Isabelle Gunning explores different mediation approaches for different cultures in the excerpt that follows.

Isabelle R. Gunning, **DIVERSITY ISSUES IN MEDIATION: CONTROLLING NEGATIVE CULTURAL MYTHS**

1995 J. Disp. Resol. 55, 83–86

Mediation, as a method of resolving disputes, has a long tradition that is not exclusively American. The American emphasis on non-intervention as the mark of neutrality is a product of the culture. Other cultures have made different choices on the "activism" of mediators. For example in both the Navajo Peacemaker Court and the Filipino Katarungang Pambarangay system, traditional methods of non-adversarial dispute resolution are kept alive which involve "mediators," called peacemakers or barangay captains, who intervene much more actively than their American counterparts even though they too are not decision-makers for the parties. In both these kinds of mediations, the mediators have confidence in their own knowledge of the community values which all participants are assumed to share. Two aspects of these mediations mark them especially: (1) the mediators openly inject concerns larger than the participants themselves; for example, community harmony and even spiritual guidance which they understand the parties share; and (2) the mediators are rarely ever strangers or unknown volunteers or professionals even though they are not to be biased towards one side or the other.

The Navajo peacemaker does not make American style claims of neutrality. He will often be a relative of the disputing parties and his role will involve teaching and even "lecturing" the parties on Navajo values and "how their behavior comports with shared values." The ground rules for a peace making session are steeped in ceremony and tradition, beginning and ending with prayers. Filipino mediators, somewhat like Navajo peacemakers, are comfortable making strong recommendations to the participants on how they should resolve their disputes. Like Navajo peacemakers, Filipino mediators often know the parties. The mediator is not likely to be a relative, but as the local barangay captain [an elected village leader] . . . they will often be familiar with the parties or their situation. Also similar to the Navajo peacemaker, the Filipino mediator, with his familiarity with the community, will have an interest in maintaining the peace within the larger community. The attitude is reflected in the practice of the mediator getting personally involved with helping the disputants achieving agreement. The session does include a spiritual component, like the Navajo Peacemaker Court, and often begins with prayer.

American mediation, in contrast, is more individualistically oriented since American culture is more individualistic than the cultures described (or indeed most cultures). But Americans cannot be said to be without concerns for the larger community and connections amongst its varied members. The non-interventionist model leaves to the parties the decision whether to discuss openly any conflicting feelings between one's individual concerns and one's communal concerns. The parties' ability to make individual, isolated decisions is augmented by the fact that in American mediation the mediator and the parties are generally unfamiliar with each other and so all are unaware of anyone's personal values or community status. However, the notion that the mediator should be a stranger to the parties is not one that is necessarily universally shared. It is an interesting comment on the amount of distance and distrust among Americans that we think that we will be more fairly treated by strangers of unknown quantities than by people we know. One can imagine that there are people who find it difficult and unnatural to discuss painful and personal matters in front of strangers, who might well prefer a mediator about whom they have some knowledge or respect or with whom they have had some contact. These aspects of American culture suggest that, as in Navajo or Filipino culture, a more interventionist style of mediation which responds more directly to needs for connectedness and community may be appropriate. On the other hand, the comparatively heavy influence of religion in these other societies' mediation forms underscore the problem of intervention. While many Americans practice some form of religion or nurture a spiritual life and increasingly feel that a religious belief system is important, not all Americans will practice their spiritual beliefs in the same way. Indeed conflicting spiritual beliefs have been and continue to be the source of much conflict between different segments of American society.

The value of respect for the individual reflected in the structure of American mediation is appropriate for our culture and its shared values on individual rights. But it is important to keep sight of the fact that connectedness and community are also values shared in American culture and that the mediation process, in other ways, very consciously nurtures and encourages those values. In a typical, even non-interventionist mediation, certain values of community are assumed to be shared; for example, connection, the ability to agree, mutual respect and peaceful resolution of conflict. Opening statements typically include remarks encouraging the parties to think in terms of their ability to agree and flagging for the parties that treating each other with respect (no name calling or interrupting) constitutes one of the few "rules" of mediation.

Notes and Questions

6.28 Phyllis Bernard highlights issues in developing countries that make the job of an international mediator highly sensitive, including complex webs of duties owed in traditional village structures, repercussions in rural areas from business transactions in cities, power structures that may not be visible to an outsider, and dangerous military realities and reactions that might lead to dire consequences. (See Phyllis Bernard, Cross-Cultural Mediation Process Skills: Understanding the Cultural Geography for Mediation, Synopsis of Comments, Panel Presentation for the ABA Section on Dispute Resolution International Conference in Washington, D.C. (Sept. 12, 2003)). Mediators and trainers cannot blithely transport their familiar process to foreign lands without care and appropriate adjustment.

6.29 From Chapter 3, recall Waldman's norm-educating and norm-enforcing variants of the mediation process, and Freshman's community-enhancing and community-enabling models. How would you characterize the traditional Navajo and Filipino approaches?

E. CO-MEDIATION

As the next excerpt describes, co-mediation — the use of two (or more) mediators for a dispute — can be helpful in a variety of situations. The strategies relevant to operating in a team, however, are challenging. Being a good partner requires study and practice, much as the strategies of serving as a mediator or a representative.

 Lela P. Love & Joseph B. Stulberg, **PRACTICE GUIDELINES FOR CO-MEDIATION: MAKING CERTAIN THAT "TWO HEADS ARE BETTER THAN ONE"**

---

13 Mediation Quarterly 179 (1996)

The difficult and delicate nature of a mediator's job argues both for and against a team approach for mediators. Where co-mediators operate in synch with one another, have the same vision of the mediation process and its goals, and have a plan that maximizes the strengths of the mediation team, their combined talents increase their capacity to respond to the myriad challenges they will face. However, when either mediator feels disrespected or underutilized in the mediation, the mediators have different visions of the goals of the process, or the mediators have no plan for or understanding of their tasks and roles vis-à-vis each other, co-mediators can be *worse* than a solo mediator, as the difficult and delicate task of trying to harmonize a dysfunctional or unprepared team is added to the usual challenges that mediators face.

Co-mediation has been routinely used in a variety of program and case situations. For example, in some programs, training needs and quality control make co-mediation advisable. Less experienced apprentice mediators are paired with more experienced mentor mediators, both to provide further training for the apprentice mediator and to ensure that disputants are well served. In some case situations, such as divorce proceedings, an attorney and a mental health professional and a male and female are recommended as the mediator team in order to address the legal and psychological complexities of such matters. Similarly, in highly specialized areas, such as intellectual property, a mediator with substantive expertise — legal, factual, or technological — might productively team with a mediator who has process expertise.

Whatever the rationale, for co-mediation to be effective, the mediators must understand its potential advantages and pitfalls. They must thoughtfully match themselves with compatible partners and must make a plan for effective teamwork, or they will lose the potential benefits.

This article will summarize the advantages and disadvantages that can be realized through co-mediation and then suggest and discuss practice guidelines designed to maximize co-mediation's advantages and minimize its risks.

An effective co-mediation team can:

- Enhance the expertise, insights, and listening capacity of the intervenors, who may possess diverse backgrounds, professions, and ethnicities.

- Increase the patience and perseverance of the mediation team by sharing the burden of being on the line.
- Create balance on the mediation team due to diversity of mediators (for example, male and female, Caucasian and African American, attorney and social worker).
- Provide a model for the parties of effective communication, cooperation, and interaction.
- Multiply the linkages that different parties can develop with the mediators, increasing the stamina and tolerance of the parties, who are given a second voice and perspective.
- Allow one mediator to take a risk, while having the other mediator available to come to the rescue.
- Make the mediation more efficient by division of tasks between the mediators.
- Create training, learning, and enrichment opportunities for mediators, who will benefit from working with each other.

To avoid potential pitfalls, co-mediators must also know the dangers of co-mediation. Possible disadvantages of co-mediation include:

- Conflict and competition among co-mediators can make mediation more difficult.
- Co-mediation can be more time-consuming than solo mediation, as mediators have to negotiate about their roles and tasks.
- Parties might try to divide and conquer the mediation team by focusing on the most sympathetic mediator, rather than having a single focus.
- Mediators, in an effort to avoid stepping on each other's toes or risking disapproval by asserting themselves, might hesitate to make moves they otherwise would make, resulting in each mediator being unduly constrained and handicapped.

[The following] practice guidelines for co-mediators . . . [are suggested] to capture co-mediation's potential advantages and to minimize the risk of its potential harms.

1. Choose a Partner with a Similar Vision of Mediation's Goal and Compatible Strategies for Executing the Mediator's Job.

Differences in fundamental goals can cause a team to pull unproductively against each other. Is the mediators' main task to assist the parties in understanding each other more fully and in facilitating dialogue aimed at resolving the negotiating issues? Or is the main task to get an agreement as quickly and efficiently as possible? Before a co-mediation begins, the mediators must discuss their goals and objectives and be sure they are a compatible team.

Co-mediators must also be sure that they share similar approaches and strategies. Are groundrules presented to the parties or are the parties invited to negotiate with each other to establish groundrules? Is the caucus used routinely in every case or only in special circumstances? Do attorneys sit at the table or away from the table? The co-mediators must be comfortable and confident concerning basic strategies they adopt.

While it may be productive to *observe* and learn from a mediator with a different orientation and basic strategies, effective partnership requires a consonance in goals, objectives, and strategies.

2.   Give Leadership Roles to Co-Mediators.

So that a power vacuum does not exist, one member of the co-mediation team should be in charge at any given point. Particularly where mediators have not co-mediated together in the past, allocating leadership roles should minimize the chance of conflict among mediators. If there is conflict, the leader gracefully takes over, and the conflict does not disrupt the session. Either one of the mediators can take the lead for the entire session or the session can take divided into discrete segments (delivering the opening statement, gathering information, articulating the issues and creating a discussion agenda, keeping track of agreements as they are reached, closing the session) with leadership changing for various segments. The latter approach can maximize particular strengths of each mediator and give the mediators a more equal voice.

3.   Strategically Use the Seating Arrangement to Maximize Opportunities for Success.

Important goals in structuring the seating arrangement include, maximizing the co-mediators' ability to communicate with each other, taking advantage of the diversity of the mediation team to balance the room, unifying the parties' focus, and providing for mediator breaks. The examples that follow illustrate how these goals may be affected by various seating configurations.

Example 1:

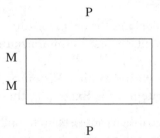

Discussion: This arrangement has the advantage of helping to unify the focus of the conversation as the parties look toward both mediators and address them when they speak. Side conversations directed toward one mediator would be minimized. Also, given their proximity to each other, the mediators can pass a note or quietly make a suggestion to each other without causing a distraction. But this configuration has drawbacks: the mediators cannot see each other easily, thereby making intrateam communication more difficult; further, sitting side by side keeps both mediators in the line of fire at all times. Example 2 avoids each of these drawbacks.

Example 2:

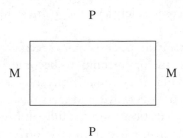

Discussion: The advantages of this arrangement address the two weaknesses of Example 1. It allows the mediators to see each other and the parties easily, and it provides some breathing space for each mediator. When the focus of the conversation is held by one mediator, the other can take a rest from the parties for creative reflection and recuperation. One challenge of this seating arrangement, however, is for the mediators to maintain a unified focus and not allow side conversations between a party and the less active mediator. This can be accomplished by the less active mediator riveting attention on the designated speaker.

Example 3:

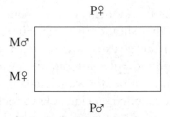

Discussion: Distributing the mediators in this manner contributes to balancing and harmonizing the room. If the female mediator were seated next to the female party and the male next to the male, it might suggest that the mediators were in advocacy roles and thereby tend to polarize the room.

These examples are not given to suggest there is one correct seating configuration, but rather to emphasize that seating arrangement, like other aspects of planning and executing an effective co-mediation, is important and must be done thoughtfully. Obviously, other table shapes than the one presented should be considered as well.

4.   Assign Specific Tasks to Each Mediator to Make the Mediation as Efficient and Productive as Possible.

Having one mediator in charge of specific tasks can facilitate the session and lighten the load on the other mediator. Therefore, assigning one person to write agreements as they emerge, manage paperwork, check on resources, or obtain special information, while the other focuses solely on the parties' interaction, can maximize mediator resources.

Whenever one mediator is not undertaking a specific task or is less active than the other, he or she should use the opportunity to become an astute process observer, tracking both the subtleties of parties' interactions and the substantive developments in the session. Having an extra pair of eyes and ears to assume this task ensures that the resources offered by a co-mediation team are fully utilized.

There is a tendency for co-mediation to take longer if it entails extensive conferencing between the mediators. This can be alleviated if the mediators use wisely the additional resources a team provides.

Note that effective planning takes time! Co-mediators must allow for planning time and then use that time to ensure they share similar goals, objectives, and strategies for the mediation process, and to discuss seating, administration, and assignment of leadership roles and specific tasks.

5.   Use the Opening Statement to Set the Right Tone for the Co-Mediation.

Most mediators begin their joint conferences by making an opening statement. When co-mediating, mediators should thoughtfully present their opening remarks in a manner that reinforces their being perceived as a team.

For example, if one mediator delivers the entire opening statement, she should close by saying to the other mediator, "Mr. (Co-Mediator), is there anything you would like to add?"

If the mediators divide the components of the opening statement so that they each participate in its delivery, they should have a transition strategy that they convey to the parties: "I will explain the goals of our session today, and then Ms. (Co-Mediator) will review the ground rules for our discussion. And, of course, we will answer any questions you have before we begin."

Also, if the mediators have assigned specific tasks to each other, they should alert the parties to their particular roles, noting that their functions might shift as the session proceeds. Such an explanation should enhance the parties' confidence that the mediators have developed a thoughtful plan. When the mediators proceed to do what they have promised, they will build more confidence and trust. Furthermore, in discussing their roles, mediators are implicitly encouraging the parties to understand the mediation process and become engaged in strategies to design productive sessions.

In delivering the opening, the pronoun *we* should be routinely used to describe the mediation team's goals, roles and groundrules, instead of the pronoun *I*.

6.   Adopt the Principle of Non-competition Among Mediators.

There is no need for one mediator to have equal time with the other mediator. In fact, one mediator might be on a roll and do 90 percent of the mediation. "Whatever works best" should be the guiding principle for determining which mediator is most active.

Mediators must be flexible. If one person, by prior arrangement, has been designated the lead mediator for a particular segment of the mediation but the other mediator is doing effective work, then the lead must step back, watch vigilantly, and be ready to take a more active role when and if a useful contribution can be made.

A caveat to this principle of non competition, (emphasized below in the discussion on using diversity to maximum advantage) is that the credibility of a co-mediator who never assumes a visibly participatory role is likely to be seriously eroded, limiting the possibility of making a contribution later in the process. Further, a seemingly inactive co-mediator who is aligned with one of the parties due to sex, age, or ethnicity might exacerbate a power imbalance between the parties by modeling such an imbalance on the mediation team. If a weaker party is already feeling overwhelmed by negotiating with a stronger party and the weaker party identifies with the inactive co-mediator due to some apparent gender, ethnicity, or age match, the inactive co-mediator's apparent nonparticipation could result in the weaker party feeling increasingly uncomfortable and disempowered. In this situation, the co-mediators may inadvertently further skew an already unlevel playing field, thereby missing an opportunity to model effective and competent interaction. Such a model might help a weaker party speak out, asserting interests and examining options that might otherwise be lost to the discussion. Co-mediators must be sensitive to such considerations. Teamwork, of course, requires more than the mere absence of competition.

7. Remember to Consult with the Other Mediator Before Making Important Decisions.

After any completed segment of the mediation, the mediator who is most active should inquire of the other mediator: "Is there anything you would like to add?" or "Is there anything we should explore further before moving on?"

Important decisions, such as structuring the discussion agenda or declaring a caucus, must be made with the consensus of the team. That consensus can be secured with a subtle nod across the table or after a mediator conference held during a recess. Mediators must work out communication signals ahead of time, including signals that address both procedural decisions (for example, when a mediator conference is necessary) and tactical moves (for example, deciding which party to caucus with first).

8. Maintain a Unified Focus so That Common Understandings Are Reached.

Mediators should not allow parties to split the conversation between the mediators. That is, while one party is addressing the active mediator, the other party should not be allowed to have a private conversation with the less active mediator. To maintain a unified focus, the less active mediator can rivet attention on the party who has the floor and refuse to be distracted by the other party. Moreover, the more active mediator can assist in maintaining a unified focus by using the pronoun *we*, rather than *I*, when describing goals and groundrules or when making suggestions to the parties.

Finally, to sustain the unified focus, when one co-mediator is exploring a topic or pursuing a line of questions, the other co-mediator must be careful not to jump in and initiate conversation on a totally different track. Co-mediators must be supportive of each other's effort to bring closure to a given angle or analysis.

At an advanced level, though, it is possible for co-mediators to maintain a unified focus even while pursuing different agendas simultaneously. For instance, there is a potential to conduct simultaneous caucuses with both (all) parties by splitting up the mediation team. If speed is a primary consideration and if the goals of the caucus are extremely clear, using this technique can be extremely effective even though it adds a layer of complexity to the communication process among the mediators.

9. Use the Diversity of the Mediation Team to Maximum Advantage.

In considering the room layout, mediators should position themselves to take greatest advantage of their diversity and not to polarize the situation in any way, as illustrated in Example 3 under the point on seating arrangements.

In situations where there is an apparent power imbalance between the parties, there should not be a matching power imbalance on the mediation team. That is, if there is a female party at a disadvantage due to a more powerful male party, the female mediator (on a male-female mediation team) should display — at a minimum — equality with her male co-mediator. In this context, the mediators might strategically plan for the female mediator to have equal floor time with the male. When structuring the mediation team in such a case, it might be particularly important for the female partner to be a strong, experienced mediator.

10. Have a Fall-Back or Fail-Safe Plan if Co-Mediation Is Not Working.

Not every team works well together. Particularly if mediators are co-mediating with each other for the first time, they must realize that it may not go smoothly. Should a mediator decide that the team is less helpful to the parties than a solo mediator would be, switch strategies. Instead of allowing the parties to suffer because the team cannot operate effectively, allow one of the mediators to conduct the session, while the other mediator observes. The lead mediator will generally be the one to take over at this point.

Should such a dysfunctional performance occur, the co-mediators should decide in their debriefing session whether they can develop a plan for a successful co-mediation in the future or whether they should simply not co-mediate. In the latter case, they may still profit from observing each other mediate.

11. Be Flexible.

Frequently, plans made by co-mediators regarding the division of responsibility, lead assignments, and the like, must be altered based on new developments in the mediation. For example, a mediator who achieves a better rapport with one or both parties, might become the more active mediator, regardless of the team's original plans. In other cases, a particular substantive expertise or industry knowledge of one of the mediators may emerge as helpful to the discussion, which results in a needed shift of mediator roles. Just as a solo mediator must be flexible and respond to shifting circumstances, a team must have a built-in principle of flexibility and be able to alter plans seamlessly when the situation requires.

12.   Debrief After Each Co-Mediation.

Among the special advantages of co-mediation is its potential to allow mediators to learn from each other. This can best be accomplished if the mediators give each other constructive feedback after each session.

Additionally, teams need to analyze their strengths and weaknesses so that future co-mediations can avoid past pitfalls and build on prior successes.

A de-briefing session should be arranged after each mediation. In such a session, each mediator should invite comments about individual and team strengths, individual and team areas for improvement, and the plan for the next mediation session. Knowing in advance that debriefing is part of co-mediation, each mediator should keep notes during the mediation targeted for the feedback session. If feedback is to be helpful, general points need to be linked to specific examples and actual quotations, both of which require notes to remember!

The debriefing session should be held at the earliest opportunity after the actual mediation session so that each mediator's recollections are fresh. Of course, observations must be made in the spirit of improving each individual's and the team's performance, rather than having a judgmental tone. Positive feedback is at least as critical as discussion of problem areas. Positive feedback highlights strengths and leads to repetition of successful behaviors. In addition, stroking and supporting your partner by recognizing strengths tends to create more receptivity to a focus on areas for improvement.

13.   Support Each Other.

It is common to have one member of the co-mediation team who is more experienced and confident than the other. Especially in such a case, the more confident mediator must allow room for the less confident one to participate, encouraging and respecting all contributions. Otherwise, the special benefits of co-mediation will not be realized. Mistake will be made by experienced and inexperienced mediators alike. The point is to recover from them smoothly and quickly; there will be time in the debriefing discussion to plan for avoiding similar pitfalls in the future.

Whenever one mediator is more active than the other, the more active mediator should regularly allow openings for the less active mediator to speak. The same way that a mediator asks parties to add to or clarify what has been said, the less active co-mediator should be invited to re-frame, reflect, and otherwise participate in the discussion. This practice minimizes the possibility of one mediator feeling disrespected or frozen out by the other.

It is essential for co-mediators to view each other as enhancing the process. Both mediators must see co-mediation as a positive mode of service and must secure a partner with whom they work effectively.

Notes and Questions

6.30 What benefits can you see in having a male and female co-mediation team in a divorce case? A therapist and lawyer team? What about situations where parties are from different cultures and speak different languages? In those cases, what protections might a co-mediation team offer? A variety of training and apprenticeship programs partner novice and experienced mediators in co-mediation teams. What are the advantages of that approach?

6.31 Can you apply the points about successful co-mediation teams to good partnerships generally? Consider the 13 guidelines in the context of giving presentations with colleagues or partnering with another attorney on a negotiation team. What guidelines might be applicable to working with friends and family?

In the next excerpt you will see a co-mediation team in action.

F. THE SELF-REFLECTIVE PRACTITIONER

Whether you are operating as the mediator or the attorney representative in mediation, an important indicia of your competence and your potential for growth is your regular practice of thoughtful reflection. While anyone can make mistakes (and everyone does), it is unfortunate to spend a lifetime making the same mistakes over and over. Consequently, viewing oneself as a lifelong learner is critical to successful performance. After each engagement, ask, "What happened and why? What did I do well? What could I improve?" See Donald Schön, The Reflective Practitioner (1983) for a model of reflective practice, now used in many professions.

In this final excerpt, Carol Liebman, a master mediator, reflects about her service as a mediator between student groups and the administration at Columbia University. The mediation succeeded in ending a student hunger strike and building takeover and in developing responsive agreements about curricula reform at Columbia. Note the mediator's capacity to be both reflective about the process and constructively self-critical.

 Carol B. Liebman, MEDIATION AS PARALLEL SEMINARS: LESSONS FROM THE STUDENT TAKEOVER OF COLUMBIA UNIVERSITY'S HAMILTON HALL

16 Negot. J. 157 (2000)

In April of 1996, a faculty colleague and I spent four days and all of one night mediating the student takeover of Hamilton Hall at Columbia University. The building takeover was the culmination of a year-long debate about whether or not Ethnic Studies should become a formal part of the university's curriculum. When I was called in (by the university) to mediate, three students had been on a hunger strike for twelve days and were approaching what I was told was the point at which they began to be in danger of long-term damage to their health. Two days earlier, the university had called the New York City Police, which resulted in the arrest of 22 demonstrators at another of the university's main buildings. In short, the debate over Ethnic Studies was rapidly escalating. . . .

THE MEDIATION . . .

The Opening Session

We started the mediation Friday evening with the traditional mediators' opening: We reviewed our understanding of the process and our role in it. . . . After our opening statement, we asked all the participants to sign the agreement to mediate. The students caucused to discuss the agreement and came back with the request that the following one-sentence paragraph be added:

> In the event that any individual or group decide to withdraw from mediation he/ she/they will communicate the reason for that withdrawal in writing to the other participants in the mediation.

At the time, my reaction was that this was just a move by the students to establish control of the process. Probably because I was extremely anxious to get all the participants to commit to the process and to start discussions, it did not occur to me at the time to use a standard mediator move of exploring what underlying interest of the student team was represented by this requested addition. I did not appreciate the value of that paragraph until after the mediation, when one of the university negotiators told me that having that requirement of a written explanation before withdrawing kept them going at times when they were ready to give up. In addition, I did not understand until after the mediation that the paragraph was a way for the members of the student negotiation team to bind themselves to each other and to the process.

Mediation as Parallel Seminars

Once the agreement was signed, Carlton [my co-mediator] and I indicated that we intended to start by having everyone who wanted to speak tell us their view of the situation. This request was greeted with a fair amount of eye rolling by members of both teams. I had the sense they were thinking they had already told their stories ad nauseam. They were right but, as in so many mediations, stories had been told but not heard. A great deal of what we did as mediators during the first few hours was basic clarification of exactly what the parties intended by various phrases or actions. We asked the students such questions as, "When you say Ethnic Studies what do you mean? Why is it important to you?" We asked the university representatives questions like, "When you say 'it (Ethnic Studies as a department) can't happen in the university,' tell us how the university works." We were really conducting two parallel seminars the whole four days, but especially that first evening. In one, the members of the university team taught us how universities are governed, how change comes about in the university, and how faculty get appointed. In the other seminar, the members of the student team taught us what they mean by Ethnic Studies, why it is important to them as a way of addressing the alienation they feel, and why it should be important to the university....

Building Trust

...While earning the trust of the student team was an underlying issue throughout the process, it became an explicit issue early in the mediation. We had taken a break so that the student team could confer. I had gone to my office in the law school, where the mediation sessions were being held. Carlton was elsewhere. The students...came to my office and asked to meet with me. One student said that they thought that I had cut him off when he tried to take the discussion in a certain direction, saying that we were not ready to talk about that topic. He charged that, fifteen minutes later, another student had brought the same topic up and I had not objected. He accused me of trying to split the student group.

Frankly, I did not remember the exchange, and said so. I also said I was sorry if I had given that impression. I acknowledged that sometimes mediators looked for differences within a negotiating team, but told them I had realized early that that was not going to be a useful approach in this situation. I paused, and then my mediator instincts took over: I addressed an underlying issue by saying to the student who had challenged me, "If what you are really asking me is, 'Have I heard about you as a controversial student?' the answer is 'Yes, I have.' I have been told that you can be pretty wild, but I haven't seen that here and I am going on what I have seen." I had felt the tension in the room go down a little when I said I was sorry if I had given the student the impression I was trying to split the group. However, when I acknowledged the underlying reputation issue, the decrease in tension was remarkable. I knew I had made a small inroad toward establishing trust. Mediators talk about the importance of addressing underlying issues. And we talk about how discussing explosive issues can make them less scary. But I was still stunned by the impact on my interactions with the students of the use of those basic techniques....

Lessons Learned and Relearned

Saturday was the kind of day most mediators would expect—joint sessions, caucuses with the mediators present, caucuses without the mediators. On Saturday, I learned one important lesson and relearned another. The lesson I learned was about the importance of food in mediation, while the lesson I relearned was about ways in which a mediator's personal stake in the outcome of a dispute can interfere with her effectiveness.

A Lesson Learned — The Role of Food.

Before the Hamilton mediation, the only time I had thought about the role of food in mediation was when a student from the Middle East mentioned, in a class discussion about cultural differences and conflict, that in his culture, if you broke bread in public with someone with whom you had been having a dispute, it was a signal that the dispute was over. When Carlton and I began the Hamilton Hall mediation, we had been authorized to order refreshments as needed. We had a local provider (the aptly named Hamilton Deli) send over soda, juice, chips, cookies, and fruit. I had been on a weight loss program for several months and decided to see if I could stick with that regime during the mediation instead of doing what would have been more typical for me — going for the chocolate and junk food. As a result, I ended up (until Monday afternoon) staying away from junk food and sweets, instead eating a piece of fruit, a yogurt, or half a sandwich every two or three hours to maintain a steady energy level. Also, in the months before the mediation, I had not been drinking much caffeine; so, when I started to drag, a Coke or cup of tea had much more than the normal impact.

Once the mediation sessions began, normal eating schedules for all the participants disappeared. I realized the first night that, when members of the negotiation teams had not eaten for a long time, their morale dropped, they became pessimistic, and it was difficult to get them to consider new options. Then they would eat and would experience a surge of energy which let us make some progress for about an hour before they began to sag again. Often the two teams were eating on different schedules. We would break for caucuses or meetings with constituents. During the break, one team would grab a bite while the other would return to the table hungry and dragging.

As mediators, we had to be aware of where the teams were in terms of their energy level. We needed to pay attention to when people were eating and manage the additional tension that was created when one team returned to the table full of energy after a meal while the other was dragging. If both teams had "refueled" at about the same time, we had the opportunity to take on tough issues and make progress. When they were eating at different times, we needed to use caucuses to take advantage of the opportunities for movement presented by the high energy team while encouraging the team that was dragging.

An Old Lesson Relearned — The Risks When the Mediator Has a Stake in the Outcome.

The principle of mediator impartiality is one of the first lessons in any basic mediation training. On Saturday afternoon, I gained new insight into the reason that an impartial mind-set can be so important. As the day progressed, I was getting resistance from both teams. At first I could not figure out what was going on. Then I realized that I had been pushing both teams too hard, and that the pushing was occurring because I had a stake in the outcome.

One of my standard "lines" to the parties when a mediation seems stuck is, "I am here to try to help you work out a solution to the situation that brought you to mediation. I have no stake in the outcome. If we work it out, I'll be pleased. If we don't work it out, you will go on living with the dispute, while I shall feel a bit sad but then just move on with the rest of my life." I finally realized that was not the situation I was in during the Hamilton mediation. As part of the university community, I had a stake in the outcome and as a result I had been pushing too hard to reach an agreement. Once I realized what was happening, I actually told the negotiators from both teams what my standard line was. However, I went on to say that this situation was different, that as a member of the university community I had a stake in finding a solution that would resolve the crisis. I told them that because I did care a great deal about finding a way to resolve the situation, I had been leaning on them, and that I would try to back off.

Articulating what was going on for me, first to myself and then to the negotiators, enabled me to back off and lower the temperature of the mediation. While the voicing of these feelings was in no way intended as a mediator tactic, in retrospect my admission did help me establish credibility, especially with the members of the student team who identified me with the administration. I simply told the truth — that I cared very much about helping find a solution. It may have built another layer of trust. . . .

The Final Day

At 6 A.M. on Monday morning, we reached a tentative agreement. . . . The student team members needed to sell the deal to the 180 demonstrators occupying Hamilton Hall, but were not prepared for that difficult role. This is another area where I think we mediators fell short. Even though it would have been difficult, given the limited trust between the mediators and the students, we should have tried to talk to the students about the difficult role they were facing, and offered to brainstorm with them about how to handle it. Those with experience in the labor field are familiar with the phenomenon where the workers are in the streets or on the picket line riled up and demonstrating. The negotiator gets the best deal she can at the bargaining table, using the noise in the streets as one of her persuasive tools. Then she has to go back and calm the troops down, tell them she has gotten far less then they were demanding, but that it is a fabulous deal. The student negotiators had no experience in this role. They were tired and, while they knew (given what they had heard during the mediation) that they had obtained a reasonable package, they went to meet with a core group of the demonstrators feeling what they had achieved was not a victory or even close to a victory. The student team met at the law school with a core group of about thirty or forty of the Hamilton demonstrators.

More on the Role of Food.

While the university team was meeting with the university leadership and the students were beginning their meeting with the core group, Carlton and I went off and bought five dozen bagels, along with juice and a big urn of coffee, and delivered it to the students. At that point, I was wishing that we had someone staffing the mediation whom we could have sent out to do the shopping. In retrospect, I think that being the person who was lugging the bagels and cream cheese to the student meeting gave a message of commitment to the students. During mediation sessions, mediators often have a nurturing function. They encourage participants to deal with underlying issues, reframe so that the parties can hear each other, and validate feelings and create a safe setting in which to wrestle with highly charged issues. Buying breakfast put us in a different sort of nurturing role which may have been another important trust-building gesture. . . .

FINAL THOUGHTS

The takeover of Hamilton ended Monday night. Wednesday morning, I had an early morning meeting on the main campus. I had to go to my office before the meeting and left the law school building at 117th Street since the main entrance at 116th was closed because of renovations. There was a gate to the main campus directly in front of me across Amsterdam Avenue. Out of habit developed during the five days of demonstrations when only the two main gates to the campus were open, I started to turn left toward the main entrance at 116th. Then I realized that the 117th Street gate was again open. It struck me that much of what we do as mediators is opening gates. When mediators help people talk to each other and hear each other and understand their own and others' interests, they symbolically aid the participants in unlocking the positional or emotional gates that have stood as a bar to settlement. . . .

Notes and Questions

6.32 What lessons about mediation does the self-reflective practitioner, Carol Lieb-man, extract from this case?

6.33 There seems little doubt that the negotiating parties could not resolve this matter alone. Can you point to specific ways in which the mediators added value to the negotiation? If you had been advising one side as an attorney, how might you add value in this situation?

Chapter 7   Legal and Policy Issues in Mediation

It must be remembered that there is nothing more difficult to plan, more doubtful of success, nor more dangerous to manage, than the creation of a new system. For the initiator has the enmity of all who would profit by the preservation of the old institutions and merely lukewarm defenders in those who would gain by the new ones.

—Niccolo Machiavelli

Mediation began as a simple, yet radical, idea of having a third party assist disputing parties to resolve issues themselves. However, the growth of mediation practice, its application in many different areas, and its relationship to the formal justice system have generated complexity, legal regulation, ethics and standards, and policy choices. As mediation has moved into the courts, the more familiar adversarial paradigm has exerted a gravitational pull, shifting mediation toward litigation with less party participation and more attorney control, and greater influence of legal norms on the processes and outcomes. Mediation's promise is to let parties decide what is best and right for them (as long as that is not otherwise unlawful). At the same time, many believe that mediated outcomes should also serve values beyond those of the parties — justice, fairness, accountability, and quality of process assurances. This chapter highlights some (not all!) of the legal and policy issues that have arisen with respect to the increased use of mediational processes in both public and private sectors. As you read each selection, you should ask yourself what underlying values are important to the commentator — party self-determination, system integrity, quality and competence of professionals, or something else. We will ask you to consider what values you think are important in legal regulation and policy choices about the uses to which mediation should be put. What role should "the rule of law" play in mediation?

A. THE INTERSECTION OF LAW, JUSTICE, AND MEDIATION

Judges and juries rely on law — the complex web of statutes and common law — to decide cases. Arbitrators apply whatever norms — law, custom, tradition, contractual, and legal rules — parties dictate in their agreement to arbitrate. Mediators, however, elicit principles and standards from the parties and cannot prescribe the governing norms or determine the outcome. Given these fundamental differences among the processes, the relationship of law and justice to mediation raises challenging questions.

1. Should the Mediator Bear Responsibility for the Quality of the Parties' Agreement?

Self-determination by the parties is the hallmark of mediation. This means that the parties' sense of fairness usually trumps other arguably applicable norms. But where mediation is taking place under the roof of a courthouse or in a context that significantly impacts public interests, there can be tension between the rule of law and party choice. For example, when a mediator helps divorcing parents negotiate parenting arrangements, should the mediator impose the legal standard of "the best interests of the child," as a judge would? Should a mediator simply alert parties to that norm and allow them to determine parenting arrangements themselves? Should a mediator elicit the guiding principles from the parties without reference to the best interests of the child? Would it make a difference if the mediator were operating in a court-sponsored program? If the program were mandatory? If the agreement were subject to court approval?

The following two excerpts explore mediator accountability for the quality of mediated outcomes. Two prominent professors (who are also practitioners) reach remarkably different conclusions.

 Lawrence Susskind, **ENVIRONMENTAL MEDIATION AND THE ACCOUNTABILITY PROBLEM**

6 Vt. L. Rev. 1, 6-8, 18, 42, 46-47 (1981)

. . . The success of most mediation efforts tends to be measured in rather narrow terms. If the parties to a labor dispute are pleased with the agreement they have reached voluntarily, and the bargain holds, the mediator is presumed to have done a good job. In the environmental field, there are reasons that a broader definition of success is needed — one that is more attentive to the interests of all segments of society.

If the parties involved in environmental mediation reach an agreement, but fail to maximize the joint gains possible, environmental quality and natural resources will actually be lost. If the key parties involved in an environmental dispute reach an agreement with which they are pleased, but fail to take account of all impacts on those interests not represented directly in the negotiations, the public health and safety could be seriously jeopardized. If the key parties to a dispute reach an agreement, but selfishly ignore the interests of future generations, short term agreements could set off environmental time bombs that cannot be defused. Although the key stakeholders in an environmental dispute may pay only a small price for failing to reach an agreement, their failure could impose substantial costs on many groups, who may be affected indefinitely. Finally, the parties to environmental disputes must be sensitive to the ways in which their agreements set precedents; even informal set-tlements have a way of becoming binding on others who find themselves in similar situations. . . .

[E]nvironmental mediators ought to accept responsibility for ensuring (1) that the interests of parties not directly involved in negotiation, but with a stake in the outcome, are adequately represented and protected; (2) that agreements are as fair and stable as possible; and (3) that agreements reached are interpreted as intended by the community-at-large and set constructive precedents. . . .

Effective environmental mediation may require teams composed of some individuals with technical backgrounds, some specialized in problem-solving or group dynamics and some with political clout. . . .

Environmental mediators ought to be concerned about (1) the impacts of nego-tiated agreements on underrepresented or unrepresentable groups in the community; (2) the possibility that joint net gains have not been maximized; (3) the long-term or spill-over effects of the settlements they help to reach; and (4) the precedents that they set and the precedents upon which agreements are based. To be effective, an environmental mediator will need to be knowledgeable about the substance of dis-putes and the intricacies of the regulatory context within which decisions are embedded. An environmental mediator should be committed to procedural fair-ness — all parties should have an opportunity to be represented by individuals with the technical sophistication to bargain effectively on their behalf. Environmental mediators should also be concerned that the agreements they help to reach are just and stable. To fulfill these responsibilities, environmental mediators will have to intervene more often and more forcefully than their counterparts in the labor-management field. Although such intervention may make it difficult to retain the appearance of neutrality and the trust of the active parties, environmental mediators cannot fulfill their responsibilities to the community-at-large if they remain passive.

 Joseph B. Stulberg, **THE THEORY AND PRACTICE OF MEDIATION: A REPLY TO PROFESSOR SUSSKIND**

6 Vt. L. Rev. 85, 85-88, 108-109, 112-115 (1981)

. . . Paradoxically, while the use of mediation has expanded, a common understand-ing as to what constitutes mediation has weakened. . . . It is important . . . to identify and clarify the principles and dynamics which together constitute mediation as a dispute settlement procedure. . . . Susskind's argument is novel in that he asserts that the mediator of environmental disputes, unlike his counterpart in labor management, community, or international disputes, should not be neutral and should be held accountable for the mediated outcome. Since most mediators believe that a commit-ment to impartiality and neutrality is the defining principle of their role, Susskind's argument carries significant consequences for mediation.

. . . Susskind's demand for a non-neutral intervenor is conceptually and prag-matically incompatible with the goals and purposes of mediation. The intervenor pos-ture that Susskind advocates is not anchored by any principles or obligations of office. The intervenor's conduct, strategies or contribution to the dispute settlement process is, therefore, neither predictable nor consistent. It is precisely a mediator's commitment to neutrality which ensures responsible actions on the part of the mediator and permits mediation to be an effective, principled dispute settlement procedure. . . .

On a substantive level, Susskind argues that the mediator must ensure that the negotiated agreements are fair. The most dramatic example of the difference between the traditional neutral mediator and Susskind's environmental mediator is the person Susskind describes and endorses as a mediator with "clout." For Susskind, the term "clout" applies to a mediator publicly committed to a particular substantive outcome with the power to move the contesting parties toward an agreement. In contrast, the traditional mediator would view that public commitment as the signal reason for disqualifying himself from service.

It is more than a mere terminological quibble to analyze whether a mediator must be someone who is committed to a posture of neutrality. Such a commitment enables both the mediation process and the mediator to operate effectively. A commitment of neutrality provides the mediator with a principled rather than opportunistic basis for service. As a result, the parties will use his services in ways that would be foreclosed to the "mediator with clout." Susskind's analysis has practical implications for mediator selection, training, scope of service, and financing of services. Clarifying this matter is of no small moment for those interested in the continued experimentation and use of mediation.

One disclaimer is in order. Arguing that a mediator's role requires a commitment to impartiality and neutrality is not to claim that Susskind's "mediator with clout" could not be an effective intervenor. There are many types of "intervenors with clout," a police officer, parent, government regulatory agency, psychologist, marriage counselor, meeting facilitator, corporate executive, and school principal. For certain kinds of dispute settings, those persons intervene with clout in much the same way that Susskind proposes for his environmental dispute mediator. Such a description does not make these persons mediators nor does it make their intervention ineffective or less effective than service rendered by a mediator. It simply constitutes a different kind of intervention posture from that of a mediator. One purpose served by conceptual analysis is to distinguish among different functions served by various types of intervenor postures, allowing those involved to become more sensitive to the types of intervention which are appropriate to different disputes.

. . . At issue is an understanding of, and respect for, what the parties to the mediation session are entitled to expect from the intervenor. Will confidences be honored? Who sets the agenda in terms of issues to be discussed? Will the order in which the issues are discussed be skewed so as to insure the mediator's desired outcome? Will meeting times be scheduled for the convenience of the parties or might they be arranged by the intervenor in order to make it difficult for some (i.e. "obstreperous") parties to attend and voice objections to the intervenor's preferred position? Will the mediator refuse to schedule meetings if the one party whose position the mediator supports demands that future meetings be conditional upon the other parties having made particular concessions? . . . Is it appropriate, for example, for the "mediator with clout" to threaten a recalcitrant party with political retaliation? If not, why not? . . . To suggest that an environmental mediator assume the responsibility of protecting the public's interest within the mediation context is comparable to suggesting that the way to avoid impasses in mediation is to authorize the mediator to impose dispositive, enforceable decisions on the parties.

Such a proposal is not simply adding a different twist to the mediation process; it is converting it from mediation to arbitration in the interest of promoting finality. Susskind has yet to meet the burden of justifying how the environmental mediator can assume this particular responsibility to the "public" without simultaneously converting the dispute settlement procedure into something other than mediation.

. . . Susskind suggests that "environmental mediators ought to be concerned . . . about . . . the possibility that joint net gains have not been maximized [and about] . . . the long-term or spillover effects of the settlements they help to reach." Susskind proposes that it is the mediator's responsibility as an objective observer to insure that the final solution secures the greatest overall net benefits for each party, without leaving any party worse off than it was in its original configuration (the Pareto-optimal principle). He further suggests that the solution agreed upon should have the least possible adverse impact on other aspects of present or future community life. Simply stating the proposed responsibility for the mediator in this way reveals how awesome the task is that Susskind is proposing for the environmental mediator. To insure that the Pareto principle is met, the environmental mediator must be able to generate, or at least guarantee, consideration of every possible technical solution to the environmental problem. He must secure demographic information on all persons affected by the dispute and factor their interests, desires, aspirations, preferences and values into the solution. He must project alternative development plans for jobs, tax bases, population trends, aesthetic values, school development and recreational needs for each possible solution. He must calculate the advantages and disadvantages of each solution against retaining the status quo, including the costs involved in using alternative dispute settlement procedures. And the list goes on.

Although these tasks might constitute a city planner's dream, they involve a host of analytical problems concerning logical theories of probability, measurement, interpersonal comparisons, and contrary-to-fact conditionals. These problems catapult the mediator's task into an intellectual war-zone which raises the serious possibility that Pareto-optimal outcomes in the context of an environmental dispute are not, in principle, possible. As such, Susskind's proposal that the mediator ought to insure such an outcome must, charitably speaking, be held in abeyance.

A more troublesome question arises, however, regarding the justification for a mediator to block an agreement that fails to meet the requirements of the Pareto principle. Who authorized the mediator to design or insure the attainment of the "optimal" outcomes so conceived? Clearly, it is preferable for persons to act as rational agents and do the "right" thing. Even conceding, however, the dubious proposition that the mediator could identify the "right" course of action as defined by the Pareto principle, on what basis does the mediator assume as an obligation of office that he help parties do only what is "right" and not necessarily that which is possible? . . .

If we were to accept the obligations of office that Susskind ascribes to the environmental mediator with regard to insuring Pareto-optimal outcomes, then the environmental mediator is simply a person who uses his entry into the dispute to become a social conscience, environmental policeman, or social critic and who carries no other obligations to the process or the participants beyond assuring Pareto-optimality. It is, in its most benign form, an invitation to permit philosopher-kings to participate in the affairs of the citizenry. . . .

The potential range of services for Susskind's environmental mediator, versus that of a traditional mediator committed to a posture of neutrality, is so importantly different that it is seriously misleading to use the same label to describe these respective intervention postures.

Notes and Questions

7.1 There has been considerable debate about the definition of mediation. See Michael L. Moffitt, Mediation, Schmediation and the Dimensions of Definition, 10 Harv. Negot. L. Rev. 69 (2005). In the exchange above, Susskind includes, among the mediator's responsibilities, accountability for a fair and optimal outcome. Do you agree with Stulberg that imposing that responsibility on mediators is inconsistent with basic principles of the process and might undermine good mediation practice? What is at stake in this debate?

7.2 Stulberg's emphasis on mediator impartiality and neutrality has been challenged in a variety of ways. Is it possible for a person to be entirely neutral? If, as a state of mind you conclude that it is not possible, is it still possible, as a professional, to maintain and display a posture of impartiality as between disputing parties? Are there differences in the concepts of neutrality, impartiality, or lack of bias? What are they?

Where the mediator does not inject his or her sense of the fair or optimal outcome, how do public values or norms come into the process? The landmark article below suggests that people do not bargain in a vacuum but rather in "the shadow of the law." Law, then, plays a significant role in mediation, as do other norms, even without the mediator being charged with injecting such norms or ensuring a "fair" settlement. Legal (and other) norms affect the assumptions, expectations, BATNAs, and proposals of bargaining parties and hence shape negotiated outcomes.

 ### Robert H. Mnookin & Lewis Kornhauser, BARGAINING IN THE SHADOW OF THE LAW: THE CASE OF DIVORCE

88 Yale L.J. 950, 968-970, 978-979 (1979)

Divorcing parents do not bargain over the division of family wealth and custodial prerogatives in a vacuum; they bargain in the shadow of the law. The legal rules governing alimony, child support, marital property, and custody give each parent certain claims based on what each would get if the case went to trial. In other words, the outcome that the law will impose if no agreement is reached gives each parent certain bargaining chips — an endowment of sorts.

A simplified example may be illustrative. Assume that in disputed custody cases the law flatly provided that all mothers had the right to custody of minor children and that all fathers only had the right to visitation two weekends a month. Absent some contrary agreement acceptable to both parents, a court would order this arrangement. Assume further that the legal rules relating to marital property, alimony, and child support gave the mother some determinate share of the family's economic resources. In negotiations under this regime, neither spouse would ever consent to a division that left him or her worse off than if he or she insisted on going to court. The range of negotiated outcomes would be limited to those that leave both parents as well off as they would be in the absence of a bargain.

If private ordering were allowed, we would not necessarily expect parents to split custody and money the way a judge would if they failed to agree. The father might well negotiate for more child-time and the mother for less. This result might occur either because the father made the mother better off by giving her additional money to compensate her for accepting less child-time, or because the mother found custody burdensome and considered herself better off with less custody. Indeed, she might agree to accept less money, or even to pay the father, if he agreed to relieve her of some child-rearing responsibilities. In all events, because the parents' tastes with regard to the trade-offs between money and child-time may differ, it will often be possible for the parties to negotiate some outcome that makes both better off than they would be if they simply accepted the result a court would impose.

Legal rules are generally not as simple or straightforward as is suggested by the last example. Often, the outcome in court is far from certain, with any number of outcomes possible. Indeed, existing legal standards governing custody, alimony, child support, and marital property are all striking for their lack of precision and thus provide a bargaining backdrop clouded by uncertainty. The almost universal judicial standard for resolving custody disputes is the "best interests of the child." Except in situations when one parent poses a substantial threat to the child's well-being, predicting who will get custody under this standard is difficult indeed, especially given the increasing pressure to reject any presumption in favor of maternal custody. Similarly, standards governing alimony and child support are also extraordinarily vague and allow courts broad discretion in disputed cases.

. . . Uncertainty has several important effects on the relative bargaining power of the parties. . . . [I]f there is substantial variance among the possible court-imposed outcomes, the relatively more risk-averse party is comparatively disadvantaged.

Notes and Questions

7.3 In Card v. Card, 706 So. 2d 409, 410 (Fla. Dist. Ct. App. 1st Dist. 1998), the court articulated a preference for party self-determination over third-party decision making for parenting decisions:

> When divorcing parents cede to the judicial branch of government the duty to decide the most intimate family issues, it is not unlikely that one or both parents will be less than satisfied with the decision. The bench and bar have

for years now encouraged divorcing parents to resolve their differences through mediation. In effect, parents have been urged to make their own law, in the hope that they can better live with a decision that is their own, rather than a decision that is externally imposed. Where attempts at mediation or other settlement fail, or are not seriously undertaken, a court must decide.

This proposition is in keeping with the notion that in mediation the fair outcome is that which the parties themselves find fair and best for their circumstances. According to this view, the application of public norms and the use of public process is the default option when parties cannot agree. How does this comport with your sense of justice?

7.4   A related topic to the role of law in mediation is informed consent. Should parties who come to court for a resolution of their dispute and who are required to attend mediation bargain without knowledge of the relevant law? This issue is less troubling when parties are represented because the burden of informing the parties rests on their attorneys. With respect to pro se parties, however, Jacqueline Nolan-Haley states that "when courts require unrepresented parties to mediate, fairness demands that they have a basic knowledge of their legal rights." Jacqueline M. Nolan-Haley, Informed Consent in Mediation: A Guiding Principle for Truly Educated Decisionmaking, 74 Notre Dame L. Rev. 775, 780 (1999).

If unrepresented parties in court-sponsored mediation should have knowledge of their rights, who should perform the service of advising them? Placing the burden on mediators to inform parties of their legal rights is fraught with problems. Such a task risks impinging on a mediator's neutrality since legal information often favors one party over another. The mediator may not be an attorney, and, even if he is, he may not have expertise in the law at issue or be positioned to do appropriate research. Finally, while mediators hope that disputing parties are informed before entering negotiations, the notion of "full information" may not be possible. Different counselors, after all, have different opinions. Joseph Stulberg points out that the "concern and passion for a party's well-being that animates the demand for informed settlement noticeably does not extend to requiring the mediator to ensure the parties' informed assessment of the proposed settlement terms on their economic, psychological, metaphysical, ethical or political rights or interests." Joseph B. Stulberg, Fairness and Mediation, 13 Ohio St. J. on Disp. Resol. 909, 938 (1998).

Would urging the parties to get legal, expert, or other counsel be sufficient to ensure informed consent? What other solutions can you think of in the context of court-annexed mediation for a pro se party?

7.5   Much has been written about mediation being a paradigm different from the adversary process, one governed by different norms and driven by different rationales. In considering what the role of law is (or should be) in mediation, consider the following perspectives:

a. "[I]n mediation — as distinguished from adjudication and, usually, arbitration — the ultimate authority resides with the disputants. The conflict is seen as unique and therefore less subject to solution by application of some general principle. The case is neither to be governed by a precedent nor to set one. Thus, all sorts of facts, needs, and interests that would be excluded from consideration in an adversary, rule-oriented proceeding could become relevant in a mediation. Indeed, whatever a party deems relevant is relevant." Leonard L. Riskin, Mediation and Lawyers, 43 Ohio St. L.J. 29, 34 (1982).

b. "Justice in adjudicative systems comes from above, from the application by a judge, jury or arbitrator of properly created standards or rules to 'facts' as determined by the adjudicator. Justice inheres in two aspects of that system — in the standards or rules that are applied, and in the process that is used to apply them. Mediation has parallel, but very different, aspects. The rules, standards, principles and beliefs that guide the resolution of the dispute in mediation are those held by the parties. The guiding norms in mediation may be legal, moral, religious or practical. In mediation, parties are free to use whatever standards they wish, not limited to standards that have been adopted by the legislature or articulated by the courts. Consequently, justice in mediation comes from below, from the parties. . . . The justice that pertains in mediation is the justice the parties themselves experience, articulate and embody in their resolution of the dispute. For individuals, public legal norms are but one factor in a constellation of norms and expectations creating a sense of correct conduct, fair procedure and a just outcome." Jonathan M. Hyman & Lela P. Love, If Portia Were a Mediator, 9 Clinical L. Rev. 157, 160-161, 164 (2002).

To what extent do you think that mediation outcomes should conform to, or "track" the law which might be applicable to the matter? See Judith Maute, Public Values and Private Justice: A Case for Mediator Accountability, 4 Geo. J. Legal Ethics 503 (1991); Nancy Welsh, Making Deals in Court-Connected Mediation: What's Justice Got to Do with It?, 79 Wash. U. L. Q. 787 (2001).

Lawyer mediators may overrate the importance of law. Therapist mediators may get stuck in theories of healing that they use in therapy. To the extent this is true, mediators who have other professions must remember to move to specific mediator responsibilities and not confuse professional roles; otherwise they may interfere with the benefits of a party-determined outcome.

2. Should the Mediator Provide Evaluations or Assessments for the Parties?

Another heated debate is whether a mediator should offer the parties legal or economic assessments about positions parties are taking. This evaluative function is clearly the domain of neutral experts engaged to provide expert opinions, arbiters, and judges. However, as mediation has been brought into the courts, the practice of evaluative mediation has grown, perhaps because lawyers and clients are most comfortable in adversarial processes and with neutrals who give opinions. Evaluative mediation is also commonly used in the market of private mediation in large commercial disputes where parties want to settle cases but want some "outside" assessment of how to do so. The Riskin grid shown in Chapter 3 depicts a mediation universe split into evaluative and facilitative spheres. An evaluative mediator, according to Leonard Riskin, does some or all of the following: develops and proposes settlement terms, urges parties to accept a particular settlement, predicts court outcomes, and assesses strengths and weaknesses of legal claims. While a facilitative mediator may be very energetic in urging parties to reevaluate their positions and legal analysis, and may supply information in an evenhanded manner, she would not give her own opinion of the merits of claims or defenses or of the likely outcome of a case. Some scholars claim that evaluative mediation is an oxymoron, just as facilitative arbitration would be. Kimberlee K. Kovach & Lela P. Love, "Evaluative" Mediation Is an Oxymoron, 14 Alternatives 31 (1996). In the excerpt that follows, Murray Levin reflects on the debate.

Murray S. Levin, THE PROPRIETY OF EVALUATIVE MEDIATION: CONCERNS ABOUT THE NATURE AND QUALITY OF AN EVALUATIVE OPINION

16 Ohio St. J. on Disp. Resol. 267, 270-271 (2001)

. . . Proponents of evaluative mediation assert that disputants [need] help in understanding the law and how their case is affected by the law, and that lawyers want mediators to provide direction regarding appropriate settlement figures. Additionally, proponents claim that because settlement negotiation takes place in the context of the alternative of litigation, the alternative outcome is highly relevant and therefore evaluation should be considered a valuable and proper component of mediation. Included within this group of proponents are commentators who do not advocate evaluative mediation, per se, but believe it should be available when chosen by the disputants.

Opponents of evaluative mediation counter that the tenor of the mediation process changes dramatically when the mediator assumes an evaluative role, because evaluation reduces mediator impartiality and disputant self-determination. When the mediator interjects an opinion, the disputant's ability to fashion a resolution based on their own needs is compromised. Understanding that the mediator will be evaluative, the disputants will not be as forthright with the mediator. A foremost goal will be a favorable mediator evaluation, and a disputant will not be willing to share information that could have an adverse effect on that evaluation. Under these circumstances it is more likely that the mediator will not learn about important information that could be relevant to assisting the disputants and should be relevant to forming a valid evaluation. This is especially likely if the mediation occurs at an early point in time prior to discovery. Evaluation turns the process away from problem solving toward an adversarial contest — sharing turns to posturing. Facilitative mediators view the potential for sharing of information through mediation as a chief means to assist the parties in recognizing opportunities to create new value and find win-win solutions. Moreover, too much emphasis on a likely legal outcome overlooks the possibility that the legal solution is not necessarily the best solution. Critics also express concern about the directive and coercive nature of the process when evaluation occurs. Some have gone so far as to characterize evaluative mediators as "Rambo mediators" who are out to "knock some sense" into the disputants by "banging their heads together" or "twisting their arms." Even if the evaluative mediator does not pressure, but merely opines, it is hard to deny a preferential effect, for there is a natural tendency to rely on the ideas, opinions, and predictions of the mediator. Undeniably, any opinion or evaluation will favor one side and disfavor the other. One may then ponder whether this influence is justified — whether the evaluative mediator's evaluation is valid and proper. . . .

Notes and Questions

7.6 Elsewhere in his article, Levin notes the lack of empirical research testing the quality or validity of mediator evaluative opinions. He points to data from studies regarding negotiation outcomes between highly regarded lawyer negotiators, case evaluations by lawyers and claims adjusters, and mock jury experiments displaying — with remarkable ranges of outcomes in a variety of studies — the difficulty of predicting negotiation or litigation outcomes. Murray S. Levin, The Propriety of Evaluative Mediation: Concerns About the Nature and Quality of an Evaluative Opinion, 16 Ohio St. J. on Disp. Resol. 267, 295 (2001). This difficulty is compounded by the fact that mediation takes place under the umbrella of confidentiality, and consequently the protections of a public process and the right of appeal are absent. Concerns about mediator opinions are allayed to some extent by the fact that such opinions are not binding on the parties. What is the impact of a mediator's opinion? Obviously, the answer is not simple and varies from case to case. Sophisticated parties, for example, may be less influenced by opinions than unsophisticated parties.

7.7 Some commentators assert that evaluation may be appropriate depending on case type. Do you agree? What cases would call for "evaluative" mediation? Cases involving constitutional or statutory rights? Commercial cases? Divorce cases? Personal injury cases? Environmental cases? For an argument that you cannot determine the propriety of evaluation from case type, see Lela P. Love & Kimberlee K. Kovach, ADR: An Eclectic Array of Processes, Rather than One Eclectic Process, 2000 J. Disp. Resol. 295; for the contrary perspective, see Jeffrey W. Stempel, The Inevitability of the Eclectic: Liberating ADR from Ideology, 2000 J. Disp. Resol. 247.

7.8 Lela Love puts forward a variety of reasons why mediators should not evaluate, including that the roles and related tasks of evaluators and facilitators are at odds; evaluation promotes positioning and polarization, which are antithetical to the goals of mediation; and ethical codes caution mediators — and other neutrals — against assuming additional roles. See Lela P. Love, The Top Ten Reasons Why Mediators Should Not Evaluate, 24 Fla. St. U. L. Rev. 937 (1997). Can you think of counter-arguments to those points? Or other reasons mediators might hesitate to give evaluations? See also Susan Oberman, Mediation Theory vs. Practice: What Are We Really Doing? Re-solving a Professional Conundrum, 20 Ohio St. J. on Disp. Resol. 775 (2005) (discussing differences in mediation models).

A Costly Evaluation

The following incident illustrates a danger of mediator evaluation:

The general counsel of a large shipping company once traveled from New York to Florida to attend a mandatory mediation conference. He went there wanting to settle the case, which involved a multi-million dollar dispute with a union. In a joint session, the court-appointed mediator, who was a federal magistrate, urged the company to be flexible, warning that the business did not have a chance of winning on appeal.

That "evaluation" shut down the negotiations. Union representatives froze in their position. The general counsel left in disgust, since his analysis of the case was so at odds with the mediator's opinion. Several years and hundreds of thousands of dollars in legal fees later, the company won a complete victory in court, which was affirmed on appeal. Both sides could have saved time and money by negotiating the outcome.

Kimberlee K. Kovach & Lela P. Love, "Evaluative" Mediation Is an Oxymoron, 14 Alternatives 31, 31 (1996).

Some commentators argue that evaluation is sometimes a necessary and beneficial tool in mediation. Many scholars and practitioners point out that mediators operate across a continuum between facilitative and evaluative, as the particular case requires. John Bickerman and Marjorie Corman Aaron, both practicing mediators and teachers, defend the practice of evaluative mediation in the brief excerpts that follow.

 John Bickerman, **EVALUATIVE MEDIATOR RESPONDS**

14 Alternatives 70 (1996)

. . . Facilitative mediation may help the parties identify interests and increase the settlement pie. However, resolving how to share the pie may require an active push from the mediator. Without sacrificing neutrality, a mediator's neutral assessment can provide participants with a much-needed reality check. Counsel will often look to a mediator to reduce a client's expectations by providing frank assessments of the risk. Parties do not lose trust in mediators or consider them biased because mediators talk frankly with them about their cases.

Sophisticated parties ought to have the freedom to choose the mediation style that best suits their needs. In their initial contacts with the parties, mediators should explain their mediation style and provide prospective participants with references of former mediation participants. Once fully informed, parties can intelligently consent to mediation.

Recently, a mediation participant confided to me his frustration with a court-appointed mediator whose facilitative style was (in his view) inappropriate for the complex, multi-party dispute at hand. Other consumers of mediation services have complained about mediators who are too judgmental (evaluative, maybe).

Parties should have the autonomy to fit the process to the case. In time, market forces may root out mediators whose overly evaluative (or overly facilitative) style inhibits settlement. Free choice — and not regulation — is the best course.

 Marjorie Corman Aaron, ADR TOOLBOX: THE HIGHWIRE ART OF EVALUATION

14 Alternatives 62 (1996)

Many mediators are uncomfortable with the idea of discussing or presenting evaluations. However, when parties reach an impasse, they often want the mediator to play an active role. In these cases, responsible use of evaluation is completely consistent with the goals of mediation.

Mediators should provide an evaluation only if there is an insurmountable settlement gap that arises from the parties' widely divergent views of what will happen if the case doesn't settle. Evaluation is not a substitute for other essential mediation tools. It is a last step, but in many cases skipping that step means missing the sole opportunity for settlement.

The primary risk of evaluation is the potential loss of perceived neutrality: the party who is the "loser" in the evaluation may come to view the mediator as an adversary. Mediators who offer evaluations need to be careful and skillful ... to reduce the risks of evaluation and increase the parties' receptiveness.

Notes and Questions

7.9   In addition to the points that Bickerman and Aaron make, scholars comment that an "eclectic" approach is in keeping with a desirable flexibility and creativity in the mediation process. For a full discussion of this perspective, see Jeffrey W. Stempel, The Inevitability of the Eclectic: Liberating ADR from Ideology, 2000 J. Disp. Resol. 247.

7.10   Deborah Hensler, interpreting findings of various leading studies, concludes that "the practice of mediation, at least as it applies to civil lawsuits other than family law cases, is generally evaluative. When designing programs, courts are more likely to offer evaluative than facilitative mediation. When given a choice, parties (or, at least, their attorneys) frequently opt for evaluative modes of mediation." Deborah R. Hensler, In Search of "Good Mediation," in Handbook of Justice Research in Law 239 (2000). It is not surprising that lawyers prefer modes of dispute resolution in which their training and experience makes them most comfortable. Robert A. Baruch Bush explains the growth of evaluative mediation in terms of its being an arbitration substitute, filling a vacuum created by arbitration becoming too formal, expensive, and "judicialized." Robert A. Baruch Bush, Substituting Mediation for Arbitration: The Growing Market for Evaluative Mediation, and What It Means for the ADR Field, 3 Pepp. Disp. Res. L.J. 111 (2002).

There is agreement that combining evaluative and facilitative dispute resolution services can be useful in particular cases where requested by informed parties. Nonetheless, the debate continues about what to call such a combination. Should evaluative mediation be called mediation or mediation *plus* the additional service? Before you dismiss this debate as one without practical import — that is, one only for academics — try to figure out why you should care — as a party, lawyer, court administrator, or mediator. An argument for careful labeling of processes follows.

 Lela P. Love & Kimberlee K. Kovach, **ADR: AN ECLECTIC ARRAY OF PROCESSES, RATHER THAN ONE ECLECTIC PROCESS**

2000 J. Disp. Resol. 295, 296-298

. . . [W]hen mediators try to resolve a controversy by providing their analysis of the legal — or other — merits, they are providing the service that judges, arbitrators and neutral experts provide. In essence, such endeavors use the neutral's judgment, award or opinion to determine or jump-start a resolution. That add-on activity to mediation should be called by its proper name. . . .

Calling the process mediation *plus* neutral evaluation (or whatever additional service is rendered) does not condemn or prohibit the activity. Instead, it lends clarity and definition to the services provided. Consumers would be more knowledgeable about what they are getting. Advocates and parties would be forewarned to consider judiciously what information to present to a neutral who will ultimately give an opinion which may well have a decisive impact on further negotiations. Of course, mediator descriptors of other sorts can be used to describe what the mediator will do, for example, "facilitative-broad" or "evaluative-narrow" [descriptors from Leonard Riskin's grid presented in Chapter 3]. However, it seems implausible that parties and advocates who are still barely educated about the differences between primary processes will be able to appreciate the implication of these confusing terms and academic distinctions. . . .

State statutes usually provide for an array of ADR processes. Often, court-connected ADR programs mandate that litigants choose among an offered menu of ADR options the court makes available prior to obtaining access to court. These options usually include mediation, neutral evaluation and nonbinding arbitration. A variety of factors have been suggested to assist in determining which process would be most beneficial for a given dispute. To have the mediation process engulf the others, where mediators provide the service of case or issue assessment, ultimately means that the multi-door courthouse would become the two-door courthouse: litigation or mediation/ADR, meaning a process that is an eclectic assortment of whatever works to resolve the dispute. Such an amorphous ADR process represents a significant back step from a rich array of alternatives, each of which can be particularly responsive to unique situations and cases and can offer very different possibilities for resolutions.

Notes and Questions

7.11 The evaluative-facilitative debate is plagued by a lack of clarity over terms. For example, would you call the following mediator questions and statements examples of "evaluative mediation" or of facilitative "reality testing"?

> Mediator to defendant in a personal injury case:
> a. "You understand that I am not a judge or an arbiter, and, in fact, no one can accurately predict what a particular judge or jury would do in a given case, but I'd like to review with you what the plaintiff's attorney just said about the question of liability. As you listen to me restate the point, please consider how a judge or jury might react."
> b. "This case is worth something between $25,000 and $35,000. Your demand for $100,000 is out of the ballpark."

Similar to a lawyer-mediator, a psychologist-mediator may be drawn to norms from their other practice (of psychology). Consider the following mediator questions:

> Mediator to father in a custody and visitation case:
> a. "Your proposal is that your child spends three days with you a week, including those weeks when school is in session. That will involve a bus commute for Danny to and from school, an hour and a half each way, when he is staying with you. Have you considered how spending three hours on a bus on school days will affect your son?"
> b. "It would be psychologically damaging for a seven-year-old child to spend three hours on a school bus he uses only once or twice a week."

For an analysis of these questions, see Lela P. Love & Kimberlee K. Kovach, ADR: An Eclectic Array of Processes, Rather than One Eclectic Process, 2000 J. Disp. Resol. 295, 303-305.

7.12 John Haynes, a pioneer in family mediation, makes a distinction between the mediator's responsibility to control the process and the mediator's responsibility to ensure that parties control the outcome. He describes questions that preserve parties' rights to make outcome decisions themselves, distinguishing them from questions that contain an imperative from the mediator.

> When asking questions, the mediator does not give advice. . . . Thus, it can be said that a major issue for a mediator is to *avoid the imperative*. In order to avoid the imperative the mediator must accept the couple's right to make the decisions — even if the decisions are not those the mediator would choose for them. . . .
> The language of the mediator is important. . . . The range of appropriateness is wide, making determination of whether a statement is an imperative less clear as the mediator moves across the range. That is, it would probably be clear that (1) "you should sell the house" is an imperative, and therefore inappropriate. But are the following imperatives? (2) "Have you considered selling the house?" (3) "You may want to consider selling the house." (4) "Do you want to consider selling the house as one of your options?" If these are not imperatives, what is the distinction between them?

Statement 1 is a clear command to act. Question 2 allows the party to consider or not consider the act. However, question 2 could also be an embedded suggestion if the client hears it as a suggestion to act; in that situation it becomes an imperative. Statement 3 is an offering to the client that places the right of selection on the client. As in 2, this may be received by the client as a suggestion/imperative. Statement 4, on the other hand, places the offer in the context of a range of options explicitly making the right of selection the clients'.

John M. Haynes, Mediation and Therapy: An Alternative View, 10 Mediation Q. 21, 26-27 (1992). Must we judge whether a mediator move is evaluative by whether a party receives it as evaluative or whether it was intended as evaluative? Do you accept the distinction between mediator control over process rather than outcome? Or do you think that some manipulation of process can have a significant effect on outcome?

7.13 If you were responsible for a panel of mediators where evaluative mediation was the norm, what impact would that have on the qualification criteria for panelists? The description of the panel's services? Accountability for erroneous conclusions of the mediators? Training for panelists? Whether you encouraged (or allowed) the use of caucuses and ex parte communications? Ethical rules?

B. MANDATORY MEDIATION

Given the benefits of mediation, both to parties and society, mediation is now routinely required as a preliminary step to getting to trial. Benefits of mandating mediation include disposing of matters clogging court dockets, overcoming the hurdle that a party's proposing mediation may be perceived as a sign of weakness by the other side, educating parties and attorneys about mediation, creating a body of skilled neutrals, providing parties who are uneducated about mediation the benefits the process can provide, and encouraging the voluntary use of mediation. However, since mediation is often described as a voluntary and consensual process that promotes party self-determination, mandated participation seems contradictory. Despite the contradiction, studies suggest that mandating mediation does not reduce the rate of settlement as compared to voluntary mediation (or does so only marginally), nor does it adversely impact the parties' experience in mediation. Indeed, some recent research by Roselle Wissler (see below and Wissler, Attorneys' Use of ADR Is Crucial to Their Willingness to Recommend It to Their Clients, Disp. Res. Mag. 36 (2000)) suggests that mandating mediation can educate parties and lawyers about the process, and those who experience mediation, even in mandated settings, may be more likely to use it again.

The next two excerpts examine this issue. Roselle Wissler addresses some concerns about mandatory mediation and concludes that, on balance, it is worthwhile. Trina Grillo raises serious concerns about mandating mediation in the context of divorce and custody cases, which is one of the arenas where mediation has been regularly required as a prerequisite to trial.

Roselle L. Wissler, THE EFFECTS OF MANDATORY MEDIATION: EMPIRICAL RESEARCH ON THE EXPERIENCE OF SMALL CLAIMS AND COMMON PLEAS COURTS

33 Willamette L. Rev. 565, 565-566 (1997)

Although parties tend to be satisfied with their experience in mediation, voluntary mediation programs consistently report low rates of utilization. In order to divert more cases from the courts and to expose more parties to the benefits associated with mediation, many states have adopted mandatory mediation programs for a variety of disputes. Critics have raised the concern that coercion *into* the mediation process translates into coercion *in* the mediation process, creating undue settlement pressures that produce unfair outcomes. In cases involving an imbalance of power, the weaker party is thought to be particularly vulnerable to such pressures. However, studies of divorce mediation that examine the effects of mandatory mediation and that explore gender differences in evaluations of the process tend not to support such concerns.

This article reports research on the effects of mandatory mediation in two different court settings: small claims courts and common pleas courts.... [I]t reports the findings of two studies that compare mandatory and voluntary mediation in terms of case outcomes and parties' and attorneys' evaluations. These studies reveal few differences between mandatory and voluntary mediation and between the assessments of male versus female litigants and white versus nonwhite litigants in mandatory mediation. Thus, there is little support for concerns about pressures to accept unfair settlements in mandatory mediation. The findings of these and prior studies suggest that costs associated with mandatory mediation are relatively few, compared to the benefits that mediation provides as an alternative to adjudication.

 Trina Grillo, THE MEDIATION ALTERNATIVE: PROCESS DANGERS FOR WOMEN

100 Yale L.J. 1545, 1549-1550, 1582-1583 (1991)

... [M]andatory mediation provides neither a more just nor a more humane alternative to the adversarial system of adjudication of custody, and, therefore, does not fulfill its promises. In particular, quite apart from whether an acceptable result is reached, mandatory mediation can be destructive to many women and some men because it requires them to speak in a setting they have not chosen and often imposes a rigid orthodoxy as to how they should speak, make decisions, and be. This orthodoxy is imposed through subtle and not-so-subtle messages about appropriate conduct and about what may be said in mediation. It is an orthodoxy that often excludes the possibility of the parties' speaking with their authentic voices.

Moreover, people vary greatly in the extent to which their sense of self is "relational" — that is, defined in terms of connection to others. If two parties are forced to engage with one another, and one has a more relational sense of self than the other, that party may feel compelled to maintain her connection with the other, even to her own detriment. For this reason, the party with the more relational sense of self will be at a disadvantage in a mediated negotiation. Several prominent researchers have suggested that, as a general rule, women have a more relational sense of self than do men, although there is little agreement on what the origin of this difference might be. Thus, rather than being a feminist alternative to the adversary system, mediation has the potential actively to harm women.

Some of the dangers of mandatory mediation apply to voluntary mediation as well. Voluntary mediation should not be abandoned, but should be recognized as a powerful process which should be used carefully and thoughtfully. Entering into such a process with one who has known you intimately and who now seems to threaten your whole life and being has great creative, but also enormous destructive, power. Nonetheless, it should be recognized that when two people themselves decide to mediate and then physically appear at the mediation sessions, that decision and their continued presence serve as a rough indication that it is not too painful or too dangerous for one or both of them to go on. . . .

Proponents of [mandatory mediation] seldom recognize that, even though an agreement might not be required, a person might agree to something because of the pressures of the situation; or that, even if no agreement is reached, the process itself might be traumatic.

It is presumptuous to assume that the state has a better idea than the parties themselves about whether mediation will work in their particular case. A party may know something the mediator does not: that her spouse is a pathological, but convincing, liar; that years of living with a man have resulted in a pattern in which the woman consistently accommodates him, even when she does not want to; that the woman will lose sight of her own needs in the attempt to appear a cooperative female; or that the woman will sacrifice many of her interests in order to end what may be a psychologically painful process. In sum, there may be an internal wisdom, one that needs to be honored, that mediation is inappropriate in a particular situation. It is true that mandatory mediation may serve the interests of women who do not wish to enter the adversary process; if opting out of mediation is permitted, some women (as well as some men) will be forced to litigate when their preference would have been to mediate. There is no way around this unfortunate situation. Either some women will be forced to litigate against their will, or some women will be forced to mediate against their will. Mediation poses such substantial dangers, and provides so few benefits to unwilling female participants, however, that to my mind it is indefensible to require mediation, notwithstanding that such a requirement would help women who do want to mediate.

Notes and Questions

7.14 Do Grillo's concerns apply outside the family context? Do carve-outs for cases with a history of domestic violence adequately address her concerns?

7.15 Grillo suggests that women are prohibited by mediation ideology or culture from fully speaking their "anger" or needs. How do we reconcile that with claims that women are "better" at emotional expression (see Deborah Tannen,

You Just Don't Understand (1995)) and that mediation is a realm of feelings and relationships, not law and rights? Is there some inconsistency here, or can these views be reconciled?

7.16 A Connecticut study, comparing 200 mediated divorce settlements with 200 adversarial divorce settlements taking into account factors such as length of marriage, children, and judicial district, concludes that women might benefit financially from mediation. Although there was no great difference in the percentage of family income women received, "women in mediated cases obtain a higher percentage of family assets, receive periodic alimony for more years than their adversarial counterparts, and obtain greater amounts of child support." Additionally, mediated settlements are more likely to include provisions for children's college education, as well as joint legal and physical custody arrangements. Mary G. Marcus, Walter Marcus, Nancy A. Stilwell & Neville Doherty, To Mediate or Not to Mediate: Financial Outcomes in Mediated Versus Adversarial Divorces, 17 Mediation Q. 143, 150-151 (1999).

7.17 While many disputants objectively see the benefits of mediation, the experience of being in a conflict can result in a belief that the other side is not rational. Consequently, parties often believe that mediation is a waste of time in *their* case. Mediators, on the other hand, who have seen parties transition from high conflict to creative problem solving, know the process is helpful in many cases (despite the parties' beliefs to the contrary). Even where there is little initial interest in mediation, parties typically report high levels of satisfaction with the process. Why do you think this is? How does it impact your view of mandatory mediation?

7.18 Carol Izumi and Homer La Rue make an interesting point about mandatory mediation:

> By funneling . . . court cases into a mediation stream, parties are dipped into a pool of vastly different values and process qualities. Mediation, in contrast to litigation, highlights subjective, party-determined standards rather than externally imposed ones, focuses on future behavior to resolve the dispute, and elevates party preference above third-party decision-making. Furthermore, mediation treats the dispute as unique and impacted by the relationship of the individuals involved. In mediation, direct action by the court is avoided by the creation of a party-crafted agreement. Thus, parties can experience "process dissonance" by this clash of incompatible values when they enter a mediation as a prerequisite to the trial process.

Carol L. Izumi & Homer C. La Rue, Prohibiting "Good Faith" Reports Under the Uniform Mediation Act: Keeping the Adjudication Camel Out of the Mediation Tent, 2003 J. Disp. Resol. 67, 92. Are the values promoted by exposing parties to mediation worth the price of the "dissonance" they may experience?

7.19 What level of participation does mandatory mediation require? How does the answer to this question affect your views on the relative advantages and disadvantages of a court-annexed program? As you read Section D on good-faith participation, keep this question in mind.

C. DIVERSITY, DISADVANTAGE, AND FAIRNESS

Trina Grillo's concerns regarding women in mandatory divorce mediation raise larger questions. Are some groups disadvantaged in mediation? If so, what is the proper response to that phenomenon? The excerpts below explore the question of various forms of unequal power and fairness in mediation. As you read this section, consider whether adjudicative processes face the same issues with respect to power imbalances, whether based on demographic (race, ethnicity, gender), economic, or other factors.

This section focuses on how differences in the gender or ethnicity of negotiating parties (and their attorneys and mediator) may come into play. Of course, in every negotiation, other differences exist among participants—hometown, education, religion, politics, affiliations, interests, age, intelligence, social class and standing, income, appearance, and height—any of which could exert more influence over negotiation behavior than gender and race. Gender and race are more visible than many characteristics, however, and can serve as surrogates for other differences that may also have an impact on the parties or the mediator.

This first excerpt discusses an empirical study of gender and negotiation using law students in a negotiation class (a group very similar to those students reading this book!).

  Charles B. Craver & David W. Barnes, **GENDER,
    RISK TAKING, AND NEGOTIATION PERFORMANCE**

> 5 Mich. J. Gender & L. 299, 320-321, 346-347 (1999)

One might reasonably expect gender-based communication stereotypes to place women at a disadvantage when facing legal negotiation exercises in the classroom. They would be likely to be perceived as less dominant and less forceful, and they would be expected to be less logical and more emotional. Nonetheless, two significant factors counterbalance these stereotypes. First, the advanced education possessed by law students and the specific training received in a legal negotiation course would minimize gender-based communication differentials. Second, the female negotiators may benefit from the established fact that women are typically more sensitive to nonverbal messages than their male cohorts. Since a significant amount of critical communication during interpersonal transactions is nonverbal, the enhanced ability of female negotiators to decode such signals could offset any disadvantage associated with latent stereotyping. . . .

Both psychological theory and empirical research suggest that women have a lower preference for risk and competition than men. If this perception is correct, more women would be inclined to take a competitive legal negotiating course on a credit/no-credit basis than men. If the women taking the course on a credit/no-credit basis were more desirous of avoiding competition than of obtaining easy credit hours, the credit/no-credit women might be expected to work more diligently on both the negotiation exercises and course papers than males who may select the credit/no-credit alternative to enable them to slack off.

The Legal Negotiating course data do indicate that a greater percentage of women take the class on a credit/no-credit basis than men, lending support for the alternative hypothesis with respect to the competition avoidance issue. Nonetheless, the data do not support the theory that the difference between the performance of graded and credit/no-credit women would be less than that between graded and credit/no-credit men.

Sociological theory also suggests that males are more acculturated to overt competition during their formative years than females, providing men with an advantage when they encounter openly competitive situations as adults. If this theory were correct, male students might be expected to achieve more beneficial results on negotiation exercises than female students. Our data found no statistically significant differences between male and female performance with respect to negotiation exercise achievement. . . .

Read together, our findings suggest that while women and men may not perform identically in negotiation settings, there is no factual basis for assuming that women are weaker or less capable negotiators. Our results directly challenge beliefs about women suggesting that female negotiators are likely to perform less proficiently than their male peers. These stereotypical perceptions have undoubtedly disadvantaged women in numerous academic and professional settings, including those seeking entry level associate positions and female associates seeking entrance to firm partnerships. We hope that legal professionals who hold gender-based beliefs such as those we have discussed will reevaluate their expectations in a manner that will diminish — if not entirely eliminate — subtle biases against women attorneys.

Notes and Questions

7.20 In an analysis of differences in effectiveness of negotiation styles in Andrea Kupfer Schneider, Shattering Negotiation Myths: Empirical Evidence on the Effectiveness of Negotiation Style, 7 Harv. Negot. L. Rev. 143 (2002), few gender differences were found. Most importantly, there is *no* statistically significant difference in *overall* effectiveness between the genders. This finding continued even when breaking down how the genders rated each other (that is, how men rated women, how women rated women, and so on). One interesting result to study further, however, is that men rated men higher than they rated women, and this "similarity" effect was statistically significant. Of the 89 adjectives in which negotiators could be rated, only 5 showed a statistically significant difference between men and women. While the overall number of similarities is impressive (84 of 89), the different ones are also interesting. Women were rated significantly higher in being "assertive" and "firm" while men were rated significantly higher in being "an avoider," "creative," "experienced," and "wise." Finally, in describing effective men and effective women, the overall adjectives did not differ, although the order of them did, as the boxed table

shows. We can hypothesize
several conclusions from
this data: (1) By the time
men and women have
significant client responsibility, childhood differences have mostly disappeared
through maturity and exp-
erience; (2) men and women
who self-select for law
school and then are trained
through law school have
few differences; and/or (3)
the differences found in
older studies no longer appear in our current society.
What do you think?

7.21 The lack of differences
between men and women
in other fields has also been
documented. In a review of
studies of male and female
managers, researchers have
concluded that men and
women do not differ in
their managerial philoso-
phy, personal values, or
management of resources.
"We've reviewed five stu-
dies involving almost 2,000
people compared on a total
of 43 scales. We've studied
matched pairs and con-
trolled for level of managerial achievement.... [W]e

Adjectives for Effective Negotiators		
ADJECTIVE	**WOMEN RANKING**	**MEN RANKING**
Ethical	1 (4.50)	1 (4.29)
Confident	2 (3.94)	5 (3.92)
Personable	2 (3.94)	3 (3.97)
Trustworthy	2 (3.94)	9 (3.77)
Experienced	5 (3.89)†	1 (4.29)
Rational	6 (3.80)	4 (3.96)
Realistic	7 (3.78)	6 (3.84)
Accommodating	8 (3.75)	12 (3.75)
Communicative	8 (3.75)	11 (3.76)
Fair-minded	10 (3.67)	16 (3.65)
Dignified	11 (3.66)	13 (3.74)
Perceptive	12 (3.64)	7 (3.83)
Adaptable	13 (3.61)	18 (3.57)*
Self-controlled	14 (3.58)	8 (3.81)
Agreeable	15 (3.56)	17 (3.63)
Astute about the law	16 (3.53)	9 (3.77)
Poised	17 (3.44)	15 (3.66)
Analytical	18 (3.42)	22 (3.45)
Careful	19 (3.41)	21 (3.47)
Sociable	20 (3.36)	14 (3.69)

† Statistically significant.
* Masculine was tied for 18 for the men.

are left with one conclusion: *Women, in general, do not differ from men, in general, in the ways in which they administer the management process.*" Susan M. Donnell & Jay Hall, Men and Women as Managers: A Significant Case of No Significant Difference, Organizational Dynamics (Spring 1980), at 76. See also Gary N. Powell, One More Time: Do Female and Male Managers Differ?, 4 Academy Mgmt. Exec. 68 (1990). On the other hand, other research suggests that there might, in fact, be significant differences, by gender, in how people negotiate, see Linda Babcock & Sara Laschever, Women Don't Ask: Negotiation the Gender Divide (2003); see also Deborah Kolb & Judith Williams, Everyday Negotiation: Navigating the Hidden Agendas in Bargaining (2003); Carrie Menkel-Meadow, Teaching About Gender and Negotiation: Sex, Truths and Video Tape, 16 Neg. J. 357 (2000); and Carol Rose, Bargaining and Gender, 18 Harv. J. L. & Pub. Poly. 547 (1995).

Despite the similarities in performance noted above for law-trained men and women, some assumptions and many stereotypes persist in society. Assumptions and stereotypes and their impact on bargaining are reflected in the study by economist and law professor Ian Ayres. Ayres conducted two studies examining how gender and race affect outcomes in car negotiations. The results are extremely troubling.

 Ian Ayres, **FAIR DRIVING**

104 Harv. L. Rev. 817, 818-819 (1991)

This article examines whether the process of negotiating for a new car disadvantages women and minorities. More than 180 independent negotiations at ninety dealerships were conducted in the Chicago area to examine how dealerships bargain. Testers of different races and genders entered new car dealerships separately and bargained to buy a new car, using a uniform negotiation strategy. The study tests whether automobile retailers react differently to this uniform strategy when potential buyers differ only by gender or race.

The tests reveal that white males receive significantly better prices than blacks and women. . . . [W]hite women had to pay forty percent higher markups than white men; black men had to pay more than twice the markup, and black women had to pay more than three times the markup of white male testers. Moreover, the study reveals that testers of different race and gender are subjected to several forms of nonprice discrimination. Specifically, testers were systematically steered to salespeople of their own race and gender (who then gave them worse deals) and were asked different questions and told about different qualities of the car.

Notes and Questions

7.22 In an expanded study Ayres confirmed his previous findings of systematic discrimination in which white males are offered lower prices than black testers. However, the second study also found that black male testers were charged higher prices than black female testers. Ian Ayres, Further Evidence of Discrimination in New Car Negotiations and Estimates of Its Cause, 94 Mich. L. Rev. 109 (1995).

7.23 Ayers suggests that "no-haggle" selling might be the most effective antidote to discrimination with respect to car sales. What advice would you give to a female or black friend looking to purchase a car? Are there other ways to make uneven tables even?

7.24 Professors Marc A. Cohen and Ian Ayres were hired as expert counsel for the plaintiffs in a class action law suit against General Motors Acceptance Corp. (GMAC). In this action, plaintiffs alleged that GMAC's automobile lending policies could harm black car buyers because the dealers "marked up" loans more frequently and aggressively with blacks than whites, in other words, charging higher interest rates to black buyers and adding to the total amount of the loan. In addition to the Ayres studies, Professor Cohen's study was also used as evidence in the case. He analyzed information on 1.5 million GMAC loans for the past four years where dealers had marked up loans. Cohen's main conclusion from this study was the blacks applying for loans paid markups of an average of $1,229, whereas whites with similar credit histories paid about $867 in markups. Amazingly, some of GM's own black employees are part of the class action suit! See Lee Hawkins, Jr., GM's Finance Arm Is Close to Setting Racial-Bias Lawsuit, Wall St. J., Jan. 30, 2004, at A1.

When reading these studies about how women and minorities are treated differently, many tend to focus on the behavior of the stereotyper and how these stereotypes can be changed. This next excerpt points out the overlooked effect that stereotypes have on the target of the stereotype.

 ### *Sharon Begley*, THE STEREOTYPE TRAP

Newsweek, Nov. 6, 2000, at 66-68

The power of stereotypes, scientists had long figured, lay in their ability to change the behavior of the person holding the stereotype. If you think women are ninnies ruled by hormonal swings, you don't name them CEO; if you think gays are pedophiles, you don't tap them to lead your Boy Scout troop. But five years ago Stanford University psychologist Claude Steele showed something else: it is the *targets* of a stereotype whose behavior is most powerfully affected by it. A stereotype that pervades the culture the way "ditzy blondes" and "forgetful seniors" do makes people painfully aware of how society views them — so painfully aware, in fact, that knowledge of the stereotype can affect how well they do on intellectual and other tasks. . . .

Steele and Aronson gave 44 Stanford undergrads questions from the verbal part of the tough Graduate Record Exam. One group was asked, right before the test, to indicate their year in school, age, major and other information. The other group answered all that, as well as one final question: what is your race? The results were sobering. "Just listing their race undermined the black students' performance," says Steele, making them score significantly worse than blacks who did not note their race, and significantly worse than all whites. But the performance of the black Stanfordites who were not explicitly reminded of their race equaled that of whites, found the scientists.

You do not even have to believe the negative stereotype to be hurt by it, psychologists find. As long as you care about the ability you're being tested on, such as golfing or math, and are familiar with the stereotype ("girls can't do higher math"), it can sink you. What seems to happen is that as soon as you reach a tough par 3 or a difficult trig problem, the possibility of confirming, and being personally reduced to, a painful stereotype causes enough distress to impair performance. . . .

Stereotypes seem to most affect the best and the brightest. Only if you're black and care about academics, or female and care about math, will you also care if society thinks you're bad at those things. . . .

Can the pernicious effects of stereotypes be vanquished? If no one reminds you of a negative stereotype, your performance doesn't suffer. It can actually improve if instead you think of a positive stereotype — Steele recommends bellowing something like "You are Stanford students!" but clearly that has limited applicability. Deception helps, too: if women are told that a difficult math test reveals no gender differences, finds Stephen Spencer of Waterloo, they perform as well as men. Otherwise, women score much lower. While such manipulations may weaken the brutal power of stereotypes, at the end of the day they remain manipulations. But until stereotypes fade away, that may be the best we can hope for.

Notes and Questions

7.25 How can the results of the Steele and Aronson study be translated into advice for representatives in mediation? For mediators? How can we avoid being trapped ourselves by stereotypes? Do you think it is helpful to know about these studies?

7.26 Stereotyping may also yield certain advantages. Phyllis Kritek writes:

> One of the nice things about being perceived as powerless at an uneven table, however, is that you have so little to lose. No one views you as having power, deserving power, or being a serious contender for power. As a nurse and a woman, I am always amazed at how blatantly people assume I'm incapable of observing the power machinations, the patronizing tones, the injustices, and the assumptions about my intellectual incapacities. What I have learned, however, is that this gives me a great deal of freedom to move the discussion to a deeper and surer place, since I usually have no dominance power or status to claim, protect, or regain. I think this is one of the really underrated dimensions of being at an uneven table. Sometimes it is even funny.

Phyllis Beck Kritek, Negotiating at an Uneven Table: A Practical Approach to Working with Difference and Diversity 193 (1994).

In the following and final excerpt in this section, the authors ask questions about the effects of ethnicity and gender on mediation outcomes. Like the Ayers study researching the effect on negotiation outcomes of gender and ethnicity, the findings obtained by LaFree and Rack raise questions about fairness in mediation. As you read this excerpt, you should note, however, the number of variables that add complexity to any attempt to systematically study the effects of race and gender on the outcomes of disputes.

Gary LaFree & Christine Rack, **THE EFFECTS OF PARTICIPANTS'
ETHNICITY AND GENDER ON MONETARY OUTCOMES IN
MEDIATED AND ADJUDICATED CIVIL CASES**

30 L. & Socy. Rev. 767, 768–772, 788–793 (1996)

Our purpose here is to report on research comparing the relative effects of disputants'
ethnicity and gender on monetary outcomes in mediated and adjudicated civil, small
claims cases. More specifically, we test the "disparity" hypothesis that minority and
female disputants will achieve poorer outcomes than nonminority and male disputants, whether their cases are mediated or adjudicated; and the "informality hypothesis" that the effects of ethnicity and gender will be greater in mediated than in
adjudicated cases. In addition, we examine the possibility that the ethnicity and
gender of the mediators and disputants interacted to affect outcomes.

SOCIOCULTURAL FACTORS IN DISPUTE RESOLUTION

As an extension of the basic conflict argument that less powerful social groups usually
do worse in a wide range of competitive situations, legal theorists and researchers
have argued that the effect of sociocultural variables on decisionmaking may depend
in part on the nature of formal institutions. Thus, some legal traditionalists have
viewed the competitive presentation of evidence in the formal adversarial system
as counteracting decisionmaker bias and producing fairer and more accurate decisions than less formal systems.

The rapid growth of alternative dispute resolution as a substitute for courtroom
adjudication has heightened interest in whether less formal processes are more susceptible than courtroom adjudication to bias. In this regard, Galanter's distinction
between "repeat" and "one-shot" players is useful. [Marc Galanter, Why the
"Haves" Come Out Ahead: Speculations on the Limits of Legal Change, 9 L. &
Socy. Rev. 95 (1974).] Galanter has argued that parties who engage in many similar
litigations over time (repeat players) enjoy an advantage over relatively less experienced one-shot players because of their greater expertise, economies of scale, and
institutional relationships, as well as their greater ability to structure outcomes, create
case precedents, and influence applicable laws. Although Galanter interprets these
advantages as pervasive, transcending forum types, the distinction he makes raises the
possibility that one-shot players may be particularly vulnerable in less formal forums.
This conclusion is supported by those who argue that the low visibility and lack of
formal rules and structures in mediation, facilitated settlement, and other relatively
informal processes reduce the rights of less powerful participants. . . .

Delgado et al. (1985) have applied similar arguments to disputes involving ethnic
minorities. They argue that prejudice springs from psychodynamic, historical (socioeconomic and political), and social-psychological variables that may be either constrained or encouraged by situational factors. Because the Anglo-American judicial
system has incorporated norms of fairness into its institutional expectations and rules
of procedure, Delgado et al. conclude that, compared with less formal dispute resolution processes, the Anglo-American system deters prejudice.

Many feminist legal theorists have also speculated that compared with men, women may settle for less in mediation because they place a higher value on relationships than on monetary goals. For example, a literature review by Bryan (1992) [Penelope E. Bryan, Killing Us Softly: Divorce Mediation and the Politics of Power, 40 Buff. L. Rev. 441] concludes that women in divorce and custody negotiations with their former spouses are disadvantaged by economic, social, and psychological power differentials.

Despite widespread concern about potential bias against minorities and women in informal dispute resolution processes, there have been surprisingly few empirical efforts to validate or disprove the existence and severity of bias. Cross-cultural studies have been restricted to surveys on procedural preference in hypothetical disputes and anthropological observations on nonindustrialized societies. Comparison of mediated and adjudicated outcomes for women have been confined mostly to divorce and custody cases, an especially personal type of dispute, and even there research findings have been contradictory....

STUDY METHODOLOGY

We collected data from the Bernalillo County Metropolitan Court in Albuquerque, New Mexico, whose 481,000 residents are 37% Hispanic in origin.... The Metropolitan Court is a state court of limited jurisdiction that has the authority to hear minor criminal and traffic cases and civil cases involving amounts in controversy of $5,000 or less....

We collected data on 323 adjudicated and 280 mediated civil small claims cases filed between September 1990 and August 1991. We included only nonjury cases that sought money judgments; that had a single individual, business, or married couple on each side; and that had been to hearing on the merits or to a mediation in which both parties were present....

Court cases were heard by one of three judges. Mediation cases were co-mediated by pairs of women, men, or mixed gender pairs; and minority, nonminority, or mixed ethnicity pairs.... Participating judges were aware of the ethnicity/gender focus of our study but were unaware of the specific hypotheses or study design. Mediators were not told of the ethnicity/gender focus of the study but participated in data collection by completing a 52-item participant observation questionnaire after each mediation....

DISCUSSION AND CONCLUSIONS

The bivariate results offer considerable support for a disparity hypothesis. Minority women received less as claimants in mediation and paid more as respondents in adjudication; minority men received less as claimants in adjudication and mediation; Anglo women received less as claimants in adjudication. In general, the bivariate disparities were more consistent for claimants than for respondents and for minorities than for Anglo women. However, the multivariate analysis showed that much of the effect of ethnicity and gender on monetary outcomes disappeared when we added case-specific and repeat-player variables to the models. Of the two remaining ethnic-gender effects, only one supported the disparity hypotheses: minority male claimants received significantly lower MORs [Monetary Outcome Ratio = relationship of initial demand to what is received] in mediation. Contrary to the disparity hypothesis, Anglo female respondents negotiated significantly . . . lower MORs in mediation.

Subsequent analysis showed that most of the bivariate effect of disputants' ethnicity and gender on monetary outcomes is explained by repeat-player variables — especially for adjudicated cases. In general, minorities and women were less likely to be in either court or mediation as repeat players: They were less likely to be in collection cases and to be represented by attorneys; they were more likely to file as individuals and to be in private cases. The main exception was for Anglo female disputants in mediation.

We found limited support for an informality hypothesis — that ethnic and gender disparities are greater in mediation than in adjudication. The multivariate analysis showed that ethnicity and gender were more important determinants of mediation than of adjudication outcomes. However, we found no significant disparity for minority female or male respondents or Anglo female claimants; and compared with Anglo males, Anglo female respondents received somewhat more favorable outcomes in mediation.

ETHNICITY AND MONETARY OUTCOMES IN MEDIATION

Overall, we found the strongest evidence of ethnic and gender disparity in the treatment of minority claimants in mediation. In the analysis including product terms, both minority male and female claimants received significantly lower MORs — even when we included the nine case-specific and repeat-player variables. Of greatest concern is the fact that this disparity was only present in cases mediated by at least one Anglo mediator. Cases mediated by two minorities resulted in lower MORs, regardless of claimant ethnicity.

We believe that these results were most likely produced by three related processes. First, we found evidence that both Anglo and minority respondents were more willing to legitimate the monetary claims of Anglo than of minority claimants. Thus, initial admitted liability was lower in minority than in Anglo claimant cases . . . , and during mediation, respondents — especially Anglo respondents — made fewer concessions to minority than to Anglo claimants. . . .

Second, Anglo mediators were more likely to assume that monetary claims brought by Anglos were nonnegotiable while claims by minorities were more open to nonmonetary resolutions or negotiations that minimized monetary outcomes. Compared with Anglo claimants, minority claimants dropped their claims nearly three times more often (16.7% vs. 5.7%). . . .

Finally, compared with Anglo claimants, minority claimants generally defined their own goals in less stringently monetary terms. A strong family, relational, and community orientation in the Hispanic/Chicano culture is a characteristic noted by many scholars. Moreover, Hispanics and others from "high-context" and collectivist cultures are more likely to have "face" needs for affiliation and honor.

Compared with Anglo claimants in our study, minority claimants settled twice as often for nonmonetary outcomes (26.1% vs. 12.5%). We also found that compared with cases resulting in monetary outcomes, minority claimants in mediation were significantly more satisfied with cases that included substantial nonmonetary outcomes . . . , a difference that was not significant for Anglo claimants. . . .

While we suspect that all three of these processes contributed to the poorer monetary outcomes of minority claimants in the mediated cases, future research should explore in greater detail the specific dynamics at work. More research on the often subtle differences in the relative contributions of mediators, claimants, and respondents to mediated outcomes would be useful. Of particular importance is our finding of no significant ethnic disparities in cases mediated by two minority mediators.

GENDER AND MONETARY OUTCOMES IN MEDIATION

While we found some evidence for disparate treatment of minority female claimants in mediation, we found no evidence that Anglo women were disadvantaged as claimants or respondents in mediated cases. In fact, Anglo females appear to have done fairly well in these mediated cases. Anglo women were more likely than others to agree to mediate . . . , were more likely to reach agreements in their mediated cases (agreement rate of 75% compared with 60% overall), and rarely accepted nonmonetary outcomes in their cases (4% compared with a mean of 10%). The main statistically significant difference between Anglo women and Anglo men in mediation was for Anglo women to pay somewhat lower MORs as respondents in mediation (i.e., receive more favorable outcomes). These findings are important in light of scholarship which argues that mediation is unfair to women. Our study shows this fear to be unfounded for Anglo women, at least in the types of small claim court disputes we have examined here. However, the results might well be different for the mediation of larger disputes in courts of general jurisdiction or for particular types of cases, such as those involving divorce or child custody. . . .

One of the implications of our findings is that prior research on mediation which has treated ethnic minorities and women as equally disadvantaged may be masking complex interaction effects. Notably, female mediators may pose some unique risks for minority disputants: In particular, our results showed that minority female claimants received significantly lower MORs in cases mediated by two women.

These results may be due in part to differences in the goals of male and female mediators. Carnevale et al. (1989) [Peter J.D. Carnevale, Donald E. Conlon, Kathy A. Hanish & Karen L. Harris, Experimental Research on the Strategic-Choice Model of Mediation, in Mediation Research: The Process and Effectiveness of Third-Party Intervention, (Kenneth Kressel & Dean G. Pruitt eds.)] found that compared with men, women/negotiator subjects in experimental settings were likely to strive harder for integrative agreements and to overestimate the common ground in disputes. Similarly, in interviews with mediators, Buldoc (1990) [D.S. Buldoc, Mediator Style Perspectives: An Innovative Look at Mediator Behavior, (unpublished master's thesis, Arizona State University)] found that compared with men, women had stronger philosophical associations with mediation, seeing it as part of an ideological commitment to peace, whereas men more often viewed mediation as a straightforward mechanism for increasing dispute processing efficiency.

We found similar patterns in our data, especially in minority claimant cases mediated by women. Compared with other mediator dyads, minority claimant cases mediated by two female mediators were more likely to end in nonmonetary outcomes. In cases mediated by two women, minority claimants reached nonmonetary agreements in 31.8% of the cases, compared with a 9.7% nonmonetary agreement rate for cases mediated by two men and a 16.3% rate for cases mediated by a man and a woman. . . .

Taken together, these results amplify research which concludes that contemporary examples of racial, ethnic, and gender disparities in the United States are often complex, indirect, or institutionalized. Thus, evidence of disparity in the treatment of minorities and women was limited mostly to minority male and female claimants in mediated cases. Minority male and female claimants did worse in cases mediated by at least one Anglo mediator; minority female claimants did worse in cases mediated by two women. Outcomes in adjudication were explained mostly by case characteristics; there was little evidence that minority and female respondents were disadvantaged in either forum.

IMPLICATIONS FOR FUTURE RESEARCH AND SMALL CLAIM MEDIATION

Our research was limited to a small claims court in Albuquerque, New Mexico, and whether the findings can be generalized to other ethnic communities in different geographic locations remains open. The minority disputants in our study were mostly Hispanic. Perhaps members of other racial and ethnic groups would fare differently in mediation than do New Mexican Hispanics. Possibly, Cuban Americans in Miami or Puerto Rican Americans in New York might achieve different results in mediation than do New Mexican Hispanics. Indeed, even Hispanics from different parts of New Mexico with different cultural backgrounds might fare differently. Thus, it will be important to replicate this study in other jurisdictions, paying particular attention to differences in mediator attitudes and behavior.

Notes and Questions

7.27 Can you think of explanations for the "findings" that are different from those offered by the authors?

7.28 What seems to be more important in terms of obtaining a fair outcome — type of process (mediation or adjudication), the gender or ethnicity of the third-party neutral(s), or the gender or ethnicity of each of the parties?

7.29 What can be said about how these same questions relate to adjudicative processes? As you will see in more depth in Chapter 14, some scholars argue that more formal processes, like litigation, may reduce prejudice. What do you think?

7.30 If dangers from stereotyping and prejudice lurk in mediation, what protections either are or could be built into the mediation process to protect from or minimize these dangers? Could any legal rules affect these phenomena?

D. GOOD-FAITH PARTICIPATION IN MEDIATION

To the extent that mediation remains a voluntary process, the concerns raised by Trina Grillo in the context of mandatory mediation and by other scholars researching the impact of diversity on bargaining and mediation are less troubling. If parties need not participate in mediation or if they can walk away without negative consequence, the downside risks seem limited.

However, as the use of court-ordered mediation and of contracts that require mediation prior to adjudication have become more common, commentators have advocated, and legislators and courts have required, "good-faith" participation in mediation. The call for good-faith in mediation is premised on the need to ensure that the court-ordered process is not a waste of time, that it is at least possible to achieve a collaborative resolution, and that mediation is not misused. Furthermore, some suggest that to the extent that courts order participation and parties devote resources to it, society should protect the integrity of the process.

One of the problems with a good-faith requirement is the difficulty in defining "good faith." It is easier to identify what is indicative of bad faith than to define good faith. That list might include: failure to attend mediation; failure to bring the client or an organizational representative with settlement authority to mediation; failure to exchange information, bring data, or bring a key expert; failure to prepare a requested pre-mediation memorandum; and failure to participate seriously or to make suitable offers in mediation. Some items on the list are objective, and others are highly subjective. Attendance arguably falls into the objective category; serious participation is certainly open to differences of opinion and thus harder to enforce.

There are other difficulties with a good-faith requirement. Placing the burden on mediators to report bad faith can compromise their facilitative role and neutral posture. It could create an incursion into mediation confidentiality since allegations or evidence of bad faith would require disclosure of otherwise confidential mediation proceedings and mediator testimony. This could increase adversarial behavior of the parties — who now have a new weapon against each other — and undermine confidence in the mediator. Similarly, creating a cause of action for bad faith could encourage satellite litigation and spawn more procedural costs and delay for litigants — an ironic outcome since mediation ideally reduces costs and delays.

Where a good-faith requirement is in place, failure to comply with such a requirement may have consequences ranging from an award of the other side's costs of participation in mediation, including attorneys' fees, to a default judgment or dismissal against the party acting in bad faith.

Advocating for a good-faith standard, Kimberlee Kovach proposed the following model rule for good faith in mediation.

Kimberlee K. Kovach, GOOD FAITH IN MEDIATION—
REQUESTED, RECOMMENDED, OR REQUIRED? A NEW
ETHIC

38 S. Tex. L. Rev. 575, 622-623 (1997)

...Model Rule for Lawyers Requiring Good Faith Participation in the Mediation Process:

Rule 1.7 Good Faith in Mediation

A lawyer representing a client in mediation shall participate in good faith.

(a) Prior to the mediation, the lawyer shall prepare by familiarizing herself with the matter, and discussing it with her client.

(b) At the mediation, the lawyer shall comply with all rules of court or statutes governing the mediation process, and counsel her client to do likewise.

(c) During the mediation, the lawyer shall not convey information that is intentionally misleading or false to the mediator or other participants.

Statutory Basis for Good Faith Requirement

Mediation Code 001.

All parties and their counsel shall participate in mediation in good faith. "Good faith" includes the following:

a. Compliance with the terms and provisions of [cite to state statute or other rule setting forth mediation ...];

b. Compliance with any specific court order referring the matter to mediation;

c. Compliance with the terms and provisions of all standing orders of the court and any local rules of the court;

d. Personal attendance at the mediation by all parties who are fully authorized to settle the dispute, which shall *not* be construed to include anyone present by telephone;

e. Preparation for the mediation by the parties and their representatives, which includes the exchange of any documents requested or as set forth in a rule, order, or request of the mediator;

f. Participation in meaningful discussions with the mediator and all other participants during the mediation;

g. Compliance with all contractual terms regarding mediation which the parties may have previously agreed to;

h. Following the rules set out by the mediator during the introductory phase of the process;

i. Remaining at the mediation until the mediator determines that the process is at an end or excuses the parties;

j. Engaging in direct communication and discussion between the parties to the dispute, as facilitated by the mediator;

k. Making no affirmative misrepresentations or misleading statements to the other parties or the mediator during the mediation; and

l. In pending lawsuits, refraining from filing any new motions until the conclusion of the mediation.

002.

"Good faith" does not require the parties to settle the dispute. The proposals made at mediation, monetary or otherwise, in and of themselves do not constitute the presence or absence of good faith.

003. Determination of Good Faith

a. In court-annexed cases, the court shall make the final determination of whether good faith was present in the mediation.

b. Where a lawsuit has not been filed, the responsibility for finding a violation of the good faith duty rests upon the mediator, who shall use the elements of this statute and context of any contract between the parties as a basis for deliberation and decision-making.

004. Consequences for the Failure to Mediate in Good Faith

If it is determined that a party or a representative of a party has failed to mediate in good faith, the following actions can be instituted at the discretion of the court or mediator:

a. The individual shall pay all fees, costs, and reasonable expenses incurred by the other participants.

b. The individual will pay the costs of another mediation.

c. The individual will be fined in an amount no greater than $5,000.00.

d. The individual, at their own cost, will attend a seminar or other educational program on mediation, for a minimum of eight (8) hours.

As a counterpoint to Kovach's proposal, John Lande argues against a good-faith rule and suggests other methods to deal with bad faith.

 John Lande, USING DISPUTE SYSTEM DESIGN METHODS TO PROMOTE GOOD-FAITH PARTICIPATION IN COURT-CONNECTED MEDIATION PROGRAMS

50 UCLA L. Rev. 69, 72-76, 139-140 (2002)

Legislatures and courts have adopted rules requiring good faith in mediation, and courts have sanctioned violators. These requirements are premised on assumptions that mediation participants would understand readily what behavior is required and would respond appropriately. . . .

The controversy over good-faith requirements is part of a larger debate over the purpose and nature of court-connected mediation programs. This debate focuses on competing program goals and ideas about what is needed to ensure the programs' integrity. On one side of the debate, people view mediation programs as mechanisms to dispose of a portion of court dockets. Courts order parties to spend time and money for mediation and want to be sure that the time and money are well-spent. Courts also want to ensure that parties and attorneys comply with their orders and cooperate with the courts' case management systems. From this perspective, a good-faith requirement seems to be the logical way to ensure the integrity of court-connected mediation programs.

On the other side of the debate, people focus on the integrity of the mediation process, defined as an adherence to mediation practice norms. Many mediators are especially concerned that people participate in mediation without coercion, take advantage of opportunities for open discussion and problem-solving, and receive assurance that courts will honor confidentiality protections. From this perspective, good-faith requirements seem to violate mediation norms and thus *undermine* the integrity of court-connected mediation programs. Although this brief summary oversimplifies the debate, it captures a real tension in the debates about the future of court-connected mediation programs.

. . . [G]ood-faith requirements should be adopted only as a last resort, after a court . . . tries other policy options, and finds that those options do not resolve significant problems of bad faith in mediation. . . . These options include collaborative education about good mediation practice, use of pre-mediation consultations and document submissions, a narrow requirement of attendance for a limited and specified time, and protections against misrepresentation. . . .

A good-faith requirement in mediation is very troublesome. Although it may deter some inappropriate conduct, it also may stimulate even more. It risks undermining the interests of *all* the stakeholder groups of court-connected mediation, especially interests in the integrity of the mediation process and the courts. . . . Actively enforcing a good-faith requirement would subject *all* participants to uncertainty about the impartiality and confidentiality of the process and could heighten adversarial tensions and inappropriate pressures to settle cases. Although such a requirement could deter and punish truly egregious behavior . . . , it would do so at the expense of overall confidence in the system of mediation. Barring evidence of a substantial number of problems of real bad faith (as opposed to loose litigation talk), the large cost of a bad-faith sanctions regime is not worth the likely small amount of benefit, especially considering the alternative policy options available.

Notes and Questions

7.31 Do you support Kovach's rule? Why or why not? Can you foresee problems with specific provisions of the rule? Do you think Lande's suggestions effectively address the problem of bad faith? While Kovach is urging a stick, Lande prefers finding carrots to offer. In your experience, which works best — stick or carrot?

7.32 Imagine the following. You agree to mediate a matter for the Equal Employment Opportunity Commission involving a government agency and a worker claiming discrimination. Government attorneys are traveling from Washington, D.C., to New York City for the mediation session. Government costs include a full day of two attorneys' time, plus travel expenses. A New York attorney representing the plaintiff says: "This meeting is a waste of time. I will come but I will not bother my client to come." As the mediator, can (or should) you require that the plaintiff attend the meeting? That the government also bring a supervisor or manager from the plaintiff's work site? That the attorneys prepare for the mediation by writing pre-mediation statements? That the plaintiff's attorney adopt a more positive and helpful attitude? No one wants to be part of a fruitless effort. What should the mediator do? How can the system at large address this problem? Can (or should) the EEOC official referring the case sanction a party for undermining the mediation effort?

Courts struggle with the tension between upholding a good-faith standard on the one hand and confidentiality on the other. In the *Foxgate* case below, the California Supreme Court overruled the Court of Appeal's decision that a mediator is allowed to report sanctionable bad-faith conduct by a party, thereby piercing statutory confidentiality. The Court of Appeal had found that the California statute creating mediation confidentiality was not intended to shield improper conduct. As you read this case, consider whether the court found the correct balance between the competing goals of promotion of good-faith conduct and protection of mediation confidentiality.

 FOXGATE HOMEOWNERS' ASSOCIATION v. BRAMALEA

25 P.3d 1117 (Cal. 2001)

The questions we address here are independent of the issues in the underlying lawsuit. Instead, we face the intersection between court-ordered mediation, the confidentiality of which is mandated by law, and the power of a court to control proceedings before it and other persons "in any manner connected with a judicial proceeding before it," by imposing sanctions on a party or the party's attorney for statements or conduct during mediation. . . .

We conclude that there are no exceptions to the confidentiality of mediation communications or to the statutory limits on the content of mediator's reports. Neither a mediator nor a party may reveal communications made during mediation. . . . We also conclude that, while a party may do so, a mediator may not report to the court about the conduct of participants in a mediation session. . . .

I. BACKGROUND

The underlying litigation is a construction defects action in which the defendants are the developers Bramalea. . . . The plaintiff is a homeowners association made up of the owners of a 65 unit Culver City condominium complex developed and constructed by defendants. In a comprehensive January 22, 1997, case management order (C.M.O.) . . . the superior court appointed Judge Peter Smith, a retired judge, as a special master to act as both mediator and special master for ruling on discovery motions. Judge Smith was given the power to preside over mediation conferences and to make orders governing attendance of the parties and their representatives at those sessions. The C.M.O. specifically provided that Judge Smith was to "set such . . . meetings as [he] deems appropriate to discuss the status of the action, the nature and extent of defects and deficiencies claimed by Plaintiffs, and to schedule future meetings, including a premediation meeting of all experts to discuss repair methodology and the mediation. . . ." Defendants were ordered to serve experts' reports on all parties prior to the first scheduled mediation session. The order confirmed that privileges applicable to mediation and settlement communications applied. The parties were ordered to make their best efforts to cooperate in the mediation process.

Bramalea . . . was (and continues to be) represented by Ivan K. Stevenson. . . . The record reflects that, on the morning of September 16, 1997, the first day of a five-day round of mediation sessions of which the parties had been notified and to which the court's notice said they should bring their experts and claims representatives, plaintiff's attorney and nine experts appeared for the session. Stevenson was late and brought no defense experts. Subsequent mediation sessions were cancelled after that morning session because the mediator concluded they could not proceed without defense experts.

Plaintiff filed its first motion . . . for the imposition of sanctions of $24,744.55 on Bramalea and Stevenson . . . for their failure to cooperate in mediation. The sanctions sought reflected the cost to plaintiff of counsel's preparation for the sessions, the charges of plaintiff's nine experts for preparation and appearance at the mediation session, and the payment to the mediator, which was no longer refundable. Plaintiff's memorandum of points and authorities and declaration of counsel in support of the motion for sanctions recited a series of actions by Bramalea and Stevenson that, plaintiff asserted, reflected a pattern of tactics pursued in bad faith and solely intended to cause unnecessary delay. The actions described included objections to the schedule and attempts to postpone the mediation sessions, and culminated with Stevenson's appearance without experts at the mediation session at which architectural and plumbing issues were to be discussed. The motion recited that when asked by plaintiffs counsel if he would have expert consultants present for the future mediation sessions, Stevenson replied that "I can't answer that." When asked why he had arrived without expert consultants, Stevenson replied: "This is your mediation, you can handle it any way you want. I'm here, you can talk to me." . . .

On September 18, two days after the aborted mediation session, Judge Smith filed the report that is the object of this dispute with the superior court. The report recited that on June 13, 1997, plaintiff's counsel requested that the mediation be continued to a later date to accommodate Stevenson. It was then continued to the September 16-22 dates. On July 16, 1997, the mediator denied as untimely a request by Stevenson for changes to the C.M.O. and for another postponement. On

August 15, 1997, Stevenson challenged the mediator pursuant to Code of Civil Procedure section 170.6. The Superior Court struck the challenge on September 8, 1997, and on September 15, 1997, Stevenson sought a writ of mandate in the Court of Appeal. That court denied Stevenson's request for stay two days later and subsequently summarily denied the petition.

The report of the mediator stated: "Mr. Stevenson has spent the vast majority of his time trying to derail the mediations scheduled for September 16 through 22, 1997. . . . On September 16, 1997, Mr. Stevenson arrived 30 minutes late. Even though the purpose of the mediation session was to have Bramalea's expert witnesses interact with plaintiff's experts on construction defect issues, Mr. Stevenson refused to bring his experts to the mediation. Mr. Stevenson stated on several occasions that he did not need experts because of his vast knowledge in the field of construction defect litigation. . . . As a result of Mr. Stevenson's obstructive bad faith tactics, the remainder of the mediation sessions were canceled at a substantial cost to all parties. . . ."

The mediator's report recommended, inter alia, that Bramalea/Stevenson be ordered to reimburse all parties for expenses incurred as a result of the cancelled September 16-22 mediation sessions. . . . Judge Smith then resigned as of the September 18, 1997, date of his report. . . .

III. DISCUSSION

. . . Section 1121 provides: "Neither a mediator nor anyone else may submit to a court or other adjudicative body, and a court or other adjudicative body may not consider, any report, assessment, evaluation, recommendation, or finding of any kind by the mediator concerning a mediation conducted by the mediator, other than a report that is mandated by court rule or other law and that states only whether an agreement was reached, unless all parties to the mediation expressly agree otherwise in writing, or orally in accordance with Section 1118."

Section 1119, subdivision (c), enacted at the same time (Stats. 1997, ch. 772, §3) provides: "All communications, negotiations, or settlement discussions by and between participants in the course of a mediation or a mediation consultation shall remain confidential." . . .

The language of sections 1119 and 1121 is clear and unambiguous, but the Court of Appeal reasoned that the Legislature did not intend these sections to create "an immunity from sanctions, shielding parties to court-ordered mediation who disobey valid orders governing their participation in the mediation process, thereby intentionally thwarting the process to pursue other litigation tactics." The court therefore crafted the exception in dispute here. As stated and as applied, the exception created by the Court of Appeal permits reporting to the court not only that a party or attorney has disobeyed a court order governing the mediation process, but also that the mediator or reporting party believes that a party has done so intentionally with the apparent purpose of derailing the court-ordered mediation and the reasons for that belief.

Appellants contend that the legislative policies codified in sections 1119 and 1121 are absolute except to the extent that a statutory exception exists. The only such exception they acknowledge is the authority of a mediator to report criminal conduct. They argue that the report of the mediator, which plaintiff submitted to the court with its motion for sanctions and which the court considered, was a form of testimony by a person made incompetent to testify by section 703.5, and violated the principle that mediators are to assist parties in reaching their own agreement, but ordinarily may not express an opinion on the merits of the case. In permitting consideration of any part of the report, the Court of Appeal has created a vague and inconsistent exception to the mandate of confidentiality, one that the Legislature did not authorize. . . .

Thus, we . . . must determine if the mediation confidentiality statutes then applicable admit of any exceptions. . . . The statutes are clear. Section 1119 prohibits any person, mediator and participants alike, from revealing any written or oral communication made during mediation. Section 1121 also prohibits the mediator, but not a party, from advising the court about *conduct* during mediation that might warrant sanctions. It also prohibits the court from considering a report that includes information not expressly permitted to be included in a mediator's report. The submission to the court, and the court's consideration of, the report of Judge Smith violated sections 1119 and 1121.

Because the language of sections 1119 and 1121 is clear and unambiguous, judicial construction of the statutes is not permitted unless they cannot be applied according to their terms or doing so would lead to absurd results, thereby violating the presumed intent of the Legislature. . . .

As all parties and *amici curiae* recognize, confidentiality is essential to effective mediation, a form of alternative dispute resolution encouraged and, in some cases required by, the Legislature. Implementing alternatives to judicial dispute resolution has been a strong legislative policy since at least 1986. In that year the Legislature enacted provisions for dispute resolution programs, including but not limited to mediation, conciliation, and arbitration, as alternatives to formal court proceedings which it found to be "unnecessarily costly, time-consuming, and complex" as contrasted with noncoercive dispute resolution. . . .

To carry out the purpose of encouraging mediation by ensuring confidentiality, the statutory scheme, which includes sections 703.5, 1119, and 1121, unqualifiedly bars disclosure of communications made during mediation absent an express statutory exception. . . .

The mediator and the Court of Appeal here were troubled by what they perceived to be a failure of Bramalea to participate in good-faith in the mediation process. Nonetheless, the Legislature has weighed and balanced the policy that promotes effective mediation by requiring confidentiality against a policy that might better encourage good faith participation in the process. Whether a mediator in addition to participants should be allowed to report conduct during mediation that the mediator believes is taken in bad faith and therefore might be sanctionable under Code of Civil Procedure section 128.5, subdivision (a), is a policy question to be resolved by the Legislature. Although a party may report obstructive conduct to the court, none of the confidentiality statutes currently makes an exception for reporting bad faith conduct or for imposition of sanctions under that section when doing so would require disclosure of communications or a mediator's assessment of a party's conduct although the Legislature presumably is aware that Code of

Civil Procedure section 128.5 permits imposition of sanctions when similar conduct occurs during trial proceedings.

. . . The Legislature has decided that the policy of encouraging mediation by ensuring confidentiality is promoted by avoiding the threat that frank expression of viewpoints by the parties during mediation may subject a participant to a motion for imposition of sanctions by another party or the mediator who might assert that those views constitute a bad faith failure to participate in mediation. Therefore, even were the court free to ignore the plain language of the confidentiality statutes, there is no justification for doing so here. . . . No evidence of communications made during the mediation may be admitted or considered.

Notes and Questions

7.33 If, as the California Supreme Court found, bad-faith conduct cannot be reported by a mediator, very little protection may exist to prevent such conduct. Is it more difficult to enforce good-faith conduct in the mediation context than in the context of other dispute resolution processes?

7.34 Where a trial court orders parties to mediation and to participate in good faith, can the court sanction a party for failing to attend? For failing to bargain in good faith? For failing to settle? See Department of Transp. v. City of Atlanta, 380 S.E.2d 265 (Ga. 1989) (holding that while a trial court can refer parties to mediation, it cannot do so under a penalty of contempt should they not settle); Graham v. Baker, 447 N.W.2d 397 (Iowa 1989) (holding that attendance alone — even for the purpose of stating that one's position is not negotiable — is sufficient to meet the good-faith requirement); and Decker v. Lindsay, 824 S.W.2d 247 (Tex. Ct. App. 1992) (holding that a court could mandate attendance but *not* good faith in negotiations).

What if parties attend the mediation but fail to submit a statement of issues to the mediator or otherwise to prepare adequately? See Francis v. Women's Obstetrics & Gynecology Group, 144 F.R.D. 646 (W.D.N.Y. 1992) (holding that mere attendance is not sufficient where the defendant did not timely submit an issue statement and had a "cavalier attitude").

What if a party fails to make a settlement offer? See Avril v. Civilmar, 605 So. 2d 988 (Fla. Dist. Ct. App. 1992) (quashing sanctions imposed by a trial court for a party's failure to make an adequate settlement offer).

John Lande, in an exhaustive summary of the status of good-faith cases, notes:

> The final court decisions in these cases generally have been quite consistent in each category. The courts have found bad faith in all the cases in which a party has failed to attend the mediation or has failed to provide a required pre-mediation memorandum. In cases involving allegations that organizational parties have provided representatives without sufficient settlement authority, the courts have split almost evenly. In virtually all of the other cases in which the courts ruled on the merits of the case, they rejected claims of bad faith. In effect, the courts have interpreted good faith narrowly to require compliance

with orders to attend mediation, provide pre-mediation memoranda, and, in some cases, produce organizational representatives with sufficient settlement authority.

John Lande, Using Dispute System Design Methods to Promote Good-Faith Participation in Court-Connected Mediation Programs, 50 UCLA L. Rev. 69, 84-85 (2002).

7.35 With respect to corporate parties, it is sometimes difficult to ascertain who is best fitted to participate in mediation. Where a court orders that a corporate representative attend "with settlement authority," is it sufficient to send an employee who has instructions to bargain within a very narrow range? Is it sufficient to have someone available by phone?

In G. Heileman Brewing Co. v. Joseph Oat Corp., 871 F.2d 648 (7th Cir. 1989), the court affirmed the district court's conclusion that the company had failed to send a representative in an appropriate position to the settlement conference. The court ruled that the corporate representative attending a pretrial conference must "hold a position within the corporate entity allowing him to speak definitively and to commit the corporation to a particular position in the litigation." Id. at 653. In that case, a corporate representative was sent with authority to speak for a party, but the only instruction he had was to make no offer. In Raad v. Wal-Mart Stores, 1998 WL 272879 (D. Neb. 1998), Wal-Mart was sanctioned — ordered to pay $4,950 representing plaintiff's costs for the mediation — for failing to bring a corporate representative to a court-ordered mediation even though the representative was available by phone. The court said:

> There are several reasons for requiring the presence of authorized represen-tatives at a settlement conference. During the conference, counsel for both sides are given an opportunity to argue their clients' respective positions to the court, including pointing out strengths and weaknesses of each party's case. In this discussion, it is often true that client representatives and insurers learn, for the first time, the difficulties they may have in prevailing at a trial. They must, during the conference, weigh their own positions in light of the statements and arguments made by counsel for the opposing parties. It is often true that as a result of such presentations, the clients' positions soften to the extent that meaningful negotiation, previously not seriously entertained, becomes pos-sible. This dynamic is not possible if the only person with authority to negoti-ate is located away from the courthouse and can be reached only by telephone, if at all. The absent decision-maker learns only what his or her attorney conveys by phone, which can be expected to be largely a recitation of what has been conveyed in previous discussions. At best, even if the attorney attempts to convey the weakness of that client's position as they have been presented by opposing counsel at the settlement conference, the message, not unlike those in the children's game of "telephone," loses its impact through repetition, and it is simply too easy for that person to reject, out of hand, even a sincere desire on the part of counsel to negotiate further. At worst, a refusal to have an authorized representative in attendance may become a weapon by which parties with comparatively greater financial

flexibility may feign a good faith settlement posture by those in attendance at the conference, relying on the absent decision-maker to refuse to agree, thereby unfairly raising the stakes in the case, to the unfair disadvantage of a less wealthy opponent. In either case, the whole purpose of the settlement conference is lost, and the result is an even greater expenditure of the parties' resources, both time and money, for naught.

Id. at 1006.

7.36 With respect to good-faith reporting by the mediator, Carol Izumi and Homer La Rue conclude:

[A] mediator good faith reporting requirement would have a deleterious effect on the mediation process. It potentially would focus the parties and their lawyers on the litigable issues of a good faith claim rather than on the interests and needs of the parties that might make resolution of the dispute possible and fair. What is potentially more troubling is that the identification of behavior that is inconsistent with good faith is for some as difficult to define as what constitutes pornography.

Carol L. Izumi & Homer C. La Rue, Prohibiting "Good Faith" Reports Under the Uniform Mediation Act: Keeping the Adjudication Camel Out of the Mediation Tent, 2003 J. Disp. Resol. 67, 92.

For other perspectives on this issue, see Wayne D. Brazil, Continuing the Conversation About the Current Status and the Future of ADR: A View from the Courts, 2000 J. Disp. Resol. 11 (warning that a good-faith participation requirement could corrupt the mediation process); Edward Sherman, Court Mandated Alternative Dispute Resolution: What Form of Participation Should Be Required?, 46 SMU L. Rev. 2079 (1993) (arguing against a good-faith participation requirement and proposing a "minimal meaningful participation" requirement); and Maureen A. Weston, Checks on Participant Conduct in Compulsory ADR: Reconciling the Tension in the Need for Good-Faith Participation, Autonomy, and Confidentiality, 76 Ind. L.J. 591, 607-609 (2001) (arguing that sanctions are needed "to compensate the aggrieved party for the costs, fees, time, and anguish").

7.37 Related to situations where courts mandate mediation and one party does not participate in good faith are situations where parties have a pre-dispute contract provision requiring mediation and one party does not want to participate. Courts have found failure to exhaust an agreed-upon remedy (mediation) precludes arbitration or litigation. In an unusual opinion, Annapolis Professional Firefighters Local 1926 v. City of Annapolis, 642 A.2d 889 (Md. Ct. Spec. App. 1994), the court noted that it would enforce an agreement to mediate "to the same extent that it would be enforced if the chosen method were arbitration." In an amusing footnote, the opinion said the court might not enforce an agreement to resolve a dispute by trial by combat or ordeal but that it did not "wish to put a straightjacket on the creative development of new forms of alternative dispute resolution that individual parties, or industries, find useful and preferable to litigation." Id. at 895.

7.38 Sanctions for bad faith can be severe. In Toon v. Wackenhut Corrections Corp., 250 F.3d 950 (5th Cir. 2001), the court found that plaintiffs' counsel violated confidentiality provisions in the mediation settlement agreement by not filing its motion to enforce under seal. The case involved abuse of young girls in a juvenile justice center and settled for $1.5 million, and the unsealed motion resulted in a newspaper article regarding the agreement. For this bad-faith conduct, plaintiffs' counsel were sanctioned as follows: their contingency fee was reduced from 40 percent to 30 percent; they were precluded from representing other plaintiffs in related claims against defendants without the leave of the court; and they were ordered to pay a $15,000 sanction to the district court. More extreme sanctions include dismissal and default judgment. See, e.g., Triad Mack Sales & Serv. v. Clement Bros. Co., 438 S.E.2d 485 (N.C. Ct. App. 1994) (defendant's failure to attend mediation without good cause resulted in a default judgment); Schulz v. Nienhuis, 448 N.W.2d 655 (Wis. 1989) (plaintiff's lack of good faith in failing to attend mediation resulted in the dismissal of the case).

7.39 Did the California Supreme Court in *Foxgate* get it right? Whatever your opinion, as the chapter that follows describes, confidentiality in mediation and exceptions to confidentiality have been at the heart of the development of mediation.

E. ENFORCEMENT OF MEDIATION AGREEMENTS

The most common issue which brings mediation questions to court is the enforcement of mediation agreements. When a mediation is successfully concluded it results in a contract. Both parties seeking enforcement of that contract and parties seeking to avoid their agreements (generally using traditional contract defenses like fraud, mistake, unconscionability) are increasingly taking their mediated cases to court for post-mediation litigation, what two scholars have aptly called, "disputing irony."

 James R. Coben & Peter N. Thompson, **DISPUTING IRONY: A SYSTEMATIC LOOK AT LITIGATION ABOUT MEDIATION**

11 Harv. Neg. L. Rev. (forthcoming, 2006)

[G]iven the oft-expressed mediation objective of providing an alternative to the traditional adversarial system, the phenomenon of mediation litigation is a "disputing irony" that warrants closer examination. Indeed, much can be learned from these "failed" mediations.

First, the sheer volume of litigation about mediation in United States courts may come as a surprise. . . . [W]e have analyzed all 1,224 state and federal court mediation decisions available on the Westlaw databases "allstates" and "allfeds" for the years 1999 through 2003. In this five-year span when general civil case loads were relatively steady or declining nationwide, mediation litigation increased 95 percent, from 172 decisions in 1999 to 336 in 2003.

Second, the mediation issues being litigated are quite diverse. . . . In a nutshell, we expected, and indeed found, large numbers of cases about enforcement of mediated settlements (569 opinions), duty to mediate (279 opinions), mediation confidentiality (153 opinions), and sanctions (143 opinions). However, we did not anticipate the significant number of decisions dealing with mediation fee and cost issues (243 opinions), ethics/malpractice (98 opinions), the intersection between mediation and arbitration (88 opinions), the procedural implications of a mediation request or participation (50 opinions), or acts or omissions in mediation as a basis for independent claims (20 opinions).

Equally surprising, was the dearth of cases addressing mediator misconduct, asserted as a contract defense only 17 times in five years. Either the concern about coercive mediators is unwarranted or the litigation process does not provide an appropriate forum to address this issue. Most of the enforcement cases raised traditional contract defenses. Indeed, one general conclusion to be drawn from the dataset is that alleged defects in the mediation process are forced by existing legal norms to be framed in litigation identically like those that plague unfacilitated party-bargaining. Thus, when parties attempt to enforce mediation settlements in court, the litigation focuses on typical contract issues such as: claims of unenforceable agreements to agree; failure to have a meeting of the minds; fraud; changed circumstances; and mistake.

Notes and Questions

7.40 Coben and Thompson found that 46 percent of all reported cases on mediation in a five year period were about enforcing agreements (close to 600 total cases). The vast majority of mediation agreements was ordered to be enforced by the courts. In five years, in all of state and federal courts, only 100 cases were reported to be unenforceable (by the acceptance of one contract defense or another). What do you make of this number? Is it low? High? Just right?

7.41 Coben and Thompson were also surprised to discover just how often courts considered information from inside the mediation, seemingly "piercing" the confidentiality veil promised in mediation (see the next chapter). In over 300 cases, courts considered mediation evidence of one kind or another without party objection, and in 67 cases mediators themselves offered testimony. This tension between enforcement and litigation about the "fairness" of mediation agreements and confidentiality is explored further in the next chapter (and see *Foxgate*, above, and Ellen Deason, Enforcing Mediated Settlement Agreements: Contract Law Collides with Confidentialiy, 35 U.C. Davis L. Rev. 33 (2001); and Peter Robinson, Centuries of Contract Law Can't Be All Wrong: Why the UMA's Exception to Mediation Confidentiality in Enforcement Proceedings Should Be Embraced and Broadened, 2003 J. Disp. Resol. 135 (2003).

7.42 How can courts scrutinize the fairness or enforceability of mediation agreements without looking at confidential information? Is it in furtherance of
traditional contract principles, consistent with court monitoring of "justice"
and fairness for courts to look inside the mediation process, or is it a violation of
the core conception of confidentiality? Is it proper for courts to ask mediators
to write reports, either of failed mediations, or to document the conditions of
successful ones in order to provide "evidence" in case there is any later conflict
about enforceability?

F. MEDIATOR LIABILITY, IMMUNITY, AND MALPRACTICE

If good-faith participation measures the legal duty of parties and lawyers in mediation, whether mediators can be held liable for what they do in mediation is rapidly
becoming an important legal issue, which we explore in greater detail at the end of
Chapter 9. So far, mediators, especially those acting in court settings, have generally
been held to be "immune" from suit for many forms of mal- or non-feasance,
because of the important "judicial-like" service they are performing for the courts,
see, e.g., Wagshal v. Foster, 28 F.3d 1249 (D.C.C. 1994). See Scott Hughes, Mediator Immunity: The Misguided and Inequitable Shifting of Risk, 83 Or. L. Rev. 107
(2004). There have been few reported cases of mediator malpractice, see Michael
Moffitt, Suing Mediators, 83 B.U. L. Rev. 147 (2003), perhaps because standards of
what constitutes good or bad performance remain unclear in this still-developing
field. On the other hand, as Professor James Coben has begun to document, reported
legal cases challenging various aspects of mediated agreements are rapidly increasing,
see, e.g., James R. Coben, Gollum, Meet Smeagol: A Schizophrenic Rumination on
Mediator Values Beyond Self-Determination and Neutrality, 5 Cardozo J. Confl.
Res. 65 (2004), n.1; and James R. Coben & Peter Thompson, Disputing Irony: A
Systematic Look at Litigation About Mediation, 11 Harv. Neg. L. Rev. (2006).
These cases represent challenges to mediated agreements based on coercive actions
of mediators, incorrect legal advice, and other alarming practices. Many, including
Professors Moffitt, Coben, and Deason, predict that cases involving mediator mis-
conduct will increase in the next few years. On the other hand, confidentiality rules
in mediation (which we study in the next chapter) may also shield mediators from
public scrutiny, see Ellen Deason, Enforcing Mediated Settlement Agreements:
Contract Law Collides with Confidentiality, 35 U.C. Davis L. Rev. 33 (2001).

Notes and Questions

7.43 We began this chapter by asking you to think about the accountability of
mediators for the agreements they "preside" over. Do you see any contradictions or policy dilemmas in the policies that protect confidentiality in mediation (see the next chapter), grant immunity or make malpractice liability
difficult to prove (in gratitude for how mediators serve the justice system),

and claims that mediation can be more fair or just for the parties than other processes? How are we to know?

7.44 With respect to mediation immunity, should it make a difference whether a mediator is serving pro bono or earning a fee?

The concerns and complexities addressed in this chapter are only a subset of all the concerns that have been raised about mediation. In Chapter 14, a variety of critiques are explored, including claims that settlement may offer peace but not justice; that mediation robs our public litigation system of opportunities to clarify the law and consequently develop public values; that power imbalances and distributional inequalities may be exacerbated in private and consensual processes; that ADR can (ironically) increase state control over private matters; that prejudice on the part of mediators and disputants can covertly pollute the process and more formal processes — like litigation — may minimize this risk; that the tendency of mediators to focus on the future (and perhaps neglect the past) undercuts justice delivery; that exporting U.S.-style ADR may have unexpected adverse consequences in other cultures and may interfere with the development of the rule of law in emerging democracies; that mediator manipulation may be unprincipled; that some of the claims of ADR in terms of efficiency, cost-savings, and relief to court dockets may be unfounded; and that mediators exert more control and direction than is advertised.

While grappling with the questions raised by these dilemmas, keep in mind the enormous promise of mediation, a process geared toward helping parties communicate more effectively, tap into human creativity, and bring about consensual and durable resolutions. As Abraham Lincoln said in his first inaugural address: "Why should there not be a patient confidence in the ultimate justice of the people? Is there any better or equal hope in the world?"

 **Chapter 8** Confidentiality in Mediation

I was angry with my friend: I told my wrath, my wrath did end. I was angry with my foe: I told it not, my wrath did grow.

— William Blake

As the Blake quote says, what you say and to whom (and then what is done with the information) can make a huge difference. When you speak with an attorney, a priest, or a doctor, you probably expect that the conversation will be kept in confidence. In most cases, those special relationships are protected by privileges recognized in law. In addition, these professionals have ethical duties not to disclose communications where privacy is expected or promised. Similarly, there are a variety of mechanisms to protect communications between parties and mediators from disclosure to those outside the mediation session and particularly to prevent disclosure to adjudicative forums.

Confidentiality is deemed necessary in relationships where parties might not otherwise share information and where furthering a particular activity, relationship, or service is important to society. Settling disputes is important to both courts and communities and since (arguably) parties would not be candid with mediators without confidentiality protections, confidentiality is thought by many to be critical to mediation. Further, calling mediators to testify raises issues about their neutrality since the mediator's testimony will most likely favor one party over another. Proponents of confidentiality point out that confidentiality also promotes protection against harassment of mediators and mediation programs, because without protection mediators and programs might be bombarded by subpoenas. Fairness considerations also argue for protections, since a more sophisticated party might use mediation to obtain information and then use it against the more forthcoming party.

Opponents of confidentiality raise important concerns. There is a tension between the public's right to obtain the "truth" or "every person's testimony" in adjudicative proceedings and the public good furthered by confidentiality. Where important matters are being resolved out of public view, concerns arise about coercion, misconduct, and a loss of societal protections for the less powerful. Confidentiality interferes with public oversight. Some have argued that confidentiality is not necessary for mediation to succeed, and indeed programs have operated successfully without confidentiality protections. Some argue that confidentiality protections in mediation make certain settlements "secret" and prevent the public from learning about information (like dangerous products) as well as the outcomes achieved in mediation. One writer has called this "the erosion of the public realm." David Luban, Settlements and the Erosion of the Public Realm, 83 Geo. L.J. 2619 (1995), see Chapter 14.

Different balances have been struck between the need for mediation confidentiality and the need for disclosure about what occurred in mediation. In striking that balance, both common law and statutes have been used to protect confidentiality as well as to delineate exceptions. The discussion that follows outlines the legal sources of confidentiality protections and exceptions to confidentiality laws and privileges. The text also reviews decisions applying statutory and common law.

A. EVIDENTIARY EXCLUSIONS

Traditionally, evidence concerning offers of settlement and compromise of disputed claims has been excluded in judicial proceedings, on the grounds that they are not probative as an admission with respect to the amount or validity of a claim. Parties, for example, might make a settlement offer simply to get rid of a claim or perhaps out of sympathy for the other side even where they do not feel legally responsible. However, statements of fact — "I am to blame because I ran the red light" — made in settlement discussions would be admissible under the common law.

Federal Rule of Evidence 408 and similar state counterparts broaden the common law protection. In addition to settlement offers, Rule 408 protects evidence of conduct or statements made in compromise negotiations as well. While Rule 408 provides more protection for settlement discussions, the protection is still quite limited. Evidence from settlement discussions may be introduced to show bias or prejudice, impeach credibility, or prove a material matter other than liability. To be excluded, the evidence must have a sufficient relationship to settlement discussions. Furthermore, the rule applies only to subsequent litigation (not administrative or legislative hearings or other types of public disclosure), and there

> **Federal Rule of Evidence 408**
>
> **COMPROMISE AND OFFERS TO COMPROMISE**
>
> Evidence of (1) furnishing or offering or promising to furnish, or (2) accepting or offering or promising to accept, a valuable consideration in compromising or attempting to compromise a claim which was disputed as to either validity or amount, is not admissible to prove liability for or invalidity of the claim or its amount. Evidence of conduct or statements made in compromise negotiations is likewise not admissible. This rule does not require the exclusion of any evidence otherwise discoverable merely because it is presented in the course of compromise negotiations. This rule also does not require exclusion when the evidence is offered for another purpose, such as proving bias or prejudice of a witness, negativing a contention of undue delay, or proving an effort to obstruct a criminal investigation or prosecution.

must be a disputed civil claim (that is, negotiations over matters that are not a legal cause of action may not be protected).

The Rule and its many exceptions do not inspire confidence about mediator confidentiality. Consider how a mediator could, in an opening statement, without undermining confidence that it is safe for the parties to speak freely, make this understandable to a non-lawyer.

B. DISCOVERY LIMITATIONS

In addition to Rule 408, mediation communications might receive protection under the Federal Rules of Civil Procedure and comparable state rules. Federal Rule of Civil Procedure 26(c), pertaining to Protective Orders, has been invoked to protect a party from harm that might be caused by divulging information learned in mediation. The Rule provides, in pertinent part, that "the court . . . may make any order which justice requires to protect a party or person from annoyance, embarrassment, oppression, or undue burden or expense."

Recently some states have limited the secrecy of discovery-produced documents and settlements themselves by amending their Rules of Civil Procedure or other rules in order to require disclosure of information that might affect "public health and safety."

 Carrie Menkel-Meadow, **PUBLIC ACCESS TO PRIVATE SETTLEMENTS: CONFLICTING LEGAL POLICIES**

11 Alternatives to the High Cost of Litigation 85-86 (1993)

Legal policy has long protected the confidentiality of negotiations designed to produce settlements. Yet a growing number of legal jurisdictions have been moving in the opposite direction—permitting, and in some cases mandating, disclosure of settlements.

The context is an ever-expanding movement to require the disclosure of settlements dealing with public health and safety, hazards, public officials, public bodies or most broadly, "public issues." To that end, more and more states are passing new laws requiring disclosure of settlements, or revising their rules of procedure to modify common practices involving confidentiality of discovery, protective orders and sealing of litigation records. Inevitably, policies allowing public access to settlements where there is a "public interest" will clash with long-standing policies that encourage settlement by providing both an atmosphere for candid discussion and the protection of a confidential or sealed settlement. . . .

Both the media and public interest groups have argued that a constitutional "right to know," derived from the First Amendment and other common law principles, provides a public right of access to any dispute that uses public institutions or fora, such as the courts. Another rationale is that there should be exceptions to the usual presumptions in favor of confidentiality when the public may be affected. Such exceptions must apply, for example, in cases involving utility rate setting, hazardous waste sites, products liability; and class actions in securities or discrimination matters. The claims here are that the public has the right to know if products are defective and likely to hurt them or that they live near hazardous waste sites or that the cost of consuming resources may rise. Although styled as individual lawsuits, the claims go, these are issues that affect us all. Some people who favor access perceive the courts as another instrument of public legal regulation, even if the parties to a given case are simply seeking to resolve their private dispute.

Efforts to make public the conduct of litigation and negotiations have been applied to discovery (challenging protective orders) and settlements (challenging the sealing of specific settlements or whole court files). For the most part, courts have continued to protect some secrecy and confidentiality interests in both the discovery and settlement contexts. They also have preferred to retain a case-by-case approach to protecting the broad scope of discovery and encouraging cooperation in both information disclosure and the settlement of cases (see Seattle Times v. Rhinehart, 467 U.S. 20 (1984); Brazil, Protecting the Confidentiality of Settlement Negotiations, 39 Hastings L.J. 955 (1988)).

When considering challenges to confidentiality, courts look to such factors as whether the common law treats a particular event as public (a trial is, a negotiation discussion isn't) or whether particular documents are public records (discovery documents are rarely filed with the courts anymore), or whether there is some important public function (like monitoring of the judicial process) being served. But there are a variety of "hybrid" situations just waiting for litigation on issues of confidentiality. These may include early neutral evaluation procedures held in private law offices under the court's aegis, or mandatory settlement conferences held in courtrooms or judges' chambers.

Case law favoring confidentiality is being challenged in a variety of ways. Some state legislatures have passed statutes mandating disclosure of information and settlements, such as Florida's Sunshine in Litigation Law. In other states, procedural rules have been modified to shift the burdens of presumption away from confidentiality in the seeking of protective orders or sealing of records. Texas, for example, in Rule 76a creates a presumption of openness applied to unfiled discovery documents and settlement agreements that "have a probable adverse effect on public health and safety."

Notes and Questions

8.1 Can you think of information, disclosed in discovery of a lawsuit, or during information exchange in a mediation, that you think should be disclosed outside of the mediation?

8.2 In Foxgate Homeowners' Asssociation v. Bramalea California, Inc. 25 P.3d 1117 (Cal. 2001), the California Supreme Court held that there were no exceptions to California's confidentiality protections in mediation (according to its evidence code Ca. Evidence Code §1119 (1997)). The court refused to permit inquiry into what occurred in a mediation, where it was alleged that some of the parties had behaved with bad faith and sanctions were demanded. This no exception to confidentiality in California has resulted in courts protecting items produced in mediation from discovery in subsequent actions, involving the same facts, see Rojas v. Superior Court, discussed in Notes and Questions 8.8.

C. CONTRACTS

In agreements to mediate, parties can (and frequently do) agree not to disclose information conveyed in the mediation and not to subpoena the mediator to testify about what happened. Mediators, both in their opening statements to parties and in agreements to mediate, typically promise not to disclose information that arose in the mediation. Such agreements may provide additional protection for confidentiality. However, courts may refuse to enforce a confidentiality agreement because suppression of evidence needed in litigation is contrary to public policy. Hence, legal protection for these agreements is not certain. Even if the confidentiality agreement is upheld for those signing it, third parties may have access to the information through discovery and subsequent use in trial.

In Simrin v. Simrin, in the context of a motion to modify a divorce decree, the court upheld a confidentiality agreement between a rabbi and a couple getting marital counseling.

 SIMRIN v. SIMRIN

43 Cal. Rptr. 376, 378-379 (Ct. App. 1965)

. . . [The] question arises from the court's ruling that a rabbi who acted as a marriage counselor for the parties need not reveal conversations with them. The wife called as a witness a rabbi, who declined to testify, not on the ground of privilege, but that he undertook marriage counseling with the husband and wife only after an express agreement that their communications to him would be confidential and that neither would call him as a witness in the event of a divorce action. He imposed the condition so they would feel free to communicate with him. After lengthy voir dire examination of the rabbi, the husband, and the wife, the court ruled that the rabbi need not relate the confidential communications. . . .

As to the agreement, appellant argues that to hold her to her bargain with the rabbi and with her husband is to sanction a contract to suppress evidence contrary to public policy. However, public policy also strongly favors procedures designed to preserve marriages, and counseling has become a promising means to that end. The two policies are here in conflict and we resolve the conflict by holding the parties to their agreement. If a husband or wife must speak guardedly for fear of making an admission that might be used in court, the purpose of counseling is frustrated. One should not be permitted, under cover of suppression of evidence, to repudiate an agreement so deeply affecting the marriage relationship. For the unwary spouse who speaks freely, repudiation would prove a trap; for the wily, a vehicle for making self-serving declarations.

A Sample Confidentiality Provision from an Agreement to Mediate

<u>Confidentiality</u>. The parties and mediator agree to the following confidentiality provisions:

a. Without the consent of all parties and an order of the court, no evidence that there has been a mediation or any fact concerning the mediation may be admitted in a trial de novo or in any subsequent proceeding involving any of the issues or parties to the mediation.
b. Statements made and documents produced in this mediation which are not otherwise discoverable are not subject to discovery or other disclosure and are not admissible into evidence for any purpose, including impeachment.
c. The mediator will not discuss the mediation process or disclose any communications made during the mediation process except as authorized by the parties, or required by law or other applicable professional codes. If either party seeks to subpoena the mediator or the mediator's records, that party shall be liable for, and shall indemnify the mediator against, any liabilities, costs or expenses, including reasonable attorneys' fees, which the mediator may incur in resisting such compulsion.

Agreement provision provided by Professor James Coben.

Notes and Questions

8.3 Mediators who breach their commitments or the parties' legitimate expectations regarding confidentiality may face civil liability for injuries caused by that breach. For a discussion of this risk, see Michael Moffitt, Ten Ways to Get Sued: A Guide for Mediators, 8 Harv. Negot. L. Rev. 81 (2003).

8.4 In *Simrin*, the court upholds the confidentiality agreement between the parties because it furthers a procedure (counseling) designed to preserve marriages, a public interest. Broadly speaking, what public interests are furthered by confidentiality agreements as they apply to mediated discussions?

D. MEDIATION PRIVILEGE

A privileged communication is protected from being divulged in court. Privileges, the strongest protection of confidentiality in mediation, can be created by courts or by statutes. The case below explores the costs and benefits of a mediation privilege and the essential elements in the creation of a privilege. In *Folb*, the plaintiff (Folb), in a discrimination action against his former employer (the Plans), is seeking information from a mediation session between the Plans and another employee (Vasquez) whom Folb allegedly sexually harassed. As you will see below, applying the federal common law of privilege, the court denied Folb access to mediation information and created a federal mediation privilege.

 ### FOLB v. MOTION PICTURE INDUSTRY PENSION & HEALTH PLANS

16 F. Supp. 2d 1164, 1167, 1170-1181 (C.D. Cal. 1998)

. . . In approximately February 1997, Vasquez and the Plans attended a formal mediation with a neutral in an attempt to settle Vasquez' potential claims against defendants arising out of the alleged sexual harassment [by Folb]. Vasquez and the Plans signed a contract agreeing to maintain the confidentiality of the mediation and all statements made in it. . . . Folb sought to compel production of (1) Vasquez' mediation brief; (2) correspondence between Vasquez' counsel and counsel for the Plans regarding mediation or other settlement discussions; and (3) notes to the file prepared by Vasquez' counsel regarding settlement communications. Folb argues that the Plans are trying to take a position in this litigation that is inconsistent with the position he believes they took in settlement negotiations with Vasquez. Folb suggests that the Plans will argue that he was properly terminated for sexually harassing Vasquez, despite the fact that they may have argued in mediation or settlement negotiations with Vasquez that she was never sexually harassed at all. . . .

FEDERAL MEDIATION PRIVILEGE

The federal courts are authorized to define new privileges based on interpretation of "common law principles . . . in the light of reason and experience." *Jaffee*, 518 U.S. at 8. . . . Nonetheless, that authority must be exercised with caution because the creation of a new privilege is based upon considerations of public policy. In general, the appropriate question is not whether a federal mediation privilege should exist in the abstract, but whether "(1) the need for that privilege is so clear, and (2) the desirable contours of that privilege are so evident, that it is appropriate for this court to craft it in common law fashion, under Rule 501." In re Grand Jury, 103 F.3d 1140, 1154 (3d Cir. 1997) (quoting *Jaffee*, 518 U.S. at 35 (Scalia, J., dissenting)), cert. denied; Roe v. U.S., 520 U.S. 1253 (1997).

The general rule is that the public is entitled to every person's evidence and that testimonial privileges are disfavored. Id. Consequently,

> we start with the primary assumption that there is a general duty to give what testimony one is capable of giving. . . . Exceptions from the general rule disfavoring testimonial privileges may be justified, however, by a "public good transcending the normally predominant principle of utilizing all rational means for ascertaining the truth." *Jaffee*, 518 U.S. at 9 (quoting *Trammel*, 445 U.S. 40 at 50).

To determine whether an asserted privilege constitutes such a public good, in light of reason and experience, the Court must consider (1) whether the asserted privilege is "rooted in the imperative need for confidence and trust[;]" (2) whether the privilege would serve public ends; (3) whether the evidentiary detriment caused by exercise of the privilege is modest; and (4) whether denial of the federal privilege would frustrate a parallel privilege adopted by the states. Id. at 9–13.

a. Need for Confidence and Trust

... To determine whether there is a need for confidentiality in mediation proceedings, the Court looks first to judicial and Congressional pronouncements on the issue. No federal court has definitively adopted a mediation privilege as federal common law under Rule 501. In one of the leading cases on the treatment of confidential communications in mediation, however, the Ninth Circuit approved revocation of a subpoena that would have required a Federal Mediation and Conciliation Service ("FMCS") mediator to testify in a National Labor Relations Board ("NLRB") enforcement proceeding. National Labor Relations Board v. Joseph Macaluso, Inc., 618 F.2d 51, 52 (9th Cir. 1980). . . .

The Ninth Circuit's conclusion that requiring a federal mediator to disclose information about the mediation proceedings would inevitably impair or destroy the usefulness of the FMCS in future proceedings is equally applicable in the context of private mediation. Admittedly, the express federal interest in preserving a labor mediation system establishes a stronger basis for a mediator privilege in the context of NLRB proceedings. Nonetheless, mediation in other contexts has clearly become a critical alternative to full-blown litigation, providing the parties a more cost-effective method of resolving disputes and allowing the courts to keep up with ever more unmanageable dockets. . . .

Whether information divulged in mediation proceedings is disclosed through the compelled testimony of a mediator or the compelled disclosure of documents conveyed to or prepared by the mediator, the side most forthcoming in the mediation process is penalized when third parties can discover confidential communications with the mediator. Refusing to establish a privilege to protect confidential communications in mediation proceedings creates an incentive for participants to withhold sensitive information in mediation or refuse to participate at all.

Today, the Court is faced with a somewhat more attenuated concern: whether the "imperative need for confidence and trust" that would support creation of a privilege protecting confidential communications with a mediator should extend so far as to protect all oral and written communications between the parties to a mediation. Before delving into the heart of the matter, we must also clarify what constitutes "mediation" for purposes of the Court's analysis today. Given the facts presented by the parties before the Court, we need only consider whether communications between parties who agreed in writing to participate in a confidential mediation with a neutral third party should be privileged and whether that privilege should extend to communications between the parties after they have concluded their formal mediation with the neutral.

Several commentators have suggested that successful mediation requires open communication between parties to a dispute. See, e.g., Alan Kirtley, The Mediation Privilege's Transition from Theory to Implementation: Designing a Mediation Privilege Standard to Protect Mediation Participants, the Process and the Public

Interest, 1995 J. Disp. Resol. 1, 8, 16 (collecting sources indicating weight of scholarly authority suggests confidentiality is essential to mediation). Kirtley argues that

> [w]ithout adequate legal protection, a party's candor in mediation might well be "rewarded" by a discovery request or the revelation of mediation information at trial. A principal purpose of the mediation privilege is to provide mediation parties protection against these downside risks of a failed mediation. Id. at 9-10.

In general, however, the academic literature provides little analysis of whether communications disclosed to the opposing party in the course of mediation proceedings should be accorded the same level of protection as private communications between one party and the mediator.

One self-described "heretical" commentator has expressed doubt over the need for a mediation privilege to protect confidentiality in mediation.

> Although most mediators assert that confidentiality is essential to the process, there is no data of which I am aware that supports this claim, and I am dubious that such data could be collected. Moreover, mediation has flourished without recognition of a privilege, most likely on assurance given by the parties and the mediator that they agree to keep mediation matters confidential, their awareness that attempts to use the fruits of mediation for litigation purposes are rare, and that courts, in appropriate instances, will accord mediation evidence Rule 408 and public policy-based protection. Eric D. Green, A Heretical View of the Mediation Privilege, 2 Ohio St. J. Disp. Resol. 1, 32 (1986) (arguing campaign to obtain blanket mediation privilege rests on "faulty logic, inadequate data, and shortsighted professional self-interest").

. . . Legal authority on the necessity of protecting confidential communications between the parties to a mediation is sparse. In an early decision by the Second Circuit, the court stated:

> [I]f participants cannot rely on the confidential treatment of everything that transpires during [mediation] sessions then counsel of necessity will feel constrained to conduct themselves in a cautious, tight-lipped, noncommital manner more suitable to poker players in a high-stakes game than adversaries attempting to arrive at a just solution of a civil dispute. This atmosphere if allowed to exist would surely destroy the effectiveness of a program which has led to settlements and withdrawals of some appeals and to the simplification of issues in other appeals, thereby expediting cases at a time when the judicial resources of this Court are sorely taxed. Lake Utopia Paper Ltd. v. Connelly Containers, Inc., 608 F.2d 928 (2d Cir. 1979). . . .

At least one district court has concluded that confidential information disclosed in alternative dispute resolution ("ADR") proceedings is privileged. See United States v. Gullo, 672 F. Supp. 99, 104 (W.D.N.Y. 1987). In *Gullo*, the court found that the confidentiality provision in New York's Community Dispute Resolution Centers Program served to ensure the effectiveness and continued existence of the program. Id. Looking to Rule 501, the court concluded, on balance, that the privilege afforded under New York law should be recognized by the federal court. Id. Having concluded that the information was protected, the *Gullo* court suppressed evidence in a criminal proceeding of all statements made during the dispute resolution process, as well as the terms and conditions of the settlement. Id. . . .

Taking the foregoing authorities en masse, the majority of courts to consider the issue appear to have concluded that the need for confidentiality and trust between participants in a mediation proceeding is sufficiently imperative to necessitate the creation of some form of privilege. This conclusion takes on added significance when considered in conjunction with the fact that many federal district courts rely on the success of ADR proceedings to minimize the size of their dockets. . . .

b. Public Ends

A new privilege must serve a public good sufficiently important to justify creating an exception to the "general rule disfavoring testimonial privileges." *Jaffee*, 518 U.S. at 9. . . . The proposed blanket mediation privilege would serve public ends by encouraging prompt, consensual resolution of disputes, minimizing the social and individual costs of litigation, and markedly reducing the size of state and federal court dockets. . . .

c. Evidentiary Detriment

In assessing the necessity of adopting a new privilege, the courts must consider whether "the likely evidentiary benefit that would result from the denial of the privilege is modest." *Jaffee*, 518 U.S. at 11-12. . . .

Where, as here, an employer is sued by one employee claiming wrongful termination based on false allegations of sexual harassment and by another employee asserting a claim for sexual harassment perpetrated by the other employee, a blanket mediation privilege might permit an unscrupulous employer to garner the benefit of the two employees' opposing positions. In open mediation proceedings, the employer would be forced to strike a balance between the two parties' positions rather than taking one employee's side in the first case and then shifting to the other side when defending against charges by the second employee. Despite the potential moral implications of fostering such duplicity, however, there is very little evidentiary benefit to be gained by refusing to recognize a mediation privilege.

First, evidence disclosed in mediation may be obtained directly from the parties to the mediation by using normal discovery channels. For example, a person's admission in mediation proceedings may, at least theoretically, be elicited in response to a request for admission or to questions in a deposition or in written interrogatories. In addition, to the extent a party takes advantage of the opportunity to use the cloak of confidentiality to take inconsistent positions in related litigation, evidence of that inconsistent position only comes into being as a result of the party's willingness to attend mediation. Absent a privilege protecting the confidentiality of mediation, the inconsistent position would presumably never come to light.

Although the Court need not, and indeed may not, address the outer limits of a federal mediation privilege, it seems appropriate to note one potential limitation here. A federal mediation privilege may be attenuated of necessity in criminal or quasi-criminal cases where the defendant's constitutional rights are at stake. In a recent decision, a California appellate court discussed the scope of acceptable evidentiary detriment created by the mediation privilege set forth in Cal. Evid. Code §1119. See Rinaker v. Superior Court of San Joaquin County, 62 Cal. App. 4th 155

(3d Dist. 1998). In the context of a juvenile delinquency proceeding, the *Rinaker* court found that

> neither the witness nor the mediator had a reasonable expectation of privacy in inconsistent statements made by the witness during confidential mediation because it has long been established that, when balanced against the competing goals of preventing perjury and preserving the integrity of the truth-seeking process of a juvenile delinquency proceeding, the interest in promoting settlements (in this case through confidential mediation of a civil harassment action against the minors) must yield to the minors' constitutional right to effective impeachment. Id. at 161. . . .

d. Mediation Privilege in the 50 States

In assessing a proposed privilege, a federal court should look to a consistent body of state legislative and judicial decisions adopting such a privilege as an important indicator of both reason and experience. *Jaffee*, 518 U.S. at 12-13. Put simply, "the policy decisions of the States bear on the question whether federal courts should recognize a new privilege or amend the coverage of an existing one." Id. Practically speaking, the confidential status accorded to mediation proceedings by the states will be of limited value if the federal courts decline to adopt a federal mediation privilege. See id. at 13. . . .

At the forefront of the inquiry, however, is the fact that every state in the Union, with the exception of Delaware, has adopted a mediation privilege of one type or another. Pamela A. Kentra, Hear No Evil, See No Evil, Speak No Evil: The Intolerable Conflict for Attorney-Mediators between the Duty to Maintain Mediation Confidentiality and the Duty to Report Fellow Attorney Misconduct, 1997 B.Y.U. L. Rev. 715. . . .

e. Contours of the Privilege

. . . On the facts presented here, the Court concludes that communications to the mediator and communications between parties during the mediation are protected. In addition, communications in preparation for and during the course of a mediation with a neutral must be protected. Subsequent negotiations between the parties, however, are not protected even if they include information initially disclosed in the mediation. To protect additional communications, the parties are required to return to mediation. A contrary rule would permit a party to claim the privilege with respect to any settlement negotiations so long as the communications took place following an attempt to mediate the dispute. . . .

CONCLUSION

. . . In short, the Court concludes that encouraging mediation by adopting a federal mediation privilege under Fed. R. Evid. 501 will provide "a public good transcending the normally predominant principle of utilizing all rational means for ascertaining the truth." *Jaffee*, 518 U.S. at 9.

Notes and Questions

8.5 The analysis in *Folb* was followed in Sheldone v. Pennsylvania Turnpike Commn., 104 F. Supp. 2d 511 (W.D. Pa. 2000). In *Sheldone*, workers and union members (plaintiffs) sought admission of statements made by their employer (defendant) in the mediation of a related matter. Plaintiffs argued that the mediation communications would show a motive for retaliation and rebut the employer's defense that it was acting in the good-faith belief that it was not violating the law. The government employer sought a protective order to preclude use of the mediation communications and documents, and the court held that the federal mediation privilege would be adopted and excluded the evidence. The *Sheldone* court noted, however, that the privilege would not protect evidence independently discoverable merely because it was presented in a mediation. How and when privileges are recognized by courts remains somewhat fuzzy, see, e.g., Carman v. McDonnell Douglas Corp., 114 F.3d 790 (8th Cir. 1997) in which the court found that there was no federal evidentiary privilege for an ombuds, who acting as a mediator, within a large corporation, attempted to settle a discrimination claim. The court ordered the ombuds to produce, in discovery of a later lawsuit, documents submitted to the ombuds during the internal company mediation.

8.6 In criminal or quasi-criminal cases, where the defendant's constitutional rights and personal liberty are at stake, there is more momentum to admit mediation communications. In Florida v. Castellano, 460 So. 2d 480 (Fla. Dist. Ct. App. 1984), the court held that privileges in Florida had to be established by the legislature and could not be judicially created. In that case, a criminal defendant in a murder case (to support a contention of self-defense), sought the testimony of a community mediator that the murder victim had made life-threatening statements to the defendant in the course of a mediation. Despite the mediator's assurance to the parties of confidentiality, the court ordered the mediator to testify and stated that: "If confidentiality is essential to the success of the CDSP [Citizens Dispute Settlement Program] program the legislature is the proper branch of government from which to obtain the necessary protection." Id. at 482. In addition to rejecting the privilege argument, the court rejected an argument that the mediation communications were protected under the Federal Rules of Evidence as "offers of compromise," noting that the "plain language of the provision only excludes evidence of an offer of compromise presented to prove liability or the absence of liability for a claim or its value. . . . [which is] simply not relevant to the situation where a mediator testifies in a criminal proceeding regarding an alleged threat made by one party to another in a prior CDSP setting." Id. at 481.

In People v. Snyder, 492 N.Y.S.2d 890 (Sup. Ct. 1985), however, where a defendant in a murder case also sought the testimony of a community mediator to support his claim of self-defense, confidentiality was upheld. A New York Supreme Court held that the statute establishing the Community Dispute Resolution Center's program provided for confidentiality, which could not be waived by parties.

Note that in Rinaker v. Superior Court of San Joaquin County, 74 Cal. Rptr. 2d 464 (Ct. App. 1998) (discussed in both *Folb* above and *Olam* below), a California appellate court found that inconsistent statements made by a witness in a confidential mediation proceeding could be admitted when balanced against the competing goals of preventing perjury and preserving the integrity of the truth-seeking process of a juvenile delinquency hearing.

8.7 In In re Grand Jury Proceedings, 148 F.3d 487 (5th Cir. 1998), the court held that mediation documents could be subpoenaed for grand jury investigation of fraud in a governmental program. Construing the Agricultural Credit Act, which provides that mediation sessions shall be confidential in order to qualify for federal funding, the court declined to infer a privilege for documents sought by a grand jury.

8.8 In Rojas v. Superior Court, 33 Cal. 4th 407 (2004), the California Supreme Court decided that evidence prepared for a mediation, including photographs, raw test data, and witness statements, was not discoverable in a subsequent action. In the first suit, owners of an apartment complex sued contractors for construction defects and settled. In the second suit, residents of the apartments sued the building owners and sought to obtain evidence the owners had compiled in the course of securing their settlement in mediation with the contractors. The Supreme Court held that the evidence was not discoverable, pursuant to California's Evidence Code, §1119(b), which provides: "No writing, as defined in section 250, that is prepared for the purpose of, in the course of, or pursuant to, a mediation . . . is admissible or subject to discovery. . . ."

The Supreme Court's decision reversed an appellate court ruling that attempted to apply the policies underlying the traditional work product doctrine to allow litigants to show substantial need to obtain otherwise protected information where that information could not otherwise be obtained. (Here, as the repairs had been made, the evidence of original problems could not be recreated.) Applying this policy, the Court of Appeals had not applied the plain language of the statute, which included as protected "writings," photographs, witness statements, and all other writings, as long as they were "prepared for the purpose of, in the course of, or pursuant to a mediation." Citing *Foxgate*, the court concluded that "confidentiality is essential to effective mediation," that the mediation privilege was an important one, that "implementing alternatives to judicial dispute resolution has been a strong legislative policy since at least 1986" (*Foxgate* at 14), and finally, that if the legislature wanted to create other exceptions for settlement agreements or evidence, it could do so in a statute. The court was not empowered to create non-statutory exceptions to mediation confidentiality or privilege.

What do you think should happen to such materials, prepared for mediation, but perhaps essential for the production of evidence in subsequent (or the same) cases? What would have happened to such documents had the parties settled without the aid of a mediator? Does it matter that the party that prepared the evidence in the first case was the defendant in the second? Who should decide such questions? The legislature? The courts, on a case-by-case basis (like work product balancing and policy tests)? How should courts decide whether evidence was prepared for mediation rather than also for litigation in the event the mediation failed? Does this matter? Do you think this sort of ruling, holding confidentiality almost inviolable, will encourage more or less mediation? Will different kinds of parties feel differently about this?

8.9 The effect of, and sanctions for, breach of confidentiality yield a range of outcomes.

In Paranzino v. Barnett Bank, 690 So. 2d 725 (Fla. Dist. Ct. App. 1997), where the plaintiff breached mediation confidentiality by divulging to a newspaper specific terms of defendant's settlement offer, the court dismissed her case with prejudice. In Bernard v. Galen Group, 901 F. Supp. 778 (S.D.N.Y. 1995), where the plaintiff's lawyer, in an unsolicited letter to the judge, divulged specific terms of settlement offers, plaintiff was fined $2,500.

In Hudson v. Hudson, 600 So. 2d 7 (Fla. Dist. Ct. App. 1992), the court held that admitting evidence about an oral mediation agreement taints the subsequent judgment and ordered a new trial where this error was made. However, in Enterprise Leasing Co. v. Jones, 789 So. 2d 964 (Fla. 2001), the Florida Supreme Court held that where a party reveals mediation settlement offers to a judge, it does not automatically disqualify the judge absent proof that the confidential communication results in actual prejudice.

While *Folb* is an example of a judicially created privilege, privileges are created also by legislatures. In *Olam* below, the court construes provisions of the California Evidence Code, which create a mediation privilege. The plaintiff, who was represented by an attorney in a court-sponsored, voluntary mediation, asserted that she had signed a Memorandum of Understanding (MOU) under duress and hence sought to avoid its enforcement. Both parties expressly waived their statutory mediation privilege. After finding that the parties' waiver of confidentiality was not a sufficient basis to order the mediator to testify, the court conducted a two-stage balancing analysis and concluded that the mediator should testify. Judge Brazil, a noted scholar in the ADR field, thoughtfully lays out pertinent considerations in the opinion.

In this case, in contrast to *Foxgate, Folb, Macaluso*, and *Sheldone*, the need for mediator testimony is found to trump the need to protect mediation confidentiality. As you read *Olam*, consider what other situations might give rise to exceptions to confidentiality and how parties and their lawyers will view confidentiality if there is always the chance that what is said in mediation may be revealed.

 OLAM v. CONGRESS MORTGAGE CO.

68 F. Supp. 2d 1110, 1118, 1131-1134, 1136-1139 (N.D. Cal. 1999)

... [P]laintiff alleges that at the time she signed the MOU she was suffering from physical pain and emotional distress that rendered her incapable of exercising her own free will. She alleges that after the mediation began during the morning of September 9, 1998, she was left *alone* in a room *all* day and into the early hours of September 10, 1998, while all the other mediation participants conversed in a nearby room. She claims that she did not understand the mediation process. In addition, she asserts that she felt pressured to sign the MOU — and that her physical and emotional distress rendered her unduly susceptible to this pressure. As a result, she says, she signed the MOU against her will and without reading and/or understanding its terms. . . .

We turn to the issue of whether, under California law, we should compel the mediator to testify — despite the statutory prohibitions set forth in sections 703.5 and 1119 of the Evidence Code. The most important opinion by a California court in this arena is Rinaker v. Superior Court, 62 Cal. App. 4th 155 (3d Dist. 1998). In that case the Court of Appeal held that there may be circumstances in which a trial court, over vigorous objection by a party and by the mediator, could compel testimony from the mediator in a juvenile delinquency proceeding (deemed a "civil" matter under California law). The defendant in the delinquency proceeding wanted to call the mediator to try to impeach testimony that was expected from a prosecution witness.

California Evidence Code §703.5

JUDGES, ARBITRATORS OR MEDIATORS AS WITNESSES; SUBSEQUENT CIVIL PROCEEDING

No person presiding at any judicial or quasi-judicial proceeding, and no arbitrator or mediator, shall be competent to testify, in any subsequent civil proceeding, as to any statement, conduct, decision, or ruling, occurring at or in conjunction with the prior proceeding, except as to a statement or conduct that could (a) give rise to civil or criminal contempt, (b) constitute a crime, (c) be the subject of investigation by the State Bar or Commission on Judicial Performance, or (d) give rise to disqualification proceedings. . . .

California Evidence Code §1119

WRITTEN OR ORAL COMMUNICATIONS DURING MEDIATION PROCESS; ADMISSIBILITY

Except as otherwise provided in this chapter:

(a) No evidence of anything said or any admission made for the purpose of, in the course of, or pursuant to, a mediation or a mediation consultation is admissible or subject to discovery, and disclosure of the evidence shall not be compelled, in any arbitration, administrative adjudication, civil action, or other noncriminal proceeding in which, pursuant to law, testimony can be compelled to be given.

(b) No writing, as defined in Section 250, that is prepared for the purpose of, in the course of, or pursuant to, a mediation or a mediation consultation, is admissible or subject to discovery, and disclosure of the writing shall not be compelled, in any arbitration, administrative adjudication, civil action, or other noncriminal proceeding in which, pursuant to law, testimony can be compelled to be given.

(c) All communications, negotiations, or settlement discussions by and between participants in the course of a mediation or a mediation consultation shall remain confidential.

That witness and the delinquency defendant had earlier participated in a mediation — and the delinquency defendant believed that the complaining witness had
made admissions to the mediator that would substantially undermine the credibility
of the complaining witness' testimony — and thus would materially strengthen the
defense. In these circumstances, the *Rinaker* court held that the mediator could be
compelled to testify if, after *in camera* consideration of what her testimony would be,
the trial judge determined that her testimony might well promote significantly the
public interest in preventing perjury and the defendant's fundamental right to a fair
judicial process.

In essence, the *Rinaker* court instructs California trial judges to conduct a
two-stage balancing analysis. The goal of the first stage balancing is to determine
whether to compel the mediator to appear at an *in camera* proceeding to determine
precisely what her testimony would be. In this first stage, the judge considers all
the circumstances and weighs all the competing rights and interests, including the
values that would be threatened not by public disclosure of mediation communications, but by ordering the mediator to appear at an *in camera* proceeding to disclose
only to the court and counsel, out of public view, what she would say the parties said
during the mediation. At this juncture the goal is to determine whether the harm
that would be done to the values that underlie the mediation privileges simply by
ordering the mediator to participate in the *in camera* proceedings can be justified — by
the prospect that her testimony might well make a singular and substantial contribution to protecting or advancing competing interests of comparable or greater
magnitude.

The trial judge reaches the second stage of balancing analysis only if the product
of the first stage is a decision to order the mediator to detail, *in camera*, what
her testimony would be. A court that orders the *in camera* disclosure gains precise
and reliable knowledge of what the mediator's testimony would be — and only
with that knowledge is the court positioned to launch its second balancing analysis.
In this second stage the court is to weigh and comparatively assess (1) the importance
of the values and interests that would be harmed if the mediator was compelled to
testify (perhaps subject to a sealing or protective order, if appropriate), (2) the magnitude of the harm that compelling the testimony would cause to those values and
interests, (3) the importance of the rights or interests that would be jeopardized if the
mediator's testimony was not accessible in the specific proceedings in question, and
(4) how much the testimony would contribute toward protecting those rights or
advancing those interests — an inquiry that includes, among other things, an assessment of whether there are alternative sources of evidence of comparable probative
value. . . .

If a party to the mediation were objecting to compelling the mediator to testify
we would be faced with a substantially more difficult analysis. But the absence of such
an objection does not mean that ordering the mediator to disclose, even *in camera*,
matters that occurred within the mediation does not pose some threat to values
underlying the mediation privileges. As the *Rinaker* court pointed out, ordering
mediators to participate in proceedings arising out of mediating imposes economic
and psychic burdens that could make some people reluctant to agree to serve as a

mediator, especially in programs where that service is pro bono or poorly compensated.

This is not a matter of time and money only. Good mediators are likely to feel violated by being compelled to give evidence that could be used against a party with whom they tried to establish a relationship of trust during a mediation. Good mediators are deeply committed to being and remaining neutral and non-judgmental, and to building and preserving relationships with parties. To force them to give evidence that hurts someone from whom they actively solicited trust (during the mediation) rips the fabric of their work and can threaten their sense of the center of their professional integrity. These are not inconsequential matters.

Like many other variables in this kind of analysis, however, the magnitude of these risks can vary with the circumstances. Here, for instance, all parties to the mediation want the mediator to testify about things that occurred during the mediation — so ordering the testimony would do less harm to the actual relationships developed than it would in a case where one of the parties to the mediation objected to the use of evidence from the mediator.

We acknowledge, however, that the possibility that a mediator might be forced to testify over objection could harm the capacity of mediators in general to create the environment of trust that they feel maximizes the likelihood that constructive communication will occur during the mediation session. But the level of harm to that interest likely varies, at least in some measure, with the perception within the community of mediators and litigants about how likely it is that any given mediation will be followed at some point by an order compelling the neutral to offer evidence about what occurred during the session. I know of no studies or statistics that purport to reflect how often courts or parties seek evidence from mediators — and I suspect that the incidence of this issue arising would not be identical across the broad spectrum of mediation programs and settings. What I can report is that this case represents the first time that I have been called upon to address these kinds of questions in the more than fifteen years that I have been responsible for ADR programs in this court. Nor am I aware of the issue arising before other judges here. Based on that experience, my partially educated guess is that the likelihood that a mediator or the parties in any given case need fear that the mediator would later be constrained to testify is extraordinarily small.

That conviction is reinforced by another consideration. As we pointed out above, under California law, and this court's view of sound public policy, there should be no occasion to consider whether to seek testimony from a mediator for the purpose of determining whether the parties entered an enforceable settlement contract unless the mediation produced a writing (or competent record) that appears on its face to constitute an enforceable contract, signed or formally assented to by all the parties. Thus, it is only when there is such a writing or record, and when a party nonetheless seeks to escape its apparent effect, that courts applying California law would even consider calling for evidence from a mediator for purposes of determining whether the parties settled the case. Surely these circumstances will arise after only a tiny fraction of mediations. . . .

[T]he kind of testimony sought from the mediator in this case poses less of a threat to fairness and reliability values than the kind of testimony that was sought from the mediator in *Rinaker*. During the first stage balancing analysis in the case at bar, the parties and I assumed that the testimony from the mediator that would be most consequential would focus not primarily on what Ms. Olam said during the mediation, but on how she acted and the mediator's perceptions of her physical, emotional, and mental condition. The purpose would not be to nail down and dissect her specific words, but to assess at a more general and impressionistic level her condition and capacities. That purpose might be achieved with relatively little disclosure of the content of her confidential communications. As conceded above, that does not mean that compelling the testimony by the mediator would pose no threat to values underlying the privileges — but that the degree of harm to those values would not be as great as it would be if the testimony was for the kinds of impeachment purposes that were proffered in *Rinaker*. And in a balancing analysis, probable degree of harm is an important consideration.

What we have been doing in the preceding paragraphs is attempting, as the first component of the first stage balancing analysis, to identify the interests that might be threatened by ordering the mediator, in the specific circumstances presented here, to testify under seal — and to assess the magnitude of the harm that ordering the testimony would likely do to those interests. Having assayed these matters, we turn to the other side of the balance. We will identify the interests that ordering the testimony (under seal, at least initially) might advance, assess the relative importance of those interests, and try to predict the magnitude of the contribution to achieving those interests that ordering the testimony would likely make (or the extent of the harm that we likely would do to those interests if we did not compel the testimony).

The interests that are likely to be advanced by compelling the mediator to testify in this case are of considerable importance. Moreover, as we shall see, some of those interests parallel and reinforce the objectives the legislature sought to advance by providing for confidentiality in mediation.

The first interest we identify is the interest in doing justice. Here is what we mean. For reasons described below, the mediator is positioned in this case to offer what could be crucial, certainly very probative, evidence about the central factual issues in this matter. There is a strong possibility that his testimony will greatly improve the court's ability to determine reliably what the pertinent historical facts actually were. Establishing reliably what the facts were is critical to doing justice (here, justice means this: applying the law correctly to the real historical facts). It is the fundamental duty of a public court in our society to do justice — to resolve disputes in accordance with the law when the parties don't. Confidence in our system of justice as a whole, in our government as a whole, turns in no small measure on confidence in the courts' ability to do justice in individual cases. So doing justice in individual cases is an interest of considerable magnitude.

When we put case-specific flesh on these abstract bones, we see that "doing justice" implicates interests of considerable importance to the parties — all of whom want the mediator to testify. From the plaintiff's perspective, the interests that the defendants' motion threatens could hardly be more fundamental. According to Ms. Olam, the mediation process was fundamentally unfair to her — and resulted in an apparent agreement whose terms are literally unconscionable and whose enforcement would render her homeless and virtually destitute. To her, doing justice in this setting means protecting her from these fundamental wrongs.

From the defendants' perspective, doing justice in this case means, among other things, bringing to a lawful close disputes with Ms. Olam that have been ongoing for about seven years — disputes that the defendants believe have cost them, without justification, at least scores of thousands of dollars. The defendants believe that Ms. Olam has breached no fewer than three separate contractual commitments with them (not counting the agreement reached at the end of the mediation) — and that those breaches are the product of a calculated effort not only to avoid meeting legitimate obligations, but also to make unfair use, for years, of the defendants' money.

Defendants also believe that Ms. Olam has abused over the years several of her own counsel — as well as the judicial process and this court's ADR program (for which she has been charged nothing). Through their motion, the defendants ask the court to affirm that they acquired legal rights through the settlement agreement that the mediation produced. They also ask the court to enforce those rights, and thus to enable the defendants to avoid the burdens, expense, delay, and risks of going to trial in this matter. These also are matters of consequence.

And they are not the only interests that could be advanced by compelling the mediator to testify. According to the defendants' pre-hearing proffers, the mediator's testimony would establish clearly that the mediation process was fair and that the plaintiff's consent to the settlement agreement was legally viable. Thus the mediator's testimony, according to the defendants, would re-assure the community and the court about the integrity of the mediation process that the court sponsored.

That testimony also would provide the court with the evidentiary confidence it needs to enforce the agreement. A publicly announced decision to enforce the settlement would, in turn, encourage parties who want to try to settle their cases to use the court's mediation program for that purpose. An order appropriately enforcing an agreement reached through the mediation also would encourage parties in the future to take mediating seriously, to understand that they represent real opportunities to reach closure and avoid trial, and to attend carefully to terms of agreements proposed in mediating. In these important ways, taking testimony from the mediator could strengthen the mediation program.

In sharp contrast, refusing to compel the mediator to testify might well deprive the court of the evidence it needs to rule reliably on the plaintiff's contentions — and thus might either cause the court to impose an unjust outcome on the plaintiff or disable the court from enforcing the settlement. In this setting, refusing to compel testimony from the mediator might end up being tantamount to denying the motion to enforce the agreement — because a crucial source of evidence about the plaintiff's condition and capacities would be missing. Following that course, defendants suggest, would do considerable harm not only to the court's mediation program but also to fundamental fairness. If parties believed that courts routinely would refuse to compel mediators to testify, and that the absence of evidence from mediators would enhance the viability of a contention that apparent consent to a settlement contract was not legally viable, cynical parties would be encouraged either to try to escape commitments they made during mediating or to use threats of such escapes to try to re-negotiate, after the mediation, more favorable terms — terms that they never would have been able to secure without this artificial and unfair leverage.

In sum, it is clear that refusing even to determine what the mediator's testimony would be, in the circumstances here presented, threatens values of great significance. But we would miss the main analytical chance if all we did was identify those values and proclaim their importance. In fact, when the values implicated are obviously of great moment, there is a danger that the process of identifying them will generate unjustified momentum toward a conclusion that exaggerates the weight on this side of the scale. Thus we emphasize that the central question is not which values are implicated, but how much they would be advanced by compelling the testimony or how much they would be harmed by not compelling it.

We concluded, after analysis and before the hearing, that the mediator's testimony was sufficiently likely to make substantial contributions toward achieving the ends described above to justify compelling an exploration, under seal, of what his testimony would be. While we did not assume that there were no pressures or motivations that might affect the reliability of the mediator's testimony, it was obvious that the mediator was the only source of presumptively disinterested, neutral evidence. The only other witnesses with personal knowledge of the plaintiff's condition at the mediation were the parties and their lawyers — none of whom were disinterested. And given the foreseeable testimony about the way the mediation was structured (with lots of caucusing by the mediator with one side at a time), it was likely that the mediator would have had much more exposure to the plaintiff over the course of the lengthy mediation than any other witness save her lawyer. . . .

In short, there was a substantial likelihood that testimony from the mediator would be the most reliable and probative on the central issues raised by the plaintiff in response to the defendants' motion. And there was no likely alternative source of evidence on these issues that would be of comparable probative utility. So it appeared that testimony from the mediator would be crucial to the court's capacity to do its job — and that refusing to compel that testimony posed a serious threat to every value identified above. In this setting, California courts clearly would conclude the first stage balancing analysis by ordering the mediator to testify *in camera* or under seal — so that the court, aided by inputs from the parties, could make a refined and reliable judgment about whether to use that testimony to help resolve the substantive issues raised by the pending motion.

The ultimate outcome in *Olam*, after Judge Brazil examined the mediator *in camera*, was admission of the mediator's testimony and a finding that the agreement was not the product of undue influence. The mediator's testimony substantially and critically differed from Ms. Olam's account of events and was particularly probative to the court.

Notes and Questions

8.10 In FDIC v. White, 76 F. Supp. 2d 736 (N.D. Tex. 1999), a party tried to avoid a mediation settlement agreement by alleging that threats of criminal prosecution made in mediation were coercive. In light of these allegations of duress, a federal district court in Texas allowed into evidence otherwise privileged mediation communications, ultimately finding that the written settlement agreement was not the result of duress.

In McKinlay v. McKinlay, 648 So. 2d 806 (Fla. Dist. Ct. App. 1995), a wife in a divorce action, in an effort to avoid a mediation settlement agreement, alleged she was badgered and intimidated by her husband's counsel, given inaccurate information and pressured by the mediator, and also pressured by her own counsel to settle. The wife also asserted she was under severe emotional distress at the time of the mediation. The court held that these allegations waived her statutory privilege to preclude mediation communications and testimony from the mediator and that it was "a breach of fair play to deny husband the opportunity to present rebuttal testimony."

8.11 A contract defense of "mutual mistake" might open the door to mediation communications. In DR Lakes Inc. v. Brandsmart U.S.A. of West Palm Beach, 819 So. 2d 971, 973 (Fla. Dist. Ct. App. 2002), where a party claimed that a settlement agreement entered into after mediation contained a $600,000 clerical error, the court allowed evidence as to what transpired in the mediation, holding that the privilege for mediation confidentiality must yield in such instances.

8.12 Courts are divided over whether evidence of oral settlement agreements should be admissible. Under contract law, oral agreements are enforceable, but confidentiality protections could effectively make an oral agreement reached in mediation impossible to prove. The Indiana Supreme Court in Vernon v. Acton, 732 N.E.2d 805 (Ind. 2000), concluded that confidentiality — the protection of Indiana Rule of Evidence 408 — would encompass oral agreements and therefore testimony about such agreements would be precluded. Similarly, in Ryan v. Garcia, 33 Cal. Rptr. 2d 158 (Cal. Ct. App. 1994), the California Court of Appeal found that the trial court erred in admitting statements made in a mediation relating to the terms of an oral settlement agreement. The result of this line of cases is that, to be enforceable, mediation agreements must be written and signed.

However, in Kaiser Found. Health Plan of the Northwest v. Doe, 903 P.2d 375 (Or. Ct. App. 1995), an oral settlement agreement reached in mediation was enforced, carving out an exception to mediation confidentiality. Similarly, in Few v. Hammack Enters., 511 S.E.2d 665 (N.C. Ct. App. 1999), testimony and other evidence arising in a mediation was found admissible solely for purposes of determining if a settlement was reached and, if so, what the terms of that settlement were.

8.13 Do you think that a claim that there was an oral settlement agreement should result in an exception to confidentiality? What about a claim of fraud or coercion? For a thorough treatment of the intersection of contract law and confidentiality, see Ellen E. Deason, Enforcing Mediated Settlement Agreements: Contract Law Collides with Confidentiality, 35 U.C. Davis L. Rev. 33 (2001). Professor Deason concludes:

> The most appropriate balance between confidentiality and other values such as enforcement [of mediated agreements] and autonomy differs depending on the nature of the claim. When the issue is whether or not the parties reached agreement, predictable confidentiality is a value that justifies requiring that mediated settlements be evidenced by a record — either a signed writing or a modern substitute — to preclude the need for testimony on the course of the mediation. Of the alternative methods for implementing this require-ment, an evidentiary privilege that accepts only written settlements is the most effective.
>
> When the issue is whether or not a mediated settlement is valid, confi-dentiality is but one very important value. It does not justify a uniform preclusion of mediation evidence that might prevent enforcement of a fraud-ulent or coerced agreement. This result would be inconsistent not only with a just outcome, but also with the consensual nature of mediation. Therefore a bright-line rule is inappropriate in this situation, and courts should instead balance the need for mediation evidence in the specific case against the harm that disclosure would cause to the purposes served by confidentiality. Legis-latures need to acknowledge the need for individualized decisions on con-fidentiality in the context of contract defenses and set an appropriately strict standard for disclosure. They should also mandate *in camera* methods, which can protect confidentiality while a court evaluates the need for mediation confidentiality in the world of contract doctrine.

Id. at 102.

8.14 Allegations of mediator misconduct have resulted in "opening the door" shut by confidentiality in order to allow a mediator to defend himself. In Allen v. Leal, 27 F. Supp. 2d 945 (S.D. Tex. 1998), the court held that a mediator could testify to defend himself against charges of misconduct. In that case, the mother of a child shot by a police officer was attempting to avoid the settlement agreement, which she claimed was coerced by the mediator. The court noted that the plaintiffs "'opened the door' by attacking the professionalism and integrity of the mediator and the mediation process, [hence] the Court was compelled, in the interests of justice, to breach the veil of confidentiality." Id. at 947.

8.15 Other questions arise in this complicated arena, for example:

   a. What is mediation itself, for purposes of analyzing whether a privilege applies? Some statutes require a court order to mediate; others require that a "mediator" have a certain amount of training and experience; others require a written agreement to mediate.

   b. When does mediation begin? Is the "beginning" in a formal session or at the first point of contact between a party and the mediator's office staff? When does mediation end?

    c. Who is covered by the mediation privilege? Typically, statements by
       parties, their attorneys, and the mediator are covered, but what about
       statements of witnesses, support persons, and other types of advocates?
    d. Are the protections of a privilege limited to court proceedings, or are
       they broader?
    e. Who holds the privilege, and who can waive the privilege? Parties only?
       Does the mediator independently hold the privilege (remember here
       the analysis in *Olam*)?

As is evident from the questions above and the different views of mediation
confidentiality, this subject is riddled with confusion and controversy. In an effort to
promote uniformity, in 2001 the National Conference of Commissioners on Uniform State Laws and the American Bar Association approved and recommended for
enactment in all states the Uniform Mediation Act (UMA). The purpose of
uniform laws is to bring coherency, consistency, and predictability to an area of
practice. The sections of the UMA creating a privilege follow (the full UMA is in
Appendix A).

THE UNIFORM MEDIATION ACT, SECTIONS 4-6

Section 4. Privilege against disclosure; admissibility; discovery

(a) Except as otherwise provided in Section 6, a mediation communication is privileged as provided in subsection (b) and is not subject to discovery or admissible in evidence in a proceeding unless waived or precluded as provided by Section 5.

(b) In a proceeding, the following privileges apply:

(1) A mediation party may refuse to disclose, and may prevent any other person
from disclosing, a mediation communication.

(2) A mediator may refuse to disclose a mediation communication, and may
prevent any other person from disclosing a mediation communication of the mediator.

(3) A nonparty participant may refuse to disclose, and may prevent any other
person from disclosing, a mediation communication of the nonparty participant.

(c) Evidence or information that is otherwise admissible or subject to discovery does
not become inadmissible or protected from discovery solely by reason of its disclosure or
use in a mediation.

Section 5. Waiver and preclusion of privilege

(a) A privilege under Section 4 may be waived in a record or orally during a proceeding if it is expressly waived by all parties to the mediation and:

(1) in the case of the privilege of a mediator, it is expressly waived by the
mediator; and

(2) in the case of the privilege of a nonparty participant, it is expressly waived by
the nonparty participant.

(b)   A person that discloses or makes a representation about a mediation communication which prejudices another person in a proceeding is precluded from asserting a privilege under Section 4, but only to the extent necessary for the person prejudiced to respond to the representation or disclosure.

(c)   A person that intentionally uses a mediation to plan, attempt to commit or commit a crime, or to conceal an ongoing crime or ongoing criminal activity is precluded from asserting a privilege under Section 4.

Section 6. Exceptions to privilege

(a)   There is no privilege under Section 4 for a mediation communication that is:

(1)   in an agreement evidenced by a record signed by all parties to the agreement;

(2)   available to the public under [insert statutory reference to open records act] or made during a session of a mediation which is open, or is required by law to be open, to the public;

(3)   a threat or statement of a plan to inflict bodily injury or commit a crime of violence;

(4)   intentionally used to plan a crime, attempt to commit a crime, or to conceal an ongoing crime or ongoing criminal activity;

(5)   sought or offered to prove or disprove a claim or complaint of professional misconduct or malpractice filed against a mediator;

(6)   except as otherwise provided in subsection (c), sought or offered to prove or disprove a claim or complaint of professional misconduct or malpractice filed against a mediation party, nonparty participant, or representative of a party based on conduct occurring during a mediation; or

(7)   sought or offered to prove or disprove abuse, neglect, abandonment, or exploitation in a proceeding in which a child or adult protective services agency is a party, unless the

[Alternative A: [State to insert, for example, child or adult protection] case is referred by a court to mediation and a public agency participates.]

[Alternative B: public agency participates in the [State to insert, for example, child or adult protection] mediation.]

(b)   There is no privilege under Section 4 if a court, administrative agency, or arbitrator finds, after a hearing *in camera*, that the party seeking discovery or the proponent of the evidence has shown that the evidence is not otherwise available, that there is a need for the evidence that substantially outweighs the interest in protecting confidentiality, and that the mediation communication is sought or offered in:

(1)   a court proceeding involving a felony [or misdemeanor]; or

(2)   except as otherwise provided in subsection (c), a proceeding to prove a claim to rescind or reform or a defense to avoid liability on a contract arising out of the mediation.

(c)   A mediator may not be compelled to provide evidence of a mediation communication referred to in subsection (a)(6) or (b)(2).

(d)   If a mediation communication is not privileged under subsection (a) or (b), only the portion of the communication necessary for the application of the exception from nondisclosure may be admitted. Admission of evidence under subsection (a) or (b) does not render the evidence, or any other mediation communication, discoverable or admissible for any other purpose.

Notes and Questions

8.16 Consider whether UMA sections 4 through 6 lend coherency and predictability to mediation confidentiality. Imagine you are a mediator explaining mediation confidentiality — the meaning of confidentiality and mediation privileges and exceptions — to parties in a mediation and their lawyers. What would you say?

8.17 What conclusions did the UMA drafters reach about piercing confidentiality where one party is alleging that an oral agreement was reached in mediation? Alleging bad-faith conduct on the part of another party? Raising a contract defense of fraud, duress, coercion, or mutual mistake?

8.18 The development of the UMA was a stormy process, and the dust has not yet settled. (As of 2005 only six states have passed the act — Illinois, Iowa, Nebraska, New Jersey, Ohio, and Washington.) One critic of the UMA, Scott Hughes, predicts that some of its provisions will "decimate predictability," which is the primary goal of a uniform law. In an article that captures the turbulent history of the Act and the difficult questions faced by the drafters, Hughes concludes:

> If it is necessary to have a privilege for mediation, certain elements should be adopted. First, the mediation process is not well served by a separate privilege for mediators. Second, clear exceptions should be drafted to cover contractual misconduct. Third, although a procedural step prior to accessing testimony (such as an *in camera* hearing or sealed proceedings) is appropriate, no substantive hurdles should hinder access to normal common law contract remedies or impair self-determination. Finally, when challenges arise to an agreement reached in mediation, the mediator should be treated like all other mediation participants — he or she should be required to testify. The UMA should not allow the artificial distinction between the mediator malpractice and the contractual misconduct exceptions.

Scott H. Hughes, The Uniform Mediation Act: To the Spoiled Go the Privileges, 85 Marq. L. Rev. 9, 76 (2001).

8.19 After your initial read of the UMA (reproduced in its entirety in Appendix A), do you understand what would and would not be protected from subsequent disclosures? If you were asked to draft a uniform law regarding mediation confidentiality, what would be your approach?

8.20 In 2003, the Commissioners on Uniform State Laws added another section to the UMA (§11) to provide for mediation privilege in international commercial matters, with the express purpose of encouraging states to adopt the UNCITRAL Model Law on International Commercial Conciliation, which was added as an appendix to the UMA.

As is evident, questions about confidentiality have caused considerable debate. The exact contours of mediation confidentiality will be developed as case law emerges. As you will see in the next chapter, equally challenging are the ethical dilemmas that surround mediation practice.

Chapter 9 Ethical Issues in Mediation

Always do right; this will gratify some people and astonish the rest.
— **Mark Twain**

This chapter focuses on ethical dilemmas raised by the use of mediation. It begins by examining questions of mediator neutrality. If mediation is premised on mediator neutrality or impartiality, is that aspiration realistic? Is such a state of being possible? Next, the chapter explores a range of ethical issues encountered in practice — first from the perspective of the attorney representative and then from the perspective of the mediator. Ethical dilemmas in mediation abound — at both the macro level of accountability for outcomes and behaviors, and the micro level of choices about behaviors inside of mediation, for mediators, representatives, and parties. Many organizations (and courts) are considering and promulgating various ethical rules and regulations, but there are still many issues not covered (or covered disparately) by these systems of rules. You should be thinking about how participants within mediation should judge their own actions — what are sources of "ethical" and good practices in mediation? The underlying values of the process? The personal or professional values of the participants?

The materials in this chapter should be read in conjunction with Appendix A (the Uniform Mediation Act) and B (the Model Standards of Conduct for Mediators).

A. NEUTRALITY

One of the important requirements for mediator acceptability is impartiality. Partiality on the part of the mediator would (and probably should) encourage the disfavored party to exit the process. Mediators, like arbitrators, are described as "neutrals." Generally, this means that the neutral does not have a stake in the outcome and is committed to being equally helpful to both sides. Do you think that "impartiality" and "neutrality" are the same thing? Some have suggested that the mediator should be "unbiased" with respect to both the parties and the issues involved in a particular case. Is this a different notion?

Whether or not an individual can be truly "neutral" — that is, have no leanings or predilections toward particular parties or to particular issues — is doubtful at best.

However, in most contexts, impartiality—as in even-handed treatment—is expected.

The next article studies mediation from an in-depth empirical analysis of a single case and the "interventions" of a particular mediator. The study raises serious questions about mediator neutrality.

 David Greatbatch & Robert Dingwall, **SELECTIVE FACILITATION: SOME PRELIMINARY OBSERVATIONS ON A STRATEGY USED BY DIVORCE MEDIATORS**

23 L. & Socy. Rev. 613, 613–618, 621–623, 626–629, 635–637, 639 (1989)

Serious criticisms have been raised about divorce mediators' claim that they act as purely neutral facilitators of party-driven agreements. This paper reports on a study, based on tape recordings of mediation in the United Kingdom, intended to describe the strategies used by mediators and clients in the attempt to resolve disputes. It identifies a technique, labeled "selective facilitation," through which clients may be steered in particular directions chosen by the mediator. This poses important questions for future evaluation studies and for the regulation of mediation practice.

I.   INTRODUCTION

At the heart of the debate over the use of mediation as an alternative to litigation in resolving the disputes of divorcing couples is the notion of the mediator as a neutral facilitator assisting clients in their search for mutually acceptable agreements. Critics of mediation, however, have cast doubt on such claims by suggesting that the process may be used to press weaker parties into accepting less than they could have expected had their case gone through traditional adversarial channels. Such criticism raises serious questions about the role of mediators and the influence they exert over the decision-making process. Is their influence really restricted to the facilitation of communication between the disputants? Or does it, as the critics tend to imply, extend beyond these bounds, with mediators seeking to guide disputants toward outcomes that they, the mediators, regard as acceptable? The study of mediation sessions reported here is intended to shed some light on these matters. Through the detailed analysis of recordings of interactions between divorce mediators and their clients, it will be possible to describe the strategies used by mediators and to differentiate them in terms of the extent to which they enhance or reduce client control of the decision-making process.

II.   MEDIATOR NEUTRALITY

One of the central arguments put forward by advocates of mediation as a method of dispute resolution in divorce is that it offers a means of settling conflicts that leaves the responsibility for outcomes in the hands of the separating couple themselves. Rather than having a decision imposed by a judge or reached by bargaining between partisan lawyers, the couple can make their own agreement based on their particular under-standing of their relative situations. . . .

[M]uch of the enthusiasm about mediation reflects the influence of libertarian arguments against state intervention. Private ordering is accordingly seen as both more efficient and morally superior to determination by some public authority.

In its pure form, however, private ordering carries with it the possibility of the strongest disputant imposing a settlement that seems grossly unfair when measured against some external standard of justice or that infringes the rights of third parties, such as the state as a provider of income support or children with their needs for economic and psychological security. These points have attracted the concern of a number of critics and have even been conceded by mediators themselves. . . .

The mediators' response is to cite their own ethical concerns. Haynes (1981: 131-132) [John M. Haynes, Divorce Mediation: A Practical Guide for Therapists and Counselors], for instance, despite his professed adherence to the empowerment of parties, insists that "the mediator does not simply facilitate a divorce: s/he does it within a value context." Since neutrality in a situation of inequality may indeed allow one party to exploit the other, he accepts that a mediator may have to act in a way that enhances the power of the weaker spouse (ibid., pp. 62-63) or to "act forcibly" to prevent the victimization of a third party, such as a child (ibid., pp. 129-132).

The tension between the professed commitment to self-determination and the imposition of an overriding ethical code remains unresolved by the mediation movement. . . .

Through the detailed analysis of recordings of interactions between divorce mediators and their clients, [this study] will identify strategies used by mediators and differentiate them in terms of the extent to which they enhance or reduce client control of the decisionmaking process. In doing so, however, it will also make available material for the pursuit of the macro-debate [about legitimacy of the process]. Much of the policy argument has so far been forced to rely on a range of sources whose information on the mediation process is limited. Any conclusions drawn from comparisons between the outcomes of traditional and mediated modes of dispute ·processing must necessarily be speculative insofar as they are used to make judgments about the nature of client experiences. Studies based on self-reports by participants have been shown in closely related settings, especially medical consultations, to be unreliable as data on the nature of the original event. Participants try to give accounts that bolster their self-presentation as competent social actors, or, in the case of me-diators, are constructed as part of the process of building demand for their services. . . .

The data reported here are taken from the pilot phase of a project that involved one of the larger and longer-established independent mediation services [in the United Kingdom]. It has played a significant role in training staff from other volun-tary agencies, and [its] practice is thought by other mediators to be broadly repre-sentative of the mainstream of the movement. . . .

DATA

The data analyzed here are drawn from one of a series of forty-five mediation sessions covering fifteen cases handled by three mediators. . . . The parties in this case are a middle-class couple, Paul and Hazel, with two children under five. They have been married for about ten years. The wife has not worked since the birth of the first child, although she says she has always intended to return to employment when the children are older. The husband is self-employed with a fluctuating income, which poses some problems for an agreement about child support.

According to the parties, their relationship has been under strain since the birth of the first child. At first they thought it was purely a result of the financial pressures from relying on a single, irregular income. However, the problems have continued and become more extensive. In the previous twelve months both parties have received counseling, which has led the wife to seek a divorce. The husband has still not fully accepted this. The wife and the two children are living in the matrimonial home, while the husband has moved out to stay temporarily with his sister and her family.

This paper is focused on a sequence of interaction, lasting approximately thirteen minutes, from the second, and as it transpires, final joint session in the case. It is fairly late in the session, and the couple has already reached agreement on custody, visitation ("access") and support payments ("maintenance"). There has been relatively little involvement by the mediator in this process, and the listener is left with the impression that it is simply a parade of decisions that have largely been made by the couple in advance. However, the previous session has identified a serious problem over the future of the matrimonial home. The husband wants an immediate sale in order to release capital to buy a new place to live, whereas the wife wants to continue living in the house with the children. In the course of this session it emerges that the couple also owns, a second property, which is rented out. . . .

The analysis of this extract from the session demonstrates that the mediator is working with notions of what kind of settlement would be desirable (a favored outcome) and what kind of settlement would be undesirable (a disfavored outcome), and seeks to guide the interaction accordingly. "Selective facilitation" is the means by which she seeks to achieve this objective. When the wife introduces the topic of the property in the context of accepting a proposal on child support, the mediator begins an active search for an agreement. What is of interest is how she proceeds to facilitate an exploration of one possible outcome while inhibiting consideration of another. Her favored outcome would involve a straight division of the two properties, with the wife retaining the matrimonial home. Her disfavored outcome is the one preferred by the husband, namely that the two properties be sold and the couple each buy somewhere else to live. While she keeps returning to the former option, and twice explicitly suggests it as an appropriate solution, the mediator systematically refrains from exploring the latter and ultimately overtly opposes it.

ANALYSIS

The Mediator Focuses on a Possible Solution

. . . [A]n option open to M [the mediator] would be to explore the pros and cons of H [the husband]'s plan. Rather than doing this, however, she chooses to address the possibility of H living in the second house (line 48), implying that this might solve his problem about obtaining a home of his own. If H were able to live in the second house, this would remove the need to sell both properties in order to release capital so he could buy another place, and W [the wife] could retain the matrimonial home.

48*M: You can't live in the house in Britvale?
49 (0.8)
50 H: er No it's let. uhm Well there is one room (.) one vacant at
51 the minute and uhm
52 M: You can't get them to leave then.
53 (0.5)
54 H: No it's tenanted, it's difficult to get the tenants out.
55 (0.8)
56 W: Well I'm [not sure] if we really wanted to before. =
57 H: [It was never —]
58 H: = It was never set up to (1.1) to sort of — (0.2) it was set up
59 to produce money for insurances for the next twenty years
60 and that's exactly what it's doing. (1.6) (Basically)
61 W: It's very underlet,
62 H: It's underlet, it's not managed properly, (0.6) or hasn't
63 been for a number of years.
64 (0.4)
65 H: [And it needs some work done on it.]
66 M: [You're sure you couldn't get the] tenant — tenancy back.
67 M: I mean if you needed it as your home.
68 (0.2)
69 H: That was one possibility (.) that did crop up. uhm You can
70 apply to evict somebody if you require it as a home.
71 M: That's right. It's what I thought.
72 H: uhm (.) You put an eviction on them and (.) get it served
73 by a court, uhm (1.0) that's — that is a possibility.
74 (0.2)
75 W: But you see I'[ve ( )]
76 H: [But you] know I think they sort of see us
77 getting na(h)sty ( ) again.

In answering M's initial question, H asserts (line 50) that he cannot live in the second property as it is rented out. He notes subsequently (lines 50-51) that one room is vacant, but the implications of this remain unexplored as, following a slight hesitation by H, M poses a supplementary question (line 52) to try to clarify what he indicated was the obstacle to his living in the Britvale property, namely that he cannot get the tenants to leave. H explains that this is so because the property does not involve fixed-period tenancies (line 54).

Subsequently, W appears to move toward endorsing the possible solution implied in M's preceding questions: a division of the properties, with H taking the rented property as his home (line 56). Referring back to a failed attempt to evict the tenants, she questions their commitment on that occasion, thereby implying

---

*[The transcript is presented in the form of formal linguistic analysis, indicating lines of dialogue and duration of pauses in conversation. M = mediator; H = husband; W = wife.]

that H may be overstating the difficulty of evicting the tenants while displaying some inclination toward attempting such a course of action again. This reading of her utterance is supported by the fact that she does not reintroduce the issue of the income the tenants generate to cover the cost of insurance policies, although she had previously proposed that the loss of this income would be an obstacle to the sale. Now, even though it is clear that if H were to live in the house, the income would be lost, she does not restate this as a problem. The issue of the insurance is, however, raised by H, who, in emphasizing the long-term planning that the rented property has involved, explains why the property is "tenanted" (instead of being occupied with short-term tenants) (lines 58-60).

This is followed by a contribution from W (line 61), "It's very underlet," which can be viewed as a further indication of incipient alignment with M in that it portrays the property in a negative light and minimizes (in contrast to her earlier statement) its importance as an income source. In responding, H agrees that the property is underlet, and further asserts that it is not managed properly (lines 62-63) and, in overlap with M's subsequent question, that it needs work (line 65). But while H's utterance factually confirms W's assertion, it gives no indication of any movement toward accepting the possibility of his living in the house as a potential solution to the dispute.

Despite this, M further pursues the possibility of his recovering the tenancy, asking if he is certain he could not repossess the house on the grounds he needs it as a home (lines 66-67). Presumably referring back to the previous attempt to evict the tenants, H accepts that this is indeed a possibility (lines 69-70). By proposing that she was aware of this (line 71), M formulates her pursuit of this option as having been based on this knowledge. H then goes on to spell out the procedure that has to be followed to evict tenants on these grounds (lines 72-73), which is serve an eviction order on them. He does not show any unwillingness to do this, but gives no indication that he would wish to live in the property and hence shows no sign of moving away from his position of wanting to sell the rental house along with the matrimonial home.

To this point, then, the mediator has pursued a line of action directed toward the possibility of the rented property providing H with a home and thus removing the need to sell the matrimonial home. For this to be possible, the tenants would have to be evicted. W has shown herself willing to explore this option, but H has been more guarded. He began by asserting that the tenants could not be evicted, but the mediator has pursued the possibility of eviction (without taking up the insurance question) and has succeeded in getting H to agree that it could be achieved. However, he has still not abandoned his opening position of wanting to sell both properties; indeed, he has not even explicitly indicated that he would in fact be willing to live in the house in Britvale. . . .

[In an omitted sequence the parties reassert their initial positions. H indicates that the Britvale property is worth substantially less than the matrimonial home, though its value would increase if it were empty. H also expresses concern over his ability to pay expenses without access to some of the capital tied up in the real estate.]

The Mediator Pursues the Possibility of a Division of the Properties

156 M: If you get could get (0.2) possession of this house
157 (0.6) would you regard that as an equal division at
158 some point, that you had one property each. (.)
159 You said give or take two f—twenty thousand
160 or [so. And that seemed to be about what—]
161 H: [No it would still mean the one in Caster] was worth
162 more than the one in Britvale.
163 M: Yes. So [:: a hefty sum]::
164 H: [By quite a large amount.]
165 (1.0)

M continues her focus on the possibility of H taking the second house and W keeping the first (lines 156-160), but now, responding to H's resistance to her prior formulation of this option, she no longer presupposes that this would involve H taking up residence in the property. Rather, she raises the possibility of the properties being divided, while leaving open what H would do with the house. In addressing the discrepancy in the value of the two properties, she begins to develop a way in which such a division might become equal (lines 159-160). She restates the differential value between the properties as formulated by H, and then appears to be going on to suggest that this difference might be approximately compatible with the additional income that W has indicated the house would generate if he were willing to sell after the tenants had been evicted. H certainly interprets M's utterance in this way, because he interrupts to indicate that he would not consider such a division to be equal since the matrimonial home in Caster would still be worth more than the rental property in Britvale, even without the tenants (lines 161-162). In overlap, both M and H then formulate the value differential as considerable (lines 163-164).

M tries to get around this impasse by introducing another factor into the equation: the fact that W's father paid off the mortgage, which might entitle W to a larger proportion of the value of the house. The implication here is that the differential value between the properties (even without the tenants) might be disregarded if W were really entitled to a larger share of the value of the matrimonial property:

166 M: I don't know w—er you—you told me I think your father
167 had paid off the mortgage [(you had).]
168 W: [mhm:]:
169 M: Yes I don't know whether that er: would entitle you to (0.7)
170 a larger (0.5) proportion?
171 W: ( ). (0.4) I don't think he would (.)
172 (laughs) want that anyway. I mean he (.) he—he gave it to
173 both of us and I think he wouldn't
174 M: hm
175 (0.5)
176 W: want that. = But on the other hand (0.3) uhm
177 (.)
178 H: Well our solicitor pointed out that I would probably have
179 to pay more (.) than Hazel. [A la]rger share anyway =

180 M: [mhm:]
181 H: = because of the children.
182 M: mhm
183 (0.2)
184 W: I mean I don't think there's any — I mean I wouldn't expect
185 to have more because it was my father.
186 M: No:. Right oh.
187 (0.2)
188 W: uhm Any more than I would expect Paul to claim more because
189 the other house was initially his. = But I mean he bought
190 it a few months before we got married and worked — worked a
191 lot on [it] while we were married. I mean it sort of—
192 M: [hm]
193 (0.2)
194 M: [You see I mean though I:] don't know the actual sums of =
195 W: [( )]
196 M: = this, but it does seem to be a: (0.6) possible division.

W initially responds by stating that she would not expect a larger share of the value of the properties (lines 171-173, 176). However, M's suggestion seems to prompt her to consider moving toward this potentially more oppositional claim as she states, "But on the other hand..." (line 176). This remains undeveloped, though, as H observes that, according to his lawyer, W would be entitled to a larger share anyway because of the children (lines 178-179, 181). With this acknowledgment of her entitlement, W reciprocates by waiving any claim to expect even more by virtue of her father's gift (lines 184-185, 188-191), noted by M at line 186.

Although her attempt to find a solution to the problem of the difference in the values of the two properties has not proved entirely successful, M has established that there could be a basis for getting each party to accept a division as a form of rough equivalence. She now pursues this possibility:

...**197 M:** I mean if you were able to have the house in Britvale and
198 Hazel ( )
199 H: Ye:s. [Well you're taking it—]
200 M: [had the other one you—]
201 H: Yes. [But you've — you've got a big] if
202 M: [you would (certainly)—]
203 (Telephone rings)
204 (.)
205 H: on this house in Britvale.
206 (Picking up of a receiver)
207 M: Hello?
208 (.)
209 M: Fine.
210 (0.5)
211 M: Well fine. Thank you.
212 (Receiver replaced)
213 H: Well it seems — seems to be a thing that's got to be worked
214 out. (.) I think.

215 W: Yeah.

216 H: uhm But I—i: the one in Britvale could take (.) it could

217 take six months or a year to empty it.

218 M: [mhm]

219 W: [Yeah] but [what's that's—that when] you're talking in

220 H: [To get an order on it.]

221 W: = terms of—

222 H: (Oh [all right what's that])

223 W: [I mean in terms of this sort of] two: years,

224 M: Well I've—it would take that time to sell. I mean

225 we were saying that just now:, it takes some time.

226 H: = It just seems to be going on and on forever. I mean it's . . .

M now openly formulates the division of the properties as an appropriate and acceptable option, implying that the lack of parity in their values is not an insoluble problem (lines 194, 196-198, 200). H, while not immediately rejecting this option, casts doubt on its credibility by underlining that the "if" in relation to the house in Britvale (that is, if he were able to gain possession of the Britvale property) is a "big if" (lines 201, 205). At this point, the interview is interrupted by a brief telephone call.

Following the call, H continues with a general statement about the need to resolve the conflict over the houses (lines 213-214), before formulating as a problem the "fact" that it could take several months to a year to empty the Britvale house (lines 216-217). Here, then, a contrast is drawn between his wanting to settle the matter of the property in the short term and the delay that the option suggested by M would involve. What appears to be implicated here is that H still wants his capital released now, but that M's option would not permit him to do so. And although first W (lines 219, 221, 223) and then M (lines 224-225) subsequently seek to minimize the significance of the delay and thus enhance the credibility of the option, H shows no sign of modifying his position as he complains about things "going on and on forever" (line 226). . . .

DISCUSSION

In analyzing this case, we have illustrated a recurrent feature of the divorce mediation sessions in the present sample. The mediators frequently conduct themselves in ways that show that they are working with notions of favored and disfavored outcomes to the disputes. In this instance, the favored outcome was a division of the two houses, with the wife retaining the matrimonial home and the husband taking the second property. The disfavored outcome was the sale of both houses, with each partner buying a new place to live.

The pressure that the mediator exerts toward the favored and against the disfavored outcome is largely managed by differentially creating opportunities to talk through the favored option rather than, for example, repeatedly producing evaluative statements about the positions of the two clients or the options open to them. This is the process that we have called selective facilitation.

It is essential to distinguish selective facilitation from the routine agenda management that goes on in any orchestrated encounter. Orchestration is one of the means by which speech exchange is ordered in multi-party encounters. The dyadic inter-actions with which conversation analysis has been mainly concerned are organized by the parties' often tacit reference to a set of conventions about taking turns to talk and to listen....

Mediation sessions are multi-party encounters in which the problems of co-ordination are compounded by the breakdown of trust between the spouses, which has made interaction under other conditions difficult or impossible. These sessions are defined in opposition to court hearings so that formal, or rule-based, methods of management are largely excluded. As a result, the mediator is inevitably likely to find herself involved in a great deal of work maintaining the orderly char-acter of talking and listening, including such matters as organizing the opening and the closing of the session, keeping the parties focused on the current topic, and managing the changes from one topic to another. Because this agenda management is directed to the process of interaction, it can be thought of as being executed in ways that are both formally and substantively neutral, although they might well lead to much longer sessions and a lower level of agreements. Selective facilitation, on the other hand, is directed toward influencing outcomes....

If ... selective facilitation turns out to be endemic in mediation and is not intro-duced with sufficient clarity for clients to be able to recognize it and choose whether to go along with it, this would contribute to the case for greater professional or legal regulation of mediators. There is no *a priori* reason why it should be regarded as illegitimate to press for particular types of resolution to particular types of matrimo-nial disputes. Client control must surely rank among the great unquestioned goods of our time. Mediator influence becomes a problem only when formal and substantive neutrality are confused so that the pressure becomes invisible or when the choice of goals remains a purely personal matter rather than one for which the practitioner may be socially accountable. Even here, one may wish to draw a distinction between mediators in private practice, who have been chosen freely by the couple, and those in court-affiliated or mandatory programs, where the philosophy of *caveat emptor* is surely unacceptable.

Until now debates about mediation have been clouded by the difficulty of establishing the exact nature of the experience and a false opposition between neu-trality and bias. This paper has shown that the methods of conversation analysis offer a powerful tool for the dissection of this type of encounter and the re-orientation of the debate around more concrete issues of policy and practice.

Notes and Questions

9.1 Reading the transcript of the session, do you feel the mediator's neutrality or impartiality was compromised? If so, indicate where.

9.2 Would it be possible for you to act as a neutral without having or developing a "preferred" outcome? Should you strive to act in this way? Recall the debate in Chapter 7 between Stulberg and Susskind. Note that "evaluative mediation" is a popular mediation variant. Do you think that evaluative mediators have preferred outcomes? Recall the norm-advocating and norm-enforcing models of mediation described by Waldman in Chapter 3. Do you think that norm-advocating and norm-enforcing mediators have preferred outcomes? If yes, describe what impact such preferences are likely to have on the dynamic.

9.3 Howard Gadlin has suggested that "neutrality" is an aspiration or ideal, imagined as a "halo-like" presence above the mediator, what the mediator attempts to convey and achieve, while acknowledging that no human being can, in fact, be totally "neutral" and step out of his or her particular demographic, cultural, or other basic characteristics. See Howard Gadlin & Elizabeth Walsh Pino, Neutrality: A Guide for the Organizational Ombudsperson, 13 Neg. J. 17 (1997). Is this a helpful image for mediators to hold while working? Do you think it is possible to achieve this "ideal" state or consciousness?

B. ETHICS

Beyond questions of neutrality lies a universe of other ethical choices and dilemmas for the attorney representative and the mediator. For example, what level of honesty is required in mediation? What information must or should be shared? Are the attorney representatives or mediators "responsible" for their actions toward others in the mediation? Others who are outside of, but affected by the mediation? When do mediators have conflicts of interests? Are mediators subject to the ethics rules of their host profession (like the Model Rules of Professional Conduct for lawyers)? Can mediators provide advice or other services to participants in mediation (like drafting agreements)? When might mediators be legally responsible for their actions (malpractice, ethics discipline, other)? These, and other, questions are explored below. Note that while many of the excerpts deal with the lawyer as negotiator, the same concerns and questions will follow the lawyer negotiator into the mediation process.

1. For the Attorney Representative

 Carrie Menkel-Meadow, **WHAT'S FAIR IN NEGOTIATION? WHAT IS ETHICS IN NEGOTIATION?**

What's Fair: Ethics for Negotiators xiii-xvi (Carrie Menkel-Meadow & Michael Wheeler eds., 2004)

What do we owe other human beings when we negotiate for something that we or our clients want? How should we behave toward our "adversaries" — opponents, partners, clients, friends, family members, strangers, third parties and future generations — when we know what we do affects them, beneficially, adversely or unpredictably? How do we think about the other people we interact with in negotiations? Are they just means to our ends or people like us, deserving of respect or aid (depending on whether they are our equals or more or less enabled than ourselves)?

How do we conceive of our goals when we approach others to help us accomplish together what we cannot do alone?

Perhaps after the question "What should I do?" in negotiation (seeking strategic or behavioral advice), the next most frequently asked question is, "What may I do?" (seeking advice, permission, or approval for particular goals, strategies, and tactics that comprise both the conceptualizations and behaviors of the human strategic interaction that we call negotiation). . . .

"What's fair" in negotiation is a complex and multi-faceted question, asking us to consider negotiation ethics on many different levels simultaneously. First, there are the concerns of the individual negotiator: What do I aspire to? How do I judge my own goals and behavior? What may I do? How will others judge me (my counterpart in a two-party negotiation, others in a multi-lateral negotiation, those with whom I might do business in the future, those who will learn of and judge my behavior or results in any negotiation that might become more public than the involved parties)? How do I calibrate my actions to those of the others with whom I am dealing? (Should I have a "relative" ethics that is sensitive, responsive, or malleable to the context, circumstances, customs or personalities of the situation at hand?) What limits are there on my goals and behavior, set from within (the "mirror" test [how do I appear to myself at the end of the day?]) or without, either informally, (the "video-tape test" [what would my mother, teacher, spouse, child or clergy person think of me if they could watch this?]) or formally (rules, laws, ethics standards, religious or moral principles to which I must or choose to adhere)? With what sensibility should I approach each negotiation I undertake?

For those who negotiate as agents, there is the added dimension of what duty is owed a client or principal. When do agent and principal goals properly align? When are they different . . . and how are differences to be reconciled? When do legal rules (like the creation of fiduciary relationships) define the limits and obligations of negotiator-principal interactions?

Third, there is the question of duty, responsibility or relationship to the Other (call him "counterpart," "opponent," "adversary," "partner," "boss" or "subordinate," spouse, lover, child or parent). . . . Do we follow some version of the Golden Rule and treat others as we would hope to be treated by them (a norm of aspirational reciprocity), or does the Golden Rule tarnish a bit on application in particular contexts? . . .

How do those outside of a negotiation judge its ethical "externalities" or social effects? Has a particular negotiation done more good than harm? For those inside the negotiation? Those affected by it (employees, shareholders, vendors and clients, consumers and the public)? And, to what extent must any negotiation be morally accountable for impacts on third parties (children in a divorce, customers in labor-management negotiation, similarly situated claimants in mass torts) and for its inter-generational effects (future generations in environmental disputes)?

In this section, we address some of the questions raised above by examining rules, standards, case law, and other sources of ethical guidance on negotiation behavior.

Formal standards, however, do not cover many situations. In the end, you will form your own ethical practice and reputation as a negotiator.

There are numerous cases in which the law has regulated negotiation behavior. Whereas existing ethics rules regarding negotiation seem to leave plenty of room for strategic behavior and deception, the negotiation lawyer who relies solely on that interpretation clearly will be in trouble. To a large degree, both law and common sense counsel truthfulness and candor in negotiation. The common law creates a cause of action for fraudulent misrepresentation.

> **RESTATEMENT (SECOND) OF TORTS §525 (1977)**
>
> **§525 Liability for Fraudulent Misrepresentation**
>
> One who fraudulently makes a misrepresentation of fact, opinion, intention or law for the purpose of inducing another to act or to refrain from action in reliance upon it, is subject to liability to the other in deceit for pecuniary loss caused to him by his justifiable reliance upon the misrepresentation.

A misrepresentation, for example, can make a contract voidable. Misrepresentation not only includes deliberate lies, but can also include uncorrected mistakes. For example, in Stare v. Tate, 21 Cal. App. 3d 432 (Cal. Ct. App. 1971) a computation error made by one side's attorney and discovered — but not reported — to the other side's attorney was sufficient to void the settlement.

Similarly, there are situations in which omissions can be misrepresentations. The law generally requires that a misrepresentation be a positive misstatement rather than an omission of information. The next excerpt, however, outlines the exceptions to this rule. Consider the four cases described by Shell below.

 G. *Richard Shell*, BARGAINING FOR ADVANTAGE: NEGOTIATION STRATEGIES FOR REASONABLE PEOPLE

208-209 (1999)

Surprisingly, there are circumstances when it may be fraudulent to keep your peace about an issue *even if the other side does not ask about it*. When does a negotiator have a duty to voluntarily disclose matters that may hurt his bargaining position? American law imposes affirmative disclosure duties in the following four circumstances:

1. *When the negotiator makes a partial disclosure that is or becomes misleading in light of all the facts.* If you say your company is profitable, you may be under a duty to disclose whether you used questionable accounting techniques to arrive at that statement. You should also update your prior statement if you show a loss in the next quarter and negotiations are still ongoing.

2. *When the parties stand in a fiduciary relationship to each other.* In negotiations between trustees and beneficiaries, partners in a partnership, shareholders in a small corporation, or members of a family business, parties may have a duty of complete candor and cannot rely on the "be silent and be safe" approach.

3. *When the nondisclosing party has vital information about the transaction not accessible to the other side.* A recent case applying this exception held that an employer owed a duty of disclosure to a prospective employee to disclose contingency plans for shutting down the project for which the employee was hired. In general, sellers have a greater duty to disclose hidden defects about their property than buyers do to disclose "hidden treasure" that may be buried there. Thus, a home seller must disclose termite infestation in her home,* but an oil company need not voluntarily disclose that there is oil on a farmer's land when negotiating to purchase it.† This is a slippery exception; the best test is one of conscience and fairness.

4. *When special codified disclosure duties, such as those regarding contracts of insurance or public offerings of securities, apply.* Legislatures sometimes impose special disclosure duties for particular kinds of transactions. In the United States, for example, many states now require home sellers to disclose all known problems with their houses.

If none of these four exceptions applies, neither side is likely to be found liable for fraud based on a nondisclosure. Each party can remain silent, passively letting the other proceed under its own assumptions.

In inquiries pertaining to fraudulent misrepresentation, facts under discussion must be "material." In negotiations in which puffing and bluffing are seen as part of the game, could a lawyer get in trouble for stretching too far? The answer is that it depends on what you are talking about and to whom you are talking in the negotiation. When the parties are of equal bargaining power, courts have permitted a certain amount of puffing and predictions of quality. In the following excerpt, taken from Vulcan Metals Co. v. Simmons Manufacturing Co., 248 F. 853, 856-857 (2d Cir. 1918), Judge Learned Hand highlights some traditional ways that courts have examined sales promises:

> When the parties are so situated that the buyer may reasonably rely upon the expression of the seller's opinion, it is no excuse to give a false one. And so it makes much difference whether the parties stand "on an equality." For example, we should treat very differently the expressed opinion of a chemist to a layman about the properties of a composition from the same opinion between chemist and chemist, when the buyer had full opportunity to examine. The reason of the rule lies, we think, in this: There are some kinds of talk which no sensible man takes seriously, and if he does he suffers from his credulity. If we were all scrupulously honest, it would not be so; but, as it is, neither party usually believes what the seller says about his own opinions, and each knows it. Such statements, like the claims of campaign managers before election, are rather designed to allay the suspicion which would attend their absence than to be understood as having any relation to objective truth. It is quite true that they induce a compliant temper in the buyer, but it is by a much more subtle process than through the acceptance of his claims for his wares. . . .

---

* See, e.g., Miles v. Perpetual Savings & Loan, Co. et. al, 388 N.E.2d 1367 (Ohio 1979).
† See, e.g., Zaschak v. Traverse Corp., 333 N.W.2d 191 (Mich. App. 1983).

In the case at bar, since the buyer was allowed full opportunity to examine the cleaner and to test it out, we put the parties upon an equality. It seems to us that general statements as to what the cleaner would do, even though consciously false, were not of a kind to be taken literally by the buyer. As between manufacturer and customer, it may not be so; but this was the case of taking over a business, after ample chance to investigate. Such a buyer, who the seller rightly expects will undertake an independent and adequate inquiry into the actual merits of what he gets, has no right to treat as material in his determination statements like these. . . . We therefore think that the District Court was right in disregarding all these misrepresentations.

As you can see from the excerpt above, courts have distinguished between opinion and fact as a way to determine when there is a material misrepresentation of fact. This distinction also applies to an attorney's own views of the strength of his client's position. A demand — "my client will only accept X" — is not deemed to be material as a matter of law. This type of statement is seen as an opinion rather than fact. Similarly, the reservation price — "my client won't settle for less than X" — is also viewed as an opinion. The comments to Model Rule 4.1, Model Rules of Professional Conduct (Appendix G), also make this point. However, other types of tactics in a negotiation could be problematic if you start to inflate (or bluff too much about) your own alternatives. Beavers v. Lamplighters Realty, Inc., 556 P.2d 1328 (Okla. 1976) provides a good example of excessive bluffing. In that case, a realtor falsely represented that another purchaser was on the verge of buying a property, and the court found that the deliberate lie was a fraudulent inducement.

Notes and Questions

9.4 In a recent case, a district attorney was sanctioned by the state disciplinary board for deception. During a hostage negotiation, when the murder suspect asked for an attorney, the district attorney pretended that he was a public defender acting on behalf of the murder suspect to encourage him to surrender. In affirming the sanctions, the Colorado Supreme Court held that "Purposeful deception by an attorney licensed in our state is intolerable. . . . " In the Matter of Paulter, 47 P.3d 1175, 1176 (Colo. 2002). If the Colorado Supreme Court would not condone deceiving a murder suspect during a hostage negotiation, do you think there is a situation where it might approve of lying?

9.5 Home buyers are generally delighted by the evolution of the law that now requires sellers (who have superior information) to reveal things about the house. See Weintraub v. Krobatsch, 317 A.2d 68 (N.J. 1974). What other elements of the home besides termite infestation should be covered under the "superior information" category? If your neighbors are unpleasant, are you required to reveal this? If your neighbors belong to a rock band that practices late into the night, are you required to reveal this? If you are selling a home in which a murder occurred, are you required to reveal this? See Reed v. King, 145 Cal. App. 3d 261 (Cal. Ct. App. 1983) (seller of a house who represented it as fit for an elderly woman living alone had a duty to disclose that the house was the site of a multiple murder ten years before).

In the excerpt that follows, Carrie Menkel-Meadow discusses some of the misrepresentation issues noted above, as well as a number of additional ethical concerns addressed by the Model Rules of Professional Conduct.

 Carrie Menkel-Meadow, ETHICS, MORALITY AND
PROFESSIONAL RESPONSIBILITY IN NEGOTIATION

in Dispute Resolution Ethics 131-139 (Phyllis Bernard & Bryant Garth eds., 2002)

Most discussions of negotiation ethics begin with Model Rule of Professional Conduct 4.1(a) and (b) which provides that a lawyer shall not, in the course of representing a client,

> Make a false statement of material fact or law to a third person; or fail to disclose a
> material fact to a third person when disclosure is necessary to avoid assisting a
> criminal or fraudulent act by a client, unless disclosure is prohibited by Model
> Rule 1.6 [client confidentiality rule].

What the black-letter rule appears to require (a fair amount of candor) is in fact greatly modified by the Comments. For example, Comment 2 states that this rule applies only to "statements of fact," and "whether a particular statement should be regarded as one of fact can depend on the circumstances." "Opinions" (of value, of interpretations of facts or of case law) are not considered "facts" under this rubric. Most significantly, the Comment goes on to exempt from the operation of the rule three particular kinds of statements made in negotiation. According to the Comment, there are "generally accepted conventions in negotiation" (a nod to the sociological phenomenology of negotiation) in which no one really expects the "truth" because these statements are not "material" statements of fact. These are (1) estimates of price or value placed on the subject of the transaction, (2) a party's intentions as to an acceptable settlement of a claim and (3) the existence of an undisclosed principal, except where non-disclosure of the principal would otherwise (by other law) constitute fraud.

Thus, the exception in the Comment defines away, as not material, several key notions of how negotiations are conducted, including inflated offers and demands (otherwise known as "puffing" and "exaggeration"), failure to disclose "bottom lines" or "reservation prices," and non-disclosure of a principal (say Donald Trump or Harvard University) where knowledge of who the principal is might raise a price or demand, on the assumption that the principal has deep pockets. In addition, as discussed more fully below, Comment 1 suggests that while a negotiating lawyer "is required to be truthful when dealing with others on a client's behalf," a lawyer does not have an *affirmative duty* to inform an opposing party of relevant facts (subject to some further qualifications that failure to act or to correct may sometimes constitute a misrepresentation and that substantive law may, in fact, sometimes require affirmative disclosure — see Comment 3).

A simple reading of these provisions demonstrates how indeterminate and unhelpful the formal rules of professional responsibility are. First, the claim that there are "generally accepted conventions" is an empirical one, without substantiation in the text of the Comments. Who, in fact, generally "accepts" these conventions? All lawyers? Lawyers who subscribe to the conventional, adversarial and distributive models of negotiation? Many lawyers would probably "accept" even more classes of "untruthful" or less-than-full-disclosure statements in negotiations. . . .

In an important test of these "generally accepted conventions," Larry Lempert asked 15 legal and ethics experts how — under these rules — they would resolve several important disclosure dilemmas, including lying about authorized limits given by the client, lying about the extent of a personal injury as a plaintiff's lawyer during a litigation negotiation, exaggerating an emotional distress claim in a torts negotiation, and failing to correct the other side's misimpression about the extent of injuries. Not surprisingly, there was relatively little consensus among the experts about how far a lawyer-negotiator could go in lying about, deceiving or misrepresenting these issues, all of which could be argued to be within the

---

MODEL RULE OF PROFESSIONAL CONDUCT

4.1 Truthfulness in Statements to Others

In the course of representing a client a lawyer shall not knowingly:

(a) make a false statement of material fact or law to a third person . . .

(b) fail to disclose a material fact to a third person when disclosure is necessary to avoid assisting a criminal or fraudulent act by a client, unless disclosure is prohibited by Rule 1.6.

COMMENT

Misrepresentation

[1] A lawyer is required to be truthful when dealing with others on a client's behalf, but generally has no affirmative duty to inform an opposing party of relevant facts. A misrepresentation can occur if the lawyer incorporates or affirms a statement of another person that the lawyer knows is false. Misrepresentations can also occur by failure to act.

Statements of Fact

[2] This Rule refers to statements of fact. Whether a particular statement should be regarded as one of fact can depend on the circumstances. Under generally accepted conventions in negotiation, certain types of statements ordinarily are not taken as statements of material fact. Estimates of price or value placed on the subject of a transaction and a party's intentions as to an acceptable settlement of a claim are in this category, and so is the existence of an undisclosed principal except where nondisclosure of the principal would constitute fraud.

Fraud by Client

[3] Paragraph (b) recognizes that substantive law may require a lawyer to disclose certain information to avoid being deemed to have assisted the client's crime or fraud. The requirement of disclosure created by this paragraph is, however, subject to the obligations created by Rule 1.6.

three "generally accepted conventions" excluded from the general non-misrepresentation rule.

Recently, I have added to this list the following negotiator's ethical dilemmas in a variety of lawyer-negotiator ethics CLE programs. Consider what you would do in the following situations, in addition to those four listed above.

1. Just before the closing of a sale of a closely held business, a major client of the business terminates a long-term commercial relationship, thereby lessening the value of the firm being purchased and you represent the seller. Do you disclose this information to the buyer?

2. On the morning of a scheduled negotiation about a litigation matter, you receive notice that your request for a summary judgment has been denied. The lawyer for the other side is coming to your office and clearly has no notice of the judge's ruling. Do you disclose it before negotiating or seek to "close the deal" quickly with an offer before the other side finds out about the summary judgment decision?

3. You receive, by mistake, a fax addressed to all of the counsel on the other side of a multi-party litigation. It contains important and damaging-to-the-other-side information that would enhance your bargaining position. What do you do? . . .

4. In a hotly contested contractual negotiation the other side demanded the inclusion of a particular clause that your client did not want to agree to but finally did when it was made a "deal-breaker." The final draft of the contract, prepared by the other side, arrives at your office without the disputed clause, which you know the other side really wants included in the final deal. What do you do? . . .

Remarkably, time after time, use of these hypotheticals reveals exactly the opposite of what Comment 2 to Model Rule 4.1 so baldly states. In my experience, there are virtually no "generally accepted conventions" with respect to what should be done in these situations. Different negotiators bring to the table different assumptions of what they are trying to do, and with those assumptions come different ethical orientations.

Thus, for those who are "tough negotiators" or who see legal negotiation as an individual maximization game, whether in the litigation or transactional context, most of the deceptions above can be justified by reference either to "expectations" about how the legal-negotiation game is played, or to the lawyer's obligation to be a zealous advocate and not to "do the work" of the other side. For those lawyers who are concerned about making a good agreement "stick" — the instrumentalists — some disclosure is considered desirable (for example, in the scenarios above that describe the omission of a contract provision or the failure to correct misimpressions) because of a concern that some failures to disclose might lead to a post-hoc attack on the agreement (fraud, negligent misrepresentation, unilateral mistake).

Still others regard negotiations as opportunities for problems to be solved and so are more likely to thoughtfully consider the later impact of doing some of the things suggested above. These lawyers ask questions such as these: What would be gained or lost by revealing to the landlord's lawyer that you know he is lying? How can you honestly return the helpful fax and honestly disclose what you now know, but perhaps shouldn't use? When should clients be consulted about these ethical choices, as Model Rule 1.2 suggests theyshould be, at least about some matters? And those who value their reputations and/or see negotiations as a method for achieving some modicum of justice outside of courtrooms or in deals would disclose (as some ethics opinions and fraud cases say they must) the omitted contract clause and the diminished value of the purchased company (is it a material matter?).

Thus, there are no "generally accepted conventions" in negotiation practice, especially as more and more lawyers and law students are trained in the newer canon of *Getting to YES,* collaborative, integrative and problem-solving negotiation models.

Model Rule 4.1, however, is not the only rule that might be seen to govern negotiation ethics. Model Rule 1.2, defining the scope of legal representation, has implications for negotiation behavior in several respects. First, Model Rule 1.2 provides for allocation of decision-making responsibility between lawyers and clients in any representation. Clients are to make decisions about the "objectives of representation," and lawyers, in consultation with clients, may make decisions about the "means" of representation. Some states now require, and others recommend, that this consultation about "means" should include counseling about and consideration of the forms of dispute resolution that should be considered in any representation, including negotiation, mediation, arbitration or other forms of "appropriate dispute resolution." Some might think that such consideration of "means" should extend to the different models of negotiation or different strategies now possible within the growing sophistication about different approaches to negotiation.

> **MODEL RULE OF PROFESSIONAL CONDUCT**
>
> **1.2 Scope of Representation**
>
> (a) A lawyer shall abide by a client's decisions concerning the objectives of representation, . . . and shall consult with the client as to the means by which they are to be pursued. A lawyer shall abide by a client's decision whether to accept an offer of settlement of a matter. . . .
>
> (d) A lawyer shall not counsel a client to engage, or assist a client, in conduct that the lawyer knows is criminal or fraudulent, but a lawyer may discuss the legal consequences of any proposed course of conduct with a client and may counsel or assist a client to make a good faith effort to determine the validity, scope, meaning or application of the law. . . .

Second, and most importantly, Model Rule 1.2 requires the lawyer to "abide by a client's decision whether to settle a matter" and thus requires the lawyer to transmit settlement offers to the client, especially in conjunction with the requirements of Model Rule 1.4(a) that a lawyer "shall keep the client reasonably informed about the status of the matter" and Model Rule 1.4(b) that a lawyer "shall explain a matter to the extent reasonably necessary to permit the client to make informed decisions regarding the representation." Model Rule 1.2(d) also admonishes lawyers not to counsel a client to engage in and not to assist the client in conduct the lawyer knows is fraudulent or criminal, and thus, once again, the Rule implicates the substantive law of fraud and crimes. Lawyers may not assist clients in such activities, and thus, what constitutes a misrepresentation in a negotiation is dependent on tort and criminal law, outside the rules of professional responsibility. The lawyer may, then, be more restricted in 1.2(d) by what other laws prohibit clients from doing than by what the lawyer might be restricted from in 4.1.

Beyond these more specific requirements, Model Rules 8.3 and 8.4 can be and have been invoked with respect to the lawyer's duty to be honest and fair in negotiation. Model Rule 8.4 states that "it is professional misconduct for a lawyer to . . . (c) engage in conduct involving dishonesty, fraud, deceit or misrepresentation," once again incorporating by reference not only substantive standards of legal fraud and misrepresentation, but also suggesting that certain forms of dishonesty or breach of trust or "serious interference with the administration of justice" (especially when a "pattern of repeated offenses" exists) may subject a lawyer to discipline for his deceptive or other fraudulent actions in negotiations. Model Rule 8.3 requires a lawyer who "knows that another lawyer has committed a violation of the Rules of Professional Conduct that raises a substantial question as to the lawyer's honesty, trustworthiness or fitness as a lawyer" to report such misconduct to the appropriate professional authority. Thus, lawyers who repeatedly deceive or play some versions of negotiation "hardball" or "hide and seek" may be subject to discipline for their professional misconduct, though such misconduct is rarely reported.

Several other ethics rules, seldom invoked, also have possible applicability to the conduct of negotiations. Model Rule 4.4 prohibits lawyers from using means that have "no substantial purpose other than to embarrass, delay, or burden a third person," and thus requires lawyers to exercise some degree of "care" toward third parties (such as opposing parties in a negotiation, whether in litigation or transactional settings).

Finally, Model Rule 5.6 prohibits any agreement "in which a restriction on the lawyer's right to practice is part of the settlement of a client controversy." This section is intended to prevent a common practice of defense counsel settling favorably with one plaintiff under the condition that the plaintiff's lawyer be barred from representing similarly situated plaintiffs, or alternatively, be prevented from using evidence or other information acquired in one representation in another, as a condition of the settlement. Despite this rule, many civil settlements, including those in class-action and mass-torts settings, have utilized such conditions. Despite this

> **MODEL RULE OF PROFESSIONAL RESPONSIBILITY**
>
> **3.3 Candor Toward the Tribunal**
>
> (a) A lawyer shall not knowingly:
>
> (1) make a false statement of fact or law to a tribunal or fail to correct a false statement of material fact or law previously made to the tribunal by the lawyer;
>
> (2) fail to disclose to the tribunal legal authority in the controlling jurisdiction known to the lawyer to be directly adverse to the position of the client and not disclosed by opposing counsel; . . .

ethics rule, a variety of case rulings now place substantial restraints on what some lawyers can negotiate for in settlements of civil matters, such as statutory attorneys fees.

Notes and Questions

9.6 How much guidance do the Model Rules provide for an attorney in negotiation? Is there a need for more? Should the same rules or standards for lawyers in negotiation apply in mediation? Why might there be any differences in expectations? Is the lawyer in a mediation appearing in a "tribunal" as contemplated in Rule 3.3? New Rule 1.0 Terminology (m) provides:

> "Tribunal" denotes a court, an arbitrator in a binding arbitration proceeding or a legislative body, administrative agency or other body acting in an adjudicative capacity. A legislative body, administrative body or other body acts in an adjudicative capacity when a neutral official, after the presentation of evidence or legal argument by a party or parties, will render a binding legal judgment directly affecting a party's interests in a particular matter.

Does this definition exclude mediation? Does this mean that lawyers in mediation have no duty to reveal adverse legal authority in a mediation setting? Have no duty to "correct a false statement of material fact or law"? How does this section interact with Rule 4.1 above?

9.7 Menkel-Meadow goes on to point out that various groups have called for more guidelines. For example, the ABA Section of Litigation has approved a set of Ethical Guidelines for Civil Settlement Negotiations. If you were on a drafting committee, how would you shape such rules?

As Carrie Menkel-Meadow writes, Rule 4.1 can be interpreted differently. The excerpt that follows examines three alternative approaches to negotiation.

 G. *Richard Shell*, BARGAINING FOR ADVANTAGE: NEGOTIATION STRATEGIES FOR REASONABLE PEOPLE

215-220 (1999)

I want to challenge you to identify what *your* beliefs are. To help you decide how you feel about ethics, I will briefly describe the three most common approaches to bargaining ethics I have heard expressed in conversation with literally hundreds of students and executives. See which shoe fits — or take a bit from each approach and construct your own.

As we explore this territory, remember that nearly everyone is sincerely convinced that they are acting ethically most of the time, whereas they often think others are acting either naively or unethically, depending on their ethical perspective and the situation. Thus, a word of warning is in order. Your ethics are mainly your own business. They will help you increase your level of confidence and comfort at the bargaining table. But do not expect others to share your ethics in every detail. Prudence pays.

THREE SCHOOLS OF BARGAINING ETHICS

The three schools of bargaining ethics I want to introduce for your consideration are (1) the "It's a game" Poker School, (2) the "Do the right thing even if it hurts" Idealist School, and (3) the "What goes around, comes around" Pragmatist School.

Let's look at each one in turn. As I describe these schools, try to decide which aspects of them best reflect your attitudes. After you figure out where you stand today, take a moment and see if that is where you ought to be. My advice is to aim as high as you can, consistent with your genuinely held beliefs about bargaining. In the pressured world of practice, people tend to slide down rather than climb up when it comes to ethical standards.

The "It's a Game" Poker School

The Poker School of ethics sees negotiation as a "game" with certain "rules." The rules are defined by the law. . . . Conduct within the rules is ethical. Conduct outside the rules is unethical.

The modern founder of the Poker School was Albert Z. Carr, a former Special Consultant to President Harry Truman. Carr wrote a book in the 1960s called, appropriately enough, *Business as a Game*. In a related article that appeared in the Harvard Business Review, Carr argued that bluffing and other misleading but lawful negotiation tactics are "an integral part of the [bargaining] game, and the executive who does not master [these] techniques is not likely to accumulate much money or power."

People who adhere to the Poker School readily admit that bargaining and poker are not exactly the same. But they point out that deception is essential to effective play in both arenas. Moreover, skilled players in both poker and bargaining exhibit a robust and realistic distrust of the other fellow. Carr argues that good players should ignore the "claims of friendship" and engage in "cunning deception and concealment" in fair, hard bargaining encounters. When the game is over, members of the Poker School do not think less of a fellow player just because that person successfully deceived them. In fact, assuming the tactic was legal, they may admire the deceiver and vow to be better prepared (and less trusting) next time.

We know how to play poker, but how exactly does one play the bargaining "game"? Stripped to its core, it looks like this: Someone opens, and then people take turns proposing terms to each other. Arguments supporting your preferred terms are allowed. You can play or pass in each round. The goal is to get the other side to agree to terms that are as close as possible to your last proposal.

In the bargaining game, it is understood that both sides might be bluffing. Bluffs disguise a weak bargaining hand, that is, the limited or unattractive alternatives you have away from the table, your inability to affect the other side's alternatives, and the arguments you have to support your demands. Unlike poker players, negotiators always attempt to disclose a good hand if they have one in a bargaining game. So the most effective bluffs are realistic, attractive, difficult-to-check (but false) alternatives or authoritative (but false) supporting standards. Experienced players know this, so one of the key skills in the bargaining game is judging when the other party's alternatives or arguments are really as good as he or she says. If the other side calls you on your bargaining bluff by walking away or giving you a credible ultimatum, you lose. Either there will be no deal when there should have been one, or the final price will be nearer to their last offer than to yours.

As mentioned above, the Poker School believes in the rule of law. In poker, you are not allowed to hide cards, collude with other players, or renege on your bets. But you are expected to deceive others about your hand. The best plays come when you win the pot with a weak hand or fool the other players into betting heavily when your hand is strong. In bargaining, you must not commit outright, actionable fraud, but negotiators must be on guard for anything short of fraud.

The Poker School has three main problems as I see it. First, the Poker School presumes that everyone treats bargaining as a game. Unfortunately, it is an empirical fact that people disagree on this. For a start, neither the idealists nor the pragmatists (more on these below) think bargaining is a game. This problem does not deter the Poker School, which holds that the rules permit its members to play even when the other party disagrees about this premise.

Second, everyone is supposed to know the rules cold. But this is impossible, given that legal rules are applied differently in different industries and regions of the world. Finally, as you now know (having read about the legal treatment of fraud), the law is far from certain even within a single jurisdiction. So you often need a sharp lawyer to help you decide what to do.

The "Do the Right Thing Even if It Hurts" Idealist School

The Idealist School says that bargaining is an aspect of social life, not a special activity with its own unique set of rules. The same ethics that apply in the home should carry over directly into the realm of negotiation. If it is wrong to lie or mislead in normal social encounters, it is wrong to do so in negotiations. If it is OK to lie in special situations (such as to protect another person's feelings), it is also OK to lie in negotiations when those special conditions apply.

Idealists do not entirely rule out deception in negotiation. For example, if the other party assumes you have a lot of leverage and never asks you directly about the situation as you see it, you do not necessarily have to volunteer the information weakening your position. And the idealist can decline to answer questions. But such exceptions are uncomfortable moments. Members of the Idealist School prefer to be candid and honest at the bargaining table even if it means giving up a certain amount of strategic advantage.

The Idealist School draws its strength from philosophy and religion. For example, Immanuel Kant said that we should all follow the ethical rules that we would wish others to follow. Kant argued that if everyone lied all the time, social life would be chaos. Hence, you should not lie. Kant also disapproved of treating other people merely as the means to achieve your own personal ends. Lies in negotiation are selfish acts designed to achieve personal gain. This form of conduct is therefore unethical. Period. Many religions also teach adherents not to lie for personal advantage.

Idealists admit that deception in negotiation rarely arouses moral indignation unless the lies breach a trust between friends, violate a fiduciary responsibility, or exploit people such as the sick or elderly, who lack the ability to protect themselves. And if the only way you can prevent some terrible harm like a murder is by lying, go ahead and lie. But the lack of moral outrage and the fact that sometimes lying can be defended does not make deception in negotiations right.

Idealists strongly reject the idea that negotiations should be viewed as "games." Negotiations, they feel, are serious, consequential communication acts. People negotiate to resolve their differences so social life will work for the benefit of all. People must be held responsible for all their actions, including the way they negotiate, under universal standards.

Idealists think that the members of the Poker School are predatory and selfish. For its part, the Poker School thinks that idealists are naïve and even a little silly. When members of the two schools meet at the bargaining table, tempers can flare.

Some members of the Idealist School have recently been trying to find a philosophical justification for bluffs about bottom lines. There is no agreement yet on whether these efforts have succeeded in ethical terms. But it is clear that outright lies such as fictitious other offers and better prices are unethical practices under idealist principles.

The big problem for the idealist is obvious: Their standards sometimes make it difficult to proceed in a realistic way at the bargaining table. Also, unless adherence to the Idealist School is coupled with a healthy skepticism about the way other people will negotiate, idealism leaves its members open to exploitation by people with standards other than their own. These limitations are especially troublesome when idealists must represent others' interests at the bargaining table.

Despite its limitations, I like the Idealist School. Perhaps because I am an academic, I genuinely believe that the different parts of my life are, in fact, whole. I aspire to ethical standards that I can apply consistently. I will admit that I sometimes fall short of idealism's strict code, but by aiming high I am leaving myself somewhere to fall that maintains my basic sense of personal integrity.

I confess my preference for the Idealist School so you will know where I am coming from in this discussion. But I realize that your experience and work environment may preclude idealism as an ethical option. That's OK. As I hope I am making clear, idealism is not the only way to think about negotiation in ethical terms.

The "What Goes Around Comes Around" Pragmatist School

The final school of bargaining ethics, the Pragmatist School, includes some original elements as well as some attributes of the previous two. In common with the Poker School, this approach views deception as a necessary part of the negotiation process. Unlike the Poker School, however, it prefers not to use misleading statements and overt lies if there is a serviceable, practical alternative. Uniquely, the Pragmatist School displays concern for the potential negative effects of deceptive conduct on present and future relationships. Thus, lying and other questionable tactics are bad not so much because they are "wrong" as because they cost the user more in the long run than they gain in the short run.

As my last comment suggests, people adhere to this school more for prudential than idealistic reasons. Lies and misleading conduct can cause serious injury to one's credibility. And credibility is an important asset for effective negotiators both to preserve working relationships and to protect one's reputation in the market or community. The latter concern is summed up in what I would call the pragmatist's credo: What goes around comes around. The Poker School is less concerned with reputation and more focused on winning each bargaining encounter within the rules of the "game."

What separates the Pragmatist School from the Idealist School? To put it bluntly, a pragmatist will lie a bit more often than will an idealist. For example, pragmatists sometimes will draw fine distinctions between lies about hard-core facts of a transaction, which are always imprudent (and often illegal), and misleading statements about such things as the rationales used to justify a position. A pragmatic car salesman considers it highly unethical to lie about anything large or small relating to the mechanical condition of a used car he is selling. But this same salesman might not have a problem saying "My manager won't let me sell this car for less than $10,000" even though he knows the manager would sell the car for $9,500. False justifications and rationales are marginally acceptable because they are usually less important to the transaction and much harder to detect as falsehoods than are core facts about the object being bought and sold.

Pragmatists are also somewhat looser within the truth when using so called blocking techniques — tactics to avoid answering questions that threaten to expose a weak bargaining position. For example, can you ethically answer "I don't know" when asked about something you know that hurts your position? An idealist would refuse to answer the question or try to change the subject, not lie by saying "I don't know." A pragmatist would go ahead and say "I don't know" if his actual state of knowledge is hard to trace and the lie poses little risk to his relationships.

Notes and Questions

9.8 Which negotiation school do you think best describes your view of negotiation? What aspects of your chosen school are most appealing?

9.9 Do you think that each school applies in different contexts? Give an example of a context in which each school would apply best.

9.10 How would each school answer the hypotheticals posed by Carrie Menkel-Meadow in the excerpt that preceded this one?

2. For the Mediator

Like attorney representatives, mediators face many ethical choices in their practice for which there are no easy answers. Dilemmas that arise often result from conflicting obligations or aspirations. For example, conflicts abound between the rule of law and the rule of party choice or the aspiration of good-faith conduct and the promise of confidentiality. Michael Moffitt describes different scenarios below that raise ethical issues for mediators and could possibly lead to mediator liability. Read these examples in light of the Model Standards of Conduct for Mediators (the Model Standards) developed by the American Bar Association, the American Arbitration Association, and the Association for Conflict Resolution. The Model Standards (reproduced in Appendix B) provide guideposts in thinking about the situations that follow. They articulate and more fully describe the following fundamental values and mediator duties: party self-determination, mediator impartiality, mediator disclosure and avoidance of conflicts of interest, mediator competence, mediator maintenance of the confidentiality and quality of the process, truth in advertising, disclosure of fees, and the mediator's duty to improve the practice of mediation. However, ethics codes rarely give bright-line boundaries and indisputable answers. Rather, they help develop a moral compass for reflective practitioners and a guide to the outer limits of permissible conduct. Pinpoint for each scenario what, if anything, about the mediator's conduct arguably violates a duty to the process or parties or society.

 Michael Moffitt, TEN WAYS TO GET SUED: A GUIDE FOR MEDIATORS

8 Harv. Negot. L. Rev. 81, 86, 95-96, 111, 113-114, 116-117, 120, 122, 125 (2003)

[Eight of ten dilemmas posed by Moffitt follow.]

[1] Melissa Mediator is a member of a small consulting firm specializing in corporate dispute resolution. One of the firm's clients is a large, multinational conglomerate. Unlike most of her colleagues, Melissa has never done work for the conglomerate. A dispute arises between one of the subsidiaries of the conglomerate and a local business. Melissa agrees to mediate the dispute and discloses nothing about the relationship between the conglomerate and her firm. . . .

[2] After considerable efforts to facilitate an agreement, and at the request of the disputants, Marjorie Mediator examines the evidence each side has compiled and develops her best assessment of a court's likely disposition of the case. The parties then quickly agree to basic settlement terms. Again at the parties' request, Marjorie drafts a formal contract to capture the terms of the parties' agreement. . . .

[3] Plaintiffs brought suit seeking injunctive relief to force a change in a particular policy at the defendant corporation and seeking modest monetary damages. During a private caucus, Marsha Mediator learns that the defendant has already decided to change the policies in question, in a way the plaintiffs will embrace. When Marsha asks defense counsel why they have not told the plaintiffs about the corporation's plans, they indicate that they hope to use the change in policies as a "trade-off concession" in order to minimize or eliminate any financial payment. In a subsequent private meeting with the plaintiffs, without the consent of the defendant, Marsha says, "Look, the defendants have already told me that they're going to make the policy change, the only issue is money." . . .

[4] Maurice Mediator learns during a conversation with a divorcing couple that the children are regularly subjected to living arrangements tantamount to abuse or neglect. Maurice mentions his concern, but both of the parents swear that the circumstances will change once they can finalize the divorce. Maurice says nothing to anyone outside of the mediation and proceeds to assist the parties in finalizing the terms of the divorce. . . .

[5] Mitchell Mediator's website touts his mediation services as "expert." In part, it says, "Over 1,000 cases of experience. Certified and sanctioned by the State and by prominent national mediation organizations." Mitchell is a former judge who presided over more than a thousand civil cases during his years on the bench. He has formally mediated, however, only a few dozen cases. Furthermore, neither the state nor the national mediation organizations to which Mitchell belongs certifies or sanctions mediators. Mitchell is simply a member of the mediation rosters each body maintains. . . .

[6] During the mediation, Muriel Mediator adopts an aggressive approach to creating settlement. As always, she had told the parties, a divorcing couple, "Bring your toothbrushes when you show up to my mediation." The divorcing wife, unrepresented by counsel, is visibly worn down by Muriel's relentless efforts at "persuasion." When the wife protests and indicates a desire to leave, Muriel threatens to report to the judge that the wife did not participate in mediation in good faith. Muriel further indicates that such a report would "all but guarantee that you'll lose your claim for custody of the children." . . .

[7] In a private caucus, the plaintiffs tell Manuel Mediator that they would be able to break this case wide open if only they could get some cooperation from a few important executives in the defendant corporation. They admit, however, that they have had no luck so far in their efforts. Manuel then sits down privately with the general counsel for the defendant and says, "Look, I spoke with the plaintiffs. They have just lined up some key insider witnesses, including a couple members of your management team. It's time for you to end this." The general counsel looks surprised but increases the defendants' offer considerably. The mediator takes the new offer to the plaintiffs, who quickly agree to it. . . .

[8] Michael Mediator misses an opportunity to improve the parties' understanding of each other and of the relevant issues. Michael creates an unhelpful agenda and refuses to adapt his approach. Michael misreads the parties' primary concerns. He makes inappropriate suggestions. Michael is unprepared. He listens horribly. Michael oversees a lengthy process that produces no agreement and worsens the parties' relationship. . . .

Wrestling with these eight scenarios should develop an appreciation of the major dilemmas that have informed the development of ethical codes. Recurring issues, many of which have no definitive resolution, include conflicts of interest that impact mediator neutrality or create the appearance of mediator bias; mediator evaluation and agreement drafting that raise questions about unauthorized practice of law; mediator responsibilities to maintain party confidences and simultaneously promote settlement; mediator duties to endangered third parties as such duties impact mediation confidentiality; consumers' rights to truthfulness in advertising and parties' rights to honesty and integrity from the mediator; the line between energizing parties to move forward and improperly pressuring them into settlement; and the contours of minimal competence. In the notes and questions below, three areas are explored further — mediator immunity, conflicts of interest, and unauthorized practice. In the early days of mediation practice, there was hope that we would find some core concepts of agreement in the ethics area. More recently, we have come to realize that with the different models and approaches to mediation summarized in Chapter 3, there are actually many different views about how to resolve some of the most important ethical dilemmas.

 Carrie Menkel-Meadow, **PROFESSIONAL RESPONSIBILITY FOR THIRD-PARTY NEUTRALS**

11 Alternatives to the High Costs of Litigation 129-131 (1993)

CORE, NON-CONTROVERSIAL ETHICS REQUIREMENTS

Virtually all of the current drafts of ethics rules contain a number of the same terms. These provisions:

- suggest that parties be fully informed about the varieties of dispute resolution options and where possible (in voluntary, not mandatory programs) that parties freely consent to the process they choose. It is the professional responsibility of the third-party neutral (and any lawyer representing a party in a dispute resolution process) to fully explain that process.
- attempt to deal with the possible conflicts of interest that third parties could have.
- provide that third-party neutrals should be disqualified from subsequent representation of any party that appears in a mediation or similar proceeding.
- prohibit third-party neutrals from taking contingency fees, or fees that would give the neutral a stake in the substantive outcome.
- prohibit mediators, arbitrators and other third-party neutrals from having a personal, financial or legal interest in or relationship to any of the parties to the dispute. (Some arbitration rules suggest that it is enough to disclose such possible conflicts and let the parties decide.)

Some drafts, including the proposed new ABA rule [Rule 2.4], suggest that under limited circumstances, such as with full party consent, third-party neutrals could mediate a dispute of a past or even present client. The argument is that often existing clients may ask their current lawyers to serve as neutrals precisely because they know and trust them and think they will be effective. This "waiver" of possible conflicts tracks the ABA's treatment of representational conflicts (MRPC 1.7-1.13).

Many of the general rules that apply to lawyers also have been applied to third-party neutrals who are lawyers. These include: rules about advertising; rules prohibiting practice with non-lawyers (somewhat problematic for lawyer-mediators who like to work with other professionals like psychologists or accountants) or assisting in the unauthorized practice of law; standards of diligence and competence (however those get defined in malpractice or disciplinary proceedings).

Most rules suggest that it is the neutral's responsibility to terminate the dispute resolution proceeding if it appears that there is coercion, unfairness or a non-consensual process. (The applicability of such a provision in situations of mandatory arbitration or mediation is less than clear.)

In addition, most rules try to develop a standard for neutrals to enforce honest information disclosure among and between the parties. However, the enforcement mechanisms for such requirements are less than clear. (One reported malpractice case was based on a theory of the neutral's failure to force a party to reveal some financial information.) Most jurisdictions would void an agreement if the failure to disclose material information could be characterized as fraud. Virtually all of the rules exhort third parties to be "neutral" and "impartial," but the actual meaning of these terms is less than clear and much law review ink has been spilled on the subject [see, e.g., Leonard L. Riskin, Toward New Standards for the Neutral Lawyer in Mediation, 26 Ariz. L. Rev. 329 (1984); Judith L. Maute, Public Values and Private Justice: A Case for Mediator Accountability, 4 Geo. J. of Leg. Ethics 503 (1991)].

CONTROVERSIAL AREAS: THE ROLE OF THE THIRD PARTY

Some of the more controversial areas of professional responsibility include the following questions: Should mediators be accountable for more than process facilitation? Should they have responsibility for ensuring a fair outcome, or does that compromise their neutrality and the philosophy that parties should be masters of their own settlements? What role should law play in judging the substantive fairness of any outcome? Are mediators, arbitrators and other third-party neutrals to be judged by a different standard than judges?

One problem for drafters of ethical guidelines is the lack of consensus about whether a mediator or other third-party neutral is a passive facilitator of party-initiated solutions or a more "aggressive" third party who makes substantive suggestions and fails to "preside" over unfair agreements [see, e.g., Susskind & Cruickshank, Breaking the Impasse (1987)]. Should a "neutral" be barred from expressing an opinion or giving an evaluation in a voluntary mediation? Should a mediator terminate a mediation that is unfair to one of the parties, or can the mediator intervene with substantive information or other techniques to correct power imbalances?

Questions like these go to the basic differences in philosophies about dispute resolution that are unlikely to be resolved by the promulgation of ethical standards. Are lawyers who represent the parties in ADR responsible for the substantive fairness of agreements they negotiate or outcomes they litigate? (Under current rules they are not. Efforts to create standards prohibiting unconscionable outcomes or unfair means were defeated in the Kutak Commission's deliberations about MRPC Rules 4.1 and 4.2.)

Issues about regulation of confidentiality and third-party privilege also prevent clear consensus in ethics regulations. Some jurisdictions have dealt with confidentiality protection for third-party neutrals and parties through legislation, in evidence codes or in rules of procedure. Efforts to make what is said in a mediation or similar proceeding completely secret are balanced against other legal standards requiring disclosure — such as in child abuse, economic fraud or other underlying regulations (for instance, those being proposed in the banking area).

Further complicating the confidentiality issue, is how communications in joint session should be treated (where both parties are present and technical attorney-client privilege would not apply) as compared to communications in separate caucus sessions. Some lawyers think that mediators should have the same evidentiary privilege as lawyers not to reveal information under any circumstances; others think non-representational relationships suggest other duties and a less absolutely protected privilege. Other commentators rest the confidentiality protection on the evidence rules (both federal and state) that prohibit disclosure of any information used in efforts to settle the case.

Perhaps most controversial is the question of whether third-party neutrals can advise the parties about their legal rights and responsibilities. The proposed ABA rule takes the position that it is all right to do so if both parties are present and have been informed that they should seek independent legal counsel. Other rules suggest that all neutrals should urge all parties to consult counsel before signing any agreement.

Commentators debate whether such rules are consumer-oriented, encouraging parties to make informed decisions about conceding important legal rights. Others see this as an effort by the bar to maintain employment of adversary lawyers against the possible competition of "neutrals." In my view this issue has been too readily applied to one of two categories: the impossibility of giving neutral legal advice, thus leading to an inevitable conflict of interest, or the suggestion that legal information, neutrally given, is not "legal advice" as an adversary lawyer would give it.

Most third parties would agree that informing parties of their legal rights and responsibilities can almost never be neutral — the law, after all, almost always requires interpretation and application to specific facts. Nevertheless, there may be an important role for the neutral third party to be sure that law (even if it advantages one party) is part of the decision-making process. The law, after all, is likely to provide the parties with some sense of their alternatives to a mediated agreement and is relevant in deciding whether to settle or to litigate.

Many third parties are concerned that mandating independent legal advice in all dispute resolution activities will render mediation and similar processes too adversarial, just as we are trying to move away from the excesses of our advocacy system. Balancing party and professional interests therefore may be difficult and far too contextual to lead to easy ethics rule drafting.

Lack of consensus about aspects of technical third-party practice also makes the development of some standards difficult. Should a third party refuse to facilitate a case when not all interested parties (for example, an insurer) are part of the process? Should a court-appointed mediator continue to mediate when it is clear that one of the parties is using the process to gain information for discovery advantage, rather than to settle the case? Do mediators of large public-policy disputes have any obligation to the public if there is no obvious representation of public interests in a particular dispute? What should a mediator do if it becomes clear that a party (or counsel) is seriously misrepresenting facts or law to the other party in the mediation? Should the mediator be an enforcer of fair negotiation practices of the parties when the ABA rules do not seem to require such standards of negotiating for lawyers (see Rule 4.1)?

A BLUEPRINT FOR CHANGE

Despite the absence of clear consensus on all issues of third-party professional responsibility, it is clear that some formal recognition of the non-representational, non-advocate dispute resolution function is long overdue in the ABA Model Rules [now recognized in new Rule 2.4, Model Rules of Professional Conduct, see below]. As the modern rules attempt to deal with the wide variety of tasks performed by lawyers — whether they be advocates, counselors, lobbyists, agents or fiduciaries — the Rules should acknowledge and authorize third-party practice....

In my view, these more complex issues can be dealt with temporarily by requiring third-party neutrals to specify in advance what

> **MODEL RULE OF PROFESSIONAL CONDUCT**
>
> **2.4 Lawyer Serving as Third-Party Neutral**
>
> **American Bar Association, Model Rules of Professional Conduct (2005)**
>
> (a) A lawyer serves as a third party neutral when the lawyer assists two or more persons who are not clients of the lawyer to reach a resolution of a dispute or other matter that has arisen between them. Service as a third party neutral may include service as an arbitrator, mediator or in such other capacity as will enable the lawyer to assist the parties to resolve the matter.
>
> (b) A lawyer serving as a third party neutral shall inform unrepresented parties that the lawyer is not representing them. When the lawyer knows or reasonably should know that a party does not understand the lawyer's role in the matter, the lawyer shall explain the difference between the lawyer's role as a third party neutral and a lawyer's role as one who represents a client.

philosophies and methods they use so that clients and consumers can select, on an informed basis, what kind of third-party neutral they want. As with all standards for ethical and professionally responsible practice, our rules will evolve from the recognition of the actual practices that are employed and analysis of how those practices affect the parties.

Notes and Questions

9.11 Moffitt's *Ten Ways to Get Sued* discusses potential causes of action against mediators in the situations he describes. However, mediators operating under the umbrella of a court-annexed or court-sponsored ADR program may be protected by quasi-judicial immunity. In Wagshal v. Foster, 28 F.3d 1249 (D.C. 1994), the court held that a mediator's actions in communicating to the judge as he recused himself from a case were within the scope of his official duties and hence entitled to absolute immunity. Generally, should mediators enjoy immunity, or would you hold them liable for malpractice? For a discussion of this question, arguing against mediator immunity, see Scott

H. Hughes, Mediator Immunity: The Misguided and Inequitable Shifting of Risk, 83 Or. L. Rev. 107 (2004).

Even absent actual immunity, there are other ways in which mediators are virtually immune from liability. Because there are no clear standards for mediator conduct, it is difficult to prove that a mediator has been negligent. A party may not be able to establish that an unfavorable settlement amounts to an actionable injury or appropriate damages for that injury. Further, parties often agree to hold mediators harmless from future actions. Finally, these hurdles are compounded by the evidentiary restrictions related to confidentiality discussed in the preceding chapter. In another article, Moffitt argues that "a mediator who engages in egregious behavior, violates contractual or statutory obligations, or breaches separately articulated duties should enjoy no legal or de facto immunity from lawsuits." Do you agree? See Michael Moffitt, Suing Mediators, 83 B.U. L. Rev. 147, 207 (2003).

9.12   In Fields-D'Arpino v. Restaurant Assocs., 39 F. Supp. 2d 412 (S.D.N.Y. 1999), the court held that counsel for defendants-employer were disqualified from representing defendants because a partner in the firm had served as a neutral mediator in trying to resolve plaintiff-employee's discrimination claim against her employer. Similarly, in Poly Software Intl. v. Su, 880 F. Supp. 1487 (D. Utah 1995), the mediator attorney who had previously settled a dispute between two parties involving the same software was disqualified from representing one of the parties, as were other members of his law firm. Can you identify the rationale for these decisions? Compare the rule on conflicts of interest in the Model Standards (Appendix B) and that of the CPR-Georgetown Commission on Ethics and Standards in ADR Proposed Model Rule of Professional Conduct for the Lawyer as Third Party Neutral (CPR-Georgetown Model Rule) (Appendix C).

9.13   The Model Standards urge mediators to "refrain from providing professional advice." (Model Standard 6 and the comments that follow in Appendix B.) This simple directive, however, is undercut by the fact that "evaluative mediation" has grown, particularly in the arena of civil court cases, and there is significant market demand for this service. How does the new Model Rule of Professional Conduct [Rule 2.4] deal with this issue?

Non-lawyer mediators have been accused of unauthorized practice of law when they provide legal information or assessments and draft settlement agreements. Several states formally prohibit lawyers from mediating cases and then drafting settlement agreements for the parties, because of the possible conflict of interest in doing work for two "adverse" parties. See, e.g., Illinois State Bar Assn. Comm. on Professional Ethics, Op. 04-03 (April 2005); Utah State Bar Ethics Advisory Op. Comm., Op. 05-03 (May 6, 2005). This is an issue on which states differ (and ethics rules are promulgated at the state level). See New York State Ethics, Op. 736 (Jan. 1, 2001). Lawyers who are not admitted in the jurisdiction where they are serving as mediators may face the same problem.

Carrie Menkel-Meadow argues that the evaluation of the merits of a case or the drafting of settlement agreements constitute the practice of law and some measures should be put into place to ensure quality and competence when these services are rendered, particularly in light of the fact that mediators often enjoy quasi-judicial immunity. Carrie Menkel-Meadow, Is Mediation the Practice of Law?, 14 Alternatives 57 (1996).

In response to the issue of unauthorized practice, the Dispute Resolution Section of the American Bar Association has promulgated a statement on mediation and the unauthorized practice of law, essentially defining away the issue. The statement asserts that mediation is *not* the practice of law and that mediators' discussions with parties about legal issues do not constitute legal advice. (A portion of this provision regarding drafting agreements is in Chapter 6.) The provision on Mediation and the Unauthorized Practice of Law was adopted by the ABA Section of Dispute Resolution on February 2, 2002, available at *http://www.abanet.org/dispute/webpolicy.html.*

Since mediation is a private process, what protection is afforded to participants for "unauthorized" or incompetent advice? Do you agree with the approach of the ABA Dispute Resolution Section? Do you think that when professionals give opinions or advice they should be held to the applicable standards of care in their respective fields? Should it make a difference if parties are represented by lawyers in mediation?

Multiple models of mediation and mediation's rapid growth raise concerns about maintaining a core consistency to the process and safeguarding consumers. At the same time, proponents of mediation want to preserve its flexibility and creativity. For one attempt to specify some general principles of ethical practice in this new field, see the credo of basic principles for mediators and neutral consensus builders or facilitators proposed in Carrie Menkel-Meadow, The Lawyer as Consensus Builder: Ethics for a New Practice, 70 Tenn. L. Rev. 63 (2002). Menkel-Meadow suggests that all third-party neutrals should insure broad party and stakeholder participation; provide opportunities for participants to agree on procedural and ground rules, as well as on decision rules for agreements; encourage participant recognition of both individual and joint needs and interests; encourage parties to express reasons and justifications for their views, needs, and offers; facilitate creative and tailored solutions to meet parties' needs and objectives; provide a place of fair hearing and respect for all parties; facilitate capacity building of parties to negotiate on their own behalf; consider the practicality and enforceability of agreements reached; be themselves free from bias and conflicts of interests; and avoid unjust, unfair, or unconscionable agreements, wherever possible.

One suggested response to these issues has been to credential or license mediators, or subject them, like other professionals, to testing, review, and certification. See Christopher Honeyman, On Evaluating Mediators, 6 Neg. J. 23 (1990). This has been controversial since the beginning, because many would prefer to permit relatively open access to the field. There is a possible tension between accessibility and openness, on the one hand, and quality control and competence, on the other. Recently, the Association for Conflict Resolution (ACR, formerly the Society for Professionals in Dispute Resolution, SPIDR) and the ABA Section of Dispute Resolution considered the creation of a national certification program for mediators, which has not been realized. Many bodies, including the private, but large, professional associations, like ACR and the ABA Section on Dispute Resolution, as well as public agencies like the Environmental Protection Agency, the Federal Mediation and Conciliation Service, and the Federal Deposit Insurance Corporation, have studied and considered the use of credentials, certification programs, and approved rosters or lists of specified mediators. See Sarah R. Cole, Certification: Has the Time Come?, 11 Disp. Resol. Mag. 7-12 (2005); Donald T. Weckstein, Mediation Certification: Why and How?, 30 U. S. F. L. Rev. 757 (1996).

Notes and Questions

9.14 Do you think mediators should be certified or licensed? On what basis? Education? Experience? Quality? Who should monitor the certification process? Professionals? Consumers of the process? Under what circumstances should a mediator be decertified or removed from a roster? (This may have constitutional implications (due process) when mediators are removed from the lists of public agencies or courts.) In assessing competence in air travel, pilots accumulate "hours of flying time" (actual experience). Is there an equivalent measure in mediation ("hours in the mediator's chair")? Or should mediators be assessed based on how many agreements they reach? What are the dangers of using a "settlement rate" as a measure of quality or competence?

9.15 For other efforts to identify, discuss, and explore ethical issues in the practice of mediation, see Sarah R. Cole, Craig A. McEwen & Nancy C. Rogers, Mediation Law, Policy, and Practice, chs. 2, 10, 11 (2001); Leonard L. Riskin, Toward New Standards for the Neutral Lawyer in Mediation, 26 Ariz. L. Rev. 329 (1984); Judith L. Maute, Public Values and Private Justice: A Case for Mediator Accountability, 4 Geo. J. Legal Ethics 503 (1991); Carrie Menkel-Meadow, The Silences of the Restatement of the Law Governing Lawyers: Lawyering as Only Adversary Practice, 10 Geo. J. Legal Ethics 631 (1997); Carrie Menkel-Meadow, Ethics and Professionalism in Non-Adversarial Lawyering, 27 Fla. St. U. L. Rev. 153 (1999); Carrie Menkel-Meadow, Ethics in ADR: The Many "C's" of Professional Responsibility and Dispute Resolution, 28 Fordham Urb. L.J. 979 (2001); Scott Peppet, ADR Ethics, 54 J. Legal Educ. (2004); Scott Peppet, Contractarian Economics and Mediation Ethics: The Case for Customizing Neutrality Through Contingent Fee Mediation, 82 Tex. L. Rev. 227 (2003); Dispute Resolution Ethics: A Comprehensive Guide (Phyllis Bernard & Bryant Garth eds., 2002); and Charles Pou, Jr., "Embracing Limbo": Thinking About Rethinking Dispute Resolution Ethics, 108 Penn. St. L. Rev. 199 (2003).

9.16 The first state to promulgate and enforce ethics standards and publish ethics opinions on the ethical practice of mediation is Florida. See Robert Moberly, Ethical Standards for Court-Appointed Mediators and Florida's Mandatory Mediation Experiment, 21 Fla. St. U. L. Rev. 701 (1994).

9.17 How much ethical guidance does the new rule (Rule 2.4, see above) for Lawyers as Third Party Neutrals actually give the lawyer who serves as a mediator? Why do you think the American Bar Association was reluctant to specify more ethical requirements for the lawyer who serves as a neutral and not as a conventional "representative"? Does this new rule provide for any guidance for the lawyer-representative in mediation or do only the rules that apply to negotiation (see above) affect the lawyer inside a mediation?

3. For the Provider of Mediators

Although ethics are most often considered a function of individual action, doctrines like *respondeat superior* and organizational or corporate liability are being imposed on organizations that provide services, see, e.g., Ted Schneyer, Professional Discipline for Law Firms?, 77 Cornell L. Rev. 1 (1991). Various regulatory bodies have taken up the issue of whether organizations that provide for or refer to mediation services can be held responsible, either through legal liability, sanctions, or discipline, for the services they provide. California, for example, recently attempted to require provider organizations and individuals to provide detailed conflict-of-interest information in the arbitration context, in the hopes of revealing repeat players with actual or potential conflicts of interests. The revisions to the Civil Procedure Code requiring disclosures (Code of Civ. Proc. §1281.85(a) and Cal. Rules of Court, appendix, div. VI) were partially overturned (at least with respect to national providers) on grounds of federal pre-emption (at least in the securities area), see Jevne v. Superior Court Los Angeles and JB Oxford Holdings, 35 Cal. 4th 935 (Cal. 2005), but many states continue to think about how to regulate provider organizations. See J. Folberg, Arbitration Ethics: Is California the Future?, 18 Ohio St. J. Dis. Resol. 343 (2003). The Center for Public Resources Institute for Dispute Resolution has published a set of Provider Principles for good ethical practice and accountability for provider organizations, see *http://www.cpradr.org/publicpolicyprojects* and see also Carrie Menkel-Meadow, Ethics Issues in Arbitration and Related Dispute Resolution Processes: What's Happening and What's Not, 56 U. Miami L. Rev. 949, 983-1007 (2002).

Notes and Questions

9.18 Would a court that referred parties to mediation (either mandatorily or suggestively) be a "provider" organization for purposes of organizational ethics?

9.19 The Federal Judicial Center has also created some ethical guidelines for courts that refer parties to mediation and other forms of ADR and some courts, such as the federal court for the Northern District of California, have promulgated their own ethical rules with respect to how mediation and other ADR services should be provided within the courts, governing such matters as conflicts of interests, confidentiality, communications between judges and third-party neutrals, and ex parte communications, see, e.g., Robert J. Niemic, Donna Stienstra & Randell E. Ravitz, Guide to Judicial Management of Cases in ADR (Federal Judicial Center, 2001); N.D. Calif. ADR R. 6-11(b). See also 28 U.S.C. §§455, 653(b), judicial disqualification and disqualification and training of court neutrals; Calif. Judicial Council, Standards of Conduct for Mediators in Court-Connected Programs for Civil Cases (2002).

As you read the next chapters, consider what ethical concerns are removed, and what new ethical issues arise in adaptations of the mediation process. Consider whether the rules change when mediation is extended to greater numbers of parties or applied to complex issues, disputes, or policy matters.

PART III APPLICATIONS OF THE MEDIATION PROCESS

Chapter 10 Mediation, Arbitration, and Other Hybrid Processes

Two roads diverged in a wood, and I—I took the one less traveled by, And that has made all the difference.

—Robert Frost

There are more ways than one to skin a cat.

—Anonymous

In counseling clients about mediation and other process options (a topic examined in Chapter 11), lawyers must understand the array of possible dispute resolution procedures. This chapter introduces a variety of alternative processes, including hybrids that use mediation in combination with another process. Understanding process options is, of course, critical for a mediator as well as an attorney representative, because the mediator helps parties explore process options when efforts to resolve substantive issues are not successful.

The first section looks at processes that can end an unresolved dispute through a final decision of a third-party neutral: an arbitrator, private judge, or private jury. These processes are shown on the left side of the map below. The second section examines processes that aid parties in evaluating their cases by providing advisory opinions and decisions to the parties: judicial settlement conferences, non-binding arbitration, summary jury trials, early neutral and expert evaluation, as well as evaluative mediation. These appear on the evaluative side of the chart under "Advisory/Evaluative."

The final section of this chapter examines mediation in a variety of specific contexts including: "restorative justice" efforts in the criminal arena: the minitrial in the corporate arena, and online mediation in cyberspace.

As you examine these processes consider the following questions:

1. What foundational (primary) processes—negotiation, mediation, arbitration, and litigation—are being used?
2. Can multiple processes be combined without sacrificing the special "morality" or "integrity" of each process?
3. What is the role of third-party neutrals? Facilitative, authoritative, evaluative, or decisional? What is the role of parties in the process? Of attorneys?
4. Who has designed the particular hybrid process? The parties themselves? A process expert? Another party or institution, such as a court or an administrative agency?

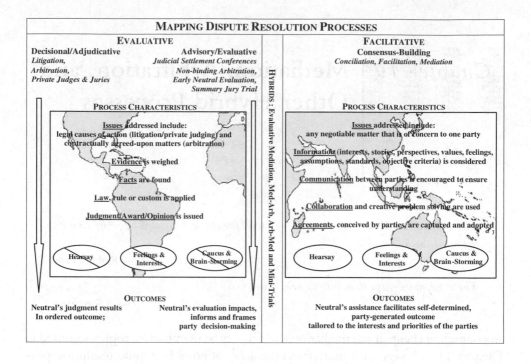

5. Is the ADR process ad hoc (designed for a particular dispute or transaction) or more formal, permanent, or institutionalized (contractual, rule-based, common practice)?

6. What is the "authority" for creation of the particular process? A contract (private ADR)? A court rule, judge's recommendation or suggestion, law, or administrative regulation (public ADR)?

7. Is entrance to the process consensual or more directed or "coerced"?

8. What are the goals or intended purposes of the process, and how might they differ from other possible processes?

9. What special areas of concern apply to the use of the process (for example, notice, fairness, ethics, inclusion, publicity, confidentiality)?

10. What other adaptations or variations of the process might be available?

One of the most attractive aspects of having various forms of dispute resolution is that individual processes can be crafted to meet the particular needs and interests of the disputants. The sections that follow discuss some combinations that are now common, but remember that the potential variations are infinite. One of the challenges in mediation when the parties cannot reach an agreement is the call to design their own special process to meet their particular needs.

A. DECISIONAL PROCESSES

Mediation cannot resolve every dispute. When parties reach an impasse, they look for a process to break the log-jam. This section explores several private adjudicative possibilities. Of course, frequently parties threaten to return to litigation (which will be more public) when mediation fails, and that option is virtually always available unless there is an agreement to use another process. But litigation may not be optimal. What other processes could be used to end a dispute? The following processes offer finality to disputants — at least when they are properly designed to do so.

1. Arbitration

Arbitration can be described most simply as a process in which a third party (or panel of third parties), who is not acting as a publicly appointed judge, renders a decision in a dispute. Arbitration has historically been used by many societies, in many contexts. Arbitration was common in ancient Rome, used by the famous merchants of Venice, and prevalent in colonial times in the United States. Arbitration is used more frequently than litigation to resolve international business disputes and to decide many other types of commercial and labor matters.

a. Variations Among the Processes Known as Arbitration

Beyond that simple definition, however, there are huge variations among processes known as arbitration. A critical distinction must be made between binding and non-binding arbitration. Binding arbitration is a process whereby the third party renders a decision that is final and binding on the disputants. Although a disputant who is dissatisfied with the award may have some opportunity to vacate that award, typically it is far more difficult to vacate an arbitral award than it is to overturn a judicial decision on appeal. In contrast, non-binding arbitral awards are merely advisory opinions. If either party is dissatisfied with the award, they can reject it and instead elect to proceed with litigation or some other form of dispute resolution. As will be discussed, however, the party who rejects the non-binding award and then does worse in court may sometimes be liable for some of the other side's costs or attorney fees or for paying the arbitrator's fee. Binding arbitration is more common than non-binding arbitration.

Another and related critical distinction must be drawn between arbitration that is elected privately by the disputing parties, most frequently in a contract before the specific dispute has arisen, and arbitration that is mandated by a statute, court rule, or treaty. In the United States, virtually all binding arbitration exists because of pre-dispute arbitration agreements that require certain future disputes to be arbitrated. As will be discussed, these pre-dispute arbitration agreements can be broken down into two subcategories: those agreements that are negotiated, knowingly, between two businesses or knowledgeable persons; and those agreements that are imposed by a business on a consumer or employee in a non-negotiable contract. Pre-dispute arbitration contracts could, but rarely do, call for non-binding arbitration, typically opting instead for binding arbitration. On the other hand, a number of U.S. statutes and court rules require disputants to use non-binding arbitration before litigating their claims. In addition, but far less often, some statutes or rules mandate binding as opposed to non-binding arbitration. As will be discussed, some would argue that state imposition of arbitration, and particularly the binding variety, is unconstitutional.

In addition to these critical distinctions, there are many other important variations in the nature of arbitration. First, there are differences depending on the choice of arbitrator(s). Sometimes a single arbitrator is used; other times a panel of three or possibly more arbitrators may be used. At times, the arbitrators may be kings, judges, former judges, or lawyers; but often the arbitrator is not a lawyer and instead is chosen on the basis of her business expertise or common sense. In some cases, the arbitrators are all expected to be completely neutral, but in other contexts (rarely outside the United States) each side picks one arbitrator who is to some degree an advocate for that side's position.

Second, the degree of formality of an arbitration varies substantially. One of the key features of arbitration is that the disputants often have the power to determine their own rules of procedure and evidence, and so it is not surprising that the nature of these rules may vary. Traditionally, arbitration was expected to be far less formal than litigation. Rules of evidence were relaxed, if used at all. Parties could represent themselves rather than rely on a lawyer for assistance. There would be minimal discovery or pre-arbitration preparation. And, arbitrators would issue few if any pre-hearing rulings. While such informality is still common in many contexts, in some business situations arbitration has instead become virtually indistinguishable from litigation. Arbitrations can involve extensive discovery; arbitrators can rule on numerous pre-hearing motions; arbitral hearings can be extremely formal, legalistic, and time-consuming; and lawyers may make arguments and introduce testimony and exhibits in an arbitration just as they might at a trial. Occasionally, class actions have even been used in arbitration. While arbitration is often a private process, it may be public as well.

Third, there is no set rule on the nature of arbitral awards. Some are oral, where others are written. Among written awards, some are extremely short and simply state which disputant prevailed (a "bare bones" award); others include lengthy reasoned analysis (a reasoned award). Similarly, whereas many arbitral awards are private, and distributed only to the disputants, others may be published.

Fourth, the way in which arbitrations are administered varies substantially. The administrator of the arbitration is the person or group who performs such tasks as helping to select the arbitrator, arranging the location, and exchanging any pre-hearing documents. Non-binding arbitration is typically administered by the parties, a court, or other governmental agency. Binding arbitration is frequently administered by a special arbitral organization. Some of the best known U.S. providers include the American Arbitration Association, JAMS,* the National Arbitration Forum, and the National Association of Securities Dealers. CPR Institute for Dispute Resolution,† while not an administrating provider, does offer rules and provide names of potential arbitrators.

b. *The Attractions of Arbitration*

Given the tremendous variation within the dispute resolution technique known as arbitration, it should be clear that disputants are attracted to arbitration for a range

---

* "JAMS" originally stood for Judicial Arbitration and Mediation Services, but the organization is now known only by its acronym.
† "CPR" originally stood for Center for Public Resources, but the organization is now known only by its acronym, or its current name CPR International Institute for Conflict Prevention and Resolution.

of reasons. In fact, arbitration is probably most popular precisely because of this flexibility. To a large extent, disputants can design exactly the process they want under the rubric of arbitration. Those disputants who are primarily looking for a speedy, low-cost dispute resolution technique can set up arbitration to meet those goals by making it quite informal and virtually non-appealable. Those disputants who seek to ensure that the decision maker has a particular background or expertise can write those requirements into the arbitration agreement. If disputants want a private non-published decision they can call for that in their agreement; but if the disputants prefer a process that is open to the public and results in a reasoned written award, that too can be arranged. In the international arena, arbitration is desirable because it allows disputants to pick a forum and decision makers who are likely more pre-disposed to be neutral than would be the home court of any disputant. Also, as a result of international treaties, arbitral awards are often more enforceable, internationally, than a court decision would be. Thus, depending on how it is structured, and depending on the context, disputants may like arbitration more than other alternative forms of dispute resolution because it can be cheap, quick, private, conducted by a neutral expert, and enforceable. The disputants can also set up a process that, as compared to litigation, is more likely to restore or improve future relationships. Binding arbitration offers the additional benefit of finality. In contrast to mediation or negotiation, which may or may not resolve a particular dispute, one can be assured that binding arbitration will result in a decision that ends the immediate controversy.

From the public standpoint, arbitration can be advantageous precisely because the disputants themselves find it desirable. In addition, to the extent that disputes are resolved privately, the public will save money it otherwise would have expended on courthouses and judges.

Notes and Questions

10.1 Arbitration is always an obvious candidate when mediation fails, although frequently, if a case is already in court, the default process is litigation. If a mediation fails, which do you think is a better process for default — arbitration or litigation? Why? Does the case type matter?

10.2 When the mediator helps the parties decide to use arbitration, there are many issues to negotiate regarding the arbitral process. From what you just read, what issues should the mediator, attorneys, and parties address?

10.3 Under the Federal Arbitration Act and most state arbitration acts, an agreement to arbitrate must be in writing to be enforceable. One agreement possibility in mediation is a written agreement to arbitrate issues left unresolved in the mediation.

2. Med–Arb and Arb–Med

One of the first-used types of hybrid processes was med-arb — mediation, followed by arbitration if the parties failed to reach agreement. This practice began in labor contexts, but it has spread to family (child custody conciliation) and commercial matters. In the original form of med-arb, the parties select an individual to facilitate the negotiation of their dispute (using all the usual ground rules of mediation, such as confidentiality and private caucusing). If and when that process fails to produce resolution, the parties have given the mediator the power of an arbitrator who then makes a decision. Med-arb can be varied in a number of interesting ways, each of which has advantages and disadvantages. In one version of med-arb, two neutrals are used. If the mediation fails to result in agreement, the mediator is replaced by a second neutral who arbitrates the dispute. In another version of med-arb, the arbitrator issues a non-binding rather than binding determination. For discussion of these and other types of med-arb, see Sherry Landry, Med-Arb: Mediation with a Bite and an Effective ADR Model, 63 Def. Couns. J. 263 (1996).

Sometimes, the order of the processes is reversed in a process known as arb-med. Here, an arbitrator hears the parties' presentations on the legal merits and makes a decision that is written down and put aside without the parties knowing the award. At the point when the arbitrator makes and puts away the decision, he loses his power to change the decision and then becomes a mediator, helping the parties settle the case. This gives the parties incentive to settle (knowing they will be subjected to the arbitrator's award if they do not), while simultaneously freeing the neutral to hear settlement information that might otherwise prejudice a decision maker. Arb-med has become common practice in many settings, including labor and employment and commercial cases. Alternatively, the arbitrator can issue a non-binding award and then allow the parties to shift to a mediation process to try to "improve" on the award. See Lawrence D. Connor, How to Combine Facilitation with Evaluation, 14 Alternatives to High Cost Litig. 15 (1996).

Some argue that combining arbitration and mediation blends the best aspects of each. The speed, efficiency, and consensual aspects of mediation are combined with the finality of arbitration. For example, some labor arbitrators find it beneficial to use mediation in situations that were formerly allocated to arbitration, such as grievances under collective bargaining agreements, because of the greater flexibility of mediation and the possibility of resolving more than a single issue at once. See Stephen B. Goldberg, Grievance Mediation: A Successful Alternative to Labor Arbitration, 5 Negot. J. 9, 11 (1989) (urging that different persons perform the mediation and arbitration roles).

However, the question of whether the same person ought to be both mediator and arbitrator is controversial. It is certainly more efficient to have the same person hear the facts of the case and interests of the parties in order to avoid duplication of effort, time, and information disclosure. On the other hand, it is not optimal from the perspective of obtaining the best evidence to have a decision maker hear from parties in caucus where the other side cannot rebut what is said. Critics also assert that the practice is problematic because mediators typically urge parties to be forthcoming and honest about their needs, interests, and facts, in settings where the disputants are assured the mediators have no power over them. If the mediators then turn into decision makers, unwary parties may find their confidences used against them. Sophisticated parties would be motivated to hide information that might sway the mediator-arbitrator. One example of this occurs in California, where family court conciliators (mediators) transform into decision-advising probation officers who sometimes reveal facts told to them in confidence during the mediation and who make arbitral-like recommendations to the court. This role switching may undermine participant trust in the whole system. At the same time, knowledge that the mediator may change roles allows savvy parties to rethink what they tell mediators, potentially undermining the effectiveness of the mediation. Similarly, critics of arb-med argue that the parties may resent the arbitrator's effort to force a "compromise" of the dispute, when what the parties seek is a clear-cut decision, assignment of liability or blame, enforcement of a rule, precedential value, or one of the other underlying reasons for choosing arbitration.

The classic work discussing "role confusion" when mediation and arbitration are combined, by Lon Fuller, is excerpted below.

 Lon L. Fuller, **COLLECTIVE BARGAINING AND THE ARBITRATOR**

in Collective Bargaining and the Arbitrator's Role: Proceedings of the Fifteenth Annual Meeting, National Academy of Arbitrators 8, 29-30, 32-33 (Mark L. Kahn ed., 1962)

Mediation and arbitration have distinct purposes and hence distinct moralities. The morality of mediation lies in optimum settlement, a settlement in which each party gives up what he values less, in return for what he values more. The morality of arbitration lies in a decision according to the law of the contract. The procedures appropriate for mediation are those most likely to uncover that pattern of adjustment which will most nearly meet the interests of both parties. The procedures appropriate for arbitration are those which most securely guarantee each of the parties a meaningful chance to present arguments and proofs for a decision in his favor. Thus, private consultations with the parties, generally wholly improper on the part of an arbitrator, are an indispensable tool of mediation.

Not only are the appropriate procedures different in the two cases, but the facts sought by those procedures are different. [There] is no way to define "the essential facts" of a situation except by reference to some objective. Since the objective of reaching an optimum settlement is different from that of rendering an award according to the contract, the facts relevant in the two cases are different, or, when they seem the same, are viewed in different aspects. If a person who has mediated unsuccessfully attempts to assume the role of arbitrator, he must endeavor to view the facts of the case in a completely new light, as if he had previously known nothing about them. This is a difficult thing to do. It will be hard for him to listen to proofs and arguments with an open mind. If he fails in this attempt, the integrity of adjudication is impaired. . . .

What, then, are the objections to an arbitrator's undertaking mediative efforts after the hearing and before rendering the award, this being often so advantageous a time for settlement? Again, the objection lies essentially in the confusion of role that results. In seeking a settlement the arbitrator turned mediator quite properly learns things that should have no bearing on his decision as an arbitrator. For example, suppose a discharge case in which the arbitrator is virtually certain that he will decide for reinstatement, though he is striving to keep his mind open until he has a chance to reflect on the case in the quiet of his study. In the course of exploring the possibilities of a settlement he learns that, contrary to the position taken by the union at the hearing, respectable elements in the union would like to see the discharge upheld. Though they concede that the employee was probably innocent of the charges made by the company, they regard him as an ambitious troublemaker the union would be well rid of. If the arbitrator fails to mediate a settlement, can he block this information out when he comes to render his award?

It is important that an arbitrator not only respect the limits of his office in fact, but that he also appear to respect them. The parties to an arbitration expect of the arbitrator that he will decide the dispute, not according to what pleases the parties, but by what accords with the contract. Yet as a mediator he must explore the parties' interests and seek to find out what would please them. He cannot be a good mediator unless he does. But if he has then to surrender his role as mediator to resume that of adjudicator, can this award ever be truly free from the suspicion that it was influenced by a desire to please one or both of the parties?

Notes and Questions

10.4 Fuller focuses on the problems that result from a single person's performing different roles. Do you find his arguments convincing? In all situations? Note that Fuller's point of view is echoed by critics of evaluative mediation in Chapter 7. What were the responses to those critiques?

10.5 To what extent are Fuller's criticisms of combining mediation and arbitration valid when different persons perform the mediation and arbitration roles?

10.6 As noted in the beginning of this section, mediation and arbitration are sometimes combined in different orders. What advantages and disadvantages do you see with how the order is established — med-arb or arb-med?

10.7 In what kinds of disputes might each variation of med-arb or arb-med be appropriate? Not appropriate? For a discussion of the use of med-arb in the international context, see James T. Peter, Med-Arb in International Arbitration, 8 Am. Rev. Intl. Arb. 83 (1997).

10.8 Robert McKersie, himself an experienced arbitrator, suggests a "conference" procedure in which the arbitrator, although empowered to resolve the dispute, first involves the parties in shaping the outcome through informal meetings in which the parties seek a mutually agreed-on outcome. The arbitrator exercises his or her decisional power only as a last resort. Is this another form of med-arb?

10.9 Recall the different models of mediation discussed in Chapter 3. Do any of these mediation models lend themselves particularly well to med-arb? Are some models less appropriate for use in med-arb or arb-med? Why?

10.10 Both bench and jury trials have been recreated in the private sector so that parties can choose their own court-like decision makers. See, e.g., Ann S. Kim, Note: Rent-a-Judges and the Costs of Selling Justice, 44 Duke L.J. 166

(1994); Stacy Lee Burns, Making Settlement Work: An Examination of the Work of Judicial Mediators (2000). Some states, like California, actually formally recognize such processes and allow appeals from a private judicial ruling, see Cal. Civ. Proc. Code §§638-645 (West Supp. 2004). Florida has also recently adopted a private judging program, known as "voluntary trial resolution." Fla. Stat. Ann. §44.104 (West 2003 and Supp. 2004). Some critics of the privatization of decisional justice argue that it is inappropriate to decide matters of public concern outside the viewing of the public. Some complain about the "vanishing trial" as more and more dispute resolution is privatized. See Symposium, The Vanishing Trial, 1 (3) J. of Empirical Studies (2003); Marc Galanter, Report to Symposium on the Vanishing Trial, Section on Litigation, American Bar Association, Dec. 2003; Ellen E. Sward, A History of the Civil Trial in the United States, 51 U. Kan. L. Rev. 347 (2003); see also Carrie Menkel-Meadow, Is the Adversary System Really Dead?: Dilemmas of Legal Ethics as Legal Institutions and Roles Evolve, in 57 Current Legal Problems 85 (Jane Holder ed., 2005). It can also be argued that it is inappropriate to tamper with the natural demographics of the jury pool and that using this private tool may erode public confidence in the public jury trial. For an article on the use of the private jury trial, see Margaret A. Jacobs, Legal Beat: Private Jury Trials: Cheap, Quick, Controversial, Wall St. J., July 7, 1997, at B1.

10.11 Should private parties be able to recreate the public justice system on a private basis? Does this recreation harm the public in any way? Does your answer depend on whether the parties recreate bench or jury trials?

10.12 What downsides, if any, are there to allowing private judicial determinations to be enforced and appealed as if they had been made by public judges?

10.13 Does a private ADR process that formally adjudicates facts, parties' rights, or legal issues raise different issues from one that attempts to facilitate settlement without deciding anything? When private parties choose to use laypeople as a mock jury focus group merely to provide an advisory opinion, what issues are raised by this choice?

10.14 If public judges can go private, either by retiring and becoming private arbitrators and mediators or by formally becoming "rent-a-judges" under California's unique rules, shouldn't laypeople be permitted to rent out their services as private jurors? Why or why not?

B. EVALUATIVE/ADVISORY PROCESSES

Courts offer a variety of processes to help litigants assess the merits of their case as an aid to settlement. When mediation fails to resolve substantive issues, these other processes may still be available. Many of these evaluative processes are offered in private settings as well. As you read the following section, which aspects of each process would be different in a private setting and which aspects can be maintained?

1. Mandatory Judicial Settlement Conferences

Many federal and state judges require disputants to attend settlement conferences or use ADR processes, and parties often find such processes useful. In issuing such orders, judges often rely on Rule 16 of the Federal Rules of Civil Procedure and its state equivalents. The initial version of Rule 16, entitled "Pre-Trial Procedures; Formulating Issues," authorized courts to require attorneys to appear before them for pretrial conferences. In 1983, the rule was amended to specify that such conferences might "facilitat[e] the settlement of the case." Fed. R. Civ. P. 16(a)(5). The current version of the rule makes even clearer that judges may "take appropriate action, with respect to . . . settlement and the use of special procedures to assist in resolving the dispute when authorized by statute or local rules." Fed. R. Civ. P. 16(c)(9). It specifically allows courts to "require that a party or its representative be present or reasonably available by telephone in order to consider possible settlement of the dispute." Fed. R. Civ. P. 16(c).

The institutionalization of settlement and other forms of dispute resolution is controversial. Judges have authority and experience that make them particularly expert in predicting probable outcomes in an evaluative context, and they are usually well respected as "wise neutrals" because of their selection process and the formal rules that govern judicial neutrality, recusals, and conflicts of interest. On the other hand, some analysts argue that judges, who are supposed to perform adjudicatory roles, should not be involved in the settlement process — most certainly when the judge at the settlement conference might be the same one to ultimately find the facts or rule on the legal issues. Judges, these critics argue, are not trained to act as facilitative mediators, and adjudication (with rules of evidentiary admissibility) should be separated from efforts to settle the case — often on grounds different from the legal merits. To some extent, this debate mirrors the concerns raised earlier in the chapter about med-arb. A second controversy surrounds the question of whether institutionalizing settlement or other forms of dispute resolution actually serves the intended purpose of saving time and money. Carrie Menkel-Meadow discusses both issues below.

 Carrie Menkel-Meadow, **FOR AND AGAINST SETTLEMENT: USES AND ABUSES OF THE MANDATORY SETTLEMENT CONFERENCE**

33 UCLA L. Rev. 485, 490-494, 497-498, 506-511, 513-514 (1985)

THE SETTLEMENT CONFERENCE: A VERY BRIEF HISTORY

Several municipal courts in the United States began utilizing both voluntary and court-structured conciliation in the early twentieth century. From what we know of this early history, the primary impulse behind these efforts seems to have been related to substantive process — producing harmony among the parties and resolving disputes with communitarian values that the court assumed were shared by the disputants. At some point in the 1920's efficiency concerns became a part of the rhetoric surrounding settlement. Judicial reformers spoke of conciliation as a method of curing court delay. . . . Conciliation or settlement methods were largely dependent on the practices and personalities of particular judges and on an informal transmission and socialization process. As is so often the case in legal reform, the debates of today reflect the two different past justifications of conciliation: substantive process values and efficient delay reduction. . . .

THE EVIDENCE ON SETTLEMENT CONFERENCES: WHAT DO THE DATA DEMONSTRATE?

. . . The first systematic study of the pretrial conference was undertaken by Maurice Rosenberg on mandatory conference, voluntary conference, and nonconference cases in New Jersey. That study reported findings, as yet uncontradicted, that mandatory pretrial conferences improved the quality of trial proceedings, but actually reduced the efficiency of the court by consuming judges' time in handling conferences, rather than in trying cases. Plaintiff "victories" were as frequent (all cases were personal injury cases) in mandatory conference cases as in other cases, though pretried cases were likely to result in higher recoveries. Most significantly, cases submitted to mandatory pretrial conferences were no more likely to result in settlements than those that were not. . . . In addition to quantitative analysis of the data collected, the Rosenberg study also consisted of interviews with and observations of judges with a variety of views on the judicial role in settlement conferences. Some judges participated as passive, neutral referees of the dispute; others were actively engaged in case management (i.e., issue clarification); still others saw settlement as one of their most useful functions. One of the most interesting and seldom noted implications of the Rosenberg study is that if parties achieve settlement with equal frequency in mandatory, voluntary, and nonconference cases, judicial settlement management may indeed be an inefficient use of judicial time. . . .

One study of the role of courts found that 75% of federal judges and 56% of state judges initiate settlement discussions in jury trials. I will explore what judges actually do in settlement conferences below, but it is instructive to note that despite all the academic criticism of the judicial settlement role, lawyers overwhelmingly seem to favor judicial intervention. In a recent study of lawyers from four federal district courts, Wayne Brazil (then law professor, now United States magistrate judge) found that a "staggering 85 percent of our respondents agree that 'involvement by federal judges in settlement discussion [is] likely to improve significantly the prospects for achieving settlement.' " A majority of these lawyers felt that settlement conferences should be mandatory. A more detailed analysis of the data reveals that most of the respondent lawyers in this study do not see the principal advantage of judicial involvement as efficiency, but as a complex web of qualities that are thought to produce better, and perhaps earlier, settlements. The lawyers valued judicial intervention in settlement proceedings most when it was analytic, active, based on the knowledge of specific facts of the case, rather than superficial formulas or simplistic compromises, and there are explicit suggestions or assessments of particular solutions. . . .

THE FUNCTIONS AND PURPOSES OF THE MANDATORY SETTLEMENT CONFERENCE: THE HOW AND WHY OF SETTLEMENT PRACTICES

As greater numbers of judges and courts use settlement conferences, our information about particular practices increases. . . . What emerges from the data is a variety of role conceptions that parallel the various conceptions of the goals of settlement. For some, efficient case management is the primary role; for others, the primary role is the facilitation of substantive or procedural justice. For others still, the primary role is simple brokering of what would occur anyway in bilateral negotiations. Some judges avoid active settlement activity because they view adjudication as their primary role. . . .

A. The Dangers of Efficiency-Seeking Settlement Techniques

For those who seek to use the settlement conference as a docket-clearing device, the conference becomes most problematic in terms of the substantive and process values (i.e., *quality* of solution) previously discussed. Judges see their role as simplifying the issues until the major issue separating the parties (usually described as money) is identified and the judge can attempt to "narrow the gap." In one study judges and lawyers were asked to report on judicial settlement activity. Seventy-two percent of the lawyers reported that they participated at least once in settlement conferences in which the judge requested the parties to "split the difference." The same study noted that when local rules require settlement conferences judges tend to be more assertive in their settlement techniques (using several techniques that some of the lawyers considered to be unethical). According to the study, jurisdictions with mandatory settlement conferences took more time in moving cases toward trial. This confirms the findings of earlier studies.

A much touted settlement technique is the use of the "Lloyds of London" formula: The settlement judge asks the parties to assess the probabilities of liability and damages and, if the figures are within reasonable range, to split the difference. The difficulty with such settlement techniques is that they tend to monetarize and compromise all the issues in the case. Although some cases are reducible to monetary issues, an approach to case evaluation on purely monetary grounds may decrease the likelihood of settlement by making fewer issues available for trade-offs. Furthermore, a wider definition of options may make compromise unnecessary. . . . The irony is that settlement managers, who think they are making settlement easier by reducing the issues, may in fact be increasing the likelihood of deadlock by reducing the issues to one. Furthermore, as I have argued at length elsewhere, using money as a proxy for other interests the parties may have, may thwart the possibilities for using party interests for mutual gain.

In addition to foreclosing a number of possible settlements, the efficiency-minded settlement officer seems prone to use coercive techniques such as suggesting a particular result, making threats about taking the case off the docket, directing meetings with clients or parties. Lawyers find these techniques problematic. Thus, the quest for efficiency may in fact be counterproductive.

B.   The Search for Quality Solutions

Some recent data seem to indicate that greater satisfaction can be achieved with a different settlement management role — the facilitator of good settlements. Brazil's survey of lawyers practicing in four federal districts reveals that lawyers favored intervention techniques that sought to produce the "best result." Lawyers favored such techniques because judges who analyzed the particular facts of the case (as opposed to those who used formulas like "Lloyds of London"), offered explicit suggestions and assessments of the parties' positions, occasionally spoke directly to recalcitrant clients, and expressed views about the unfairness of particular results. Brazil's data are interesting in that they point to variations in the desirability of particular settlement techniques, depending on size of case, case type, defense or plaintiff practice, and other demographic factors.

What emerges from Brazil's data is that lawyers want different things in different cases. Thus, a routinized settlement agenda is not likely to be successful in satisfying their desires. More significantly, the data show that lawyers do not perceive judges' settlement role as significantly different from their adjudicative role when the judges employ the more favored settlement techniques. In alternative dispute resolution parlance, the lawyers of Brazil's study seek a hybrid of the adjudicator — the "med-arb" (mediator-arbitrator):

> They prefer that judges express opinions, offer suggestions, or analyze situations much more than they value judges asking the attorneys to make a presentation or conduct an analysis. Our respondents consistently give higher effective ratings to settlement conference procedures that revolve around inputs by judges than those that feature exposition by counsel. Thus, the lawyers' assessments of specific techniques reinforce the major theme that what litigators want most from judges in settlement conferences is *an expression of analytical opinion.* . . .

[Wayne A. Brazil, Settling Civil Cases: What Lawyers Want from Judges, Judges' J., Summer 1984, at 14, 16.]

To the extent that settlement procedures are used to achieve substantive outcomes that are better than court-defined remedies, they have implications for how the settlement conference should be conducted and who should conduct it. First, those with knowledge about the larger implications of the litigation — the parties — should be present (this is the principle behind the mini-trial concept with business personnel in attendance) to offer or accept solutions that involve more than simple money settlements. Second, such conferences should be managed by someone other than the trial judge so that interests and considerations that might effect a settlement but would be inadmissible in court will not prejudice a later trial. Some argue for a separate "settlement officer" because the skills required for guiding negotiations are different from those required for trying cases. Third, some cases in which issues should not be traded off should not be subjected to the settlement process at all. For example, in employment discrimination cases, parties should not be asked to accept monetary settlements in lieu of a job for which they are qualified. Finally, a more traditional mediator's role may be more appropriate when the substantive process (i.e., direct communication between the parties) may be more important than the substantive outcome (i.e., employer-employee disputes, some civil rights cases).

CONCLUSION

... The settlement conference is a process that can be used to serve a number of different ends. How we evaluate its utility depends on whether we are looking at the individual dispute being settled, the numbers of cases on the docket, the quality of the results (measured against cases that would have settled anyway and cases that would have gone on to trial), the effect of the number and types of settlements on the number and types of cases that remain in the system, or the alternatives available. These considerations do not all point in the same direction. The evaluation of settlement conferences is something we will have to keep watching. . . .

Can judges, who are historically neutral rule declarers, fact finders, and expeditors, perform this new function without a new socialization process? As settlement conferences become mandatory, socialization of settlement officers and research and evaluation of the settlement process must be conducted simultaneously. If many judges use the sorts of "Lloyds of London" formulas described above, additional training will be necessary to expose settlement officers to the problematic aspects of these practices. Settlement officers will have to learn not how to commodify and monetarize all issues, but rather how to identify alternative issues that the parties may value differently, in the hope of reaching settlements that are fair, perhaps norm-based, and that take account of the parties' needs. To the extent that I have criticized the limited remedial imagination of courts, the settlement conference provides an opportunity to temper the rigidity of win/loss trials with flexible solutions.

Notes and Questions

10.15 The line between ADR and more purportedly "traditional" forms of dispute resolution (litigation and administrative agency processes) has never been as sharp as some might think. There have always been judges and lawyers who encouraged settlement. Similarly, some jurisdictions adopted non-binding arbitration programs over one hundred years ago.

The recent emphasis on alternatives to litigation has brought these alternatives right into the traditional litigation system and into governmental and administrative processes that were once handled on a more adversarial basis. This institutionalization of ADR can be linked to the 1976 Pound Conference, discussed in Chapter 1.

The institutionalization of alternative approaches can also be linked to several important pieces of federal legislation. The Civil Justice Reform Act of 1990 encourages all federal courts to reduce cost and delay. As part of this effort, the Act authorizes each district court to "refer appropriate cases to alternative dispute resolution programs that . . . have been designated for use in a district court; or the court may make available, including mediation, minitrial, and summary jury trial." 28 U.S.C. §473(a)(6) (2000). Two other important pieces of legislation were also passed in 1990 to encourage the use of ADR in the administrative context. The Negotiated Rulemaking Act of 1990, 5 U.S.C. §§561-570 (2000), permits federal agencies to bring together public and private entities and individuals to draft federal regulations. The Administrative Dispute Resolution Act of 1990, 5 U.S.C. §§571-584 (2000), permits and encourages federal agencies to use mediation, arbitration, and other alternative processes to resolve disputes quickly and informally. Finally, the Alternative Dispute Resolution Act of 1998, 28 U.S.C. §§651-658 (2000), focuses again on the courts, but this time mandates, rather than encourages, the use of alternative processes. In particular, the Act requires "[e]ach United States district court . . . to authorize, by local rule . . . the use of alternative dispute resolution processes in all civil actions. . . . " 28 U.S.C. §651(b) (2000).

10.16   Do you think there should be uniformity in how judges and courts approach settlement and other ADR practices, or is it appropriate for there to be local variation and discretion (whether at the level of court or individual judge)? See John Maull, ADR in the Federal Courts: Would Uniformity Be Better?, 34 Duq. L. Rev. 245 (1996). What arguments favor each approach?

As the Model Code of Judicial Conduct is being revised, there have been demands for a uniform rule prohibiting judges who preside over settlement talks to preside over any subsequent trial of the same matter. Some have argued that such a rule should not be uniform because of the dearth of judges in some less populous areas of the country who might have to perform several roles within their courts. Others suggest that distinctions should be drawn between bench trials and jury trials. See ABA Joint Commission to Evaluate the Model Code of Judicial Conduct, Proposed Model Rule 2.08, Hearings, June 3, 2005, 73 U.S.L.W. 2783. (June 28, 2005). What do you think the rule should be with respect to judicial participation in settlement proceedings and subsequent trials? Why?

10.17   Although it has been clear since 1993 that Rule 16 permits courts to order represented parties, as well as their lawyers, to attend settlement conferences, this was not always the case. In G. Heileman Brewing Co. v. Joseph Oat Corp., 871 F.2d 648 (7th Cir. 1989), the Seventh Circuit, *en banc*, considered whether, under an earlier version of the rule, a court was justified in sanctioning a company $5,860 (opposing party's fees and costs) for failing to comply with the court's order to send a principal of the company to a pretrial conference. The court held that "the action taken by the district court in this case constituted the proper use of inherent authority to aid in accomplishing the purpose and intent of Rule 16." 871 F.2d at 652-653. At the same time, the majority opined that a representative required to attend with "authority to settle" did not mean that the representative must settle "on someone else's terms, but only that they come to court in order to consider the possibility of settlement." Id. at 653. Why do you suppose courts have been eager to require parties, as opposed to just their attorneys, to attend settlement conferences? For an extensive discussion of the *Heileman* case and this issue, see Leonard L. Riskin, The Represented Client in a Settlement Conference: The Lessons of *G. Heileman Brewing Co. v. Joseph Oat Corp.*, 69 Wash. U. L.Q. 1059 (1991), and the discussion of *Heileman* in Chapter 7.

10.18   Pre-trial conferences, in one form or another, have been around for decades. What is different about the modern pre-trial conference is its emphasis not on pre-trial preparation and narrowing of trial issues but on efforts to encourage (some would say coerce) settlement. To what extent are pre-trial conferences that seek to narrow issues for trial different from settlement conferences that broaden the number of issues in order to increase the likelihood of trades between differentially valued items, as negotiation theory suggests? If pre-trial conferences have different purposes or draw on different techniques, as is suggested above, who should conduct them? Should there be different conferences for different purposes? How is a pre-trial conference different from mediation?

10.19 In a variant on the settlement conference, some courts have a "settlement week." During a specified period of time, regular trial assignments are suspended for an entire courthouse, and judges, magistrates, and often volunteer lawyers spend the entire period meeting with lawyers and parties in "settlement conferences" that may resemble either mediation, in its facilitative or evaluative forms, or non-binding arbitration. As you might imagine, some argue that this suspension of the trial docket for judges to perform other roles is *ultra vires* judicial roles and unauthorized by statutes or court rules. Despite such objections, many courts (mostly at the state level) still pursue this settlement device in an effort not only to settle particular cases and reduce court caseloads (the efficiency criterion) but also to educate lawyers and parties about negotiation, mediation, and other settlement techniques and theories (the qualitative approach). What do you think of the practice? What advantages and disadvantages do you see?

2. Non-binding Arbitration

In non-binding arbitration, the arbitrator's award becomes binding only if it is accepted voluntarily by the disputants. Here, the purpose of the arbitration is not to guarantee a final resolution of the dispute, but rather to give the disputants a good prediction of how the claim would be resolved if it went to trial. The hope is that once the disputants learn of this prediction, and have the opportunity to go through a process that is similar to what they might obtain in court, they will voluntarily abide by the arbitrator's decision. Although non-binding arbitration can be and sometimes is agreed to contractually, most non-binding arbitration that takes place in the United States occurs pursuant to court order or rule.

Many courts have adopted non-binding arbitration programs with the hope that they will afford a quicker, cheaper form of justice than does litigation. Certain jurisdictions, such as Pennsylvania, have used mandatory court-supervised arbitration for quite a few years. For a discussion of the history of the Pennsylvania program, founded in the 1800s, see Jerold S. Auerbach, Justice Without Law? at 48 (1983). Other state and federal jurisdictions adopted mandatory non-binding arbitration programs more recently, in the 1980s and 1990s. Many of the federal programs were established in response to the Civil Justice Reform Act of 1990. At present, over half of the states have rules allowing non-binding arbitration. See John D. Feerick, Toward Uniform Standards of Conduct for Mediators, 38 S. Tex. L. Rev.

455, 456 (1997). About a quarter of the federal district courts have a non-binding arbitration program. Elizabeth Plapinger & Donna Stienstra, Source Book on Federal District Court ADR and Settlement Procedures (Federal Judicial Center 1996). However, a number of federal court programs have replaced their mandatory non-binding arbitration programs with mediation. Lisa B. Bingham, Why Suppose? Let's Find Out: A Public Policy Research Program on Dispute Resolution, 2002 J. Disp. Resol. 101, 120.

Court-connected arbitration programs require that certain categories of disputes be heard by arbitrators before they can be aired in court. For example, Local Rule 53.2 of the Eastern District of Pennsylvania requires that virtually all suits brought for less than $150,000 proceed initially to non-binding arbitration. Nevada Arbitration Rule 3 provides that, with certain exceptions, all civil cases brought for $40,000 or less must be handled first through non-binding arbitration.

In most programs, the arbitrators are local attorneys or retired judges, but how they are chosen and conduct the arbitration varies substantially. Some programs assign the arbitrators to a case and afford the litigants little or no opportunity to choose or even reject arbitrators, whereas other programs allow disputants to select their own arbitrators. In addition, in some programs arbitrators sit in panels, as in Pennsylvania, and hear several cases in a day. But, in Nevada, court-annexed arbitrators hear cases individually and typically hear only a single matter in a day.

The economics of court-annexed arbitration also vary. In some jurisdictions, the program is free to disputants, and the arbitrators serve on a volunteer basis or receive a small honoraria such as $100 per case. But, in other jurisdictions, such as Nevada, the disputants are required to pay for court-annexed arbitration. The Nevada Arbitration Rules require disputants to pay arbitrators $100 per hour to a maximum of $1,000 per case (unless otherwise authorized by the arbitration commissioner) and further require payment of up to $250 in costs to the arbitrator. These fees and costs are shared between the disputants.

Most court-annexed arbitration rules provide that the ordinary rules of evidence may be "relaxed" and that the arbitrators also have discretion to modify the types and timing of discovery from that which would be permitted in court. These rules are intended to make the process speedier and cheaper than litigation would be.

The non-binding arbitration rules of many jurisdictions provide that the arbitration award shall become final and binding unless either party demands a trial *de novo* within a short period of time, such as 30 days. Thus, although the award is non-binding, it can easily become binding. Some jurisdictions seek to discourage parties from seeking a trial *de novo* by providing that a party who seeks trial *de novo* and secures a result less favorable than the arbitrator's award must pay a significant amount. See Cal. Civ. Proc. Code §1141.21 (2002) (requiring party, less successful on appeal, to pay opposing party's court costs and expert fees, and also to reimburse county or opposing party for fees paid to arbitrator); Nevada Arbitration Rule 20 ("Where the arbitration award is $20,000 or less, and the party requesting the trial *de novo* fails to obtain a judgment that exceeds the arbitration award by at least 20 percent of the award, the no-requesting party is entitled to its attorneys fees [to a maximum of $10,000] and costs associated with the proceedings following the request for trial *de novo*"). In other jurisdictions, the risk is far less, since the party who unsuccessfully pursued a trial *de novo* will only lose the arbitrator fees of $100 or so. E.D. Pa. Local Rule 53.2(7)(E).

Many policy issues surround the use of mandatory court-annexed non-binding arbitration, including questions of constitutionality. Although court-mandated non-binding arbitration remains popular in some jurisdictions, it is unclear whether these programs meet the goal of resolving disputes more cheaply and quickly than they would have been resolved through a combination of litigation and negotiation. Some books and articles discussing non-binding arbitration include Jane W. Adler et al. Simple Justice: How Litigants Fare in the Pittsburgh Court Arbitration Program (1983); Lisa Bernstein, Understanding the Limits of Court-Connected ADR: A Critique of Federal Court-Annexed Arbitration Programs, 141 U. Pa. L. Rev. 2169 (1993); Deborah R. Hensler, What We Know and Don't Know About Court-Administered Arbitration, 69 Judicature 270 (1986); Barbara S. Meierhoefer, Court-Annexed Arbitration in Ten District Courts (Federal Judicial Center 1990); Judge William P. Lynch, Problems with Court-Annexed Mandatory Arbitration: Illustrations from the New Mexico Experience, 32 N. Mex. L. Rev. 181 (2002); Note, L. Christopher Rose, Nevada's Court-Annexed Mandatory Arbitration Program: A Solution to Some of the Causes of Dissatisfaction with the Civil Justice System, 36 Idaho L. Rev. 171 (1999).

Notes and Questions

10.20 Non-binding arbitration can also be agreed to privately by parties (outside the context of a litigated case). Note that non-binding arbitration avoids the risk of finality on the one hand, but on the other hand may not end the dispute.

10.21 As you consider these evaluative processes, consider whose evaluation you would value most as a party — a judge's, a respected "expert" arbitrator, a jury's, an expert's. Of course, if you are using an evaluative process in the hope of ending a dispute, you would want an advisory opinion that would also be persuasive to the other side.

3. The Summary Jury Trial

As the ADR movement gained momentum, judges began to use new procedural techniques more creatively. The private mini-trial, described later in this chapter, was so successful in the late 1970s and early 1980s that federal judge Thomas Lambros of Ohio imported aspects of it for use in federal courts. The practice spread to state courts as well. See Thomas D. Lambros, The Summary Jury Trial and Other Alternative Methods of Dispute Resolution: A Report to the Judicial Conference of the United States Committee on the Operation of the Jury System, 103 F.R.D. 461 (1984). In summary jury trials, used in jury cases containing contested factual or legal liability questions, lawyers present shortened versions of their cases (usually no more than part of a day), drawing on argument, testimony, or summarized depositions and documentary evidence. The audience, members of a regular jury venire who don't actually serve as jurors, deliberates and offers what is ultimately only an advisory verdict. The verdict is then communicated to the parties to encourage more realistic negotiations. This process was credited with providing lodestar damage assessments in some kinds of repeat cases, such as those involving asbestos, reducing caseloads, and offering individualized assessments in cases with conflicting lawyer or party demands. This process also creates controversy because of its mandatory nature, its unorthodox use of jurors (who often don't know they are not "real" jurors), and its use of public courtrooms to facilitate private settlements. See Richard Posner, The Summary Jury Trial and Other Methods of Alternative Dispute Resolution: Some Cautionary Observations, 53 U. Chi. L. Rev. 366 (1986) (suggesting evaluative criteria for judging the effectiveness and legality of the summary jury trial as a substitute for formal adjudication).

Notes and Questions

10.22 Can you think of categories of cases that summary jury trials particularly suit? Does it matter if the conflicts between the parties are factual or legal ones? If witness credibility is at issue? If the law is unclear?

10.23 Do judges have authority to create processes that are not formally contemplated by the applicable rules of procedure? What is the source of the judge's authority to order participation in such processes? Recall that the Seventh Circuit held in *G. Heileman Brewing* that courts had the "inherent power" to require parties to attend settlement conferences. Is or should this power be unlimited? Should the state pay (for jurors and courtroom usage) to assist in what ultimately amounts to a negotiation process?

10.24 Can private parties who have filed complaints in court privately contract for some other kind of dispute processing while their case remains pending? If so, should they have to tell the court about their private pursuits? Explain your answer.

10.25 Should summary jury trials that take place in a public courtroom be open to the public, or can the parties claim they are merely engaged in a "private" negotiation session that is not open to the public? The Sixth Circuit faced this question in Cincinnati Gas & Elec. Co. v. General Elec. Co., 854 F.2d 900 (6th Cir. 1988). It held that courts "have the power to conduct summary jury trials under either Fed. R. Civ. P. 16, or as a matter of the court's inherent power to manage its cases." Id. at 903 n. 4. It then went on to reject the idea that the public or press had a right to observe the summary jury trial under the First Amendment, reasoning that summary jury trials are analogous to settlement negotiations that are shielded from the public eye. Do you think this is a good analogy? Why or why not?

10.26 The question of whether a court may mandate parties' participation in the summary jury trial was also examined by the Seventh Circuit, in Strandell v. Jackson County, Ill., 838 F.2d 884 (7th Cir. 1987). Coming to the opposite conclusion as did the Sixth Circuit, the Seventh Circuit found that Rule 16 did not permit courts to mandate the use of a summary jury trial. Id. at 887.

Note also that the Seventh Circuit had earlier approved the use of mandatory settlement conferences in _Heileman._ In your view, are these divergent results reconcilable? Why or why not?

10.27 Following the criticisms of the summary jury trial on the theoretical, policy, doctrinal, and empirical grounds suggested by Judge Posner and the _Strandell_ court, James Alfini studied the reception of summary jury trials in both state and federal courts. His 1989 article drew on data collected from interviews of lawyers in two Florida federal and state jurisdictions. He concluded that the process was viewed more favorably by lawyers in the voluntary state court program than by lawyers in the mandatory federal court program. James J. Alfini, Summary Jury Trials in State and Federal Courts: A Comparative Analysis of the Perceptions of Participating Lawyers, 4 Ohio St. J. on Disp. Resol. 213, 233 (1989). Even in the state court program, the lawyers interviewed believed that the process was not appropriate for cases in which liability was disputed based on divergent views of the facts. Id. at 217.

10.28 Consider the concern that, if the purpose of the summary jury trial is to give parties a more realistic assessment of the value of their claims, other decision makers might be more appropriate than an involuntarily "conscripted" federal or state jury. In fact, there has been a little experimentation with another form based on the summary jury trial, called the summary judge or summary bench trial, in which essentially the same procedures as the summary jury trial are used. However, in a summary bench trial, a magistrate judge or a judge other than the one formally assigned to the case issues a non-binding verdict to assist in settlement negotiations. Do you think this summary judge trial is more or less problematic than the summary jury trial? Why?

4. Early Neutral Evaluation

Instead of using jurors or judges to facilitate a settlement within the court system, some courts have developed hybrids that draw on mediation, arbitration, and case management and valuation practices. Early Neutral Evaluation (ENE) uses volunteer or paid lawyers to help parties assess the value of a case before trial and, in some cases, assist in fact development and discovery issues. ENE was first developed in the federal courts in the Northern District of California (San Francisco), while a similar system, called "Michigan mediation," was developed in the state trial courts there. In both settings, the practice involves shortened case presentations (with varying degrees of documentary or witness evidence, discovery completion, and argumentation) to either a single lawyer (California federal practice) or a panel of three lawyers (in Michigan), who then evaluate the case. The evaluation may suggest either substantive strengths or weaknesses in the case or attach a numerical value to what a likely verdict would be. This non-binding evaluation is then used to facilitate settlement negotiations by the parties and their lawyers. In some cases, if the evaluation does not result in a settlement, the neutral evaluators may assist the parties with other matters, such as developing a discovery schedule, streamlining issues for trial, or planning other settlement events.

The Federal District Court for the Northern District of California sets out its process on its Web site, *http://www.cand.uscourts.gov*. It explains that the goals of ENE are to:

- Enhance direct communication between the parties about their claims and supporting evidence
- Provide an assessment of the merits of the case by a neutral expert
- Provide a "reality check" for clients and lawyers
- Identify and clarify the central issues in dispute
- Assist with discovery and motion planning or with an informal exchange of key information
- Facilitate settlement discussions, when requested by the parties.

The district court Web site explains that "settlement is not the major goal of ENE, but the process can lead to settlement." Under the district court's plan, the evaluator provides a written assessment (samples are provided on the Web site), and parties are given the opportunity to negotiate a resolution either prior or subsequent to hearing the evaluation. The neutral may also help facilitate these negotiations. Attendance at the ENE is mandatory not only for the lead trial attorney for each side but also for "clients with settlement authority and knowledge of the facts" and for "insurers of parties," if their agreement would be necessary for a settlement to occur. Id.

For further discussion of the ENE process, see generally W.D. Mich. L. Civ. R. 16.4; Wayne D. Brazil, A Close Look at Three Court-Sponsored ADR Programs: Why They Exist, How They Operate, What They Deliver, and Whether They Threaten Important Values, 1990 U. Chi. Legal F. 303; Robert J. Niemic, Donna Stienstra & Randall E. Ravitz, Guide to Judicial Management of Cases in ADR (2001); Elizabeth Plapinger & Donna Stienstra, ADR and Settlement in the Federal District Courts: A Sourcebook for Judges & Lawyers (1996).

Notes and Questions

10.29 In the Northern District of California, ENE neutrals are lawyers who have 15 years of experience in practice, experience with federal court litigation, expertise with respect to the substantive law pertinent to the case, and court training. Do you think those credentials are appropriate? Would you impose different or additional requirements? What kind of training should courts provide to such neutrals? Should courts monitor the performance of such neutrals?

10.30 Assuming it is appropriate for courts to help parties settle their cases, through such programs as ENE, court-sponsored mediation and arbitration, summary jury trials, or judicially managed settlement conferences, should the courts provide these services for free, or should the parties pay for them? List factors that support your conclusion.

10.31 The extent to which communications made in the course of an ENE session are confidential is critically important. In the Northern District of California, communications made in ENE sessions are generally confidential, meaning they cannot be conveyed to the judge, subject to certain exceptions. N.D. Cal. ADR L. R. 5-12. What exceptions do you think might be necessary?

C. MEDIATION AND HYBRIDS USED IN SPECIFIC ARENAS

1. Restorative Justice: Mediation in Criminal Contexts

Although most people think of using ADR only with respect to civil disputes, it is also used to handle conflicts arising in the criminal context. "Victim-offender" mediation and "restorative justice" aim to make the victim whole (or at least more whole), to instill some sense of remorse and responsibility in the offender, and, more generally, to heal the conflict and restore the fabric of communities torn apart by crime. While some programs focus on caseload reduction, most programs focus on the broader themes of forgiveness and reconciliation, with reconciliation being sought not only for its own sake but to prevent vengeance and vigilantism. These forms of ADR are used in settings ranging from neighborhood disputes and minor misdemeanors all the way up the criminal ladder to serious felonies and murder. Proponents of restorative justice advocate approaching crime and punishment from more than just a legalistic perspective.

One of the leading figures in the restorative justice movement is a social worker in Minneapolis, Mark Umbreit. Mark S. Umbreit, Mediation of Victim-Offender Conflict, 1988 J. Disp. Resol. 85. The movement has now spread to many different jurisdictions around the country, see, e.g., David Lerman, Restoring Justice, Tikkun (Sept.-Oct. 1999), at 13, and exists in a number of countries outside the United States as well.

 Marty Price, **PERSONALIZING CRIME: MEDIATION PRODUCES RESTORATIVE JUSTICE FOR VICTIMS AND OFFENDERS**

7 Disp. Resol. Mag. 8, 8-11 (2000)

Our traditional criminal justice system is a system of retributive justice — a system of institutionalized vengeance. The system is based on the belief that justice is accomplished by assigning blame and administering pain. If you do the crime, you do the time. If you do the time, then you've paid your debt to society and justice has been done. But justice for whom?

In our system, crime is defined as an act against the state (e.g., State v. John Jones) rather than an act against individuals and their community. The prosecutor is the attorney for the state, not the harmed individuals. Victims may be viewed, at worst, as impediments to the prosecutorial process — at best, as valuable witnesses for the prosecution of the state's case. Only the most progressive prosecutor's offices view crime victims as their clients and prioritize the needs of victims.

The criminal justice system is offender-centered, placing its emphasis upon guilt, punishment and the rights of the accused. Crime victims' so-called rights are violated as often as they are honored. In most victims' rights amendments and statutes, these are rights without remedies.

Incarceration may be said to serve functions other than retribution: incapacitation, deterrence and rehabilitation. Public safety requires incapacitation of the minority of incarcerated offenders who are violent and dangerous. Intuitively, incarceration (or the threat of incarceration) may seem like a deterrent, but its proven deterrent effects are extremely limited. It is generally agreed that some rehabilitation programs work (notably, drug treatment), but rehabilitation as a goal of imprisonment has been widely abandoned by the corrections system in the United States since the 1970s. Although it is difficult to justify empirically on a broad scale, punishment appears to be a societal value in and of itself. Politicians cry out for more and longer prison terms; the building of prisons has become a major growth industry. In some states, the corrections budget exceeds the education budget.

PUNISHMENT OFTEN UNSATISFYING FOR MANY VICTIMS OF CRIME

Because our society defines justice in terms of guilt and punishment, crime victims often seek the most severe possible punishment for their offenders. Victims believe this will bring them justice, but it often leaves them feeling empty and unsatisfied. Retribution cannot restore their losses, answer their questions, relieve their fears, help them make sense of their tragedy or heal their wounds. And punishment cannot mend the torn fabric of the community that has been violated.

FOCUS ON INDIVIDUALS, HEALING

Restorative justice has emerged as a social movement for justice reform. Virtually every state is implementing restorative justice at state, regional and/or local levels. A growing number of states that have officially adopted restorative justice principles and policies require any justice program that receives state funding to adhere to these principles.

Instead of viewing crime as a violation of law, restorative justice emphasizes one fundamental fact: crime damages people, communities and relationships. Retributive justice asks three questions: who did it, what laws were broken and what should be done to punish or treat the offender? Contrast a restorative justice inquiry, in which three very different questions receive primary emphasis. First, what is the nature of the harm resulting from the crime? Second, what needs to be done to "make it right" or repair the harm? Third, who is responsible for the repair?

Traditionally, accountability has been viewed as compliance with program rules or as taking one's punishment. But accepting punishment is passive, requiring nothing from the offender. A restorative justice system holds the offender accountable by facilitating and enforcing reparative agreements, including restitution. Restorative justice recognizes that we must give offenders the opportunity to right their wrongs and redeem themselves, in their own eyes and in the eyes of the community.

A DIFFERENT PARADIGM

Restorative justice is not any one program. It is a different paradigm for understanding and responding to issues of crime and justice. Restorative justice takes its most familiar forms in victim-offender mediation (VOM) programs and victim-offender reconciliation programs (VORP). Other restorative justice responses to crime include family group conferencing, community sentencing circles, neighborhood accountability boards, reparative probation, restitution programs, restorative community service, victim and community impact statements and victim awareness panels.

As the most common application of restorative justice principles, VOM/VORP programs warrant examination in detail. These programs bring offenders face to face with the victims of their crimes, with the assistance of a trained mediator, usually a community volunteer. Victim participation is always voluntary; offender participation is voluntary in most programs.

In mediation, crime is personalized as offenders learn the human consequences of their actions, and victims have the opportunity to speak their minds and their feelings to the one who most ought to hear them, contributing to the victim's healing. Victims get answers to haunting questions that only the offender can answer. The most commonly asked questions are "Why did you do this to me? Was this my fault? Could I have prevented this? Were you stalking or watching me?" Victims commonly report a new peace of mind, even when the answers to their questions were worse than they had feared.

Offenders take meaningful responsibility for their actions by mediating a restitution agreement with the victim to restore the victims' losses in whatever ways possible. Restitution may be monetary or symbolic; it may consist of work for the victim, community service or other actions that contribute to a sense of justice between the victim and offender.

FULFILLING RESTITUTION

VOM programs have been mediating meaningful justice between crime victims and offenders for more than 25 years. There are now more than 300 programs in the United States and Canada and more than 700 in England, Germany, Scandinavia, Eastern Europe, Australia and New Zealand. Remarkably consistent statistics from a cross-section of the North American programs show that about two-thirds of the cases referred resulted in a face-to-face mediation. More than 95 percent of the cases mediated resulted in a written restitution agreement. More than 90 percent of those restitution agreements are completed within one year. In contrast, the rate of payment of court-ordered restitution is typically only from 20-to-30 percent. Recent research has shown that juvenile offenders who participate in VOM subsequently commit fewer and less serious offenses than their counterparts in the traditional juvenile justice system. . . .

CAREFUL PREPARATION REQUIRED

Mediation is not appropriate for every crime, every victim or every offender. Individual, preliminary meetings between mediator and victim, mediator and offender permit careful screening and assessment according to established criteria. Pre-meetings are essential to case development, allowing for thorough preparation of participants to assure safe and successful mediation. In situations as emotionally charged as crimes, it would be difficult — in many cases impossible — to bring victims and offenders into dialogue if not for the trust each builds with the mediator.

At their best, mediation sessions focus upon dialogue rather than the restitution agreement (or settlement), facilitating empathy and understanding between victim and offender. Ground rules help assure safety and respect. Victims typically speak first, explaining the impact of the crime and asking questions of the offender. Offenders acknowledge and describe their participation in the offense, usually offering an explanation and/or apology. The victim's losses are discussed. Surprisingly, a dialogue-focused (rather than settlement-driven) approach produces the highest rates of agreement and compliance.

Agreements the victim and offender make together reflect justice that is meaningful to them, not limited by narrow legal definitions. In multistate and international (United States, Canada and United Kingdom) studies, the overwhelming majority of participants — both victims and offenders — have reported in post-mediation interviews and questionnaires that they obtained a just and satisfying result. Victims who feared re-victimization by the offender before the mediation typically report this fear is now gone.

Forgiveness is not a focus of VOM, but the process provides an open space in which participants may address issues of forgiveness if they wish. Forgiveness is a process, not a goal, and it must occur according to the victim's own timing, if at all. For some victims, forgiveness may never be appropriate.

Restorative justice requires an offender who is willing to admit responsibility and remorse to the victim. Where a defendant maintains a not guilty plea in contemplation of a genuine defense — "I didn't do it," self-defense, diminished capacity, etc. — there is no place for mediation until such issues are resolved. Where a defendant maintains a pro forma not guilty plea only to preserve the possibility for plea negotiations, a restorative justice process may be appropriate. (Such a situation may raise issues regarding the confidentiality of the mediation. These concerns are beyond the scope of this article.)

DIFFERENT CONCEPT OF NEUTRALITY

. . . VOM requires specialized training beyond the basic skills of conflict resolution. Mediators are trained to guide the sensitive process of preparing victims and offenders to come face to face. Further advanced training is needed to mediate in crimes involving severe violence. Most victim-offender programs limit their service to juvenile offenses, crimes against property and minor assaults, but a growing number of experienced programs have found that a face-to-face encounter can be invaluable even in heinous crimes.

A number of programs have now mediated violent assaults, including rapes, and mediations have taken place between murderers and the families of their victims. Mediation has been helpful in repairing the lives of surviving family members and the offender in drunk-driving fatalities. In severe crime mediations, case development may take a year or more before the mediation can take place.

VOM may be useful at any stage of the criminal justice process. For young offenders and first- or second-time offenders, mediation may provide diversion from prosecution. In these cases, charges may be dismissed if the offender mediates an agreement with the victim and complies with its terms. After a guilty plea or a conviction, a court may refer an offender to VOM as a part of the sentence or as a term of probation. In cases of severely violent crime, VOM has not been a substitute for a prison sentence, and prison terms have seldom been reduced following mediation. Mediations have even taken place in prison. Impending release of an offender may motivate victims to seek mediation, and mediations have taken place after release from prison.

THE POWER OF REMORSE

As societal values, we want those who offend to "fess up, make amends and change their ways." Ironically, our adversarial criminal justice system conspires against these values. A defendant's role in the system is to assist his attorney in denying responsibility and avoiding consequences. The defense attorney properly advises the client to "admit nothing, say nothing." The understandable anger and bitterness that crime victims feel is often exacerbated because the defendant's stance (silence, avoidance of eye contact) communicates denial of responsibility and lack of remorse. Sadly, in many cases the defendant has, on advice of counsel, stifled a sincere desire to approach the victim in apology and contrition.

After the criminal justice system has validated such behavior as a defendant's proper role, the defendant may eventually negotiate a guilty plea or be found guilty. The issue of guilt resolved, we as a society now want the offender to shift gears and admit responsibility for the offense. Not surprisingly, such admissions are not often forthcoming.

WHAT CAN WE LEARN?

What can attorneys and other dispute resolution professionals learn from the philosophy and successes of restorative justice? Our system, which settles most cases without trial, does so with adversarial assumptions as its foundation. Each attorney is expected to maximize her client's win at the expense of the other attorney's client's loss. In the majority of cases, the clients of both attorneys (and often the attorneys, as well) feel like losers in the settlement.

The most important lesson learned from restorative justice practice may be the realization that the key to justice is found not in laws but in the recognition and honoring of human relationships. If the application of restorative justice principles can bring justice and healing to some of the most grievous losses that human beings can suffer, the potential for more effective conflict resolution in other arenas must be considered. If crimes or disputes are not resolved with relationship values guiding the process, it is predictable that all parties may walk away feeling like losers or like victims — feeling that justice has not been done.

When lawyers are viewed as healers of conflicts, it will be a clear indicator that our justice system has become restorative in its assumptions, goals and priorities. Regrettably, there will always be a need for adversarial processes for resolution of the situations where, sadly, the conflicts cannot be healed restoratively. In these intractable cases, we will employ the adversarial contest as the means for "alternative dispute resolution."

Notes and Questions

10.32 How do you react to a restorative justice model that uses mediation in a criminal context? Do you see this process as a supplement to or substitute for the traditional criminal justice system? As another variation on the restorative justice theme, there are now over 300 "problem solving courts" in the United States, which use rehabilitation, acknowledged responsibility, and monitored treatment, sometimes in combination with punishment, instead of more conventional adjudication, see Greg Berman & John Feinblatt, Good Courts: The Case for Problem-Solving Justice (2005). Judges in these courts often see themselves more "holistically," serving as mediation-like social workers, with a judicial "edge" or power lurking in the background. See Judith S. Kaye, Changing Courts in Changing Times: The Need for a Fresh Look at How Courts Are Run, 48 Hastings L.J. 851 (1997). Like all hybrid processes, these new courts are controversial. See Anthony C. Thompson, Courting Disorder: Some Thoughts on Community Courts, 10 Wash. U. J. L. & Poly. 63 (2002). Can you think of objections that could be made to these new forms of courts?

10.33 Are there particular kinds of cases that you think are appropriate or inappropriate for this form of dispute resolution? Why?

10.34 Is restorative justice possible in a world of determinate sentencing? Mediation and restorative justice require discretion, flexibility, and degrees of "softness" in the system, qualities that determinate sentencing seeks to remove for reasons of justice and equity. How do we resolve these tensions?

10.35 The use of a restorative justice approach raises interesting legal questions. For example, as Price observes, the question as to whether confidentiality is afforded can be critically important to the offender. While the offender's guilt has typically been established for the crime at issue in the mediation, what should happen if the offender confesses to other past or planned crimes during the course of a VOM? The answer depends on the law of the particular jurisdiction.

10.36 Questions can also be raised regarding the constitutionality of restorative justice processes. See Joan W. Howarth, Toward the Restorative Constitution: A Restorative Justice Critique of Anti-Gang Public Nuisance Injunctions, 27 Hastings Const. L.Q. 717, 744-754 (2000); Mary Ellen Reimund, Mediation in Criminal Justice: A Restorative Approach, 46 Advocate (Idaho B.J.) 22, 24-25 (May 2003).

10.37 Numerous analysts have criticized restorative justice. Some argue that there is either no community left to be restored in modern America or that community justice may be coercive. Robert Weisberg, Restorative Justice and the Danger of "Community," 2003 Utah L. Rev. 343. Others suggest that power imbalances between the victim and the offender (with the state casting a deep shadow) remove the very premises of equality and voluntarism in mediation models. Are these critiques valid in your view? How might defenders of the programs respond? Can you think of other reasons that make restorative justice objectionable? On a systemwide basis? In individual cases? Should restorative justice be optional and individually chosen, or is there some social benefit in establishing systemwide or community-based programs? See Shari Tickell & Kate Akester, Restorative Justice: The Way Ahead (2004), for a review of restorative justice practices in a variety of different legal jurisdictions.

2. The Mini-Trial: A Hybrid Process in the Corporate Context

In 1977, a group of creative lawyers were faced with a complex and expensive patent infringement lawsuit that threatened to cost millions of dollars and to publicly reveal trade secrets.* These lawyers designed a special new legal process called the "mini-trial." The process took several months to plan but only two days to conduct. A settlement in principle was reached within a half hour after the proceeding ended. What the parties arranged was an informal (private, outside of the pending litigation) process that combined elements of many different dispute resolution processes. Through a negotiated agreement on procedural rules, the parties in Telecredit, Inc. v. TRW, Inc. engaged in expedited discovery for several months, deposed key witnesses, and exchanged a limited number of documents. During the two-day proceeding, retained counsel presented, in structured but abbreviated time, their "best case" in arguments along with their supporting evidence to the top management of both companies. The proceeding was presided over by a neutral advisor, former Federal Court of Claims Judge James Davis, an expert in patent infringement matters. His official duties, as negotiated by the parties, were to moderate the proceedings and to keep order, but not to rule in any way on the outcome. As the parties agreed in advance, if they did not reach a negotiated agreement at the end of the information exchange, Judge Davis was to supply a non-binding opinion discussing the strengths and weaknesses of each party's case and predict how a court might rule on the merits. The parties agreed that everything exchanged during this special proceeding would be inadmissible at any subsequent trial. Parties, lawyers, and the neutral advisor all asked questions of each other, and all participants later disclosed that they learned new things from the proceeding. After the information exchange, the top management officials negotiated without their lawyers. Management resolved the matter according to business interests, not just legal principles.

As described above, the mini-trial uses negotiation, non-binding evaluation (arbitration), and some aspects of mediation (in the role of the neutral advisor). What is most unusual about the mini-trial is that top management negotiates directly without lawyers. These negotiations are founded on the companies' business interests, as well as the executives' perspectives on their litigation prospects. They form their view of these prospects after hearing the positions of the other side directly from the other side, rather than as filtered through their own lawyers.

---

* This description of the process is taken from The CPR Legal Program Mini-Trial Handbook, in 1982 CPR Corporate Dispute Management, at MH-5 (Eric D. Green et al. eds., 1982). For further analysis of *Telecredit* by some of the lawyers involved, see Eric D. Green, Jonathan B. Marks & Ronald L. Olsen, Settling Large Case Litigation: An Alternative Approach, 11 Loy. L.A. L. Rev. 493 (1978).

For some years after this first mini-trial, the process was used often in high stakes cases. It was particularly attractive in cases where the parties sought to avoid the high costs of litigation, get informal advice from noted experts, keep the subject matter of their disputes private, or avoid the inevitable vagaries of having issues resolved by lay juries or judges who were presumed not to know enough about complex business disputes or complicated legal issues. The mini-trial was especially valued for getting clients (especially CEOs or high-level government officials) to pay close attention to a particular matter. In part, the idea was that concentrated and focused attention at an early stage of a dispute would prevent economic waste by avoiding protracted discovery, longer trials, expensive expert witnesses, and lost management time from company officials spending time in court. Advocates of the mini-trial, such as Eric Green, formalized its use in a "Mini-Trial Handbook" and other procedural protocols.

Over time, however, use of the mini-trial has diminished, perhaps because if high-level officials spend too much time in "direct and focused" attention on disputes, they spend too much time at mini-trials and not enough time managing. Some also think mini-trials are quite expensive to run, after taking into account attorneys' fees, high neutral advisor fees, and lost work time for key corporate or government officials.

Perhaps the greatest strength of the mini-trial is indirect, in that it demonstrates that parties can develop alternatives to both courts and the more conventional alternatives to courts on an informal, ad hoc basis. The concept of a negotiated process resulting in a dispute resolution agreement or protocol, crafted for a particular purpose, dispute, or transaction, continues to be an important part of ADR. As you will see in later chapters, professionals in dispute resolution now counsel clients about the appropriateness of particular processes for their matters, tailor-make processes for single matters, or serve as "system designers" who develop dispute resolution mechanisms for classes of disputes or for whole entities, including government agencies, corporations, and other organizations.

Notes and Questions

10.38 Given the enormous expense of litigating or arbitrating large commercial disputes, it is curious that mini-trials, and the business-oriented solutions they produce, are not on the rise. What might account for this phenomenon?

10.39 One reported example of a business-oriented resolution coming from a mini-trial is connected with a dispute between Texaco and Borden over natural gas supplies. The case involved claims for $200 million and complex contract and anti-trust questions. In a several week mini-trial, the companies negotiated a different gas-supply contract and made new arrangements for gas transportation. No money changed hands. See Texaco-Borden Antitrust Mini-Trial Sets Record, Alternatives to the High Cost of Litigation, March 1983 at 1, as discussed in Out of Court: The Mini Trial, CPR Institute for Dispute Resolution (1987).

3. Online Dispute Resolution Mechanisms: Taking Mediation into Cyberspace

Some of the most innovative forms of dispute resolution are those developed for use on the Internet. Variously called EDR (electronic dispute resolution) or ODR (online dispute resolution), these online processes vary tremendously. Some ODRs directly involve the Internet (such as claims relating to sales made on the Internet or relating to rights over Web site addresses). Other ODRs resolve disputes having nothing to do with the Internet, such as automobile accidents. Sometimes the ODR consists simply of taking conventional forms of mediation or arbitration and conducting the process through words and e-mails rather than face-to-face. At other times, more unusual methods are used, including auctions, blind-bidding, or a "behind the screen" mediation conducted by an unseen moderator, either in real time or with sequential discussion. ODR will change quickly as technology changes. For example, as Web-based cameras become more common, the line between online and live hearings may become fuzzier. For an excellent overview of ODR, see *http://www.odr.info* (The Center for Information Technology and Dispute Resolution). Some of the best-known online providers include *http://www.squaretrade.com* (which handles many disputes relating to eBay); *http://www.cybersettle.com* (which uses a double-blind bidding system to resolve many personal injury claims involving insurance); *http://www.hamaar.com* (which handles insurance and other commercial disputes); and the World Intellectual Property organization, *http://arbiter.wipo.int* (which handles intellectual property disputes). You can view decisions pertaining to conflicts over domain name ownership at *http://www.icann.org/udrp*. For a book providing a general discussion of online dispute resolution, see Ethan Katsh & Janet Rifkin, Online Dispute Resolution: Resolving Conflicts in Cyberspace (2001).

The use of ODR raises unique issues of both over- and under-use of technology. Does the absence of a "real" person, whether neutral or participant, incite parties to more conflict, or does the necessity of using written words slow down communication and require people to think before they write, encouraging more rational discourse than might occur in person? Does this particular medium encourage parties to overemphasize narrowly defined aspects of the dispute? Can an electronic written dispute really ever be confidential, even with encryption and other protections? Does this form of communication prevent significant human connection from occurring? Does dispute resolution on the Web make resources for creative solutions more immediately available to a broader audience? Will parties participate more actively in the drafting of their agreements when they can easily see and utilize each other's words? Will middlemen and brokers, such as lawyers and agents, become less useful when people use the Internet to communicate with each other directly? How or why should ODR be regulated when the rest of the Web is largely unregulated? Are there particular issues in ODR that are *sui generis* to technology, or are the issues essentially the same as in other forms of dispute resolution?

In the following article, psychologist and law professor Janice Nadler examines some of the psychological issues raised by replacing in-person dispute resolution with ODR.

Janice Nadler, **ELECTRONICALLY-MEDIATED DISPUTE RESOLUTION AND E-COMMERCE**

17 Negot. J. 333, 337–340, 342–346 (2001)

TRUST AND EMOTION ON-LINE

When dispute resolution occurs face-to-face, people have available to them a wide range of interpersonal cues that facilitate understanding that we often take for granted. Politeness rituals, such as smiling, nodding, making direct eye contact, and verbal acknowledgments (e.g., "uh-huh," "ok"), help communicate both positive emotion and also indicate that the other person's message is understood. But on-line dispute resolution takes place in a socially impoverished environment. As a result of the absence of important cues, on-line communication is more difficult, and the process of resolving the dispute can deteriorate quickly.

In on-line communication, humor, an important social lubricant, can be misinterpreted or simply absent. In addition, expression of positive emotion is often cumbersome — we can't rely on smiling, eye contact, or verbal markers of understanding. In an on-line dispute environment, people may be tempted to use the strategy of being a squeaky wheel — using negative emotion tactics to extract the desired concessions from the opponent. . . . Disputes arising from on-line auction transactions may be particularly prone to negative emotion, because the parties are strangers during the transaction, and they are now angry about the dispute.

The electronic medium can itself contribute to an atmosphere where the disputants view the mediator and each other with suspicion. In electronic communication where the absence of social cues leads to feelings of social distance, we tend to attribute malevolent motives to the other person. Negative emotion, blaming, and sinister attributions can quickly get out of control and escalate in on-line communication, more so than in a face-to-face situation. As a Squaretrade executive recently observed, the vulnerability of on-line consumers to initial feelings of hostility and mistrust lead them to suspect: "I am a scam victim!" . . . Indeed, this proposition has been borne out in empirical studies. . . .

Flaming and other expressions of negative emotions are more likely to erupt over electronic media, in part because people pay less attention to etiquette in this context, and in part because people perceive the squeaky wheel strategy as the best method for getting their preferred outcomes from the dispute. In fact, one study found that people are eight times more likely to flame in electronic discussion than in face-to-face discussion. To help e-mail communicators combat this phenomenon through self-regulation, the makers of Eudora 5.0, a popular e-mail program, have incorporated a feature called "Moodwatch" into the program. Moodwatch acts as an "emotion monitor" for the e-mail writer and flags any message that is "aggressive, demeaning, or rude." The program rates messages containing questionable language and marks them with one, two, or three chili peppers to indicate the level of an e-mail's emotional hotness. The Moodwatch feature is designed to let the writer know that they are about to send an e-mail message that they might later regret. . . . Participants in on-line mediation or arbitration are also likely to find that conflicts escalate more quickly than they do face-to-face, and this process of conflict escalation frequently functions as a roadblock in the process of information exchange required for a mutually beneficial decision or settlement.

On the other hand, the same remoteness that prompts flaming and suspicion also can allow cooler heads to prevail. Emotion might be diffused more easily on-line than face-to-face because disputants have more time to think and cool down. In an electronic setting, the person who made you so angry initially is not physically in front of you to make you more angry. The third party can use the asynchronous nature of the exchange to encourage cooler heads. It is therefore important in an on-line dispute resolution context to give people the opportunity to vent their frustrations and negative attributions. This exercise makes people feel better and also gives the third party an opportunity to understand where the deal went wrong and what negative attributions parties are making, and thereby successfully identify a solution that will satisfy both sides. For example, the Squaretrade "direct negotiation" process is structured so that participants are provided an opportunity to communicate their frustrations, but only after they are first greeted with a screen that provides encouraging information about the on-line dispute resolution procedure they would be using ("Over 80 percent of [users] . . . said they would use the service again."). . . .

TEMPORAL ASYNCHRONY

When disputants meet face-to-face with a mediator, or appear in person before an arbitrator, they can explain their concerns verbally, and wait to see the third party's reaction to their side of the story. In addition, any questions about the process that a disputant might have can be posed in such a face-to-face meeting and answered on the spot. In a face-to-face arbitration, disputants have an opportunity to present their side of the story verbally to the arbitrator, and they ordinarily have the opportunity to hear the other side's story at the same time. In simple disputes, the entire process frequently takes place over the course of one meeting or hearing. Conversations that occur in a face-to-face setting also benefit from the natural verbal back-and-forth rhythm present in a normal conversation.

When dispute resolution occurs on-line, by contrast, the communication is necessarily asynchronous. . . .

Typically in face-to-face conversation, we take turns speaking so that we develop a conversational rhythm. This pattern of synchronous rhythm gives us an opportunity to anticipate our turn to speak, acknowledge understanding, request clarification, or express a reaction or a new idea. By contrast, in on-line communication, we do not have the opportunity to engage in the same kind of instantaneous clarifications and spontaneous reactions that we have in face-to-face communications. Instead, on-line communicators tend to rely on longer, more complex messages without being interrupted by the other person. . . . In a mediation context, this allows for the conveyance of more semantic information in a given message, but at the same time, it does not allow for brief, on-line verbal interjections to check understanding ("so what you're saying is . . ."). Moreover, participants in on-line mediation are missing other cues, such as tacit ongoing requests for clarification (e.g., facial expressions of puzzlement, or a verbal "hmm?"), and brief contemporaneous indications of understanding (e.g., head nods or a verbal "uh-huh").

Empirical research on the effects of on-line dispute resolution is just beginning. However, we can expect that the result of electronically mediated dispute resolution and its attendant missing signals would be a greater potential for misunderstanding and, ultimately, a greater likelihood of impasse in e-mediation compared to face-to-face mediation. Empirical research on e-negotiation supports this hypothesis. Compared to face-to-face negotiators, people who negotiate using email become frustrated with the inability to ask for information repeatedly and receive immediate responses. Delays in receiving replies can quickly become a source of irritation, as negotiators attempt to unilaterally force progress by jumping to final proposals rather than letting them emerge naturally (e.g., "If I don't get your answer by tomorrow, then I assume that you agree with my proposal"). In general, e-negotiators have less trust than face-to-face negotiators that their opponent is bargaining in good faith. Mutual distrust, breakdown of communication, and impasse are often the consequence. It is therefore imperative in an on-line dispute resolution context that the parties are provided clear expectations at the outset about the ground rules and pace of the process, and of the importance of clear and explicit statements of fact and responses to minimize the misunderstandings that arise from the impoverished on-line medium. . . .

These procedural differences raise questions regarding the aftermath of the dispute. . . . Do the unique procedural features of electronic dispute resolution make any difference to disputants' satisfaction after settlement is reached? Of course, these questions are best answered with data gleaned from empirical investigation. Because new communication technologies have only recently been used in dispute resolution systems, few (if any) empirical investigations of e-disputant attitudes toward settlement have been undertaken to date. We can, however, set forth hypotheses about the effects of electronic communication technology on disputants' acceptance of and satisfaction with dispute resolution outcomes, on the basis of existing theory and research in the social psychology of procedural justice.

PROCEDURAL JUSTICE AND DISPUTE RESOLUTION

[Nadler here summarizes the procedural justice literature that we have discussed previously, emphasizing that disputants' decisions about whether to accept or reject dispute resolutions depend crucially on the extent to which the procedures used are perceived as fair: whether the disputant's views were fully considered, the disputant was treated with respect, and the disputant was treated in an evenhanded, nondiscriminatory way by behaving in an open, fact-based fashion.]

If electronic dispute resolution systems lack many interpersonal and institutional cues that signal inclusion, esteem, respect, and dignity, then disputants may come away feeling like the process was not fair. As a result, they may be less satisfied with the outcome, and less likely to comply with the settlement or decision. . . . It must be noted, however, that while the concerns raised here are hypothesized based upon established theory in the face-to-face context, empirical investigations of the consequences of electronically-mediated dispute resolution on participants' fairness perceptions are in the very early stages. It is not until empirical data are made available that we will have a good understanding of these phenomena. . . .

Despite the concerns raised here, electronic dispute resolution appears to be a viable alternative to traditional systems of dispute resolution. Although on-line dispute resolution is still a new phenomenon, there are nonetheless numerous examples of successful mediation and arbitration systems that operate in cyberspace . . . suggesting the possibility that on-line dispute resolution systems incorporate certain successful aspects of traditional dispute resolution, as well as uniquely successful characteristics of the on-line environment that compensate for the deficits described earlier. We must keep in mind, however, that at this early stage, we do not yet have the benefit of empirical evidence upon which to base these hypotheses; until such empirical research is done, any discussion regarding the relative success of on-line and off-line dispute resolution systems, and the factors underlying such success remains speculative.

Notes and Questions

10.40 The next time you make a less-than-pleasing purchase on the Internet, try contacting one of the ODR services and keep a record of your interactions. Does dispute resolution over the Internet feel different from in-person dispute resolution? Do you have any way of knowing how many people were involved in the dispute? For additional readings on the psychology of ODR, see Michael W. Morris, Janice Nadler, Terri Kurtzberg & Leigh L. Thompson, Schmooze or Lose: Social Friction and Lubrication in E-Mail Negotiations, 6 Group Dynamics 89-100 (2002); Leigh L. Thompson & Janice Nadler, Negotiating via Information Technology: Theory and Application, 58 J. Soc. Issues 109 (2002).

10.41 One can view the Internet as a world unto itself that offers unique opportunities for dispute resolution. One commentator suggests that cyberspace is different from real space in that (1) it creates a virtual community based on interests rather than proximity; (2) communications transcend time, space, and reality; and (3) it tends to eliminate the significance of geographic and political boundaries. Robert C. Bordone, Electronic Online Dispute Resolution: A Systems Approach — Potential Problems, and a Proposal, 3 Harv. Negot. L. Rev. 175, 177-183 (1998). Given these fundamental differences between the physical and online worlds, Bordone goes on to propose a system of ODR that might be used to resolve disputes regarding online communications between persons residing in cyberspace. His system depends on a Web page staffed by a dispute diagnostic specialist who would create a private chat room for the dispute and then determine what kind of ODR process would be best. What do you think of this proposal? Do instant messaging and chat rooms eliminate Nadler's concerns with asynchronous communication? If you were designing a system for resolving disputes arising from online communications, what would your goals be? What kind of system might you design? For further readings on dispute system design, see Chapter 11.

The possibilities for creating processes responsive to the needs of parties in particular disputes are limited only by the imagination. We have not covered all of the possibilities here. The next chapter addresses how lawyers and mediators can help parties to select processes for particular disputes, both when a dispute has arisen and planning for disputes before they occur.

 **Chapter 11** | Counseling and Planning for Mediation

Plan the dive and dive the plan.

— Anonymous

Counseling clients about appropriate dispute processes, including mediation, is an attorney task that precedes entry into mediation proper. Sometimes, of course, mediation is not the most appropriate process for a dispute. This chapter begins by examining client counseling about process choice. Mediators are also counselors, in that they help parties examine and re-examine alternative approaches for resolving a dispute. Counseling skills and theories about matching particular controversies to the best process stay central even in mediation.

Mediation is most often used when disputes are already underway. In the second section, this chapter shows how attorneys and parties can think about the use of mediation and other processes to avoid conflicts through advance planning, and to establish optimal methods of addressing conflicts when they arise. This is known as dispute system design. Dispute system design not only creates prevention and planning strategies; it also educates the parties about constructive dispute resolution approaches. It is increasingly common for lawyers, working both for individuals and for organizations, to be called on to design systems of dispute resolution, sometimes called "integrated dispute resolution." As you will see, mediation plays a major role in disputing systems; on the other hand, it is only one of several approaches. The way it is placed in a dispute system will affect its usefulness. To illustrate how to use dispute system design principles, the chapter concludes with advice about appropriate dispute resolution clauses in diverse settings.

A. COUNSELING ABOUT DISPUTE RESOLUTION OPTIONS

How do lawyers counsel their clients about dispute resolution processes? How do mediators help parties explore process options? This section examines these questions. The counseling process rarely occurs in a linear fashion. As a lawyer counsels a client about dispute resolution processes, the lawyer's and client's understanding of the problem evolves. Initial discussions about the client's interests and options are then modified and analyzed as the lawyer and the client attempt to resolve the problem. And as a mediation progresses, an understanding of individual and common interests among the parties and mutually attractive options evolves and shifts. As a result of this movement, there is ongoing analysis concerning optimal procedure.

The lawyer and mediator must understand the array of dispute resolution processes, and they also must be able to make those processes—and the opportunities and risks they represent—clear to the parties. The lawyer is the primary translator of legal processes for the client. The vast majority of clients, facing a dispute for the first time, have little knowledge of how dispute resolution fits within our legal system. While some clients will have gained exposure to litigation from television, movies, or books, very few will have gained knowledge of other dispute resolution processes. The burden to inform and educate, let alone advise and counsel, may actually be greater when dealing with alternatives to litigation than with litigation itself. Counseling about dispute resolution should reflect the same values that problem solving itself promotes—self-determination, voice, and client empowerment.

This section begins by examining the importance of a client's interests (looking beyond the legal merits of a situation) and of distinguishing interests from positions. The chapter then turns to the actual skills of client interviewing and counseling, focusing on how to obtain critical information and then how to advise the client. The listening techniques covered in Chapter 5 would be appropriate to review at this time. Next is a discussion of different approaches in choosing among dispute resolution processes. How does one evaluate the strengths and weaknesses of each process based on the particular conflict and the interests of the client? Finally, this chapter discusses the primary public policy issue related to dispute resolution counseling: whether lawyers should be required to counsel about alternative dispute resolution processes.

1. Learning Your Client's Interests

The first excerpt discusses the importance of uncovering the legal *and* nonlegal concerns of your client, *as the client defines them.* Of course, helping the client be reflective and insightful about underlying interests is part of the job of a counselor. To study the skills necessary to learn about clients' needs and interests more systematically see David Binder, Paul B. Bergman, Susan Price & Paul K. Tremblay, Lawyers as Counselors: A Client-Centered Approach (2d ed. 2004).

 Warren Lehman, **THE PURSUIT OF A CLIENT'S INTEREST**

77 Mich. L. Rev. 1078, 1079, 1088-1090 (1979)

Clients come to lawyers for help with important decisions in their business and private lives. How do lawyers respond to these requests, and how ought they? Doubtless many clients, thinking they know what they want—or wishing to appear to know—encourage the lawyer to believe he is consulted solely for a technical expertise, for a knowledge of how to do legal things, for his ability to interpret legal words, or for the objective way he looks at legal and practical outcomes. . . .

What I want to discuss in the balance of this article is how utilitarianism in specific kinds of familiar counseling situations leads to giving clients bad advice, advice that sacrifices their humanity in the name of seemingly self-evident goods.

My father-in-law, Charles Wooster, tells of clients of his, a husband and wife, who had been moved to give a sizeable gift to a friend who had shown them care and love. Mr. Wooster encouraged them to put off giving until the next year because a gift given that year would have been taxed less heavily. The following January, husband and wife were killed in the same accident, before the gift was delivered; there was thereafter no way to transfer the gift. The intended donee had lost out because of Mr. Wooster's tax advice. So, too, the donors had been denied the pleasure of bestowing the gift. The event suggests to a nice conscience that perhaps the advice had been wrong in the first place. Mr. Wooster was unhappy with the result, but could see nothing else — with the clients alive before him and no crystal ball — that would have been right for him to have done. . . .

A practicing lawyer, call him Doe, who also teaches client counseling, said that he is very concerned, in doing estate matters, with the possibility that a client will be overborne by information about tax consequences. His tactic to avoid that result is to persuade his client — before there is any mention of those consequences — to expand in as much detail as possible upon what it is he wants to do. Only after that does Doe point out costs and mention ways the client's plan could be changed to save money. In teaching as well as practice, Doe is trying to take account of the power a lawyer has to impress upon a client the importance of his lawyerly considerations. The progress represented by Doe's concerned approach is the recognition that the client's values may not be the lawyer's, or more precisely, that the real, live client's interests may not match those of the "standard client" for whom lawyers are wont to model their services. . . .

I told Doe of a friend of mine, a widow recovering from alcoholism, who is fifty-four years old. Her house has become a burden to her, perhaps even a threat to her sobriety, although it might seem overly dramatic to say as much to a stranger. If she waits until she is fifty-five, the better part of a year, the large capital gain on the house will be tax free. She decided she did not want to go to a lawyer for fear he might talk her into putting off the sale. I asked Doe if that were realistic. He said her fear was well grounded; a lawyer might well give her the impression that another year in the house ought to be suffered for the tax saving. (I expect a lawyer's inclination to press the merits of his money-saving advice reflects, among other things, a desire to feel that his expertise is really useful. We may know no other way to judge our own usefulness.)

One possible analysis of these cases is that suggested by Doe: that the lawyer needs to be careful to discover what it is the client is really about, to give fullest possible opportunity for her interests to be explored, and to avoid the over-bearing assertion of simple money saving. . . .

Notes and Questions

11.1 Lehman notes that most lawyers use a morally neutral utilitarian model in counseling their clients. From a utilitarian approach, lawyers give advice based on practicality or long-run consequences rather than morality. Lehman argues that such an approach is problematic for a number of reasons. First, the lawyer considers a hypothetical, standardized client rather than the specific client. This results in advice that does not account for particular interests (e.g., recognizing a friendship or maintaining sobriety). Second, the lawyer may encourage the client to put off present gratification to the future. The result is that the client does not realize his own interests because the lawyer views the alternative act as more rational. Why is giving utilitarian advice appealing? Why might it be dangerous?

11.2 How should lawyers value non-legal concerns compared to legal ones? How should lawyers help their clients compare these?

11.3 The alternative to an approach that solicits client interests and client-centered decisions is often called the hierarchical approach to lawyer-client relations. For example, the Wisconsin Bar Association in 1959 offered this advice:

> Most lawyers spend too much time in interviewing clients. This is very wasteful and costly to the lawyer. . . . Get at the client's problem immediately and stick to it. Don't bother to explain the reasoning processes by which you arrive at your advice. The client expects you to be an expert. This not only prolongs the interview, but generally confuses the client. The client will feel better and more secure if told in simple straightforward language what to do and how to do it, without an explanation of how you reached your conclusions.

Quoted in Joseph Goldstein & Jay Katz, The Family and the Law: Problems for Decision in the Family Law Process 87 (1965). What are the advantages to you as a lawyer of the hierarchical approach? What are the advantages and disadvantages to the client?

2. Interviewing Skills

Interviewing skills are critical in helping clients choose a dispute resolution process and, once representation is underway, in making sure client goals and needs are being met. To ensure this, regular communication with the client is necessary. The lawyer who either assumes she knows what the client wants or, even more troublesome, substitutes her own judgment for the client's, fails the client. Yet communication between lawyer and client does not always occur as often or as well as it should. Recall the material in Chapters 5 and 6 on listening. Listening is difficult. It is both a science and an art.

In working with a client, in addition to ascertaining a client's interests, a lawyer must develop rapport — a good relationship and client confidence in his competence. Competent lawyers in initial interviews engage in ice-breaking to make clients comfortable; problem identification, often gleaned from responses to open-ended questions; and amassing a detailed overview — often chronological — of the situation leading to the problem. Getting the facts is important and is not as easy as calling for them. One must consider how to get information flowing, whether the information concerns a thoughtful assessment of interests and feelings, how to develop an accurate factual picture, and how to ask the client to help generate options. This challenge of obtaining information occurs not only in initial interviews, but also in subsequent interviews and mediation sessions. For a good review of techniques for questioning clients, using facilitators, and avoiding inhibitors of good information gathering and rapport developing, see David Binder, Paul B. Bergman, Susan Price & Paul K. Tremblay, Lawyers as Counselors: A Client-Centered Approach (2d ed. 2004).

Notes and Questions

11.4 Attorneys can find communicating with their client difficult, sometimes more difficult than conversations with the other side. Here again, mediators have an important role to play in drawing out clients so they can be understood more fully by their attorney and by their counterpart.

11.5 In addition to difficulties attorneys experience in uncovering their client's interests, attorneys also complain that it is hard to make clients adopt a realistic picture of their BATNA. How might you (as attorney) enlist the mediator in the counseling task of making a client appreciate his BATNA?

11.6 This section is primarily addressed to lawyers interviewing clients. How is the advice on lawyer interviewing and counseling relevant to mediators as well?

3. Choosing Among Dispute Resolution Processes

Once a client's interests are known, how can attorneys help clients meet their interests by utilizing the appropriate or optimal process? Or once a mediator sees that she is not going to be able to resolve all the issues in a dispute, how does the mediator help parties decide what procedural options are best? Or, during a mediation, can the mediator and the attorneys uncover processes that might be used in conjunction with mediation (for instance, obtaining a neutral evaluation or expert opinion) that might make the mediation more productive.

The following analysis by Frank Sander and Stephen Goldberg is considered the standard in how to advise clients about dispute resolution options and to ensure that clients' problems are addressed in the most appropriate process.

As you read this, consider what processes are most comfortable for you. Does this affect how you would advise your client? Should the courts or you as an attorney have a default process you recommend? What do these authors suggest? The second part of their article addresses some of the psychological barriers to negotiation (discussed in Chapter 2) and shows how different dispute resolution processes could overcome them. The last part of the article deals with the situation of a multidoor courthouse where a public official might be in the position of assigning a dispute to a particular process. Should the selection process be any different in that instance?

Frank E.A. Sander & Stephen B. Goldberg, **FITTING THE FORUM TO THE FUSS: A USER-FRIENDLY GUIDE TO SELECTING AN ADR PROCEDURE**

10 Negot. J. 49 (1994)

CLIENT GOALS

In the hypothetical [sexual harassment] case with which we began this article, how do you, as [her] attorney, prepare for your initial interview with your client? Is she eager to remain at the company (perhaps because alternative employment opportunities are scarce) and hence wants to resolve this situation with the least disruption and fuss? Or is she so angry that she is determined to have some outside neutral pronounce her "right," and thus vindicate her position?

Answers to questions like these are critical in determining what dispute resolution procedure is appropriate in this case. The fact that [she] has decided to come to an attorney indicates that she is dissatisfied with the present posture of the dispute. But should she file a lawsuit or seek some other way of resolving the problem? If she has an emotional need for vindication, she will have to resort to some form of adjudication, either in court or — if the company is willing — through private means, such as arbitration or private judging. Private adjudication, in addition to assuring confidentiality, is often faster and cheaper than a court decision. In arbitration and private judging, there is also an opportunity to participate in the selection of the adjudicator and thus to obtain particular expertise. In addition, arbitration almost guarantees finality, since a reviewing court will hardly ever overturn an arbitrator's decision. If [she] wants public vindication, however, or a binding precedent, only court will do....

These, then, are some of the considerations that lawyers and clients must examine with regard to processes that might meet client objectives. The value of various procedures in meeting specific client objectives is set forth in [see the table on next page].

An important point to note is that the values assigned to each procedure in [the table] ... are not based on empirical research but rather upon our own experience, combined with the views of other dispute resolution professionals. Moreover, the numerical values assigned to each procedure are not intended to be taken literally, but rather as a shorthand expression of the extent to which each procedure satisfies a particular objective....

The next step in the analysis is to list the client's goals in order of priority. If the client is primarily interested in a prompt and inexpensive resolution of the dispute that also maintains or improves the parties' relationship — which is typical of *most* clients in *most* business disputes — mediation is the preferred procedure. Mediation is the only procedure to receive maximum scores on each of these dimensions — cost, speed, and maintain or improve the relationship — as well as on assuring privacy, another interest which is present in many business disputes. It is only when the client's primary interests consist of establishing a precedent, being vindicated, or maximizing (or minimizing) recovery that procedures other than mediation are more likely to be satisfactory....

Procedures						
Non-binding			Binding			
OBJECTIVES	MEDIATION	MINITRIAL	SUMMARY JURY TRIAL	EARLY NEUTRAL EVALUATION	ARBITRATION/ PRIVATE JUDGING	COURT
Minimize costs	3	2	2	3	1	0
Speed	3	2	2	3	1	0
Privacy	3	3	2	2	3	0
Maintain/ improve relationship	3	2	2	1	1	0
Vindication	0	1	1	1	2	3
Neutral opinion	0	3	3	3	3	3
Precedent	0	0	0	0	2	3
Maximizing/ minimizing recovery	0	1	1	1	2	3

0 = Unlikely to satisfy objective
1 = Satisfies objective somewhat
2 = Satisfies objective substantially
3 = Satisfies objective very substantially

One final point concerning client goals: Some contend that ADR should be avoided altogether when one party will be sure to win if the matter is litigated. We disagree. First, the likely loser may be persuaded, through the use of one of the evaluative ADR procedures, to concede, thus sparing both parties the costs of litigation. An agreed-upon outcome is also more likely to be fully complied with than a court order. Alternatively, the likely loser may offer, in ADR, a settlement that is better in non-monetary terms than what could be achieved in litigation; such a settlement preserves, and often enhances, the parties' relationship. Thus, the prospect of a victory in litigation is not reason enough for avoiding ADR.

IMPEDIMENTS TO SETTLEMENT AND WAYS OF OVERCOMING THEM

In some circumstances, a settlement is not in the client's interest. For example, the client may want a binding precedent or may want to impress other potential litigants with its firmness and the consequent costs of asserting claims against it. Alternatively, the client may be in a situation in which there are no relational concerns; the only issue is whether it must pay out money; there is no pre-judgment interest; and the cost of contesting the claim is less than the interest earned on the money. In these and a small number of other situations, settlement will not be in the client's interest.

Still, a satisfactory settlement typically is in the client's interest. It is the inability to obtain such a settlement, in fact, that impels the client to seek the advice of counsel in the first place. The lawyer must consider not only what the client wants but also why the parties have been unable to settle their dispute, and then must find a dispute resolution procedure that is likely to overcome the impediments to settlement. . . .

Poor Communication

The relationship between the parties and/or their lawyers may be so poor that they cannot effectively communicate. Neither party believes the other, and each searches for hidden daggers in all proposals put forth by the other. An inability to communicate clearly and effectively, which impedes successful negotiations, is often, but not always, the result of a poor relationship. . . .

The Need to Express Emotions

At times, no settlement can be achieved until the parties have had the opportunity to express their views to each other about the dispute and each other's conduct. . . .

Different Views of Facts

Did the defendant engage in the conduct that forms the basis of the plaintiff's complaint? Whose version of the facts is the finder of fact likely to believe? The greater the parties' disagreement on these matters, the more difficult settlement is likely to be. . . .

Different Views of Legal Outcome if Settlement Is Not Reached

Disputants often agree on the facts but disagree on their legal implications. The plaintiff asserts that, on the basis of the agreed-upon facts, he has a 90 percent likelihood of success in court; the defendant, with equal fervor, asserts that she has a 90 percent chance of success. While there may be a legitimate dispute over the likely outcome, both these estimates cannot be right. . . .

Issues of Principle

If each of the disputing parties is deeply attached to some "fundamental" principle that must be abandoned or compromised in order to resolve the dispute, then resolution is likely to be difficult. Two examples: a suit challenging the right of neo-Nazis to march in a town where many Holocaust survivors live; and a suit by a religious group objecting to the withdrawal of life support systems from a comatose patient. . . .

Constituency Pressures

If one or more of the negotiators represents an institution or group, constituency pressures may impede agreement in two ways: different elements within the institution or group may have different interests in the dispute, or the negotiator may have staked her political or job future on attaining a certain result. . . .

Linkage to Other Disputes

The resolution of one dispute may have an effect on other disputes involving one or both parties. If so, this linkage will enter into their calculations, and may so complicate negotiations as to lead to an impasse. . . .

Multiple Parties

When there are multiple parties, with diverse interests, the problems are similar to those raised by diverse constituencies and by issue linkages. . . .

Different Lawyer/Client Interests

Lawyers and clients often have divergent attitudes and interests concerning settlement. This may be a matter of personality (one may be a fighter, the other a problem solver) or of money. An attorney who is paid on an hourly basis stands to profit handsomely from trial, and may be less interested in settlement than the client. On the other hand, an attorney paid on a contingent fee basis is interested in a prompt recovery without the expense of preparing for or conducting a trial, and may be more interested in settlement than is the client. It is in part because of this potential conflict of interest that most processes that seek to promote settlement provide for the client's direct involvement. . . .

The "Jackpot" Syndrome

An enormous barrier to settlement often exists in those cases where the plaintiff is confident of obtaining in court a financial recovery far exceeding its damages, and the defendant thinks this is highly unlikely. . . .

A Rule of Presumptive Mediation

Mediation will most often be the preferred procedure for overcoming the impediments to settlement. It has the greatest likelihood of overcoming all impediments except different views of facts and law, and the jackpot syndrome. . . .

The presumption in favor of mediation would be overcome when the goals of one or both parties could not be satisfied in mediation, or mediation was clearly incapable of overcoming a major impediment to settlement. The most common situation in which this could occur would be when either party has a strong interest in receiving a neutral opinion, obtaining a precedent, or being vindicated, and is unwilling to consider any procedure that forecloses the possibility of accomplishing that objective.

The Public Perspective

For either a judge or a court employee responsible for recommending an ADR procedure, the question regarding barriers to settlement and how they can be overcome is the same as it is for individual disputants. The other question concerning goals is similar, but with a broader perspective. In lieu of asking what are the objectives one party wishes to achieve, as would counsel, the question is what both parties want to achieve. Under an ADR program in the Superior Court of the District of Columbia, for example, each party is asked to select, in order of importance, three goals for the processing of its case. These goals can then be considered in making an ADR recommendation.

When a process selection is made from a public perspective, the public interest must also be considered. If the dispute is one in which a trial is likely to be lengthy, and so consume precious court time, there may be a public interest in referring the dispute to *some* form of ADR. Beyond that, one must ask if there is a public interest in having the dispute resolved pursuant to a *particular* procedure. For example, the referral of child custody disputes to mediation is required by law in several jurisdictions. The disputing parents may believe that they have no interest in a better relationship, but only in vindication, and hence prefer court to mediation. However, many states believe that a better relationship between the parents serves the public interest by improving the life of the child, and so mandate that child custody disputes go first to mediation.

The final question that must be asked in the public context is whether the public interests will be better served by a court decision than by a private settlement. If, for example, the dispute raises a significant question of statutory or constitutional interpretation, a court resolution might be preferable to a private settlement. While a court normally has no power to prevent parties from settling their own dispute, it does not follow that the court, as a public agency, should encourage or assist settlement in such a case.

Litigation may also serve the public interest better than mediation in cases of consumer fraud, which are often handled by the consumer protection division of an attorney general's office. Here not only the issue of *precedent*, but also the related issue of *recurring violations*, is key. The establishment of a general principle or a class remedy, by means of a class action, is clearly preferable to a series of repetitive and inconsistent mediations. . . .

Finally, two more situations may militate against any use of ADR. First, *one or more of the parties may be incapable of negotiating effectively*. An unsophisticated pro se litigant, for example, may be vulnerable to exploitation in an ADR process. (On the other hand, such an individual, if not represented by a lawyer, may not fare better in court.) Second, court process may be required for some other reason: for example, *when serious issues of compliance or discovery are anticipated*.

Conclusion

In addressing the problem of "fitting the forum to the fuss," we have suggested two lines of inquiry: What are the disputants' goals in making a forum choice? And, if the disputants are amenable to settlement, what are the obstacles to settlement, and in what forum might they be overcome?

The fact that these inquiries rarely lead to a clear answer to the question of forum selection does not, we think, indicate that the analysis is faulty. Rather, it indicates that the question of forum selection ultimately turns on the extent to which the interests of the disputing parties (and sometimes of the public) will be met in various forums. Thus, the most that analysis can offer is a framework that clarifies the interests involved and promotes a thoughtful weighing and resolution of those interests.

Moreover such an inquiry concerning goals and impediments is often independently helpful in clarifying the dimensions of the basic dispute. When it then comes to exploring the ADR implications of that analysis, a sophisticated ADR user might well ask: "If these are my goals and my impediments, what kinds of third-party help do I need, and how can I design a procedure that provides that kind of help?"

Notes and Questions

11.7 How do you determine your client's true interests? What if those interests — and their relative priorities for the client — seem misguided?

11.8 Which impediments to settlement might be the hardest to overcome? Why?

11.9 Examine the Sander and Goldberg table. Do you agree with all of the assigned numbers?

11.10 How would you advise your client if her goals were different from public policy goals? In addition to a divorce case, what other examples can you think of where individual and public policy goals might diverge?

The next writer adds another dimension to the analysis, interweaving therapeutic jurisprudence into dispute process choice. Advocates of therapeutic jurisprudence argue that lawyers must look at the emotional and mental impact of legal processes. Andrea Schneider encourages attorneys to examine the emotional or therapeutic impact of each dispute resolution process, arguing that this broader approach is more consistent with the ideals of dispute resolution itself.

 Andrea Kupfer Schneider, **BUILDING A PEDAGOGY OF PROBLEM-SOLVING: LEARNING TO CHOOSE AMONG ADR PROCESSES**

5 Harv. Negot. L. Rev. 113, 123-127, 131-132 (2000)

A NEW MODEL FOR CHOOSING AMONG THE ADR PROCESSES

Therapeutic jurisprudence and preventive law [TJPL] provide a coherent methodology for choosing among the ADR processes of negotiation, mediation and arbitration. Given that ADR was developed with the goal of increasing parties' satisfaction, ADR practitioners should be advising their clients on that basis. An intellectual framework for choosing the process could achieve the qualitative-justice advantages that ADR's founders intended. This approach adds a needed layer to the current analysis of ADR choices by explicitly adding emotional and psychological concerns to that of the traditional legal and financial analysis. TJPL can help us look at additional factors in order to make a fully educated and beneficial choice for the client. . . .

APPLYING THE MODEL

To demonstrate the usefulness of applying TJPL, [we assume the following facts, outlined in Leonard Riskin, James Westbrook & James Levin, Instructor's Manual to Accompany Dispute Resolution and Lawyers 119 (1998)] . . .

Dr. John Roark sued the *Daily Bugle*, its editor, and reporter Terry Ives for defamation. Terry Ives wrote a front page article about a fire in slum housing owned by Dr. John Roark. The article reports that a source in the Fire Marshall's office has indicated that the office is not ruling out the possibility of arson. The article also alleges that it is not uncommon for owners of tenements to intentionally burn their properties to collect insurance. When Roark called to complain, the editor said he stood by the story.

Roark insists that the reporter was negligent because property records show that Roark was only a limited partner in a group owning the property. Roark also believes that the reporter acted with malice because Ives had once before written a story about Roark's youngest son when the son was arrested for drug possession. Roark seeks $250,000 in actual damages for harm to his reputation, lost income in his medical practice, aggravation of a serious health problem, and mental anguish. He also seeks punitive damages of $1 million.

A.   Step One: Counseling & Interviewing — Identifying Emotional Concerns

As part of the initial meeting with Roark, the lawyer should discuss, in addition to legal and financial concerns, the emotional impact of various dispute resolution processes. These concerns could range from broad issues applicable to every client to the more specific concerns that Roark might have in this case. The lawyer should first determine general issues such as how much Roark would like to participate in resolving the dispute, whether he is comfortable in formal settings, and how at ease he is with the legal process in general. The lawyer should review Roark's desire to tell his story and determine whether he (a) wishes to confront the other side; (b) wants to tell his story to a neutral third party; (c) would want to testify (and would be good at testifying) in a courtroom; or (d) would like to detach from the process as much as possible.

The lawyer should also look for emotional concerns particular to this client. In a defamation case with a claim of mental anguish, these issues should not be ignored. . . .

First, Roark's feelings of anger at the paper and hurt at his subsequent treatment need to be considered. . . . Second, this event has aggravated Roark's medical condition. . . . Finally, Roark could have more general emotional concerns. He might be worried about the impact of this situation on his reputation. He might be concerned about the impact that dealing with this situation would have on his quality of work and his quality of life. . . .

B. Step Two: Choosing a Process — Determining Legal Procedures That Would Be Therapeutic

In light of Roark's emotional concerns, each of the ADR processes should be assessed in terms of their ability to provide therapeutic, or emotionally beneficial, results. They should also be judged by whether any of these processes could also have nontherapeutic, or emotionally harmful, effects.

Again, this analysis is intended to augment, not supplant, traditional consideration of legal and financial ramification. Indeed, given the facts of this particular claim, it is plausible that only litigation would vindicate Dr. Roark's desires. Defamation is a complex legal claim and he might trust a court to better apply the relevant standards. . . .

1. Negotiation

Negotiation has the advantage of allowing clients to be more detached from legal proceedings because most negotiations occur solely between the lawyers outside the presence of the clients. Thus, if the client is relatively uninterested in participating, negotiation [without clients present] may provide the most therapeutic effects.

A problem-solving approach to negotiation can also have therapeutic effects on both lawyers and the clients. Since problem solving focuses on the interests of the client, the client must be more involved in the preparation of the case. . . .

2. Mediation

Mediation can have excellent therapeutic effects for clients. Numerous articles on mediation have discussed the value of being heard or meeting face-to-face to resolve disputes. The strength of mediation lies in providing the client the opportunity to tell her story in a setting that is safe and helpful. The opportunity to be heard is cathartic for many clients. Also, simply sitting across from the person whom the client perceives as having wronged him can be helpful in resolving and overcoming the dispute. Mediation allows parties the opportunity to face one another and to have a true conversation together. In addition, the ability to hear the plaintiff's story, perhaps even apologize, and to tell the other side of the dispute can be important for the defendant as well. . . .

In the *Daily Bugle* example, mediation would allow Roark to tell his story. A face-to-face meeting with the editor who ignored him could be of great psychological benefit. It might also provide the opportunity for the editor or reporter to apologize. Nevertheless, an unproductive mediation could be even more aggravating to Roark. If the editor is intransigent or the reporter admits no fault, Roark could leave even more infuriated.

3. Arbitration

Arbitration provides a different array of therapeutic advantages and disadvantages. Roark might want the whole world to know what has happened. If Roark feels that the paper has a history of sloppy reporting, he might opt for litigation to obtain a public ruling condemning their actions.

He might, however, be content with a private adjudication of his rights. In arbitration, a decision is made on the merits of the case, but with more speed and confidentiality than litigation. This might be a great benefit to him and his family given the situation between Roark and his son, as well as the family's general desire to keep its name out of the paper. . . .

C. Step Three: Looking to Settlement — Implementing Preventive Law for Therapeutic Outcomes

1. *Negotiation & Mediation*

Negotiation and mediation . . . can implement ideas from preventive law by looking beyond the specific litigation issue. If the goal is to prevent further disputes between the parties, then the ability of mediation to deal with these issues is more likely to work to clients' benefit than litigation. Settlements can be structured so that all of the elements of the dispute are discussed, evaluated, and dealt with in a final agreement. . . .

In Roark's case, the settlement agreement should be written with an eye toward the future. If payment is agreed upon, the settlement should specify how and when that payment will arrive. What if payment does not occur? If a public apology or retraction is part of the settlement, the settlement should include details such as timing and placement of such retraction. Is the apology on behalf of the paper, or will the apology come from the reporter? The settlement might include internal changes within the paper — a punishment for the reporter or new procedures for fact-checking. The where, when, and how of each of these elements should be covered in the settlement agreement. By dealing with these issues as part of the ADR process and settlement, Roark's lawyer can help him avoid disturbing legal problems down the road.

2. *Arbitration*

Arbitration can provide different preventive law opportunities, although there is often little opportunity to do so in the process. Frequently, individual arbitrators feel constrained to keep to the dispute at hand and not look down the road. This, however, should not prevent the parties from doing so. The parties can do this in two ways. First, they can agree to widen the scope of the questions presented to the arbitrator or perhaps give the arbitrator broader remedial powers. This would allow the arbitrator to employ preventive law ideas in crafting the decision by examining future interactions between the parties.

Notes and Questions

11.11 Having a clear destination is critical to arriving at a desired place. Is it consistent to extend the notion of zealous advocacy to zealous pursuit of a client's best interests — broadly defined by the client herself?

11.12 Are there disadvantages in including this type of interest-based analysis in client counseling? Is the lawyer being asked to be a therapist?

4. Counseling Skills

After a lawyer interviews a client, it is time to use the legal and nonlegal information learned to help the client decide which legal process makes sense. You and your client might conclude that one of the processes discussed thus far is most helpful.

You both might also conclude that pursuing litigation would be most useful for your client. It is important that well-constructed and well-planned conversations take place between lawyers and clients, to ensure that the client makes the best possible choices. Mediators (especially if there are no lawyers representing the parties) will also counsel clients about particular outcomes in mediation and help them to evaluate what is a good solution. Mediators call this part of counseling, "reality testing."

Preparation for Counseling

Step 1. Research the law and investigate the facts....

Step 2. Clarify your goals for the counseling session....

Step 3. Scan your research, investigation, and experience to identify alternatives for the client....

Step 4. Note the positive and negative consequences of each alternative to ensure that the client fully considers the total impact of his or her decision. Your explanation should include legal and nonlegal consequences....

Step 5. Plan for in-session probing to accomplish three interrelated objectives...: (a)...clarify the client's priorities, (b) ascertain the client's reactions to the possible consequences of the identified alternatives, and (c) cure informational gaps and ambiguities....

Step 6. Plan the format for the counseling session....

Step 7. Think through what [communication] techniques might be appropriate during the counseling session....

Step 8. Prepare visual aids for the client.

Robert M. Bastress & Joseph D. Harbaugh, Interviewing, Counseling and Negotiating 237-240 (1990).

Notes and Questions

11.13 Assume that you have just started practicing law and a client, Xander, comes through your door with a seemingly straightforward problem that appears to have a litigable solution. Xander has always admired a certain antique clock that his aunt owned. Unfortunately, his aunt has recently passed away leaving a will that decreed her few remaining possessions "to be divided evenly among my remaining family members." Xander's uncle was in charge of distributing these few items, and before Xander could stake a claim, Xander's half-sister, Yolanda, took the clock as her own. He has tried to talk to Yolanda about the clock, but all she has to say is "first come first serve." He has tried to talk to his uncle as well, but his uncle is somewhat senile and hard to communicate with. You are aware that in your jurisdiction the law says that the courts must aid the execution of the will if the executor's competency can reasonably be called into question. No such process has taken place, and you are confident that if Xander brought suit you could have the aunt's possessions seized and redistributed. You are not confident, however, that Xander would be the one to eventually end up with the clock. You also feel that such an action could further strain family relations.

    a. What are you going to say to Xander to make him understand some of these implications?

   b. What other kinds of possible solutions can you and Xander come up
      with by yourselves?

   c. What kinds of possible solutions can Xander and Yolanda come up
      with if they brainstorm together in a negotiation session? Why would
      having both parties brainstorm like this be beneficial?

   d. If, on further questioning, you learn that Yolanda is struggling for
      money, that Xander is quite wealthy, and that Yolanda never really
      liked the clock anyway, how would this change the options available?

   e. What kind of information would you like to know more about? Does it
      matter how close Xander and his half-sister Yolanda were growing up?

   f. How would the information in (e) affect how you counsel your client,
      and what would you suggest he do even if familial relations were already
      strained?

   g. Given all of these factors, is this a situation where the introduction of a
      third party to the negotiation (i.e., mediation) is appropriate? If not at
      first, what kind of a breakdown in negotiation would lead you to want
      to introduce a third party?

   h. At what point would you want to scrap the dispute resolution process
      altogether and commence your lawsuit? (This may not be as obvious as
      it seems. What is really important to Xander, the clock, or Yolanda?)

5. Ethics and Public Policy

The final section on counseling focuses on the primary public policy issue relating
to counseling about mediation and appropriate dispute resolution — whether this
counseling should be required. The Model Rules of Professional Responsibility
have no explicit rule requiring the discussion of appropriate dispute resolution,
although this requirement could be inferred. Some states' ethics rules and codes
require counseling about appropriate dispute resolution. Furthermore, some state
bar opinions hold that lawyers must counsel their clients about appropriate dispute
resolution. With some requirements unclear and others evolving, this part of the
chapter reviews policy arguments on this requirement, some of the theories under-
pinning proposed requirements, and how a change to the Model Rules might look.

The first excerpt that follows is from a debate over whether counseling about the
appropriate dispute resolution process should be required. It summarizes the policy
pros and cons of mandatory counseling.

 **PROFESSIONAL RESPONSIBILITY: SHOULD THERE BE A
DUTY TO ADVISE OF ADR OPTIONS?**

76 A.B.A. J. 50 (1990)

YES: AN AID TO CLIENTS
by Frank E.A. Sander

[A]lthough many lawyers already are explaining the potential risks and benefits of
dispute resolution options to their clients, many others are not. Why? For one thing,

many lawyers are unfamiliar with the subject. Such unfamiliarity causes growing problems as more and more courts advocate ADR options. . . .

Some lawyers may be uncomfortable with involving a client with what they perceive as strategy. But if, as we repeatedly assert, our mission is to help clients find the best way to handle their disputes — not merely by litigation but also by a variety of other available techniques — why shouldn't it be part of our explicit professional obligation to canvass those options with clients? How would we feel about a doctor who suggested surgery without exploring other possible choices?

Perhaps a number of lawyers are not now fulfilling this responsibility because of fear — because of the nagging thought that to do so may hurt them financially.

Choosing Wisely

Some attorneys also insist that their clients want to win rather than settle or mediate, but it is the client who should make that decision after being fully informed of all the available options. We might be surprised by the choices some clients will make when they are candidly told the costs and benefits of pursuing various courses.

How might such an obligation be implemented? There are many possible approaches. Attorneys could be required to hand out a brochure that describes the most common alternatives and to discuss these options with their clients and opponents. Then, as part of the attorneys' pretrial submissions, they could be required to certify compliance with that obligation. . . .

Another alternative is to have the lawyer write a letter canvassing the possible options, and then have this letter signed by the client, much as is now done with contingent fee agreements.

In the final analysis, the question may come down not to whether to recognize such an obligation, but who should do it. For surely if lawyers themselves do not take this step, others will do it for them. There are already rumblings in Congress. . . . And one can readily envision a court holding a lawyer liable for malpractice because he failed to apprise his client of possibly cheaper, faster and less polarizing ways of achieving his objectives than via litigation.

NO: AN UNREASONABLE BURDEN
by Michael L. Prigoff

I agree with Professor Sander that we as lawyers have a professional obligation to advise our clients of all relevant information and options about the objectives of the representation, including disputes. In many cases, among these issues may be various dispute resolution methodologies.

However, I vigorously oppose what I suspect the real issue is: "Should an obligation to advise clients of dispute resolution options be a basis for professional discipline or malpractice liability?"

The argument for a disciplinary or malpractice standard is purely functional and bears no relation to traditional ethics or malpractice analysis. The rationale seems to be that ADR is "good"; not enough clients are aware of it; the best way to inform clients is to have their lawyers do it; the most efficient way to motivate lawyers to do so is to penalize them if they don't. Q.E.D.

Let's look at the concept in practice. A comes into my office and asks me to sue B on a note. Even with such a simple factual pattern, there are a myriad of tactical decisions possible, even without considering ADR methodologies: Do we attempt settlement before suit? Do we file in state or federal court, and in which jurisdiction? Do we ask for a jury, and so forth.

If, instead of explaining each of these options to clients and letting them make these choices (which do not involve "the objectives of the representation," RPC 1.2(a)), I make the choices for them, is there anything that would be a basis for professional discipline or malpractice liability? I think not. . . .

What differences would the proposed obligation make in our approach? For one, we would feel constrained to provide written information about "available" options to each litigation client to protect against the allegation that we hadn't complied with the anticipated rule or standard. This, together with the time required to properly explain all options in every dispute, would add some cost to each representation, which would be more of a factor in smaller disputes.

Much as the ethical requirement of a written fee agreement for every matter is absurd in some circumstances, so would the proposed requirement be counterproductive to the goal of providing more satisfactory dispute resolution at an affordable price.

While the bar and public should be better informed about ADR, the proposal to make this responsibility a matter of professional discipline or malpractice liability is overkill and unfair micromanagement of the practice of law. In the real world of clients and lawyers, it unfairly burdens the bar and will prove counterproductive to the goals sought by ADR, at least with respect to smaller disputes.

Notes and Questions

11.14 What are Sander's primary arguments? What are Prigoff's primary arguments? How do you think their arguments are affected by their background, the first as one of the primary advocates of ADR and the second as a practicing attorney?

11.15 With which writer do you agree? Which of his arguments do you find most persuasive? Which arguments do you find most persuasive on the other side? What major drawbacks do you see to implementing your position on this issue?

11.16 When considering whether it is an ethical violation not to inform a client about dispute resolution options, it is useful to examine other considerations that influence the attorney's decision. As you can probably surmise, attorneys who are familiar with a procedure are more likely to suggest it to their clients. A study done in Ohio discovered that training and exposure to a specific type of ADR increased the likelihood of its use. This study also revealed that the factors that had the greatest impact on the attorney's decision to use ADR were either the attorney's participation as a third-party neutral in the past or his having actually represented another client in the process on an earlier occasion. One possible implication of this finding is the importance of becoming familiar with ADR processes from the perspective of an attorney or a neutral. Roselle Wissler, Attorneys' Use of ADR Is Crucial to Their Willingness to Recommend It to Clients, Disp. Resol. Mag., 36 Winter 2000.

The next excerpt, by Marshall Breger, states relevant rules from the *Model Rules of Professional Conduct* and explains their implication for counseling about ADR options. The latter part of the article (not excerpted here) recommends a national approach and a change to the *Model Rules* that would explicitly require ADR counseling from all lawyers.

 Marshall J. Breger, **SHOULD AN ATTORNEY BE REQUIRED TO ADVISE A CLIENT OF ADR OPTIONS?**

13 Geo. J. Legal Ethics 427, 429-430 (2000)

Consideration of the issue begins with four relevant *Model Rules of Professional Conduct,* which is the operative "model" text for state ethics rules.

1. *Model Rule* 1.2(a) provides that "[a] lawyer shall abide by a client's decisions concerning the objectives of representation . . . *and shall consult with the client as to the means by which they are to be pursued* (emphasis added)."
2. *Model Rule* 1.4(b) provides that "[a] lawyer shall explain a matter to the extent reasonably necessary to permit the client to make informed decisions regarding the representation."
3. *Model Rule* 3.2 provides that "[a] lawyer shall make reasonable efforts to expedite litigation consistent with the interest of the client."
4. Finally, *Model Rule* 2.1 provides that "[i]n representing a client, a lawyer shall exercise independent professional judgment and render candid advice. In rendering advice, a lawyer may refer not only to law but to other considerations such as moral, economic, social and political factors, that may be relevant to the client's situation."

As the above texts make clear, the *Model Rules* do not provide explicit guidance regarding the mandatory quality of an ADR requirement. For many, however, the language of the *Model Rules* creates an implicit obligation to advise a client regarding ADR options. After all, the *Model Rules* require that an attorney "consult with the client" to "explain a matter," to expedite litigation and to "render candid advice" on relevant matters, all seemingly consonant with the duty to consult with a client regarding ADR options. . . .

Notes and Questions

11.17 As you read these model rules, do you believe a rule of consultation regarding process options already exists? If not, should there be such a rule?

11.18 If you were drafting a rule requiring ADR consultation, what would it say? Would it be part of a "lawyer's creed" — aspirational goals added to codes of professional behavior — or a mandatory rule? What would be the result of failure to comply? Bar discipline? Malpractice liability?

11.19 Breger's article concludes with the following drafting recommendation:

> In considering revisions to the *Model Rules,* whether to *Model Rule* 2.1 or *Model Rule* 1.4, the ABA ought to adopt a formulation like that found in the

ABA Section of Dispute Resolution Proposed Draft One which provides: "[a] lawyer has a duty to inform his client about the availability and applicability of alternative dispute resolution procedures that are reasonably appropriate under the circumstances." . . .

If one were to use the Comment approach, I would add a proposed Comment, to *Model Rule* 1.4, as follows:

> A lawyer should take into consideration, in relevant and appropriate circumstances, alternatives to litigation that may further the client's interests and provide the client with this information in order to assist the client in making an informed decision as to what avenue should be pursued to achieve the legal objective sought. In some circumstances, providing notice of the availability of alternatives to litigation may be sufficient and, in other cases, the applicability of alternatives may need to be discussed in greater detail. . . .

As one commentator has suggested, "not only is ADR here but it is becoming a standard way of resolving legal disputes." The rules of ethics ought to recognize this change.

11.20 The ABA has yet to adopt such a rule. Why do you think this is? Why are states individually adopting rules to advise clients? What is the problem with different requirements in different states?

11.21 Should lawyers be held to the same counseling standard as doctors? As Jacqueline Nolan-Haley outlines, the medical standard of informed consent could provide some lessons for mediation participation: "At a minimum, the principle of informed consent requires that parties be educated about the mediation process before they consent to participate in it, that their continued participation in mediation be voluntary, and that they understand and consent to the outcomes reached in mediation." Jacqueline M. Nolan-Haley, Informed Consent in Mediation: A Guiding Principle for Truly Educated Decision-making, 74 Notre Dame L. Rev. 775, 778 (1990). If informed consent is the appropriate standard, in what kind of counseling must lawyers engage?

11.22 Do you think that different types of cases should have different requirements? In other words, should we require counseling about ADR in family disputes and neighborhood disputes but not in commercial disputes or personal injury disputes?

11.23 Robert Cochran, Jr., advocates that "courts require lawyers to allow clients to make those choices which a reasonable person, in what the lawyer knows or should know to be the position of the client, would want to make. If a lawyer's failure to allow a client to make such decisions results in a loss to the client, the lawyer should be subject to malpractice liability. Courts should also continue to identify specific choices that as a matter of law are for the client." This right to choose would include the right to choose to pursue mediation. Robert F. Cochran, Jr., Legal Representation and the Next Steps Toward Client Control: Attorney Malpractice for the Failure to Allow the Client to Control Negotiation and Pursue Alternatives to Litigation, 47 Wash. & Lee L. Rev. 819, 823 (1990). Do you agree with Cochran?

B. PLANNING FOR DISPUTES

1. Dispute System Design

Paralleling efforts to counsel clients regarding processes to address and resolve existing disputes, attorneys and providers of dispute resolution services to organizations can design dispute resolution systems to help prevent conflicts and manage disputes before they ripen into full-scale grievances or lawsuits. Organizations face both internal disputes and grievances, such as in labor-management relations, and external disputes, with either one-shot or repeat customers, suppliers, vendors, or constituents. For some organizations, these disputes are now referred to as "streams of disputes" because they involve large numbers of people (for example, in matters of defective products, employment discrimination, and price fixing). Claimants may experience one-shot or repeat disputes. The challenge is to create processes that treat individual complaints nonbureaucratically and also deal fairly and efficiently with repetitive issues.

Good dispute system designers recognize that one size does not fit all and that a tiered system is often optimal. Tiered systems may begin with informal conversation and negotiation, then use consensual mediation with a third party, and finally offer a system for hearing arguments and legal rights claims, with appropriate remedial possibilities (for example, non-binding arbitration). Ultimately, when consensus-based processes fail to provide a resolution, adjudication — either private or public — must be available. Of course, dispute mechanisms vary, according to the relationship between the disputants and the issues that arise.

William Ury, Jeanne Brett, and Stephen Goldberg pioneered the principles of dispute system design by designing a grievance and mediation system for a labor union and its management counterpart, and then moving on to other organizations. In their book, Getting Disputes Resolved: Designing Systems to Cut the Costs of Conflict (1988), they distinguish among three approaches to resolving disputes. The first, familiar to you from the negotiation and mediation chapters, focuses on *underlying interests* (the needs, desires, concerns, and fears that bring people into conflict). The second focuses on *rights*, independent standards or entitlements granted by contracts, laws, or socially accepted standards. Finally, some disputes are resolved by simple assertion of *power*, defined by the ability to get someone else to do what you want them to do because you have more physical, economic, political, or even emotional "control" than the other person or situation. In their work on dispute system design, based in labor relations and organizational management, Ury, Brett, and Goldberg reorient parties to focus on a multitiered, interest-based system of resolving often recurrent or repetitive disputes. Such a system will lead to rights-based adjudication, providing loop-backs to consensual interest-based processes whenever possible.

Notes and Questions

11.24 For other perspectives on system design, see Cathy A. Costantino & Christina Sickles Merchant, Designing Conflict Management Systems (1996); David B. Lipsky, Ronald L. Seeber & Richard Fincher, Emerging Systems for

Managing Workplace Conflict: Lessons from American Corporations for Managers and Dispute Resolution Professionals (2003); Karl Slaikeu, Designing Dispute Resolution Systems in the Health Care Industry, 5 Negot. J. 395 (1989).

11.25 What role does context play in designing a system? Design dispute resolution systems for (1) grade disputes at your school, (2) employment grievances at your workplace, (3) disputes within your living unit or family. How do your systems differ? Why? What values are expressed in each? Who are the decision makers or third-party neutrals in each system? How much direct negotiation or interaction have you designed for the principal disputants? What type of mediation does your system embrace?

2. Drafting Mediation and ADR Clauses

Whether seen from a dispute prevention, conflict management, or transactional perspective, one of the most important skills of the lawyer is the ability to help parties work together, whether in one-shot contracts, longer-term transactions, or permanent organizational settings. Foreseeing the inevitability of conflicts and knowing the importance of a thoughtful system for dealing with disputes, sophisticated lawyers are designing tailor-made dispute resolution clauses in a variety of settings. These clauses often incorporate mediation and provide back-up adjudicatory processes in case mediation fails. For example, estate attorneys are inserting clauses in wills calling for mediation should disputes arise among beneficiaries. In housing cooperatives, bylaws and house rules reflect attention to dispute resolution, sometimes requiring that residents mediate matters before proceeding to an adjudicative forum. Reflecting the growing importance of dispute resolution clauses and the planning they represent, the CPR Institute for Dispute Resolution created a Drafter's Deskbook. In the excerpts below, Kathleen Scanlon emphasizes the need for a thoughtful and creative approach to drafting dispute resolution clauses, and Terry Trantina provides practical advice to drafters.

 Kathleen M. Scanlon, **CPR INSTITUTE FOR DISPUTE RESOLUTION, DRAFTER'S DESKBOOK FOR DISPUTE RESOLUTION CLAUSES**

§§1.4-1.5 (2002)

Dispute resolution planning . . . involves creating a framework to anticipate, avoid and manage disputes. Such planning is becoming a critical function of corporate law departments, law firms and public sector legal departments. Powerful economic incentives, increased emphasis on risk management and the growing complexity of dispute resolution options are among the numerous reasons compelling private and public sector lawyers to engage in dispute resolution planning. . . .

A multi-step dispute resolution clause provides for sequential stages of dispute resolution. Multi-step clauses typically provide for a period when the parties engage in a consensual process, such as negotiation or mediation, before resorting to an adjudicatory process, such as arbitration and litigation. The rationale underlying such an approach is that the negotiation or mediation stage affords the parties an opportunity to develop creative, business-oriented solutions before investing time and money in an adversarial process such as arbitration or litigation. More and more leading companies are including multi-step clauses in business-to-business agreements. . . . Many practitioners contend that the best time for business parties to decide how to resolve any future disputes between them is before they occur. . . . A complex series of choices exist when drafting a dispute resolution clause. Special drafting issues exist for a multi-step clause. In all practice areas, counsel are incorporating dispute resolution clause drafting into their master set of skills.

 Terry L. Trantina, **HOW TO DESIGN ADR CLAUSES THAT SATISFY CLIENTS' NEEDS AND MINIMIZE LITIGATION RISK**

19 Alternatives to High Cost Litigation 137, 137, 145-146 (2001)

Too often attorneys take ADR for granted or as essentially "lawless" and begin by offering clients a boilerplate ADR clause or a clause taken from another client's contract. The dispute resolution process that can be imposed on a client by using a boilerplate clause may permanently sour them on ADR when they experience just as many — or worse — problems as they did in the courts. In fact, they may be subjected to the worst of both worlds and end up spending inordinate time both in court and in ADR and unhappy with the lawyer that suggested ADR. . . .

As interpreted by the U.S. Supreme Court, the FAA [Federal Arbitration Act] allows the drafter of a pre-dispute arbitration provision to dictate every aspect of the dispute resolution process and have that provision enforced by both state and federal courts precisely as written. Furthermore, the FAA preempts any state law that would interfere with that enforcement as long as the provision is not unconscionable, i.e., the process is substantively and procedurally fair. Fundamental fairness does not require a guarantee of a jury, a publicly subsidized decision judge, class actions, the rules of evidence, boundless discovery or an appeal. Fundamental fairness is, again, a simple matter. The process simply cannot give advantage to one party or deprive a party of a timely, merit-based inquiry and decision by a neutral third party and the availability of the remedies available at law or in equity. The requirement of fundamental fairness does not restrict process design, only abuse. . . .

How do you achieve client satisfying results through ADR? First, take some time to understand the client's business needs: i.e., the nature of likely or significant, but less likely, disputes; the nature of the business relationships or environments that may cause these disputes; what the client dislikes most about resolving disputes in court; and what, in affirmative terms, will be required in a process or the background of the neutral to produce a merits-based, cost-effective and timely resolution.

Second, become familiar with the state and federal case law that have identified flaws in other ADR clauses. The basic principle flowing through all of the decisions interpreting ADR provisions subject to the FAA or individual state arbitration acts is that ADR provisions are to be given effect and enforced precisely as the parties expressly provide in their arbitration provision. There are a number of decisions where the court laments that "if the clause had only expressly provided for it, the court would have had no choice but to enforce it," but because the ADR clause was vague or silent on the issue, the court could not grant the party's post-dispute request for relief from the effects of the boilerplate arbitration clause.

Third, don't confidently copy another ADR clause that was custom-designed for another client. That actually may be worse than using the boilerplate clause or having no clause at all.

Fourth, use an up-to-date issues checklist when drafting ADR clauses. Each time you run across another court decision that addresses a flaw in someone else's ADR clause or adds a new gloss on an old issue, modify the check list.

Trantina's checklist has 89 subparts! Here are the first 7:

Clause Drafting Checklist

Specify the Type and Combinations of ADR

1. Select number and type of ADR steps
   a. Mandatory pre-litigation negotiation only.
   b. Mandatory pre-litigation mediation only.
   c. Arbitration only.
   d. Negotiation and arbitration.
   e. Mediation and arbitration.
   f. Negotiation, mediation and arbitration.
   g. Incorporate other ADR types (e.g., med/arb, fact-finding, mock trial).
2. Good faith, face-to-face negotiation
   a. Between same players with stake in outcome.
   b. Escalate above players to "big-picture executives" (recommended approach).
   c. Require presence of a person with authority to bind. The minimum acceptable is a "reachable" decision maker.
   d. This step slows process down. (Is time an issue? Desirable?)
3. Mediation by neutral third party
   a. Almost always a good idea; successful a majority of the time.
   b. Require presence of a person with authority to bind. The minimum acceptable is a "reachable" decision maker.
   c. This step slows process down. (Is time an issue? Desirable?)
4. Arbitration
   a. Binding (preferred).
   b. Nonbinding (operates to give both sides a view of how a court may decide the issues and facilitate settlement, but may give losing party an idea of how to improve arguments. It's risky, often taken less seriously, time consuming, and an added expense).
5. Other binding processes, e.g., minitrial with mock judge and jury; med/arb.
6. Provide how each step is initiated and whether the prior step must be abandoned for the next step to commence, e.g., arbitration demand may not be made until after mediation abandoned.
7. Provide whether new disputes, e.g., counterclaims, may be raised for the first time at a subsequent step or must go through entire process.

Notes and Questions

11.26 Trantina provides a comprehensive checklist for drafting ADR clauses (see box on previous page). He assumes (and many lawyers recommend) the incorporation of established ADR rules into the clause (such as the American Arbitration Association's Commercial Arbitration Rules and Mediation Procedures or the CPR Rules for Non-Administered Arbitration). Among other things, the drafters must determine the types and sequence of ADR processes; the participants and the nature of their involvement; the preconditions for each step of the process; the qualifications of and the resources available to the neutral(s); the location for each step; the issues that each process may address; the law, rule, or custom that a neutral adjudicator should apply; the procedural time limits; the reviewability (or finality) of decisions and awards; the confidentiality of each process; the limits of discovery; the neutral's fees; the remedies available to an arbitrator, including awarding attorneys' fees; and so on. The checklists are long, much longer than this abbreviated list.

Both the AAA and CPR also publish checklists and ADR clause drafting aids. See AAA's at *http://www.adr.org* and CPR's at *http://www.cpradr.org*.

11.27 What are the advantages and disadvantages of these kinds of checklists? What or whom else should an ADR clause drafter consult?

11.28 One of the authors of this casebook drafted her own "Partnering and Dispute Review Board" clause in a house renovation project:

> Should a conflict, dispute or difference of interpretation or opinion arise as to the meaning of a term of this contract, a design, materials, labor, deadline or any other issue in connection with the performance and completion of this contract, one representative of the Owner, the Architect and the Contractor (with or without relevant sub-contractors) shall convene within 24 hours on the site of the contract performance and resolve the issue among these three representatives within 24 hours.

Note that this clause does not specify a decision rule such as a majority vote or an appeals process, nor does it indicate what happens when an agreement cannot be reached. It simply requires a "meet and resolve" session on site. During six months of construction, the process was used about 20 times, and all disputes were amicably resolved within the 24-hour time period or with agreed-to extensions. As a result, the project was satisfactorily concluded on time. The contractor placed a similar clause in subsequent home renovation contracts. Would you draft a different clause? Which issues and participants might you take into account?

11.29 In addition to variations among industries, corporate cultural differences exist within industries. See, for example, the Center for Public Resources MAPP series of dispute resolution clauses for particular industries, available at *http://www.cpradr.org*, covering such areas as franchising, construction, energy, multiparty, transnational, banking, and employment. For useful empirical studies of differences in particular corporate cultures of disputing, see Calvin Morrill,

The Executive Way: Conflict Management in Corporations (1996); Craig A. McEwen, Managing Corporate Disputing: Overcoming Barriers to the Effective Use of Mediation for Reducing the Cost and Time of Litigation, 14 Ohio St. J. on Disp. Resol. 1 (1998).

Chapter 12 Multiparty Mediation, Consensus Building, and Facilitated Processes

It has been said that Democracy is the worst form of government except all those other forms that have been tried from time to time.

— Winston Churchill

Making the whole greater than the sum of its parts.

— Anonymous

The assumption that disputes involve two parties (for example, a plaintiff and a defendant), three parties (two disputants and a "neutral" intervener), or sometimes five parties (two disputants, two lawyers, and a third-party neutral) is often inaccurate. Increasingly, those who study and practice dispute resolution analyze how what they know about negotiation and mediation might have to be adapted when there are more than two or three parties. Many new forms of conflict resolution are specially designed to deal with multiparty situations, both in public and in private disputes. Indeed, the use of conflict resolution theory and practice has created not just new processes but whole new institutions. These include negotiated rule making ("reg-neg") in the administrative context and consensus-building forums for public policy and intractable disputes (such as in environmental siting or community disputes). When they are made more complex by multiple parties, these processes, like traditional mediation, have unique dynamics and raise new issues, for both the parties and their representatives and the neutral serving as mediator or facilitator.

This chapter explores some of these processes and considers what new concepts are needed when multiple parties are involved in a conflict. With more than two players, the dynamics change: two may align against one, and coalitions may radically change the interactions. "Defections" and new alliances introduce another form of instability to what is already a dynamic process. In addition, processes with multiple parties are more complex and difficult to organize and, for that reason, need more formal management than other processes. In addition to exploring theory and new organizational structures for multiparty processes, this chapter examines practice and skill sets relevant to meeting management, group process, and facilitation generally.

Finally, when multiparty processes are used to settle legal disputes, make public policy, and resolve complex social issues, they raise important jurisprudential and philosophical issues about the separation of powers in our constitutional government, the kinds of "discourse" that are permitted in these proceedings, and their relation to democracy and formal rules of governance. Our concrete forms of democracy, as expressed in the institutions we create, are themselves forms of dispute resolution. The chapter examines how both new and old forms of democratic dispute resolution are being analyzed as legitimate processes in our particular constitutional form of government.

A. WHY MULTIPARTY PROCESSES DIFFER

The readings in this section suggest some of the important ways in which multiparty dispute resolution differs from two-person (negotiation) or three-person (mediation) processes. As you read these excerpts, consider the implications for both representatives and mediators in multiparty mediations.

 Robert H. Mnookin, STRATEGIC BARRIERS TO DISPUTE RESOLUTION: A COMPARISON OF BILATERAL AND MULTILATERAL NEGOTIATIONS

159 J. Institutional & Theoretical Econ. 199, 199-201 (2003)

Why do negotiations so often fail even when there are possible resolutions that would better serve disputants than protracted struggle? And why, when resolutions are achieved, are they so often sub-optimal for the parties, or are achieved only after heavy and avoidable costs? . . . [I have begun] to think through and compare the barriers to the negotiated resolution of conflict in bilateral and multilateral negotiations. For this initial foray, I will primarily focus on what I have previously called *strategic barriers* — those, which arise from the efforts of "rational" bargainers to maximize individual returns, but may preclude the achievement of the greatest possible "gains in trade" at the lowest cost. In other words, strategic barriers are those that can cause rational-self-interested disputants to act in a manner that proves to be both individually and collectively disadvantageous. . . .

I suggest that Pareto-criterion may not provide an appropriate standard to evaluate issues of efficiency in multiparty bargaining. In a two party case, any negotiated deal presumably better serves the parties than the *status quo*. The same could be said in a multiparty negotiation only if the consent of *every party* were necessary. A requirement of unanimity in multilateral negotiation, however, creates potential holdout problems that may pose severe strategic barriers to resolution. This problem can be mitigated if the consent of less than all the parties can permit action. But other problems may arise. If conditions of less than all are able to change the *status quo*, this necessarily means that a party left out of a coalition may potentially be made worse off.

A variety of procedural rules may permit decision-making without unanimity in multiparty negotiations. Majority voting is but one of many possible mechanisms to allocate decision-making authority. The outcome of any multilateral negotiation can be profoundly affected by these procedural rules and various decisions concerning agenda. [Another part of this paper] briefly explores the application of an unusual procedural rule — the "sufficient consensus" standard — that was employed in the multiparty "constitutional" negotiations in South Africa and in Northern Ireland. . . .

Leigh L. Thompson, **THE MIND AND HEART OF THE NEGOTIATOR**

189-194, 198-203 (3d ed. 2005)

KEY CHALLENGES OF MULTIPARTY NEGOTIATIONS

There are several challenges at both the cognitive (mind) and the emotional (heart) level that crop up in multiparty negotiations. We present four key challenges of multiparty negotiations and follow with some practical advice [on dealing with coalitions, formulating trade-offs, voting and majority rule, and communication breakdowns].

Dealing with Coalitions

A key difference between two-party and group negotiations is the potential for two or more parties within a group to form a coalition to pool their resources and have a greater influence on outcomes. A **coalition** is a (sub)group of two or more individuals who join together in using their resources to affect the outcome of a decision in a mixed-motive situation involving at least three parties. For example, parties may seek to maximize control over other members, maximize their status in the group, maximize similarity of attitudes and values, or minimize conflict among members. Coalition formation is one way that otherwise weak group members may marshal a greater share of resources. Coalitions involve both cooperation and competition: Members of coalitions cooperate with one another in competition against other coalitions, but compete against one another regarding the allocation of rewards the coalition obtains. . . .

Formulating Trade-Offs

Integrative agreements are more difficult to fashion in multiparty negotiations because the trade-offs are more complex. In a multiparty negotiation, integrative trade-offs may be achieved either through circular or reciprocal logrolling. **Circular logrolling** involves trade-offs that require each group member to offer another member a concession on one issue while receiving a concession from yet another group member on a different issue. A circular trade-off is typified by the tradition of drawing names from a hat to give holiday gifts to people. People receive a gift from one person and give a gift to yet another person. Ideally, we give gifts that are more appreciated by the recipient than by the giver. In contrast, **reciprocal trade-offs** are fashioned between two members of a larger group. Reciprocal tradeoffs are typified in the more traditional form of exchanging presents. Circular trade-offs are more risky than reciprocal trade-offs because they involve the cooperation of more than two group members.

Voting and Majority Rule

Groups often simplify the negotiation of multiple issues among multiple parties through voting and decision rules. However, if not used wisely, decision rules can thwart effective negotiation, both in terms of pie expansion and pie slicing. There are a number of problems associated with voting that we will now describe.

Problems with Voting and Majority Rule

Voting is the procedure of collecting individuals' preferences for alternatives on issues and selecting the most popular alternative as the group choice. The most common procedure used to aggregate preferences of team members is **majority rule**. However, majority rule presents several problems in the attainment of efficient negotiation settlements. Despite its democratic appeal, majority rule fails to recognize the strength of individual preferences. One person in a group may feel very strongly about an issue, but his or her vote counts the same as the vote of someone who does not have a strong opinion about the issue. Consequently, majority rule does not promote integrative trade-offs among issues. In fact, groups negotiating under unanimous rule reach more efficient outcomes than groups operating under majority rule.

Although unanimity rule is time consuming, it encourages group members to consider creative alternatives to expand the size of the pie and satisfy the interests of all group members. Because strength of preference is a key component in the fashioning of integrative agreements, majority rule hinders the development of mutually beneficial trade-offs. Voting in combination with other decision aids, such as agendas, may be especially detrimental to the attainment of efficient outcomes because it prevents logrolling.

There are other problems with voting. Group members may not agree upon a method for voting; for example, some members may insist upon unanimity, others may argue for a simple majority rule, and still others may advocate a weighted majority rule. Even if a voting method is agreed upon, it may not yield a choice. For example, a group may not find a majority if there is an even split in the group. Voting does not eliminate conflicts of interest, but instead, provides a way for group members to live with conflicts of interest; for this reason, majority rule decisions may not be stable. In this sense, voting hides disagreement within groups, which threatens long-term group and organizational effectiveness.

Voting Paradoxes

Consider a three-person (Raines, Warner, and Lassiter) product development team. The three are in conflict over which design to use — A, B, or C.

The preference ordering is depicted . . . [in the following table]. Everyone is frustrated, and the group has argued for hours. As a way of resolving the conflict, Warner suggests voting between designs A and B. In that vote A wins, and B is tossed in the trash. Warner then proposes that the group vote between A and C. In that vote, C wins. Warner then declares that design C be implemented. Lassiter concludes that the group vote was fair and agrees to develop design C. However, Raines is perplexed and suggests taking another vote. Warner laughs and says "We just took a vote and you lost — so just accept the outcome!" Raines glares at Warner and says, "Let's do the vote again, and I will agree to accept the outcome. However, this time I want us to vote between B and C first." Warner has no choice but to go along. In this vote B is the clear winner, and C is eliminated. Next, the vote is between A and B, and A beats B. Raines happily declares A the winner. Lassiter then jumps up and declares that the whole voting process was fraudulent, but cannot explain why.

Managers' Preferences for Product Designs

MANAGER	DESIGN A	DESIGN B	DESIGN C
Raines	1	2	3
Warner	2	3	1
Lassiter	3	1	2

Raines, Warner, and Lassiter are victims of the **condorcet paradox**. The condorcet paradox demonstrates that the winners of majority rule elections will change as a function of the *order* in which alternatives are proposed. Alternatives that are proposed later, as opposed to earlier, are more likely to survive sequential voting. Thus, clever negotiators arrange to have their preferred alternatives entered at later stages of a sequential voting process.

The unstable voting outcomes of the product development team point to a larger concern, known as the **impossibility theorem**, which states that the derivation of group preference from individual preference is indeterminate. Simply put, there is no method of combining group members' preferences that guarantees that group preference has been maximized when groups have three or more members and there are three or more options. That is, even though each manager's preferences are transitive, the group-level preference is intransitive.

Strategic Voting

The problem of indeterminate group choice is further compounded by the temptation for members to **strategically misrepresent** their true preferences so that a preferred option is more likely to be favored by the group. For example, a group member may vote for his least-preferred option to ensure that the second choice option is killed. Raines could have voted strategically in the first election to ensure that his preferred strategy was not eliminated in the first round.

Consensus Decisions

Consensus agreements require the consent of all parties to the negotiation before an agreement is binding. However, consensus agreements do not imply unanimity. For an agreement to be unanimous, parties must agree inwardly as well as outwardly. Consensus agreements imply that parties agree *publicly* to a particular settlement, even though their *private* views about the situation may be in conflict.

Although consensus agreements are desirable, there are several problems with them. They are time consuming because they require the consent of all members, who are often not in agreement. Second, they often lead to compromise, in which parties identify a lowest common denominator acceptable to all. Compromise agreements are an extremely easy method of reaching agreement and are compelling because they appear to be fair, but they are usually inefficient because they fail to exploit potential Pareto-improving trade-offs.

Communication Breakdowns

Most people take communication for granted in their interactions with multiple parties. In a perfect communication system, a sender transmits or sends a message that is accurately received by a recipient. There are at least three points of possible error: The sender may fail to send a message; the message may be sent, but is inaccurate or distorted; or an accurate message is sent, but is distorted or not received by the recipient. In a multiparty environment, the complexity grows when several people are simultaneously sending and receiving messages.

Private Caucusing

When groups grow large, communication among all parties is difficult. One way of simplifying negotiations is for negotiators to communicate in smaller groups, thereby avoiding full-group communication. Group members often form private caucuses for strategic purposes. However, private caucusing may cause problems. Full-group communication is more time consuming but enhances equality of group members' outcomes, increases joint profitability, and minimizes perceptions of competition. However, there is a caveat to the benefits of full communication. When the task structure requires group members to logroll in a reciprocal fashion (as opposed to a circular fashion), restricted communication leads to higher joint outcomes than full communication. . . .

Perspective-Taking Failures

People are remarkably poor at taking the perspective of others. For example, people who are privy to information and knowledge that they know others are not aware of nevertheless act as if others are aware of it, even though it would be impossible for the receiver to have this knowledge. This problem is known as the **curse of knowledge**. For example, in a simulation, traders who possessed privileged information that could have been used to their advantage behaved as if their trading partners also had access to the privileged information. Perspective-taking deficiencies also explain why some instructors who understand an idea perfectly are unable to teach students the same idea. They are unable to put themselves in their students' shoes to explain the idea in a way the students can understand. . . .

Multiple Audience Problem

In some negotiation situations, negotiators need to communicate with another person in the presence of someone who should not understand the message. For example, consider a couple selling a house having a face-to-face discussion with a potential buyer. Ideally, the couple wants to communicate information to one another in a way that the spouse understands but the buyer does not—better yet, in such a way that the buyer is not even aware that a surreptitious communication is taking place. [This is called] the **multiple audience problem**. . . .

COALITIONS

Coalitions face three sets of challenges: (1) the formation of the coalition, (2) coalition maintenance, and (3) the distribution of resources among coalition members.

Next, we take up these challenges and provide strategies for maximizing coalition effectiveness.

KEY CHALLENGES OF COALITIONS

Optimal Coalition Size

What is the ideal size for a winning coalition? Ideally, coalitions should contain the minimum number of people sufficient to achieve a desired goal. Coalitions are difficult to maintain because members are tempted by other members to join other coalitions, and agreements are not enforceable.

Trust and Temptation in Coalitions

Coalitional integrity is a function of the costs and rewards of coalitional membership; when coalitions are no longer rewarding, people will leave them. Nevertheless, there is a strong pull for members of coalitions to remain intact even when it is not rational to do so. According to the **status quo bias**, even when a new coalition structure that offers greater gain is possible, members are influenced by a norm of **coalitional integrity**, such that they stick with their current coalition. The implication is that negotiators should form coalitions early so as to not be left without coalitional partners.

Dividing the Pie

The distribution of resources among members of coalitions is complex because a normative method of fair allocation does not exist (Howard Raiffa, The Art and Science of Negotiation, 1982). To illustrate this consider the following example. Lindholm, Tepe, and Clauson are three small firms producing specialized products, equipment, and research for the rehabilitation medicine community. This area has become a critical, high-growth industry, and each firm is exploring ways to expand and improve its technologies through innovations in the research and development (R&D) divisions. Each firm has recently applied for R&D funding from the National Rehabilitation Medicine Research Council (NRMR).

The NRMR is a government agency dedicated to funding research in reha-bilitation medicine and treatment. The NRMR is willing to provide funds for the proposed research, but because the firms' requests are so similar, they will fund only a **consortium** of two or three firms. The NRMR will not grant funding to Lindholm, Tepe, or Clauson alone.

The largest of the three firms is Lindholm, followed by Tepe, and then Clauson. The NRMR took a variety of factors into consideration when they set caps on funding [as shown next page].

Maximum Funding Caps as a Function of Parties in Consortium

ORGANIZATIONS IN CONSORTIUM	CAP FOR R&D FUNDING
Lindholm alone	0
Tepe alone	0
Clauson alone	0
Lindholm and Tepe	$220,000
Lindholm and Clauson	$190,000
Tepe and Clauson	$150,000
Lindholm, Tepe, and Clauson	$240,000

The NRMR has strictly stipulated that for a consortium of firms to receive funding, the parties in the consortium (either two or three firms) must be in complete agreement concerning the allocation of resources among firms.

If you are Lindholm, what consortium would you consider to be the best for you? Obviously, you want to be in on some consortium, with either Tepe or Clauson or both, to avoid being left out in the cold. But what is the best division of resources within each of those consortiums? Suppose that you approach Tepe about a two-way venture, and Tepe proposes that she receive half of the $220,000 or $110,000 for herself. You argue that because you are bigger, and bring more synergy to the agreement, you should earn more. You demand $200,000 for yourself, leaving $20,000 for Tepe. At this point, Tepe threatens to leave you and approach Clauson. Tepe argues that she and Clauson can command $150,000 as a consortium without you, and each can receive $75,000. At this point, you argue that you can outbid her offer to Clauson with $80,000 and keep $110,000 for yourself. Just as Tepe is threatening to overbid you for Clauson, Clauson steps in and tells Tepe that she would want at least $100,000 of the $150,000 pie that she and Tepe could command. Tepe is frustrated, but relents.

You get nervous in your role as Lindholm. You certainly do not want to be left out. You could attempt to get Clauson or Tepe in a consortium. But, then, a thought occurs to you: Maybe all three of you can be in a consortium. After all, all three firms command the greatest amount of funding ($240,000). But how should the $240,000 be divided [among] the three of you? You are the biggest firm, so you propose that you keep half of the $240,000 (or $120,000), that Tepe get $80,000, and that Clauson get $40,000. This strikes you as fair. At this point, Clauson gets upset and tells you that she and Tepe can go it alone and get $150,000. She thinks that your share is unfair and should be reduced to something less than $90,000. You then remind Clauson that you and Tepe can get $190,000 together, of which you certainly deserve at least half, which is better than the $90,000 offer. Then the three of you are at it again in a vicious circle of coalition formation and demolition.

The negotiation between Lindholm, Tepe, and Clauson illustrates the unstable nature of coalitions. In this example, the left-out party is always able to approach one of the two parties in the coalition and offer him or her a better deal, which can then be beaten by the remaining party, ad infinitum. Furthermore, splitting the pie three ways seems to offer no obvious solution. So, what should the three parties do? Is there a solution? Or are the parties destined to go around in circles forever?

Getting Out of the Vicious Circle

As a way out of the vicious circle, let's conceptualize the problem as a system of simultaneous equations to solve. . . . [Three different conceptual mathematical models are explored to resolve the dilemma and each results in a different allocation to the three parties. The authors conclude:] Is there an optimal way for multiple parties to allocate resources so that group members are not tempted to form coalitions that may hinder group welfare? Usually not. Whereas there are several defensible ways to allocate resources among coalition members, there is no single best way.

STRATEGIES FOR MAXIMIZING COALITIONAL EFFECTIVENESS

Make Your Contacts Early

Because of the commitment process, people tend to feel obligated to others with whom they have made explicit or implicit agreements. For this reason, it is important to make contact with key parties early in the process of multiparty negotiation before they become psychologically committed to others.

Seek Verbal Commitments

One of the most effective strategies for enhancing coalitional effectiveness is to obtain verbal commitments from people with whom you want to develop trust and follow-through. Most people feel obligated to follow through with promises they make to others, even when verbal commitments are not legally binding in any sense.

Allocate Resources Among Coalitional Members Fairly

If one or more members of the coalition regard the proposed allocation of resources to be unfair, the coalition will be less stable and they will be likely to renege. To the extent to which coalitional members feel that the distribution of the coalition pie is fair, they are more likely to resist persuasion from others to break away from the coalition.

Notes and Questions

12.1 If you were mediating among Raines, Warner, and Lassiter with respect to the product design the team is responsible for, how would you use your knowledge about the condorcet paradox and the impossibility theorem?

12.2 Imagine that Lindholm, Tepe, and Clauson engaged you to mediate the funding allocation conundrum they face. How would you approach the problem?

The question of how people behave in groups, whether forming coalitions or seeking to achieve something as a group, has long been the subject of study by sociologists and social psychologists. Not surprisingly, scholars have differed on whether people within a group become more solidified in their views (Irving L. Janis, Groupthink (2d ed. 1982); Robert B. Cialdini, Influence: The Psychology of Persuasion, (rev. ed. 1993)), especially as "against" other groups, or whether individuals within groups resist collective thinking. This has important implications for forming coalitions among individuals and is even more complex when one tries to bring groups, organizations, or nations together for multiple-party negotiations in the political, commercial, policy, or international arenas. Legal scholar Cass Sunstein explores some of the implications of this research.

 Cass R. Sunstein, DELIBERATIVE TROUBLE? WHY GROUPS GO TO EXTREMES

110 Yale L.J. 71, 73-76, 113-116 (2000)

... Every society contains innumerable deliberating groups. Church groups, political parties, women's organizations, juries, legislative bodies, regulatory commissions, multimember courts, faculties, student organizations, those participating in talk radio programs, Internet discussion groups, and others engage in deliberation. It is a simple social fact that sometimes people enter discussions with one view and leave with another, even on moral and political questions. Emphasizing this fact, many recent observers have embraced the traditional American aspiration to "deliberative democracy," an ideal that is designed to combine popular responsiveness with a high degree of reflection and exchange among people with competing views. But for the most part, the resulting literature has not been empirically informed. It has not dealt much with the real-world consequences of deliberation, and with what generalizations hold in actual deliberative settings, with groups of different predispositions and compositions.

The standard view of deliberation is that of Hamilton and Rawls.... Group discussion is likely to lead to better outcomes, if only because competing views are stated and exchanged. Aristotle spoke in similar terms, suggesting that when diverse people

> all come together.... they may surpass—collectively and as a body, although not individually—the quality of the few best.... [W]hen there are many [who contribute to the process of deliberation], each has his share of goodness and practical wisdom.... Some appreciate one part, some another, and all together appreciate all.

But an important empirical question is whether and under what circumstances it is really true that "some appreciate one part, some another, and all together appreciate all."

My principal purpose in this essay is to investigate a striking but largely neglected statistical regularity—that of group polarization—and to relate this phenomenon to underlying questions about the role of deliberation in the "public sphere" of a heterogeneous democracy. In brief, group polarization means that members of a deliberating group predictably move toward a more extreme point in the direction indicated by the members' predeliberation tendencies. "Like polarized molecules, group members become even more aligned in the direction they were already tending." ... Notably, groups consisting of individuals with extremist tendencies are more likely to shift, and likely to shift more; the same is true for groups with some kind of salient shared identity (like Republicans, Democrats, and lawyers, but unlike jurors and experimental subjects). When like-minded people are participating in "iterated polarization games" — when they meet regularly, without sustained exposure to competing views — extreme movements are all the more likely.

Two principal mechanisms underlie group polarization. The first points to social influences on behavior and in particular to people's desire to maintain their reputation and their self-conception. The second emphasizes the limited "argument pools" within any group, and the directions in which those limited pools lead group members. An understanding of the two mechanisms provides many insights into deliberating bodies. Such an understanding illuminates a great deal, for example, about likely processes within multimember courts, juries, political parties, and legislatures — not to mention ethnic groups, extremist organizations, criminal conspiracies, student associations, faculties, institutions engaged in feuds or "turf battles," workplaces, and families. At the same time, these mechanisms raise serious questions about deliberation from the normative point of view. If deliberation predictably pushes groups toward a more extreme point in the direction of their original tendency, whatever that tendency may be, is there any reason to think that deliberation is producing improvements?

One of my largest purposes is to cast light on *enclave deliberation* as simultaneously a potential danger to social stability, a source of social fragmentation, and a safeguard against social injustice and unreasonableness. Group polarization helps explain an old point, with clear constitutional resonances, to the effect that social homogeneity can be quite damaging to good deliberation. When people are hearing echoes of their own voices, the consequence may be far more than support and reinforcement. An understanding of group polarization thus illuminates social practices designed to reduce the risks of deliberation limited to like-minded people. Consider the ban on single-party domination of independent regulatory agencies, the requirement of legislative bicameralism, and debates, within the United States and internationally, about the value of proportional or group representation. Group polarization is naturally taken as a reason for skepticism about enclave deliberation and for seeking to ensure deliberation among a wide group of diverse people.

But there is a point more supportive of enclave deliberation: Participants in heterogeneous groups tend to give least weight to the views of low-status members — in some times and places, women, African Americans, less-educated people. Hence enclave deliberation might be the only way to ensure that those views are developed and eventually heard. Without a place for enclave deliberation, citizens in the broader public sphere may move in certain directions, even extreme directions, precisely because opposing voices are not heard at all. The ambivalent lesson is that deliberating enclaves can be breeding grounds both for the development of unjustly suppressed views and for unjustified extremism, indeed fanaticism. . . .

THE PUBLIC SPHERE AND APPROPRIATE HETEROGENEITY

. . . For a deliberative democracy, a central question is how to ensure *appropriate* heterogeneity. For example, it would not make sense to say that in a deliberating group attempting to think through issues of affirmative action, it is important to allow exposure to people who think that slavery was good and should be restored. The constraints of time and attention call for limits to heterogeneity; and — a separate point — for good deliberation to take place, some views are properly placed off the table, simply because time is limited and they are so invidious, or implausible, or both. This point might seem to create a final conundrum: To know what points of view should be represented in any group deliberation, it is important to have a good sense of the substantive issues involved, indeed a sense sufficient to generate judgments about what points of view must be included and excluded. But if we already know that, does deliberation have any point at all?

The answer is that we often do know enough to see which views count as reasonable, without knowing which view counts as right, and this point is sufficient to allow people to construct deliberative processes that should correct for the most serious problems potentially created by group polarization. What is necessary is not to allow every view to be heard, but to ensure that no single view is so widely heard, and reinforced, that people are unable to engage in critical evaluation of the reasonable competitors.

Of course, the provision of diverse views does not guarantee good deliberation. Among other things, most people are subject to "confirmation bias," in accordance with which exposure to a competing position will not dislodge and may even strengthen the antecedently held position. On questions of morality and fairness, and undoubtedly other questions as well, those who listen to diverse opinions may well emerge from the experience with an enhanced belief in the soundness of their original commitment. But this is not a universal phenomenon, and at least an understanding of competing views is likely to weaken the forms of fragmentation and misunderstanding that come from deliberation among the like-minded.

The final excerpt in this section explores the use of new "deliberative democracy" enhancing processes to resolve political and policy issues involving multiple stakeholders. Since multiparty situations themselves pose a variety of new challenges, good process design in this arena is necessarily complicated and challenging.

 Carrie Menkel-Meadow, **THE LAWYER'S ROLE(S) IN DELIBERATIVE DEMOCRACY**

5 Nev. L.J. 347, 352-53, 357 (2005)

To the extent that participation remains a cornerstone of democratic theory, new forms of participation (whether direct or mediated by agents or representatives) may require the creation of new institutions or modifications of old forms to permit optimum and appropriate levels of participation for effective and legitimate outcomes. Whether tied to traditional constitutional and legal institutions, like courts, legislatures, and administrative agencies, or created new out of the particularities of specific situations (as in negotiated consensus building fora), lawyers have knowledge, skills, craft and wisdom (if effectively employed) to help craft and manage such institutions. . . .

Turning away from substantive discussions of the just and the good does not eliminate theoretical or practical debate — the terrain has shifted to what kinds of processes or procedures may best facilitate either partial or more global "agreements" about the good and the just. What is fair becomes the principal concern in these process-oriented theories. Thus, some political theorists look to "reasoned deliberation" focused on rationality, principled and rational discourse, others on explicit models of bargaining and interest or preference trading or negotiation and still others, on the recognition of emotional or subjective sensibilities (such as empathy and "imaginative identification") in the processes by which modern political actors must get things done. Some insist that foundational principles like American constitutionalism are essential to the legitimacy and fairness of any dispute resolution and political governance system, while others suggest that constitutionalism is too rigid and prevents important procedural flexibility from letting process rules be negotiated along with substantive outcomes, as particular parties and problems require. Modern political theorists seek to describe, elaborate and in some cases, prescribe "ideal speech conditions," "ideal proceduralism," "procedural justice," "fairness in procedure as an invariable value" or "discourse ethics" at various levels of theoretical complexity. Others have focused on "new institutions" or new understandings or reconfigurations of existing governmental institutions or structures, like courts, legislatures and agencies, often by focusing on new public and private collaborations. Still others suggest that new forms of participation will themselves generate new substantive solutions or at least contingent accommodations, recognizing that the tools used to solve problems may influence the resolutions. . . .

If there is only one thing . . . theorists seem to have in common, it is a belief that greater, wider and deeper participation in democracy and political and legal decision making will be better for our society, as well as for individuals. . . . The unifying theme is one of articulating a vision of collaborative, cooperative social processes, in opposition to the more adversarial and competitive assumptions of Hobbesian and Madisonian theories of contest and factionalism in human deliberation. And, in other respects, the claims for deliberative democracy recapitulate old dualisms between liberalism (individualism) and democracy (republican and representative forms). . . .

Notes and Questions

12.3 From these descriptions of the complexities of multiparty decision-making processes, imagine how you might structure a mediation process to facilitate the following:

    a. The best possible process for a "good" decision;

    b. The best possible process for "maximum stakeholder participation";

    c. The best possible process to avoid bad "group polarization" and promote optimal heterogeneity in participation.

Do different values suggest different process designs?

12.4 From these readings, what do you think about the role of stability of coalitions, groups, or even individuals within decision-making settings? How can disputes be resolved when there is instability? When there is too much stability (rigid adherence to a particular view, such as within an "enclave" as Sunstein describes it)?

12.5 What goals do you think are important to achieve in multiparty processes? Are those goals different from those in two-party or three-party disputes?

12.6 Have you ever been involved in a multiparty dispute? What issues were being resolved? What process was used? What would you like to have changed about the process? How might changing the process have changed the outcome?

12.7 Think about a major multiparty dispute in the public arena now (domestic or international). How would you structure a process to effectively deal with the issues and parties?

12.8 Consider whether there are or ought to be differences in process design for public multiparty disputes (governmental, international) versus private ones.

12.9 What are the implications for conducting multiparty mediations in joint session only? In caucus sessions only? What purposes might selective caucusing serve?

B. APPLICATIONS OF MULTIPARTY PROCESSES

Different kinds of problems call up different kinds of participants, who may speak in different "languages" (for example, appeals to principles, reasons, logic, emotions, utilitarian interests or preferences, moral, ethical, or religious suasion). To make conflict resolution legitimate and effective in a wide variety of public and private settings, we have to marry conflict resolution theory and its process pluralism to political theory. The political scientist Jon Elster compares the processes of public-open and plenary processes, which employ highly principled and politicized rhetoric (as was used in the French constitutional process) to the more "secret," committee-based, and "pragmatic bargaining" rhetoric of the American constitutional process, suggesting that sometimes "second-best processes" (less transparent, more compromising, and less "principled") make for more robust outcomes or conclusions. (The American Constitution, even after the Civil War and numerous amendments, has lasted far longer than the French.) See Jon Elster, Strategic Uses of Argument, in Kenneth J. Arrow et al. eds., Barriers to Conflict Resolution (1995). From this work of Elster's, Carrie Menkel-Meadow has elaborated a taxonomy of different modes of processes to use in conflict resolution and political deliberation. Her work describes and separates modes of discourse with different structures of process and different kinds of parties. She then provides examples of different kinds of group process and decision making. Following her taxonomy, Lawrence Susskind and Liona Zion describe ideal conditions for consensus building in multi-party disputes.

Carrie Menkel-Meadow, **INTRODUCTION: FROM LEGAL DISPUTES TO CONFLICT RESOLUTION AND HUMAN PROBLEM SOLVING**

in Dispute Processing and Conflict Resolution (2003), at xi, xxxi

MODES OF CONFLICT RESOLUTION*

MODE OF DISCOURSE	PRINCIPLED (REASONS)	BARGAINING (INTERESTS)	PASSIONS (NEEDS/ EMOTIONS/RELIGION)
FORMS OF PROCESS:			
Closed	Some court proceedings; arbitration	Negotiation-U.S. Constitution; diplomacy	Mediation (e.g., divorce)
Open	French Constitution; courts; arbitration	Public negotiations; some labor	Dialogue movement
Plenary	French Constitution	Reg-neg	Town meetings
Committees	Faculty committees; task groups	U.S. Constitution/ U.S. Congress	Caucuses-interest groups
Expert/Facilitator	Consensus building	Mini-trial	Public conversations
Naturalistic (Leaderless)			Grassroots organizing/ WTO protests
Permanent	Government; institutions	Business organizations; unions	Religious organizations; Alcoholics Anonymous; Weight Watchers
Constitutive	UN, national constitution	National constitutions/professional associations	Civil justice movements; peace movement
Temporary/Ad Hoc	Issue organizations/ social justice	Interest groups	Yippies; New Age; vigilantes

Principles = reasons, appeals to universalism, law
Bargaining = interests, preferences, trading, compromises

Open = public or transparent meetings or proceedings
Closed = confidential, secret process or even outcomes (settlements)

Plenary = full group participation, joint meetings
Committees = task groups, caucuses, parts of the whole

Expert-facilitator = led by expertise (process or substantive or both)
Naturalistic = leaderless, grassroots, ad hoc

Permanent = organizational, institutional
Constitutive = constitutional
Temporary = ad hoc groups or disputants

Some predicted effects of process on outcome:

Closed (confidential) proceedings allow more expression of interests, needs and passions = more "honest" and "candid, " allow more "trades, " less posturing, open to vulnerability
Open (transparent) proceedings require more principled/reasons justifications, produce more rigidity

---

*Partially derived from catagories specified by Jon Elster, Strategic Uses of Argument, in Kenneth Arrow et al. eds., Barriers to Conflict Resolution (1995).

Lawrence Susskind & Liora Zion, **STRENGTHENING THE DEMOCRATIC PROCESS IN THE UNITED STATES: AN EXAMINATION OF RECENT EXPERIMENTS**

(2002) (unpub. manuscript — see *http://www.susskind.info/content/contributions/ democracy.pdf.*)

...The current structure and practice of representative democracy in the United States falls short of our ideals in numerous ways:

1. Too few people are involved in a meaningful way in most decisions that affect them and their communities.
2. There is an excessive reliance on majority rule, and a lack of emphasis on forging political consensus. So, the concerns of certain groups are constantly ignored.
3. Very little effort has been made to increase the capacity of people who disagree or come from disparate schools of thought to interact in ways that encourage deeper understanding or resolution of differences. It is almost as if we have resigned ourselves to the idea that people who disagree will never change their views, no matter what evidence or arguments are presented.
4. There is too much dependence on electing representatives to speak on behalf of those whom they serve.
5. Seldom do we experiment with new technologies or new approaches to involving citizens more directly in decisions that affect them.

Towards a More Inclusive and Responsive Democracy

Under ideal circumstances, the democratic process ought to "direct the exercise of political rights toward the satisfaction of interests." In this paper, we suggest that by working to satisfy individual interests through professionally facilitated dialogue, it is possible to enhance our democratic process and produce public policy results that are viewed as fairer by those affected, more efficient from the standpoint of independent policy analysts, more stable over time, and wiser when the participants look back on the knowledge that was actually available at the time decisions had to be made. We also argue in this paper that by working to satisfy interests in the right way, we can, as a society, achieve better public policy outcomes. The key is to create new problem-solving forums that operate by consensus.

The basis for our claims is found within the theory of deliberative democracy, which has emerged within the last decade as a means of addressing the inadequacies of current democratic practices. Essentially, deliberation provides an opportunity for the public to determine the legitimacy of particular public policy choices. Proponents and opponents of each decision must justify their claims in terms that the public as a whole can accept. The critical assumption behind deliberation is that individuals must be able to reflect upon conflicting arguments, because individual preferences will evolve as different ideas and facts emerge during the dialogue....

[I]n order to realize democratic ideals in today's America, new forms of deliberation that seek informed consensus are required. We conclude that the most effective model of deliberation is a consensus building approach that has the following features: (1) it includes key stakeholder representatives, selected by the relevant groups themselves, in both fact-finding and decision-making; (2) it involves transparent public discourse, organized and managed by a neutral party according to rules that are made, in part, by those who will be affected; (3) it involves the search for mutual gains among the parties, rather than a zero sum outcome; and (4) it seeks to generate agreements that can be implemented (and does not settle for just conversation). We argue that these elements are necessary to ensure practical and effective deliberations that can yield policy decisions that will ultimately be judged fairer, more efficient, more stable, and wiser than the other procedural options available. . . .

CONSENSUS BUILDING

Consensus building is an approach to decision-making that brings all stakeholders together to jointly seek solutions or to develop a shared approach to a problem. The stakeholders, with the help of a neutral facilitator, strive to produce a mutually beneficial "package" that must then be approved by the relevant elected or appointed officials. The goal is to reach an informed consensus.

In the words of John Stuart Mill, "the success of democratic arrangements can be measured in two ways, by the quality of its decisions and the quality of the citizens it produces." Consensus building enhances democratic practice by involving those directly affected by decisions in the process of deciding what to do. As a consequence, such decisions are easier to implement. Also, since deliberation is a fundamental part of consensus building, the stakeholders learn more about the issue under discussion, are able to refine their own ideas and learn more about each other's interests, perceptions, and world-views. The process enables stakeholders to establish new contacts in their community while increasing the knowledge base of the players in the network. Thus, consensus building enhances the quality of the decisions that have to be made while increasing the capabilities of the citizens involved. It can also be a tool for building social capital.

Consensus building is not just another form of deliberation (that seeks agreement through compromise or by suppressing conflict). Quite the opposite. Consensus building requires an exploration and understanding of all stakeholders' interests, fears, and perceptions to produce a fair, efficient, stable and wise agreement. This means that conflict airing often needs to be a part of consensus building. Consensus building brings elected officials into negotiations as stakeholders, encourages the involvement of lay experts, puts a premium on joint fact finding, and restructures the relationship between dialogue and decision-making. . . .

STAKEHOLDER INVOLVEMENT: DEALING WITH QUESTIONS OF WHO TO INCLUDE AND DEGREES OF INVOLVEMENT

Ideally, a consensus building process should include all parties with a stake in the outcome. Practical matters on the ground may cause difficulties in meeting this ideal.

INTRODUCING PROFESSIONAL FACILITATION AND MEDIATION

Although the tasks and strategies of facilitators and mediators are varied, facilitation and mediation are tools that can generally be used to support a consensus building process in complex public policy-making situations. In order to be effective, a group of individuals working collaboratively should have a clear mandate or mission. Moreover, to achieve results in a reasonable time, they should be well organized, technically competent, and motivated to work together. Unfortunately, groups formed to address issues of public interest rarely possess these characteristics. Because this is so often the case, a facilitator or mediator is needed to assist. . . .

CONCLUSIONS

How can one be sure that the interests of all stakeholders will be protected and incorporated into a consensus agreement? There are several well-defined procedures to ensure that this occurs. Firstly, consensus building begins with a neutral party undertaking a "conflict assessment" before anyone comes to the table. During this prenegotiation stage, the "assessor" is responsible for seeking out all legitimate stakeholders (including elected and appointed officials) and documenting their concerns. Stakeholder groups then choose their own representatives to participate in the ad hoc dialogue. Through discussions with each set of stakeholders, the assessor must uncover all of the issues of concern to each party. This ensures that the agenda, timetable, ground rules, and work plan proposed by the neutral will be acceptable to all the parties. Following the assessment, stakeholder interests continue to be protected and incorporated in explicit ways. An experienced mediator ensures that the dialogue is at least as transparent as existing legislative, judicial or executive decision-making processes. Moreover, use of joint fact-finding procedures ensures that all stakeholders have access to the technical information they need to present their views effectively. . . . Finally, as mentioned above, the dialogue is managed by the mediator to maximize joint gains, and provide a written explanation, that makes sense to all participants, for how "value" will be distributed.

The properly constructed and managed consensus building process addresses concerns about power imbalance (although it cannot transform them). . . . [W]e recognize that full political equality is virtually impossible in a deliberative context. However, while a dire lack of material resources can certainly detract from a party's ability to affect deliberated outcomes, equality in resources is not essential to effective consensus building. If political equality is, as Dryzek [Deliberative Democracy and Beyond, 2000] defines it, "the presumption that all participants in a process have an equal chance of affecting the outcome," then a consensus building process may actually improve the degree of political equality among stakeholders by providing weaker parties with an opportunity to employ alternative sources of (negotiating) power. . . .

Dryzek states that "we should rely on mechanisms endogenous to deliberation to achieve an appropriate and acceptable balance between private and public interests, partial and impartial concerns." By contrast, we believe that the public interest is, by definition, the product of a decision-making process that incorporates all the elements we have discussed above: inclusion and active involvement of all stakeholders both in decision-making and in fact-finding; integrative bargaining to maximize joint gains; and professional facilitation that ensures transparency and fair management of negotiation dynamics. These elements ensure that the products of a deliberative decision-making process will be considered fairer by the parties, more efficient by independent analysts, more stable, and ultimately wiser when considered in retrospect by independent technical analysts. Consensus building, which embodies all of these elements, provides an organized means for ensuring both a more attentive and a more effective democracy.

Notes and Questions

12.10 As you read about "deliberative democracy" and new processes or institutions of multiparty problem solving, think about both the process and legal issues that are implicated in their use, remembering Lon Fuller's exhortation to consider the "moral integrity" and separate justifications of each process. When we use privately facilitated consensus-building processes to deal with public problems such as resource allocation, environmental siting, governmental budgeting, school programming, and interracial and community governance issues, what is the relationship of the state to the negotiators, facilitators, and decision makers? You are reading this text as a soon-to-be-lawyer — what are the legal issues implicated in the use of these processes?

12.11 How does private decision making (such as in commercial development or environmental waste siting) interact with public law requirements (such as zoning and regulation)? Must there be formal legal authority (the constitution, zoning laws) to use these processes antecedent to their use, or can the outcomes be legitimized or ratified post hoc after "good" decisions are reached? See Alejandro Esteban Camacho, Mustering the Missing Voices: A Collaborative Model for Fostering Equality, Community Involvement and Adaptive Planning in Land Use Decisions, Installment One, 24 Stan. Environ. L.J. 3 (2005); Installment Two, 24 Stan. Environ. L.J. 269 (2005) for a rich discussion of these issues.

12.12 Who should convene these processes? Skilled process experts? Interested stakeholders? The government? How should they be evaluated?

12.13 Is it a good thing to "let a thousand flowers bloom" (Chairman Mao) in permitting many forms of decentralized decision making and processes ("devolution of power" to some), or should our government require equality (as in sameness) of process for decisions that affect many people in many different regions of the country? How are dispute resolution processes related to federalism and separation of powers?

12.14 Compare the tasks of a facilitator in consensus-building processes and a mediator. Are there meaningful differences?

Philip Harter made the first effort to combine the insights of problem-solving dispute resolution theory with the formal governmental processes used in multiparty disputes and public policy settings. His concept of negotiated rule making ("reg-neg") put into practice the theory of formally recognizing negotiation theory in multiparty processes and granted governmental legitimacy to "alternative" processes based on negotiation and party participation. Following Harter's publication of the article below, Congress permitted these processes in the Negotiated Rulemaking Act of 1990, 5 U.S.C. §§561-570 (2000), and multiparty negotiations in the form of reg-neg began to be employed in a variety of regulatory settings (occupational health and safety, food and drug administration, and environmental, to name a few). In 1996, these processes were more formally legitimated in the Administrative Dispute Resolution Act, 5 U.S.C. §§571-584 (2000). Although Harter's path-breaking work has been influential primarily in federal policy making, many states have employed these processes. For some examples, see Consensus Building Institute, *http://www.cbuilding.org*, and Policy Consensus Institute, *http://www.policyconsensus.org*. Variations on this use of multiparty participation have also been used in private disputes, such as those over land use or development and racial or ethnic conflicts.

 Philip J. Harter, **NEGOTIATING REGULATIONS: A CURE FOR MALAISE**

71 Geo. L.J. 1, 7, 28, 30-31, 112-113 (1982)

This article proposes that a form of negotiation among representatives of the interested parties, including administrative agencies, would be an effective alternative procedure to the current rulemaking process. Although virtually every rulemaking includes some negotiation, it is almost never the group consensus envisioned here. Negotiations among directly affected groups, conducted within both the existing policies of the statute authorizing the regulation and the existing policies of the agency, would enable the parties to participate directly in the establishment of the rule....

THE ADVANTAGES OF RULEMAKING BY NEGOTIATION

Negotiating has many advantages over the adversarial process. The parties participate directly and immediately in the decision. They share in its development and concur with it, rather than "participate" by submitting information that the decision maker considers in reaching the decision. Frequently, those who participate in the negotiation are closer to the ultimate decisionmaking authority of the interest they represent than traditional intermediaries that represent the interest in an adversarial proceeding. Thus, participants in negotiations can make substantive decisions, rather than acting as experts in the decisionmaking process. In addition, negotiation can be a less expensive means of decision making because it reduces the need to engage in defensive research in anticipation of arguments made by adversaries....

Rulemaking by negotiation can reduce the time and cost of developing regulations by emphasizing practical and empirical concerns rather than theoretical predictions. In developing a regulation under the current system, an agency must prove a factual case, at least preliminarily, and anticipate the factual information that will be submitted in the record. Because the agency lacks direct access to empirical data, the information used is often of a theoretical nature derived from models. In negotiations, the parties in interest decide together what information is necessary to make a reasonably informed decision. . . .

Negotiation also can enable the participants to focus on the details of a regulation. In the adversary process, the big points must be hit and hit hard, while the subtleties and details frequently are overlooked. Or, even if the details are not overlooked, the decision maker may not appreciate their consequences. In negotiations, however, interested parties can directly address all aspects of a problem in attempting to formulate workable solutions.

Overarching all the other benefits of negotiations is the added legitimacy a rule would acquire if all parties viewed the rule as reasonable and endorsed it without a fight. Affected parties would participate in the development of a rule by sharing in the decisions, ranking their own concerns and needs, and trading them with other parties. . . .

[Harter goes on to discuss ground rules, the importance of participants committing to a "rule of reason" or principle of good faith; and the delicate balancing of special confidentiality concerns relevant to government-related deliberation and decision-making. He concludes:]

CONCLUSION: WORTH A TRY

Regulatory negotiation holds promise for success when the issues are relatively well defined, when there are a limited number of parties with sufficient power to prevent the others from emerging victorious, and when it is inevitable that some decision is imminent. . . . [T]he potential theoretical benefits of negotiation are attractive. Experience with negotiating solutions to complex policy questions indicates that, at least in some circumstances, many of those benefits can indeed be realized. The malaise of administrative law, which has marched steadily toward reliance on the judiciary to settle disputes and away from direct participation of affected parties, could be countered with a participatory negotiation process. Regulatory negotiations would provide the legitimacy currently lacking in the regulatory process.

Notes and Questions

12.15 Since Harter's original suggestion, many reg-negs have occurred and are now the subject of heated academic and evaluative debate about their effectiveness and ability to accomplish the goals that Harter and others have set for them. See, e.g., Cary Coglianese, Assessing Consensus: The Promise and Performance of Negotiated Rulemaking, 46 Duke L.J. 1255 (1997); Jody Freeman, Collaborative Governance in the Administrative State, 45 UCLA L. Rev. 1 (1997); Jody Freeman & Laura I. Langbein, Regulatory Negotiation and the Legitimacy Benefit, 9 N.Y.U. Envtl. L.J. 60 (2000); Philip J. Harter, Assessing the Assessors: The Actual Performance of Negotiated Rulemaking, 9 N.Y.U. Envtl. L.J. 32 (2000).

12.16   Harter uses the Fisher and Ury model of principled negotiation (see Chapter 2) as his suggested form of negotiated rule making. Do the more general theories of negotiation, such as principled negotiation or integrative bargaining, work the same way in dyadic two-party negotiation as in multiple party negotiation in this context? Are public governmental negotiations the same as dyadic private ones? Consider confidentiality as it intersects with government or public issues negotiations (such as requirements of the Sunshine Act or Freedom of Information Act).

12.17   What evaluative criteria would you use to assess whether stakeholder negotiations, held before formal rule making, are more or less successful than the more conventional draft rule, publish notice and comments, promulgation of regulation, and litigation model of administrative law (see Administrative Procedure Act, 5 U.S.C. §§551 et seq. (2000))? How can we evaluate different kinds of processes when the subject matter of each process may be different, and, unlike experimental evaluation, we cannot assign the same "issue" to several different treatments simultaneously for evaluation?

12.18   Is negotiation appropriate among formal governmental processes about public matters? Isn't this how laws are made in Congress, as well as in the administrative process? Which processes are more transparent? Is transparency the only goal? Must negotiations be "principled" to be legitimate?

12.19   How does government decision making about regulatory matters satisfy requirements for democracy? What does democracy mean here — a majority vote? Plurality? Supermajority? Unanimity? What is consensus in these contexts? Must all policy making be "democratic"? What about dispute resolution in the public sphere? Does democracy mean only those "affected by a decision" should participate, as Jürgen Habermas suggests (that the "acted upon" should participate in decisions that affect them)? Or that all citizens should have some input into governmental decision making? How do we evaluate whether democracy has been part of a decision-making process?

12.20   Is it undemocratic to use "process experts," as facilitators or substantive experts in such processes? Is mediation or facilitated dialogue more or less democratic than other decision-making processes? More or less participatory? Is participation synonymous with democracy? What are the possible ethical issues implicated in serving as a third-party facilitator in a regulatory forum? How might professional and ethical duties here compare to those of a third-party neutral in a private forum?

12.21   What additional tasks and skills must a neutral intervener undertake to be of good service in a reg-neg forum, as contrasted to a mediator of a dispute between a plaintiff and a defendant in the context of a civil litigation?

C.   SKILLS AND PROCEDURES FOR MULTIPARTY PROCESSES

Because multiparty processes occur in so many different subject areas and formats, it is much harder to specify in advance what a multiparty process does or should do. As you learned from reading the preceding excerpts, professionals — ranging from social psychologists to economists to lawyers — all offer important insights into what happens when the already dynamic processes of negotiation and mediation are "opened out" to include multiple parties. The practical result of all these scholars' work is a new field within dispute resolution formed to develop structures, procedures, rules, protocols, and training models to guide both formal and informal multiparty negotiations and mediations.

As you have read, parties and their representatives inside multiparty decision making fora face additional issues as contrasted with advocates in simpler negotiations or mediations. Such issues as coalition formation, trust, sequencing and ordering of interactions, and alliance creation become important. This section first examines the importance of sequencing for the attorney (or other) representative and then introduces facilitation skills for the mediator.

1. Sequencing

The excerpt below, on sequencing, is one of the classics in the emerging field of multiparty negotiation analysis. It is written by a scholar who is also a skilled participant in many complex international and commercial multiparty negotiations.

 James K. Sebenius, **SEQUENCING TO BUILD COALITIONS: WITH WHOM SHOULD I TALK FIRST?**

> in **Wise Choices: Decisions, Games and Negotiations 324, 324-329; 332-333, 335, 337-338, 344-345 (Richard J. Zeckhauser, Ralph L. Keeney & James K. Sebenius eds., 1996)**

Surprisingly little systematic consideration has been given to the processes by which negotiators build coalitions, the logic behind their tactical choices, and how these actions matter to outcomes. This essay explores one part of the issue: what David Lax and I have called "strategic sequencing," or the choice of which parties are approached, in what order, openly or secretly, separately or together. Sequencing choices can be a prominent feature of coalition building, an implicit logic governs the tactics employed, and these tactics may significantly affect the results.

For example, the 1985 Plaza accords represent a virtuoso example of sequencing. When James Baker became U.S. Treasury Secretary in 1985, the strong dollar was taking a severe toll on American industry and generating powerful protectionist reactions. The United States, under former Treasury Secretary Donald Regan, then Chief of Staff at the Reagan White House, had for some time spurned international economic cooperation to bring the dollar down. Baker's efforts to build a domestic and international coalition committed to a coordinated effort to accomplish this goal initially relied on secrecy. According to one insider's account,

> "Reagan knew of the [Plaza Hotel ministerial] meeting in advance, of course, but was apprised of the full scope of Baker's plan only two days beforehand. Devaluation

was sold to the President as necessary to stem the protectionist tide in Congress," says a Baker intimate. "It was sold to Don Regan as being consistent with an earlier call he had made for an international conference to discuss exchange rates. To this day, I don't think Don understood what we were about to do. We managed [Federal Reserve Chairman Paul] Volcker . . . because we had carefully split his board. Paul had no alternative but to go along."

Armed with this domestic "mandate," Baker used the Plaza Hotel meeting to build the necessary international coalition both to act and to make it very difficult for his domestic rivals to later reverse the resulting policy course. As one finance minister said, "At first he split us just like he split the Fed. He began by using the U.S. and Japan against West Germany. Then he combined those three to bring along the whole Group of Five [including Britain and France]."

Baker carefully sequenced his actions to build the coalition of finance ministers committed to implementing his preferred agreement. The de facto coalition was larger, encompassing both domestic and international players. Secrecy and ambiguity, divide-and-conquer tactics, and a tight deadline were used domestically to gain Baker the right to move into the actual Plaza process. There, with the initial concurrence of the Japanese — whose economic interests and bargaining position on the dollar were firmly allied with that of the United States — it was possible to get German agreement. Then this powerful three-way coalition could press the others into the final agreement. To see the potential importance of sequencing here, imagine other possible orders of approach; for example, suppose that the Germans had in advance forged an ironclad coalition with the British, French, and others against the likely American proposal.

Baker's coalitional machinations are fairly typical of one broad class of sequencing actions intended to create an irreversible commitment to a preferred agreement. They suggest a number of analytic and prescriptive issues. For example, under what conditions does sequencing matter? Why are some potential sequences preferred to others? When are natural allies likely to be approached first and when is the process most likely to commence among potentially blocking interests? How and why does the openness or secrecy of the process matter? Are there characteristic negotiation sequences when both internal and external actors are involved? . . .

While game theory has neglected sequencing issues, folk wisdom has not. For example, one standard admonition is to "get your allies on board first." Obviously, this sensible approach is the product of much experience and makes eminent sense in many situations; for example, Baker did just this with the Japanese in the international phase of the Plaza accord process. However, there are striking counterexamples to "allies on board first." For example, as the United States sought to build a global anti-Iraq coalition following the Kuwait invasion, many observers would have argued that Israel was its strongest regional ally. Yet the Israelis were pointedly excluded from the growing coalition: Israel's formal membership would have greatly complicated, if not precluded, numerous Arab states' joining.

A related bit of folk wisdom and standard diplomatic practice when preparing "your side" to negotiate with an "external" party is to "get your own house in order first," or "hammer out a common internal position." Ambassadors and bargaining agents often see a required first step for eventual external dealings as thrashing out a consensus internally on negotiating instructions. Evidently, this represents time-honored and often good advice. Yet in preparing for the Gulf War, President George Bush [Senior] did anything but get the U.S. house in order first and then negotiate externally. Instead, he committed U.S. troops to the region, and then exhaustively built up — in part by virtuoso sequential diplomacy — an external international U.N. coalition behind a Security Council Resolution authorizing "all necessary means" to eject Iraq from Kuwait. Only then did the Bush administration begin negotiating seriously for Congressional authorization to use force in the Gulf. Of course, the prior commitment of U.S. troops along with hard-won international backing for the use of force made it vastly harder for Congress to withhold approval. Had Bush started by seeking the approval of a deeply skeptical U.S. Congress, agreement would have been unlikely at best and, given Congressional refusal, any subsequent American-led international coalition-building enterprise would have been hobbled.

Exceptions to maxims — such as "allies first" or "internal consensus before external negotiation" — only raise more basic questions: when are they right and when are they wrong and why? This essay explores such questions, proposes a more general model for sequencing choices, and concludes with a few observations. In contrast with the "structure implies outcome" tradition, the "path effects" of different sequences will play a central role in the analysis.

PATH EFFECTS I: SEQUENCING TO EXPLOIT "PATTERNS OF DEFERENCE"

A common problem for the would-be coalition builder is that approaching the most difficult — and perhaps most critical — party offers slim chances for a deal. One approach is to discern what we will define as the "patterns of deference" involving the "target player." An illustration comes from observing the successful sequencing tactic of Bill Daley, President Clinton's key strategist for securing Congressional approval of the controversial North American Free Trade Agreement (NAFTA).

> News might arrive that a representative who had been leaning toward yes had come out as a no. "Weenie," [Daley would] say. When he heard the bad news, he did not take it personally. He'd take more calls. "Can we find the guy who can deliver the guy? We have to call the guy who calls the guy who calls the guy."

More formally, suppose that the subjective probability of Party A saying yes if asked independently is less than the conditional probability of Party A saying yes given that A is informed that Party B has already said yes. In symbols, P(A says Yes/B says Yes) > P(A says Yes). A's deference to B might be due to several factors: B's perceived greater expertise, status, or reputation for having the same values as A; B may have done A a favor and A might feel the tug of reciprocity; or B's yes may "cover" A's choice and lessen the risk for A of agreement. In all these cases, we could say that "A tends to defer to B," or that a pattern of deference exists. Deference may be weak, strong, or absolute, depending on the situation and the magnitudes of the probabilities.

With such a pattern of deference, sequence matters; there is an optimal sequence that maximizes the probability of the desired winning coalition, and the coalitional outcome can be said to be path dependent. If B is the "easier" party in the sense that P(B says Yes) > P(A says Yes), then we might call the B-then-A sequence a "bootstrapping" approach to coalition building. The process of working out the sequence from this structure could be called "backward mapping" or reasoning from the hardest ultimate target to the easiest. . . .

Does this mean that the most-likely-to-agree party should always be approached first? Not at all. Suppose A is the "harder" party in that P(A says Yes) = .4, while P(B says Yes) = .5, but that B defers to A, or P(B says Yes/A says Yes) = .9, while A shows no deference to B. Approaching the easy party (B) first yields a success probability of $(.5)(.4) = .2$, while the reverse order yields a higher value $(.4)(.9) = .36$. This "harder first" result is driven by the extent of B's deference to A. The path effect of sequence A-B over B-A equals the probability increment, .16, of successful coalition building. . . .

Prescriptive advice for would-be coalition builders in such cases suggests first, enumerating actual and potential parties relevant to the target coalition; second, assessing their interests, their likely position on joining the target coalition, and their likely alternatives to agreement; third, evaluating potential patterns of deference among the players; and fourth, constructing an optimal sequence by mapping backward from the target coalition to exploit deference patterns. . . .

PATH EFFECTS II: SEQUENCING TO CHANGE NO-AGREEMENT ALTERNATIVES

Considerable evidence suggests that a party is more likely to agree to a proposal, and on less attractive terms, the worse his or her no-agreement alternatives (disagreement utility) appears. An extreme version of this observation would be the Godfather's "offer you can't refuse" with its implied "or else." Popular negotiation accounts have enshrined the acronym BATNA (Best Alternative to Negotiated Agreement) as a standard part of prescriptive advice. In a multiparty negotiation aimed at securing the ultimate agreement of several parties, earlier agreement among some of the players may worsen the no-agreement alternatives of later players. Rather than face the status quo ante, later players may face the prospect of a growing coalition. Often the risk of being left out of such a coalition is quite undesirable, thus increasing the chances of the later players joining the growing coalition. Sequencing actions, therefore, may lead to higher agreement probabilities and more attractive terms from the point of view of the coalition builder. . . .

Worsening No-Agreement Alternatives of Internal Blocking Coalitions in Two-Level Games

Despite the conventional wisdom of negotiating "internally" first in order to present a united front in later "external" negotiations, the reverse sequence is often employed when internal would-be blockers are too strong. For example, of the Bush Administration decision to negotiate internationally first for the right to use force against Iraq, National Security Advisor General Brent Scowcroft observed:

There has been some criticism of us for, in effect, pressuring Congress by building an international coalition and then making the argument, "You mean, Congressman, you're not going to support the President, but the president of Ethiopia is supporting him?" But I don't think we should be apologetic about it. You build consensus in whatever way you can, and when this thing first started, we didn't have support from Congress, and we didn't have support from the American people. We couldn't have gotten the Congress earlier, I don't think, and if there had been no coalition and no UN vote, we would never have gotten Congress. . . .

In [this example] — an internal faction may well have functioned as a successful blocking coalition to the initiative favored by the protagonist. By choosing to negotiate with outsiders first, the protagonists in these cases hoped to generate an irreversible commitment to a preferred deal. The path effects could overcome the internal blockers and improve the terms of the deal. By examining a number of such instances, the likelihood and effects of an "outside-in" (or, more accurately, a "small inside, then outside, then larger inside") approach may be better assessed in situations with this structure.

PATH EFFECTS III: SHAPING OUTCOME EXPECTATIONS

Beyond patterns of deference and worsening no-agreement alternatives, a bootstrapper may seek to progressively shape the expectations of later players through the actions taken with earlier ones. Social psychological research points up the potent effects that parties' expectations of the outcome can have on bargaining results. An extraordinary story illustrating this class of path effects on the expected value of subsequent bargaining is how labor organizer Ray Rogers broke the anti-union board coalition at J.P. Stevens, a textile firm.

Although organized labor had sought to gain recognition from Stevens for almost 20 years, frontal bargaining assaults, consumer boycotts, demonizing publicity, and legal action had failed to achieve the union's goals. The first step of Rogers's bootstrapping approach was a highly publicized demonstration at Stevens's annual meeting, which raised the salience of the new campaign. Rogers's second step was to use labor's clout and sizable business in New York with Manufacturer's Hanover bank to oust Stevens's chairman and another Stevens board member from the Manufacturer's Hanover Board. The surprise success of this effort greatly enhanced the credibility of Rogers's approach both internally at the union, where there was considerable hesitancy about the approach, and with subsequent targets.

The next target was the New York Life Insurance Company, a Stevens creditor that also wrote many union life and health insurance contracts and managed sizable union pension funds. A New York state insurance law permits a sufficient number of policy holders to contest board elections. Rogers threatened New York Life with such an election and that inherently risk averse institution agreed to eject Stevens's chairman from its board.

Next, Rogers targeted Metropolitan Life, a much larger insurance company that, like New York Life, was a major Stevens creditor, wrote many union life and health policies, and managed substantial union pension funds. Rogers's threat to contest the board election at MetLife, combined with the credibility that his campaign had amassed with victories over both Manufacturer's Hanover and New York Life, predisposed MetLife to exert great pressure on J.P. Stevens to make a deal with the union. The anti-union coalition including the Stevens board and management was broken, the union recognized, and a new contract negotiated.

As with deference patterns and worsened no-agreement alternatives, this sequencing strategy depended on early moves to boost Rogers's credibility and share expectations of the outcome for later targets. By starting with the easiest target, Manufacturer's Hanover, raising credibility both internally and externally, and favorably shaping subsequent outcome expectations, Rogers's bootstrapping approach succeeded.

An oft-noted coalitional dynamic, the "bandwagon," normally operates by a combination of worsened no-agreement alternatives and reshaped expectations of the outcome. In getting classic bandwagons rolling, one seeks to get the easy parties on board first and to create the impression of inevitability of the desired final coalition — ideally facing later parties with the choice of (profitably) saying yes to joining or of saying no and being isolated in an undesirable, no-agreement alternative. . . .

CONCLUSIONS

Although sequential tactics have been the focus of the essay, a prior question has been lurking in the background: when should one avoid sequencing and attempt a fully open, collective route to consensus? After all, many sequential moves appear to be — and often are — sneaky, manipulative, deceptive, coercive, and even plainly unethical. It is thus important to think them through both for their ethical *and* their prudential implications. In principle, the choice of a simultaneous or sequential process can be unraveled by specifying and weighing the relevant path effects. Such effects associated with a simultaneous process might include a greater sense of legitimacy and "ownership" of agreement, the possibility of new options generated by brainstorming, as well as altered roles of deference patterns and different possibilities for blocking coalitions to form or to be thwarted. . . .

Notes and Questions

12.22 Can you think of particular situations in which you would "get your allies on board first"? Situations in which you would go "outside" before inside? Assuming a situation in which a mediator plays a role, how should decisions about caucus sequence be made?

12.23 Think of a current multiparty dispute (either domestic or international), and see if you can draw a "backward map" of the "deference patterns" of the parties.

2. Facilitation

> **Facilitation = to make easy**

The preceding excerpt is addressed principally to those participating in multiparty negotiations or decision-making processes as parties or party representatives.

Switching to the perspective of the neutral intervener, what organizational principles and practices emerge?

In the more formal multiparty processes, organizing rules and protocols focus on both *rules of process* or *procedure* and *rules of decision* (such as voting procedures, definitions of key terms such as *consensus*, or majority rules). In informal processes too, including those in which "resolution" is not a goal (for example, facilitated dialogues about controversial issues such as abortion or gun control), protocols or guided questions organize what potentially are complex and unstructured multiparty processes.

One of the founders of this new field, Lawrence Susskind, professor of urban planning at MIT and founder of the Consensus Building Institute, has pioneered the development of these facilitated processes in complex public policy matters and disputes. In a handbook for this new practice, Susskind and several colleagues develop guidelines for conducting facilitated processes in both formal and ad hoc settings.

 Lawrence Susskind, **AN ALTERNATIVE TO ROBERT'S RULES OF ORDER FOR GROUPS, ORGANIZATIONS, AND AD HOC ASSEMBLIES THAT WANT TO OPERATE BY CONSENSUS**

in The Consensus Building Handbook: A Comprehensive Guide to Reaching Agreement 3, 3-13, 20-35, 55-56 (Lawrence Susskind, Sarah McKearnan & Jennifer Thomas-Larmer eds., 1999)

Let's compare what this "Short Guide" has to say with what *Robert's Rules of Order* requires. Assume that a few dozen people have gotten together, on their own, at a community center because they are upset with a new policy or program recently announced by their local officials. After several impassioned speeches, someone suggests that the group appoint a moderator to "keep order" and ensure that the conversation proceeds effectively. Someone else wants to know how the group will decide what to recommend after they are done debating. "Will we vote?" this person wants to know. At this point, everyone turns to Joe, who has had experience as a moderator. Joe moves to the front of the room and explains that he will follow *Robert's Rules of Order.* From that moment on, the conversation takes on a very formal tone.

Instead of just saying what's on their mind, everyone is forced to frame suggestions in the cumbersome form of *motions.* These have to be *seconded.* Efforts to *move the question* are proceeded by an explanation from Joe about what is and isn't an acceptable way of doing this. Proposals to *table* various items are considered, even though everyone hasn't had a chance to speak. Ultimately, all-or-nothing votes are the only way the group seems able to make a decision.

As the hour passes, fewer and fewer of those in attendance feel capable of expressing their views. They don't know the rules, and they are intimidated. Every once in a while, someone makes an effort to restate the problem or make a suggestion, but the person is shouted down ("You're not following *Robert's Rules*!").

No one takes responsibility for ensuring that the concerns of everyone in the room are met, especially the needs of those individuals who are least able to present their views effectively. After an hour or so, many people have left. A final proposal is approved by a vote of 55 percent to 45 percent of those remaining.

If the group had followed the procedures spelled out in this "Short Guide to Consensus Building," the meeting would have been run differently and the result would probably have been a lot more to everyone's liking. The person at the front of the room would have been a trained facilitator or mediator—a person adept at helping groups build consensus—not a moderator with specialized knowledge about how motions should be made or votes should be taken. His or her job would have been to get agreement at the outset on how the group wanted to proceed. Then, the facilitator would have focused on producing an agreement that could meet the underlying concerns of everyone in the room: no motions, no arcane rituals, and no vote at the end. Instead, the facilitator might have pushed the group to brainstorm (e.g., "Can anyone propose a way of proceeding that meets all the interests we have heard expressed thus far?"). After as thorough a consideration of options as time permitted, the facilitator would ask, "Is there anyone who can't live with the last version of what has been proposed? If so, what improvement or modification can you suggest that will make it more acceptable to you, while continuing to meet the interests of everyone else with a stake in the issue?" The group would have likely developed a proposal that everyone—or nearly everyone—in the room could support. And participants would leave satisfied that their opinions and needs had been heard, understood, and taken into account.

WHAT'S WRONG WITH *ROBERT'S RULES*?

Robert's Rules of Order was first published in 1870. It was based on the rules and practices of Congress, and presumed that parliamentary procedures (and majority rule) offered the most appropriate model for any and all groups. The author presumed that the *Rules of Order* would "assist an assembly in accomplishing the work for which it was designed" by "restraining the individual" so that the interests of the group could be met.

In the more than 125 years since *Robert's Rules* was first published, many other approaches to group work and organizational activity have emerged. The goal of this "Short Guide" and the full *Handbook* is to codify the best possible advice to groups and organizations that prefer to operate with broad support, by consensus, rather than simply by majority rule. We believe that something greater than a bare majority achieved through voting is almost always more desirable than majority rule. Moreover, the formalism of parliamentary procedure is particularly unsatisfying and often counterproductive, getting in the way of commonsense solutions. It relies on insider knowledge of obscure rules of the game. It does not tap the full range of facilitative skills of group leaders. And it typically leaves many stakeholders (often something just short of a majority) angry and disappointed, with little or nothing to show for their efforts. . . .

DEFINITIONS

Consensus Building (An Agreement-Seeking Process)

Consensus building is a process of seeking unanimous agreement. It involves a good-faith effort to meet the interests of all stakeholders. Consensus has been reached when everyone agrees they can live with whatever is proposed after every effort has been made to meet the interests of all stakeholding parties. Thus, consensus building requires that someone frame a proposal after listening carefully to everyone's concerns. Participants in a consensus building process have both the right to expect that no one will ask them to undermine their interests and the responsibility to propose solutions that will meet everyone else's interests as well as their own.

Most consensus building efforts set out to achieve unanimity. Along the way, however, there are sometimes *holdouts*: people who believe that their interests are better served by remaining outside the emerging agreement. Should the rest of the group throw in the towel? No, this would invite blackmail (i.e., outrageous demands by the holdouts that have nothing to do with the issues under discussion). Most dispute resolution professionals believe that groups or assemblies should seek unanimity, but settle for overwhelming agreement that goes as far as possible toward meeting the interests of all stakeholders. This effort to meet the interests of all stakeholders should be understood to include an affirmative responsibility to ensure that those who are excluded really are holdouts and are rejecting the proposal on reasonable grounds that would seem compelling to anyone who found themselves in the holdouts' shoes. It is absolutely crucial that the definition of success be clear at the outset of any consensus building process.

Facilitation (A Way of Helping Groups Work Together in Meetings)

Facilitation is a meeting management skill. When people are face-to-face, they need to talk and to listen. When there are several people involved, especially if they don't know each other or they disagree sharply, getting the talking-listening-deciding sequence right is hard. Often, it is helpful to have someone who has no stake in the outcome assist in managing the conversation. Of course, a skilled group member can, with the concurrence of the participants, play this role, too. As the parties try to collect information, formulate proposals, defend their views, and take account of what others are saying, a facilitator reminds them of the ground rules they have adopted and, much like a referee, intervenes when someone violates the ground rules. The facilitator is supposed to be nonpartisan or neutral.

There is some disagreement in various professional circles about the extent to which an effective facilitator needs to be someone from outside the group. Certainly in a corporate context, work teams have traditionally relied on the person "in charge" to play a facilitative role. The concept of facilitative leadership is growing in popularity. Even work teams in the private sector, however, are turning more and more to skilled outsiders to provide facilitation services. In the final analysis, there is reason to worry that a stakeholder might use facilitative authority to advance his or her own interests at the expense of the others. . . .

Before the parties in a consensus building process come together, mediators (or facilitators) can play an important part in helping to identify the right participants, assist them in setting an agenda and clarifying the ground rules by which they will operate, and even in "selling" recalcitrant parties on the value of participating. Once the process has begun, mediators (and facilitators) try to assist the parties in their efforts to generate creative resolution of differences. During these discussions or negotiations, a mediator may accompany a representative back to a meeting with his or her constituents to explain what has been happening. The mediator might serve as a spokesperson for the process if the media are following the story. A mediator might (with the parties' concurrence) push them to accept an accord (because they need someone to blame for forcing them to back off some of the demands they made at the outset). Finally, the mediator may be called on to monitor implementation of an agreement and reassemble the parties to review progress or deal with perceived violations or a failure to live up to commitments.

Facilitation and *mediation* are often used interchangeably. We think the key distinction is that facilitators work mostly with parties once they are at the table, while mediators do that as well as handle the prenegotiation and postnegotiation tasks described above. Also, mediators tend to be called on in particularly conflictual situations. In addition, some facilitators do not necessarily strive for agreement as mediators always do, but rather seek to ensure productive deliberation. Some professionals have both sets of skills; many do not. Neither form of consensus building assistance requires stakeholders to give up their authority or their power to decide what is best for them.

Recording (Creating a Visual Record of What a Group Has Discussed and Decided)

Recording involves creating a visual record that captures the key points of agreement and disagreement during a dialogue. Some facilitators (and mediators) work in tandem with a recorder. Recording can be done on large sheets of paper, often called flip charts, tacked up in front of a room. With the introduction of new computer and multimedia technologies, this can be done electronically as well. The important thing is to have an ongoing visual representation of what the group has discussed and agreed. Unlike formal minutes of a meeting, this "group memory" may use drawings, illustrations, maps, or other icons to help people recall what they have discussed. Visual records prepared by a recorder ultimately need to be turned into written meeting summaries. Like minutes, these summaries must be reviewed in draft by all participants to ensure that everyone agrees with the review of what happened.

Convening (Bringing Parties Together)

Convening, or the gathering together of parties for a meeting or a series of meetings, is not a skill that depends on training. An agency or organization that has decided to host a consensus building process (and wants to encourage others to participate) can play an important convening role. In a private firm, for example, a senior official might be the convenor. In the public arena, a regulatory agency might want to convene a public involvement process. There is some disagreement about whether or not the convenor or the convening organization is obliged to stay at the table as the conversation proceeds. In general, convening organizations want to be part of the dialogue, but we do not feel they must commit to ongoing participation in a consensus building process.

Someone has to finance a consensus building process. When it takes place inside an existing organization, financial arrangements are reasonably straightforward. When consensus building involves a wide range of groups in an ad hoc assembly, it is much less obvious who can and will provide the financial support. If costs are not shared equally by the parties, for example, and if they are covered by the convening organization, special steps must be taken to ensure that the facilitator or mediator has a contract with the entire group, and not just the convenor, and that the organization(s) providing the financing do not use that sponsorship to dictate the outcome.

Conflict Assessment (An Essential Convening Step)

A conflict assessment is a document that spells out what the issues are, who the stakeholding interests are, where they disagree, and where they might find common ground. It is usually prepared by a neutral outsider based on confidential interviews with key stakeholders. There is some disagreement over whether the same neutral who prepared the conflict assessment should then be the one to facilitate or mediate, if the process goes forward. Typically, after interviewing a wide range of stakeholders, a neutral party will suggest whether or not it makes sense to go forward with a consensus building process and, if so, how the process ought to be structured. . . .

Circles of Stakeholder Involvement (A Strategy for Identifying Representative Stakeholders)

Stakeholders are persons or groups likely to be affected by (or who think they will be affected by) a decision — whether it is their decision to make or not. When we talk about "circles of stakeholders," we are talking about individuals or groups that want or ought to be involved in decision making, but at different levels of intensity. Some stakeholders may be involved in a core negotiating team, others may have their interests represented on that team, and still others may choose to observe the process from the sidelines.

Some stakeholders are very hard to represent in an organized way. Think about "future generations," for example. Who can represent them in a dialogue about sustainable development? In the law, various strategies have evolved so that surrogates or stand-ins can represent hard-to-represent groups (such as the members of a class of consumers who have been hurt by a certain product or children who have no capacity to speak for themselves in a court proceeding).

Sometimes, it is necessary to caucus all the groups or individuals who think they represent a certain set of stakeholders for the purposes of selecting a representative for a particular dialogue or problem-solving purpose. Such meetings typically need to be facilitated by an outside party. Finally, there are various statutes that govern who may and who must be invited to participate in various public and private dialogues. Ad hoc consensus building processes must take these laws into account.

Section I. Helping an Ad Hoc Assembly Reach Agreement

We have identified five steps in the consensus building process: convening, clarifying responsibilities, deliberating, deciding, and implementing agreements. The key problems for ad hoc assemblies (as opposed to permanent entities) are organizational. Selecting the relevant stakeholders, finding individuals who can represent those interests effectively, getting agreement on ground rules and an agenda, and securing funding are particularly difficult when the participants have no shared history and may have few, if any, interests in common. . . .

[The authors proceed to provide basic rules (in Appendix D) together with a roadmap for facilitation and a full elaboration on how to implement the rules.]

Section II: Helping a Permanent Group or Organization Reach Agreement

The same five consensus building steps apply when dealing with permanent groups, although there is a sixth step—organizational learning—that needs to be emphasized. Permanent groups and organizations are likely to have well established decision-making procedures. This can be an advantage in that less time should be needed to reach agreement on how the group should operate. At the same time, resistance to change may be a new source of difficulty. An organization that has historically operated in a top-down management style may have a hard time adapting to a consensus building approach. A shared commitment to the long term well-being of the organization, however, can provide common ground on which to build. . . .

Section III: Dealing with the Barriers to Consensus Building

Both ad hoc and permanent groups and organizations are likely to encounter certain predictable obstacles to consensus building. It is important that participants handle these obstacles with great care.

7.0 Respond to Disruptive Behavior.

If a participant or an observer of a consensus building process acts in a disruptive manner, the facilitator, mediator, or chair—whoever is managing the meeting—should remind that individual of the procedural ground rules he or she signed. If that does not result in the desired change in behavior, other participants with the closest ties to the disruptive party should be asked to intercede on behalf of the group. If that, too, fails to deter the disruptive individual, it may be advisable to adjourn the meeting temporarily and allow the group as a whole to convince the disruptive person to either alter his or her behavior or leave. If that fails as well, participants should not be afraid to contact the relevant civil authorities and ask for assistance in removing the individual involved.

8.0 Accept an Advisory Role if That Is All That Is Allowed.

In many instances, both in the public arena and in private organizations, consensus building groups are often granted only advisory and not decision-making authority. Formal decision making may still reside with elected or appointed officials or officers. This need not diminish the contribution that a consensus building effort can make. From the standpoint of a decision maker, it is always helpful to know which options or packages are likely to have the full support of all the relevant stakeholders. Moreover, if those with decision-making authority are involved in a consensus building effort—or, at least, kept apprised of its progress—they may feel sufficiently comfortable with the result to endorse it.

9.0 Clarify the Presumed Liability of the Participants.

If the participants in a consensus building process are dealing with confidential or proprietary information that could create legal liability, the scope of this liability should be stated in the invitation to participate extended by the convenor, and be explained in the ground rules governing the groups' operations.

10.0 Clarify Confidentiality Arrangements.

There are legitimate reasons for consensus building processes, however public they may be, to adopt confidentiality arrangements. Both the arrangements and the rationale for adopting them should be spelled out in the groups' ground rules. These arrangements must take account of open-meeting and sunshine laws if public officials are involved.

11.0 Clarify Legal Obligations if the Participants Are Simultaneously Involved in Pending Litigation.

If a consensus building effort is meant to resolve issues that are simultaneously the subject of litigation, the participants in the informal dialogue should be apprised (by counsel) of their legal rights and the impact that informal consensus building conversations might have on the legal proceedings, and vice versa. They should also approach the judge or adjudication body to talk about the best way of coordinating the two processes.

Notes and Questions

12.24 Consider whether participants or facilitators should set ground rules. Should rules be "laid down" or negotiated? What might be the consequences (both on the process and on ultimate outcomes) of ground rule setting by the parties versus the facilitators? Is this issue (developing ground rules) the same for a mediator of a two-party dispute? What are the pros and cons generally of a mediator's proposing ground rules versus inviting the parties to negotiate about conversational guidelines?

12.25 Have you ever assumed the convenor's or facilitator's role (in relation to student or organizational governance, for example)? Which of Susskind's points resonate with your own experience?

In addition to Susskind's suggested protocols for managing a formal consensus-building event, modern lawyers and mediators also need to know how to manage meetings that are preparatory to group or organizational negotiations or that later become part of a more formal negotiation process. Here are a few other suggested guidelines for effectively managing such meetings.

❖❖ *David A. Straus*, **MANAGING MEETINGS TO BUILD CONSENSUS**

in The Consensus Building Handbook: A Comprehensive Guide to Reaching Agreement 287, 289-292, 302-304, 310-311, 313-314, 321-322 (Lawrence Susskind, Sarah McKearnan & Jennifer Thomas-Larmer eds., 1999)

THE VALUE OF FACE-TO-FACE MEETINGS

Some models of mediation call for keeping opposing parties separate, minimizing their interactions, and engaging in *shuttle diplomacy*. In consensus building, on the other hand, most of the work of building agreements is accomplished in face-to-face, facilitated meetings. In these meetings, participants' interests are articulated and acknowledged so they can be discussed, understood, and used as the basis for seeking mutually agreeable solutions. The commitments that parties make to each other in meetings are built on a wide base of shared effort and learning—a base that brokered agreements developed through shuttle diplomacy often lack.

Participants sometimes find that effective meetings, in which opposing parties begin with strongly entrenched, opposing positions and then build consensus step-by-step, can actually be a transforming experience. They learn constructive ways of working together and communicating. They become empowered by the experience of being understood by, and understanding, their adversaries. They are often surprised at what they all have in common, and this realization can help them to see ways to meet everyone's needs. Indeed, in well-facilitated meetings, participants can develop agreements that they can enthusiastically support and help implement, for which they have not compromised their basic values, and that they can present to their constituents (those they represent) as worthy of support. Even when consensus is not achieved, the process of respectful, face-to-face exploration helps people to better understand each other's points of view and makes future attempts at consensus building more likely to succeed.

THE IMPORTANCE OF WELL-RUN MEETINGS

Meetings can be evaluated in terms of three dimensions of success.

- *The results achieved.* Was the meeting productive? Did the group reach its goals? Did the participants produce a high-quality product?
- *The process used.* Were participants satisfied with the way the meeting was run? Did they feel in control of the meeting and not manipulated in any way? Did the facilitator employ effective and efficient consensus building techniques?
- *The relationships built.* Are participants able to communicate with each other more constructively as a result of the meeting? Do they feel that their viewpoints and concerns were acknowledged and understood by their fellow participants?

Effective meetings achieve positive results in all three dimensions. They are conducted according to proven principles of collaboration, include clear roles and responsibilities for participants and organizers, and offer carefully managed opportunities for discussion and decision making. In effective meetings, facilitators and participants are well prepared. Facilitators use effective problem-solving skills and tools, plan workable agendas, and model appropriate conflict resolution behaviors. They clearly delineate between content (*what* is to be discussed) and process (*how* to proceed with discussions). Participants recognize that the meeting's success depends on their positive, productive input; they do not rely on a facilitator to do it all for them. The atmosphere is safe and stimulating. Time is used well. There is little repetitious arguing, "speechifying," or personal gossip or attacks. Often, agreements are reached. People leave such meetings energized to implement decisions and, in fact, are eager to meet again to report on their efforts and take up new assignments. . . .

BEFORE A MEETING: SETTING UP FOR SUCCESS

Effective meetings do not just happen; they require considerable preparation and planning. To set up a meeting to succeed, the meeting planner(s) must consider and make conscious choices about every factor that could influence the outcome of the meeting. In particular, they must think through and make decisions about

- the purpose of the meeting,
- who should be involved and how,
- the desired outcomes,
- the agenda,
- the roles and responsibilities of participants and organizers,
- what ground rules will guide discussions,
- how group decisions will be made, and
- where the meeting will be held. . . .

Drafting Proposed Ground Rules

Meeting planners must develop a list of proposed ground rules. Ground rules, in a single-meeting setting, typically set forth behavioral norms that participants are expected to follow. In multimeeting consensus building processes, by contrast, ground rules are often quite detailed. They may describe, for example, the issues to be discussed in the process, the range of interests represented, the decision rule to be used, the goals of the process, and so forth. . . .

For ground rules governing a single meeting, we suggest guidelines such as the following.

- One person speaks at a time.
- No side conversations.
- No personal attacks (i.e., criticize ideas, not people).
- Listen as an ally.
- Respect agreements about time (e.g., return from breaks promptly).
- Turn off beepers and cell phones.

Draft ground rules should be presented to a group at the outset of a meeting and revised according to participants' suggestions. When process problems arise during a meeting that are not covered by the ground rules, participants should be asked to suggest additional ground rules to prevent the problems from recurring.

Determining the Decision Rule

Meeting planners must be prepared to suggest a decision rule for the meeting, that is, to recommend *how* a group will make decisions (e.g., by consensus, by majority vote). Their recommendation should be discussed with group members at the beginning of the meeting. When people have had a role in determining how decisions are to be made, they are more likely to support the outcomes of a process. When consensus building is the prevailing method of decision making, a group must agree on a definition of *consensus*. Participants in one meeting may want it to mean that everyone in the group must actively support a decision, for example. Those in another meeting might agree to move forward with an agreement even if there are one or two holdouts.

Meeting planners and participants should also clarify what will happen if consensus can't be reached, that is, who the fallback decision makers will be. In a hierarchical organization, the fallback is usually an individual; in a horizontal organization, a majority vote; and in public sector consensus building efforts, the fallback is often a formal decision-making body (such as a public agency or a court). It is often the threat of having to rely on the fallback method of decision making that keeps participants engaged in the search for mutually agreeable solutions.

FACILITATIVE TOOLS: PREVENTIONS AND INTERVENTIONS

The most useful sets of tools a facilitator possesses are what we call *preventions* and *interventions*. Preventions are the actions a facilitator takes before and during meetings to head off potential obstacles to success. Interventions are actions a facilitator can take to help a group get back on track during a meeting, after difficulties have occurred. The most skillful facilitators rely primarily on preventions; in a way, this makes their facilitation "invisible." After a meeting in which a facilitator was very skillful, participants will often leave saying, "That was a great meeting. I'm not sure we needed a facilitator." When a facilitator does not prepare well or makes mistakes, and then uses interventions to get back on track, participants are more aware of the role of facilitation and may compliment the facilitator on a job well done. Thus, a facilitator's best work may go unrecognized.

Preventions

The preventions described below include reaching key agreements with participants at the outset of a meeting, making process suggestions, and checking for agreement.

Up-Front Agreements.   Facilitators have no formal power to control a group. It is only by building agreements among participants on various process decisions and then holding them to those agreements (at least until they choose to change them) that facilitators develop a measure of control—and even then always as a servant to the group. So, at the outset of a meeting, a facilitator must seek agreement on

- who is playing which roles in the meeting,
- the basic "contract" between the group and the facilitator and recorder,
- the desired outcomes for the meeting,
- the agenda (i.e., the flow or sequence of agenda items),
- the decision-making rule to be used, and
- the ground rules to govern the meeting. . . .

Interventions

The interventions described in this section include reflecting questions back to a group, refocusing a group, using body language, employing escalating levels of intervention, and allowing a group to "ebb and flow."

Reflect Questions Back to the Group. One of the most useful interventions a facilitator can employ is the *boomerang*, the technique of reflecting a group's questions back to itself. A facilitator can use the boomerang technique when he or she is asked to offer an answer to a specific question or problem, particularly those relating to the overall direction of the group (i.e., "When are we going to be meeting again?" or even "Isn't Option A really the only feasible way to go?"). Rather than directly responding to the group's query, an effective facilitator will "boomerang" the question back to the group: "I can't answer that question for you; what do *you* think?" or "Who might have an idea about that?" This technique keeps group members focused on the fact that they are responsible for the meeting, rather than thinking of the facilitator as an expert.

Refocus the Group. A second common intervention is to refocus a discussion that has gone astray. For example, a facilitator may need to refocus a group if too many side conversations are taking place at one time. Simply saying, "Just a moment, one person at a time" or "Let's hear Janet before Joe" sets the norm of holding a single conversation among group members during a meeting. A facilitator may also need to intervene to enforce any process agreements that have been made, such as time limits on presentations or staying focused on one substantive issue at a time. Also, comments about a group's general "demeanor" can help a group clarify difficulties, refocus, and move on. A facilitator might say, for example, "It's very quiet right now, what's going on?" And humor, of course — though never at anyone's expense — enables group members to relax and get back on track.

Use Body Language Consciously. The conscious use of body language is a powerful intervention. When a facilitator goes from sitting to standing up, or from standing in front of a group to walking into the semicircle, group members suddenly become more aware of him or her and, consciously or not, begin to pay more attention to their own behavior. If a facilitator believes someone has spoken too long or too often, for example, a move toward the person often makes him or her aware of the situation and more likely to stop. Taking a few steps toward the group memory sheets encourages participants to reorient themselves to the task at hand.

Escalate the Levels of Intervention.   As a rule, facilitators should choose less confrontational interventions first, and escalate them as needed. For example, if an individual is dominating the discussion or intimidating others, a facilitator can first try to make eye contact with the person — a brief glare or a slightly raised eyebrow might be enough. If it isn't, the facilitator could stand up, which is usually sufficient to get someone's attention, or even walk partway toward the area where that individual is seated. If necessary, the facilitator could walk right up to the individual. If there is still no response, the facilitator could gently invite the person to stop (e.g., "Could you hold back for a moment while somebody else speaks?") At the highest levels of intervention, the facilitator could give the person feedback at a break, and, as a last resort, confront the issue directly and firmly in front of the group.

AFTER THE MEETING

Most consensus building processes involve a sequence of meetings, in which each meeting builds on the work of the previous one. For a group to avoid backsliding and spending excessive time reviewing what happened before, meeting organizers should provide participants with a record of each meeting. We have found the most useful documentation to be the group memory itself. The handwritten sheets of newsprint contain "memory hooks" to remind meeting attendees of what was said at each point in the meeting. The diagrams, the placement of comments on the page, and even the misspellings all carry clues that jog participants' memories. Because the group memory was created in front of all the participants, it is hard to dispute its accuracy. . . .

In addition to the group memory or meeting minutes, it is often useful to organize the "data" produced during one meeting to assist with problem solving in the next. For example, a facilitator might sort all the agreements that have been made previously, or organize and restate all of the definitions of the problem. This information can be charted and presented at the beginning of the following meeting for review and revision, serving as a strong foundation for the next steps in the consensus building process.

It is also helpful, after a meeting is over, for the facilitator to call the convenor, group leader, and several key participants to get their thoughts on how the meeting went. Were they satisfied with what was accomplished? What did they think went well? What did not go well? What would they like to see done differently next time? Feedback on these kinds of questions can help a facilitator continually improve his or her craft.

Notes and Questions

12.26 Do facilitators Susskind and Straus offer the same ground rules or suggestions for facilitating consensus-building meetings? Where do they differ? What might be the underlying reasons, purposes, or goals for differences in their treatment of some issues?

12.27 Can Straus's processes be used in settings if the parties do not formally commit to them in advance?

12.28 For what kind of issue or dispute would you advise a client, an organization, or a community group to use this kind of process? Does it make a difference if the issue involves parties internal to the organization rather than parties external to it? Why and how?

12.29 Can you think of particular ground rules you would want to have in any process you were a part of? As a participant? As a facilitator? Why? Would you want the protocols, guidelines, or rules laid down, or suggested, by the process facilitator or arrived at by the parties themselves? Why and how might it matter who suggested particular ground rules?

12.30 These excerpts contemplate a very particular kind of process, a relatively formal multiparty negotiation, mediation, or policy-setting consensus-building environment. There are many other ways to organize multiparty negotiations, running from no rules at all to very formal rules of speaking and participation. Similarly, there are many schools of thought about how to be an effective third-party neutral in facilitating such meetings, depending on whether a decision or action is required at the end or whether a group is being convened for different purposes, such as to foster understanding across divisive value differences. For some other sources on how to facilitate such negotiations or group discussions, see, e.g., Center for Conflict Resolution, Manual for Group Facilitators (1977); Donald Hackett & Charles L. Martin, Facilitation Skills for Team Leaders (1993); Tim Hindle, Managing Meetings (1998); Public Conversations Project, Constructive Conversations About Challenging Times: A Guide to Community Dialogue (3d ed. 2003), at *http://www.publicconversations.org/pcp/UploadDocs/CommunityGuide3.0/pdf*; Roger Schwarz, The Skilled Facilitator (2d ed. 2002).

In the final excerpt in this section, Lela Love and Joseph Stulberg reflect on additional skills that mediators need in complex, multiparty disputes. They point to facilitation skills, as well as to the importance of strategic partnering. As you read, note how the skills discussed can mitigate some of the additional complications present in multiparty mediations.

 Lela P. Love & Joseph B. Stulberg, **PARTNERSHIPS AND FACILITATION: MEDIATORS DEVELOP NEW SKILLS FOR COMPLEX CASES**

9 Disp. Resol. Mag. 14, 14-17 (2003)

... To provide a context for analysis and application, imagine the following scenarios:

Case A: Tenants and Landlords.   A large group of residential and commercial tenants who live in a building in a large urban setting are threatening both rent strikes and lawsuits against the landlord. The issues include: asbestos and lead paint in the building; the adequacy of windows and ventilation; the ovens used by commercial tenants as part of a restaurant and bakery business and the timing, safety and legality of baking-related activities; the parking of commercial vehicles; the payment of both overdue and future rent.

The parties' impasse on various issues has been exacerbated by ethnic divisions and tensions. The building manager is from South America, the landlord is Jewish and the tenants are from mixed ethnic backgrounds, including African-American.

Racial slurs have encouraged polarized and positional approaches. The situation has been reported in the press. The parties agree to participate in mediation.

Case B: The Suicide.   *A mother, father and son arrive at their home in a suburban community to discover that their daughter (and sister) has committed suicide by shooting herself in the head. The family is distraught, and the son/brother calls 911.*

Instead of an ambulance, a SWAT team arrives on the scene and mistakes the family members for perpetrators. The grief-stricken family members, trying to get medical attention for their loved one, are thrown on the ground and handcuffed. As a result, they suffer multiple injuries, both physical and psychological.

The family brings a civil action against the police department and the town. The case is referred to mediation.

What partnering and facilitation skills are relevant to intervening in such situations?

Partnering Skills

A mediator may choose to use partners in multiple ways. Some common partnerships involve co-mediators, interpreters and resource experts. Whoever the partner, several principles must guide these partnering relationships:

1. To the extent possible, the team must be neutral. That is, the mediator's partner must not have a partisan affiliation with any party. Put another way, all partners must be acceptable to all parties.
2. The team must share a similar goal or vision of the task.
3. There should be no more partners than are necessary to perform the tasks.
4. Partners should reflect diverse, complementary and relevant resources for the situation.
5. Partners must develop and follow a plan.

How do these principles apply to the cases described above? In *Case A*, the mediator is undertaking a significant challenge in simply managing the conversational project in a manner that is both efficient and responsive to stakeholder needs.

The diversity of the parties' interests and backgrounds would prompt the prudent mediator to be cautious in assuming that his or her knowledge of the legal, business and cultural/religious norms are sufficiently comprehensive to service the participants. Hence, in order to promote efficiency, as well as match expertise to the challenge, a mediator might consider working with a partner.

Minimally, he or she would consider using a resource team of language translators (assuming one or more of the many parties did not speak English), and credible professionals (in this case, for example, architects were very useful) whose expertise might help provide all participants with a common understanding of the various norms and requirements that might impact resolution of the conflict. A co-mediator whose professional background, language ability or ethnicity might balance the team should also be considered.

Case B's challenges are more nuanced. The family's psychological trauma is significant and sustained. A mediator who pays no attention to those matters in the discussion would disserve the parties. Most lawyer-mediators, though, are not trained professionally in the helping professions.

Therefore, a mediator who partners with a trained psychologist would send an immediate signal to all participants that the appropriate discussion range for this situation could be more extensive than simply venting and translating all concerns into money damages.

It is important for partners to work collaboratively, but collaboration is not accomplished by accident. Partners must: confirm they have a shared vision of the goals of the mediation process and the strategies they will use, assign specific tasks in a manner designed to make the mediation efficient and productive, act in a supportive, noncompetitive manner and develop fail safe plans and "exit strategies" to ensure that an ineffective partnership does not sabotage the parties' well-being.

Considerations with respect to neutrality and optimal performance are important for anyone on the mediation team or assisting in the mediation effort. An interpreter, for example, must be physically positioned to reinforce a neutral role, must develop a plan with the mediator to ensure adequate breaks so that the interpreter can function at maximum capacity and must alternate between simultaneous and consecutive translation, depending on whether speed or accuracy is most critical at that precise moment.

These features of a successful collaboration do not happen by accident. They require attentive discussion by both the mediator and her partner.

TIPS FOR WORKING WITH AN INTERPRETER

- Ensure that the seating arrangement allows the interpreter to have a clear line of vision to parties for whom she must translate.
- Position the interpreter so that eye contact naturally flows to the mediator and the other parties to enhance communication and connection.
- Use consecutive translation, in which each sentence or idea is translated after it is spoken, when accuracy is critical (e.g., the opening statement or reviewing the final agreement). Use simultaneous translation, in which the interpreter speaks a beat behind the speaker for whom she is translating, when a natural flow of conversation is most important (e.g., when parties are telling their stories).
- Orient the interpreter to the mediation process by providing her with copies of relevant documents.
- Develop an understanding about accuracy versus diplomacy. Generally, the interpreter should not soften or reframe harsh language, but rather give an accurate summary of what is said.
- If resources allow, use two interpreters who can help each other when it is clear that translation will be needed throughout the process. If using only one interpreter, ensure the interpreter receives adequate breaks.
- Ensure that the interpreter remains neutral and does not become partisan for the party who is most dependent on translation.
- Minimize or eliminate cross-talk or interruptions, as translating more than one person at a time is too difficult.

Facilitation Skills

The conventional facilitation process involves two significant roles, a facilitator and a recorder, although in many practical contexts one person serves both roles. Typical facilitation settings have the following features: (1) multiple stakeholders, but not crystallized "parties"; (2) fluid agenda of issues and concerns; (3) multiple relationships among the stakeholders, with some being hierarchical and others horizontal; and (4) decisionmaking time frames that may vary significantly by particular topic. Given this context, the facilitator's role is to enhance discussion, promote clarity and keep the group on track toward reaching its goals.

In traditional intervener roles, the facilitator focuses primarily on process matters. The facilitator highlights for groups the different ways in which group members might discuss a given topic, generate options, rank preferences and make decisions.

The recording function is a critical component for advancing discussion. Contrary to a dispute setting in which each party is taking its own notes, the recorder produces a public, visible memory of the group's discussion, ideas and proposals.

> **CRITICAL FACILITATOR SKILLS**
>
> - Creating a dynamic, positive tone and environment.
> - Maintaining the group memory.
> - Keeping the group on task and within applicable time frames.
> - Offering and managing methods to generate options (i.e., brainstorming techniques).
> - Offering and managing procedures to gain consensus and make decisions.
> - Capturing the outcome of sessions and closing in a positive manner.

The recorder captures the dialogue in language that is accurate but neutral, writes in a quick, legible style and keeps the medium on which the notes are recorded in a place that is easily and readily visible to all participants. Doing all this effectively requires significant multitasking skills.

The facilitator contributes both a focus on process issues and a public memory of the discussion. Together, these tools produce a constructive tone and organized analysis in situations otherwise ripe for dissension and wasted effort. . . .

How might these skills help a mediator service the cases noted above?

In *Case B* (the Suicide), the parties frame the legal issues when filing their lawsuit. But this appears to be a situation in which the mediator, when inviting the plaintiffs to describe their concerns, should explicitly encourage them to discuss their plight in a manner that illuminates the multilayered drama of this tragic human situation.

One can imagine the plaintiffs' lawyer wanting to be the sole spokesperson for the family's concerns. Instead of that potentially adversarial format, the mediator should encourage a rich description of the family's plight by inviting all family members (and any support personnel) to actively participate.

Similarly, the defendant should be invited and encouraged to communicate with the plaintiffs in unconventional ways. Various officials, both elected and appointed, might constructively be present to express both concern for the plaintiffs' well-being and support for the officials' employees. Such officials may well be open to hearing the plaintiffs' ideas about how such occurrences could be prevented in the future.

How would the mediator invite the participation of each of these persons? This is a significant challenge. If the mediator treats some or all of these participants as witnesses, or wants to have the parties' attorneys focus sharply on exchanging and bargaining over positional monetary demands, then she is imposing a rigid, insensitive box on each person's participation.

The challenge must be met instead by leading a discussion among all participants targeted on gaining agreement about appropriate methods for sharing narratives and identifying concerns. That is, the intervener must explicitly facilitate a discussion among the participants that focuses on who should talk, in what sequence, for how long, under what circumstances, with what goals and with what (if any) recording mechanism. The process that the parties agreed on might (predictably) look considerably different from what has become a very conventional courtroom presentation of opening mediation statements made exclusively by lawyers.

In *Case A* (Tenants and Landlords), while various persons have agreed to participate in what was labeled a "mediation," the situation is, in fact, much more fluid. Getting the appropriate stakeholders together for discussion — not simply those initially identified — is the intervener's first task. By facilitating and recording this important dialogue, the intervener helps the participants construct an effective problem-solving framework to address the situation's multiple ambiguities and to provide a mechanism for ongoing relationships.

Once the appropriate parties convene, one can imagine a series of monthly meetings in which parties identify concerns, make provisional agreements and return to examine the success and challenges in the last month. In fact, the case upon which this hypothetical is based involved many meetings over the course of nine months.

There, the mediators gradually worked themselves out of a job by demonstrating the structure of an effective problem-solving process and generating experiences of success, month by month, so that parties could identify issues, develop proposed solutions and garner a variety of commitments to move forward within targeted time frames. Success created goodwill, and ultimately the meetings had a social, as well as a business, component. The most important tool the mediators conveyed to the parties was the ability to facilitate their own meetings. . . .

Notes and Questions

12.31 Imagine you are a mediator called by the landlord's agent in Case A. He describes the situation and asks the following questions: Can you handle this situation? What are your fees? If the tenants will not participate in paying the mediator's fees, is there any problem with the landlord paying the entire fee? How long will the mediation take? May a lawyer be sent as the sole representative of the landlord? How can you insure that the tenants will not interpret an invitation to mediation as a sign of weakness? Is the telephone conversation with you confidential? How can the press be kept out of the mediation? Should there be separate mediations for the commercial and residential tenants? In answering these questions, what principles guide you?

12.32 Suppose you are a mediator called by a town selectman in Case B. She suggests that you meet with the attorney for each side to "hammer out a settlement." Would you simply follow the party's lead with respect to this idea?

12.33 Suppose you are an attorney for the plaintiffs in Case B, serving on a contingency fee basis. If your clients express a desire for an apology from the town, and you fear an apology, if given, might result in your clients' willingness to accept a lower financial settlement, what would you do?

D. LEGAL ISSUES IN THE USE OF MULTIPARTY CONSENSUS-BUILDING PROCESSES

As this chapter's selections indicate, there is rapid growth in the development of different kinds of multiparty processes — from more informal negotiations, "public conversations," and "dialogue groups" to more formal and governmentally recognized negotiated rulemaking and consensus building or collaborative problem-solving fora. With the increased use of such processes, the relation of "convened" processes to formal regulation and governmental action is important for all lawyers engaged in ADR work to understand. We conclude this chapter with one of the first attempts to catalog some of these issues.

 Dwight Golann & Eric E. Van Loon, **LEGAL ISSUES IN CONSENSUS BUILDING**

> in The Consensus Building Handbook: A Comprehensive Guide to Reaching
> Agreement 495, 495-497 (Lawrence Susskind, Sarah McKearnan & Jennifer
> Thomas-Larmer eds., 1999)

... With so many state legislatures, courts, and systems of legal rules in the United States, it is impossible to offer a single answer to most legal questions. Responses are likely to depend on the state(s) in which a consensus building effort takes place and the terms of the ground rules that govern a process. Precise answers are also difficult for the more fundamental reason that lawmakers themselves are sometimes unclear; the laws they pass and the rules they write often create more ambiguities than they resolve. For some issues, no statute or regulation exists, forcing individual courts to make law on an ad hoc basis. As a result, it can take decades before a particular issue is addressed in the legal system — and even then the answer may vary from one place to another.

Despite these limitations, it *is* possible to provide general guidance on legal challenges that may arise in the course of consensus building. We have identified six categories of challenges. Many of the issues within these categories proceed from the fact that consensus processes often involve public officials, who are subject to special constraints because of their role in government.

    1. Relationship to Government Agencies and the Courts.   Disputes that are the subject of consensus building are sometimes simultaneously the focus of legal proceedings before agencies or courts. This raises the question of how the two processes should be coordinated.

    2. Procedural Requirements Imposed by Laws and Regulations.   Government employees often must follow specific procedures, which may prevent them from making binding commitments during a negotiation. For example, agency officials usually cannot commit to change regulations as part of a settlement, because they must first consider comments from the general public.

    3. Substantive Restrictions on the Power of Government Representatives.   Some limitations on government negotiators cannot be resolved even by following the right procedures because they arise from fundamental constraints embedded in the U.S. system of government. An example is the concept of separation of powers. The head of a federal agency, for example, cannot make commitments that bind Congress to take action. Similarly, state agencies are limited in how they can control the activities of municipalities on topics such as education or zoning.

    4. Disclosure Requirements and Confidentiality Protections.   Participants in sensitive negotiations often prefer to hold their discussions in private, and many states bar participants from revealing what was said during a mediation process. Other statutes, however, require that meetings in which public officials participate be open to citizens and the press. Because consensus building is a mediative process that often involves public officials, both sets of laws may apply, creating confusion.

    5. Liability Considerations.   Mediators and facilitators can be held legally liable for their actions in a consensus-based process and should therefore take appropriate precautions. Certain risky behaviors should be avoided, for example, and liability insurance should be obtained.

    6. Implementation Concerns.   Once an agreement has been reached, everyone involved presumably wants to see it carried out. Nonetheless, implementation problems may arise over time, prompting two legal questions. One concerns the minimum requirements for a contract to be legally binding. For instance, must an agreement be written in "legalese" to be enforceable? The other question involves how to structure the terms of an agreement so that, if necessary, it can be enforced by court order . . . .

Notes and Questions

12.34 Can you think of any other legal issues that might arise in the use of both formal and informal multiparty negotiation processes?

12.35 The use of class action settlements in the areas of mass torts, consumer actions, securities cases, and similar cases has now raised a host of complex legal, procedural, and ethical issues involving both private and court-assisted settlements in major, multiparty litigation. See, e.g., Ortiz v. Fibreboard Corp., 527 U.S. 815 (1999) (disapproving the use of Rule 23 class action settlements of mass torts claims on both procedural and ethical grounds); Amchem Prods., Inc. v. Windsor, 521 U.S. 591 (1997); John C. Coffee, Jr., Class Wars: The Dilemma of the Mass Tort Class Action, 95 Colum. L. Rev. 1343 (1995); Robert H. Klonoff & Edward K.M. Bilich, Class Actions and Other Multi-Party Litigation: Cases and Materials ch. 8 (2000); Carrie Menkel-Meadow, Ethics and the Settlements of Mass Torts: When the Rules Meet the Road, 80 Cornell L. Rev. 1159 (1995); Nancy Morawetz, Bargaining, Class Representation, and Fairness, 54 Ohio St. L.J. 1 (1993).

12.36 As in so many areas of alternative dispute resolution, there is a tension between the use of more flexible, solution-seeking, informal processes and the requirements of legality, transparency, and formality. Does the fact that situations discussed in this chapter involve more than two parties affect your views on how the balance between public law requirements and private flexible settlements should be drawn? How do formal public processes and informal private processes affect each other?

Chapter 13 International Mediation

There never was a good war or a bad peace.

— Benjamin Franklin

I recall a statement — probably something I read in the memoirs of a diplomat — that if the secret files of all nations could be opened we would find that the politeness, the good manners, the civility of diplomats and statesmen avoided more wars than all the generals ever won. Unprovable or not, I am prepared to believe that.

— Warren Burger

Much of this book focuses on uses of mediation in the United States. Mediation, however, existed in various social and historical forms long before its reinvention and use here. Modern American mediation has been influenced greatly by African moots (informal community mediation processes, using kinsmen or elders as mediators), see P.H. Gulliver, Disputes and Negotiations (1979); Confucian principles of social harmony, Stanley Lubman, Dispute Resolution in China After Deng Xiaoping: Mao and Mediation Revisited, 11 Colum. J. Asian L. 229 (1997); and a variety of religious and community forms of problem solving, Jerold Auerbach, Justice Without Law (1983). In short, mediation is not new and it is not exclusively American. Various forms of dispute resolution have been used by other nations, cultures, and multinational organizations for thousands of years.

Modern global interdependence makes international conflict resolution increasingly urgent. The twentieth century's deadly wars led to the formation of the United Nations. Many other multinational and nongovernmental organizations seek to foster peace as the twenty-first century explodes in new forms of concerted and randomized violence and terrorism. As life in an ever-shrinking world becomes both more prosperous (for some) and more dangerous for most, new forms of international conflict resolution are invented. To deal with economic and legal aspects of globalization or internationalization, dispute resolution techniques are used to seek peace, ensure stability, and promote reconciliation and coexistence in a diverse world with conflicting values and objectives.

This chapter explores various forms of international dispute resolution interventions. International mediation is used in many contexts, between nations, between citizens of different nations, in commercial trade, in diplomacy, and in pre- and post-conflict situations. The parties and the mediators can be individuals, organizations, or nations, working either directly or through representatives. As you study the international arena, consider the following questions:

1. Does mediation — or some forms of mediation — take for granted or assume particular cultural norms, goals, or uses of conflict resolution techniques?
2. Is mediation an American ethnocentric export?
3. Is the American talking cure of mediation dependent on a particular verbalized approach to problem solving?
4. Do Americans seek conflict and file lawsuits more than others? Do they also aim to "solve" more problems, with their own forms of technological, verbal, or legal solutions?
5. Is problem solving itself a cultural construct?
6. Can dispute resolution processes be developed that can work across borders or cultures?
7. Are dispute resolution processes culturally based? Substantively based?
8. Does what works in the international trade arena have any influence on international peace and diplomacy? What about on disputes and violence in local communities?
9. Is it possible to create a *lingua franca* out of some forms of dispute resolution that work effectively across cultures?
10. What correspondences are there between issues in domestic dispute resolution and international dispute resolution?

A. CULTURAL CONSIDERATIONS IN INTERNATIONAL CONFLICT

What is culture? Much of the literature on international conflict resolution assumes that culture is "out there" — something for lawyers and parties in disputes to consider, adapt to, and be sensitive to when dealing with someone from a different country or ethnic group. The premise here is that a person from another culture may behave differently because her culture has different expectations and goals about negotiation or because individual behaviors are culturally structured. The individual may not even know that her behavior is culturally influenced.

> **Culture** is the total accumulation of many beliefs, customs, activities, institutions and communication patterns of an identifiable group of people.
>
> C.H. Dodd, Dynamics of Intercultural Communication (1987).

This view of culture may be too limited. All of us are in cultures, but most of us are like fish who live in water but don't know they are wet. Culture surrounds and is "in" all of us. At the same time, culture is not uniformly or universally distributed. You may be an American, come from a state, be male or female, have an ethnic/racial heritage, a family, a religion, and an age, and are now entering a profession. Is your culture American, Texan or Californian, southern or midwestern, Catholic or Jewish, white or black, progressive or conservative, or lawyer-like or student-like?

People hold several social statuses or roles at any one time, and nationality or ethnic identification is only one aspect of a multifaceted cultural identity. Indeed, as the U.S. Census now finally recognizes, individuals may consider themselves to be part white, black, Latino, and Native American. Different situations bring out different parts of demographic and behaviorally salient characteristics.

Whether the dispute resolution profession itself has become an international culture is a hotly debated question. This book asks you to think about your cultures, whatever those might be, as you think about others' cultures in the creation and use of international dispute resolution processes.

Advice on dealing with cultural differences in negotiation runs the risk of either being too simplistic (don't cross your legs in certain cultures) or being so general that it is not helpful (there may be different assumptions about how negotiations are conducted). This section steers through these alternatives by providing both some general and more specific advice. Obviously, if one were planning on conducting extensive negotiations in another country, this brief foray into cultural differences would be insufficient. This section points out only some common cultural differences in negotiation, while also reminding negotiators that cultural differences may or may not explain any one individual's approach to negotiations. Much like gender and race, culture can be an obvious difference between negotiators but perhaps not the determining one in how each party approaches the negotiation.

The following excerpt highlights some of the dangers of too easily categorizing or stereotyping your negotiation counterpart.

> Cold realities continually remind us of groups of people, nations, continents, and a world divided not merely by political boundaries but by cultural barriers. For example, during a nationwide news interview in 1978, Barbara Walters interviewed the Prime Minister of India, who explained a cultural practice of imbibing one's liquid waste. He described its salutary effects, it ceremonial significance, and its widespread practice. In 1979 and the early 1980s, dissenters to the resurgence of a Muslim nation, during the turmoil of Iran's political life, left a trail of executions; like thieves, their hands were chopped off as a means of social control. Perhaps such a practice of law should be no more shocking than practices in portions of the United States, not so many years ago, where men were hung for stealing a horse, but released or mildly punished for taking a life. The mass suicide of over nine hundred persons in a religious cult in Jonestown, Guyana, also reminds us that we live in a world of cultural differences.
>
> C.H. Dodd, Dynamics of Intercultural Communication (1987), 37-49.

 Jeffrey Z. Rubin & Frank E.A. Sander, **CULTURE, NEGOTIATION, AND THE EYE OF THE BEHOLDER**

7 Negot. J. 249, 251-253 (1991)

The purpose of this brief column is to draw attention to several considerations that should be borne in mind in any analysis of culture and negotiation. Our thesis is that, although differences in culture clearly do exist and have a bearing on the style of negotiation that emerges, some of the most important effects of culture are felt even before the negotiators sit down across from one another and begin to exchange offers. Culture, we believe, is a profoundly powerful organizing prism, through which we tend to view and integrate all kinds of disparate interpersonal information. . . .

Robert Rosenthal and his colleagues have demonstrated the power of expectations and labels in an important series of experimental studies. In one of these experiments,[*] teachers were told that some of the children in their elementary school classes had been identified as "intellectual bloomers," children who were likely to grow and develop substantially in the coming year. About other children (who had been privately matched with the "bloomers" in terms of measured aptitude) nothing was said. When an achievement test was administered at the end of the academic year, a shocking and important discovery was made: those children who had been labeled as intellectual bloomers scored significantly higher than those with whom they had been matched. In explanation, the researchers hypothesized that children who were expected to do very, very well were given more attention by their teachers; this increased attention, organized by hypothesis that the child in question was a talented individual, created a self-fulfilling prophecy.

The label of culture may have an effect very similar to that of gender or intellectual aptitude; it is a "hook" that makes it easy for one negotiator (the perceiver) to organize what he or she sees emanating from that "different person" seated at the other side of the table. To understand how culture may function as a label, consider the following teaching exercise, used during a two week session on negotiation. . . . During one class session, the fifty or so participants were formed into rough national groups, and were asked to characterize their national negotiating style — as seen by others. That is, the task was *not* to describe true differences that may be attributable to culture or nationality, but to characterize the stereotypic perceptions that others typically carry around in their heads.

This exercise yielded a set of very powerful, albeit contradictory, stereotypic descriptions of different nationalities. To give a couple of examples, British participants characterized others' stereotypic characterization of the British as "reserved, arrogant, old-fashioned, eccentric, fair, and self-deprecating." . . . And a cluster of Central Americans listed others' stereotypes of them as negotiators as "idealistic, impractical, disorganized, unprepared, stubborn in arguments, and flowery in style."

Now imagine that you have begun to negotiate with someone from another culture, who at some point in the proceedings simply insists that he or she can go no further, and is prepared to conclude without an agreement if necessary; in effect, says this individual, his BATNA has been reached, and he can do just as well by walking away from the table. How should you interpret such an assertion? If you share the general cluster of stereotypes described by the students, your interpretation will probably depend on the other person's culture or nationality. Thus, if the other negotiator is British, and (among other things) you regard the British as "fair," you may interpret this person's refusal to concede further as an honest statement of principle. The same behavior issuing from a Central American, however

---

[*] Robert Rosenthal & Lenore Jacobson, Pygmalion in the Classroom (1968).

(someone you suspect of being "stubborn in arguments"), may lead you to suspect your counterpart of being stubborn and perhaps deceitful. Wouldn't you therefore be more likely to strike an agreement with a British than a Central American negotiator — despite the fact that each has behaved in the identical way?

If there is any truth to our surmise, you can see how powerful the effects of culture may prove to be, leading us (even before we have had a chance to gather information about our counterpart) to hold a set of expectations that guide and inform our judgments. Moreover, once our "hypotheses" about others are in place, it becomes very difficult to disprove them. We tend to gather interpersonal information in such a way that we pay attention only to the "facts" that support our preconceived ideas, ignoring or dismissing disconforming data....

[P]robably the wisest thing any of us can do to prepare for such negotiations is to: be aware of our biases and predispositions; acquire as much information as possible about our counterpart as an individual; and learn as much as we can about the norms and customs (of all kinds) that are to be found in our counterpart's home country.

Notes and Questions

13.1 Other often cited differences among cultures include relationship to time; the comfortable or appropriate spatial distance and loudness (or volume) between people talking with each other; customs regarding food and drink; the meaning of nonverbal behavior (including the appropriateness of eye contact); the expected level of formality; the relationship of individuals to others, including family, community, and the world; belief systems; and greetings and farewells. Understanding cultural norms, a culture's history, art, literature, religion, and beliefs can be critically important to successful negotiation and mediation.

13.2 What is the authors' primary message to any negotiator? Is this helpful to you? How is it or isn't it?

13.3 Perform the same exercise Rubin and Sander write about. Identify yourself culturally (or regionally or by other identifying characteristics). What are the typical stereotypes of your culture? Do they apply to you? For another description of cultural differences in negotiation, see Jeanne Brett, Negotiating Globally (2001) (describing differences in styles of confrontation, motivation, information strategies, individualism versus collectivism, equalitarian versus hierarchical orientations, and low context versus high context cultures). See also Frank L. Acuff, How to Negotiate Anything with Anyone Anywhere Around the World (1997).

13.4 In an empirical study, international law professor Jeswald Salacuse examined how culture, profession, and gender affect different aspects of negotiation style. The ten factors he studied were goals, attitudes, personal styles, communication, time sensitivity, emotionalism, agreement form, agreement building, team organization, and risk taking. Depending on the factor studied, he found that culture, profession, and gender all influenced negotiation style in different ways. Jeswald W. Salacuse, Ten Ways That Culture Affects Negotiating Style: Some Survey Results, 14 Negot. J. 221 (1998).

13.5 One example that shows creativity and cultural differences in negotiation is that in which Nigerian women successfully negotiated with Chevron Texaco for more jobs and better schools while Nigerian men had been unsuccessful and the strikes were typically violent. The Nigerian women successfully negotiated by occupying and striking against an export terminal. They also used a particularly persuasive threat that was unique to their culture. "When several days had passed without success in negotiations, they threatened to take off their clothes if their demands were not met. In the culture of the Niger Delta, women bring great shame upon men by stripping naked in front of them." Nigerian Women Show Power, at *http://www.news24.com* (July 19, 2002).

13.6 In a study of archaeological digs in Syria, an anthropologist discovered a very interesting phenomenon:

> It quickly became evident that gender is a key pivot in the power relations at the site when, in sharp contrast to the common sense notions of most Westerners, the workers excavate squares headed by female volunteers much more quickly and smoothly than squares run by male volunteers. This disparity is clearly visible to all observers through the amount of soil removed from an excavation square which thus becomes an approximate and readily measurable index of social competence and authority of the volunteer.
>
> The following journal excerpt, written by an undergraduate volunteer in June 1988 after her first day of digging, illustrates this dynamic. "I was so nervous before we started up to the tell [archaeological site] that I could hardly speak or eat, but actually it went pretty well once I reached my square. . . . I just took a big breath; pointed to the area I had outlined with my trowel, looked the pickman in the eyes, smiled and said *men fadluk* (please). That's all I had to do. . . . By the time we stopped for second breakfast at nine o'clock my whole square was dug down ten centimeters below the surface. This drove Dick crazy. His workers had barely scratched the surface of his square; in fact none of the guys had gotten their squares dug deeper than mine. . . . The more Dick yells and screams the slower his workers seemed to go. I just try to be polite and not interfere too much. So far it seems to be working."
>
> The greater success of the female volunteers, in terms of soil excavated from their squares, persisted throughout the eight-week digging season and has generally remained true for each succeeding season (1988-1996).

Sharon Doerre, Negotiating Gender and Authority in Northern Syria, 6 Intl. Negot. J. 251, 255-266 (2001). Does this story surprise you? Why? What assumptions are you making? What advice would you give a male friend participating in the dig? To a female friend?

13.7 In the example above, to really learn from this experience, the writer had to have both knowledge of the Syrian culture, knowledge about the particular business (archaeological digs), and knowledge of negotiation theory. What can you do if you do not possess such expertise and are about to go negotiate in another culture? How can you research this information?

B. INTERNATIONAL NEGOTIATION PRINCIPLES AND PRACTICES

This section examines some issues of practice for negotiators in international settings, followed by targets and techniques for mediators. To some extent, if negotiators performed at peak capacity, they might not need mediators. From another angle, mediators are negotiation coaches, so it is important for representatives to understand what behaviors will be productive in negotiation and mediation.

The following article from political science professor Robert D. Putnam discusses how negotiators must deal with both their negotiation counterpart and their external constituency.

 Robert D. Putnam, **DIPLOMACY AND DOMESTIC POLITICS: THE LOGIC OF TWO-LEVEL GAMES**

> in **Double-Edge Diplomacy: International Bargaining and Domestic Politics**
> **436-442, 459-460 (1993)**

TWO-LEVEL GAMES: A METAPHOR FOR DOMESTIC-INTERNATIONAL INTERACTIONS

The politics of many international negotiations can usefully be conceived as a two-level game. At the national level, domestic groups pursue their interests by pressuring the government to adopt favorable policies, and politicians seek power by constructing coalitions among those groups. At the international level, national governments seek to maximize their own ability to satisfy domestic pressures, while minimizing the adverse consequences of foreign developments. Neither of the two games can be ignored by central decision-makers, so long as their countries remain interdependent, yet sovereign.

Each national political leader appears at both game boards. Across the international table sit his foreign counterparts, and at his elbows sit diplomats and other international advisors. Around the domestic table behind him sit party and parliamentary figures, spokesmen for domestic agencies, representatives of key interest groups, and the leader's own political advisors. The unusual complexity of this two-level game is that moves that are rational for a player at one board (such as raising energy prices, conceding territory, or limiting auto imports) may be impolitic for that same player at the other board. Nevertheless, there are powerful incentives for consistency between the two games. Players (and kibitzers) will tolerate some differences in rhetoric between the two games, but in the end either prices rise or they don't.

The political complexities for the players in this two-level game are staggering. Any key player at the international table who is dissatisfied with the outcome may upset the game board; and conversely, any leader who fails to satisfy his fellow players at the domestic table risks being evicted from his seat. . . .

TOWARD A THEORY OF RATIFICATION: THE IMPORTANCE OF "WIN-SETS"

Consider the following stylized scenario that might apply to any two-level game. Negotiators representing two organizations meet to reach an agreement between them, subject to the constraint that any tentative agreement must be ratified by their respective organizations. The negotiators might be heads of government representing nations, for example, or labor and management representatives, or party leaders in a multi-party coalition, or a finance minister negotiating with an IMF team, or leaders of a House-Senate conference committee, or ethnic-group leaders in a consociational democracy. For the moment, we shall presume that each side is represented by a single leader or "chief negotiator," and that this individual has no independent policy preferences, but seeks simply to achieve an agreement that will be attractive to his constituents.

It is convenient analytically to decompose the process into two stages:

1. Bargaining between the negotiators, leading to a tentative agreement; call that Level I.
2. Separate discussions within each group of constituents about whether to ratify the agreement; call that Level II.

This sequential decomposition into a negotiation phase and a ratification phase is useful for purposes of exposition, although it is not descriptively accurate. In practice, expectational effects will be quite important. There are likely to be prior consultations and bargaining at Level II to hammer out an initial position for the Level I negotiations. Conversely, the need for Level II ratification is certain to affect the Level I bargaining. In fact, expectations of rejection at Level II may abort negotiations at Level I without any formal action at Level II. For example, even though both the American and Iranian governments seem to have favored an arms-for-hostages deal, negotiations collapsed as soon as they became public and thus liable to de facto "ratification." In many negotiations, the two-level process may be iterative, as the negotiators try out possible agreements and probe their constituents' views. In more complicated cases . . . the constituents' views may themselves evolve in the course of the negotiations. Nevertheless, the requirement that any Level I agreement must, in the end, be ratified at Level II imposes a crucial theoretical link between the two levels. . . .

For two quite different reasons, the contours of the Level II win-sets are very important for understanding Level I agreements.

First, *larger win-sets make Level I agreement more likely, ceteris paribus.* By definition, any successful agreement must fall within the Level II win-sets of each of the parties to the accord. Thus, agreement is possible only if those win-sets overlap; and the larger each win-set, the more likely they are to overlap. Conversely, the smaller the win-sets, the greater the risk that the negotiations will break down. For example, during the prolonged prewar Anglo-Argentine negotiations over the Falklands/Malvinas, several tentative agreements were rejected in one capital or the other for domestic political reasons; when it became clear that the initial British and Argentine win-sets did not overlap at all, war became virtually inevitable. . . .

The second reason why win-set size is important is that the relative size of the respective Level II win-sets will affect the distribution of the joint gains from the international bargain. The larger the perceived win-set of a negotiator, the more he can be "pushed around" by the other Level I negotiators. Conversely, a small domestic win-set can be a bargaining advantage: "I'd like to accept your proposal, but I could never get it accepted at home." Lamenting the domestic constraints under which one must operate is (in the words of one experienced British diplomat) "the natural thing to say at the beginning of a tough negotiation." . . .

A Third World leader whose domestic position is relatively weak (Argentina's Alfonsin?) should be able to drive a better bargain with his international creditors, other things being equal, than one whose domestic standing is more solid (Mexico's de la Madrid?). The difficulties of winning Congressional ratification are often exploited by American negotiators. During the negotiation of the Panama Canal Treaty, for example, "the Secretary of State warned the Panamanians several times . . . that the new treaty would have to be acceptable to at least sixty-seven senators," and "Carter, in a personal letter to Torrijos, warned that further concessions by the United States would seriously threaten chances for Senate ratification." Precisely to forestall such tactics, opponents may demand that a negotiator ensure himself "negotiating room" at Level II before opening the Level I negotiations. . . .

CONCLUSION

The most portentous development in the fields of comparative politics and international relations in recent years is the dawning recognition among practitioners in each field of the need to take into account entanglements between the two. Empirical illustrations of reciprocal influence between domestic and international affairs abound. What we need now are concepts and theories that will help us organize and extend our empirical observations.

Analysis in terms of two-level games offers a promising response to this challenge. Unlike state-centric theories, the two-level approach recognizes the inevitability of domestic conflict about what the "national interest" requires. . . .

This theoretical approach highlights several significant features of the links between diplomacy and domestic politics, including:

- the important distinction between voluntary and involuntary defection from international agreements;
- the contrast between issues on which domestic interests are homogeneous, simply pitting hawks against doves, and issues on which domestic interests are more heterogeneous, so that domestic cleavage may actually foster international cooperation;
- the possibility of synergistic issue linkage, in which strategic moves at one game-table facilitate unexpected coalitions at the second table;
- the paradoxical fact that institutional arrangements which strengthen decision-makers at home may weaken their international bargaining position, and vice versa;
- the importance of targeting international threats, offers, and side-payments with an eye toward their domestic influence at home and abroad;
- the strategic uses of uncertainty about domestic politics, and the special utility of "kinky win-sets";
- the potential reverberation of international pressures within the domestic arena;

- the divergences of interest between a national leader and those on whose behalf he is negotiating — and in particular, the international implications of his fixed investments in domestic politics.

Notes and Questions

13.8 Think of a recent international negotiation. Who were the Level II players? Who were the Level I players? Which negotiation was more difficult?

13.9 What are domestic examples of two-level bargaining games?

This section's final excerpt, by Robert Mnookin, examines situations in the international arena where parties are best served by refusing to negotiate. Are there some people with whom we should never negotiate? Does the answer depend, to some degree, on culture?

 Robert H. Mnookin, **WHEN NOT TO NEGOTIATE: A NEGOTIATION IMPERIALIST REFLECTS ON APPROPRIATE LIMITS**

74 U. Colo. L. Rev. 1082-1083, 1088-1090, 1095-1096, 1106-1107 (2003)

. . . [S]ometimes *it is better not to negotiate*. What considerations are and should be taken into account in deciding whether to negotiate at all? In various contexts, where a party refuses to negotiate, what reasons are typically used to justify that decision? How should a party think about and decide whether to enter into or begin a negotiation at all? . . .

My framework poses six questions that should be addressed, four of which draw from negotiation analysis. Negotiation imperialists — myself included — suggest that in preparing for a negotiation a party should identify its own interests and those of the other parties; think about each side's BATNA (best alternative to negotiated agreement); try to imagine options that might better serve the negotiators' interests than their BATNAs; and ensure that commitments made in any negotiated deal have a reasonable prospect of actually being implemented. These same considerations are equally valid in informing an individual's decision whether one should enter into a negotiation. In addition, one must also consider the expected costs — both direct and indirect — of engaging in the negotiation process, as well as issues of legitimacy and morality. . . .

What considerations of legitimacy and morality should be taken into account? In considering the benefits and costs of the decision whether to negotiate, there is no avoiding questions of legitimacy and morality. One aspect was mentioned earlier: when thinking about alternatives to negotiation, one must consider the legitimacy of those alternatives. A bigger child may have the power to grab the toy of a younger and smaller sibling, but most parents would prefer that the child not exercise that alternative but instead ask to use the toy. A self-help alternative to negotiation may not be considered legitimate, at least without some institutional approval. Few doubted the capacity of the U.S. to bring about a regime change in Iraq, but many have questioned the legitimacy of the American resort to force in the absence of U.N. Security Council authorization.

The mere process of negotiation with a counterpart is perceived as conferring some recognition and legitimacy on them. Providing a counterpart with "a place at the table" acknowledges their existence, actions, (and to some degree) the validity of their interests. To avoid validation of interests or claims, countries have often refused to negotiate with rebels or insurgent groups, denying them any recognition or legitimacy. Thus, for decades, Israel refused to negotiate with the Palestinian Liberation Organization, Britain denied any status for the Irish Revolutionary Army, the Spanish would not negotiate with the Basque separatist rebels, Peru would not engage in a dialogue with the Tupac Amaru, and Russia announced an absolute policy of not negotiating with the Chechen rebels. . . .

The policy of refusing to negotiate with terrorists derives not only from the fear of conferring legitimacy or recognition, but also from aversion to *rewarding past bad behavior*. When previous interactions have failed to satisfy the claims of a party, satisfying its claims under the pressure of violence implies that violence was indeed worthwhile. This consideration, of course, is problematic. Although most of the national liberation movements around the world have employed violence in their struggle to gain independence or self-determination (among very few Gandhi-like exceptions), once violence is employed it usually entrenches political rivals, at least in the short term following violence.

Perhaps the most renowned example of a refusal to negotiate for moral considerations is Sir Winston Churchill's refusal to negotiate directly or indirectly with Adolph Hitler in May of 1940. For Churchill, the refusal derived not only from the questionable effectiveness of such negotiations, given the dismal history of Hitler's negotiations with Chamberlain, or the potential effects of failed negotiations on his fellow citizens, but also from a strong moral aversion to "*doing business with the devil.*" Churchill truly believed that Britain had a deep moral obligation, on behalf of itself as well as the rest of the world, to fight Nazi Germany. In relation to British advocates of appeasement, he said: "An appeaser is one who feeds a crocodile — hoping it will eat him last.". . .

The members of the Taliban were not innocent bystanders. They had been given advance warning by the U.S. government: according to a State Department official who had testified before Congress in the summer of 2000, the U.S. had let the Taliban "know, in no uncertain terms, that we will hold [the Taliban] responsible for any terrorist acts undertaken by bin Laden." There could be little doubt that the Taliban harbored thousands of Islamic terrorists from around the world and allowed its territory to serve as a training ground for armed secret agents capable of terrorist acts in the U.S. and elsewhere.

Under these circumstances, there would be moral costs associated with negotiating with the Taliban. Negotiating a deal that would save the Taliban regime would be tantamount to rewarding it for its flagrant defiance of the U.S. and the international community regarding its responsibility for *al Qaeda's* operations in Afghanistan. Moreover, it would have required the U.S. to negotiate with an intolerant and repressive regime that the U.S. had been unwilling officially to recognize heretofore and which the U.S. had already declared it would hold directly responsible for any future *al Qaeda* attack. Finally, although negotiation with the Taliban did take place after the 1998 bombing of the U.S. embassies, the nature, magnitude, and horror of the September 11th attacks brought many to feel that there would be something repulsive in negotiating the fate of the chief perpetrator of the attacks with the regime that was complicit.

To conclude, analyzed through the framework offered here, and specifically, by weighing the interests, the probability of a good negotiated outcome, the available BATNAs, and the costs associated with negotiating, I believe President Bush's decision not to negotiate with the Taliban, and instead, to use force to achieve U.S. goals, was correct. To negotiate with the Taliban would have imposed substantial costs:

1. in deterring future terrorists and those who might harbor them;
2. in maintaining credibility and self-respect;
3. in legitimizing a regime that the U.S. had not previously recognized;
4. in building and sustaining a broad international coalition and maintaining domestic political support; and
5. in allowing heinous acts to be the occasion for dialogue with a party that the U.S. believes is at least partially responsible for such acts.

Because of the combined weight of these costs, the lack of Taliban credibility, and improbability of a negotiated outcome that would serve American interests, the U.S. refusal to negotiate with the Taliban was justified. However, taken individually these costs should not be considered determinative of the decision whether to negotiate. For example, there may be cases where the costs of negotiating with a regime that the U.S. has not previously recognized would be outweighed by substantial benefits. . . .

My basic preference in favor of negotiation remains. For any number of reasons, disputants may tend to exaggerate the potential costs of entering into negotiations and may underestimate the possible benefits in comparison with more coercive alternatives. Indeed, it would be useful to explore both theoretically and empirically this possibility, which if true, might go some distance in justifying the preference of negotiation imperialists. But even if true this would do no more than justify a presumption in favor of using negotiation to resolve conflict. This presumption must be rebuttable.

For too long, negotiation imperialists have implicitly assumed that negotiation always makes sense. This is, of course, nonsense. Such a conclusion would require that the expected net benefits of negotiation are always greater than the expected net benefits of any alternative form of dispute resolution. Negotiation is not without costs, and my primary purpose in writing this article is to suggest a framework for the analysis of not only the expected benefits but also the expected costs of entering into negotiation.

Notes and Questions

13.10 What do you think about Mnookin's conclusion? To whom else would "no negotiation" apply? Who should decide this?

13.11 How does this analysis affect whether or not mediation services should be proposed in international crises?

13.12 Are attorneys who refuse to negotiate with the other side simply making strategic judgments? Strategic errors? Is their behavior ever justifiable in the framework Mnookin offers? In other ways?

C. INTERNATIONAL MEDIATION

As in domestic negotiations, when the parties themselves fail to accomplish their goals, they may call on a third party for help. In the international arena, the disputants can seek an informal mediator, an institutionally appointed arbitrator or mediator, or they can appeal to a number of formal international institutions established to help resolve particular kinds of disputes or issues between citizens of different nations (as in commercial trade disputes), between governments and private parties (as in international investments), and between and among nations and other international groups (formal institutions such as the UN or nongovernmental organizations such as Search for Common Ground). A number of international and national organizations, both governmental and nongovernmental, provide technical assistance and training in dispute resolution processes both for internal "rule of law" and justice system development and for international development activities. These programs — from organizations such as the World Bank, USAID, the U.S. State Department, and the Consensus Building Institute — are often challenged as being ethnocentric (American or Anglo-American in origin) or culturally imperialistic (see Laura Nader & Elisabetta Grande, in Chapter 14) in suggesting that other nations should follow "our" approaches to conflict resolution. (Of course, this criticism could also apply to our efforts to promote constitutionalism, rule of law, democracy, and separation of powers.)

It is useful to ask whether mediation in the international context is different from domestic mediation. It seems fairly obvious that the answer is yes. Third parties have attempted interventions in nation-to-nation, international, and multinational conflicts for thousands of years, with many very different role conceptions in mind. Often such intervenors did not think of themselves as mediators in the sense this book uses that term. Third-party intervenors in the international context often are not neutral but quite interested in the relations between other parties, such as in peacekeeping efforts, trade disputes, boundary disputes, and economic or political alliances. The phrase "muscle mediation" was probably first used in international contexts where mediators with strong political or economic power are able to control, persuade, or cajole disputing parties to agree by using implicit or explicit threats, promises of aid and benefits, or threats of sanctions and withholding of benefits. The phrase "shuttle diplomacy," too, usually refers to disputes of international origin. Used by such mediators as Secretary of State Kissinger and President Jimmy Carter at Camp David, shuttle diplomacy involves moving from party to party, using nothing but caucuses and confidential meetings to broker a settlement. In this form of mediation, the parties are almost never together, and the solutions or agreements are much more likely to be suggested by the mediators than developed in direct negotiations between the parties. (Contrast the mediation efforts at

President Carter's and President Clinton's respective Camp David peace talks on the Mideast (1978 and 2000, respectively) with the Oslo peace accords.)

At present, mediation is much more common in diplomatic and peace-seeking efforts, but its use is increasing in commercial and private dealings with multinational actors. See Ellen Deason, Procedural Rules for Complementary Systems of Litigation and Mediation Worldwide, 80 Notre Dame L. Rev. 553 (discussing parallel developments in domestic and international relationships of mediation to litigation and the development of rules for the conduct of both). Fortunately for dispute resolution students and analysts, many of those who have participated in international mediations, both successful and unsuccessful, have written post hoc case studies or memoirs of their activities, and third-party scholars have reported on conflict interventions, so it is possible to analyze what interventions or techniques have been successful or not in particular settings. See, e.g., Jacob Bercovitch, Resolving International Conflicts: The Theory and Practice of Mediation (1996); Jimmy Carter, Keeping Faith (1982); Chester Crocker, Fen Osler Hampson & Pamela Aall, Herding Cats: Multi-Party Mediation in a Complex World (1999); Henry Kissinger, The White House Years (1979); Hugh Miall, The Peacemakers: Peaceful Settlement of Disputes Since 1945 (1992); George Mitchell, Making Peace (1999); Turbulent Peace: The Challenges of Managing International Conflict (Chester A. Crocker et al. eds., 2001); Words over War: Mediation and Arbitration to Prevent Deadly Conflict (Melanie Greenberg et al. eds., 2000).

This section first looks at a broad definition of third-party intervention, and then narrows its focus to international mediation. Finally it reviews some case studies.

1. Third-Party Intervention

The first excerpt broadly discusses international conflict and what third parties need to look for when intervening. Economist and aid worker Mary Anderson

---

PEACE BUILDING

Recognizing that multiple types of intervening are occurring in conflict areas, some practitioners and theorists have started to think about how to coordinate all of these ongoing interventions. Furthermore, the new thinking recognizes that for a conflict to be resolved, the political, social, and structural problems all need to be addressed. After graduating from law school, Robert Ricigliano began working for Conflict Management Group (CMG), a nonprofit organization that works on training and intervention in international conflicts. CMG was founded by Roger Fisher, author of *Getting to YES*, and applies the same problem-solving skills you learned earlier to conflicts around the world. Professor Ricigliano writes that peacebuilding can occur only through "networks of effective action" in which intervenors need to promote information exchange between the political, social, and structural actors all working on a specific conflict, between official and unofficial actors, and between international actors and local partners. In addition, intervenors need to take an iterative approach to peacebuilding, combining all the political, social, and structural activity addressing the conflict, rather than trying to find a "global" settlement for the problems. See Robert Ricigliano, Networks of Effective Action: Implementing an Integrated Approach to Peacebuilding (Security Dialogue 34 (4) (2003)).

writes for the aid community, but her insights apply to the conflict resolution field as well.

 Mary B. Anderson, **DO NO HARM: HOW AID CAN SUPPORT PEACE — OR WAR**

23-29, 31 (1999)

Conflict situations are characterized by intergroup tensions and divisions. Everyone knows this, expects it, and focuses on it.

More interesting is the fact that conflict situations are also characterized by local capacities for peace and by connectors that interlink the people who fight. This surprises many people — indeed, it surprised us as we became familiar with numerous conflict situations. . . .

In all civil war situations some things connect the people who fight. In all societies there are capacities for peace.

Too often, when international assistance providers arrive in a conflict area, they are so overwhelmed by the violence that they fail to see or recognize the capacities for peace. The loud and compelling terms of war — violence, danger, and expressions of hatred — are accepted as the only reality. As a result, aid is often provided in relation to the divisions in the society rather than in relation to and support of the connectors. Aid can thus inadvertently reinforce conflict and miss remarkable opportunities for helping people to rediscover and strengthen the aspects of their lives that connect them to each other. . . .

CAPACITIES FOR PEACE AND CONNECTORS

Even in virulent warfare, more people do not fight than do so. More individuals do not kill their neighbors than do so. . . . More would-be leaders fail to arouse people to violence than succeed in doing so. More people strive to correct their societies' systems of marginalization and injustice through nonwar means than through warfare.

People generally tend at least as much to avoid and avert violence as they do to seek and pursue it. Even in today's troubled world, peace is more widespread than war.

The Local Capacities for Peace Project found that even in societies where civilian-based civil war rips daily patterns apart, many aspects of life continue to connect people rather than divide them. Common history, culture, language, and experience; shared institutions and values; economic and political interdependence; and habits of thinking and acting exist in all societies, including those embroiled in civil war.

In addition, all societies have systems for handling disagreements and tensions without violence. Often they designate specific categories of people, such as elders or women, as negotiators or reconcilers. All have systems for limiting and ending violence if it erupts, and all have individuals who assert the values of peace even when prevalent warfare makes such positions unpopular and dangerous.

All of these elements constitute local capacities for peace. They exist prior to war and often avert open violence. Obviously, they are not always sufficient to prevent war. But even when war erupts, local capacities for peace exist; in fact, some are aroused by the experience of war. Peace capacities are important because they provide the base on which future peace can and must be built. They are the existing — and potential — building blocks of systems of political and economic interaction that can ensure stable, peaceful, and just futures for societies once in conflict.

We have identified five categories of peace capacities and the connectors...: systems and institutions, attitudes and actions, shared values and interests, common experiences, and symbols and occasions. These are not airtight, mutually exclusive categories; rather, they often overlap or run into each other. We include all five categories to illustrate the range of connectors found to exist. We hope to raise awareness among aid workers of where to look for peace capacities and how to recognize opportunities to support them.

SYSTEMS AND INSTITUTIONS

In all societies in which civil war breaks out, markets continue to connect people across the lines of the fighting. Sometimes a system of interenemy trade is formalized involving contracts and third-country bank accounts. . . .

Infrastructure also continues to connect people in civil war societies. Electrical, water, and communications systems and roads can connect warring people who jointly depend on them and thus let them remain even in the midst of war. . . .

ATTITUDES AND ACTIONS

A second category of connectors is found in people's nonwar attitudes and actions. In the midst of war, some individuals and groups continue to express tolerance, acceptance, and even love or appreciation for people on the other side. They refuse to demonize or stereotype the "others," and they recognize the failures and wrongdoing of their own side. . . . In Somalia a young man tells of a time when two clans began to fight. He and his friends, who did not want to take part in the battle because they saw it as meaningless, simply "walked" — that is, they announced their "membership" in a third clan that was not at war with either of the others. They were able to make this shift because over the years there had been so many intermarriages that people actually "belonged" to a number of different clans. They could thus change clans to avoid a foolish fight. . . .

These nonwar attitudes and actions may be taken consciously by an individual or a group in protest against the conflict. Or they may simply be expressed in the course of daily living because in the immediate sense they seem "normal" or "right."

SHARED VALUES AND INTERESTS

When people have an interest in continuing a system (even when it is also used by the enemy), as in the examples of electric and health services cited earlier, or when they share a common value, such as a love for children, these commonalities can represent connectors in conflict societies. . . .

COMMON EXPERIENCES

A shared experience — even the experience of war — can provide a basis for linkage and connection among people on differing sides of a conflict. Women often empathize with women on the other side, citing the commonalities of their and their families' suffering. In Central America one NGO started a postwar production plant in which workers were recruited from among the wounded fighters in the recently ended war. One employee commented, "Once you've lost a leg, you're all alike. It doesn't matter anymore what side you fought on." . . .

SYMBOLS AND OCCASIONS

National art, music, and literature and historic anniversaries, monuments, and ceremonies all provide connections in societies torn apart by civil war.

Notes and Questions

13.13   How can awareness of these "peace capacities" help third-party intervenors?

13.14   Anderson's statement that "more people do not fight than do so. More individuals do not kill their neighbors than do so" is very similar to international law professor Louis Henkin's observation that most countries follow most of the laws most of the time. Louis Henkin, How Nations Behave 47 (1979). Are these writers overoptimistic? What are their ideas based on?

13.15   Intervenors in conflict may find that peacemaking goals are often at odds with one another. John Paul Lederach writes of four traditional dilemmas in peacemaking: (1) Is social change fundamentally a process of personal or systemic transformation? (2) Should we seek justice (through prosecution, for example), or should we grant mercy (and move on)? (3) Should we empower individuals or create community? (4) Should we focus on process or on outcome? Lederach suggests that transformative peacemaking embraces both sides of these paradoxes in order to truly resolve conflict. John Paul Lederach, Preparing for Peace: Conflict Transformation Across Cultures 19-22 (1995). What do you think about these paradoxes? Can you think of any recent international conflicts where these dichotomies have been raised?

The next excerpt starts by outlining broad roles third parties can take in a conflict and concludes by discussing a type of mediation strategy called the "One-Text Process."

 Roger Fisher, Elizabeth Kopelman & Andrea Kupfer Schneider, BEYOND MACHIAVELLI: TOOLS FOR COPING WITH CONFLICT

123-131 (1994)

Players who are not principals in a conflict can play a wide range of constructive roles. Third-party interventions can contribute to problem-solving by making sure that disputants attack the problem rather than each other, and by keeping the focus on interests rather than on positions. Some roles are purely administrative, such as the functions associated with hosting a Devising Session or a conference. Other roles engage the third party in the substance of the dispute.

In a world filled with ready-made dispute-resolution procedures, it is important to look beyond the labels of "alternative dispute resolution," "negotiation," "mediation," and "arbitration" when considering useful roles for third parties. Chart 31 illustrates a variety of roles that third parties can play, ranging from primarily process-oriented ones, such as hosting a diplomatic conference, to primarily substance-oriented ones, such as monitoring compliance after an agreement. In any action plan involving the participation of a third party, what is most important is to design a role for the third party that addresses the particular diagnosis of why a given conflict has not been settled. . . .

31. Some Third-Party Roles for Coping with a Conflict

RANGE OF ROLES	EXAMPLES	WHO MIGHT PLAY THEM
Primarily process-oriented roles	Hosting a diplomatic conference	Another government
	Developing tools for the parties to use in diagnosing their conflict	Academic institutions
	Facilitating a brainstorming session	A trained facilitator
Mixed process and substantive roles	Holding a devising session to develop a range of options for the parties' consideration	A nonprofit foundation
	Facilitating a one-text procedure	A prominent international figure
	Providing peace-keeping forces to maintain a ceasefire while negotiations continue	The U.N. or a regional group such as the OAS
Primarily substance-oriented roles	Providing neutral evaluation of the merits of parties' claims	A professional association or specialized arbitration organization
	Providing a binding decision for outstanding issues in a dispute	The World Court

One way in which third parties often try to assist the parties is in mediating between them. The mediation technique perhaps most commonly used by third parties — concession hunting — often fails because it does not address the underlying interests of the disputants that have impeded a settlement. Focusing on positions rather than interests, this strategy tries to persuade the parties to give up bits of their opposing positions piece by piece. The goal is to edge the parties' positions toward each other until they eventually converge. . . .

Most players, in anticipation of this common strategy, adopt extreme positions from which they will later be able to make concessions without giving up anything important. Unfortunately, the "fat" that was originally included in order to pad a position is likely, through the process of public debate and commitment to one's constituents, to harden into "bone" that is now difficult to cut away. . . .

It is easy to see how this process encourages foot-dragging and haggling. This concession-hunting process tends to foreclose the possibility of generating creative options — the possibility that the pie can be enlarged through joint problem-solving.

A better process can change the choice. Rather than talking about two plans that reflect extreme partisan perceptions, it is usually better to talk about one plan that reflects some third party's judgment of what options might be acceptable to both sides. Consider how a lawyer might help two business professionals work out an agreement to become partners. One approach would be to ask each of them to draw up a separate plan, and then to ask each for concessions until a common plan could be reached. A better way would be for the lawyer to listen to the two parties discuss their individual and joint interests, and then to produce a rough draft of points that might be included in a partnership agreement. This draft would not be "the lawyer's proposal" but rather an open draft for all to discuss. . . .

Parties engaged in a conflict also need such a "business plan" of how they are going to deal with each other. Presenting disputants with a single draft that has been generated by the mediator and asking, "What would be wrong with doing it this way?" is more likely to garner a constructive response than asking for a concession. It is typically difficult to give something away and to make commitments, especially when we are uncertain about what we will receive in return. It is always easy to criticize. . . . Over the ensuing days and weeks, the mediator refines the draft by circulating among the parties, learning of concerns they may still have, and drafting new language designed to meet them as best he can. When the mediator feels that they cannot improve the draft any further — that it is fair, workable, and reconciles their conflicting interests as well as possible — he polishes the text and presents a final document to the parties for their approval. . . .

The One-Text Process was used by President Carter and Secretary of State Cyrus Vance at the 1978 Camp David negotiations between President Anwar Sadat of Egypt and Prime Minister Menachem Begin of Israel. The U.S. negotiating team prepared some twenty-three consecutive drafts or redrafts of parts of a text over ten days, each responding to some point raised by a party. On the last day, President Carter decided that this was the best he could do and asked each party to agree. A few hours later, the Camp David Accords were signed.

Some differences between the widely used strategy of hunting for concessions and the One-Text procedure are summarized in Chart 35 (see next page).

---

35. Two Ways of Generating a Draft Proposal

CONCESSION-HUNTING	ONE-TEXT
Ask the parties for their positions and proposals.	Ask the parties about their interests and concerns.
Focus discussion on each party's position.	Focus discussion on a single text aimed at reconciling conflicting interests and developing joint gains.
In turn, ask each party for a concession.	Ask each party to criticize the text wherever it fails to meet a legitimate interest.
Communicate the concessions obtained.	Prepare a revised single text in light of criticism and suggestions.
Repeat the process of pressing first one and then the other party for more concessions.	Repeat the process of revision until [you] have the best draft you can prepare.
Press one party or the other for a final concession to produce an agreement between the original positions of the parties.	Ask each party to accept the final draft if the other will. The final agreement may bear no relationship to the parties' original positions.

In some cases a mediator might want to employ a variation on the One-Text Process by producing two alternative drafts. These would not reflect partisan positions but, starting from different assumptions, would seek to meet as well as possible the interests of both parties. An architect, for example, might develop in parallel two alternative plans for his client, one a single-story house, the other a two-story house. Or a mediator working on a long-term settlement of the Palestinian-Israeli conflict might similarly develop in parallel drafts of two possible treaties. One would seek to meet Palestinian interests in acceptance, equality, self-government, and so forth without establishing a wholly independent sovereign Palestinian state. The other might start with such a state and then consider how best to meet Israeli interests, particularly in security, through provisions about neutrality, mutual inspection, restrictions on weapons, and so on. If the parties became unable to choose between the two texts, they might go to the Security Council for its recommendation or decision. . . .

Notes and Questions

13.16 Why isn't this One-Text Process more widely used in domestic mediation? Should it be? What disadvantages does this procedure embody?

13.17 Who should play the role of drafter in a One-Text Process? Is this issue relevant only in a mediation? If not, how would this procedure work in the absence of third parties?

13.18 What other third-party roles do the authors of *Beyond Machiavelli* suggest? Can you think of examples of these roles in action?

13.19 How do the suggestions in *Beyond Machiavelli* relate to Mary Anderson's advice to build "peace capacities"?

13.20 In an effort to develop variations on the themes of mediation, many international peace workers and theorists have developed "hybrid" forms of proceedings, including "problem-solving workshops," John Burton, Resolving Deep Rooted Conflicts: A Handbook (1987), Herbert C. Kelman, "The Problem Solving Workshop in Conflict Resolution," in Communication in International Politics (R.L. Merritt ed., 1972), and "public peace processes" that are intended to bring second-tier diplomats, policy makers, and some NGO participants together for limited periods of time to work together and learn from each other, without necessarily formally signing particular peace agreements. Much of this work is based in communication and group process theory. Advocates hope that strong ties and bonds, formed by activities, workshops, and interpersonal interaction, will build trust and longer-term relationships across disputing boundaries, relationships that can then be drawn from in times of acute crisis as well as for longer-term peace planning.

2. Theories of International Mediation

This next section outlines more specifically some of the theories and debates in international mediation. International mediation, as opposed to the broader concept of third-party intervention, is quite similar to the idea of domestic mediation already studied in this book. As you read, however, start to note important differences between the two contexts.

The following article explores the dimensions of mediation that are peculiar to international disputes, when and how mediation can be used, what its rationales are, and the specific tensions and issues that can develop when one individual or nation seeks to intervene in the disputes of "others." These issues involve conflicts of interest at both the individual and national levels, as well as concerns about authority for acting and whether mediators should be the international equivalents of facilitators or evaluators. Consider whether, in order to maintain mediator neutrality, international mediation should always be conducted by some transnational or international organization.

 Jacob Bercovitch, **THE STRUCTURE AND DIVERSITY OF MEDIATION IN INTERNATIONAL RELATIONS**

in Mediation in International Relations 4, 7-10, 12-14 (Jacob Bercovitch & Jeffrey Z. Rubin eds., 1996)

International disputes are not static or uniform events. They vary in terms of situations, parties, intensity, escalation, response, meaning and transformation.

The context in which a dispute occurs affects its process and outcome. Mediation too will be shaped by the context and characteristics of the situation. The specific rules, beliefs, attitudes, behaviors and symbols that make up international conflict, impinge on, perhaps even govern, the process of mediation. Mediating a dispute between two friendly states requires different forms, different settings, different resources and different strategies to that required when the representatives of two antagonistic states seek to have their dispute mediated. The structure and practice of mediation reflects the context of the situation and the nature of the parties. As a social process, mediation may be as variable as the disputants themselves. Mediation is, above all, adaptive and responsive. It reflects different problems, different parties and different situations. To assume otherwise is to mistake wishful thinking for reality. . . .

THE RATIONALE FOR MEDIATION

As a form of conflict management, mediation has become increasingly important in international relations. Article 33(1) of the United Nations Charter exhorts all member-states to settle their disputes through mediation. Empirical data indicates that states are more than happy to do so. International mediation has become almost as common as conflict itself. It is carried on by such heterogeneous actors as private individuals, government officials, religious figures, regional or international organizations, *ad hoc* groupings, small states and large states. Each actor brings to the mediation situation its own interests, perceptions and resources, and the behavior of each may encompass a spectrum that ranges from very passive, through facilitative, to the highly active. The form and character of mediation in a particular international dispute will be determined by the interaction between contextual variables and the identity of the mediator. The importance of this reciprocal influence can hardly be overemphasized.

As a form of international conflict management having high control over the process and low control over the outcome, mediation is likely to be used when (a) a dispute is long, drawn out and complex, (b) the parties' own conflict management efforts have reached an impasse, (c) neither party is prepared to countenance further costs or loss of life, and (d) both parties are prepared to cooperate to break their stalemate. . . .

From the point of view of an individual, unofficial mediator, the motives for initiating mediation may include: (a) a desire to be instrumental in changing the pattern of a long-standing conflict, (b) a desire to observe, analyze and influence an actual international conflict, (c) a desire to gain access to political leaders, (d) a desire to put into practice a set of ideas on conflict management, and, some might argue, (e) a desire to spread one's ideas and enhance personal standing and professional status. The co-presence of one or more of these motives (and they may be conscious or unconscious) with an opportune situation provides a very strong rationale for initiating individual informal mediation.

Where a mediator is an official representative of a government or an organization, another set of motives may prevail. As political actors such individuals may wish to initiate mediation because (a) they have a clear mandate to intervene in disputes (e.g. the constitutions of the Arab League, the Organization of African Unity and the

Organization of American States all contain an explicit clause mandating its members to mediate in regional disputes); (b) they may want to do something about a dispute whose continuance could adversely affect their own political interests; (c) they may be approached directly by one or both parties and asked to mediate; (d) they may wish to preserve intact a structure of which they are a part (e.g. the frequent mediation attempts by the United States between Greece and Turkey, two NATO member-states); or finally, (e) they may see mediation as a way of extending and enhancing their influence by becoming indispensable to the parties in dispute, or by gaining the gratitude (and presumably political allegiance) of one or both protagonists. Mediators, like other political actors, engage in mediation and expend resources, because they expect to gain something from it.

What then of the parties? Why would they seek or accept mediation? Disputing parties too may have a number of reasons for believing that a mediator's presence will be helpful. The parties may want to initiate mediation in the hope that (a) this low-risk and flexible form of conflict management will actually help them understand their conflict, reduce some of its risks and get them closer toward settling it; (b) each party may embrace mediation in the expectation that the mediator might nudge or influence the other; (c) both parties may see mediation as a public expression of their commitment to genuine conflict management; (d) the parties may want an outsider to take much of the blame for failure; and (e) the parties may desire mediation because a mediator can be used to monitor, verify and guarantee any eventual agreement. One way or another, disputing parties and a mediator have pretty compelling reasons for initiating, and engaging in, mediation. . . .

MEDIATORS IN INTERNATIONAL RELATIONS

Individuals

The traditional image of international mediation, one nurtured by the media and popular accounts, is that of a single, usually high-ranking, individual, shuttling from one place to another trying to search for understanding, restore communication between hostile parties or help settle their conflict. This image is only partly accurate. The individual mediator who engages in such behavior is normally an official representing his/her government in a series of formal interactions with high-level officials from the disputing countries. The interactions may be of an individual kind (as most political interactions ultimately are), but we must not lose sight of the consequences of formal representation. . . .

By individual mediation I mean mediation that is carried on by individuals who do not fulfill an official, representative function. As individuals *qua* individuals, mediators may differ with respect to the nature and level of their capabilities and resources, ability to perform the tasks required, knowledge, skills, experience and other attributes. They may also hold different beliefs, values, and attitudes. These affect the objectives they seek and their range of options in mediation. The strategies and mediation of individuals are more directly related to their capabilities and subjective experiences than to the external and contextual stimuli that impinge on them. Individual mediation can therefore exhibit greater flexibility and experimentation than mediation by political incumbents. . . .

States

Individual mediation, although significant, is not all that common in international relations. Most mediation activity is carried on by two kinds of actors, states (or to be more accurate, their representatives) and international organizations.

As a political actor the state is one of the most successful and enduring forms of social and political organization.... Often they get into conflicts with other states pursuing similar objectives. When this happens, representatives of states get together in any of the myriad of international forums to articulate their concerns and search for a settlement — through mediation or other means.

Notwithstanding the increase in, and importance accorded to, various transnational entities (e.g. multinational corporations, international organizations), states are still widely regarded as the most significant actors in international politics....

When a state is invited to mediate a dispute, or initiates mediation itself, it normally engages the services of one of its top decision makers. In these cases figures such as Dr. Henry Kissinger, President Carter, Secretary of State Baker or Lord Carrington fulfill a mediatory role, in the full glare of the international media, as salient representatives of their countries. International mediation by such individuals depend on (a) the position they hold in their own country, (b) the leeway given to them in determining policies, and (c) the different resources, capabilities and political orientations of their countries....

Institutions and Organizations

The complexity of the international environment is such that states and nations can no longer facilitate the pursuit of human interests, nor satisfy their demands for an ever-increasing range of services. Consequently we have witnessed a phenomenal growth in the number of international, transnational and other non-state actors, all of whom affect issues of war and peace, knowledge and responsibility and environment and survival. These functional systems of activities or organizations have become, in some cases, more important providers of services than states. They have also become, in the modern international system, very active participants in the search for institutions and proposals conducive to peace. We would expect such organizations to play their full part in the mediation of international disputes.

Three kinds of organizations are important to our understanding of international politics. These are: (a) regional organizations, (b) international organizations, and (c) transnational organizations. Regional and international organizations represent local or global collections of *states* signifying their intention to fulfill the obligations of membership as set forth in their formal treaty. Transnational organizations represent *individuals* across countries who have similar feelings, cognitions, knowledge, skills or interests, who meet together on a regular basis to promote the special interests of their members. Whereas regional and international organizations are "governmental" in origin, imbued with political purposes, and largely staffed by official representatives, transnational organizations are "non-governmental" in origin, and insofar that they are not really "public" organizations, they can afford to be more creative and less inhibited in the policy positions they advocate than international organizations.

Transnational organizations, operating independently of states, embody many of the elements commonly associated with impartiality. Does this suggest that transnational organizations are best likely to maximize the potential of successful mediation? Or would their mediatory role be somewhat circumscribed by the lack of an adequate resource-base? And, come to that, how do regional and international organizations accept and enact their mediatory role? Do discrepancies in context and formal structure affect mediation, or are we really suggesting that there exists a uniform pattern of mediation irrespective of actors?

Notes and Questions

13.21 What differences do you see between international and domestic mediation?
13.22 What are the respective advantages and disadvantages of each type of intervenor?

This next excerpt, from international relations researcher and former FBI analyst Matthew Levitt, begins to outline one of the primary differences between domestic and international mediation — neutrality.

 Matthew A. Levitt, KILOMETER 101: OASIS OR MIRAGE? AN ANALYSIS OF THIRD-PARTY SELF-INTEREST IN INTERNATIONAL MEDIATION

15 Mediation Q. 2, 155–161 (1997)

In reality, the myth of the scrupulously neutral mediator is just that — a myth. Parties that accept mediation as a means of resolving conflict, whether individuals, companies, or states, are not well served by the maintenance of this myth. . . .

UNORTHODOX INTERNATIONAL MEDIATION

The term *international mediation* immediately conjures up images of the Middle East, and is practically synonymous with the Arab-Israeli conflict. Among the numerous third parties to trudge through the negotiation process in this complex region, Henry Kissinger stands out as the most dynamic, and until recently the most successful. One aspect of Kissinger's famed disengagement negotiations in the aftermath of the 1973 Yom Kippur War, however, highlights a facet of international mediation that demands further analysis.

Immediately following the cease-fire, Egyptian and Israeli generals met at Kilometer 101 on the Cairo-Suez road, under U.N. auspices, for military talks on a permanent disengagement. Despite the progress produced, Kissinger sabotaged these backstage desert talks in favor of an international peace conference, center stage, in Geneva. Typically, negotiation experts classify direct negotiations between the disputants as the ideal model, and rate third-party intervention as a second-string alternative, usually focused on bringing the parties to the table. As Pruitt and Rubin note, "Third-party intervention is probably best likened to a strong medicine that may have undesirable side effects and that should therefore be employed with caution and some reluctance. The best, most effective third party is the one who becomes involved *only when needed* and who is so successful at helping the principals find a settlement and develop a working relationship with each other that they no longer need or want his or her services."

In light of this, why would Kissinger seek such a drastic change of venue? The negotiations at Kilometer 101 were producing concrete results, were insulated from the drawbacks of public diplomacy such as negotiating in front of the media, and, above all, constituted direct negotiations between the parties. In the words of one negotiation analyst, "from the perspective of mediation theory, this was and is most unorthodox behavior." The answer to this contradiction lies in a deeper analysis of the roles third parties play, especially in international mediation.

Who decides how and when Pruitt and Rubin's "only when needed" test applies? Kilometer 101 provides a prime example of when the seemingly black-and-white answer to this question drifts into a hazy gray area that should alarm all students of negotiation and its related fields. Kilometer 101 fell victim to the Geneva Conference because Geneva provides Kissinger with a venue more suitable for the realization of U.S. interests. Although Kilometer 101 indeed proved to hold the key to an Israeli-Egyptian disengagement, the mediator let his own self-interests dictate his actions to the detriment of the parties themselves. . . .

BIAS, BAGGAGE, AND BALANCE

The interdependence of the three parties (the two disputants and the mediator) in a triangular relationship offsets the mediator's fear of losing trust in the eyes of one or both parties. The disputants expect *balance*, not neutrality. As Roger Fisher colorfully explains, a neutral third party would have to be a "eunuch from mars." A mediator with absolutely no prior baggage might be hard to come by, but one that behaves in a balanced manner should not be hard to find. Often in mediation, and especially in international affairs, the disputants expect the mediator to apply leverage. They calculate that they will be subjected to no more pressure than the other party and accept the mediation despite their perceptions of bias. As Saadia Touval notes, "A would-be mediator's acceptability depends on the parties' expectations of the consequences of the mediator's intervention, and the relative advantages and disadvantages of acceptance or rejection. These expectations were usually closely related to the tactical considerations of the moment, and not to the mediator's reputation of impartiality."

Jonah [a member of the U.N. team] opines that impartiality is not synonymous with neutrality. Like Fisher, he contends that neutrality lies beyond the scope of tenable conditions for mediation. For Jonah, however, while impartiality represents a cardinal law of mediation, it simultaneously allows for an activism that prevents third parties from becoming "political or diplomatic celibates." Jonah, a member of the U.N. team at Kilometer 101, claims that one of the key factors that enabled the United Nations to intervene effectively at Kilometer 101 was its balance. Still, to affect the mediation positively, balance must not only apply to the application of mediator activism in the form of sticks and carrots but also to the prioritization of the interests that produce such inducements. Mediator activism can only agree with impartiality if the applied leverage aims to bring the parties to a settlement based on their interests, not those of the mediator. This becomes a particularly acute issue in light of the semi-imposed character of superpower mediation in the Middle East. As Touval notes, a superpower's offer to mediate a conflict represents an offer that cannot be refused: better to accept the superpower's mediation than risk it aligning itself with the enemy.

Notes and Questions

13.23 Is Levitt right? Do international mediators inevitably have their own agenda?

13.24 If the mediator is not neutral, is the process still mediation? If not, what is this process?

13.25 Assuming Levitt is correct that Kissinger's approach was influenced by U.S. interests, was that legitimate or illegitimate? Was the United States a party to the dispute? Does this matter in your analysis?

13.26 Think of other examples when the United States or the United Nations has served as a mediator to an international conflict. Was the mediator neutral? How do you define neutrality?

13.27 Are there times where the mediator cannot or should not be neutral in domestic mediation? Recall the Susskind/Stulberg debate over the responsibility of the mediator in Chapter 7.

The following two excerpts from I. William Zartman and John Paul Lederach are a point-counterpoint debate on the importance of timing and "ripeness" in helping parties settle a dispute. Some suggest that there are special opportunities for settling cases, and they come, in the international context, from the potential of a "hurting stalemate" in Zartman's terms or the danger of violent conflict. Such conditions create a necessary "ripe moment" for mediation. The case study of Northern Ireland, which we will read later, is often cited as an example of "ripeness." John Paul Lederach, on the other hand, emphasizes the long-term nature of peace-building. See which argument seems more persuasive to you.

 I. *William Zartman*, THE TIMING OF PEACE INITIATIVES: HURTING STALEMATES AND RIPE MOMENTS

in Contemporary Peacemaking: Conflict, Violence, and Peace Processes 19-20, 24, 26 (John Darby & Roger MacGinty eds., 2003)

While most studies on peaceful settlement of disputes see the substance of the proposals for a solution as the key to a successful resolution of conflict, a growing focus of attention shows that a second and equally necessary key lies in the timing of efforts for resolution. Parties resolve their conflict only when they are ready to do so — when alternative, usually unilateral, means of achieving a satisfactory result are blocked and the parties feel that they are in an uncomfortable and costly predicament. At that ripe moment, they grab onto proposals that usually have been in the air for a long time and that only now appear attractive. . . .

The concept of a ripe moment centers on the parties' perception of a mutually hurting stalemate (MHS), optimally associated with an impending, past or recently avoided catastrophe. The concept is based on the notion that when the parties find themselves locked in a conflict from which they cannot escalate to victory and this deadlock is painful to both of them (although not necessarily in equal degree or for the same reasons), they seek an alternative policy or way out. The catastrophe provides a deadline or a lesson indicating that pain can be sharply increased if something is not done about it now; catastrophe is a useful extension of MHS but is not necessary either to its definition or to its existence. Using different images, the stalemate has been termed the plateau, a flat and unending terrain without relief, and the catastrophe the precipice, the point where things suddenly and predictably get worse. If the notion of mutual blockage is too static to be realistic, the concept may be stated dynamically as a moment when the upper hand slips and the lower hand rises, both parties moving towards equality, with both movements carrying pain for the parties. . . .

Ripeness is necessarily a perceptual event, and as with any subjective perception, there are likely to be objective referents to be perceived. These can be highlighted by a mediator or an opposing party when they are not immediately recognized by the party itself, and resisted so long as the conflicting party refuses or is otherwise able to block out their perception. But it is the perception of the objective condition, not the condition itself, that makes for an MHS. If the parties do not recognize "clear evidence" (in someone else's view) that they are in an impasse, an MHS has not (yet) occurred, and if they do perceive themselves to be in such a situation, no matter how flimsy the "evidence," the MHS is present.

The other element necessary for a ripe moment is less complex and also perceptional: a way out. Parties do not have to be able to identify a specific solution, only a sense that a negotiated solution is possible and that the other party shares that sense and the willingness to search too. Without a sense of a way out, the push associated with the MHS would leave the parties with nowhere to go. Spokespersons often indicate whether they do or do not feel that a deal can be made with the other side and that requitement — i.e. the sense that concessions will be reciprocated, not just banked — exists, particularly when there is a change in that judgment.

Ripeness is only a condition, necessary but not sufficient, for the initiation of negotiations. It is not self-fulfilling or self-implementing. It must be seized, either directly by the parties or, if not, through the persuasion of a mediator. Thus, it is not identical to its results, which are not part of its definition, and is therefore not tautological. Not all ripe moments are so seized and turned into negotiations, hence the importance of specifying the meaning and evidence of ripeness so as to indicate when conflicting or third parties can fruitfully initiate negotiations. . . .

IMPLICATIONS

In itself, the concept explains the difficulty of achieving pre-emptive conflict resolution and preventive diplomacy, even though nothing in the definition of the MHS requires it to take place at the height of the conflict or at a high level of violence. The internal (and unmediated) negotiations in South Africa between 1990 and 1994 stand out as a striking case of negotiations opened (and pursued) on the basis of an MHS perceived by both sides on the basis of impending catastrophe, not of present casualties. However, the greater the objective evidence, the greater the subjective perception of the stalemate and its pain is likely to be, and this evidence is more likely to come late, when all other courses of action and possibilities of escalation have been exhausted. In notable cases, a long period of conflict is required before the MHS sinks in. Yet given the infinite number of potential conflicts which have not reached "the heights," evidence would suggest that perception of an MHS occurs either (and optimally) at a low level of conflict, where it is relatively easy to begin problem-solving in most cases, or, in salient cases, at rather high levels of conflict. . . .

Unripeness should not constitute an excuse for second or third parties' inaction, even if one or both of the conflicting parties are mired in their hopes of escalation and victory. Crocker states very forcefully (in boldface in the original) that "the absence of 'ripeness' does not tell us to walk away and do nothing. Rather, it helps us to identify obstacles and suggests ways of handling them and managing the problem until resolution becomes possible."

 John Paul Lederach, **CULTIVATING PEACE: A PRACTITIONER'S VIEW OF DEADLY CONFLICT AND NEGOTIATION**

in Contemporary Peacemaking: Conflict, Violence, and Peace Processes
33–35, 37 (John Darby & Roger MacGinty eds., 2003)

RIPENESS SEES MEDIATOR ACTION AS CHERRY PICKING

When I played basketball many years ago our coach had a phrase with which he provoked us whenever we missed an easy shot, "I can't believe you missed that cherry picker." Essentially it meant that a lot of work had gone into place and then just when everything was right and a giveaway opportunity was presented, the basket was missed.

There are times when I have the impression that the metaphor of ripeness leads towards an emphasis on mediator action as if it were "cherry picking." The impression emerges from two understandings about mediation that I believe have significant limitations and implications. . . .

What the ripeness metaphor does not provide is a sense of the long-term nature of the process, the building and sustaining of the relationships, nor the multiplicity of roles, activities and functions that may be necessary to make a sustained dialogue and change in the relationships possible. . . .

It is not a metaphor that provides a vision of cultivating the soil, planting the seeds or nourishing the seedling in the face of winds, burning sun or icy storms, all of which speak to process, relationship and sustainability rather than a momentary action. . . .

CULTIVATION: THE BUILDING OF LONG-TERM AUTHENTIC RELATIONSHIPS

The cultivation metaphor suggests that a deep respect for, and connection to, the context is critical for sustaining a change process that is moving from deadly expressions of conflict to increased justice and peace in relationships. The context of protracted deadly conflict, like soil, is the people, commonly shared geographies but often sharply differing views of history, rights and responsibilities, and the formation of perception and understandings based on cultural meaning structures. Cultivation is recognizing that ultimately the change process must be taken up, embraced and sustained by people in these contexts. The cultivator, as a connected but outside element in the system, approaches this soil with a great deal of respect, the suspension of quick judgment in favor of the wisdom of adaptation, and an orientation towards supporting the change process through highs and lows, ebbs and flows of violence and thawing of tensions, whether or not the situation appears ripe. The cultivator gives attention to the well-being of the ecosystem, not just the quick production of a given fruit. . . .

EPILOGUE

So what do I say when the journalist asks, "And do you really believe it is possible to talk about negotiation and peace when war is raging?" I say hope is not negotiated. It is kept alive by people who understand the depth of suffering and know the cost of keeping a horizon of change as a possibility for their children and grandchildren. Quick fixes to long-standing violent conflict are like growing a garden with no understanding of seeds, soils and sweat. This conflict traces back across decades, even generations. It will take that long to sort out.

Journalists generally do not quote me in their papers. Sound bites about ripeness, people coming to their senses, and the need for realism and pressure seem to find their way into print more often. But I believe in cultivation. Cultivation as a metaphor suggests that the core of the peacebuilding work — fostering and sustaining committed, authentic relationships across the lines of conflict over time — does not rise and fall with the temporal ups and downs of the conflict cycles. It answers the question — is it possible to pursue peace when things are bad — with a resounding "Yes!" just as it also suggests that when things are suddenly headed towards an agreement the work is hardly over. It has only begun.

Notes and Questions

13.28 Are these two visions of ripeness at odds with one another? Can they be reconciled?

13.29 Can you think of examples that fit under these theories?

13.30 How does the idea of ripeness work (or not work) in domestic mediation or negotiation?

13.31 Consider this exhortation to learn from different models:

> If "third party intervention" and "deadline" setting or "ripeness" look different in different contexts we will have learned something. Lawsuits, even the longest ones, usually settle more quickly than centuries of inter-racial or inter-ethnic conflict. The threat of an authoritative decision maker may hasten voluntary settlement over situations where there is no enforcing authority, but agreements reached consensually when there is no outside threat of decision may be longer-lasting and more easily complied with. Learning to live with differences within national boundaries or regional trade zones may provide a variety of "exemplars" for different modes of co-existence. If we are truly looking for "solutions" to domestic and international conflicts, disputes and problems, than we should be open to as many different and contextually specific ideas as it will take. Though I doubt there is a single theory to fit all human problems for decision, I think we can get better at it by "comparing and contrasting" specifics, rather than assuming uniformity or generality. I urge you to find your favorite conflict resolution idea, model or concept and try it out in a few different places. Our theory and our practice will be all the richer and deeper for it.

Carrie Menkel-Meadow, Correspondences and Contradictions in International and Domestic Conflict Resolution: Lessons from General Theory and Varied Contexts, 2003 J. Disp. Resol. 319, 352 (2003).

3. Case Studies

As you read the following case studies, keep in mind the metaphors of mutually hurting stalemate versus cultivation and harvesting. Also remember the question of the role and objectivity of the mediator. Finally, do these case studies help draw out larger lessons about effective mediation? Are these lessons translatable to other conflicts? Other contexts?

Business school professors Daniel Curran, James Sebenius, and Michael Watkins compare the interventions of Richard Holbrooke in Bosnia-Herzegovina and George Mitchell in Northern Ireland.

 Daniel Curran, James K. Sebenius & Michael Watkins, **CASE ANALYSIS: TWO PATHS TO PEACE: CONTRASTING GEORGE MITCHELL IN NORTHERN IRELAND WITH RICHARD HOLBROOKE IN BOSNIA-HERZEGOVINA**

20 (4) Neg. J. 513-531 (October 2004)

In August 1995, Richard Holbrooke stepped in to lead a new, aggressive attempt to negotiate peace [in Bosnia-Herzegovina], ultimately backed up by North Atlantic Treaty Organization (NATO) air assaults and economic sanctions. After three months of frenetic shuttle diplomacy, Holbrooke and his team were able to negotiate a series of agreements on basic principles and a cease-fire that ultimately led to the Dayton Accords, ending the bloodiest European conflict since World War II; in total, the Balkan wars caused more than 100,000 deaths.

At roughly the same time, George Mitchell was agreeing to chair a British-Irish effort to break the deadlock on the issue, which had become the most significant roadblock to peace in Northern Ireland — the decommissioning of weapons by both sides in the conflict. In 1995, Mitchell was about to step into a three-hundred-year-old feud between a largely Catholic nationalist minority, which wanted the province to become part of Ireland, and the mainly Protestant unionist majority, which wanted the province to remain part of the United Kingdom. Paramilitary groups on both sides had been conducting terrorist attacks since the late 1960s in this slow-burning conflict that had cost more than three thousand Catholic and Protestant lives. Ten parties and two governments were involved in the peace process. Many of these parties refused to talk with each other, in some cases, those on the same side attacked each other, and a virtual chasm yawned between the negotiating positions on major issues. . . . An excruciating two-year process to define the rules and agenda for the talks ensued while the participants slowly disentangled the contentious issues. Finally, the parties made a two-week sprint to a final agreement by the self-imposed deadline of Easter 1998.

At least superficially, the efforts of George Mitchell in Northern Ireland and Richard Holbrooke in Bosnia offer strong similarities. Two white, male, Democratic, U.S. citizens assumed third-party roles in ethnic and religious conflicts in Europe in the latter half of the 1990s. Each man took actions leading to what most observers would regard as a provisional success — at least over the short to medium term, and certainly relative to violent alternatives. Yet, the personalities of these two men could hardly be more different nor could they have taken more divergent approaches to their roles. . . .

THEORETICAL APPROACH

. . . Third parties face three fundamental and early decisions: First, they have to determine their *basic objectives*. At first blush, seeking to foster an agreement among the warring parties might appear to be the obvious basic objective, but more subtle goals are possible: transforming relationships, modeling a more constructive process, delaying the conflict, and others. Second, they have to choose their *fundamental role* (e.g., neutral, advocate for one party or outside player, etc.). Third, they have to consider their best *means of influence* on the situation (e.g., forceful, persuasive, facilitative, and so forth). Along with these three key choices, the third party must, at least implicitly, formulate a strategy to form a "winning coalition" on behalf of the chosen objective. Supporting this *coalition strategy* are three concurrent and overlapping strands: (1) An *issues strategy* with respect to the substantive aspects of the agreements sought, (2) a *process strategy* with respect to the choices of process for the mediation, and (3) a *timing strategy* with respect to the timing of their efforts. These are neither independent from each other nor always equal in their influence on the negotiations. While many other formulations are possible, these dimensions at least capture major elements of the choices made by third parties. We will use this framework to compare the approaches of Mitchell and Holbrooke.

COMPARISONS OF FUNDAMENTAL CHOICES

Basic Objectives

Richard Holbrooke's evident objective was to stop the violent and bloody war in Bosnia —and he needed to do it quickly. He wanted an immediate and comprehensive deal that would end the killing and create a new Bosnia. His approach was deal-oriented, focused on the substantive issues at stake, and transactional.... Holbrooke was less focused on its long-term sustainability, and more interested in "getting the deal done." It took a scant three months from the time he became centrally involved in the conflict until the signing of the Dayton Accords.

George Mitchell's objective in Northern Ireland was also to end the conflict. He found party leaders from both sides who were articulate in their understanding that unemployment and violence were inextricably linked and that a durable peace rested on a foundation of trust and prosperity. Yet, their hatred for one another remained and they were unable to act to realize shared interests. Mitchell was amazed to find that, although the party leaders had lived together in the same community all of their lives, many of them literally did not talk with each other.

By contrast with Holbrooke, Mitchell's approach had the apparent objective of helping the political leadership of the warring factions of Northern Ireland to begin to cooperate in a rudimentary way in creating an institutional and constitutional framework in which the parties could govern Northern Ireland for the future. From the start of the all-party talks, he took almost two years in a highly process-oriented, relationship-focused effort at transforming the working and political relationships among key players.

Fundamental Role

The roles of Mitchell and Holbrooke were well aligned with their objectives. Holbrooke assumed the role of an advocate with substantial potential clout from both the U.S. and NATO. He had an unambiguous mandate and could claim strong powers to punish and reward. He and his team became "active engineers" in the process to meet a clear national interest of the U.S. to stop the violence as expeditiously as possible. The U.S. was already practicing maneuvers for a possible UN withdrawal from Bosnia involving 25,000 U.S. troops.... [T]hey... faced a high cost of failure. Their plan for reaching a comprehensive settlement based on assertive diplomacy put U.S. credibility on the line.

Thus, their actions could be interpreted both as "solving" problems and tactical "manipulation." Throughout Holbrooke's shuttle diplomacy, for example, Serbian President Slobodan Milosevic would press Holbrooke for economic sanctions relief. But Holbrooke planned to save that incentive for an eventual peace conference. "I would tell him that it wasn't in my authority, that's Washington's. But I was always playing a game," Holbrooke recalled. Likewise, Holbrooke viewed the Balkan leaders as the most difficult he had ever dealt with. "They're thugs, they're murderers, they're entrenched," he declared....

By contrast, George Mitchell assumed the role of a neutral mediator on behalf of an agreement among the parties. The situation in Northern Ireland was of relatively peripheral concern to U.S. policy makers, although it had entangled a key ally (Britain) and served as something of a test bed for U.S. influence on post–Cold War ethnic conflicts. Mitchell first became involved in Northern Ireland in early 1995 when President Clinton announced his intention to sponsor a White House Conference on Trade and Investment in Northern Ireland and asked Mitchell to help organize the conference. . . .

Although the British government had long been reluctant to involve outsiders in what it saw as a domestic political matter, its leaders came to the conclusion that a peace settlement in Northern Ireland could benefit from a detached third-party role. Mitchell arrived without a strong interest in the final substance of the negotiated deal but with a desire that the needs of parties be met. He had an unclear mandate and no powers to tangibly reward or punish. Over time, he blamed the problems of the province on the situation rather than the people. Mitchell viewed the leaders of Northern Ireland differently than Holbrooke viewed the Balkan leaders. "I was impressed by the energy and intelligence of the people. They are productive, literate, and articulate," he said. . . .

Means of Influence

In Bosnia, Holbrooke arguably adopted an approach of "whatever it takes to force a deal." In the language of negotiation, it was a best alternative to a negotiated agreement (BATNA)-focused approach of lowering the value of no-agreement alternatives and influencing the dynamics to impose ever higher costs on the various parties who refused to play. Holbrooke had the might of the U.S. and NATO to back up his mediation. He could greatly shape and manipulate the situation through bombing and promised aid and sanctions. . . .

By contrast to this BATNA-lowering approach, George Mitchell followed a strategy that focused on joint gains, continually alluding to the political and economic value of a deal. Mitchell had no formal power and only had a few carrots and sticks with which to influence negotiators and their constituents. "I felt, throughout the discussion, that ultimately my ability to be effective would depend more upon gaining the participants' trust and confidence than on the formal description of my authority," Mitchell said. . . .

Mitchell sought to model constructive future dealings among the parties to show that, in living together in the future, they would be more productive and secure. Arguably, by analogy, Holbrooke was affecting a workable divorce while Mitchell was engaged in relationship therapy.

COMPARISONS OF STRATEGIES: COALITIONAL, PROCESS, ISSUE, AND TIMING

Coalition Strategy: Minimum Necessary Versus Maximum Feasible

Holbrooke's strategy in Bosnia, with respect to the various parties, consisted of four basic steps. First, he sought to simplify the overall decision making within the U.S., NATO, and the European Union (EU). He took steps to disentangle the U.S.-NATO-EU process from that of the UN with his efforts to do away with the infamous "dual key" arrangement requiring the approval of both UN and NATO officials to authorize air strikes.

Second, Holbrooke acted to take advantage of, and foster, the simplification of the hitherto fragmented Balkan parties. This was accomplished, in part, through exploiting the fortuitous actions of Milosevic in obtaining the "Patriarch Paper," which ensured that, in all negotiations, the interests of the Bosnian Serbs would be represented by Milosevic himself. Holbrooke's support of the strengthened Muslim-Croat Federation furthered the simplification process.

Third, he sought to apply considerable pressure on the Serbs to weaken their thus-far dominant position. . . . Finally, when Bosnian Muslims began to press their new found advantage on the battlefield, Holbrooke took steps to isolate the Bosnian Muslims, to block further battlefield progress by this group, and effectively to force a settlement.

In seeking an agreement, Holbrooke wanted the narrow participation of the minimum necessary number of parties, hardly a broad-based stakeholder effort (as was the case, for example, with the ten political parties who played roles in the all-party Northern Irish talks). His tightly defined mediation team then discouraged direct communication between the parties in favor of themselves acting as the conduit of information. Holbrooke had co-opted potential spoilers to the agreement, such as Serbian President Slobodan Milosevic, through enticements and later pushed them to make concessions. . . .

When Holbrooke finally got the leaders together in Dayton, they were edgy, angry, and distrustful. But, drawing on his careful nurtured reputation as a wielder of great power, he kept them there by threatening that the alternative to agreement would be dire, and convincing them that he and his team provided the best opportunity for success.

By contrast with Holbrooke's sequential, divide-conquer-and-force approach and desire to limit participation, George Mitchell carefully built an outwardly rippling, relatively inclusive, coalition of the center against the extremes. . . . Mitchell fostered the creation of a center and helped to give it voice in a manner that significantly displaced the prior political influence of the extremes.

He sought a wide participation of parties by first recommending the election to a negotiating forum and later allowing all parties to remain involved as long as they adhered to the "Mitchell Principles" of democracy and nonviolence. Throughout the negotiations, Mitchell and his loosely organized team encouraged the parties to communicate among themselves. . . . Mitchell effectively reduced the influence of potential spoilers to the agreement by allowing extremists from both sides to leave of their own accord. . . .

Process Strategy: Control Versus Consensus

Holbrooke essentially imposed a negotiation process by fiat. He engineered and manipulated representation in the talks and undertook his shuttles and summits to meet what he saw as the requirements of rapid closure. He apparently worried very little about explicitly defining a clear strategy for the negotiation process and disliked sharing his thoughts with others outside of his team. . . .

Holbrooke was a master at artfully concealing and revealing information in his actions. He frequently kept the international Contact Group in the dark, claiming that it was necessary to exclude the Europeans until the last moment due to their internal divisions. Having to accommodate extraneous demands was something Holbrooke was anxious to avoid. He paid close attention, however, to the details of the process by dictating the precise dimensions of negotiation tables at the summits and carefully arranging the accommodations at Dayton. . . .

As part of the process, Holbrooke used the press to further the idea of an "abyss" in the event of no-deal and he consistently sought to lower expectations for the results he sought at each stage. . . . Yet, when progress was made, Holbrooke trumpeted the publicity to lock in gains. . . . Holbrooke also used the press and the process as tools to build perceptions in the minds of the players of his personal credibility and power.

By contrast, Mitchell acted as the steward of a deliberate process of principled inclusion. The delegates were formally elected to a comprehensive forum and had to endorse the "Mitchell Principles" of democracy and nonviolence in order to enter the talks and continue participating. At first, Mitchell's chairmanship was not even accepted by the unionist parties. . . . To gain acceptance, Mitchell agreed to dispense with the process and agenda created in advance by the Irish and British governments. Instead, he agreed to negotiate his role, the rules, the agenda, and the procedures of the talks; including the principle of "sufficient consensus," which gave veto power to all of the largest players and ensured the reality of power sharing. For months, he and his team sought proposals from parties, provided comparative tables to guide discussion, and used bilateral meetings to ease things forward. . . . Throughout the talks, Mitchell kept the process going at all costs—however threadbare it seemed at any given time. He and the other chairmen were routinely called upon to speak to the press. Mitchell used the press to hold out a "pot of gold" waiting at the end of a negotiated settlement. He felt a need to optimistically assess the state of the talks. But it grew difficult. . . .

Mitchell's process was highly transparent and, even in despairing moments, he found positive ways to interpret the talks' future potential to the parties and the press. Unlike Holbrooke, whose process actions built perceptions of personal credibility and power, which could be deployed to force a deal, Mitchell used the process to build perceptions of fairness, respect, dedication, and credibility.

When Mitchell decided to set a deadline for the talks, he negotiated it with the two governments and met with representatives of each of the parties several times, refining his proposal at each meeting. The proposal included a process for the preparation of two drafts that would allow all parties to object and make proposals for the final version so that there would be no last minute surprises. He effectively modeled the means of debate and governance that would be required by the institutions established under the Good Friday Agreement.

Issue Strategy: Substance Versus Procedure

Richard Holbrooke placed more emphasis on substance than procedure in the Bosnian negotiations. His agenda for discussion changed frequently and always revolved around substantive issues. It was highly sequential, using shuttles and late-night diplomatic pressure to explore concessions and then hold summits to lock in gains and build momentum towards a larger package. At these summits, Holbrooke consistently sought a series of agreed-upon *principles* followed by *specifics on the issues*. His seven member team artfully concealed and revealed information in order to benefit the process.

The first summit was "a tense affair with hostile officials clustered tightly around the custom-built table," but Holbrooke emerged with a list of agreed basic principles that recognized Bosnia's existing borders, created two entities within Bosnia, and allowed each entity the right to establish ties with neighboring countries. The second summit, three weeks later, resulted in another contentious list of principles defining the structures of government such as a parliament, a presidency, a constitutional court, and a commitment to elections.

Holbrooke deferred for a later time toxic issues such as the map with boundaries and delimitations of the postconflict country, which he deemed to be "too hard." . . . Still, Holbrooke sought to leave no issues that could be negotiated untouched. By the time the leaders arrived in Dayton, the U.S. State Department presented them with a comprehensive Framework Peace Agreement complete with annexes covering military issues, elections, the constitution, human rights, and an international police task force. The idea was to present them with a complete package and ram it through by way of an intensive negotiations process to be completed as rapidly as humanly possible.

By contrast, George Mitchell deferred the difficult substantive issues until the very end of his involvement in favor of focusing on negotiations over the procedures and agendas themselves. His early discussions slogged through arcane debates about rules. He not only negotiated the process and procedures for the all-party talks, but he negotiated a preliminary agenda, then a more detailed agenda with the parties — all of which took more than a year. This extreme procedural focus was a mirror image of Holbrooke's extreme substantive focus.

When Mitchell did deal with substantive issues, he methodically separated them into three strands for the parties to discuss the nuances of each issue. His team shared information widely in an effort to avoid surprises or misunderstandings. The parties canvassed their various proposals, concepts, and models but, more importantly, they explored each other's ideas, seeking further explanations or offering explanations for their own reservations or objections. . . .

Mitchell later repackaged the issues in the final agreement for mutual gain. Mitchell progressively isolated and deferred the hardest issue, decommissioning of IRA weapons, in the hope that enough of a relationship would be built up among the parties to tackle it later in a more productive way.

Timing Strategy: Forcing Versus Fostering

Holbrooke's timing strategy called for building momentum by gaining early wins through agreements on principles. He then accelerated the pace with a series of partial agreements and forcible actions to prevent backsliding on promises.

He used several imposed deadlines — backed with the threat of bombing — to forge agreements. He also made well-timed persuasive arguments — backed by intelligence data — to force parties to back down....

By contrast, Mitchell's patient strategy used time, not only to begin to foster a more constructive relationship among the parties, but to increase their sense of respect, obligation, liking, and credibility toward him. Mitchell, in turn, used his credibility — and only his credibility — to create a culminating event in December 1997 when he felt further interaction was pointless.

> Much has been said about my patience. I have a lot of it, but I felt I had just about used it up. Rarely in my life have I felt as frustrated and angry. We had been meeting for a year and a half. For hundreds and hundreds of hours I had listened to the same arguments. Very little had been accomplished. It had taken two months to get an understanding on the rules to be followed once the negotiations began. Then it took another two months to get agreement on a preliminary agenda. Then we had tried for fourteen more months to get an accord on a detailed final agenda. We couldn't even get that, and we were about to adjourn for the Christmas break. Our failure...would be crushing...I began to think about a deadline. (Mitchell, Making Peace, 1999: 126)

Mitchell deployed his hard-earned credibility on the final deadline, which he carefully negotiated with the parties and governments at the talks. To emphasize that this would be the parties' last clear chance for agreement, and that his participation was at an end, he stated at the outset of the final talks, "I am Humpty Dumpty. I can only jump once."

The remarkable differences between Holbrooke and Mitchell are summarized in Table One, which outlines their fundamental choices and Table Two, which compares the strategies they each chose to employ. While suggestive, these categories of choice are neither mutually exclusive nor collectively exhaustive. In many respects, these two superficially similar third-party episodes could scarcely be more different, once critically examined.

Table One
Differences Between Holbrooke and Mitchell Approach

	HOLBROOKE BOSNIA-HERZEGOVINA	MITCHELL NORTHERN IRELAND
Fundamental objectives	Deal-oriented Substantive Transactional	Process-oriented Relationship Transformational
Fundamental interest/role	Mediator/advocate (with clout)	Mediator/neutral
Fundamental influence strategy	BATNA-focused "Whatever it takes"	Joint gains-focused Model-future dealings

Table Two
Strategies Employed by Holbrooke and Mitchell

STRATEGIC ELEMENT	HOLBROOKE BOSNIA-HERZEGOVINA	MITCHELL NORTHERN IRELAND
Coalition strategy	Simplify structure Equalize core parties Sequence	Coalition of center against extremes
Issue strategy	Process by fiat	Process an issue for negotiation
	Principles, then specifics	Procedure, then substance
	Sequential, then lock in gains	Separate into three strands, then package
	Defer deal-breakers	Decouple decommissioning
Process strategy	Engineer/manipulate representation	Principled inclusion (Mitchell Principles, "sufficient consensus")
	Sequence shuttles and summits	Keep going at all costs ("variable geometry")
	Conceal/reveal information	Highly transparent
	Use press to paint abyss/ lower expectations, yet lock in gains	Relentlessly positive press spin
	Use process to build perceptions of personal credibility and power	Use process to build perceptions of fairness, dedication, and respect
Timing strategy	As fast as possible	As long as it takes
	Build "momentum" by early wins, accelerating series of partial agree- ments, forcible actions, and process choices	Use time to bootstrap sense of respect, obligation, liking, and credibility Expend personal credibility on final deadline

THE MEN AND THEIR MISSION: WERE THEIR PERSONALITIES, EXPERIENCE, AND APPROACHES A "FIT"?

The relatively bloodless comparisons of strategies and approaches in Tables One and Two largely sidestep the question of the specific individuals involved along with the "fit" between the person and the situation. Indeed, arguably as a function of the actors themselves, these twin cases—at least in their central tendencies—contrast force with tact, acting with listening, and manipulation with process stewardship. While Holbrooke turned to coercive means to forge a peace, Mitchell first created and then presided over a "Senate" in Northern Ireland.

Richard Holbrooke possessed one of the most assertive personalities in Washington. He could be bombastic and brash. Some considered him a "showman" and he had a reputation for being unpredictable and often difficult. He had served on the U.S. delegation to the Paris peace talks with the Vietcong in 1968 and, as Assistant Secretary of State for East Asian and Pacific Affairs, he had conducted difficult negotiations with the Chinese and with former Filipino President Ferdinand Marcos.... Holbrooke was not only blunt and impatient, but he also used all the means at his disposal to force agreements....

George Mitchell, on the other hand, had a reputation for being diligent, cautious, and levelheaded. He had served for fourteen years in the U.S. Senate, seven of those years as Democratic Majority Leader. Throughout his political career, he displayed a fairness and calm temperament that made him a natural intermediary between senators, administration officials, and staff. As a legislator, Mitchell was quiet and judicious. He massaged details and soothed tempers, always seeking consensus over mundane issues.... Mitchell developed a sense of patience and timing in the U.S. Senate where passion was more effective in opposition than when in the majority. Yet a restrained style did not imply an unwillingness to exert power; indeed, Mitchell could be fiercely partisan. In his early career, he learned when to use this passion.... He frequently allowed room for events to unfold....

It would be too easy to caricature and exaggerate the extent of the personality differences between Holbrooke and Mitchell, when in fact, observers have also remarked on Mitchell's toughness and Holbrooke's empathy and charm. Yet the contrasting central personality attributes and prior experiences of the two men were strongly consistent with the nature of the approaches they chose to the two conflicts. Perhaps ironically, the character of the two negotiated outcomes also seemed to differ along similar lines.

Representatives of the Republic of Bosnia and Herzegovina, the Republic of Croatia, and the Federal Republic of Yugoslavia hastily initialed Holbrooke's General Framework Agreement for Peace in Bosnia and Herzegovina. Even at the signing ceremony, however, Izetbegovic and the rest of his delegation described it as "a bitter and unjust peace" and called it a "brutal process." Maintenance of the peace hinged on the ongoing presence of outside military forces with many participants asserting that "if they were removed, the parties would be back killing each other the next day."

By contrast, the representatives of eight political parties, including the largest Catholic party, SDLP; and the largest Protestant party, UUP; and representatives of the Irish and British governments, signed Mitchell's Belfast Agreement. At the signing ceremony, UUP leader David Trimble and John Hume of SDLP called it a "principled compromise" forged in "learning and understanding."...

CONCLUDING THOUGHTS

To sharpen the contrasts between these two men and the episodes in which they played central roles, consider the following thought experiment: Imagine the likely process and outcome in each case if Holbrooke had been assigned to Northern Ireland and Mitchell to Bosnia. While each man might have flexibly adapted to radically different situations, it is clear that simply juxtaposing the two approaches would sharply lower the chances of success in each case....

Perhaps the most important contribution of this comparison of the sharply divergent approaches taken in Northern Ireland and Bosnia is the challenge it poses to easy generalizations about effective mediation. Holbrooke's results may confound those who see the essence of successful mediation as scrupulous neutrality buttressed by patient, interest-based, empathetic joint problem solving to find mutually beneficial solutions. For others who may see the coercive diplomacy of Holbrooke as the essential ingredient to cutting through intractable and violent situations, the success of Mitchell's low-key, even-handed, endlessly persistent style may seem almost magical. Yet, in the course of their respective efforts, both men helped forge peace agreements in two immensely challenging situations that had defeated many prior attempts. While two data points do not a theory make, these twin cases highlight the range of tactical and strategic dimensions required of any candidate theory of third party action.

Notes and Questions

13.32 In Mitchell's case, the deadline worked. On Good Friday 1998, the parties agreed to sign a peace accord, now known as the "Good Friday Accord," which, as of this writing, has more or less worked, with a few challenges to its legitimacy and robustness. On the other hand, efforts to use a "deadline" of the end of President Clinton's term as president, together with the fragile leadership of Israel's Prime Minister Barak in the summer of 2000 talks at Camp David, doomed those talks to failure in the eyes of some commentators. See, e.g., Robert Malley & Hussein Agha, Camp David: Tragedy of Errors, N.Y. Review of Books, Aug. 8, 2001, at 59. So, efforts to claim that some intervention strategies like "setting a firm deadline" ("setting a firm trial date" in the domestic context) should be effective in most, if not all, settings, may be wrong in the great variety of real-world international disputing contexts.

13.33 What might distinguish negotiating and mediating contexts in Northern Ireland and the Mideast? Many international mediators who have worked in both places have attempted to get each of the parties in one of these conflicts to think about the other conflict. What might be learned by contrasting different disputes and attempts to resolve them by those who are inside the disputes as negotiators or mediators?

13.34 Would it be accurate to call Holbrooke a "negotiator" and Mitchell a "mediator," or were they both mediators engaged in two different types of mediation?

13.35 Different contexts will each pose different challenges. Raymond Shonholtz, President of Partners for Democratic Change, writes about conflict and dispute resolution in emerging democracies:

> In the pre-democratic period [in former communist countries], issues became conflicts when they were managed through forms of repression, violence, avoidance or ideology. Issues become disputes when they are managed through transparent rule of law systems. The difference is that the latter system is designed to resolve differences peacefully, while the former system is designed to manipulate or suppress them at all costs.

Shonholtz goes on to discuss the importance of relationship building in arenas where there is no trust between individuals and government or between ethnic groups divided by a bitter past against each other. Such a relationship-building phase must precede addressing substantive issues through mediation. He also emphasizes the importance of building "in-country" capacity for democracy building: "Democracy and its mechanics for dispute management is not something one can just import. It is a social process, not a mechanical process." Raymond Shonholtz, Constructive Responses to Conflict in Emerging Democracies, Partners for Democratic Change/UNDP Conference Paper (2/14/01).

Shonholtz and Kinga Göncz, in another article, conclude that in the context of emerging democracies and market economies in Central and Eastern Europe:

> "Facilitation" seems less threatening to formal entities in the new democracies than "mediation," which is associated with compromise, power imbalances, and third party power tactics. While drawing on negotiation and mediation techniques during the course of a cooperative planning or problem solving process, facilitation strengthens the imagery of responsible parties as decision makers and reduces the impression that the "third party" is authorized to promote any resolution of differences.

Kinga Göncz & Raymond Shonholtz, Applying Collaborative Processes in Former Communist Countries, IAP2 (First Quarter 2000).

D. INTERNATIONAL MEDIATION IN COMMERCIAL OR TRADE SETTINGS

Increasingly, as individuals and corporations do business together across borders, disputes about contracts or commercial dealings must be resolved in multinational settings, implicating complicated issues of choice of forum, choice of law, and jurisdiction. To avoid these complicated issues of litigation, most commercial disputes are now handled by a group of international commercial arbitration tribunals, including the International Chamber of Commerce in Paris, the London Court of International Arbitration, the American Arbitration Association, which have their own rules and which, when activated, produce arbitral awards which are enforceable in domestic courts by the power of an international treaty and the New York Convention on Recognition and Enforcement of Foreign Arbitral Awards (in the United States this law is codified in the Federal Arbitration Act, FAA, 9 U.S.C. §§1-307 (1994)). See Yves Dezalay & Bryant Garth, Dealing in Virtue: International Commercial Arbitration and the Construction of a Transnational Legal Order (1996).

In recent years, many of these international bodies, as well as the UN itself, through UNCITRAL (the United Nations Commission on International Trade Law), have promulgated rules and procedures for the use of mediation or conciliation processes, for many of the same reasons litigants in domestic settings have moved from litigation and arbitration to mediation of their disputes — party control and determination over process and outcome and more tailored solutions to problems and disputes, especially in cases where business relationships are best preserved. See

UNCITRAL Model Law for International Commercial Conciliation (2002). (Now proposed to be added to the Uniform Mediation Act.)

This development in private international law has been echoed in public international law, where both regional and world trade organizations have now added mediation or conciliation processes to their more adjudicative or arbitral processes, see Andrea K. Schneider, Getting Along: The Evolution of Dispute Resolution Regimes in the International Trade Organizations, 20 Mich. J. Intl. L. 697 (1999), and Andrea K. Schneider, Public and Private International Dispute Resolution, in The Handbook of Dispute Resolution (Michael L. Moffitt & Robert C. Bordone eds., 2005) at 438.

As with domestic uses of mediation, arbitration, and other dispute resolution processes, important questions of procedure, conflicts of interests, fairness, and enforceability have arisen (without the protection of "default" laws of a particular sovereign), resulting in the call for international standards, procedures, and ethics codes for third-party neutrals in these international contexts. See, e.g., Catherine Rogers, Fit and Function in Legal Ethics: Developing a Code of Conduct for International Arbitration, 23 Mich. J. Intl. L. 341 (2002).

Notes and Questions

13.36 Can you think of particularly difficult or unique ethics issues that could arise from having mediators in an international commercial or trade dispute? What might the role of culture be in mediating such disputes? Is it possible to think about an international ethical culture for third-party neutrals?

13.37 What differences and similarities, in terms of process choices, roles, and available tools confront the international mediator of public, political disputes, compared to private, commercial disputes?

E. MEDIATION TOOLS IN POST-CONFLICT SITUATIONS

While dispute resolution tools traditionally have been used to prevent future conflicts or resolve ongoing disputes, similar techniques are increasingly being used in post-conflict efforts to seek peace, some form of coexistence, and even reconciliation. South Africa's Truth and Reconciliation Commission (TRC) is the premier example of a form of dispute resolution used to try to mend communal ties. By the time the TRC was established, apartheid had been abolished and a new government was in control. Yet, many in South Africa, on all sides, felt the need to do more to get beyond the problems of the past.

As with "problem-solving workshops" and "public peace processes," post-conflict dispute resolution processes focus on narrative, listening, and communicating rather than on reaching concrete agreements or full adjudication. They can be contrasted, for example, to the various war crimes tribunals, which are an adjudicative form of dispute resolution in the international context. The theories behind processes such as the TRC are that victims must be able to tell their stories and to hear why those who have harmed them have done so (some taking of responsibility) before new nation building and peaceful coexistence can be achieved. See Antonia Chayes & Martha Minow, Imagine Co-Existence: Restoring Humanity After Violent Conflict (2003), Martha Minow, Between Vengeance and Forgiveness (1998), for examples of such efforts in a wide variety of contexts and settings. See also Carrie Menkel-Meadow, Remembrance of Things Past: The Future and Past in Mediation, 5 Cardozo J. Conflict Resol. 97 (2004). Other attempts to mend ties in a post-conflict context include the film *Promises* (Justin Shapiro & B.Z. Goldberg, 2002) (depicting the encounter of Israeli and Palestinian children in Israel, before the current *intifada)* and the camp Seeds for Peace, which has brought children together in recreational settings, across dispute and cultural boundaries, in hopes of "seeding" nonviolence and peaceful, respectful, and tolerant relationships across deep divides.

The use of these processes remains controversial. Many believe that prosecution and punishment for murders and other human rights violations are necessary to reinstall the rule of law before real "healing" can begin for post-conflict societies. Others fear that too much punishment continues the retributive impulse and fosters generations of ethnic, political, racial, or class conflict. Some question whether all the "truth" is told and all responsible for the harm have come forward to make amends. Some recent empirical work suggests that those who participated in the TRC have a greater belief in the ability to establish a human rights culture and are less cynical about the rule of law, perhaps challenging the notion that truth and reconciliation (or mediation) and law or rights-based processes are antithetical to each other. See James L. Gibson, Truth, Reconciliation, and the Creation of a Human Rights Culture in South Africa, 38 L. & Socy. Rev. 5 (2004).

The following excerpt by a clinical psychologist who worked with South Africa's TRC gives insight into how other forms of mediation are used.

 Pumla Gobodo-Madikizela, **A HUMAN BEING DIED THAT NIGHT: A SOUTH AFRICAN STORY OF FORGIVENESS**

117-120, 126-129 (2003)

Although forgiveness is often regarded as an expression of weakness, the decision to forgive can paradoxically elevate a victim to a position of strength as the one who holds the key to the perpetrator's wish. For just at the moment when the perpetrator begins to show remorse, to seek some way to ask forgiveness, the victim becomes the gatekeeper to what the outcast desires — readmission into the human community. And the victim retains that privileged status as long as he or she stays the moral course, refusing to sink to the level of the evil that was done to her or to him. In this sense, then, forgiveness is a kind of revenge, but revenge enacted at a rarefied level. . . .

The question is no longer *whether* victims can forgive "evildoers" but whether we — our symbols, language, and politics, our legal, media, and academic institutions — are creating the conditions that encourage alternatives to revenge. We have come to rely too narrowly on retribution as the only legitimate form of justice and on the Nuremberg trial model as the only one capable of adequately addressing

state-orchestrated atrocities. Tell-
ingly, recent international tribunals
such as the International Criminal
Tribunal on the genocide in
Rwanda and the tribunal in The
Hague on the former Yugoslavia
have run into problems. In
Rwanda, for example, victims
have felt largely excluded from a
process that is supposed to help
heal their wounds and restore
some normality in their society.
Our knowledge of the dynamic
between victims and perpetrators
has further been influenced by
narratives from the Holocaust
experience. Although a few Jewish
German groups have been established to try to build positive relationships between children of
Holocaust survivors and descen-
dants of Nazi perpetrators, Holo-

Truth and Healing

"If the affirmative case for truth commissions
rests on the goal of healing, then the working
hypothesis is that testimony of the victims and
perpetrators, offered publicly to a truth commission, affords opportunities for individuals
and the nation as a whole to heal. With the aim
of producing a fair and thorough account of
the atrocities, a truth commission proceeds on
the assumption that it helps individuals to tell
their stories and to have them acknowledged
officially. Also assumed here is the premise
that a final report can create a framework for
the nation to deal with its past. Echoing
assumptions of psychotherapy, religious confession, and journalistic muckraking, truth
commissions presume that telling and hearing truth is healing."

Martha Minow, Between Vengeance and
Forgiveness 61 (1998).

---

caust discourse has sometimes emphasized remembering but not so clearly
dialogue, which is critical if victims are to live again with perpetrators in the same
society, or indeed if they are to live in greater harmony with themselves.

Dialogue, of course, will not solve every problem faced by a society that has
suffered sustained violence on a large scale. But dialogue does create avenues for
broadening our models of justice and for healing deep fractures in a nation by
unearthing, acknowledging, and recording what has been done. It humanizes the
dehumanized and confronts perpetrators with their inhumanity. Through dialogue,
victims as well as the greater society come to recognize perpetrators as human beings
who failed morally, whether through coercion, the perverted convictions of a
warped mind, or fear.

Far from relieving the pressure on them, recognizing the most serious criminals
as human intensifies it, because society is thereby able to hold them to greater moral
accountability. Indeed, demonizing as monsters those who commit evil lets them off
too easily. . . . Sustained, engaged, ordered dialogue thus forces an offender to
unearth what moral sensibilities he has buried under a façade of "obedience to
orders" or righteous "duty to my country" and to face what he has done, not in
the heady climate of the period of mayhem but in the sobering atmosphere of
reflection on ordinary human lives now shattered. But it also thereby invites him,
if he can, if he dares, to negotiate the chasm between his monstrousness and the world
of the forgiven. It thus encourages him to stop denying the suspected truth: that all
along, he knew that he was human and knew right from wrong. The act of

humanizing is therefore at once both punishment and rehabilitation. Finally, dialogue creates the possibility of setting the person's actions, through testimony and witnessing, in the broader framework of the political-ideological context that may have supported and even directed his deeds. It is this component of the crime, the one that resides at the systemic, institutional, and policy levels rather than at a personal level, that is notoriously difficult to substantiate within the strict evidentiary rules of a purely judicial process. Thus the politics of abuse that were enshrined in the policies of an oppressive system can be acknowledged and confirmed in ways that the more rigid, adversarial relationship of courtroom exchanges cannot. . . .

What enables some victims to forgive heinous crimes? What distinguishes them from those who feel unable to do so? In addition to an external context that makes reconciliation normative through the language of restoration — a truth commission, for example, or a counseling agency that focuses on victim-offender encounters, or a national dialogue that begins to put in place the symbols and vocabulary of forgiveness and compromise — there are internal psychological dynamics that impel most of us toward forming an empathic connection with another person in pain, that draw us *into* his pain, regardless of who that someone is. The possibility of making an empathic connection with someone who has victimized us, as a response to the pain of his remorse, stems significantly from this underlying dynamic. The power of human connectedness, of identification with the other as "bone of my bone" through the sheer fact of his being human, draws us to "rescue" others in pain, almost as if this were a learned response embedded deep in our genetic and evolutionary past. . . .

This is not a statement about whether it "makes sense" for the victimized to respond with empathy, nor an evaluation of the propriety of extending forgiveness. It is a tracing of what makes it possible for enemies to connect in a way that might otherwise seem unimaginable.

There is another dimension to the internal dynamic that motivates many to connect with those who have victimized them. A broad consensus exists in the literature that in order to torture, kill, and maim, perpetrators must first exclude their victims from the moral obligations they feel toward the world in general and, in particular, toward those with whom they are socially and politically connected. Moral exclusion of a victim from the community of those who deserve to be treated humanely, in effect, effaces his pain. . . . When perpetrators express remorse, when they finally acknowledge that they can see what they previously could not see, or did not want to, they are revalidating the victim's pain — in a sense, giving his or her humanity back. Empowered and revalidated, many victims at this point find it natural to extend and deepen the healing process by going a step further: turning around and conferring forgiveness on their torturer.

The motivation to do this does not stem only from altruism or high moral principles. The victim in a sense *needs* forgiveness as part of the process of becoming rehumanized. The victim needs it in order to complete himself or herself and to wrest away from the perpetrator the fiat power to destroy or to spare. . . . Reciprocating with empathy and forgiveness in the face of a perpetrator's remorse restores to many victims the sense that they are once again capable of affecting a profound difference in the moral community.

Notes and Questions

13.38 Is the language of healing compatible with notions of justice? Can therapeutic mediation substitute for adjudication when terrible human rights violations have occurred? Is truth-telling enough for building coexistence, a new nation, and a new culture? Do the different vocabularies or techniques of mediation, therapy, and adjudication, as well as the different remedies produced by these different processes, limit what each process can offer? Is it possible for the same events, both within nations, and between nations, to be processed in different ways? Some TRCs promise amnesty for some acknowledgment of responsibility for different "levels" of human rights violations or crimes; see also Jason Strain & Elizabeth Keyes, Accountability in the Aftermath of Rwanda's Genocide, in Accountability for Atrocities: National and International Responses (Jane Stromseth ed., 2003).

13.39 How do the theories behind the TRCs relate to the goals behind transformative mediation or understanding-based mediation? Contrast these goals with evaluative mediation (which is more aligned with a law- or rights-based approach).

13.40 Disputing across legal and cultural boundaries raises issues different from those raised in domestic disputes. What processes, for example, work effectively across systems, cultures, and nations? Some argue that the complex differences across cultures, legal systems, and nation-states make alternative forms of dispute resolution particularly appropriate for development across those boundaries and differences. Do you agree? See The Handbook of Negotiation and Culture (Michele Gelfand & Jeanne M. Brett eds., 2004).

Now that you have read this chapter, consider what principles apply in both domestic and international conflict resolution. Do different contexts require different knowledge and process design? As the field of international dispute resolution continues to evolve, broader questions will include the neutrality of a third party; the benefits of negotiation or diplomacy versus mandatory arbitration; and economic support for disadvantaged parties on both the domestic and international level. As in the domestic context, consider whether a backdrop of "the rule of law" and default enforcement by formal institutions is necessary for the effectiveness of more informal processes in the international arena. See Tom Ginsburg & Richard H. McAdams, Adjudicating in Anarchy: An Expressive Theory of International Dispute Resolution, 45 Wm. & Mary L. Rev. 1229 (2004).

Chapter 14 Thinking Critically About Mediation

It was only a small dream of the Golden World, now you trot off to bed.
—John Berryman

Humans are always seeking something better. As a result, all human processes are (and should be) evaluated regularly by their creators. Mediation and related problem-solving processes are no exception. Mediation has grown in popularity — in part to address injustices, inflexibilities, high costs, and increased time delays in the traditional litigation system — and now it is subject to various critiques. Many of these criticisms are described in this chapter. They include claims that settlement through non-adjudicatory processes does not permit enough elaboration of the law to clarify important public values, that inequalities of parties are exacerbated in informal settings without judicial control, and that too much ADR means too much state control of private matters. In addition, critiques are included that are related to prejudice, to mediator manipulation, to mediation's focus on the future and consequent neglect of past injustices, and to the export of "American" modes of mediation. Finally, some of the claims of mediation proponents regarding the impact of mediation on the cost and speed of litigated matters are challenged.

The field of dispute resolution is intended to be flexible and responsive to issues, problems, and criticisms. Thoughtful responses to valid criticisms and the development of new solutions and ideas are the goal. To encourage active engagement with the readings in this chapter and to stimulate your own critical thinking, keep the following questions in mind while reading these excerpts:

1. What are the authors' stated (explicit) and unstated (implicit) criticisms? Are they criticizing mediation only or a variety of ADR processes?
2. What are the sources of support (for instance, data, case law, analysis, theory) for the authors' claims?
3. Are you persuaded of the dangers, disadvantages, or concerns expressed?
4. What responses, rebuttals, or other reactions do you have to these claims or arguments? What is the evidence for your response?
5. Do you see other criticisms of mediation that are not expressed here? What are they, and why do they concern you?
6. What can be done to deal with some of these concerns and issues?

7. How can we develop good tools for assessing these claims? Are dispute processes always subject to quantitative metrics? How might qualitative measures be taken and evaluated?

8. Some of the critiques levied against mediation could be made against litigation as well. As you read these various critiques, you should be asking: Compared to what? (known as the "baseline" problem in evaluation research).

A. CRITIQUES OF MEDIATION: IN THEORY

Among the most dramatic critiques of mediation (and negotiation), insofar as it resolves cases in the litigation system, are that it robs the public of important precedents and hence impoverishes the development of law. Critics of settlements achieved by negotiation, mediation, or other alternative processes also point to power imbalances that sometimes make bargaining unfair. An underlying assumption of this reasoning is that settlement involves compromises that do not serve "justice." As you read Owen Fiss's famous critique below, recall the underlying justice rationales of mediation, and develop your own analysis of this question. See also Nancy Welsh, Remembering the Role of Justice in Resolution: Insights from Procedural and Social Justice Theories, 54 J. Legal Educ. 49 (2004).

The second critic, David Luban, agrees in some important respects with Fiss but adds another facet to the discussion. If every case were litigated, our system would break down from overload. Luban endorses the need for the development of precedent—hence litigation—but urges a careful balancing of settlement and litigation.

Finally, Richard Abel raises questions about the impact of introducing less formal mechanisms for dispute resolution. Are mediation and other ADR programs one means for government, like Big Brother in George Orwell's *1984*, to extend its tentacles into our private domains and gain more control over individual lives? In a critique focusing on the implications of the development and expansion of government and court-connected dispute resolution programs, Abel argues that programs offering informal justice, which ostensibly give power to individual disputants, actually extend state power.

 Owen M. Fiss, **AGAINST SETTLEMENT**

93 Yale L.J. 1073, 1075-1078, 1085-1090 (1984)

The advocates of ADR . . . exalt the idea of settlement more generally because they view adjudication as a process to resolve disputes. They act as though courts arose to resolve quarrels between neighbors who had reached an impasse and turned to a stranger for help. Courts are seen as an institutionalization of the stranger and adjudication is viewed as the process by which the stranger exercises power. The very fact that the neighbors have turned to someone else to resolve their dispute signifies a breakdown in their social relations; the advocates of ADR acknowledge this, but nonetheless hope that the neighbors will be able to reach agreement before the stranger renders judgment. Settlement is that agreement. It is a truce more than a true reconciliation, but it seems preferable to judgment because it rests on the consent of both parties and avoids the cost of a lengthy trial.

In my view, however, this account of adjudication and the case for settlement rest on questionable premises. I do not believe that settlement as a generic practice is preferable to judgment or should be institutionalized on a wholesale and indiscriminate basis. It should be treated instead as a highly problematic technique for streamlining dockets. Settlement is for me the civil analogue of plea bargaining: Consent is often coerced; the bargain may be struck by someone without authority; the absence of a trial and judgment renders subsequent judicial involvement troublesome; and although dockets are trimmed, justice may not be done. Like plea bargaining, settlement is a capitulation to the conditions of mass society and should be neither encouraged nor praised.

THE IMBALANCE OF POWER

By viewing the lawsuit as a quarrel between two neighbors, the dispute-resolution story that underlies ADR implicitly asks us to assume a rough equality between the contending parties. It treats settlement as the anticipation of the outcome of trial and assumes that the terms of settlement are simply a product of the parties' predictions of that outcome. In truth, however, settlement is also a function of the resources available to each party to finance the litigation, and those resources are frequently distributed unequally. Many lawsuits do not involve a property dispute between two neighbors, or between AT&T and the government (to update the story), but rather concern a struggle between a member of a racial minority and a municipal police department over alleged brutality, or a claim by a worker against a large corporation over work-related injuries. In these cases, the distribution of financial resources, or the ability of one party to pass along its costs, will invariably infect the bargaining process, and the settlement will be at odds with a conception of justice that seeks to make the wealth of the parties irrelevant.

The disparities in resources between the parties can influence the settlement in three ways. First, the poorer party may be less able to amass and analyze the information needed to predict the outcome of the litigation, and thus be disadvantaged in the bargaining process. Second, he may need the damages he seeks immediately and thus be induced to settle as a way of accelerating payment, even though he realizes he would get less now than he might if he awaited judgment. All plaintiffs want their damages immediately, but an indigent plaintiff may be exploited by a rich defendant because his need is so great that the defendant can force him to accept a sum that is less than the ordinary present value of the judgment. Third, the poorer party might be forced to settle because he does not have the resources to finance the litigation, to cover either his own projected expenses, such as his lawyer's time, or the expenses his opponent can impose through the manipulation or procedural mechanisms such as discovery. It might seem that settlement benefits the plaintiff by allowing him to avoid the costs of litigation, but this is not so. The defendant can anticipate the plaintiff's costs if the case were to be tried fully and decrease his offer by that amount. The indigent plaintiff is a victim of the costs of litigation even if he settles. . . .

Of course, imbalances of power can distort judgment as well: Resources influence the quality of presentation, which in turn has an important bearing on who wins and the terms of victory. We count, however, on the guiding presence of the judge, who can employ a number of measures to lessen the impact of distributional inequalities. He can, for example, supplement the parties' presentations by asking questions, calling his own witnesses, and inviting other persons and institutions to participate as *amici*. These measures are likely to make only a small contribution toward moderating the influence of distributional inequalities, but should not be ignored for that reason. Not even these small steps are possible with settlement. There is, moreover, a critical difference between a process like settlement, which is based on bargaining and accepts inequalities of wealth as an integral and legitimate component of the process, and a process like judgment, which knowingly struggles against those inequalities. Judgment aspires to an autonomy from distributional inequalities, and it gathers much of its appeal from this aspiration. . . .

JUSTICE RATHER THAN PEACE

The dispute-resolution story makes settlement appear as a perfect substitute for judgment, as we just saw, by trivializing the remedial dimensions of a lawsuit, and also by reducing the social function of the lawsuit to one of resolving private disputes. In that story, settlement appears to achieve exactly the same purpose as judgment — peace between the parties — but at considerably less expense to society. The two quarreling neighbors turn to a court in order to resolve their dispute, and society makes courts available because it wants to aid in the achievement of their private ends or to secure the peace.

In my view, however, the purpose of adjudication should be understood in broader terms. Adjudication uses public resources, and employs not strangers chosen by the parties but public officials chosen by a process in which the public participates. These officials, like members of the legislative and executive branches, possess a power that has been defined and conferred by public law, not by private agreement. Their job is not to maximize the ends of private parties, nor simply to secure the peace, but to explicate and give force to the values embodied in authoritative texts such as the Constitution and statutes: to interpret those values and to bring reality into accord with them. This duty is not discharged when the parties settle.

In our political system, courts are reactive institutions. They do not search out interpretive occasions, but instead wait for others to bring matters to their attention. They also rely for the most part on others to investigate and present the law and facts. A settlement will thereby deprive a court of the occasion, and perhaps even the ability, to render an interpretation. A court cannot proceed (or not proceed very far) in the face of a settlement. To be against settlement is not to urge that parties be "forced" to litigate, since that would interfere with their autonomy and distort the adjudicative process; the parties will be inclined to make the court believe that their bargain is justice. To be against settlement is only to suggest that when the parties settle, society gets less than what appears, and for a price it does not know it is paying. Parties might settle while leaving justice undone. The settlement of a school suit might secure the peace, but not racial equality. Although the parties are prepared to live under the terms they bargained for, and although such peaceful coexistence may be a necessary precondition of justice, and itself a state of affairs to be valued, it is not justice itself. To settle for something means to accept less than some ideal. . . .

THE REAL DIVIDE

To all this, one can readily imagine a simple response by way of confession and avoidance: We are not talking about *those* lawsuits. Advocates of ADR might insist that my account of adjudication, in contrast to the one implied by the dispute-resolution story, focuses on a rather narrow category of lawsuits. They could argue that while settlement may have only the most limited appeal with respect to those cases, I have not spoken to the "typical" case. My response is twofold.

First, even as a purely quantitative matter, I doubt that the number of cases I am referring to is trivial. My universe includes those cases in which there are significant distributional inequalities; those in which it is difficult to generate authoritative consent because organizations or social groups are parties or because the power to settle is vested in autonomous agents; those in which the court must continue to supervise the parties after judgment; and those in which justice needs to be done, or to put it more modestly, where there is a genuine social need for an authoritative interpretation of law. I imagine that the number of cases that satisfy one of these four criteria is considerable; in contrast to the kind of case portrayed in the dispute-resolution story, they probably dominate the docket of a modern court system.

Second, it demands a certain kind of myopia to be concerned only with the number of cases, as though all cases are equal simply because the clerk of the court assigns each a single docket number. All cases are not equal. The Los Angeles deseg-regation case, to take one example, is not equal to the allegedly more typical suit involving a property dispute or an automobile accident. The desegregation suit consumes more resources, affects more people, and provokes far greater challenges to the judicial power. The settlement movement must introduce a qualitative per-spective; it must speak to these more "significant" cases, and demonstrate the pro-priety of settling them. Otherwise it will soon be seen as an irrelevance, dealing with trivia rather than responding to the very conditions that give the movement its greatest sway and saliency.

Nor would sorting cases into "two tracks," one for settlement and another for judgment, avoid my objections. Settling automobile cases and leaving discrimination or antitrust cases for judgment might remove a large number of cases from the dockets, but the dockets will nevertheless remain burdened with the cases that consume the most judicial resources and represent the most controversial exercises of the judicial power. A "two track" strategy would drain the argument for settle-ment of much of its appeal. I also doubt whether the "two track" strategy can be sensibly implemented. It is impossible to formulate adequate criteria for prospectively sorting cases. The problems of settlement are not tied to the subject matter of the suit, but instead stem from factors that are harder to identify, such as the wealth of the parties, the likely post-judgment history of the suit, or the need for an authoritative interpretation of law. . . .

Someone like [former Harvard University President Derek] Bok sees adjudication in essentially private terms: The purpose of lawsuits and the civil courts is to resolve disputes, and the amount of litigation we encounter is evidence of the needlessly combative and quarrelsome character of Americans. Or as Bok put it, using a more diplomatic idiom: "At bottom, ours is a society built on individualism, competition, and success." I, on the other hand, see adjudication in more public terms: Civil litigation is an institutional arrangement for using state power to bring a recalcitrant reality closer to our chosen ideals. We turn to the courts because we need to, not because of some quirk in our personalities. We train our students in the tougher arts so that they may help secure all that the law promises, not because we want them to become gladiators or because we take a special pleasure in combat.

To conceive of the civil lawsuit in public terms as America does might be unique. I am willing to assume that no other country—including Japan, Bok's new paragon—has a case like Brown v. Board of Education in which the judicial power is used to eradicate the caste structure. I am willing to assume that no other country conceives of law and uses law in quite the way we do. But this should be a source of pride rather than shame. What is unique is not the problem, that we live short of our ideals, but that we alone among the nations of the world seem willing to do something about it. Adjudication American-style is not a reflection of our combativeness but rather a tribute to our inventiveness and perhaps even more to our commitment.

 David Luban, **SETTLEMENTS AND THE EROSION OF THE PUBLIC REALM**

83 Geo. L.J. 2619, 2621-2626, 2642-2646, 2648-2649, 2662 (1995)

THE NORMATIVE VALUE OF ADJUDICATION

Learned Hand once wrote, "I must say that as a litigant I should dread a lawsuit beyond almost anything short of sickness and death." This is conventional wisdom. Lawsuits are expensive, terrifying, frustrating, infuriating, humiliating, time-consuming, perhaps all-consuming. Small wonder, then, that both judges and litigants prefer settlements, which are cheaper, quicker, less public, and less all-or-nothing than adjudications. In an aphorism recently cited by Samuel Gross and Kent Syverud, a trial is a failed settlement. Though trials and judgments may sometimes be necessary, they are like surgeries: painful last resorts for otherwise incurable ailments, which are likely to place the patient in a weakened condition at least temporarily and almost certain to leave lasting scars. Pursuing this metaphor, settlements provide the noninvasive alternate therapy that, if successful, is invariably better than surgery. . . .

ADJUDICATION AS A PUBLIC GOOD

Some years ago, University of Chicago economist William M. Landes and then-law-professor Richard A. Posner wrote an article entitled *Adjudication as a Private Good*

[8 J. Legal Stud. 235 (1979)] in which they consider our courts as though they were private vendors of a service — dispute resolution — in competition with other purveyors of the same service, such as commercial arbitrators. Landes and Posner argue that treating adjudication as a private good is perfectly coherent, and that economic competition could increase the efficiency of the judicial system. After all, litigants hiring their own judges would create an incentive for quick and cheap dispute resolution as well as for judicial fairness, because litigants would refuse to hire an inefficient or biased judge. If public courts couldn't compete, litigants would switch to alternative providers.

However, Landes and Posner continue, our court system not only resolves disputes, but also produces rules and precedents. Though private judges may well be efficient purveyors of dispute resolution, they are terribly inefficient producers of rules. Why would litigants who engage the services of a rent-a-judge want to pay extra for a reasoned opinion enunciating a rule that benefits only future litigants? Future litigants, after all, would receive the benefits of the rule for free. Landes and Posner thus conclude that because the private market would systematically underproduce rules and precedents, the state should control the provision of judicial services.

The Landes-Posner objection to private adjudication is an objection to settlements as well, a point that Jules Coleman and Charles Silver have elaborated: settlements, like private adjudications, produce no rules or precedents binding on nonparties. Rules and precedents, in turn, have obvious importance for guiding future behavior and imposing order and certainty on a transactional world that would otherwise be in flux and chaos. Even those who favor settlement over adjudication generally rank order and certainty very high on the scale of legal values. Indeed, one of Fiss's criticisms of the alternative dispute resolution (ADR) movement is that its proponents value peace over justice. Settlements bring peace whereas adjudication, though perhaps more just, creates disruption. Regardless of whether Fiss is right that to be prosettlement is to value peace over justice, the present argument yields a surprising result: adjudication may often prove superior to settlement for securing peace because the former, unlike the latter, creates rules and precedents.

Economists define a public good as a beneficial product that cannot be provided to one consumer without making it available to all (or at least many others). The textbook example is a lighthouse: if one shipper erects a lighthouse, she cannot prevent other ships navigating the same waters from using it for free. The Landes/Posner/Coleman/Silver analysis shows that precedents and legal rules are public goods. Although the original litigants of the cases "purchase" the rules, future litigants use these rules without paying. This exemplifies a more general economic precept: absent public intervention, private economic actors often have inadequate incentives to produce public goods, because it is individually rational to be a free rider.

Civil adjudication can create other public goods besides rules and precedents. For example, it may develop the advocacy skills of litigating attorneys. Kevin McMunigal has noted that, as the number of civil trials declines, litigators' advocacy skills tend to atrophy [Kevin C. McMunigal, The Costs of Settlement: The Impact of

Scarcity of Adjudication on Litigating Lawyers, 37 UCLA L. Rev. 833 (1990)].
Ironically, this degeneration may distort not only trials but the settlement process
as well: litigators without adequate trial experience are less able to evaluate cases
accurately and are more likely to settle out of fear of their own inadequacy. If
McMunigal is correct, the attorney skills developed through trials are a public
good that will lead to settlements that better reflect the value of a case. McMunigal's
argument presumably applies to the skills of trial judges as well: if a judge tries only a
handful of cases each year, then crucial trial skills such as ruling on objections will
atrophy. . . .

   To take another example, the discovery and publicizing of facts, which may
subsequently be used by political actors, ordinary citizens, or other agents in the legal
system (litigants as well as lawyers), is a public good created by adjudication. In a
world of private settlements, such facts would most likely be underproduced. . . .

   Even the authority of courts may be conceptualized as a public good furthered by
adjudication. Whenever disputants rely on the final and public judgment of a court to
resolve their controversy, they enhance the courts' claim as an authoritative resolver
of controversies. However, when disputants turn elsewhere for resolution — private
arbitration, nonjudicial government agencies, or private bargaining — the salience of
adjudication fades and the authority of courts weakens. Each litigant who proceeds to
judgment and acquiesces in it thereby subsidizes a judicial authority that is available
for future litigants.

SETTLEMENTS AND PUBLIC BADS

A second instrumental argument against settlement focuses not on the public goods
it fails to create, but on the "public bads" it may inflict. The point is simple: two
parties trying to apportion a loss are most likely to reach agreement if they can find
a way to shift the burden to a third party who is not present at the bargaining table.
For example, the parties to an environmental dispute may settle it through an
agreement that a chemical company will dispose of waste at sites purchased in a
remote community with no political clout. Similarly, a law firm may settle a
malpractice claim with the Resolution Trust Corporation by agreeing not to
contest liability provided that the settlement is within the firm's insurance limits,
or a labor union and an employer may settle a controversy by passing the losses on
to consumers. Adjudication may make such agreements impossible because the
terms are no longer in the parties' hands, or because the public character of a trial
makes it impossible for the parties to pass along their losses without scandal and
protest. . . .

LAW AT THE BRINK OF BABEL

It is not hard to see where expanding the judicial system takes us: more trial courts
generate more law, along with more inconsistent decisions, more appeals, more
efforts by higher courts to reconcile inconsistencies, and — in short — a
buzzing, blooming confusion of legal information. What began as the Tree of

Life ends as the Tower of Babel. In the speculation of a recent Judicial Conference report:

> [T]he year is 2020. . . . In the United States Court of Appeals for the 21st Circuit, Lower Tier, a recently appointed federal judge arrives at her chambers, planning to consult the latest electronic advance sheets in Fed 7th in order to determine the applicable law of her Circuit and the upper tier court of appeals for her region. With nearly a thousand court of appeals judges writing opinions, federal law in 2020 has become vaster and more incoherent than ever.

This scenario is by no means preposterous, though Fed 7th may be an exaggeration. The Judicial Conference continues: "[T]he vision of coherence and consistency in decisional law likely would be a chimera. Federal law would be babel, with thousands of decisions issuing weekly and no one judge capable of comprehending the entire corpus of federal law, or even the law of his or her own circuit."

The danger if the rate of adjudications were to rise is that judges would devote less time to thoughtful decisionmaking in each case — something of which judges already complain bitterly. Even if the judges are exaggerating about how hard they work (why should judges be different in this respect from the rest of us?), they are unlikely to respond to the expanding caseload with a Stakhanovite speedup. Already, judges respond to heavy caseloads with an unseemly large number of unpublished opinions, which often have no precedential value. A common criticism of unpublished opinions is that they represent hastier and sloppier judicial work than writing for publication. Unpublished opinions and nonprecedential decisions represent the *opposite* of the public-life conception of adjudication.

If the number of adjudications increases, then worse craftsmanship, worse thinking, and worse law will likely result. From the standpoint of the public-life conception, bad adjudication is substantially worse than no adjudication: a settlement before judgment removes one opportunity for the law to work itself pure, but a bad adjudication reverberates until its precedent is overruled. One particular kind of bad law should be especially disturbing to the Friends of Adjudication — overwhelmed judges may craft rules of law calculated to dump categories of cases out of the courts. . . .

SECRET SETTLEMENTS

The opacity of settlements is particularly troubling when their terms are secret. Kant once wrote: "All actions relating to the right of other human beings are wrong if their maxim is incompatible with publicity." This publicity principle lies at the core of democratic political morality. Although the principle has exceptions because political morality cannot dispense with all forms of secrecy and confidentiality, these exceptions are themselves governed by the publicity principle. That is, awarding officials the discretion to keep secrets or grant confidentiality is itself a policy that should be able to withstand public scrutiny. . . . [T]he widespread practice of secret settlements carves out an unacceptable area of exceptions to democratic publicity. . . .

We cannot really be against settlements; nor can we really be against settlements that vastly outnumber adjudications. But we can be against the wrong settlements.

The public-life conception of legitimacy, with its naive Enlightenment faith in the public realm, offers one set of criteria for deciding which settlements are wrong.

 Richard L. Abel, **THE CONTRADICTIONS OF INFORMAL JUSTICE**

in 1 The Politics of Informal Justice: The American Experience 270-272 (Richard L. Abel ed., 1982)

Informal justice can extend the ambit of state control. Here I am talking only about those institutions that are somehow implicated in the state apparatus (although the boundaries are often amorphous). Informalism permits this expansion, in the first instance, by reducing or disguising the coercion that both stimulates resistance and justifies the demand for the protection of formal due process. Coercion is indeed relaxed: parties are often "referred" to informal institutions rather than arrested; the police are involved briefly, if at all; the symbols of state authority that so dominate the courtroom — a male judge, in black robes, on a raised dais, supported by security personnel — are all banished from the mediation center; and that epitome of force, the prison, is almost never threatened. Even more important, coercion is disguised. In place of prosecution, we find the forms of civil litigation, arbitration, or mediation; staff go to great lengths to make participants feel comfortable; the mediator is often female, dressed like the parties, and seated with them round a table; even the language is different, stressing help rather than threats, speaking about a respondent rather than an accused — the velvet glove has largely hidden the iron fist. Penalties are far milder: restitution rather than fines, the promise of behavioral change rather than imprisonment. Because coercion is less extreme and less visible the state can seek to control more behavior: deviance that was too trivial to interest officials (police, prosecutors), justify cumbersome formal procedures, or warrant severe sanctions. Because informal justice generally requires lower state expenditures per case, more intervention is possible within the same budget. The lower level of coercion (whether real or apparent) also obviates the need for the full panoply of procedural and constitutional protections, making it both easier and less expensive to extend control. One index of expanded control is that informal institutions virtually never dismiss a case — everyone needs, and deserves, help. When comparable behavior is presented to formal institutions — domestic violence, for instance — dismissal is the modal response. Indeed, a controlled comparison of cases that could have been brought to the neighborhood justice center but were instead prosecuted in formal courts revealed that in half the charges were dropped prior to the hearing and that only a quarter of the remaining half that were tried were found guilty; in other words, seven out of every eight respondents referred to informal institutions would have gone scot-free had they been prosecuted.

But if coercion is minimized for strategic reasons, it is by no means eliminated. It would be naive to expect otherwise: State action cannot avoid using force; social control cannot function without it. Coercion serves to "persuade" parties to submit to informal justice, to "agree" to the outcome, and to comply with it. The modus *operandi* is similar to the police interrogation in which the suspect is alternately confronted with a "bad" cop, who is large, unpleasant, and threatening, and a "good" cop, who promises to protect the suspect if he will cooperate. Informal justice offers a haven from the formal system: from its lengthy, costly, humiliating process and threat of prison. . . .

Because informal state institutions reduce or disguise coercion they can seek to review behavior that presently escapes state control. They are not limited to acting in situations where a party has violated a formal law, civil or criminal. Indeed, whereas the formal institutions of the liberal state punish or reward specified *acts* with the object of channeling behavior that is believed to be governed by a rational, utilitarian calculus, informal institutions engage in covert manipulation that seeks to modify the *character* of a person whose behavior is viewed as an expression of irrational impulses. Unlike trial courts of limited jurisdiction, informal institutions often are unconstrained by any upper boundary (amount in controversy, magnitude of crime); instead, their competence is defined by the nature of the relationship between the parties and the type of accusation or claim. If they stigmatize one party less by redesignating the accused as "respondent," they render the other more vulnerable to criticism by recharacterizing the victim as a "complainant." This allows, indeed encourages, informal institutions to ask whether, perhaps, the complainant provoked the conflict or perhaps is being hypersensitive; the parallel to the way formal courts treat rape victims is not coincidental, for informal institutions have a larger number of women complainants than do formal.

Notes and Questions

14.1 To support his thesis, Abel points to a variety of factors. More informal institutions increase "the quantum of state resources devoted to social control." As informal institutions provide relief for courts, courts themselves can do more. Additionally, community mediation programs and the like have been targeted toward the poor, and consequently state control increases disproportionately with respect to the already oppressed. Some proponents of mediation argue that offering mediation programs is a service that enhances the quality of life in communities. Can that view be squared with the concern about the growth and imposition of state control (or Big Brother)? Do you see the growth of state intervention in the form of courts and ADR programs as a danger to individual liberty?

Abel concludes his critique by reviewing the values that support informalism: "the preference for harmony over conflict, for mechanisms that offer equal access to the many rather than unequal privilege to the few, that operate quickly and cheaply, that permit all citizens to participate in decision making rather than limiting authority to 'professionals,' that are familiar rather than esoteric, and that strive for and achieve substantive justice." Does his appreciation of these values lend gravity to his critique?

14.2 Review the questions at the beginning of the chapter. Are you persuaded by Fiss's argument against settlement? By Luban's concerns? By Abel's warnings that state control is increasing? What do the critiques leveled by Fiss, Luban, and Abel have in common? Upon what data do they rely? At the other end of Abel's spectrum are critics who say that the less powerful or economically advantaged have less access to justice when they have less access, not only to courts, but also to the newer forms of dispute resolution, see, e.g., Robert Rubinson, A Theory of Access to Justice, 29 J. of the Leg. Profession 89 (2004-2005).

14.3 Research by Marc Galanter indicates that the rate of trials is dramatically decreasing in both federal and state courts despite an increase in filings. Marc Galanter, The Vanishing Trial: An Examination of Trials and Related Matters in Federal and State Courts, 1 J. Empirical Legal Stud. 459 (2004). Does that affect your analysis of Fiss, Luban, or Abel's concerns?

B. CRITIQUES OF MEDIATION: IN PRACTICE

1. The Problem of Prejudice

Several critiques of ADR in practice were introduced in Chapter 7. Recall Trina Grillo's argument that mediation, particularly when it is mandated, disadvantages women. Women may be more relational than men and hence willing to accept less in exchange for "harmony." It may be especially difficult for women to stand up for their rights, and when they do, Grillo argues, they should not be forced into a process where rights are undervalued. Ayres and LaFree and Rack raise questions about disadvantages that women and minority groups might face in negotiation and mediation. In Chapter 9 a challenge was made to the notion that mediators can always be neutral and impartial. In the excerpt below, Grillo points to ways in which mediators are subject to their own prejudices, which they may visit upon disputants. While the norm of neutrality or impartiality is the goal of most mediators, a variety of factors can create hurdles to achieving that objective: personality traits, family background, cultural and ethnic differences, and so on.

 Trina Grillo, **THE MEDIATION ALTERNATIVE: PROCESS DANGERS FOR WOMEN**

100 Yale L.J. 1545, 1585-1587 (1991)

Mediators . . . exert a great deal of power. When two people are in conflict, having a third, purportedly neutral person take the viewpoint of one or the other results in a palpable shift of power to the party with whom the mediator agrees. The mediator also can set the rules regarding who talks, when they may speak, and what may be said. The power of the mediator is not always openly acknowledged but is hidden beneath protestations that the process belongs to the parties. This can make the parties feel less, not more, in control of the process and its consequences for their lives. There is much room for, but little acknowledgment of, the possibility of the mediator's exhibiting partiality or imposing a hidden agenda on the parties. . . .

George, a Black man, is in the process of divorcing Michelle, a white woman. During the course of the mediation, the mediator asks a number of times whether there is a history of domestic violence. She seems not to believe George or his wife when each insists that although Michelle occasionally has attacked George, he has never fought back.

Elaine is a Black woman, who has worked herself up in the ranks of the local telephone company from an entry level position to her new job, in which she supervises a number of employees. She handles herself with calm and poise, but also a certain coolness. Joe, her husband, who is also Black, is a friendly, gregarious man who has not been reliable in meeting his support obligations or in taking regular responsibility for their two sons. In mediation, Elaine immediately senses that the mediator favors her husband and does not like her. This intuition is confirmed when the mediator permits her husband to interrupt her constantly, but quickly stops her with a sharp lecture when she tries to interrupt him. At one point, the mediator turns to her and says, "I was a single parent too, and I did not have the luxury of an ex-husband who was willing to help me with the children." Five minutes later, the mediator repeats the same statement. When Elaine mentions her debilitating health problems, the mediator laughs and says, "You don't have to act sick to get what you want."

George and Elaine are encountering extreme examples of what is, to some degree, a troublesome aspect of any mediation: the process introduces a third party who is held out to be, but is not, impartial. George's mediator is racially prejudiced; she has some preconceived ideas, sturdy enough to withstand mutual denials, about the likelihood that a Black husband has battered a white wife. Elaine's mediator is clearly partial to Elaine's husband. Whether this partiality is based on racial prejudice, Elaine will never know. Elaine's mediator has also projected some of her own conflicts onto Elaine. Because the mediator feels that her own situation as a single parent was so difficult, it is hard for her to empathize with a woman who has a seemingly lighter burden, but who is still not appreciative.

Partiality comes in many forms. In its most virulent form it results from prejudice in favor of or against a person because of his race, gender, sexual orientation, disability, religion, or class. It may also arise, however, from a personal disposition to favor certain outcomes or even from a positive or negative reaction to a particular personality. It is no surprise that mediators are not completely impartial, for, in a very fundamental way, impartiality is a myth. It cannot exist in anything approaching a pure form, although we would like it to, and often we pretend that it does. The concept of impartiality is based on the notion of an observer without a perspective. But any observer inevitably sees from a particular perspective, whether that perspective is acknowledged or not. Mediators, like all other human beings, have biases, values, and points of view. They have all had experiences in their lives that influence how they react to others, independent of anything the others might do.

Notes and Questions

14.4 Many issues can be raised about mediator neutrality, for example: What about cases where mediators get business from repeat customers (such as insurance companies and law firms) and want to please those repeat players? What about in-house mediators who might have institutional loyalties that influence them? What about situations where one party is paying the bill? See Carrie Menkel-Meadow, Do the Haves Come Out Ahead in Alternative Judicial Systems? Repeat Players in ADR, 15 Ohio St. J. on Disp. Resol. 19 (1999).

14.5 One might comment that the mediators in the cases of George and Elaine are simply bad mediators and should (at the very least) go back to school. If you served on an ethics committee applying the Model Standards of Conduct for Mediators (see Appendix B), would you sanction the mediators for the conduct that Grillo describes?

14.6 Grillo argues elsewhere in her article that the "past" and "blame" are banished from discussion in some forms of mediation where a "focus on the future" is paramount. She contends this mediator strategy may be at odds with the needs of women who are trying to come to terms with wrongs they have experienced. See Trina Grillo, The Mediation Alternative: Process Dangers for Women, 100 Yale L.J. 1545, 1563 (1991). Is this accurate? If it is, what, if anything, should be done about it? See Carrie Menkel-Meadow, Remembrance of Things Past? The Relationship of Past to Future in Pursuing Justice in Mediation, 5 Cardozo J. Conflict Resol. 97 (2004).

The following critique raises additional concerns about the relationship of mediation processes to possible prejudice or discrimination.

 Richard Delgado, Chris Dunn, Pamela Brown, Helena Lee & David Hubbert, **FAIRNESS AND FORMALITY: MINIMIZING THE RISK OF PREJUDICE IN ALTERNATIVE DISPUTE RESOLUTION**

1985 Wis. L. Rev. 1359, 1367, 1375, 1387-1391, 1402-1404 (1985)

Virtually absent from previous discussions of ADR is consideration of the possibility that ADR might foster racial or ethnic bias in dispute resolution. . . .

This [article] examines theories of prejudice and their relation to ADR. Though based primarily on studies of prejudice among whites toward blacks, many of the findings are also applicable to prejudice against Hispanics, Indians, women, and other groups, as well as interethnic group prejudice. After surveying the leading theories of how prejudice develops and is expressed, we examine prejudice in relation to the "American Creed." According to a leading school of thought, many persons suffer from a "moral dilemma" which arises from a conflict between socially espoused precepts of both equality and humanitarianism, and personal attitudes that are less egalitarian. The manner in which these conflicts are resolved depends largely on situational factors. Certain settings tend to foster prejudiced behavior, while others tend to discourage it. We apply these findings to the formalism/informalism dichotomy and find that formal dispute resolution is better at deterring prejudice than informal adjudication. . . .

THE OPTIMAL SETTING FOR THE REDUCTION OF PREJUDICE: FORMAL VS. INFORMAL DISPUTE RESOLUTION

The selection of one mode or another of dispute resolution can do little, at least in the short run, to counter prejudice that stems from authoritarian personalities or historical currents. Prejudice that results from social-psychological factors is, however, relatively controllable. Much prejudice is environmental — people express it because the setting encourages or tolerates it. In some settings people feel free to vent hostile or denigrating attitudes toward members of minority groups; in others they do not.

Our review of social-psychological theories of prejudice indicates that prejudiced persons are least likely to act on their beliefs if the immediate environment confronts them with the discrepancy between their professed ideals and their personal hostilities against out-groups. According to social psychologists, once most persons realize that their attitudes and behavior deviate from what is expected, they will change or suppress them.

Given this human tendency to conform, American institutions have structured and defined situations to encourage appropriate behavior. Our judicial system, in particular, has incorporated societal norms of fairness and even-handedness into institutional expectations and rules of procedure at many points. These norms create a "public conscience and a standard for expected behavior that check overt signs of prejudice." They do this in a variety of ways. First, the formalities of a court trial — the flag, the black robes, the ritual — remind those present that the occasion calls for the higher, "public" values, rather then the lesser values embraced during moments of informality and intimacy. In a courtroom trial the American Creed, with its emphasis on fairness, equality, and respect for personhood, governs. Equality of status, or something approaching it is preserved — each party is represented by an attorney and has a prescribed time and manner for speaking, putting on evidence, and questioning the other side. Equally important, formal adjudication avoids the unstructured, intimate interactions that, according to social scientists, foster prejudice. The rules of procedure maintain distance between the parties. Counsel for the parties do not address one another, but present the issue to the trier of fact. The rules preserve the formality of the setting by dictating in detail how this confrontation is to be conducted. . . .

Formality and adversarial procedures thus counteract bias among legal decision-makers and disputants. But it seems likely that those factors increase fairness in yet [another] way — by strengthening the resolve of minority disputants to pursue their legal rights. . . .

DISPUTE RESOLUTION AND THE MINORITY DISPUTANT

Early in life, minority children become aware of themselves as different, especially with respect to skin color. This awareness is often not merely neutral, but associated with feelings of inferiority. Separate studies by psychologists Kenneth Clark and Mary Goodman in which minority children were presented with dolls of various colors illustrate this graphically. For example, when asked to make a choice between a white and black doll, "the doll that looks like you," most black children chose the white doll. A black child justified his choice of the white doll over the black doll as friend because "his feet, hands, ears, elbows, knees, and hair are clean." In another experiment, a black child hated her skin color so much that she "vigorously lathered her arms and face with soap in an effort to wash away the dirt." As minority children grow, they are "likely to experience a long series of events, from exclusion from play groups and cliques to violence and threats of violence, that are far less likely to be experienced by the average member of the majority group." Against a background of "slights, rebuffs, forbidden opportunities, restraints, and often violence . . . the minority group member shapes that fundamental aspect or personality — a sense of oneself and one's place in the total scheme of things."

Discriminatory treatment can trigger a variety of responses. Writers identify three main reactions: avoidance, aggression, and acceptance. A minority group member may display one or more of these responses, depending on the setting. In some situations, victims of discrimination are likely to respond with apathy or defeatism; in others, the same individuals may forthrightly and effectively assert their interests. In general, when a person feels "he is the master of his fate, that he can control to some extent his own destiny, that if he works hard things will go better for him, he is then likely to achieve more. . . ." That is, minority group members are more apt to participate in processes which they believe will respond to reasonable efforts. They are understandably less likely to participate in proceedings where the results are random and unpredictable.

Thus, it is not surprising that a favored forum for redress of race-based wrongs has been the traditional adjudicatory setting. Minorities recognize that public institutions, with their defined rules and formal structure, are more subject to rational control than private or informal structures. Informal settings allow wider scope for the participants' emotional and behavioral idiosyncrasies; in these settings majority group members are most likely to exhibit prejudicial behavior. Thus, a formal adjudicative forum increases the minority group member's sense of control and, therefore, may be seen as the fairer forum. This perception becomes self-fulfilling: minority persons are encouraged to pursue their legal rights as though prejudice were unlikely and thus the possibility of prejudice is in fact lessened. . . .

STRIKING THE BALANCE: PROTECTING AGAINST PREJUDICE WITHOUT SACRIFICING THE BENEFITS OF ADR

[T]he risk of prejudice is greatest when a member of an in-group confronts a member of an out-group; when that confrontation is direct, rather than through intermediaries; when there are few rules to constrain conduct; when the setting is closed and does not make clear that "public" values are to preponderate; and when the controversy concerns an intimate, personal matter rather than some impersonal question. Our review also indicated that many minority participants will press their claims most vigorously when they believe that what they do and say will make a difference, that the structure will respond, and that the outcome is predictable and related to effort and merit.

It follows that ADR is most apt to incorporate prejudice when a person of low status and power confronts a person or institution of high status and power. In such situations, the party of high status is more likely than in other situations to attempt to call up prejudiced responses; at the same time, the individual of low status is less likely to press his or her claim energetically. The dangers increase when the mediator or other third party is a member of the superior group or class. Examples of ADR settings that may contain these characteristics are prison and other institutional review boards, consumer complaint panels, and certain types of cases referred to an ombudsman. In these situations, minorities and members or other out-groups should opt for formal in-court adjudication, and the justice system ought to avoid pressuring them to accept an alternate procedure. ADR should be reserved for cases in which parties of comparable power and status confront each other.

ADR also poses heightened risks of prejudice when the issue to be adjudicated touches a sensitive or intimate area of life, for example, housing or culture-based conduct. Thus, many landlord-tenant, inter-neighbor, and intra-familial disputes are poor candidates for ADR. When the parties are of unequal status and the question litigated concerns a sensitive, intimate area, the risks of an outcome colored by prejudice are especially great. If, for reasons of economy or efficiency ADR must be resorted to in these situations, the likelihood of bias can be reduced by providing rules that clearly specify the scope of the proceedings and forbid irrelevant or intrusive inquiries, by requiring open proceedings, and by providing some form of higher review. The third-party facilitator or decisionmaker should be a professional and be acceptable to both parties. Any party desiring one should be provided with an advocate, ideally an attorney, experienced with representation before the forum in question. To avoid atomization and lost opportunities to aggregate claims and inject public values into dispute resolution, ADR mechanisms should not be used in cases that have a broad societal dimension, but [they should] forward them to court for appropriate treatment.

Notes and Questions

14.7 Many proponents of mediation value its capacity to bridge ethnic, racial, and other differences *because* it is personal, less formal, and focused on individual interests and perceptions. These aspects of mediation worry Delgado and his colleagues. Do the checks of a formal adversarial process safeguard against prejudice or tend to entrench parties in their positions? Explain your answer.

14.8 How accurate do you think the descriptions of the formal trial process are here? Are people more likely to act without prejudice in formal settings? In informal settings when they are face to face with others? For a recent and comprehensive study of how plaintiffs in employment discrimination cases fare in formal adjudication (not well), see Kevin M. Clermont & Stewart J. Schwab, How Employment Discrimination Plaintiffs Fare in Federal Court, 1 J. of Empirical Legal Studies 429 (2004).

2. Mediator Manipulation

The next article raises another ethical concern, that of unprincipled mediator manipulation. In Chapter 6, a variety of techniques that mediators use to promote constructive dialogue, option development, and party agreement were introduced. Such techniques include creating a conducive environment, listening and reframing strategies, controlling the agenda, generating doubt about positions and assumptions, and using caucus and joint sessions to manage information flow. James Coben asks whether these mediator "moves" interfere with party self-determination. If you agree with Coben that many mediator techniques are manipulative, is it ethical to use them?

 James R. Coben, **MEDIATION'S DIRTY LITTLE SECRET: STRAIGHT TALK ABOUT MEDIATOR MANIPULATION AND DECEPTION**

2 J. Alternative Disp. Resol. Emp. 4, 4-6 (2000)

[M]ediation's dirty little secret is the degree to which mediators . . . routinely and unabashedly engage in manipulation and deception to foster settlements, albeit under the rationale of fostering self-determination. Sophisticated consumers have come to know and expect it. Unsophisticated consumers are not so lucky. . . .

Think back on your last few employment mediations. You may have heard a mediator reframe a plaintiff's demand for $100,000 as a request for substantial compensation. The plaintiff's ultimatum that an alleged harasser be fired was transformed into recognition that there be "consequences for unacceptable workplace behavior." The mediator most likely brought a box of Kleenex to the table and strategically used empathy to connect with an injured worker. At some point, the mediator may have orchestrated an awkward period of silence to help encourage options generation. Perhaps the mediator used neuro-linguistic programming to mirror the speech patterns of the company's human resource manager in a way that maximized that person's comfort.

In an early caucus, the mediator may have enthusiastically over-reported the extent of progress being made to encourage you to press on. Conversely, in a later caucus, the mediator pessimistically reported the threat of stalemate precisely when settlement was close at hand to encourage you to make the final necessary compromises. How many times has a mediator agreed to take a proposal to the other side as his or her own in order to help you save face? The list could go on and on.

. . . All of these mediator techniques are consistent with the basic observation from one oft-cited mediation treatise that "mediators, although neutral in relationship to the parties and generally impartial toward the substantive outcome, *are directly involved in influencing disputants toward settlement*" (emphasis added).[2] . . . [S]houldn't we be troubled that these tools of the trade are used by mediators working with consumers who are often unaware that a technique is being used at all? Such "control or play upon by artful, unfair, or insidious means so as to serve one's purpose" is the very definition of manipulation.

---

[2] Christopher W. Moore, The Mediation Process: Practical Strategies for Resolving Conflict 327 (1986).

The fact that mediators justify their interventions as necessary to foster parties' self-determination does not mean the interventions are no longer manipulative. And, surely one must question if a settlement is ever truly self-determined, when it is the product of manipulative tactics (no matter how well intentioned).

Moreover, mediator manipulation/deception is not always so benign. At a continuing education event last March sponsored by the Minnesota State Bar Association, I was stunned by the high percentage of mediators who answered "yes" when asked if strongly encouraging parties to skip lunch (to keep the pressure on) was a good tactic. Furthermore, how do you react to these two examples? Taken from John Cooley's entertaining "encyclopedia" of mediator magic, consider:

1. the mediator who conveys a false demand to a side which can be dropped at any time to obtain closure; or
2. the mediator who implies to a proposing side that a proposal was communicated to the other side when it was not.[4]

Wait a minute, you might ask, surely these mediator techniques (or perhaps you would pejoratively label them ploys) cross the line of permissible behavior? . . .

Notes and Questions

14.9 Many of the tools of the trade that Coben describes as "manipulation" are tasks that mediators are trained to perform. Other tactics are arguably unethical. Which is which? Why? Does the Model Code of Conduct help answer the question (see Appendix B)? For another tool of the trade that can lead to manipulation, see Michael Moffitt, Will This Case Settle? An Exploration of Mediators' Predictions, 16 Ohio St. J. on Disp. Resol. 39 (2000) (exploring how mediators' predictions of likely outcomes can manipulate parties' negotiations and agreements in mediation).

14.10 When patients seek help from psychologists or physicians, don't they hope and expect they will be "manipulated" into a better state of psychological or physical health? Can mediators be compared to those other professionals with respect to parties in conflict?

14.11 Where mediators have a fee agreement that is contingent on their obtaining a settlement, the type of manipulation described by Coben seems particularly egregious, since it serves the financial interests of the mediator. Note that Model Standard 8 (see Appendix B) states that a mediator should not enter into a contingent fee arrangement. Compare this to the CPR-Georgetown Model Rule (see Appendix C), which allows contingent fees with certain safeguards. For an interesting argument about how to use conditional fees in contractual mediation, see Scott Peppet, Contractarian Economics and Mediation Ethics: The Case for Contingent Fee Mediation, 82 Tex. L. Rev. 227 (2003).

---

[4] John W. Cooley, Mediation Magic: Its Use and Abuse, 29 Loy. U. Chi. L.J. 1 (1997).

3. Mediator's Focus on the Future

In the excerpt that follows Carrie Menkel-Meadow raises important questions about the frequently used mediator technique of asking parties to "focus on the future."

 Carrie Menkel-Meadow, REMEMBRANCE OF THINGS PAST? THE RELATIONSHIP OF PAST TO FUTURE IN PURSUING JUSTICE IN MEDIATION

5 Cardozo J. Conflict Resol. 97, 97-115 (2004)

The process [of the Truth and Reconciliation Commission in South Africa] was backward-looking in the sense of being expected to document and deal with the gross human rights violations of the past, but it was forward-looking in trying to prevent future tyranny.

—James L. Gibson, Truth, Reconciliation, and the Creation of a Human Rights
Culture in South Africa

What must be remembered and acknowledged before we can move forward to create a future together, whether individually or collectively? Or, as Avishai Margalit has recently put it, is there an ethics of memory — must some things be remembered; what can be forgiven or forgotten in a moral sense? I have long been worried about the emphasis in mediation to focus on the future, to seek "solutions" to problems in which the parties are guided to "move forward," even while "reorienting the parties to each other," in crafting a more productive relationship. With the growing use and adaptation of mediative-like processes in collective, political, and nation-state conflicts, as well as individualized conflicts in divorce, commercial, employment and criminal matters, this worry has grown into a larger concern about the role of the past in achieving justice in such settings. . . .

There are many descriptions and purposes claimed for the mediation process. Whether mediation is used to solve problems, transform parties, while acknowledging and recognizing their issues with each other, settle lawsuits, facilitate legal rule-making, or create new entities, a large part of the ideology of mediation that informs its raison d'etre or sensibility is to focus on the future and to "make the world anew." Mediation is offered in contrast to more traditional legal processes, particularly adjudication, but also arbitration, precisely because it can craft future relationships and does not have to find facts, assign fault and blame, or issue judgments or awards about the past. Structurally and functionally, this is one of mediation's defining characteristics — mediation is not required to deal with the past; it asks the parties to look to their futures and remake their duties and responsibilities toward each other.

In contrast to mediation, adjudication, and to a lesser extent arbitration, requires the participants to bring evidence of what happened in the past so that a third party decision-maker can assign blame and fault, and assess damages and order remediation, in forms of cash payments, punishments, or sometimes injunctions about future behavior (usually, but not always, negative), typically using legal or other laid-down principles such as a collective bargaining agreement. For a long time adjudication has been the process thought to provide "justice." . . . [L]awyers in particular, and some political theorists and philosophers, see justice as located in the courts. . . . I have not been among those, arguing instead that legal justice (as ordered by a court) is not co-extensive with "human" justice, and mediation can often offer a more tailored, particularized, and more "just" outcome (as well as process) for parties that choose to use it. As I have argued extensively elsewhere, mediated solutions are not always compromises; but even if they sometimes are, compromises are often more fair and just than "winner take all" outcomes. Mediation offers the opportunity for participating parties to have more authentic dialogues and make decisions about what is fair and just to them than when an outsider applies rules that have been enacted by a legislature for some generalized mean, rather than for particularized human individuals. . . .

Nevertheless, despite my generally appreciative and productive participation in the mediation movement, both in theory development and in practice, I want to express some concerns in the hopes we might "reorient" our own process to seek more sophisticated and nuanced ways to achieve justice in mediative processes. . . .

THE FUTURE ORIENTATION IN MEDIATION THEORY AND PRACTICE

Consider the critique of mediation made so movingly by Trina Grillo in *The Mediation Alternative: Process Dangers for Women*, where she outlines one of mediation's animating principles — prospectivity. Citing some of the early training materials and writings about mediation, Grillo points out that mediators often "police" the acceptability of particular narratives by reminding the parties that "in mediation the past history of the participants is only important in relation to the present or as a basis for predicting future needs, intentions, abilities, and reactions to decisions." Early ground rules, especially in divorce mediation, suggested that the focus should be on future needs (particularly of children) and not on "fighting and arguing about the past," which was regarded as unproductive, preventing agreement, and not useful for the parties. For Grillo, writing from her own experiences as a mediator and then as a divorcing parent herself, too much focus on the future and elimination of discourse about the past eliminated the context in which a particular issue, conflict, or dispute was located. Assumptions in mediation of prospectivity, equality of participation and responsibility, "controlling of emotions," espoused values of self-determinism and contextualism in the face of differential experiences and unequal power all enable, in her view, a process intended to do good and empower parties, but that instead does great harm by cutting off experiences of past wrongs and banishing rights-based consciousness of legitimate entitlements. . . .

Recent treatments of mediation purposes, skills, techniques and processes focus more on party satisfaction while meeting underlying needs and interests, wherever those needs and interests might come from, and also acknowledge the importance of party expressions of emotions as part of the mix of what is "permitted" in the stylized discourse of mediation. I still worry, however, that mediation as a process is too associated with an instrumental need to "move forward," whether it be in the more material aspects of case settlements, agreements, contracts and payments made, or in the more psychological realm of acknowledgment and recognition of the existential reality and intersubjective experience of others. Mediation remains an instrumental tool of propulsion into a better state in the future. I have no real quibble with this as an aspiration, as long as we take full account of and time for what else we might be losing in the process, if for no other reason, than to make room for other things at the mediation table, such as some appreciation of the importance of the past. . . .

JUSTICE IN MEDIATION? THE PAST OR THE FUTURE?

. . . Given the new uses of mediative-like techniques and approaches in new processes and institutions (which I generally applaud as evidence of our evolutionary development in legal and conflict processes), I want to reflect on how these new processes, like Truth and Reconciliation Commissions, with their documentation of the past "truth," teach us new lessons in the quest for justice in mediation.

First, *the past is an essential part of justice.*

Second, *how the past is treated is an essential part of the justice of any dispute resolution process, including both mediation and the newer forms of "mediation-like" processes.*

Third, *the past is no more knowable or stable than the future, so there are likely to be many "pasts" and "mediation-like" processes have both a special ability and a special disability to deal with this. Mediation permits several realities to "co-exist." Mediation cannot adjudicate or judge the past or "find a truth." It can enable relevant parties to "mediate" their own stories and realities of the past.*

Fourth, *the past must be acknowledged and responsibility taken in mediative-like processes if they are to be considered legitimate and "just" processes. The past cannot be banished or proscribed from mediation. Different kinds of outcomes in such processes must be clearly understood — ranging from amnesty, forgiveness, restitution, restoration, recompense, and punishment.*

Fifth, *mediation and various kinds of the "mediation-like" processes must be made more variable and accountable for their different purposes and to their different constituencies, including both those inside and outside of the processes.*

Consider this thought experiment. Imagine if you can, that you are not a mediator, but a person who feels grievously wronged — a terminated employee, an abandoned spouse, a victim of an urban American police beating, a victim of economic, if not physical, discrimination in apartheid South Africa, a released political prisoner from an opposition party in Guatemala, El Salvador, Chile or Argentina, a family member of a murdered Tutsi in Rwanda, a property owner in a formerly Communist regime in Eastern or Central Europe, a displaced resident of East Timor or Kosovo, an aged Korean comfort woman or a survivor of the German Holocaust. In any or all of these cases, whether by virtue of an overwhelming caseload (Rwanda, East Timor, South Africa) or because of an innovative design for forging new governments and new processes (South Africa, American employment or civil rights dispute panels, Rwanda) or because documentation of claims may be stale or unavailable (Eastern and Central Europe and Holocaust victims, comfort women), you are asked to participate in a community dispute and grievance panel, an organizational mediation or dispute resolution program, a Truth and Reconciliation

Commission hearing or a traditionally adapted community justice process. . . . How would you decide if you had been treated justly? All of these processes, recently designed, do things differently than courts. For example, most cannot punish, though some can order remuneration or compensation of some kind. Some offer nothing more than an opportunity to "testify" about wrongs done — what kind of process creates justice? . . .

I suggest that anyone inside any of these grievous wrongs would not be totally comfortable with a process that asked them only to "think of the children" or to "move forward" in the spirit of national peace and reconciliation or world peace. Whether testimony, stories, and narratives to create a "record" of remembering is enough will likely vary from person to person and group to group, and some social science evidence suggests that it is not only degree of injury that affects such judgments. Even among the most scarred by the Holocaust, some were able to lead what others call "productive" lives, expressing what one writer has called a *"carpe diem* energy," while others become totally disabled by painful memories of experiences. Some will want retribution, some "payment," some "righting" of wrongs to mark the losses suffered, both for individual relief and for human legacies to be left. In Margalit's words again, "must some things be remembered?;" and if so, what does mediation do to erase or preserve such "ethical memories"?

From a victim's (or party's) perspective what is likely most wanted is some sense of restoration (of self, of the moral order, of the status quo ante to the extent that is possible) and acknowledgment by someone outside of the self (the "perpetrator" of wrongdoing, a third party neutral, a witness) that injury has been suffered, that wrong has been committed. Consider the abandoning, but truthful, spouse who says, "I admit I did wrong, I had an affair, but I love another person." This is painful and causes harm to the spouse (and perhaps to children), but it is sadly honest and acknowledges wrongdoing. What should flow from that acknowledgment remains complicated and problematic (especially after the elimination of fault divorce). Acknowledgment may be far easier in such settings of individual harm than in the larger mass or group harms that constitute my other examples. Traditional mediation can be adapted to deal with the past "injustices" of failed familial, commercial, or employment relationships. Mediators and parties can "stay with" the past longer, recounting, restating, and understanding both facts (establishing the "facticity" of wrongs is crucial to any justice process) and the more interpretive and hermeneutic and personal meanings of those facts. Indeed, mediation may be especially appropriate for allowing non-evidence based narratives to be told, heard, repeated, clarified, and understood, if not "agreed to" or formally adjudicated. . . .

The point here is that mediators need to reorient their practices to allow, tolerate, and perhaps "structure" stories of what happened and the meanings of the past, rather than hurrying the parties on to "future-oriented" creative problem-solving when it is too premature. We must not be fearful of the past, even if some conflicts, disagreements and arguments arise from its retelling. I fear that too often conflict-aversive mediators suggest the parties move on; "talk about the future," "talk about your plans . . . ," and, "what would you like to see happen" are often used as a way of managing what they fear will be contests about the past. With skillful communication and facilitation, mediation may be just the most appropriate place for telling narratives about the past meanings and hurts. Further, mediation, at least in such "thick" settings, usually, though not always, permits negotiation of restorative, restitutionary, or compensatory, if not "punitive" outcomes. . . .

Without a full airing of our past sufferings, we cannot move on. To suffer is human — so is to share and seek acknowledgment of our pain so we can move on. The pessimistic story of humankind is that we will destroy each other; the more optimistic story is the one that recognizes our resiliency and lets some, if not all of us, build again. If we have learned anything from the mass violence of the twentieth century it is that we must find new ways to seek understanding across differences. Mediation is one such way, but as a process, it cannot abjure the past. Even the most conventional mediation process must focus more on the experience of the past, as suffered by the parties, if they are to go forward and find new relationships or agreements.

LESSONS FOR MEDIATION: RECOGNIZING THE PAST, TAKING AND MAKING RESPONSIBILITY AND CHANGING OUR PRACTICES

[W]e, who participate in mediation, both as parties and as mediators, need to be more mindful of what we ask parties and ourselves to do and say. To say such things as "we don't need to decide who is right or wrong to move on to a solution," or "this is not a court to assign blame," or "you don't have to admit anything to participate in this process" may contribute to the widespread perception that mediative processes are ones which do not provide justice, but only traded preferences or instrumental bargaining. To expand on what I think the more controversial obligations of mediation could be, recognition and responsibility are not just about apprehending the intersubjective reality of another person in interpersonal terms, but recognition and taking responsibility for harms caused or injuries delivered, whether intentionally or not.

When mediation is conducted in the same spirit as Truth and Reconciliation Commissions — seeking "truth" as well as reconciliation — we can learn to forgive without forgetting; for the hurts, harms, and injuries we bring to mediation are real and often are constitutive of who we are, both as individuals and in our affiliations, chosen or given, in particular identities or groups. Mediators' desires to remain neutral, never to assess blame or to call into account the responsibility of parties (which can of course be both or more than one) preserve several elements of classic mediation — its detached, neutral and facilitative forms. But, if the mediator is too passive, if the mediator excludes "past" testimony, if the mediator encourages the parties to "just get over it" and tries to resolve the problem without proper respect for their relative histories, then I fear mediation will continue to have a mixed reputation, as well as fail to perform some of its most valuable functions of encouraging authentic encounters of human beings who seek to make better what has gone wrong. . . .

In my career, I have most often defended mediation against attacks made by the litigation romanticists who tend to see conventional adjudicative processes and the "rule of law" as the only measure of justice. Mediation offers an often better process, by providing direct party engagement, open dialogue unrestricted by rigid rules of evidence and the possibilities that parties can craft their own solutions. To the extent that this process has all too often restricted discussion of the past in its promise to "move forward constructively," I now think it is time for us to reconsider some of our dogmas and doctrines to see whether mediation is as adaptive and fair as we have claimed. My hope in suggesting that we look at constructive ways to bring the past and future together in mediation, both in ideology and conception and in our practices, is that we might then create a truly sacred place in mediation for truth, human understanding, and justice to co-exist. As they say, without peace there will be no justice, but with no justice, there will be no peace.

Notes and Questions

14.12 Victim-offender mediation gives victims an opportunity to determine what will make them whole, to understand the offense more fully, and to receive apologies. Offenders are educated about the cost of their actions and have an opportunity to make amends. Like Truth and Reconciliation Commissions, such processes allow for dialogue about the past that might be restorative to victims and offenders alike. In many senses these processes are at least equally about the past and the future.

14.13 Menkel-Meadow also suggests that mediation must be flexible enough to adapt to situations where a record might be needed to preserve the past or where more transparency is desirable than in the traditional "confidential" mediation process.

C. MEDIATION AND ADR ABROAD

The following commentaries address the export of American mediation. Are American forms of ADR in developing countries another form of cultural imperialism? What are the implications of taking processes that work in one place and transplanting them to another? Laura Nader and Elisabetta Grande argue that North American ADR might be quite dangerous in Third World countries. Neal Milner responds to their thesis in the subsequent excerpt.

 Laura Nader & Elisabetta Grande, **CURRENT ILLUSIONS AND DELUSIONS ABOUT CONFLICT MANAGEMENT — IN AFRICA AND ELSEWHERE**

27 L. & Soc. Inquiry 573, 574, 578-582, 589-591 (2002)

In recent decades, U.S.-style dispute resolution (ADR) techniques have been exported to and imposed on communities in other parts of the world. ADR approaches such as mediation may have immediate appeal, appearing to foster harmonious and consensual resolution of conflict. However, they can in fact do more harm than good when forced on communities in which underlying understandings and situations do not fit well with the assumptions and epistemology that undergird ADR. In addition, the use of ADR has power dimensions that have not been adequately analyzed or understood. An accurate and sophisticated analysis would consider these problems as well as the input of nationalism; of political, economic, and religious processes; and of the wide range of players involved — politicians, businessmen, missionaries, arms dealers, ethnic groups, and victims. In short, policy initiatives in this area must proceed from a thorough understanding of conflict management in grounded contexts. This more careful, respectful, and contextual analysis might at times favor constraint over consensus, or more formal law over lawlessness or informal dispute resolution techniques. . . .

Today, tradition is up for grabs by any person or group interested in garnering power, and anthropologists are analyzing the many ways tradition is "reinvented" for current contexts and purposes. Again in the Native American context, it has been noted that federal officials and native advocates actively use linguistic, ethical, moral, cultural, and political traditions to sell nuclear waste disposal to Native Americans by means of ADR. In Africa and elsewhere, traditional symbols and institutions are regularly used by politicians to reach both rural and urban populations. If politicians can manipulate tradition or reinvent tradition, so might strategists in conflict management.

A central dilemma revolves around the observation that experts generally look for standardized solutions, while traditional conflict resolution is often particularistic or situational. For example, in a recent note "Are Alternative Dispute Resolution (ADR) Programs Suitable for Africa?" anthropologist Laurel Rose (1996) [in Africa Notes 5-7] addresses some of the conceptual problems of reinvented tradition by comparing contemporary American ADR with conflict resolution in African communities. Rose points out that modern mediators are formally trained, are strangers to the disputants, and are expected to be neutral, private, formal, and structured. By contrast, African communities use mediators informally trained through "life experience," who are known to the disputants, are not expected to be neutral, and operate collectively within a council of elders in a public setting. While the American ADR specialists operate with a limited range of relevance, the African process is characterized by a wide range of relevance, with full communication and public disclosure. Consensus between the parties is not what is sought; rather, the ideal outcome satisfies the whole community, usually placing community interests before the disputants' personal interests.

Under the auspices of the US AID program, Rose visited postwar Rwanda in 1994 to conduct research into the condition of the local justice system (customary institutions known as the *gacaca*) as preparation for a larger ADR research team. The long-term goal was to support a Rwandan ADR initiative to train mediators in the (temporary) absence of courts. Rose found that the *gacaca* survived the war, that people were seldom without operational *gacaca*, and that they adapted to circumstances of refugee camps or other temporary or permanent circumstances. Rose also noted that the *gacaca* took on functions beyond dispute resolution, such as the resettlement of large numbers of displaced persons. Those *gacaca* implicated in war-related events suffered a loss of legitimacy; nevertheless, Rose makes the point that

Rwanda's "customary institution" had risen to the challenges of their war-ravaged country and that an ADR initiative, even one making use of traditional institutions like the *gacaca*, would weaken local self-management or customary law. Rose refers to the cultural baggage that travels with American ADR, even when (or especially when) it is tied to a restructuring of indigenous systems. Moreover, she addresses the important issues of tradition and power, raising questions about an American ADR style that has much the flavor of earlier missionizing efforts of religious evangelists....

THE POWER DIMENSION

If any single generalization has emerged from the anthropological research on disputing processes, it is that mediation and negotiation require conditions of relatively equal power. In other words, negotiation and mediation cannot be used for all disputes and all conflicts. The adversary model was created to deal with uneven playing fields, made even by each party having an advocate in a court of law. In real life things are not so neat. In Africa and elsewhere, there are courts where mediation predominates or at least where a third party can judge whether to mediate, negotiate, or adjudicate a case.

In Euro-American societies, harmony law models recently have been valorized over adversary models — a reversal of the earlier trend, as we mentioned in our historical survey of the literature. But history is clear on one point. During the heyday of European colonialism, courts were valorized over moots, and the colonized were reminded regularly that the rule of law was a most important sign of civilized society. Its presence indicated the right to participate in the international law of nations. The presence of courts was a sign of development and social complexity. The World Court was a standard of civilized behavior. Yet, in the later part of the twentieth century, harmony legal models began to be thought of as more civilized than courts. Now that the "primitives" have courts, practitioners often value ADR or international negotiations as more "civilized." In this worldview, the "civilized" first worlders who wish to go to court are "barbarians," while "primitives" and the natives are considered a model of what it is to be truly human....

A review of the role of adjudication and negotiation in international river disputes (the Ganges, Jordan, Colorado, Duoro and Danube rivers) characterized by power asymmetry and upstream-downstream issues reveals preference by the less powerful nations for World Court adjudication, while the more powerful countries prefer negotiation. In light of the skewing effects of power asymmetries on informally negotiated outcomes, it is understandable why powerful parties have preferred negotiation and ADR over the International Court of Justice....

We need to think about these issues before recommending any policies — national or otherwise — for the peoples of Africa. If the spread of ADR is born of a contempt for law and if the International Court is to be replaced by international negotiation, using justifications of efficiency or stability, then what hope is there for the justice issues that should be foundational here?...

Stronger constituencies, such as multinational corporations, are practically unaffected by the state, since they mostly carry on their transactions outside state jurisdiction. Under such conditions, it becomes tempting for the state to avoid performing functions related to dispute resolution. The substitution of the confrontational model with a nonadversarial technique (whether in the United States or in the Horn) becomes in practice a complete loss of protection for poor litigants: They cannot rely on the market to buy protection (as the wealthy can), and they have given up the protection of a group that simply is considered irrelevant as far as state law is concerned.

The unevenness of power between litigants becomes once again relevant, and the weak individual finds himself not only without the effective protection of a group but also without the protection of individual rights, a consideration that, in theory, he has received for giving up the group. . . .

Clearly any ADR scheme needs careful study of the social conditions in which it may operate. The rhetoric of harmony law models is attractive. But the idea that in a conciliatory model, people do not fight but rather harmoniously agree about a common solution is fiction. So also is the belief that such a harmony model exists in "primitive" and idyllic societies. Similarly we need to understand the real dynamics of power that are at play when foreign systems are transplanted.

Notes and Questions

14.14 What are the critiques of ADR leveled by Grillo, Delgado et. al., and Nader and Grande? What do they have in common? Are these critiques supported by the data in LaFree and Rack (see Chapter 7)?

14.15 Critics point to an ideology of ADR that concerns them. What does it mean to have a harmony ideology? A justice ideology? Are the two inconsistent or incompatible in some ways? How?

14.16 To the extent that many of the critiques denounce power disparities in mediation, how do they compare to the power disparities that occur in other processes, such as adjudication? Are there fewer power disparities there? In governmental, formal, institutional, and agency decision making? What are the baselines for comparisons?

14.17 Are all power inequalities the same? Class and economic resources? Access to lawyers? Ability to express anger and emotion? Race and ethnicity? Access to power? Are domestic power inequalities the same as or analogous to international power disparities (the United States versus the rest of the world)? The same as or analogous to internal issues in countries or cultures not our own? How can we know?

14.18 How do you react to Nader and Grande's argument that ADR is a more or less "dangerous" U.S. export in the international aid arena that threatens the rule of law or justice in developing nations? Is the rule of law any more "indigenous" to other nations than ADR? How should we evaluate what processes or ideologies are appropriate for ourselves? For others?

14.19 Can you think of responses, in theory, ideology, or practice, to these critiques? How would you change ADR processes to respond to these critiques?

Neal Milner, **FROM THE TRENCHES AND THE TOWERS:**
ILLUSIONS AND DELUSIONS ABOUT CONFLICT
MANAGEMENT — IN AFRICA AND ELSEWHERE

27 L. & Soc. Inquiry 621, 621-622, 624-626 (2002)

What propels "Current Illusions and Delusions About Conflict Management" is this claim: "In spite of growing awareness of consequences, ADR ideology is intact and diffusing worldwide, in hegemonic splendor."

Laura Nader and Elisabetta Grande fail to support this assertion. They present little evidence of ADR's consequences, particularly its impact on developing countries during its recent evolution. . . .

The same is true about their claim that ADR ideology is "intact." Other than very general discussions of ADR and harmony ideology, the paper says little about what this ideology entails, much less how it has evolved as it encounters new settings. There is every reason to be skeptical that the movement is as homogeneous or intact as they claim, particularly in light of the very literatures Nader and Grande correctly rely on for their general orientation. This influential literature's thrust is toward diversity and heterogeneity. It stresses that colonial law's consequences are products of the interaction between the universal and the local. Certainly English colonial administrators in Kenya and India shared an overall legal ideology, but their differing colonial encounters reduced the intactness of this ideology as the ideas confronted particular circumstances. Whatever law's power and the violence associated with colonials, law did not remain "intact" in these encounters, and there is no reason to expect that ADR has either.

Their paper has far too little evidence to support their assertion that ADR has a "universal paradigm" for conflict management. This is something that generally is asserted far more than it is investigated. Nader and Grande's problems again emanate from their willingness to assume or assert homogeneity when the law and social science research they cite suggests otherwise. Contemporary social science shows that claims for universality should be viewed skeptically. Our understanding of law increased vastly as we began to fathom the nuances of the relationship between law and locale. These discoveries of variance and contextual differences are the very things that have made the more recent research on law and colonialism so valuable. It seems counter to this understanding to think that ADR stays intact, and there is every reason to expect that similar variations occur with ADR from place to place. . . .

Nader and Grande have an idealized view of law. To them, "the rule of law" and "justice" appear to have universally understood meanings. . . . But when Nader and Grande criticize ADR, their grounded, subtle, and skeptical stance toward law disappears. The law then takes on a Solomon-the-Wise aura. Discussing the inability of "locals" to deal with disparities of power, they argue that dealing with "grossly unequal power" [is] a "role for national and international law, if we are civilized that is." They talk of the power of the "just rule of law" as if the meaning of this is clear and universally accepted. Isn't this the same rule of law that their own lessons of African colonial history taught us to be skeptical about? Isn't it odd to be using the word *civilized* this way when Nader and Grande both recognize the powerful role law played in earlier "civilizing" projects that created repression throughout the colonial world?

Trina Grillo's warning about gender inequity in American ADR may be a useful warning for Bangladeshi women, but the "rule of law" the American women have available to them is quite different from their Bangladeshi counterparts. Nader's argument that informal justice is just only if formal institutions advocating the rule of law are also available is easy to accept in regard to the United States, but the argument does not travel well. What does the rule of law mean in weak states with no autonomous judiciary or in kleptocracies where justice goes to the highest bidder? Does Rwanda, with its legal institutions overwhelmed by genocide cases that are so numerous and so tied into the fabric of Rwandan society, offer an opportunity for a strong and useful rule of law? These are not rhetorical questions. People in such places have to encounter and answer them every day.

Nader and Grande show the same odd faith in international law. They exaggerate the availability and influence of international forums. For the sake of argument, I will reluctantly accept their sweeping assertion that the "International Court [of Justice] is to be replaced by international negotiation." Even if that were the case, what is the big loss here? Since when were these tribunals such saviors of justice? Maybe, as they say, ADR is part of "the trivialization of international adjudication," but these tribunals were not very central in the first place.

Nader and Grande's extraordinary faith in law is clear in their description of and response to the Sahel famine that decimated Senegal. . . . Here is what they offer as a response to that problem: "All the alternative dispute mechanisms in the world will not replace the just rule of law (state or international) in such a situation." Without a doubt ADR would be ineffectual and deceptive in this case. But what is it about the rule of law that is supposed to save these people from starvation? The government of Senegal demonstrated its notions about the rule of law by selling out to the lettuce companies, bringing in the police, and no doubt defining the government's idea of justice by asserting some fulsome claims defending the sanctity of private property. Given these responses and the colonial history of law, there's no reason to be so optimistic about the rule of law. And where exactly in the international legal order is there an effective forum for dealing with the plight of starving people getting chased off their land while Americans in Cleveland get inexpensive salad fixings all-year round? This is a problem that far transcends the rule of law, and advocating it even as a partial solution smacks too much of the historically misplaced faith the West has had in bringing order to an unruly world. This view of law is the mirror image of the uncritical ADR advocate.

This is not to dismiss totally the potential of the rule of law either in the national or international arena. Important new international and pan-national human rights forums are emerging. These institutions resonate with claims to rights and the rule of law that people in many parts of the world risk their lives to make.

Notes and Questions

14.20 Milner speaks critically elsewhere in his article of those belonging to the "ADR Church." He calls for more research, analysis, and interaction among ADR advocates, scholars, and practitioners. While ADR romanticism may be dangerous, do you find a tendency toward litigation (or rule of law) romanticism in any of the critics?

14.21 What is the relationship of ADR to the "rule of law"? Must there be effective law and formal legal institutions behind a more informal system for mediation to work? See Tom Ginsburg & Richard H. McAdams, Adjudicating in Anarchy: An Expressive Theory of International Dispute Resolution, 45 Wm. & Mary L. Rev. 1229 (2004) (exploring the effects of unenforceable sanctions of international adjudication tribunals on international dispute resolution).

D. EMPIRICAL EVALUATION OF ADR CLAIMS

The use of mediation is controversial. Over the years, there have been claims about the advantages and disadvantages of different forms of ADR and some efforts to examine these claims empirically. There is not yet consensus on whether the various alternative processes or adjudication have demonstrated the validity of their various claims. Below is one example of empirical research designed to test some of the claims about ADR, both critical and supportive. As you read this excerpt, consider how you would test whether particular processes are meeting the needs of the parties and the demands of our justice system. This example uses and illustrates a particular method — the analysis of aggregate data, collected from court files, as well as interviews with lawyers and participants; it depends on accurate matching of different kinds of case types and courts for reliable and valid comparisons of case processing information over time. Compare this approach with that of LaFree and Rack (analyzing the party reactions and outcomes in a range of mediated and litigated Small Claims cases in Chapter 7) and Greatbatch and Dingwall (doing a single case sociolinguistic analysis of a mediation transcript in Chapter 9). Consider which methods of empirical analysis are valid for which kinds of conclusions about the effectiveness of a process, and what methods provide a better picture of what is actually happening in a process.

The study excerpted below is a U.S. government-funded, multimillion dollar research project examining the use of various dispute resolution techniques in the federal courts, primarily to measure "efficiency" in costs and time saved when mediation, arbitration, early neutral evaluation, and other case management devices were used. The RAND study found no substantial savings in economic costs or time saved when these alternative processes were used. The RAND study spawned an ongoing debate about the appropriate measurement tools, categories, and analyses that should be used when measuring a process that has both quantitative and qualitative impacts. Other studies have found evidence of both cost and time reduction in other federal courts (see, e.g., N&Q 14.22). A growing body of research, attempting more rigorous empirical analysis of a greater variety of significant variables and input and output measures, is now exploring many ways of developing appropriate metrics to understand the effectiveness of these processes of conflict resolution in a variety of settings.

James S. Kakalik, Terence Dunworth, Laural A. Hill, Daniel McCaffrey, Marian Oshiro, Nicholas M. Pace & Mary E. Vaiana, **AN EVALUATION OF MEDIATION AND EARLY NEUTRAL EVALUATION UNDER THE CIVIL JUSTICE REFORM ACT**

v, xxvii–xxxiv (1996)

This report is one of four RAND reports evaluating the pilot program of the Civil Justice Reform Act (CJRA) of 1990. . . . The study was undertaken at the request of the Judicial Conference of the United States. . . .

The Civil Justice Reform Act (CJRA) of 1990 emerged from a multi-year debate about ways to reduce delay and litigation costs in federal courts. The legislation required each federal district court to develop a case management plan to reduce costs and delay. . . .

This study's objective is to assess the implementation, costs, and effects of mediation and neutral evaluation programs for civil cases in the six CJRA pilot and comparison federal district courts that had mediation or neutral evaluation programs in 1992-93 involving a sufficient number of cases to permit detailed evaluation. The districts studied were California (Southern), New York (Eastern), New York (Southern), Pennsylvania (Eastern), Oklahoma (Western), and Texas (Southern).

CHARACTERISTICS OF THE ADR PROGRAMS

[K]ey design features of the programs . . . assessed . . . vary considerably on a number of dimensions, including whether the program is mandatory or voluntary, the point in the litigation at which referral occurs, the purpose of the program, the length of sessions, the type of provider, and the cost to parties. . . .

DESIGN OF THE EVALUATION

We selected approximately 150 representative cases that were referred to the ADR program in each district and a comparison group of about 150 cases in the same district. . . .

We analyzed each district separately. Within each district, we compared the cases referred to ADR with the comparison group, using both bivariate tabulations and multivariate statistical analyses.

The primary measures used to evaluate the cases were:

- Time to disposition, defined as the interval from first filing of the case to case closing;
- Cost of litigation, defined primarily as lawyer work hours per litigant, but also including monetary legal fees and costs and litigant hours spent on the case;
- Cost to the court for administering the ADR program;
- Monetary outcomes;
- Provider, litigant, and lawyer views of satisfaction with case management that includes ADR; and
- Provider, litigant, and lawyer views of the fairness of case management that includes ADR.

Table S.1
Characteristics of ADR Programs Studied

DISTRICT PROGRAM	TYPE OF REFERRAL	WHEN REFERRED	PROGRAM EMPHASIS	CASES INCLUDED	TYPICAL SESSION	ADR PROVIDER	MEDIAN FEE
Mediation							
NY(S)	Mandatory	After mgmt. track is assigned	Settlement	Random experimental design	5 hours over 2 days	Lawyers	None
PA(E)	Mandatory	90 days from filing	Case issues, settlement	Random experimental design	Single 90-minute session	Lawyers	None
OK(W)	Voluntary; or mandatory at judicial discretion	Initial pretrial conference	Settlement	All cases required to have pretrial conference	Single 4-hour session	Lawyers	$660, split by parties
TX(S)	Voluntary, tougher cases encouraged; or mandatory at judicial discretion	Initial pretrial conference or later	Settlement	All cases required to have pretrial conference	Single 8-hour session	Lawyers	$1,800, split by parties
Neutral Evaluation							
CA(S)	Mandatory	Before initial pretrial conference	Evaluation, settlement	All cases required to have pretrial conference	2.5 hours over 2 days	Magistrate judges handling pretrial case mgmt.	None
NY(E)	Mandatory at judicial discretion; or voluntary	Initial pretrial conference or later	Settlement	Any eligible case with value >$100,000	Single 3.5-hour session	Lawyers	None

The evaluation draws on subjective and objective case-level data from the period January 1991 through December 1995, depending on the district. We followed the cases from filing to termination, or until December 1995 when our data collection stopped if they were still open then. Data sources include:

- Court records, including summary data on each of the sample cases;
- Records and reports of CJRA advisory groups;
- Pilot and comparison districts' cost and delay reduction plans;
- Detailed case processing and complete docket information on our samples of cases;
- Mail surveys of ADR providers on the sample of ADR cases selected;
- Mail surveys of attorneys and litigants on closed ADR and comparison cases about costs, time, satisfaction and views of the fairness of the process; and
- Personal interviews with judges, court staff, lawyers, and ADR providers during site visits to each of the six districts.

About two-thirds of the ADR providers, half of the lawyers, and one-ninth of the litigants responded to our surveys. Because so few litigants responded, we excluded litigant data from our statistical analyses and view these data as merely supportive of our other analyses.

OVERVIEW OF PRIOR RESEARCH ON COURT-RELATED ADR

It is useful to view the results of the current study in the broader context of previous research on court-related ADR of all types.

The rationale for ADR programs is the hope that they will be faster, cheaper, and/or more satisfactory to participants than formal court adjudication. Although past research has not confirmed all of these putative benefits, it does seem to suggest that litigants are more satisfied when ADR has taken place, even if they do not settle their case at that time.

Unfortunately, sound empirical research on various ADR mechanisms is quite thin. Much of the literature is descriptive and, often, hortatory, with the latter tending to rely on anecdotal data or individual experiences, which may or may not be representative. Court-related arbitration and family mediation programs have been most extensively studied, using accepted academic research methods, including randomized experimentation. Early neutral evaluation has also been the subject of some field experimentation. Mediation outside of the family law context has not often been examined, nor have most private ADR programs been scrutinized closely.

The previous empirical research on court-annexed arbitration suggests that these programs have, at best, modest contributions to make to managing civil litigation more expeditiously and more economically. However, they offer litigants a more satisfying form of justice than is accorded through the combination of bilateral negotiation and judicially facilitated settlement that is their practical alternative in today's trial courts.

Previous empirical research on other forms of court-annexed ADR such as mediation and neutral evaluation is much more limited in volume than research on arbitration; the available findings do not provide an adequate basis on which to make definitive policy recommendations.

KEY FINDINGS OF THIS STUDY

Time to Disposition

We have no strong statistical evidence that time to disposition is significantly affected by mediation or neutral evaluation in any of the six programs studied.

There was no statistically significant difference in the time to disposition between the ADR sample cases and the comparison cases in five of the six ADR programs. TX(S) referrals to ADR were significantly slower (by about three months) to terminate than comparison cases. We believe the ADR cases terminate more slowly because judges encourage cases that appear more difficult to settle to volunteer for mediation.

Costs of Litigation

We have no strong statistical evidence that lawyer work hours are significantly affected by mediation or neutral evaluation in any of the six programs studied. . . .

As we discussed above with respect to time to disposition, TX(S) cases that appear tougher to settle receive more judicial encouragement to volunteer for mediation; these more difficult cases may have higher costs.

There are also confounding factors at work in CA(S). In addition to instituting a policy of early neutral evaluation, this district expanded the role of magistrate judges for civil cases and increased the use of early management. Policy changes other than neutral evaluation could have increased lawyer work hours. For example, in our main CJRA evaluation, we found that early management was associated with significantly increased lawyer work hours. Because of these other potential influences on the time that lawyers spend, we do not believe that the data from CA(S) provide any clear evidence that neutral evaluation, by itself, will necessarily lead to increased lawyer work hours.

Cost to Court for ADR Program Administration

The court's cost for ADR program administration includes the startup and recurring personnel cost of providing the program (including clerk's office personnel and judicial officer time), and any non-personnel costs such as for training programs, telephone, reproduction, and mailing. For CA(S), the cost of the magistrate judge's time spent providing the early neutral evaluation must also be included. Personnel time estimates include all full-time-equivalent (FTE) personnel actually working on the specific ADR program, whether they are paid by CJRA funds or not. Cost estimates, measured in 1995 dollars, include salaries, fringe benefits, and operations and maintenance expenses. . . .

The annual number of FTE court personnel devoted to ADR ranges from 0.8 to 3.15 for the six programs. . . .

The total annual cost to the district court of providing the ADR program being evaluated ranges from about $47,000 for 100 referred cases in NY(E) to about $384,000 for 1,070 referred cases in CA(S)....

These totals translate into a cost per case referred ranging from $130 to $490.... About $500, the highest administrative cost per case referred to ADR, contrasts with the substantially higher median cost of litigation per litigant, which ranges from $5,000 to $17,000....

The total startup cost to district courts ranged from $10,000 to $69,000....

MONETARY OUTCOME

Money appears more likely to change hands when mediation or neutral evaluation is involved. ADR cases in all six programs have a higher percentage of monetary outcomes than comparison cases have. The difference in the likelihood of a monetary outcome is statistically significant in three of four mediation programs and nearly significant in the fourth.

A plausible explanation for this pattern is that the mediation process is designed to facilitate settlement and does indeed increase the number of cases that settle. When parties reach an agreement and settle the case, that disposition is likely to involve a monetary outcome.

SETTLEMENT AS A RESULT OF MEDIATION OR NEUTRAL EVALUATION

The likelihood that a case referred to mediation or neutral evaluation settles just before or as a result of the ADR session ranges from 31 percent to 72 percent across the six districts. There appears to be a correspondence between settlement and when the session is held: Settlement is more likely to occur just before or after the ADR session when the session is held later in the life of the case. The programs ranked from lowest to highest percentage of ADR-related settlements are PA(E), CA(S), OK(W), TX(S), NY(E), and NY(S). We obtain the same sequence of programs if we rank them from the shortest to longest time from case filing to holding the ADR session. Discovery may be completed and cases may be more ready to settle by the time of the later sessions; thus, the fact that the lawyers and parties must meet for mediation or neutral evaluation may be the precipitating event required to finalize agreement.

PERCEPTIONS OF FAIRNESS

There was no statistically significant difference in lawyers' perception of how fairly the cases were managed. Lawyers on about nine out of ten cases in all programs felt that the mediation or neutral evaluation process was fair. A slightly lower percentage of litigants agreed, but the low completion rate for our litigant surveys does not allow us to confidently make statistical inferences from the litigant data.

SATISFACTION

We found no statistically significant effects for *mediation* referral in terms of lawyer satisfaction with case management.

Overall, a smaller percentage of litigants than lawyers report being satisfied with case management. However, in three of the four mediation districts studied, a greater percentage of litigants from mediation cases report satisfaction than from the comparison cases.

Our findings with respect to litigant and lawyer satisfaction with case management that includes *neutral evaluation* are inconclusive. As noted above, the difference between our two CA(S) samples might be attributed to other factors, including the increased role of magistrate judges and the wider use of early management. We cannot distinguish between these confounding effects. . . .

Focusing on the ADR session itself, only a minority of the respondents were dissatisfied with ADR; the majority were either neutral or satisfied.

OPINIONS AND RECOMMENDATIONS OF PARTICIPANTS

We asked mediation and neutral evaluation program participants (litigants, lawyers, and ADR providers) for their opinions on a variety of topics, including the appropriateness and timing of the ADR session, possible problems, and the session's effects.

Participants in these programs are generally supportive of them. Most of the lawyers involved feel the programs are worthwhile in general as well as valuable for their individual cases. Only a small percentage in any district thought the referral to ADR was inappropriate or that the program should be dropped.

Litigants also generally thought that referral to mediation or neutral evaluation was appropriate for their case and that the program should be retained. However, they were a little less positive than lawyers, and up to one-fourth of the litigants in some programs felt that referral was inappropriate or that the program should be dropped.

The vast majority of lawyers in every program were satisfied with the ADR process itself and thought it was handled fairly. In no district did we find a local bar that strongly opposed a program of mediation or neutral evaluation.

This general satisfaction with the ADR process does not mean that it was perfect. The problem cited most often by lawyers and ADR providers was that the parties were not ready to settle. The timing of the ADR session could be a major factor in this lack of "readiness." It may be best to conduct the sessions in an atmosphere where at least the basic facts and positions on issues are known to both sides and the ADR provider as well. Substantial numbers of lawyers in some districts felt that the sessions were held too early to be useful. Lawyers and ADR providers also thought that in a minority of cases, settlement eluded them because critical persons with authority to settle did not participate in the session.

ASSESSMENT

Our evaluation provided no strong statistical evidence that the mediation or neutral evaluation programs, as implemented in the six districts studied, significantly affected time to disposition, litigation costs, or attorney views of fairness or satisfaction with case management. The low completion rate for our litigant surveys does not allow us to confidently make statistical inferences from the litigant data. Our only statistically significant finding is that the ADR programs appear to increase the likelihood of a monetary settlement.

We conclude that the mediation and neutral evaluation programs as implemented in these six districts are not a panacea for perceived problems of cost and delay, but neither do they appear to be detrimental. We have no justification for a strong policy recommendation because we found no major program effects, either positive or negative. This lack of a demonstrated major effect on litigation cost and delay is generally consistent with the outcomes of prior empirical research on court-related ADR. . . .

Given that most mediation and neutral evaluation programs have been in place in federal court for only a few years, refinements should be expected as time progresses. The problems noted by the participants in the ADR sessions suggest the need to consider ensuring that each side has some basic information about the other side's case before the session is held, adjusting the timing of the session to maximize its utility for the case, and enforcing the requirement that the sessions involve not only the lawyers but also those who hold the keys to the litigation's resolution.

Notes and Questions

14.22 At the time that the RAND studies were completed, to evaluate the effects of various forms of court reform under the Civil Justice Reform Act (the Cost and Delay Reduction Act of 1990), the Federal Judicial Center also completed a study of five courts' experience with ADR. That study found there was some cost and delay reduction in several of the court-sponsored ADR programs. See Donna Stienstra et al., A Study of the Five Demonstration Programs Established Under the Civil Justice Reform Act of 1990 (1997). The somewhat contradictory, or less than consistent, findings on the question of whether ADR processes increased court "efficiency" led to a spirited debate about evaluation studies and their outcomes in the literature and at policy and judicial conferences. See, e.g., Craig A. McEwen, Mediation in Context: New Questions for Research, 3 Disp. Resol. Mag. 16 (1996); Craig A. McEwen & Elizabeth Plapinger, RAND Report Points Way to Next Generation of Research, 3 Disp. Resol. Mag. 10 (1997); Francis E. McGovern, Beyond Efficiency: A Bevy of ADR Justifications, 3 Disp. Resol. Mag. 12 (1997); Carrie Menkel-Meadow, When Dispute Resolution Begets Disputes of Its Own: Conflicts Among Dispute Professionals, 44 UCLA L. Rev. 1871 (1997).

14.23 In a more recent evaluation of the RAND — and other — studies, Deborah Hensler concludes:

> To date, there is no evidence that introducing ADR, including mediation, into the litigation process after a suit is filed, will consistently result in lower transaction costs and shorter time to disposition, compared to settling cases without third-party involvement. Nor is there evidence that facilitative mediation is more likely than evaluative mediation to produce such results,

> or that the converse is true. Where court-connected mediation programs
> result in shorter time to disposition, the explanation appears to lie in the
> combination of early referral times and high settlement rates. Just how early
> is too early to achieve high settlement rates is unclear from the available data.

Deborah R. Hensler, In Search of "Good" Mediation in Handbook of Justice
Research in Law 258 (Joseph Sanders & V. Lee Hamilton eds., 2001). What is
becoming clear is that more research is needed on virtually every front!

Controversies abound about how to collect data, how to categorize inputs and
outputs, how to evaluate inside processes, how to define program and process objectives (cost savings to systems versus party satisfaction or self-determination for individuals), and how to find appropriate baseline comparisons of alternative treatments.
It is difficult to measure ultimate consequences for parties inside a dispute, as well as
the larger systems or societies in which particular disputes or dispute processing
systems are located. There may also be "bystander" effects on other users of dispute
resolution systems or on those who stand near or are affected by a particular dispute
or outcome.

Because the evaluation of "success" of such processes entails both objective and
quantitative measures (time and cost savings, transaction costs of systems used, number of cases settled) and qualitative and more subjective assessments (client satisfaction, better ongoing relationships, greater worker productivity, self-determination,
and development of better human skill sets for communication), it is difficult to reach
agreement about how to develop metrics in the field. This is an important ongoing
project since increasingly funding agencies, both public and private, seek objective
demonstrations of the effectiveness of these processes and programs. Below is a list of
possible metrics that various studies have used to measure these aspects of dispute
resolution processes. Developing a sound evaluation and research protocol requires
some conceptualization of more "composite" formulas and measurement tools in
order to capture both the quantitative and qualitative richness of what conflict
resolution processes both promise and actually deliver. No single program evaluation
has made use of all of these possible metrics (collection of all of this kind of data would
be prohibitively expensive). Some possible variables and criteria for measurement are
listed below.

QUANTITATIVE OR "OBJECTIVE" MEASURES

- Number of conflicts or disputes in relevant "universe" (which and how many
  form into formal claim or complaint)
- Number of contacts or cases (in a particular process, as compared to the full
  "universe" of possible cases or comparable cases in another process)
- Numbers of issues
- Number of cases resolved/settled/closed/disposed of ("settlement rates")
- Number of cases referred to another process
- Number of cases dropped

- Case types (categories within systems, e.g., employment promotion, dismissal, communication, etc.)
- Numbers of parties
- Types of agreements, resolutions, outcomes
- Time to process case
- Cost of processing case — to parties, third-party neutrals, to program or system
- Comparisons (where possible) of all of the above of comparable cases in different systems
- Comparisons of pre-conflict resolution program claiming (grievance systems, litigation) or violence with post-programmatic claiming
- Comparisons of rates of compliance with agreements, judgments, or orders
- Durability/longevity of outcomes
- Longitudinal comparisons of changes in usage, time for processing, case types, etc.
- Demographic data on users, third-party neutrals, and other facilitators or professionals
- Variations in usage, outcomes, solutions by demographics, and differential characteristics of disputants and third-party neutrals, such as "experience" ratings
- Awareness of ability to choose different processes (an attitudinal measure)

QUALITATIVE OR SUBJECTIVE MEASURES

- Client satisfaction
- Criteria for selecting particular processes
- Improved relationships (post-conflict societies (such as Rwanda), families, workplaces, commercial relations)
- Improved communication
- Enhanced workplace productivity
- Learned conflict resolution/communication/relational skills ("transformative" mutual intersubjective understandings or learned use of new processes, such as lawyers using mediation and other forms of problem solving)
- "Better" outcomes (more creative, individually tailored, deeper solutions)
- Perceived self-determination/autonomy/control over decision making
- Compliance with national, systemic, family, company, workplace, contractual norms/rules when legitimacy is less questioned
- Perceptions of fairness, justice, and legitimacy of process
- Trust in institutions, both dispute processing and others
- Resolution of systemic issues (proactive conflict resolution, policy changes)
- "Value added" to organization or institution

Can you think of any other criteria? How would you combine both quantitative and qualitative measures to develop an accurate assessment of how a particular process is working (in comparison to others)?

Notes and Questions

14.24 Select one of the critiques made about mediation from the articles you have read in this chapter. Consider the critical claim and any implicit or explicit comparisons being drawn to another kind of process. Now develop a research design for evaluating that claim.

14.25 Does it make a difference whether the process is one in the public domain (in a court) or in the private domain?

14.26 What obstacles might there be to actually mounting your study (aside from costs), such as party consent, case matching, or commensurability? Consider, for example, the discomfort you might feel about being critical of someone who had participated voluntarily in your study.

14.27 How should individual decisions (about whether to employ a particular process) or policy choices (whether to institutionally support a particular program) be made without valid and reliable empirical studies?

14.28 Since ADR processes were first used, there has been a strong desire to evaluate the effectiveness of these processes. Researchers want to compare ADR processes to other baseline processes such as formal litigation, dispute avoidance, formal grievance systems, and traditional hierarchical decision making. Scholars hope to determine whether ADR processes achieve their often-stated objectives: party autonomy and self-determination, more productive workforces, better communication in ongoing relationship settings, more creative and individually tailored solutions, more durable agreements, greater efficiency, cost effectiveness, time savings, and interpersonal transformation and "conflict competence." The ability to measure the inputs, processes, outcomes, and systemic or programmatic consequences of these processes has been hindered by an inability to construct social scientific "experimental" conditions of control groups to compare several "treatments" of the same conflict in the same case, as well as lack of uniformity in data collection, coding, interpretations of data, and in many cases (due to the special promises of confidentiality in some of these processes), the unavailability of data at all (especially in private contexts). Probably the first rigorous studies that were conducted compared the consequences and robustness of mediation agreements reached in divorce and family settings to those reached in litigation. Jessica Pearson & Nancy Thoennes, Divorce Mediation: Reflections on a Decade of Research, 9 Med. Res. 19 (1989). Other studies reviewed compliance with small claims court mediation, as compared to court-ordered judgments. Craig A. McEwen & Richard J. Maiman, Small Claims Mediation in Maine: An Empirical Assessment, 33 Me. L. Rev. 237 (1981). See generally Kenneth Kressel et al., Mediation Research (1989).

E. TRENDS: THE FUTURE OF MEDIATION IN THE LEGAL ARENA

A final alarm about mediation is sounded below by Nancy Welsh, who suggests that the robust and simple vision of mediation as a process to foster party participation and self-determination is "thinning." To put the concern more boldly, some feel mediation is being gutted as it is adopted into the adversarial world of attorneys and courts. Think about how the "better" side of mediation can be encouraged and preserved as mediation is increasingly institutionalized.

 Nancy A. Welsh, **THE THINNING VISION OF SELF-DETERMINATION IN COURT-CONNECTED MEDIATION: THE INEVITABLE PRICE OF INSTITUTIONALIZATION**

6 Harv. Negot. L. Rev. 1, 4-5, 25-27 (2001)

[A]s mediation has been institutionalized in the courts and as [mediator] evaluation has become an acknowledged and accepted part of the mediator's function, the original vision of [party] self-determination is giving way to a vision in which the disputing parties play a less central role. The parties are still responsible for making the final decision regarding settlement, but they are cast in the role of consumers, largely limited to selecting from among the settlement options developed by their attorneys. Indeed, it is the parties' attorneys, often aided by mediators who are also attorneys, who assume responsibility for actively and directly participating in the mediation process, invoking the substantive (i.e., legal) norms to be applied and creating settlement options. Thus, even as most mediators and many courts continue to name party self-determination as the "fundamental principle" underlying court-connected mediation, the party-centered empowerment concepts that anchored the original vision of self-determination are being replaced with concepts that are more reflective of the norms and traditional practices of lawyers and judges, as well as the courts' strong orientation to efficiency and closure of cases through settlement....

Perhaps inevitably, current evidence strongly suggests that the "legitimacy handed to [the ADR movement] by its assimilation into the court system" has come at a price. Court-connected mediation of non-family civil cases is developing an uncanny resemblance to the judicially-hosted settlement conference. In certain types of cases, such as personal injury and medical malpractice, the defendants regularly fail to attend mediation sessions. Even when all of the clients do attend, their attorneys are likely to do much, if not all, of the talking, particularly in joint sessions. An increasing number of mediators are abandoning or greatly minimizing the joint session, preferring to move quickly to caucuses. The attorneys are choosing mediators who, like judges, are expected to have the knowledge and experience which would permit them to comment on the parties' legal arguments. Indeed, mediators now often focus on the legal issues and opine regarding the strengths and weaknesses of each party's case and appropriate settlement ranges. Finally, it appears that few mediators now actively promote the search in mediation for creative, non-monetary settlements.

To a large extent, the presence of lawyers, as advocates and as mediators, explains why court-connected mediation now looks like a judicial settlement conference. First, attorneys have long operated within an "adversary culture." As they were ordered to participate with their clients in the mysterious process called "mediation," they brought with them a "standard philosophical map," assumptions regarding their relationship with their clients, and expectations and tactics that they had honed in their prior experience with traditional judicial settlement conferences. Second, as more and more attorneys and retired judges were attracted to mediation as a remunerative activity, they brought to the role of mediator the skills and knowledge that had served them well in their careers, as well as certain assumptions about "the role of the [quasi-]judicial host." Parties and their attorneys began to select mediators who could and would provide reasoned evaluation. Increasingly, mediators were willing to provide it.

Notes and Questions

14.29   Do you agree that this "thinning" of the mediation process — its conversion toward an adversarial paradigm — is inevitable? Is it desirable? In a study of Maine mediation in family law, researchers Craig McEwen and Nancy Rogers found that even mandatory mediation programs in divorce could change the legal culture and way that divorce conflicts were resolved, both by parties and by their lawyers, see Craig McEwen & Nancy Rogers, Bring the Lawyers into Divorce Mediation, 1994 Disp. Resol. Mag. 8.

14.30   What measures could be taken to identify mediation as distinct from judicial settlement conferences or neutral evaluation?

The critiques of mediation in this chapter demonstrate that the process is not a panacea for all the challenges that beset the disputing world. Most good things come with a cost, and mediation is no exception. The process of mediation — both in theory and in practice — offers many great goods, while simultaneously raising new concerns and issues.

It is unrealistic to think we will ever reach a fixed stasis in the world of dispute processes. Rather the goal should be a dynamic evolutionary development of both mediation and adjudication — a development that keeps pace with the disputes that we collectively face. Mediation, and its sister adjudicative processes, must support both the goals of enhanced human communication and collaboration and of fairness, stability, and the rule of law. As the mediation process adapts and develops — like a sail that is constantly adjusted to the vagaries of the wind — designers and practitioners must keep in mind the unique purposes of mediation: to achieve higher levels of human understanding, constructive interaction, creative problem solving, and agreement.

Appendix A UNIFORM MEDIATION ACT, SECTIONS 1–13

National Conference of Commissioners on Uniform State Laws and UNCITRAL Model Law on International Commercial Conciliation

SECTION 1. Title. This [Act] may be cited as the Uniform Mediation Act.

SECTION 2. Definitions. In this [Act]:

(1) "Mediation" means a process in which a mediator facilitates communication and negotiation between parties to assist them in reaching a voluntary agreement regarding their dispute.

(2) "Mediation communication" means a statement, whether oral or in a record or verbal or nonverbal, that occurs during a mediation or is made for purposes of considering, conducting, participating in, initiating, continuing, or reconvening a mediation or retaining a mediator.

(3) "Mediator" means an individual who conducts a mediation.

(4) "Nonparty participant" means a person, other than a party or mediator, that participates in a mediation.

(5) "Mediation party" means a person that participates in a mediation and whose agreement is necessary to resolve the dispute.

(6) "Person" means an individual, corporation, business trust, estate, trust, partnership, limited liability company, association, joint venture, government; governmental subdivision, agency, or instrumentality; public corporation, or any other legal or commercial entity.

(7) "Proceeding" means:

(A) a judicial, administrative, arbitral, or other adjudicative process, including related pre-hearing and post-hearing motions, conferences, and discovery; or

(B) a legislative hearing or similar process.

(8) "Record" means information that is inscribed on a tangible medium or that is stored in an electronic or other medium and is retrievable in perceivable form.

(9) "Sign" means:

(A) to execute or adopt a tangible symbol with the present intent to authenticate a record; or

(B) to attach or logically associate an electronic symbol, sound, or process to or with a record with the present intent to authenticate a record.

SECTION 3. Scope.

(a) Except as otherwise provided in subsection (b) or (c), this [Act] applies to a mediation in which:

(1) the mediation parties are required to mediate by statute or court or administrative agency rule or referred to mediation by a court, administrative agency, or arbitrator;

(2) the mediation parties and the mediator agree to mediate in a record that demonstrates an expectation that mediation communications will be privileged against disclosure; or

(3) the mediation parties use as a mediator an individual who holds himself or herself out as a mediator, or the mediation is provided by a person that holds itself out as providing mediation.

(b) The [Act] does not apply to a mediation:

(1) relating to the establishment, negotiation, administration, or termination of a collective bargaining relationship;

(2) relating to a dispute that is pending under or is part of the processes established by a collective bargaining agreement, except that the [Act] applies to a mediation arising out of a dispute that has been filed with an administrative agency or court;

(3) conducted by a judge who might make a ruling on the case; or

(4) conducted under the auspices of:

(A) a primary or secondary school if all the parties are students or

(B) a correctional institution for youths if all the parties are residents of that institution.

(c) If the parties agree in advance in a signed record, or a record of proceeding reflects agreement by the parties, that all or part of a mediation is not privileged, the privileges under Sections 4 through 6 do not apply to the mediation or part agreed upon. However, Sections 4 through 6 apply to a mediation communication made by a person that has not received actual notice of the agreement before the communication is made.

SECTION 4. Privilege Against Disclosure; Admissibility; Discovery.

(a) Except as otherwise provided in Section 6, a mediation communication is privileged as provided in subsection (b) and is not subject to discovery or admissible in evidence in a proceeding unless waived or precluded as provided by Section 5.

(b) In a proceeding, the following privileges apply:

(1) A mediation party may refuse to disclose, and may prevent any other person from disclosing, a mediation communication.

(2) A mediator may refuse to disclose a mediation communication, and may prevent any other person from disclosing a mediation communication of the mediator.

(3) A nonparty participant may refuse to disclose, and may prevent any other person from disclosing, a mediation communication of the nonparty participant.

(c) Evidence or information that is otherwise admissible or subject to discovery does not become inadmissible or protected from discovery solely by reason of its disclosure or use in a mediation.

SECTION 5. Waiver and Preclusion of Privilege.

(a) A privilege under Section 4 may be waived in a record or orally during a proceeding if it is expressly waived by all parties to the mediation and:

(1) in the case of the privilege of a mediator, it is expressly waived by the mediator; and

(2)   in the case of the privilege of a nonparty participant, it is expressly waived by the nonparty participant.

(b)   A person that discloses or makes a representation about a mediation communication which prejudices another person in a proceeding is precluded from asserting a privilege under Section 4, but only to the extent necessary for the person prejudiced to respond to the representation or disclosure.

(c)   A person that intentionally uses a mediation to plan, attempt to commit or commit a crime, or to conceal an ongoing crime or ongoing criminal activity is precluded from asserting a privilege under Section 4.

SECTION 6. Exceptions to Privilege.

(a)   There is no privilege under Section 4 for a mediation communication that is:

(1)   in an agreement evidenced by a record signed by all parties to the agreement;

(2)   available to the public under [insert statutory reference to open records act] or made during a session of a mediation which is open, or is required by law to be open, to the public;

(3)   a threat or statement of a plan to inflict bodily injury or commit a crime of violence;

(4)   intentionally used to plan a crime, attempt to commit a crime, or to conceal an ongoing crime or ongoing criminal activity;

(5)   sought or offered to prove or disprove a claim or complaint of professional misconduct or malpractice filed against a mediator;

(6)   except as otherwise provided in subsection (c), sought or offered to prove or disprove a claim or complaint of professional misconduct or malpractice filed against a mediation party, nonparty participant, or representative of a party based on conduct occurring during a mediation; or

(7)   sought or offered to prove or disprove abuse, neglect, abandonment, or exploitation in a proceeding in which a child or adult protective services agency is a party, unless the

[Alternative A: [State to insert, for example, child or adult protection] case is referred by a court to mediation and a public agency participates.]

[Alternative B: public agency participates in the [State to insert, for example, child or adult protection] mediation.]

(b)   There is no privilege under Section 4 if a court, administrative agency, or arbitrator finds, after a hearing in camera, that the party seeking discovery or the proponent of the evidence has shown that the evidence is not otherwise available, that there is a need for the evidence that substantially outweighs the interest in protecting confidentiality, and that the mediation communication is sought or offered in:

(1)   a court proceeding involving a felony [or misdemeanor]; or

(2)   except as otherwise provided in subsection (c), a proceeding to prove a claim to rescind or reform or a defense to avoid liability on a contract arising out of the mediation.

(c)   A mediator may not be compelled to provide evidence of a mediation communication referred to in subsection (a)(6) or (b)(2).

(d)   If a mediation communication is not privileged under subsection (a) or (b), only the portion of the communication necessary for the application of the exception from nondisclosure may be admitted. Admission of evidence under subsection (a) or (b) does not render the evidence, or any other mediation communication, discoverable or admissible for any other purpose.

SECTION 7. Prohibited Mediator Reports.

(a)   Except as required in subsection (b), a mediator may not make a report, assessment, evaluation, recommendation, finding, or other communication regarding a mediation to a court, administrative agency, or other authority that may make a ruling on the dispute that is the subject of the mediation.

(b)   A mediator may disclose:

(1)   whether the mediation occurred or has terminated, whether a settlement was reached, and attendance;

(2)   a mediation communication as permitted under Section 6; or

(3)   a mediation communication evidencing abuse, neglect, abandonment, or exploitation of an individual to a public agency responsible for protecting individuals against such mistreatment.

(c)   A communication made in violation of subsection (a) may not be considered by a court, administrative agency, or arbitrator.

SECTION 8. Confidentiality.

Unless subject to the [insert statutory references to open meetings act and open records act], mediation communications are confidential to the extent agreed by the parties or provided by other law or rule of this State.

SECTION 9. Mediator's Disclosure of Conflicts of Interest; Background.

(a)   Before accepting a mediation, an individual who is requested to serve as a mediator shall:

(1)   make an inquiry that is reasonable under the circumstances to determine whether there are any known facts that a reasonable individual would consider likely to affect the impartiality of the mediator, including a financial or personal interest in the outcome of the mediation and an existing or past relationship with a mediation party or foreseeable participant in the mediation; and

(2)   disclose any such known fact to the mediation parties as soon as is practical before accepting a mediation.

(b)   If a mediator learns any fact described in subsection (a)(1) after accepting a mediation, the mediator shall disclose it as soon as is practicable.

(c)   At the request of a mediation party, an individual who is requested to serve as a mediator shall disclose the mediator's qualifications to mediate a dispute.

(d)   A person that violates subsection [(a) or (b)][(a), (b), or (g)] is precluded by the violation from asserting a privilege under Section 4.

(e)   Subsections (a), (b), [and] (c), [and] [(g)] do not apply to an individual acting as a judge.

(f)   This [Act] does not require that a mediator have a special qualification by background or profession.

[(g) A mediator must be impartial, unless after disclosure of the facts required in subsections (a) and (b) to be disclosed, the parties agree otherwise.]

SECTION 10. Participation in Mediation.

An attorney or other individual designated by a party may accompany the party to and participate in a mediation. A waiver of participation given before the mediation may be rescinded.

SECTION 11. International Commercial Mediation.

(a) In this section, "Model Law" means the Model Law on International Commercial Conciliation adopted by the United Nations Commission on International Trade Law on 28 June 2002 and recommended by the United Nations General Assembly in a resolution (A/RES/ 57/18) dated 19 November 2002 [Appendix A below], and "international commercial mediation" means an international commercial conciliation as defined in Article 1 of the Model Law.

(b) Except as otherwise provided in subsections (c) and (d), if a mediation is an International commercial mediation, the mediation is governed by the Model Law.

(c) Unless the parties agree in accordance with Section 3(c) of this [Act] that all or part of an international commercial mediation is not privileged, Sections 4, 5, and 6 and any applicable definitions in Section 2 of this [Act] also apply to the mediation and nothing in Article 10 of the Model Law derogates from Sections 4, 5, and 6.

(d) If the parties to an international commercial mediation agree under Article 1, subsection (7), of the Model Law that the Model Law does not apply, this [Act] applies.

Legislative Note. The UNCITRAL Model Law on International Commercial Conciliation may be found at *www.uncitral.org/en-index.htm.* Important comments on interpretation are included in the Draft Guide to Enactment and Use of UNCITRAL Model Law on International Commercial Conciliation. The States should note the Draft Guide In a Legislative Note to the Act. This is especially important with respect to interpretation of Article 9 of the Model Law.

SECTION 12. Relation to Electronic Signatures in Global and National Commerce Act.

This [Act] modifies, limits, or supersedes the federal Electronic Signatures in Global and National Commerce Act, 15. U.S.C. Section 7001 et seq., but this [Act] does not modify, limit, or supersede Section 101(c) of that Act or authorize electronic delivery of any of the notices described in Section 103(b) of that Act.

SECTION 13. Uniformity of Application and Construction.

In applying and construing this [Act], consideration should be given to the need to promote uniformity of the law with respect to its subject matter among States that enact it.

APPENDIX A

(Model Law as adopted by the United Nations Commission on International Trade Law — UNCITRAL at its 35th session in New York on 28 June 2002 and approved by the United Nations General Assembly on November 19, 2002)

UNCITRAL Model Law on International Commercial Conciliation (footnotes omitted)

Article 1. Scope of application and definitions

(1) This Law applies to international commercial conciliation.

(2)   For the purposes of this Law, "conciliator" means a sole conciliator or two or more conciliators, as the case may be.

(3)   For the purposes of this Law, "conciliation" means a process, whether referred to by the expression conciliation, mediation or an expression of similar import, whereby parties request a third person or persons ("the conciliator") to assist them in their attempt to reach an amicable settlement of their dispute arising out of or relating to a contractual or other legal relationship. The conciliator does not have the authority to impose upon the parties a solution to the dispute.

(4)   A conciliation is international if:

(a)   The parties to an agreement to conciliate have, at the time of the conclusion of that agreement, their places of business in different States; or

(b)   The State in which the parties have their places of business is different from either:

(i)   The State in which a substantial part of the obligations of the commercial relationship is to be performed; or

(ii)   The State with which the subject matter of the dispute Is most closely connected.

(5)   For the purposes of this article:

(a)   If a party has more than one place of business, the place of business is that which has the closest relationship to the agreement to conciliate;

(b)   If a party does not have a place of business, reference is to be made to the party's habitual residence.

(6)   This Law also applies to a commercial conciliation when the parties agree that the conciliation is international or agree to the applicability of this Law.

(7)   The parties are free to agree to exclude the applicability of this Law.

(8)   Subject to the provisions of paragraph (9) of this article, this Law applies irrespective of the basis upon which the conciliation is carried out, including agreement between the parties whether reached before or after a dispute has arisen, an obligation established by law, or a direction or suggestion of a court, arbitral tribunal or competent governmental entity.

(9)   This Law does not apply to:

(a)   Cases where a judge or an arbitrator, in the course of judicial or arbitral proceedings, attempts to facilitate a settlement; and

(b)   [reserved]

Article 2. Interpretation

(1)   In the Interpretation of this Law, regard is to be had to its international origin and to the need to promote uniformity in its application and the observance of good faith.

(2)   Questions concerning matters governed by this Law which are not expressly settled in it are to be settled in conformity with the general principles on which this Law is based.

Article 3. Variation by agreement

Except for the provisions of article 2 and article 6, paragraph (3), the parties may agree to exclude or vary any of the provisions of this Law.

Article 4. Commencement of conciliation proceedings

(1)   Conciliation proceedings in respect of a dispute that has arisen commence on the day on which the parties to that dispute agree to engage in conciliation proceedings.

(2)   If a party that invited another party to conciliate does not receive an acceptance of the invitation within thirty days from the day on which the invitation was sent, or within such other period of time as specified in the invitation, the party may elect to treat this as a rejection of the invitation to conciliate.

Article 5. Number and appointment of conciliators

(1)   There shall be one conciliator, unless the parties agree that there shall be two or more conciliators.

(2)   The parties shall endeavour to reach agreement on a conciliator or conciliators, unless a different procedure for their appointment has been agreed upon.

(3)   Parties may seek the assistance of an institution or person in connection with the appointment of conciliators. In particular:

(a)   A party may request such an institution or person to recommend suitable persons to act as conciliator; or

(b)   The parties may agree that the appointment of one or more conciliators be made directly by such an institution or person.

(4)   In recommending or appointing individuals to act as conciliator, the institution or person shall have regard to such considerations as are likely to secure the appointment of an independent and impartial conciliator and, where appropriate, shall take into account the advisability of appointing a conciliator of a nationality other than the nationalities of the parties.

(5)   When a person is approached in connection with his or her possible appointment as conciliator, he or she shall disclose any circumstances likely to give rise to justifiable doubts as to his or her impartiality or independence. A conciliator, from the time of his or her appointment and throughout the conciliation proceedings, shall without delay disclose any such circumstances to the parties unless they have already been informed of them by him or her.

Article 6. Conduct of conciliation

(1)   The parties are free to agree, by reference to a set of rules or otherwise, on the manner in which the conciliation is to be conducted.

(2)   Failing agreement on the manner in which the conciliation is to be conducted, the conciliator may conduct the conciliation proceedings in such a manner as the conciliator considers appropriate, taking into account the circumstances of the case, any wishes that the parties may express and the need for a speedy settlement of the dispute.

(3)   In any case, in conducting the proceedings, the conciliator shall seek to maintain fair treatment of the parties and, in so doing, shall take into account the circumstances of the case.

(4)   The conciliator may, at any stage of the conciliation proceedings, make proposals for a settlement of the dispute.

Article 7. Communication between conciliator and parties

The conciliator may meet or communicate with the parties together or with each of them separately.

Article 8. Disclosure of information

When the conciliator receives information concerning the dispute from a party, the conciliator may disclose the substance of that information to any other party to the conciliation. However, when a party gives any information to the conciliator, subject to a specific condition that it be kept confidential, that information shall not be disclosed to any other party to the conciliation.

Article 9. Confidentiality

Unless otherwise agreed by the parties, all information relating to the conciliation proceedings shall be kept confidential, except where disclosure is required under the law or for the purposes of implementation or enforcement of a settlement agreement.

Article 10. Admissibility of evidence in other proceedings

(1)   A party to the conciliation proceedings, the conciliator and any third person, including those involved in the administration of the conciliation proceedings, shall not in arbitral, judicial or similar proceedings rely on, introduce as evidence or give testimony or evidence regarding any of the following:

(a)   An invitation by a party to engage in conciliation proceedings or the fact that a party was willing to participate in conciliation proceedings;

(b)   Views expressed or suggestions made by a party in the conciliation in respect of a possible settlement of the dispute;

(c)   Statements or admissions made by a party in the course of the conciliation proceedings;

(d)   Proposals made by the conciliator;

(e)   The fact that a party had indicated its willingness to accept a proposal for settlement made by the conciliator;

(f)   A document prepared solely for purposes of the conciliation proceedings.

(2)   Paragraph (1) of this article applies irrespective of the form of the information or evidence referred to therein.

(3)   The disclosure of the information referred to in paragraph (1) of this article shall not be ordered by an arbitral tribunal, court or other competent governmental authority and, if such information is offered as evidence in contravention of paragraph (1) of this article, that evidence shall be treated as inadmissible. Nevertheless, such information may be disclosed or admitted in evidence to the extent required under the law or for the purposes of implementation or enforcement of a settlement agreement.

(4)   The provisions of paragraphs (1), (2) and (3) of this article apply whether or not the arbitral, judicial or similar proceedings relate to the dispute that is or was the subject matter of the conciliation proceedings.

(5)   Subject to the limitations of paragraph (1) of this article, evidence that is otherwise admissible in arbitral or judicial or similar proceedings does not become inadmissible as a consequence of having been used in a conciliation.

Article 11. Termination of conciliation proceedings

The conciliation proceedings are terminated:

(a)   By the conclusion of a settlement agreement by the parties, on the date of the agreement;

(b)   By a declaration of the conciliator, after consultation with the parties, to the effect that further efforts at conciliation are no longer justified, on the date of the declaration;

(c)   By a declaration of the parties addressed to the conciliator to the effect that the conciliation proceedings are terminated, on the date of the declaration; or

(d)   By a declaration of a party to the other party or parties and the conciliator, if appointed, to the effect that the conciliation proceedings are terminated, on the date of the declaration.

Article 12. Conciliator acting as arbitrator

Unless otherwise agreed by the parties, the conciliator shall not act as an arbitrator in respect of a dispute that was or is the subject of the conciliation proceedings or in respect of another dispute that has arisen from the same contract or legal relationship or any related contract or legal relationship.

Article 13. Resort to arbitral or judicial proceedings

Where the parties have agreed to conciliate and have expressly undertaken not to initiate during a specified period of time or until a specified event has occurred arbitral or judicial proceedings with respect to an existing or future dispute, such an undertaking shall be given effect by the arbitral tribunal or the court until the terms of the undertaking have been complied with, except to the extent necessary for a party, in its opinion, to preserve its rights. Initiation of such proceedings is not of itself to be regarded as a waiver of the agreement to conciliate or as a termination of the conciliation proceedings.

Article 14. Enforceability of settlement agreement

If the parties conclude an agreement settling a dispute, that settlement agreement is binding and enforceable . . . *[the enacting State may insert a description of the method of enforcing settlement agreements or refer to provisions governing such enforcement].*

MODEL STANDARDS OF CONDUCT FOR MEDIATORS

American Bar Association, American Arbitration Association, and Association for Conflict Resolution (2005)

August 2005

The *Model Standards of Conduct for Mediators* was prepared in 1994 by the American Arbitration Association, the American Bar Association's Section of Dispute Resolution, and the Association for Conflict Resolution.[1] A joint committee consisting of representatives from the same successor organizations revised the Model Standards in 2005.[2] Both the original 1994 version and the 2005 revision have been approved by each participating organization.[3]

Preamble

Mediation is used to resolve a broad range of conflicts within a variety of settings. These Standards are designed to serve as fundamental ethical guidelines for persons mediating in all practice contexts. They serve three primary goals: to guide the conduct of mediators; to inform the mediating parties; and to promote public confidence in mediation as a process for resolving disputes.

Mediation is a process in which an impartial third party facilitates communication and negotiation and promotes voluntary decision making by the parties to the dispute.

Mediation serves various purposes, including providing the opportunity for parties to define and clarify issues, understand different perspectives, identify interests, explore and assess possible solutions, and reach mutually satisfactory agreements, when desired.

Note on Construction

These Standards are to be read and construed in their entirety. There is no priority significance attached to the sequence in which the Standards appear.

---

[1] The Association for Conflict Resolution is a merged organization of the Academy of Family Mediators, the Conflict Resolution Education Network and the Society of Professionals in Dispute Resolution (SPIDR). SPIDR was the third participating organization in the development of the 1994 Standards.

[2] Reporter's Notes, which are not part of these Standards and therefore have not been specifically approved by any of the organizations, provide commentary regarding these revisions.

[3] Approved in 2005 by the ABA, the AAA and ACR.

The use of the term "shall" in a Standard indicates that the mediator must follow the practice described. The use of the term "should" indicates that the practice described in the standard is highly desirable, but not required, and is to be departed from only for very strong reasons and requires careful use of judgment and discretion.

The use of the term "mediator" is understood to be inclusive so that it applies to co-mediator models.

These Standards do not include specific temporal parameters when referencing a mediation, and therefore, do not define the exact beginning or ending of a mediation.

Various aspects of a mediation, including some matters covered by these Standards, may also be affected by applicable law, court rules, regulations, other applicable professional rules, mediation rules to which the parties have agreed and other agreements of the parties. These sources may create conflicts with, and may take precedence over, these Standards. However, a mediator should make every effort to comply with the spirit and intent of these Standards in resolving such conflicts. This effort should include honoring all remaining Standards not in conflict with these other sources.

These Standards, unless and until adopted by a court or other regulatory authority do not have the force of law. Nonetheless, the fact that these Standards have been adopted by the respective sponsoring entities, should alert mediators to the fact that the Standards might be viewed as establishing a standard of care for mediators.

STANDARD I. Self-Determination

(A) A mediator shall conduct a mediation based on the principle of party self-determination. Self-determination is the act of coming to a voluntary, uncoerced decision in which each party makes free and informed choices as to process and outcome. Parties may exercise self-determination at any stage of a mediation, including mediator selection, process design, participation in or withdrawal from the process, and outcomes.

(1) Although party self-determination for process design is a fundamental principle of mediation practice, a mediator may need to balance such party self-determination with a mediator's duty to conduct a quality process in accordance with these Standards.

(2) A mediator cannot personally ensure that each party has made free and informed choices to reach particular decisions, but, where appropriate, a mediator should make the parties aware of the importance of consulting other professionals to help them make informed choices.

(B) A mediator shall not undermine party self-determination by any party for reasons such as higher settlement rates, egos, increased fees, or outside pressures from court personnel, program administrators, provider organizations, the media or others.

STANDARD II. Impartiality

(A) A mediator shall decline a mediation if the mediator cannot conduct it in an impartial manner. Impartiality means freedom from favoritism, bias or prejudice.

(B) A mediator shall conduct a mediation in an impartial manner and avoid conduct that gives the appearance of partiality.

(1) A mediator should not act with partiality or prejudice based on any participant's personal characteristics, background, values and beliefs, or performance at a mediation, or any other reason.

(2) A mediator should neither give nor accept a gift, favor, loan or other item of value that raises a question as to the mediator's actual or perceived impartiality.

(3) A mediator may accept or give de minimis gifts or incidental items or services that are provided to facilitate a mediation or respect cultural norms so long as such practices do not raise questions as to a mediator's actual or perceived impartiality.

(C) If at any time a mediator is unable to conduct a mediation in an impartial manner, the mediator shall withdraw.

STANDARD III. Conflicts of Interest

(A) A mediator shall avoid a conflict of interest or the appearance of a conflict of interest during and after a mediation. A conflict of interest can arise from involvement by a mediator with the subject matter of the dispute or from any relationship between a mediator and any mediation participant, whether past or present, personal or professional, that reasonably raises a question of a mediator's impartiality.

(B) A mediator shall make a reasonable inquiry to determine whether there are any facts that a reasonable individual would consider likely to create a potential or actual conflict of interest for a mediator. A mediator's actions necessary to accomplish a reasonable inquiry into potential conflicts of interest may vary based on practice context.

(C) A mediator shall disclose, as soon as practicable, all actual and potential conflicts of interest that are reasonably known to the mediator and could reasonably be seen as raising a question about the mediator's impartiality. After disclosure, if all parties agree, the mediator may proceed with the mediation.

(D) If a mediator learns any fact after accepting a mediation that raises a question with respect to that mediator's service creating a potential or actual conflict of interest, the mediator shall disclose it as quickly as practicable. After disclosure, if all parties agree, the mediator may proceed with the mediation.

(E) If a mediator's conflict of interest might reasonably be viewed as undermining the integrity of the mediation, a mediator shall withdraw from or decline to proceed with the mediation regardless of the expressed desire or agreement of the parties to the contrary.

(F) Subsequent to a mediation, a mediator shall not establish another relationship with any of the participants in any matter that would raise questions about the integrity of the mediation. When a mediator develops personal or professional relationships with parties, other individuals or organizations following a mediation in which they were involved, the mediator should consider factors such as time elapsed following the mediation, the nature of the relationships established, and services offered when determining whether the relationships might create a perceived or actual conflict of interest.

STANDARD IV. Competence

(A) A mediator shall mediate only when the mediator has the necessary competence to satisfy the reasonable expectations of the parties.

(1) Any person may be selected as a mediator, provided that the parties are satisfied with the mediator's competence and qualifications. Training, experience in mediation, skills, cultural understandings and other qualities are often necessary for mediator competence. A person who offers to serve as a mediator creates the expectation that the person is competent to mediate effectively.

(2) A mediator should attend educational programs and related activities to maintain and enhance the mediator's knowledge and skills related to mediation.

(3) A mediator should have available for the parties information relevant to the mediator's training, education, experience and approach to conducting a mediation.

(B) If a mediator, during the course of a mediation, determines that the mediator cannot conduct the mediation competently, the mediator shall discuss that determination with the parties as soon as is practicable and take appropriate steps to address the situation, including, but not limited to, withdrawing or requesting appropriate assistance.

(C) If a mediator's ability to conduct a mediation is impaired by drugs, alcohol, medication or otherwise, the mediator shall not conduct the mediation.

STANDARD V. Confidentiality

(A) A mediator shall maintain the confidentiality of all information obtained by the mediator in mediation, unless otherwise agreed to by the parties or required by applicable law.

(1) If the parties to a mediation agree that the mediator may disclose information obtained during the mediation, the mediator may do so.

(2) A mediator should not communicate to any non-participant information about how the parties acted in the mediation. A mediator may report, if required, whether parties appeared at a scheduled mediation and whether or not the parties reached a resolution.

(3) If a mediator participates in teaching, research or evaluation of mediation, the mediator should protect the anonymity of the parties and abide by their reasonable expectations regarding confidentiality.

(B) A mediator who meets with any persons in private session during a mediation shall not convey directly or indirectly to any other person, any information that was obtained during that private session without the consent of the disclosing person.

(C) A mediator shall promote understanding among the parties of the extent to which the parties will maintain confidentiality of information they obtain in a mediation.

(D) Depending on the circumstance of a mediation, the parties may have varying expectations regarding confidentiality that a mediator should address. The parties may make their own rules with respect to confidentiality, or the accepted practice of an individual mediator or institution may dictate a particular set of expectations.

STANDARD VI. Quality of the Process

(A) A mediator shall conduct a mediation in accordance with these Standards and in a manner that promotes diligence, timeliness, safety, presence of the appropriate participants, party participation, procedural fairness, party competency and mutual respect among all participants.

(1) A mediator should agree to mediate only when the mediator is prepared to commit the attention essential to an effective mediation.

(2) A mediator should only accept cases when the mediator can satisfy the reasonable expectation of the parties concerning the timing of a mediation.

(3) The presence or absence of persons at a mediation depends on the agreement of the parties and the mediator. The parties and mediator may agree that others may be excluded from particular sessions or from all sessions.

(4) A mediator should promote honesty and candor between and among all participants, and a mediator shall not knowingly misrepresent any material fact or circumstance in the course of a mediation.

(5) The role of a mediator differs substantially from other professional roles. Mixing the role of a mediator and the role of another profession is problematic and thus, a mediator should distinguish between the roles. A mediator may provide information that the mediator is qualified by training or experience to provide, only if the mediator can do so consistent with these Standards.

(6) A mediator shall not conduct a dispute resolution procedure other than mediation but label it mediation in an effort to gain the protection of rules, statutes, or other governing authorities pertaining to mediation.

(7) A mediator may recommend, when appropriate, that parties consider resolving their dispute through arbitration, counseling, neutral evaluation or other processes.

(8) A mediator shall not undertake an additional dispute resolution role in the same matter without the consent of the parties. Before providing such service, a mediator shall inform the parties of the implications of the change in process and obtain their consent to the change. A mediator who undertakes such a role assumes different duties and responsibilities that may be governed by other standards.

(9) If a mediation is being used to further criminal conduct, a mediator should take appropriate steps including, if necessary, postponing, withdrawing from or terminating the mediation.

(10) If a party appears to have difficulty comprehending the process, issues, or settlement options, or difficulty participating in a mediation, the mediator should explore the circumstances and potential accommodations, modifications or adjustments that would make possible the party's capacity to comprehend, participate and exercise self-determination.

(B) If a mediator is made aware of domestic abuse or violence among the parties, the mediator shall take appropriate steps including, if necessary, postponing, withdrawing from or terminating the mediation.

(C) If a mediator believes that participant conduct, including that of the mediator, jeopardizes conducting a mediation consistent with these Standards, a mediator shall take appropriate steps including, if necessary, postponing, withdrawing from or terminating the mediation.

STANDARD VII. Advertising and Solicitation

(A) A mediator shall be truthful and not misleading when advertising, soliciting or otherwise communicating the mediator's qualifications, experience, services and fees.

(1) A mediator should not include any promises as to outcome in communications, including business cards, stationery, or computer-based communications.

(2) A mediator should only claim to meet the mediator qualifications of a governmental entity or private organization if that entity or organization has a recognized procedure for qualifying mediators and it grants such status to the mediator.

(B) A mediator shall not solicit in a manner that gives an appearance of partiality for or against a party or otherwise undermines the integrity of the process.

(C) A mediator shall not communicate to others, in promotional materials or through other forms of communication, the names of persons served without their permission.

STANDARD VIII. Fees and Other Charges

(A) A mediator shall provide each party or each party's representative true and complete information about mediation fees, expenses and any other actual or potential charges that may be incurred in connection with a mediation.

(1) If a mediator charges fees, the mediator should develop them in light of all relevant factors, including the type and complexity of the matter, the qualifications of the mediator, the time required and the rates customary for such mediation services.

(2) A mediator's fee arrangement should be in writing unless the parties request otherwise.

(B) A mediator shall not charge fees in a manner that impairs a mediator's impartiality.

(1) A mediator should not enter into a fee agreement which is contingent upon the result of the mediation or amount of the settlement.

(2) While a mediator may accept unequal fee payments from the parties, a mediator should not allow such a fee arrangement to adversely impact the mediator's ability to conduct a mediation in an impartial manner.

STANDARD IX. Advancement of Mediation Practice

(A) A mediator should act in a manner that advances the practice of mediation. A mediator promotes this Standard by engaging in some or all of the following:

(1) Fostering diversity within the field of mediation.

(2) Striving to make mediation accessible to those who elect to use it, including providing services at a reduced rate or on a pro bono basis as appropriate.

(3) Participating in research when given the opportunity, including obtaining participant feedback when appropriate.

(4) Participating in outreach and education efforts to assist the public in developing an improved understanding of, and appreciation for, mediation.

(5) Assisting newer mediators through training, mentoring and networking.

(B) A mediator should demonstrate respect for differing points of view within the field, seek to learn from other mediators and work together with other mediators to improve the profession and better serve people in conflict.

 *Appendix C* **MODEL RULE OF PROFESSIONAL CONDUCT FOR THE LAWYER AS THIRD-PARTY NEUTRAL**

CPR-Georgetown Commission on Ethics and Standards in ADR (2004)

1.1.1. Proposed Model Rule of Professional Conduct for the Lawyer as Third-Party Neutral

The Commission on Ethics and Standards in ADR (sponsored by Georgetown University and CPR Institute for Dispute Resolution) has drafted this proposed Rule for adoption into the Model Rules of Professional Conduct. We offer here a framework or architecture for consideration by the appropriate bodies of the American Bar Association and any state agency or legislature charged with drafting lawyer ethics rules.

The proposed Model Rule addresses the ethical responsibilities of lawyers serving as third-party neutrals, in a variety of Alternative Dispute Resolution (ADR) fora (arbitration, mediation, early neutral evaluation, etc.). As an initial jurisdictional matter, the proposed Rule does not address the ethical requirements of non-lawyers performing these duties or the ethical duties of lawyers acting in Alternative Dispute Resolution proceedings as representatives or advocates.

1.1.2. Proposed New Model Rule of Professional Conduct Rule 4.5 for the Lawyer as Third-Party Neutral

1.1.3. Preamble

As client representatives, public citizens and professionals committed to justice and fair and efficient legal process, lawyers should help clients and others with legal matters pursue the most effective resolution of legal problems. This obligation should include pursuing methods and outcomes that cause the least harm to all parties, that resolve matters amicably where possible, and that promote harmonious relations. Modern lawyers serve these values of justice, fairness, efficiency and harmony as partisan representatives and as third-party neutrals.

This Rule applies to the lawyer who acts as third-party neutral to help represented or unrepresented parties resolve disputes or arrange transactions among each other. When lawyers act in neutral, non-representative capacities, they have different duties and obligations in the areas addressed by this Rule than lawyers acting in a representative capacity. The current Model Rules are silent on lawyer roles as third-party neutrals*, which are

---

* Model Rule of Professional Responsibility 2.4 (see Appendix G) now provides some recognition of the lawyer as third-party neutral.

different from the representational functions addressed by the Model Rules of Professional Conduct and judicial functions governed by the Judicial Code of Conduct.

Contemporary law practice involves lawyers in a variety of new roles within the traditional boundaries of counselors, advocates and advisors in the legal system. Lawyers now commonly serve as third-party neutrals, either as facilitators to settle disputes or plan transactions, as in mediation, or as third-party decision makers, as in arbitration. Such proceedings, including mediation, arbitration and other hybrid forms of settlement or decision-making, occur both as adjuncts to the litigation process (either through a court referral or court-based program, or by agreement of the parties) and outside litigation via private agreement. These proceedings are commonly known as "ADR" processes. Some state ethics codes, statutes or court rules now require or strongly suggest that lawyers have a duty to counsel their clients regarding ADR means.

When lawyers serve as ADR neutrals they do not have partisan "clients," as contemplated in much of the Model Rules, but rather serve all of the parties. Lawyer neutrals do not "represent" parties, but have a duty to be fair to all participants in the process and to execute different obligations and responsibilities with respect to the parties and to the process. Nor do the rules which apply to judges, such as the Judicial Code of Conduct, adequately deal with many issues that confront lawyer neutrals. For example, lawyers who act as third-party neutrals in one case may serve as representational counsel in other matters and thus confront special conflicts of interest, appearance of impropriety, and confidentiality issues as they switch roles. *See Poly Software International, Inc. v. Su*, 880 F. Supp. 1487 (D. Utah, 1995). Unlike the judge or arbitrator who remains at "arms-length" distance from the parties and who hears information usually when only both parties are present, mediators have different ethical issues to contend with as they hear private, proprietary facts from both sides, in caucuses and ex parte communications. *See Cho v. Superior Court*, 45 Cal. Rptr. 2d 863 (1995).

While there continues to be some controversy about whether serving as a mediator or arbitrator is the practice of law or may be covered by the ancillary practice Rule 5.7, it is clear that lawyers serving as third-party neutrals need ethical guidance from the Model Rules with respect to their dual roles as partisan representatives and as neutrals. The drafters believe that it is especially important to develop clear ethical rules when the lawyer, commonly conceived of as a "partisan" representative, takes on the different role of "neutral" problem-solver, facilitator or decision-maker.

Lawyers may be disciplined for any violation of the Model Rules or misconduct, regardless of whether they are formally found to be serving in lawyer-like roles. Accordingly, while other associations provide guidance within specific contexts, *see*, e.g., the Code of Ethics for Arbitrators in Commercial Disputes (American Arbitration Association (AAA)-American Bar Association (ABA), 1977, revised 2004), when lawyers serve as mediators or arbitrators their ethical duties and discipline under the Model Rules of Professional Conduct may be implicated. For these reasons, this proposed Rule is submitted to provide guidance for lawyers who serve as third-party neutrals, and to advise judicial officers and state discipline counsel who enforce lawyer ethical or disciplinary standards.

1.1.4. Scope of the Model Rule

The proposed Model Rule is drafted to govern lawyers serving in the full variety of ADR neutral roles, as arbitrators, mediators, evaluators and in other hybrid processes. (See definitions which follow.) The Drafting Committee believes that a general rule governing lawyers serving in all third-party neutral roles is appropriate because the proposed Rule addresses core ethical duties that apply to virtually all neutral roles. Where different neutral roles give rise to different duties and obligations, the proposed Rule so provides in text or comment. A single rule is also consistent with the generally transsubstantive approach of the Model Rules. As the Model Rules recognize increasing diversity of lawyer roles, *see* Rule 3.8, Special Responsibilities of Lawyer as Prosecutor; Rule 2.1, Lawyer as Advisor; Rule 1.13, Organization as Client, separate rules for lawyers as mediators or arbitrators may be appropriate in the future.

The proposed Rule applies only to lawyers serving as third-party neutrals. Many other professionals now serve as arbitrators, mediators, conciliators, evaluators or ombuds, and other bodies have promulgated transdisciplinary ethical rules relating to those services. When a lawyer serves as a third-party neutral in a capacity governed by multiple sets of ethical standards, the lawyer must note that the Model Rules of Professional Conduct govern his/her duties as a lawyer-neutral and that discipline *as a lawyer* will be governed by the Model Rules. Nor does the Rule govern lawyers in their capacity as representatives or advocates within ADR proceedings. When a lawyer serves as an advocate, representative or counselor to a party in an ADR proceeding, he or she is governed by such other rules as are applicable to lawyer conduct, either before tribunals (Rule 3.3) or in relation to all other third parties (Rule 4.1).

The proposed Rule, where possible, uses the same language and definitions of other lawyer and judicial standards, including formulations from the Model Rules of Professional Conduct, the Judicial Code of Conduct, the Code of Ethics for Arbitrators in Commercial Disputes (American Arbitration Association-American Bar Association, 1977, revised 2004) and the Restatement of the Law Governing Lawyers (2000). As the Preamble to the Model Rules states, these rules are not to be used as liability standards for malpractice or other purposes. On the other hand, the Restatement of the Law Governing Lawyers recognizes that ethical rules and standards are often used for civil liability, as well as for discipline, and this proposed Rule has been drafted accordingly.

1.1.5. Definitions

This Rule is intended to be applied to the duties and responsibilities of lawyers who act as third-party neutrals in the following processes:

I. Adjudicative

Arbitration—A procedure in which each party presents its position and evidence before a single neutral third-party or a panel, who is empowered to render a resolution of the matter between the parties. Arbitrators may be chosen jointly by all parties, by contractual arrangements, under court or other rules, and in some cases, may be chosen specifically by each side. Arbitrators chosen separately by each party to a dispute may be considered "partisan" arbitrators or "neutral" arbitrators, depending on the rules governing the arbitration. If the parties agree in advance, or applicable law provides, the award is binding and is enforceable in the same manner as any contractual obligation or under applicable statute (such as the Federal Arbitration Act or state equivalents). Agreements by the parties or applicable law may provide rules for whether the award must be in writing and what recourse the parties may have when the arbitration is not binding.

II. Evaluative

Neutral Evaluation — A procedure in which a third-party neutral provides an assessment of the positions of the parties. In a neutral evaluation process, lawyers and/or parties present summaries of the facts, evidence and legal principles applicable to their cases to a single neutral or a panel of neutral evaluators who then provide(s) an assessment of the strengths, weaknesses and potential value of the case to all sides. By agreement of the parties or by applicable law, such evaluations are usually non-binding and offered to facilitate settlement. By agreement of the parties or by applicable law or practice, if the matter does not reach a settlement, the neutral evaluator may also provide other services such as case planning guidance, discovery scheduling, or other settlement assistance. By agreement of the parties or applicable law, the neutral evaluator(s) may issue fact-finding, discovery and other reports or recommendations.

Mediation — A procedure in which a third-party neutral facilitates communications and negotiations among the parties to effect resolution of the matter by agreement of the parties. Although often considered a facilitative process (see below) in which a third-party neutral facilitates communication and party negotiation, in some forms of mediation, the third-party neutral may engage in evaluative tasks, such as providing legal information, helping parties and their counsel assess likely outcomes and inquiring into the legal and factual strengths and weaknesses of the problems presented. By agreement of the parties or applicable law, mediators may sometimes be called on to act as evaluators or special discovery masters, or to perform other third-party neutral roles.

III. Facilitative

Mediation — A procedure in which a neutral third-party facilitates communication and negotiations among the parties to seek resolution of issues between the parties. Mediation is non-binding and does not, unless otherwise agreed to by the parties, authorize the third-party neutral to evaluate (see above), decide or otherwise offer a judgment on the issues between the parties. If the mediation concludes in an agreement, that agreement, if it meets otherwise applicable law concerning the enforceability of contracts, is enforceable as a contractual agreement. Where authorized by applicable law, mediation agreements achieved during pending litigation may be entered as court judgments.

IV. Hybrid Processes

Minitrial — A procedure in which parties and their counsel present their matter, which may include evidence, legal arguments, documents and other summaries of their case, before a neutral third-party and representatives of all parties, for the purpose of defining issues, pursuing settlement negotiations or otherwise sharing information. A neutral third-party, usually at the parties' request, may issue an advisory opinion, which is non-binding, unless the parties agree otherwise.

Med-Arb — A procedure in which the parties initially seek mediation of their dispute before a third-party neutral, but if they reach impasse, may convert the proceeding into an arbitration in which the third-party neutral renders an award. This process may also occur in reverse in which during a contested arbitration proceeding, the parties may agree to seek facilitation of a settlement (mediation) from the third-party neutral. In some cases, these third-party neutral functions may be divided between two separate individuals or panels of individuals.

Other — Parties by agreement, or pursuant to court rules and regulations, may create and utilize other dispute resolution processes before third-party neutral(s) in order to facilitate settlement, manage or plan discovery and other case issues, seek fact-finding or concilia-tion services, improve communication, simplify or settle parts of cases, arrange transac-tions or for other reasons. Such processes may be decisional (adjudicative) or facilitative or a hybrid of the two, and they may be binding or non-binding as party agreements or court rules or statutes provide.

Lawyers who provide neutral services as described above shall be subject to the duties and obligations as specified below.

Rule 4.5.1. Diligence and Competence

(a) A lawyer serving as a third-party neutral should act diligently, efficiently and promptly, subject to the standard of care owed the parties as required by applicable law or contract.

(b) A lawyer serving as a third-party neutral should decline to serve in those matters in which the lawyer is not competent to serve.

COMMENT

Diligence

[1] Like its equivalent in representational work (*see* Model Rule 1.3, discussing diligence in the lawyer–client relationship), this Rule requires the ADR neutral to act diligently, efficiently and promptly, subject to the duty of care owed the parties by applic-able law or contract. Other rules or specifications of timeliness and standards of care may be specified in agreements of the parties, rules provided by relevant organizations or by applicable case law dealing with mediator or arbitrator civil liability. The standard of care to be applied to the work of mediators and arbitrators is currently evolving in practice and case law.

[2] The lawyer–neutral should commit the time necessary to promote prompt resolu-tion of the dispute and should not let other matters interfere with the timely and efficient completion of the matter. If a lawyer–neutral cannot meet the parties' expectations for prompt, diligent and efficient resolution of the dispute, the lawyer–neutral should decline to serve.

[3] While settlement or resolution is the goal of most ADR processes, the primary responsibility for the resolution of the dispute and the shaping of a settlement in mediation and evaluation rests with the parties. Accordingly, when serving in a facilitative or eval-uative process (*see* definitions), the lawyer–neutral should not coerce or improperly influ-ence a party to make a decision, to continue participating in the process, or to reach settlement or agreement. *See* Proposed Florida Rules for Certified and Court–Appointed Mediators, Rule 10.031.

[4] When serving in an adjudicative or evaluative capacity, the lawyer–neutral should decide all matters justly, exercising independent judgement, without permitting outside pressure to affect the decision. The lawyer–neutral serving in adjudicative or evaluative roles should be guided by judicial standards of diligence and competence, *see* Model Code of Judicial Conduct, Canon 3B, and other concurrent ethical standards, *see*, e.g., Code of Ethics for Arbitrators in Commercial Disputes (AAA–ABA, 1977) (currently under revision).

Competence

[5] A lawyer should decline appointment as a neutral when such appointment is beyond the lawyer's competence. A lawyer-neutral should serve "only in cases where the neutral has sufficient knowledge [and skill] regarding the process and subject matter to be effective." *Ethical Standards of Professional Responsibility for the Society of Professionals in Dispute Resolution*, adopted June 2, 1986.

[6] In determining whether a lawyer-neutral has the requisite knowledge and skill to serve as neutral in a particular matter and process, relevant factors may include: the parties' reasonable expectations regarding the ADR process and the neutral's role, the procedural and substantive complexity of the matter and process, the lawyer-neutral's general ADR experience and training, legal experience, subject matter expertise, the preparation the lawyer-neutral is able to give to the matter, and the feasibility of employing experts or co-neutrals with required substantive or process expertise. In many instances, a lawyer-neutral may accept a neutral assignment where the requisite level of competence can be achieved by reasonable preparation.

Rule 4.5.2. Confidentiality

(a) A lawyer serving as a third-party neutral shall maintain the confidentiality of all information acquired in the course of serving as a third-party neutral, unless the third-party neutral is required or permitted by law or agreement of all the parties to disclose or use any otherwise confidential information.

(1) A third-party neutral should discuss confidentiality rules and requirements with the parties at the beginning of any proceeding and obtain party consent with respect to any ex parte communication or practice.

(2) As between the parties, the third-party neutral shall maintain confidentiality for all information disclosed to the third-party neutral in confidence by a party, unless the party agrees or specifies otherwise.

(3) A lawyer who has served as a third-party neutral shall not thereafter use information acquired in the ADR proceeding to the disadvantage of any party to the ADR proceeding, except when the information has become publicly known or the parties have agreed otherwise or except when necessary under (b) below or to defend the neutral from a charge of misconduct.

(b) A third-party neutral may use or disclose confidential information obtained during a proceeding when and to the extent the third party believes necessary to prevent:

(1) death or serious bodily injury from occurring; or

(2) substantial financial loss from occurring in the matter at hand as the result of a crime or fraud that a party has committed or intends to commit.

(c) Before using or disclosing information pursuant to section (b), if not otherwise required to be disclosed, the third-party neutral must, if feasible, make a good faith effort to persuade the party's counsel or the party, if the party is unrepresented, either not to act or to warn those who might be harmed by the party's action.

COMMENT

[1] ADR confidentiality is distinctly different from lawyer-client confidentiality, which is defeated when adverse parties reveal information to each other or in the presence of a third party. The extent of ADR confidentiality protections can be determined by contract, court rules, statutes or other professional norms or rules. This Rule addresses the confidentiality responsibilities of the lawyer-neutral and delineates the neutral's duties

to the parties, the process, and the public. *See Poly Software International, Inc. v. Su*, 880 F. Supp. 1487, 1494; *Cho v. Superior Court*, 45 Cal. Rptr. 2d 863 (1995); Symposium, *Confidentiality in Mediation*, Dispute Resolution Magazine (Winter 1999).

[2] Principles of confidentiality are given effect in the laws of evidence (which govern evidentiary uses, restrictions and privileges) and in ethics rules (which establish professional ethical obligations). Privileges apply in judicial and other proceedings in which the lawyer neutral may be called as a witness or otherwise required to produce evidence regarding an ADR process. The rule of confidentiality in professional ethics applies in situations other than those where evidence is sought from the lawyer-neutral through compulsion of law. This Rule is intended to provide the ADR neutral and parties with confidentiality protections for ADR processes, where privacy of the process and unguarded, candid communications are central to their use and effectiveness.

[3] Since there is no attorney-client relationship between parties and lawyer neutrals, and because most disclosures of information in most forms of ADR occur in the presence of the other party, the confidentiality protection guaranteed to clients by their representational lawyers by Rule 1.6 (as well as the evidentiary privilege of attorney-client) does not apply in most ADR settings.

[4] The general rule that lawyers may divulge confidences to facilitate law practice within the firm is not applicable in ADR confidentiality, especially mediation. "Since the essence of mediation is the preservation of confidential communications, most lawyer-mediators are scrupulous not to disclose such confidential information to anyone, even attorneys in their own firm. Mediators may discuss fact patterns or mediation issues with other mediators within the firm or the community of mediators. As a matter of routine, most mediators will screen such comments to ensure that they never reveal names or confidential information." James E. McGuire, *Conflicts in Subsequent Representation*, Dispute Resolution Magazine 4 (Spring 1996).

[5] This rule imposes an ethical duty of confidentiality on the ADR neutral to protect the ADR process and the parties. The rule's confidentiality standards can be altered by agreement of all parties or applicable law.

Many jurisdictions and courts provide confidentiality protections to parties and ADR neutrals as a matter of law. While some statutes are narrowly evidentiary in nature (and govern only the use of information in a court proceeding), other mediation confidentiality provisions include both evidentiary restrictions and broader prohibitions against disclosure. *See* Nancy Rogers and Craig McEwen, *Mediation: Law, Policy and Practice* (Clark, Boardman & Callaghan, 2nd ed., 1994 (state legislatures have enacted over 200 mediation statutes); Elizabeth Plapinger and Donna Stienstra, *ADR and Settlement in the Federal District Courts: A Sourcebook for Judges and Lawyers* (Federal Judicial Center and CPR Institute for Dispute Resolution, 1996) (federal district courts provide for confidentiality of ADR processes by local rule or court orders). Additionally, confidentiality is often provided by contract among parties and neutrals in private forums. *See, e.g., CPR Mediation Procedure*, confidentiality provision at para. 9, in CPR MAPP Series, 1998; *CPR Model Confidentiality Agreement*, in CPR MAPP Series, Confidentiality, 1998.

[6] Since ADR confidentiality can be governed by different and sometimes conflicting sources of law and ethical duties, it is important that the parties and the neutral understand the extent and uncertainties of the ADR confidentiality protections. Accordingly, section (1) requires the third-party neutral to discuss the applicable confidentiality rules with the parties and counsel at the beginning of the process.

Statutory or common law privileges, evidence codes, protective orders issued by courts under discovery or other statutes, as well as party contracts and court rules all can affect the scope of confidentiality for the parties, the third-party neutral and others outside of the particular matter. *See* Rogers and McEwen, supra, at ch.8, Confidentiality. Some states, for example, require mediators to disclose certain information, like the occurrence of child abuse or domestic violence. *See, e.g.*, Cal. Penal Code section 11164. Additionally this Rule, like the ABA's Ethics 2000 Commission's proposed revision of Model Rule 1.6 and the forthcoming Restatement of the Law Governing Lawyers section 117, permits disclosure of information to prevent imminent bodily harm or substantial financial loss. *See* Comment [10] below.

[7] In addition to advising the parties about the scope of confidentiality protections under law and applicable agreement, section (1) also requires the neutral to discuss and obtain party consent regarding the nature of ex parte communications, if any, contemplated by the process. In some mediation processes, for example, parties meet separately with the mediator and share information confidentially. In arbitration processes, ex parte communications with partisan arbitrators may be permitted under certain rules and prohibited under others. *See, e.g.*, Code of Ethics for Arbitrators in Commercial Disputes (AAA-ABA, 1977) (Canon VII.C(2), permitting ex parte communications between the non-neutral arbitrator and the party who appointed them); *cf. CPR Rules for Non-Administered Arbitration*, Rule 9.3, in CPR MAPP Series, Arbitration, 1998 (prohibiting ex parte communications with neutral or party-appointed arbitrators).

[8] Given the extensive use in mediation of separate, ex parte meetings or caucuses with the mediator, parties and their lawyers may reveal information in caucus that is not to be disclosed to the other party without permission. Section (2) establishes that the neutral shall maintain the confidentiality of all information disclosed to the third party in confidence, unless the party agrees or specifies otherwise. In effect, all information revealed in confidence in ex parte sessions or through other confidential means, is to be considered confidential, absent a specific statement or agreement by the party otherwise.

[9] Section (3) prohibits the use by the neutral of any information acquired in the ADR proceeding to the disadvantage of any party, subject to the exceptions stated in the rule. This formulation tracks the current Model Rule 1.9(c)(1) for conflicts of interest for representational attorneys and former clients. Particularly in mediation or other ADR fora where ex parte sessions are used, the third-party neutral may hear information or settlement facts that may not be legally relevant but that are highly sensitive or proprietary. Under this rule, the lawyer-neutral is prohibited from using this information in subsequent neutral or representational work to the disadvantage of the former ADR party.

[10] Like the ABA's Ethics 2000 Commission's proposed version of Model Rule 1.6 and the forthcoming Restatement of the Law Governing Lawyers section 117, this rule permits disclosure by the neutral third party of information to prevent death or serious bodily harm to anyone on the basis of any information learned, and disclosure to prevent substantial financial loss from occurring in the manner at hand, as a result of a crime or fraud one of the parties has committed or intends to commit. Several states, notably New Jersey and Florida, require (not just permit) lawyers to reveal information to prevent death or serious bodily harm, as well as to avoid some criminal acts or fraud on the tribunal, even when learned in an otherwise confidentially protected situation. *See, e.g.*, N.J. Rule of Professional Conduct 1.6.

In many jurisdictions, third-party neutrals are already under an obligation to reveal such information under separate statutes or case law, *see, e.g.*, Cal. Penal Code sec. 11164 (West 1992) (requiring child abuse to be reported); Idaho Rules of Evid. Section 507(4) (West 1998) (child abuse learned about in mediation is not a protected confidence); *cf. Tarasoff v. The Regents of the University of California*, 17 Cal. 3d 425 (1976) (placing an affirmative duty on psychologist to inform patient's intended victim of danger).

Rule 4.5.3. Impartiality

(a) A lawyer who serves as a third-party neutral should be impartial with respect to the issues and the parties in the matter.

(1) A lawyer who serves as a third-party neutral should conduct all proceedings in an impartial, unbiased and evenhanded manner, treating all parties with fairness and respect. If at any time the lawyer is unable to conduct the process in an impartial manner, the lawyer shall withdraw, unless prohibited from doing so by applicable law.

(2) A lawyer serving in a third-party neutral capacity should not allow other matters to interfere with the lawyer's impartiality.

(3) When serving in an adjudicative capacity, the lawyer shall decide all matters fairly, with impartiality, exercising independent judgment and without any improper outside influence.

(b) A lawyer who serves as a third-party neutral should:

(1) Disclose to the parties all circumstances, reasonably known to the lawyer, why the lawyer might not be perceived to be impartial. These circumstances include (i) any financial or personal interest in the outcome, (ii) any existing or past financial, business, professional, family or social relationship with any of the parties, including, but not limited to, any prior representation of any of the parties, their counsel and witnesses, or service as an ADR neutral for any of the parties, (iii) any other source of bias or prejudice concerning a person or institution which is likely to affect impartiality or which might reasonably create an appearance of partiality or bias, and (iv) any other disclosures required of the lawyer by law or contract.

(2) Conduct a reasonable inquiry and effort to determine if any interests or biases described in section (b)(1) exist, and maintain a continuing obligation to disclose any such interests or potential biases which may arise during the proceedings,

(3) Decline to participate as a third-party neutral unless all parties choose to retain the neutral, following all such disclosures, unless contract or applicable law require participation. If, however, the lawyer believes that the matters disclosed would inhibit the lawyer's impartiality, the lawyer should decline to proceed;

(c) All disclosures under (b) extend to those of the lawyer, members of his or her family, his or her current employer, partners or business associates.

(d) After accepting appointment and while serving as a neutral, a lawyer shall not enter into any financial, business, professional, family or social relationship or acquire any financial or personal interest which is likely to affect impartiality or which might reasonably create the appearance of partiality or bias, without disclosure and consent of all parties.

COMMENT

Impartiality

[1] Impartiality means freedom from favoritism or bias either by word or action, and a commitment to serve the process and all parties equally. Section (a) codifies established concepts of neutrality and neutral conduct.

Disclosure

[2] Understanding that absolute neutrality is unobtainable even under the best circumstances, this rule establishes a broad and continuing standard of disclosure by

lawyer-neutrals with the possibility of waiver by the parties. The rule describes the circumstances which should be disclosed in determining whether the neutral third party is without impermissible partiality and bias to serve in the particular matter. This form of disclosure is accepted practice in ADR proceedings, including both arbitration and mediation.

A lawyer, as prospective neutral, should err on the side of disclosure because it is better that the relationship or other matter be disclosed at the outset when the parties are free to reject the prospective neutral or to accept the person with knowledge of the relationship. *See Commonwealth Coatings Corp. v. Continental Co.*, 393 U.S. 145, 151-52 (1968) (concurring opinion). While there is often disagreement over what may reasonably constitute a potential conflict, the growing acceptance of the principle of disclosure acts as some reassurance that potentially disadvantaged parties will be given an opportunity to object or at least investigate further. *See* Christopher Honeyman, *Patterns of Bias in Mediation*, J. of Dis. Res. 141 (1985). Conversely, it allows all parties to select a neutral after full disclosure, where the parties knowingly decide to go forward.

[3] Where possible, best practices suggest that the disclosures should be in writing, as should any subsequent waivers or consents. While the ABA's Ethics 2000 Commission revision of MRPC 1.7 currently requires written disclosures of all representational conflicts and waivers, this section advises, but does not require, the preparation of written disclosures and consents. *Cf.* Calif. arbitration statute, Cal. Code Civ. Proc. section 1281.9 (requires all conflicts disclosures in writing).

[4] What constitutes reasonable inquiry and effort by the lawyer-neutral to uncover interests or relationships requiring disclosure depends on the circumstances. Typically, in matters where the parties are represented, this will involve the prospective lawyer-neutral obtaining from the parties a complete identification of the parties, their representatives, insurers, lawyers, witnesses and attendees at the ADR process and submitting that list to the prospective neutral's conflicts system. *See Al-Harbi v. Citibank*, 85 F.3d 680, 681-683 (D.C. Cir. 1996). We note that there may be a tension under the law between the duty to disclose prior matters, clients, financial holdings etc., and the confidentiality required to be maintained with respect to ongoing or concluded representations and ADR proceedings.

The rule defines the scope of required disclosure to include immediate family members and business partners and associates as defined in Model Rule of Professional Conduct 1.8(I). It also follows Rule 1.10 and Restatement of the Law Governing Lawyers section 203 for definitions of business associations and law firm associations. The rule does not follow the Judicial Code of Conduct Canon 3(E)(1)(d).

[5] Where a lawyer-neutral volunteers to act as a neutral at the request of a court, public agency or other group for a *de minimis* period and *pro bono publico*, section (b)(2) recognizes that there may not be opportunity for full inquiry, disclosure or disqualification challenge. In such circumstances, a third-party neutral may have to proceed with the minimal inquiry and disclosure which may be reasonable under the circumstances. If the lawyer from memory recognizes an interest or relationship relevant to the case, the lawyer should identify that interest or relationship. Otherwise the lawyer should disclose the general nature of the lawyer-neutral's practice and affiliations with law firms or other associations, or other known disqualifying circumstances. *See also* Rule 4.5.4(b).

[6] In general, parties may elect to retain a lawyer as neutral after the latter's disclosure of reasons why the lawyer reasonably might be perceived not to be neutral. However, section (b)(3) imposes on the lawyer-neutral the obligation to decline to serve if the lawyer-neutral believes that the matters disclosed or other circumstances would inhibit the lawyer's impartiality or otherwise impugn the integrity of the process. In such instances,

the lawyer-neutral should decline to serve even if the parties consent to the lawyer's retention as a neutral.

[7] Section (d) tracks language from the Code of Ethics for Arbitrators in Commercial Disputes (AAA–ABA, 1977) (currently under revision) and is intended to prevent partiality from developing through the acquisition of future business during the pendency of an ADR proceeding. The parties may consent to waive this provision. The consent provision may prevent difficulties for third-party neutrals engaged to mediate or arbitrate a number of disputes with the same party, either through contractual appointment predispute or through multiple, simultaneous appointments or appointments during the pendency of a particular case.

Rule 4.5.4. Conflicts of Interest

(a) Disqualification of Individual Third-Party Neutrals

(1) A lawyer who is serving as a third-party neutral shall not, during the course of an ADR proceeding, seek to establish any financial, business, representational, neutral or personal relationship with or acquire an interest in, any party, entity or counsel who is involved in the matter in which the lawyer is participating as a neutral, unless all parties consent after full disclosure.

(2) A lawyer who has served as a third-party neutral shall not subsequently represent any party to the ADR proceeding (in which the third-party neutral served as neutral) in the same or a substantially related matter, unless all parties consent after full disclosure.

(3) A lawyer who has served as a third-party neutral shall not subsequently represent a party adverse to a former ADR party where the lawyer-neutral has acquired information protected by confidentiality under this Rule, without the consent of the former ADR party.

(4) Where the circumstances might reasonably create the appearance that the neutral had been influenced in the ADR process by the anticipation or expectation of a subsequent relationship or interest, a lawyer who has served as a third-party neutral shall not subsequently acquire an interest in or represent a party to the ADR proceeding in a substantially unrelated matter for a period of one year or other reasonable period of time under the circumstances, unless all parties consent after full disclosure.

(b) Imputation of Conflicts to Affiliated Lawyers and Removing Imputation

(1) If a lawyer is disqualified by section (a), no lawyer who is affiliated with that lawyer may knowingly undertake or continue representation in any substantially related or unrelated matter unless the personally disqualified lawyer is adequately screened from any participation in the matter, is apportioned no fee from the matter and timely and adequate notice of the screening has been provided to all affected parties and tribunals, provided that no material confidential information about any of the parties to the ADR proceeding has been communicated by the personally disqualified lawyer to the affiliated lawyer or that lawyer's firm.

(c) A lawyer selected as a partisan arbitrator of a party in a multi-member arbitration panel is not prohibited from subsequently representing that party, nor are any affiliated lawyers.

(d) If a lawyer serves as a neutral at the request of a court, public agency or other group for a *de minimis* period and *pro bono publico*, the firm with which the lawyer is associated is not subject to imputation under 4.5.4(b).

COMMENT
Conflicts

[1] ADR conflicts policy, like all conflicts regulation, has two main objectives: to protect the parties from actual harm suffered by conflicts of interest, and to protect the process, the public, and the parties from the "appearance" of improper influences. In the ADR context, it is essential that conflicts rules protect against both actual harm and the appearance of self-interest.

Modern law practice is increasingly characterized by lawyer mobility, both externally where lawyers move among law firms and organizations, and internally where lawyers on a case-by-case basis move from representative to neutral roles within their law firm and through association with other private or public organizations (such as court or bar volunteer ADR programs). This Rule strives to protect against both actual harm from lawyer role changes, and to protect the ADR processes, the lawyer-neutrals, the parties and the public against the corrosive but less tangible "appearance of impropriety" or "public" harms which threaten the integrity of these processes, the neutrality of the lawyer-neutrals, and the public's confidence in these dispute resolution procedures.

[2] Section (a)(1) governs conflicts which may arise during the pendency of an ADR process and is intended to be a bar against using the ADR process to obtain additional employment or other benefit. Conflicts arising under this section can be consented by all parties after full disclosure.

[3] Section (a)(2) prohibits future representational roles by lawyer-neutrals in the same or substantially related matters, absent disclosure and consent by all parties. This section codifies the rule established in *Poly Software*: "Where a mediator has received confidential information in the course of a mediation, that mediator should not thereafter represent anyone in connection with the same or a substantially factually related matter unless all parties to the mediation consent after disclosure." *Poly Software*, 880 F. Supp. at 1495. We believe that the logic behind *Poly Software*'s prohibition of future representational relationships in the same or substantially related cases also applies to adjudicative processes such as arbitration. Accordingly, under this Rule, a neutral arbitrator is subject to the same restrictions as a mediator, although a partisan arbitrator is excepted from these restriction by Rule 4.5.4(c).

[4] Conflicts may exist when lawyer-neutrals, who have facilitated disputes and learned confidential and proprietary information about the disputing parties, are asked to represent a party adverse to a former ADR party. When trying to facilitate solutions, third-party neutrals may learn significant "settlement facts"—proprietary information about entities or individuals learned within the neutral setting that may not be legally relevant but that affect the possibility of settlement. *See* Menkel-Meadow, *The Silences of the Restatement of the Law Governing Lawyers* 10 Geo. J. Legal Ethics 631 (1997). In this situation, the conflicts issue is whether an ADR neutral who learned facts (e.g., about financial solvency, human relations, product development, acquisitions or entity future plans) during the ADR would or could use those facts against the former ADR party in the subsequent representation. Section (a)(3) addresses this situation by prohibiting a lawyer-neutral from representing a party adverse to a former ADR party where the lawyer-neutral has acquired settlement facts or other information protected by this rule's confidentiality provision, Rule 4.5.2, absent consent by the former ADR party.

[5] Section (a)(4) addresses potential future representational or other relationships between the lawyer-neutral and a party to the prior ADR in unrelated cases. These relationships are often referred to by the bar as "downstream conflicts." The section is designed to protect against the appearance or the actuality that an expectation of a beneficial future relationship or interest has influenced the neutral's conduct in the preceding ADR

process. The language in this section is derived from Canon I.D. of the Code of Ethics for Arbitrators in Commercial Disputes (AAA–ABA, 1977) (currently under revision).

Imputation and Screening

[6] This rule follows the trend of the Restatement of the Law Governing Lawyers and the draft revisions by the Ethics 2000 Commission to Rule 1.10 to provide for screening of lawyer-neutrals disqualified under section (a) in unrelated or substantially related matters. This formulation continues to impute disqualification to the whole firm for the same matter, *see Cho*, (screening not sufficient to defeat law firm's disqualification when the judge who heard the action and presided over confidential, ex parte settlement conferences joined the opposing party's law firm). This rule is premised, in part, on the different confidentiality obligations of third-party neutrals and lawyer representatives. Unlike lawyers representing clients, lawyer-neutrals generally should not share information with other lawyers in their firm, and thus are particularly well-suited for screening. *See* Comment [4] to Rule 4.5.2, Confidentiality, *supra*.

An alternative formulation, which the Drafting Committee rejected, would apply the current non-screen, imputation formulation of Model Rule 1.10. This rule would read: "Unless all affected parties consent after disclosure, in any matter where a lawyer would be disqualified under section (a), the restrictions imposed therein also restrict all other lawyers who are affiliated with that lawyer under Rule 1.10." We believe that a no-screen imputation rule is contrary to the trend in the law, as noted above, and would inappropriately limit the growth of mixed neutral and representational roles for lawyers, with its attendant benefits to both the practice and the public.

[7] Screening in the ADR context involves the same actions as screening in other contexts. *See, e.g.*, Model Rule of Professional Conduct 1.11(a)(1), which permits the law firm of a former government lawyer to undertake or continue representation in a matter in which the former government lawyer participated personally and substantially if the lawyer is screened from further participation in it, including receipt of fees from it; *see also* Restatement of the Law Governing Lawyers. The Annotated Model Rule 1.11 states that: "An effective screen commonly includes the following factors: (1) the disqualified lawyer does not participate in the matter, (2) the disqualified lawyer does not discuss the matter with any member of the firm, (3) the disqualified lawyer represents through sworn testimony that he or she had not imparted any confidential information to the firm, (4) the disqualified lawyer does not have access to any files or documents relating to the matter; and (5) the disqualified lawyer does not share in any of the fees from the matter." *Annotated Model Rules of Professional Conduct* at 186 (3rd ed.). In addition, under the proposed rule, notice of the screening must be provided to all affected parties and tribunals.

[8] Section (c) excepts partisan, party-appointed arbitrators from the restrictions on future representational work under section (a), and from imputation and screening under section (b). We note, however, the lack of consensus regarding the role and practices of partisan arbitrators, and suggest that if "partisan" arbitrators become more like neutral arbitrators, section (c) will need to be amended.

[9] Section (d) excepts lawyer-neutrals and their affiliated lawyers from the imputation and screening rule when the lawyer-neutral volunteers his or her services at the request of a court, other public agency, or institution and serves for a de minimis period.

Rule 4.5.5. Fees

(a) Before or within a reasonable time after being retained as a third-party neutral, a lawyer should communicate to the parties, in writing, the basis or rate and allocation of the fee for service, unless the third-party neutral is serving in a no-fee or pro bono capacity.

(b) A third-party neutral who withdraws from a case should return any unearned fee to the parties.

(c) A third-party neutral who charges a fee contingent on the settlement or other specific resolution of the matter should explain to the parties that such an arrangement gives the third-party neutral a direct financial interest in settlement that may conflict with the parties' possible interest in terminating the proceedings without reaching settlement. The third-party neutral should consider whether such a fee arrangement creates an appearance or actuality of partiality, inconsistent with the requirements of Rule 4.5.3.

COMMENT

[1] This rule requires a written communication specifying the basis, rate and allocation of fees to all parties, unless the third-party neutral is serving in a no-fee or pro bono capacity.

[2] It has become relatively common to use contingent fee or bonus compensation schemes to provide an incentive to participate in ADR or to reward the achievement of an effective settlement. Section (3) of the rule does not prohibit contingent fees (which some jurisdictions or provider organizations do) but requires the third-party neutral to explain what the effects of such a fee arrangement may be, including conflicts of interest. This rule imposes two obligations on the neutral. The lawyer-neutral is required to assess the possible conflicts attendant to use of contingent fees and whether the appearance or actuality of partiality prohibits its use under Rule 4.5.3, Impartiality. If use of the compensation arrangements is not prohibited under that standard, the neutral is required to disclose the possible consequences of this fee arrangement to the parties.

Rule 4.5.6. Fairness and Integrity of the Process

(a) The lawyer serving as third-party neutral should make reasonable efforts to determine that the ADR proceedings utilized are explained to the parties and their counsel, and that the parties knowingly consent to the process being used and the neutral selected (unless applicable law or contract requires use of a particular process or third-party neutral).

(b) The third-party neutral should not engage in any process or procedure not consented to by the parties (unless required by applicable law or contract).

(c) The third-party neutral should use all reasonable efforts to conduct the process with fairness to all parties. The third-party neutral should be especially diligent that parties who are not represented have adequate opportunities to be heard and involved in any ADR proceedings.

(d) The third-party neutral should make reasonable efforts to prevent misconduct that would invalidate any settlement. The third-party neutral should also make reasonable efforts to determine that the parties have reached agreement of their own volition and knowingly consent to any settlement.

COMMENT

[1] While ethical rules cannot guarantee the specific procedures or fairness of a process, this rule is intended to require third-party neutrals to be attentive to the basic values and goals informing fair dispute resolution. These values include party autonomy; party choice of process (to the extent permitted by law or contract); party choice of and consent to the choice of the third-party neutral (to the extent permitted by law or contract); and fairness of the conduct of the process itself. This rule is concerned not only with specific harms to

particular participating parties but with the appearance of the integrity of the process to the public and other possible users of these processes.

[2] This section requires third-party neutrals to make reasonable efforts to determine that the parties have reached an agreement of their own volition, one which is not coerced. While some have suggested that third-party neutrals should bear some moral accountability or legal responsibility for the agreements they help facilitate, *see* Lawrence Susskind, *Environmental Mediation and the Accountability Problem*, 9 Vt. L. Rev. 1 (Spring 1981), these Rules do not make the third-party neutral the guarantor of a fair or just result. (The Kutak Commission rejected an earlier effort to prevent lawyers from facilitating negotiated agreements which would be held unconscionable as a matter of law, *see* Proposed Rule 4.3, Draft Model Rules, 1980.)

[3] This section of the Rule is designed to prevent harm not only to parties engaged in dispute resolution processes, but to the appearances presented to the general public of how legal processes are conducted. Although this section of the Rule may suffer from the same complaints about vagueness as the former Canon 9 "appearance of impropriety" did under the old structure of the Code of Professional Conduct, the drafters believe that where lawyers "switch" sides and roles, from partisan to neutral, it is important to provide for basic criteria of fairness to be monitored in the process for the acceptability and legitimacy of the process and the lawyers within it.

 *Appendix D* AN ALTERNATIVE TO ROBERT'S RULES OF ORDER FOR GROUPS, ORGANIZATIONS, AND AD HOC ASSEMBLIES THAT WANT TO OPERATE BY CONSENSUS

Lawrence Susskind, in
A Comprehensive Guide
to Reaching Agreement
(Lawrence Susskind, Sarah
McKearnan & Jennifer
Thomas–Larmer eds., 1999)

[THE ALTERNATIVE RULES]

STEP 1: Convening

1.1 Initiate a Discussion About Whether to Have a Consensus Building Dialogue.

1.2 Prepare a Written Conflict Assessment.

    1.2.1 Assign responsibility for preparing the conflict assessment.

    1.2.2 Identify a first circle of essential participants.

    1.2.3 Identify a second circle of suggested participants.

    1.2.4 Complete initial interviews.

    1.2.5 Prepare a draft conflict assessment. A draft conflict assessment ought to include a clear categorization of all the relevant stakeholders, a summary of the interests and concerns of each category (without attribution to any individual or organization), and—given the results of the interviews—a proposal as to whether the assessor thinks it is worth going forward with a consensus building process. If the assessor believes such a process should be organized, he or she also ought to recommend a possible agenda, timetable, and budget for the process.

    1.2.6 Prepare a final conflict assessment. Every interviewee ought to receive a copy of the draft conflict assessment and be given adequate time to offer comments and suggestions. The assessor ought to use this period as an occasion to modify the conflict assessment in a way that will allow all the key stakeholders to agree to attend at least an organizational meeting, if a recommendation to go forward is accepted by the convening entity. If key stakeholding groups refuse to participate, the process should probably not go forward. The final conflict assessment ought to include an appendix listing the name of every individual and organization interviewed. In appropriate instances, especially those involving public agencies, the final conflict assessment ought to become a public document.

    1.2.7 Convene an organizational meeting to consider the recommendations of the conflict assessment.

1.3 If a Decision Is Made to Proceed, Identify Appropriate Representatives.

    1.3.1 Identify missing actors likely to affect the credibility of the process.

    1.3.2 Use facilitated caucusing, if necessary.

    1.3.3 Use proxies to represent hard-to-represent groups.

    1.3.4 Identify possible alternate representatives.

1.4 Locate the Necessary Funding.

STEP 2: Clarifying Responsibilities

2.1 Clarify the Roles of Facilitators, Mediators, and Recorders.

    2.1.1 Select and specify responsibilities of a facilitator or a mediator.

    2.1.2 Select and specify the responsibilities of a recorder.

    2.1.3 Form an executive committee.

    2.1.4 Consider appointing a chair.

2.2 Set Rules Regarding the Participation of Observers.

2.3 Set an Agenda and Ground Rules.

    2.3.1 Get agreement on the range of issues to be discussed.

    2.3.2 Specify a timetable.

    2.3.3 Finalize procedural ground rules. The final version of the conflict assessment should contain a set of suggested ground rules. These should address procedural concerns raised in the interviews undertaken by the assessor. The suggested ground rules should be reviewed and ratified at the opening organizational meeting. Most ground rules for consensus building cover a range of topics including (a) the rights and responsibilities of participants, (b) behavioral guidelines that participants will be expected to follow, (c) rules governing interaction with the media, (d) decision making procedures, and (e) strategies for handling disagreement and ensuring implementation of an agreement if one is reached.

    2.3.4 Require all participants to sign the ground rules.

    2.3.5 Clarify the extent to which precedents are or are not being set.

2.4 Assess Computer-Based Communication Options.

2.5 Establish a Mailing List.

STEP 3: Deliberating

3.1 Pursue Deliberations in a Constructive Fashion.

    3.1.1 Express concerns in an unconditionally constructive manner.

    3.1.2 Never trade interests for relationships.

3.1.3 Engage in active listening.

3.1.4 Disagree without being disagreeable.

3.1.5 Strive for the greatest degree of transparency possible.

3.2 Separate Inventing from Committing.

3.2.1 Strive to invent options for mutual gain.

3.2.2 Emphasize packaging.

3.2.3 Test options by playing the game of "what if?"

3.3 Create Subcommittees and Seek Expert Advice.

3.3.1 Formulate joint fact-finding procedures. If left to their own devices, participants in a consensus building process will produce their own versions of the relevant facts (or technical data) consistent with their definition of the problem and their sense of how the problem or issue should be handled. This often leads to what is called adversary science. It is better if all participants can agree on the information that ought to be used to answer unanswered or contested questions. An agreement on joint fact-finding should specify (a) what information is sought, (b) how it should be generated (i.e., by whom and using which methods), and (c) how gaps or disagreements among technical sources will be handled. It is perfectly reasonable for there to be agreement on facts while substantial disagreement on how to interpret such facts remains.

3.3.2 Identify expert advisers.

3.3.3 Organize drafting or joint fact-finding subcommittees.

3.3.4 Incorporate the work of subcommittees or expert advisers.

3.4 Use a Single-Text Procedure.

3.4.1 Draft preliminary proposals.

3.4.2 Brainstorm.

3.4.3 Withhold criticism.

3.4.4 Avoid attribution and individual authorship. Consensus building is best viewed as a group enterprise. When individuals or a single group insists on claiming authorship of a particular proposal (i.e., in an effort to enhance its standing with its own constituents), they are likely to provoke criticism or counter proposals. Consensus is much more likely to emerge if participants avoid attributing or claiming authorship of specific ideas or packages.

3.4.5 Consolidate improvements in the text. As the dialogue proceeds, participants should focus on "improving" a consolidated single text prepared by a drafting subcommittee or a neutral party. Avoid competing texts that seek to maximize the interests of one or just a few parties. When changes to a text are made, do not indicate where they originated. All revisions to the single text need to be acceptable to the group as a whole.   .

3.4.6 Search for contingent options. As the discussion proceeds, participants should search for ways of bridging differences by suggesting contingent agreements. Using an "if...then" format is likely to be helpful. That is, if a set of participants is opposed to the prevailing draft of a recommendation or a consolidated agreement, then the set of participants should suggest the changes necessary for it to accept that proposal.

3.5 Modify the Agenda and Ground Rules (if necessary).

3.5.1 Reconsider the responsibilities, obligations, and powers of sponsoring agencies and organizations. During the course of a consensus building process, it is not inappropriate to revisit the assignment of responsibilities and obligations of sponsoring agencies and organizations set by the participants at the outset. Changes should be made only if consensus can be reached on suggested revisions.

3.5.2 Consider the obligations and powers of late arrivals. During the course of a consensus building process, as unanticipated issues or concerns arise, it may be desirable to add new participants. With the concurrence of the group, representatives of new stakeholding groups—attracted or recruited because of the emerging agreement or shifts in the agenda—can be added. The obligations and powers of latecomers (especially with regard to requesting that issues already covered be reconsidered) should be considered by the full group upon the arrival of new participants. Changes in the agenda or the ground rules should be made only with the concurrence of all parties.

3.6 Complete the Deliberations.

STEP 4: Deciding

4.1 Try to Maximize Joint Gains.

4.1.1 Test the scope and depth of any agreement. The results of every effort to maximize joint gains should be continuously assessed. This is best accomplished by having a neutral party ask whether the participants can think of any "improvements" to the proposed agreement. In addition, it is important to ask whether each representative is prepared to "sell" the proposal to his or her constituents and whether each can "live with" the group's recommendation.

4.1.2 Use straw polls.

4.1.3 Seek unanimity.

4.1.4 Settle for an overwhelming level of support. It is appropriate to settle for an overwhelming level of support for final recommendations or decisions, if unanimity cannot be achieved within the agreed-on time frame. While it is not possible to specify an exact percentage of support that would constitute an overwhelming endorsement, it would be hard to make a claim for consensus having been reached if fewer than 80 percent of the participants in a group were not in agreement.

4.1.5 Make every effort to satisfy the concerns of holdouts. Prior to making its final recommendations or decisions, a consensus building group should make one final attempt to satisfy the concerns of any remaining holdout(s). This can be done by asking those who can't live with the final recommendations or decisions to suggest modifications to the package or tentative agreement that would make it acceptable to them without making it less attractive to anyone who has already expressed support for it.

4.2 Keep a Record.

4.2.1 Maintain a visual summary of key points of agreement and disagreement.

4.2.2 Review written versions of all decisions before they are finalized. A written draft of the final report of a consensus building process should be circulated to all participants before they are asked to indicate support or opposition. Initial drafting responsibility may be allocated to the neutral, but ultimately all parties must take responsibility for a final report if one is produced.

4.2.3 Maintain a written summary of every discussion for review by all participants.

STEP 5: Implementing Agreements

    5.1 Seek Ratification by Constituencies.

        5.1.1 Hold representatives responsible for canvassing constituent responses to a penultimate draft.

        5.1.2 Hold representatives responsible for signing and committing to a final agreement in their own name.

        5.1.3 Include the necessary steps to ensure that informal agreements are incorporated or adopted by whatever formal mechanisms are appropriate. Often, the results of a consensus building process are advisory. Sometimes they must be ratified by a set of elected or appointed officials. Any agreement resulting from a consensus building process should contain within it a clear statement of the steps that will be taken (and who they will be taken by) to ensure that the informal agreement will be incorporated or adopted by whatever formal means are appropriate. For example, informally negotiated agreements can be stipulated as additional conditions when a permit is granted by a government agency or the head of an organization. This must be done according to the rules of the permitting agency or the organization.

        5.1.4 Incorporate appropriate monitoring procedures.

        5.1.5 Include reopener and dispute resolution procedures.

        5.1.6 Evaluate.

Appendix E ADA MEDIATION GUIDELINES

Introduction

The ADA Mediation Guidelines for mediation providers are the product of a national Work Group convened to develop mediation practice Guidelines unique to conflicts arising under the Americans with Disabilities Act (42 USC Sec.12101-12213) ("ADA") and similar laws promoting the eradication of discrimination against persons with disabilities.

The ADA Mediation Guidelines were developed between January 1998 and January 2000 by a Work Group comprised of 12 mediation practitioners, trainers and administrators: Judith Cohen, *Work Group Coordinator*; Melissa Brodrick; Samuel H. DeShazer; Art Finkle; Winnie M. Hargis; David Hoffman; Laura L. Mancuso; Kathryn McCarty; Alice Norman; Elizabeth Plapinger; Anne B. Thomas; and Doug Van Epps.

The Guidelines address ADA mediation issues in the areas of Program & Case Administration, Process, Training, and Ethics. A Draft, and later, the Interim Standards, were widely distributed for public comment during the development period. The final Guidelines could not have been developed at all were it not for the tremendous collaboration and valuable comments contributed by many mediators, stakeholders and advocates. The Work Group expresses its appreciation to the many people who contributed to this effort.

The term "ADA mediation," as used in this document, applies to programs mediating claims arising under the Americans with Disabilities Act and other disability civil rights statutes, such as the Rehabilitation Act of 1973, the Fair Housing Amendments Act of 1988, and comparable state and local civil rights laws. The mediation of special education disputes raises issues that are not addressed here.

The Guidelines provide direction for mediators, administrators, funders and consumers of ADA mediation. They also provide direction for disability access in any type of mediation involving persons with disabilities, such as family, commercial or labor mediation. The Guidelines are available to be followed voluntarily by individual mediators and mediation provider organizations who wish to signal to potential parties and mediation participants their familiarity with disability issues and their commitment to high quality ADA mediation services.

In developing the Guidelines, the Work Group reviewed existing mediator codes of conduct and other relevant documents to ensure that the Guidelines were in keeping with already developed work in the field. The ADA Mediation Guidelines address only issues that are unique to resolving disability-related disputes. The Guidelines do not include basic mediation ethics, general principles of administering a mediation program or educational information about ADA regulations, compliance or disability access. Codes and resources that informed the development of the Guidelines are available to persons seeking additional information on integrating the Guidelines into mediation practice.

Public policy and legal issues often arise in ADA mediations. These Guidelines do not constitute legal advice. Persons interested in ADA mediation are encouraged to consult with attorneys and legal resources for substantive interpretation of the ADA and related disability civil rights statutes and regulations.

The Work Group wishes to thank the Kukin Program for Conflict Resolution at Benjamin N. Cardozo School of Law, under the direction of Lela P. Love, for providing an institutional home for the ADA Mediation Guidelines, published in the Cardozo Journal of Conflict Resolution.

An ongoing discussion of issues related to the ADA mediation and to the Guidelines is posted at *www.adamediation.org/forum.*

February 16, 2000

CONTENTS

1. PROGRAM AND CASE ADMINISTRATION

This section of the Guidelines refers to the administration of mediation programs and to the administration of cases by mediation providers, both mediation provider organizations (any entity that manages or administers mediation services) and private mediators.

a)   **Program Development**

1.   Providers, staff and volunteers involved in ADA mediation in any capacity should be trained in disability-related issues and ADA compliance requirements, according to their particular program's needs and structure.

2.   Mediation providers should be responsive to their constituents. The input of people with disabilities and other stakeholders should be considered in program development and evaluation.

b)   **Disability Access to Mediation**

Mediation providers have obligations to make their services accessible to persons with disabilities. These obligations are articulated in the ADA Title III (Public Accommodations) under which mediation providers would be considered as "Service Establishments," in Title II (Public Service) if they are state or local government entities such as publicly funded court or community mediation programs, and in Title I (Employment) for internal employment dispute resolution programs. Mediation provider organizations and private mediators may not charge the individual with the disability for any expenses relating to making the session accessible.

1.   ADA mediation providers should make all aspects of mediation — ranging from training to mediation sessions — accessible to persons with disabilities, including parties and other mediation participants, staff, volunteers, and mediators. For these purposes, the broadest definition of disability should be applied, including chronic conditions, episodic symptoms and temporary disabilities. This is in keeping with generally accepted mediation principles that the parties be able to participate fully in the process. Persons conducting intake or case development should notify the mediator of a case of any disability accommodation required to enable a party's participation in the mediation.*

2.   Mediation provider organizations should have in place policies and procedures concerning accessibility for persons with disabilities. Essential components include procedures for requesting a disability accommodation, for grieving the denial of accommodations, and a non-discrimination policy that includes disability. The policies and procedures should be communicated to the parties, to mediation participants, to mediators and to staff and volunteers.

c)   **Mediator Recruitment and Selection**

1.   ADA mediation presents complex issues, and mediation provider organizations that provide ADA mediator training should select mediators who have mediation experience in addition to training.

2.   Mediation provider organizations that do not provide ADA mediator training should select as mediators only persons who have completed advanced ADA Mediation Training as set out in Section III of these Guidelines, or who have equivalent knowledge.

3.   Provider organizations should have a diverse pool of mediators. Diversity recruiting efforts should include seeking out qualified mediators who have disabilities.

d)   **Party Capacity**

1.   In order for the mediation process to work, the parties must be able to understand the process and the options under discussion and to give voluntary and informed consent to any agreement reached. Mediators and provider organizations therefore should determine whether the parties in a mediation have the capacity to do

so. In making such determinations, neither the mediator nor the provider organization should rely solely on a party's medical condition or diagnosis. Instead, they should evaluate a party's capacity to mediate on a case by case basis, if and when a question arises regarding a party's capacity to engage in the mediation process and enter into a contract.

2.   This evaluation should be based on several factors. The mediator should ascertain that a party understands the nature of the mediation process, who the parties are, the role of the mediator, the parties' relationship to the mediator, and the issues at hand. The mediator should determine whether the party can assess options and make and keep an agreement. An adjudication of legal incapacity is not necessarily determinative of capacity to mediate.* However, a mediation agreement signed by a person without legal capacity may require co-signing by a surrogate to ensure its enforceability.

3.   Capacity is a decision-specific concept. Capacity to mediate may not be the same as capacity to make financial or health care decisions, to vote, marry, or drive. A party with a judicial determination of incapacity may still be able to participate in mediation. Conversely, a party without such a determination may not have the ability or understanding to participate. If a party appears to have diminished capacity or if a party's capacity to mediate is unclear, the provider organization or the mediator should determine whether a disability is interfering with the capacity to mediate and whether an accommodation will enable the party to participate effectively. If so, the provider organization or the mediator should offer such an accommodation.

4.   The provider organization or mediator should also determine whether the party can mediate with support. If a representative, such as attorney or support person, is present or participating, the party with diminished capacity remains the decision-maker in any agreement.

5.   If, despite support, a party lacks capacity to participate in the mediation, mediation should not proceed unless a surrogate participates in the process to represent the interests of the party and make the mediation decisions in place of the party. Surrogates are defined according to state law, and might be agents under durable and health care powers of attorney, guardians, or family members. The surrogate and the person represented by the surrogate should be present and participate when possible. The mediator should encourage the surrogate to express the party's interests, values and preferences.

e) **Party Preparedness**

1.   Provider organizations and mediators should encourage the parties to become aware of their legal rights and responsibilities under the ADA prior to the mediation so that the parties participate meaningfully and make informed decisions.

2.   While providers may supply parties with educational materials, such as booklets on ADA rights and responsibilities, this information is not a substitute for legal representation. Before the mediation session, and at the outset of the session, parties should be advised that they may obtain independent legal or other representation. Parties in an ADA mediation should also be advised of the risks of not being represented by counsel or of not having a potential agreement reviewed by counsel. The provider or mediator may refer parties to resources to seek representation.

f) **Referral of Cases to Mediators**

The provider organization should provide the mediator with sufficient information about the case to permit the mediator to plan and conduct the mediation competently. Such information may also be conveyed to the mediator directly by the parties, or their representatives, if they are represented. Disability-related information will ordinarily be provided by the parties, and other appropriate mediation participants (particularly representatives and resource persons) during the course of the mediation. However, prior knowledge may be critical to the mediator's effective management of the mediation process. Prior knowledge may also alert the mediator to the need for the participation of a resource person in the session, if the parties or their representatives have not already raised this issue.

2. MEDIATION PROCESS

a) **Mediation Techniques or Methods**

1.   These Guidelines do not advocate a particular mediator orientation, strategies or techniques, except as those may impact disability-related issues.

2.   In ADA cases where reasonable accommodations are an issue, the joint session provides an opportunity for the parties to engage in the "interactive process" (favored by the EEOC, courts and commentators) to identify and evaluate accommodation alternatives (42 USC 12101-1630.9). However, when this process is taking place in the context of mediation, it must be clear that anything said or done — even as part of the interactive process — will remain confidential and inadmissible as evidence in any legal proceeding unless otherwise agreed to by the parties.

b) **Other Mediation Participants**

The role of some mediation participants may overlap. However, the role of mediation participants should be as clearly defined as possible.

1.   Representatives

a. The parties may bring a representative of their choice to the mediation session. A representative is an individual who serves as an agent and advocate for the party, advising, counseling, or presenting the party's views. Unlike a surrogate, who is legally authorized to make decisions on behalf of the party, a representative does not make decisions on the party's behalf. The representative may be a disability rights advocate, expert, vocational rehabilitation counselor, job coach, family member, attorney, union representative, or other person.

b. A party may bring a support person, as a representative or in addition to the representative, to assist the person throughout the mediation process, for example by providing emotional or moral support.

c. Where representation might serve the interests of the parties to ensure effective participation and thoughtful decision-making, the mediator may suggest that the parties (or one party) obtain representation.

d. The roles of support person, surrogate, and representative may vary, depending on the circumstances of the parties, a case or a mediation.

2.   Neutral experts and resource persons

Supplementary disability-related information might be critical to the resolution of a dispute. The parties may engage experts, or with the parties' permission, the mediator may invite a neutral expert to educate the mediator and the parties about the disability and to assist in developing options.

3.   Personal assistants

Persons with disabilities may be accompanied by a personal assistant (PA) who is supervised by the person with a disability and provides physical aid or other assistance. The PA should not speak on behalf of the person with the disability or assist with his/her communication, unless requested to do so by that individual.

4.   Interpreters

A qualified sign language or oral interpreter has the dual role of being a "disability accommodation" for persons who are deaf, hard of hearing, or who have speech disabilities, and of facilitating communication between these persons and other participants in the session. The mediator should allow the interpreter to confer with the individual with a disability to clarify terms before and during the mediation.

3. MEDIATOR TRAINING

a)   ADA Mediator Training Contents

At a minimum, ADA mediator training should include:

1.   Substantive law and procedural issues

a. ADA or other applicable federal or state statutes and/or local ordinances

b. State and federal regulations and policy statements

c. Court decisions applying these legal principles

d. Other related laws (e.g., Family and Medical Leave Act of 1993, Workers Compensation, Age Discrimination in Employment Act, Social Security Disability)

e. Mediating in a unionized setting (for employment mediation training)

f. The administrative processes for handling disability cases in federal, state and local agencies and the courts, where appropriate

g. Settlement/release and employee benefits options (for resolutions where the employee does not return to work)

2.   Disability awareness

a. Disability etiquette* (appropriate ways to interact with people with disabilities) and terminology*

b. Addressing one's own biases about disability*

c. Common disabilities, their impact on persons' functioning, and accommodation options

d. Planning and running an accessible session

e. Disability resources, including sources of information and technical assistance

3.   Practical application

a. Common ADA dispute issues and options in the area to be handled by the mediators (e.g., employment, public accommodations, and housing)

b. Adaptation of mediation techniques to ADA mediation and unique circumstances of people with particular disabilities

c. Ethical considerations

d. ADA Mediation Guidelines

b) **ADA Mediator Training Logistics**

1. ADA mediator training—for already trained, experienced mediators—should be a minimum of fourteen (14) hours in length. The following time guidelines are advisory only, as some subject areas may require more time, based on the needs of the program, and some areas may be combined.

> a. Substantive law and procedural issues—three hours. However, more time may be required, depending on the legal issues covered and the extent of prior legal training of the trainees. Discussion and activities, such as case studies, should be included, in addition to lectures. Legal issues are also covered throughout the entire training through discussion, role-plays, and other practical application activities.

> b. Disability awareness—three hours.

> c. Practical application—eight hours. In addition to presentation of practical ADA mediation skills, this should include role-plays, discussion and other participatory activities. Role-play exercises should be designed to reflect the types of disability-related disputes in which the trainees will likely be involved as mediators.

2. Training should include at least one opportunity for participants to interact personally with a person who has a disability.

3. Each training participant should participate in role-plays of ADA disputes, including role-play as a mediator, and to debrief and receive feedback.

4. A trainer skilled in ADA mediation must be present throughout the training. The section on substantive law and procedural issues may be presented by a non-mediator, and the disability awareness section may be presented by persons with disabilities who do not have mediation expertise.

5. ADA mediation training manuals should include a copy of the laws and regulations applicable to cases that mediators will be mediating, a list of national and local disability-related resources, and basic information about reasonable accommodations and disability etiquette and terminology.

6. Some mediation provider organizations provide ADA mediator training and offer trainees who successfully complete the training opportunities to mediate. Such organizations should require that training participants demonstrate, through an evaluated performance, sufficient competency in the areas of ADA mediation practice addressed in training, before providing mediation services. This may be done after an apprenticeship period, but before the mediator conducts an unsupervised mediation. ADA mediator training programs that do not provide mediation services do not have an obligation to evaluate training participants.

c) **Post-Training/Mediator Support**

1. To ensure quality mediation services, mediator feedback and ongoing support and skills development are recommended. Mediator apprenticeship should include observing actual ADA mediation sessions conducted by experienced ADA mediators, conducting ADA mediations with, or observed by, a skilled ADA mediator, and participating in follow-up debriefing with the observing mediator or co-mediator, including an evaluation of the apprentice's performance.

2. Mediators need to keep abreast of developments in ADA and in the ADA mediation field. ADA mediation provider organizations should require that ADA

mediators fulfill a certain minimal number of continuing education hours annually addressing ADA and other disability-related topics. ADA mediation continuing education may include non-mediation areas such as disability-related public hearings, workshops provided by Independent Living Centers and other disability organizations, or attending workshops on disability issues.

4. ETHICS

The following ethical guidelines are minimum guidelines unique to ADA mediation that mediation provider organizations and mediators should follow. These Guidelines should be considered in conjunction with basic ethical standards of mediation, which are not addressed here.

a) **Mediator Competency**

1.   Mediators should have knowledge of disabilities, disability access, and disability law. This includes being aware of general ADA case law developments and guidance issued by regulatory agencies. The ADA mediator needs to have information about the status of the law to work with the parties effectively in exploring the range of settlement options, and to know if the parties are making informed decisions and enforceable agreements.

2.   ADA mediators should not accept cases for which they are not qualified. Where particular background information is required for ADA mediations, mediators should acquire legal or disability-related information in order to have sufficient knowledge to mediate the case competently.

b) **Fair Process**

1.   The mediator should encourage parties to seek information and advice from relevant sources during the course of the mediation. Agreements should be based on a clear understanding of the issues, options and facts of the particular case. Agreements should never be coerced by the mediator or by the mediation provider organization. The mediator should make every effort to ascertain whether the parties have a sufficient understanding of their rights and obligations under the ADA, and the implications of any (a) agreement that they reach, or (b) decision to reject an offer of settlement.

2.   Where the mediator believes that a party(ies) does not understand the implications of a contemplated agreement, the mediator should encourage the parties to consult appropriate sources of information and advice.

3.   The mediator should terminate the mediation if s/he believes that the parties' agreement would be inconsistent with principles of mediation ethics (such as those listed here and those articulated in the standards of practice listed in Appendix I).

4.   The mediator should ask whether the parties have considered the impact of parties who are not at the table, such as a labor union, on the enforceability, successful implementation or durability of the agreement.

c) **Legal and Disability-Related Information**

ADA Mediators should use their knowledge of the law and disability issues to assess when unrepresented parties need legal or other counsel, or when the participation of an expert or resource person would be advisable. Mediators may encourage one or more of the parties to consider obtaining such assistance where needed. However, such encouragement should be given in a manner that protects the mediation process. Discussing matters of this kind in a private caucus session of the mediation is often preferable to doing so in a joint session.

d) **Confidentiality**

1.   Mediators should maintain confidentiality with respect to disability-related information in arranging access and when conducting the mediation. While the person with the disability may have disclosed his/her disability, there still may be information that the person does not wish to reveal, such as the diagnosis or the severity of his/her limitations or health problems. Where a mediator believes that disclosure of such information would enhance the mediation process or would otherwise be beneficial to the parties, the mediator should invite disclosure by the person with a disability during private caucus, but may not disclose the information without the person's permission.

2.   If a mediator withdraws from a case because the mediator believes that one or more of the parties does not understand the implications of the agreement or the terms of a potential agreement, or for any other reason, s/he should do so in a manner that protects the confidentiality of the parties' communications in the mediation to the fullest extent legally possible.

Note: These Guidelines are not intended to be used in litigation involving the practice of mediation — either as evidence of a standard of due care for ADA mediators or as a measure of "reasonable accommodation" for purposes of establishing liability on the part of mediators. Instead, these Guidelines represent a set of aspirational principles and practices that the Work Group recommends to ADA mediators and mediation providers. The Work Group is not a governmental organization. Therefore, its views on the matters addressed in these Guidelines do not have the force of law in any jurisdiction unless they are adopted by rule or statute by a governmental body.

CPR INTERNATIONAL INSTITUTE FOR CONFLICT PREVENTION AND RESOLUTION MEDIATION PROCEDURE

(Revised and effective as of April 1, 1998)

1. Agreement to Mediate

The CPR Mediation Procedure (the "Procedure") may be adopted by agreement of the parties, with or without modification, before or after a dispute has arisen. The following provisions are suggested:

A. Pre-Dispute Clause

The parties shall attempt in good faith to resolve any dispute arising out of or relating to this Agreement promptly by confidential mediation under the [then current] CPR Mediation Procedure [in effect on the date of this Agreement], before resorting to arbitration or litigation.

B. Existing Dispute Submission Agreement

We hereby agree to submit to confidential mediation under the CPR Mediation Procedure the following controversy:

(Describe briefly)

2. Selecting the Mediator

Unless the parties agree otherwise, the mediator shall be selected from the CPR Panels of Neutrals. If the parties cannot agree promptly on a mediator, they will notify CPR of their need for assistance in selecting a mediator, informing CPR of any preferences as to matters such as candidates' mediation style, subject matter expertise and geographic location. CPR will submit to the parties the names of not less than three candidates, with their resumes and hourly rates. If the parties are unable to agree on a candidate from the list within seven days following receipt of the list, each party will, within 15 days following receipt of the list, send to CPR the list of candidates ranked in descending order of preference. The candidate with the lowest combined score will be appointed as the mediator by CPR. CPR will break any tie.

Before proposing any mediator candidate, CPR will request the candidate to disclose any circumstances known to him or her that would cause reasonable doubt regarding the candidate's impartiality. If a clear conflict is disclosed, the individual will not be proposed. Other circumstances a candidate discloses to CPR will be disclosed to the parties. A party may challenge a mediator candidate if it knows of any circumstances giving rise to reasonable doubt regarding the candidate's impartiality.

The mediator's rate of compensation will be determined before appointment. Such compensation, and any other costs of the process, will be shared equally by the parties unless they otherwise agree. If a party withdraws from a multiparty mediation but the procedure continues, the withdrawing party will not be responsible for any costs incurred after it has notified the mediator and the other parties of its withdrawal.

Before appointment, the mediator will assure the parties of his or her availability to conduct the proceeding expeditiously. It is strongly advised that the parties and the mediator enter into a retention agreement. A model agreement is attached hereto as a Form.

3. Ground Rules of Proceeding

The following ground rules will apply, subject to any changes on which the parties and the mediator agree.

a. The process is non-binding.

b. Each party may withdraw at any time after attending the first session, and before execution of a written settlement agreement, by written notice to the mediator and the other party or parties.

c. The mediator shall be neutral and impartial.

d. The mediator shall control the procedural aspects of the mediation. The parties will cooperate fully with the mediator.

   i. The mediator is free to meet and communicate separately with each party.

   ii. The mediator will decide when to hold joint meetings with the parties and when to hold separate meetings. The mediator will fix the time and place of each session and its agenda in consultation with the parties. There will be no stenographic record of any meeting. Formal rules of evidence or procedure will not apply.

e. Each party will be represented at each mediation conference by a business executive authorized to negotiate a resolution of the dispute, unless excused by the mediator as to a particular conference. Each party may be represented by more than one person, e.g. a business executive and an attorney. The mediator may limit the number of persons representing each party.

f. Each party will be represented by counsel to advise it in the mediation, whether or not such counsel is present at mediation conferences.

g. The process will be conducted expeditiously. Each representative will make every effort to be available for meetings.

h. The mediator will not transmit information received in confidence from any party to any other party or any third party unless authorized to do so by the party transmitting the information, or unless ordered to do so by a court of competent jurisdiction.

i. Unless the parties agree otherwise, they will refrain from pursuing litigation or any administrative or judicial remedies during the mediation process or for a set period of time, insofar as they can do so without prejudicing their legal rights.

j. Unless all parties and the mediator otherwise agree in writing, the mediator and any persons assisting the mediator will be disqualified as a witness, consultant or expert in any pending or future investigation, action or proceeding relating to the subject matter of the mediation (including any investigation, action or proceeding which involves persons not party to this mediation).

k. If the dispute goes into arbitration, the mediator shall not serve as an arbitrator, unless the parties and the mediator otherwise agree in writing.

l. The mediator may obtain assistance and independent expert advice, with the prior agreement of and at the expense of the parties. Any person proposed as an independent expert also will be required to disclose any circumstances known to him or her that would cause reasonable doubt regarding the candidate's impartiality.

m. Neither CPR nor the mediator shall be liable for any act or omission in connection with the mediation, except for its/his/her own willful misconduct.

n. The mediator may withdraw at any time by written notice to the parties (i) for serious personal reasons, (ii) if the mediator believes that a party is not acting in good faith, or (iii) if the mediator concludes that further mediation efforts would not be useful. If the mediator withdraws pursuant to (i) or (ii), he or she need not state the reason for withdrawal.

4. Exchange of Information

If any party has a substantial need for documents or other material in the possession of another party, or for other discovery that may facilitate a settlement, the parties shall attempt to agree thereon. Should they fail to agree, either party may request a joint consultation with the mediator who shall assist the parties in reaching agreement.

The parties shall exchange with each other, with a copy to the mediator, the names and job titles of all individuals who will attend the joint mediation session.

At the conclusion of the mediation process, upon the request of a party which provided documents or other material to one or more other parties, the recipients shall return the same to the originating party without retaining copies.

5. Presentation to the Mediator

Before dealing with the substance of the dispute, the parties and the mediator will discuss preliminary matters, such as possible modification of the procedure, place and time of meetings, and each party's need for documents or other information in the possession of the other.

At least 10 business days before the first substantive mediation conference, unless otherwise agreed, each party will submit to the mediator a written statement summarizing the background and present status of the dispute, including any settlement efforts that have occurred, and such other material and information as the mediator requests or the party deems helpful to familiarize the mediator with the dispute. It is desirable for the submission to include an analysis of the party's real interests and needs and of its litigation risks. The parties may agree to submit jointly certain records and other materials. The mediator may request any party to provide clarification and additional information.

The parties are encouraged to discuss the exchange of all or certain materials they submit to the mediator to further each party's understanding of the other party's viewpoints. The mediator may request the parties to submit a joint statement of facts. Except as the parties otherwise agree, the mediator shall keep confidential any written materials or information that are submitted to him or her. The parties and their representatives are not entitled to receive or review any materials or information submitted to the mediator by another party or representative without the concurrence of the latter. At the conclusion of the mediation process, upon request of a party, the mediator will return to that party all written materials and information which that party had provided to the mediator without retaining copies thereof or certify as to the destruction of such materials.

At the first substantive mediation conference each party will make an opening statement.

6. Negotiations

The mediator may facilitate settlement in any manner the mediator believes is appropriate. The mediator will help the parties focus on their underlying interests and concerns, explore resolution alternatives and develop settlement options. The mediator will decide when to hold joint meetings, and when to confer separately with each party.

The parties are expected to initiate and convey to the mediator proposals for settlement. Each party shall provide a rationale for any settlement terms proposed.

Finally, if the parties fail to develop mutually acceptable settlement terms, before terminating the procedure, and only with the consent of the parties, (a) the mediator may submit to the parties a final settlement proposal; and (b) if the mediator believes he/she is qualified to do so, the mediator may give the parties an evaluation (which if all parties choose, and the mediator agrees, may be in writing) of the likely outcome of the case if it were tried to final judgment, subject to any limitations under any applicable mediation statutes/rules, court rules or ethical codes. Thereupon, the mediator may suggest further discussions to explore whether the mediator's evaluation or proposal may lead to a resolution.

Efforts to reach a settlement will continue until (a) a written settlement is reached, or (b) the mediator concludes and informs the parties that further efforts would not be useful, or (c) one of the parties or the mediator withdraws from the process. However, if there are more than two parties, the remaining parties may elect to continue following the withdrawal of a party.

7. Settlement

If a settlement is reached, a preliminary memorandum of understanding or term sheet normally will be prepared and signed or initialed before the parties separate. Thereafter, unless the mediator undertakes to do so, representatives of the parties will promptly draft a written settlement document incorporating all settlement terms. This draft will be circulated, amended as necessary, and formally executed. If litigation is pending, the settlement may provide that the parties will request dismissal of the case. The parties also may request the court to enter the settlement agreement as a consent judgment.

8. Failure to Agree

If a resolution is not reached, the mediator will discuss with the parties the possibility of their agreeing on advisory or binding arbitration, "last offer" arbitration or another form of ADR. If the parties agree in principle, the mediator may offer to assist them in structuring a procedure designed to result in a prompt, economical process. The mediator will not serve as arbitrator, unless all parties agree.

9. Confidentiality

The entire mediation process is confidential. Unless agreed among all the parties or required to do so by law, the parties and the mediator shall not disclose to any person who is not associated with participants in the process, including any judicial officer, any information regarding the process (including pre-process exchanges and agreements), contents (including written and oral information), settlement terms or outcome of the proceeding. If litigation is pending, the participants may, however, advise the court of the schedule and overall status of the mediation for purposes of litigation management. Any written settlement agreement resulting from the mediation may be disclosed for purposes of enforcement.

Under this procedure, the entire process is a compromise negotiation subject to Federal Rule of Evidence 408 and all state counterparts, together with any applicable statute protecting the confidentiality of mediation. All offers, promises, conduct and statements, whether oral or written, made in the course of the proceeding by any of the parties, their agents, employees, experts and attorneys, and by the mediator are confidential. Such offers, promises, conduct and statements are privileged under any applicable mediation privilege and are inadmissible and not discoverable for any purpose, including impeachment, in litigation between the parties. However, evidence that is otherwise admissible or discoverable shall not be rendered inadmissible or non-discoverable solely as a result of its presentation or use during the mediation.

The exchange of any tangible material shall be without prejudice to any claim that such material is privileged or protected as work-product within the meaning of Federal Rule of Civil Procedure 26 and all state and local counterparts.

The mediator and any documents and information in the mediator's possession will not be subpoenaed in any such investigation, action or proceeding, and all parties will oppose any effort to have the mediator or documents subpoenaed. The mediator will promptly advise the parties of any attempt to compel him/her to divulge information received in mediation.

CPR Model Agreement for Parties and Mediator

Agreement made (date) _____, _____

between _____

represented by _____

and _____

represented by _____

and (the Mediator) _____

A dispute has arisen between the parties (the "Dispute"). The parties have agreed to participate in a mediation proceeding (the "Proceeding") under the CPR Mediation Procedure [as modified by mutual agreement] (the "Procedure"). The parties have chosen the Mediator for the Proceeding. The parties and the Mediator agree as follows:

A. Duties and Obligations

1. Mediator and each of the parties agree to be bound by and to comply faithfully with the Procedure, including without limitation the provisions regarding confidentiality.
2. The Mediator has no previous commitments that may significantly delay the expeditious conduct of the proceeding and will not make any such commitments.
3. The Mediator, the CPR Institute for Dispute Resolution (CPR) and their employees, agents and partners shall not be liable for any act or omission in connection with the Proceeding, other than as a result of its/his/her own willful misconduct.

B. Disclosure of Prior Relationships

1. The Mediator has made a reasonable effort to learn and has disclosed to the parties in writing (a) all business or professional relationships the Mediator and/or the Mediator's firm have had with the parties or their law firms within the past five years, including all instances in which the Mediator or the Mediator's firm served as an attorney for any party or adverse to any party; (b) any financial interest the Mediator has in any party; (c) any significant social, business or professional relationship the Mediator has had with an officer or employee of a party or with an individual representing a party in the Proceeding; and (d) any other circumstances that may create doubt regarding the Mediator's impartiality in the Proceeding.
2. Each party and its law firm has made a reasonable effort to learn and has disclosed to every other party and the Mediator in writing any relationships of a nature described in paragraph B.1. not previously identified and disclosed by the Mediator.
3. The parties and the Mediator are satisfied that any relationships disclosed pursuant to paragraphs B.1. and B.2. will not affect the Mediator's independence or impartiality. Notwithstanding such relationships or others the Mediator and the parties did not discover despite good faith efforts, the parties wish the Mediator to serve in the Proceeding, waiving any claim based on said relationships, and the Mediator agrees to so serve.
4. The disclosure obligations in paragraphs B.1. and B.2. are continuing until the Proceeding is concluded. The ability of the Mediator to continue serving in this capacity shall be explored with each such disclosure.

C. Future Relationships

1. Neither the Mediator nor the Mediator's firm shall undertake any work for or against a party regarding the Dispute.

2. Neither the Mediator nor any person assisting the Mediator with this Proceeding shall personally work on any matter for or against a party, regardless of specific subject matter, prior to six months following cessation of the Mediator's services in the Proceeding.

3. The Mediator's firm may work on matters for or against a party during the pendency of the Proceeding if such matters are unrelated to the Dispute. The Mediator shall establish appropriate safeguards to insure that other members and employees of the firm working on the Dispute do not have access to any confidential information obtained by the Mediator during the course of the Proceeding.

D. Compensation

1. The Mediator shall be compensated for time expended in connection with the Proceeding at the rate of $_____, plus reasonable travel and other out-of-pocket expenses. The Mediator's fee shall be shared equally by the parties. No part of such fee shall accrue to CPR.

2. The Mediator may utilize members and employees of the firm to assist in connection with the Proceeding and may bill the parties for the time expended by any such persons, to the extent and at a rate agreed upon in advance by the parties.

_____   _____
Party   Party

by   by

_____   _____
Party's Attorney   Party's Attorney

_____
Mediator

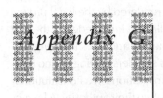

Appendix G MODEL RULES OF PROFESSIONAL CONDUCT (2004) (SELECTED RULES AND COMMENTS)

American Bar Association

PREAMBLE: A Lawyer's Responsibilities

[1] A lawyer, as a member of the legal profession, is a representative of clients, an officer of the legal system and a public citizen having special responsibility for the quality of justice.

[2] As a representative of clients, a lawyer performs various functions. As advisor, a lawyer provides a client with an informed understanding of the client's legal rights and obligations and explains their practical implications. As advocate, a lawyer zealously asserts the client's position under the rules of the adversary system. As negotiator, a lawyer seeks a result advantageous to the client but consistent with requirements of honest dealings with others. As an evaluator, a lawyer acts by examining a client's legal affairs and reporting about them to the client or to others.

[3] In addition to these representational functions, a lawyer may serve as a third-party neutral, a nonrepresentational role helping the parties to resolve a dispute or other matter. Some of these Rules apply directly to lawyers who are or have served as third-party neutrals. See, e.g., Rules 1.12 and 2.4. In addition, there are Rules that apply to lawyers who are not active in the practice of law or to practicing lawyers even when they are acting in a nonprofessional capacity. For example, a lawyer who commits fraud in the conduct of a business is subject to discipline for engaging in conduct involving dishonesty, fraud, deceit or misrepresentation. See Rule 8.4.

[4] In all professional functions a lawyer should be competent, prompt and diligent. A lawyer should maintain communication with a client concerning the representation. A lawyer should keep in confidence information relating to representation of a client except so far as disclosure is required or permitted by the Rules of Professional Conduct or other law.

[5] A lawyer's conduct should conform to the requirements of the law, both in professional service to clients and in the lawyer's business and personal affairs. A lawyer should use the law's procedures only for legitimate purposes and not to harass or intimidate others. A lawyer should demonstrate respect for the legal system and for those who serve it, including judges, other lawyers and public officials. While it is a lawyer's duty, when necessary, to challenge the rectitude of official action, it is also a lawyer's duty to uphold legal process.

[6]   As a public citizen, a lawyer should seek improvement of the law, access to the legal system, the administration of justice and the quality of service rendered by the legal profession. As a member of a learned profession, a lawyer should cultivate knowledge of the law beyond its use for clients, employ that knowledge in reform of the law and work to strengthen legal education. In addition, a lawyer should further the public's understanding of and confidence in the rule of law and the justice system because legal institutions in a constitutional democracy depend on popular participation and support to maintain their authority. A lawyer should be mindful of deficiencies in the administration of justice and of the fact that the poor, and sometimes persons who are not poor, cannot afford adequate legal assistance. Therefore, all lawyers should devote professional time and resources and use civic influence to ensure equal access to our system of justice for all those who because of economic or social barriers cannot afford or secure adequate legal counsel. A lawyer should aid the legal profession in pursuing these objectives and should help the bar regulate itself in the public interest.

[7]   Many of a lawyer's professional responsibilities are prescribed in the Rules of Professional Conduct, as well as substantive and procedural law. However, a lawyer is also guided by personal conscience and the approbation of professional peers. A lawyer should strive to attain the highest level of skill, to improve the law and the legal profession and to exemplify the legal profession's ideals of public service.

[8]   A lawyer's responsibilities as a representative of clients, an officer of the legal system and a public citizen are usually harmonious. Thus, when an opposing party is well represented, a lawyer can be a zealous advocate on behalf of a client and at the same time assume that justice is being done. So also, a lawyer can be sure that preserving client confidences ordinarily serves the public interest because people are more likely to seek legal advice, and thereby heed their legal obligations, when they know their communications will be private.

[9]   In the nature of law practice, however, conflicting responsibilities are encountered. Virtually all difficult ethical problems arise from conflict between a lawyer's responsibilities to clients, to the legal system and to the lawyer's own interest in remaining an ethical person while earning a satisfactory living. The Rules of Professional Conduct often prescribe terms for resolving such conflicts. Within the framework of these Rules, however, many difficult issues of professional discretion can arise. Such issues must be resolved through the exercise of sensitive professional and moral judgment guided by the basic principles underlying the Rules. These principles include the lawyer's obligation zealously to protect and pursue a client's legitimate interests, within the bounds of the law, while maintaining a professional, courteous and civil attitude toward all persons involved in the legal system.

[10]   The legal profession is largely self-governing. Although other professions also have been granted powers of self-government, the legal profession is unique in this respect because of the close relationship between the profession and the processes of government and law enforcement. This connection is manifested in the fact that ultimate authority over the legal profession is vested largely in the courts.

[11]   To the extent that lawyers meet the obligations of their professional calling, the occasion for government regulation is obviated. Self-regulation also helps maintain the legal profession's independence from government domination. An independent legal profession is an important force in preserving government under law, for abuse of legal authority is more readily challenged by a profession whose members are not dependent on government for the right to practice.

[12] The legal profession's relative autonomy carries with it special responsibilities of self-government. The profession has a responsibility to assure that its regulations are conceived in the public interest and not in furtherance of parochial or self-interested concerns of the bar. Every lawyer is responsible for observance of the Rules of Professional Conduct. A lawyer should also aid in securing their observance by other lawyers. Neglect of these responsibilities compromises the independence of the profession and the public interest which it serves.

[13] Lawyers play a vital role in the preservation of society. The fulfillment of this role requires an understanding by lawyers of their relationship to our legal system. The Rules of Professional Conduct, when properly applied, serve to define that relationship.

SCOPE

[14] The Rules of Professional Conduct are rules of reason. They should be interpreted with reference to the purposes of legal representation and of the law itself. Some of the Rules are imperatives, cast in the terms "shall" or "shall not." These define proper conduct for purposes of professional discipline. Others, generally cast in the term "may," are permissive and define areas under the Rules in which the lawyer has discretion to exercise professional judgment. No disciplinary action should be taken when the lawyer chooses not to act or acts within the bounds of such discretion. Other Rules define the nature of relationships between the lawyer and others. The Rules are thus partly obligatory and disciplinary and partly constitutive and descriptive in that they define a lawyer's professional role. Many of the Comments use the term "should." Comments do not add obligations to the Rules but provide guidance for practicing in compliance with the Rules.

[15] The Rules presuppose a larger legal context shaping the lawyer's role. That context includes court rules and statutes relating to matters of licensure, laws defining specific obligations of lawyers and substantive and procedural law in general. The Comments are sometimes used to alert lawyers to their responsibilities under such other law.

[16] Compliance with the Rules, as with all law in an open society, depends primarily upon understanding and voluntary compliance, secondarily upon reinforcement by peer and public opinion and finally, when necessary, upon enforcement through disciplinary proceedings. The Rules do not, however, exhaust the moral and ethical considerations that should inform a lawyer, for no worthwhile human activity can be completely defined by legal rules. The Rules simply provide a framework for the ethical practice of law.

[17] Furthermore, for purposes of determining the lawyer's authority and responsibility, principles of substantive law external to these Rules determine whether a client-lawyer relationship exists. Most of the duties flowing from the client-lawyer relationship attach only after the client has requested the lawyer to render legal services and the lawyer has agreed to do so. But there are some duties, such as that of confidentiality under Rule 1.6, that attach when the lawyer agrees to consider whether a client-lawyer relationship shall be established. See Rule 1.18. Whether a client-lawyer relationship exists for any specific purpose can depend on the circumstances and may be a question of fact.

[18] Under various legal provisions, including constitutional, statutory and common law, the responsibilities of government lawyers may include authority concerning legal matters that ordinarily reposes in the client in private client-lawyer relationships. For example, a lawyer for a government agency may have authority on behalf of the government to decide upon settlement or whether to appeal from an adverse judgment. Such

authority in various respects is generally vested in the attorney general and the state's attorney in state government, and their federal counterparts, and the same may be true of other government law officers. Also, lawyers under the supervision of these officers may be authorized to represent several government agencies in intragovernmental legal controversies in circumstances where a private lawyer could not represent multiple private clients. These Rules do not abrogate any such authority.

[19] Failure to comply with an obligation or prohibition imposed by a Rule is a basis for invoking the disciplinary process. The Rules presuppose that disciplinary assessment of a lawyer's conduct will be made on the basis of the facts and circumstances as they existed at the time of the conduct in question and in recognition of the fact that a lawyer often has to act upon uncertain or incomplete evidence of the situation. Moreover, the Rules presuppose that whether or not discipline should be imposed for a violation, and the severity of a sanction, depend on all the circumstances, such as the willfulness and seriousness of the violation, extenuating factors and whether there have been previous violations.

[20] Violation of a Rule should not itself give rise to a cause of action against a lawyer nor should it create any presumption in such a case that a legal duty has been breached. In addition, violation of a Rule does not necessarily warrant any other nondisciplinary remedy, such as disqualification of a lawyer in pending litigation. The Rules are designed to provide guidance to lawyers and to provide a structure for regulating conduct through disciplinary agencies. They are not designed to be a basis for civil liability. Furthermore, the purpose of the Rules can be subverted when they are invoked by opposing parties as procedural weapons. The fact that a Rule is a just basis for a lawyer's self-assessment, or for sanctioning a lawyer under the administration of a disciplinary authority, does not imply that an antagonist in a collateral proceeding or transaction has standing to seek enforcement of the Rule. Nevertheless, since the Rules do establish standards of conduct by lawyers, a lawyer's violation of a Rule may be evidence of breach of the applicable standard of conduct.

[21] The Comment accompanying each Rule explains and illustrates the meaning and purpose of the Rule. The Preamble and this note on Scope provide general orientation. The Comments are intended as guides to interpretation, but the text of each Rule is authoritative.

RULE 1.0. Terminology

(a) **"Belief" or "believes" denotes that the person involved actually supposed the fact in question to be true. A person's belief may be inferred from circumstances.**

(b) **"Confirmed in writing," when used in reference to the informed consent of a person, denotes informed consent that is given in writing by the person or a writing that a lawyer promptly transmits to the person confirming an oral informed consent. See paragraph (e) for the definition of "informed consent." If it is not feasible to obtain or transmit the writing at the time the person gives informed consent, then the lawyer must obtain or transmit it within a reasonable time thereafter.**

(c) **"Firm" or "law firm" denotes a lawyer or lawyers in a law partnership, professional corporation, sole proprietorship or other association authorized to practice law; or lawyers employed in a legal services organization or the legal department of a corporation or other organization.**

(d) "Fraud" or "fraudulent" denotes conduct that is fraudulent under the substantive or procedural law of the applicable jurisdiction and has a purpose to deceive.

(e) "Informed consent" denotes the agreement by a person to a proposed course of conduct after the lawyer has communicated adequate information and explanation about the material risks of and reasonably available alternatives to the proposed course of conduct.

(f) "Knowingly," "known," or "knows" denotes actual knowledge of the fact in question. A person's knowledge may be inferred from circumstances.

(g) "Partner" denotes a member of a partnership, a shareholder in a law firm organized as a professional corporation, or a member of an association authorized to practice law.

(h) "Reasonable" or "reasonably" when used in relation to conduct by a lawyer denotes the conduct of a reasonably prudent and competent lawyer.

(i) "Reasonable belief" or "reasonably believes" when used in reference to a lawyer denotes that the lawyer believes the matter in question and that the circumstances are such that the belief is reasonable.

(j) "Reasonably should know" when used in reference to a lawyer denotes that a lawyer of reasonable prudence and competence would ascertain the matter in question.

(k) "Screened" denotes the isolation of a lawyer from any participation in a matter through the timely imposition of procedures within a firm that are reasonably adequate under the circumstances to protect information that the isolated lawyer is obligated to protect under these Rules or other law.

(l) "Substantial" when used in reference to degree or extent denotes a material matter of clear and weighty importance.

(m) "Tribunal" denotes a court, an arbitrator in a binding arbitration proceeding or a legislative body, administrative agency or other body acting in an adjudicative capacity. A legislative body, administrative agency or other body acts in an adjudicative capacity when a neutral official, after the presentation of evidence or legal argument by a party or parties, will render a binding legal judgment directly affecting a party's interests in a particular matter.

(n) "Writing" or "written" denotes a tangible or electronic record of a communication or representation, including handwriting, typewriting, printing, photostating, photography, audio or videorecording and e-mail. A "signed" writing includes an electronic sound, symbol or process attached to or logically associated with a writing and executed or adopted by a person with the intent to sign the writing.

COMMENT

Confirmed in Writing

[1] If it is not feasible to obtain or transmit a written confirmation at the time the client gives informed consent, then the lawyer must obtain or transmit it within a reasonable time thereafter. If a lawyer has obtained a client's informed consent, the lawyer may act in reliance on that consent so long as it is confirmed in writing within a reasonable time thereafter.

Firm

[2] Whether two or more lawyers constitute a firm within paragraph (c) can depend on the specific facts. For example, two practitioners who share office space

and occasionally consult or assist each other ordinarily would not be regarded as constituting a firm. However, if they present themselves to the public in a way that suggests that they are a firm or conduct themselves as a firm, they should be regarded as a firm for purposes of the Rules. The terms of any formal agreement between associated lawyers are relevant in determining whether they are a firm, as is the fact that they have mutual access to information concerning the clients they serve. Furthermore, it is relevant in doubtful cases to consider the underlying purpose of the Rule that is involved. A group of lawyers could be regarded as a firm for purposes of the Rule that the same lawyer should not represent opposing parties in litigation, while it might not be so regarded for purposes of the Rule that information acquired by one lawyer is attributed to another.

[3] With respect to the law department of an organization, including the government, there is ordinarily no question that the members of the department constitute a firm within the meaning of the Rules of Professional Conduct. There can be uncertainty, however, as to the identity of the client. For example, it may not be clear whether the law department of a corporation represents a subsidiary or an affiliated corporation, as well as the corporation by which the members of the department are directly employed. A similar question can arise concerning an unincorporated association and its local affiliates.

[4] Similar questions can also arise with respect to lawyers in legal aid and legal services organizations. Depending upon the structure of the organization, the entire organization or different components of it may constitute a firm or firms for purposes of these Rules.

Fraud

[5] When used in these Rules, the terms "fraud" or "fraudulent" refer to conduct that is characterized as such under the substantive or procedural law of the applicable jurisdiction and has a purpose to deceive. This does not include merely negligent misrepresentation or negligent failure to apprise another of relevant information. For purposes of these Rules, it is not necessary that anyone has suffered damages or relied on the misrepresentation or failure to inform.

Informed Consent

[6] Many of the Rules of Professional Conduct require the lawyer to obtain the informed consent of a client or other person (e.g., a former client or, under certain circumstances, a prospective client) before accepting or continuing representation or pursuing a course of conduct. See, e.g., Rules 1.2(c), 1.6(a) and 1.7(b). The communication necessary to obtain such consent will vary according to the Rule involved and the circumstances giving rise to the need to obtain informed consent. The lawyer must make reasonable efforts to ensure that the client or other person possesses information reasonably adequate to make an informed decision. Ordinarily, this will require communication that includes a disclosure of the facts and circumstances giving rise to the situation, any explanation reasonably necessary to inform the client or other person of the material advantages and disadvantages of the proposed course of conduct and a discussion of the client's or other person's options and alternatives. In some circumstances it may be appropriate for a lawyer to advise a client or other person to seek the advice of other counsel. A lawyer need not inform a client or other person of facts or implications already known to the client or other person; nevertheless, a lawyer who does not personally inform the client or other person assumes the risk that the client or other person is inadequately informed and the consent is invalid. In determining whether the information and explanation provided are reasonably adequate, relevant factors include whether the client or other person is experienced in legal matters generally and in making decisions of the type involved, and whether the client

or other person is independently represented by other counsel in giving the consent. Normally, such persons need less information and explanation than others, and generally a client or other person who is independently represented by other counsel in giving the consent should be assumed to have given informed consent.

[7] Obtaining informed consent will usually require an affirmative response by the client or other person. In general, a lawyer may not assume consent from a client's or other person's silence. Consent may be inferred, however, from the conduct of a client or other person who has reasonably adequate information about the matter. A number of Rules require that a person's consent be confirmed in writing. See Rules 1.7(b) and 1.9(a). For a definition of "writing" and "confirmed in writing," see paragraphs (n) and (b). Other Rules require that a client's consent be obtained in a writing signed by the client. See, e.g., Rules 1.8(a) and (g). For a definition of "signed," see paragraph (n).

Screened

[8] This definition applies to situations where screening of a personally disqualified lawyer is permitted to remove imputation of a conflict of interest under Rules 1.11, 1.12 or 1.18.

[9] The purpose of screening is to assure the affected parties that confidential information known by the personally disqualified lawyer remains protected. The personally disqualified lawyer should acknowledge the obligation not to communicate with any of the other lawyers in the firm with respect to the matter. Similarly, other lawyers in the firm who are working on the matter should be informed that the screening is in place and that they may not communicate with the personally disqualified lawyer with respect to the matter. Additional screening measures that are appropriate for the particular matter will depend on the circumstances. To implement, reinforce and remind all affected lawyers of the presence of the screening, it may be appropriate for the firm to undertake such procedures as a written undertaking by the screened lawyer to avoid any communication with other firm personnel and any contact with any firm files or other materials relating to the matter, written notice and instructions to all other firm personnel forbidding any communication with the screened lawyer relating to the matter, denial of access by the screened lawyer to firm files or other materials relating to the matter and periodic reminders of the screen to the screened lawyer and all other firm personnel.

[10] In order to be effective, screening measures must be implemented as soon as practical after a lawyer or law firm knows or reasonably should know that there is a need for screening.

CLIENT-LAWYER RELATIONSHIP
RULE 1.2. Scope of Representation and Allocation of Authority Between Client and Lawyer

(a) Subject to paragraphs (c) and (d), a lawyer shall abide by a client's decisions concerning the objectives of representation and, as required by Rule 1.4, shall consult with the client as to the means by which they are to be pursued. A lawyer may take such action on behalf of the client as is impliedly authorized to carry out the representation. A lawyer shall abide by a client's decision whether to settle a matter. In a criminal case, the lawyer shall abide by the client's decision, after consultation with the lawyer, as to a plea to be entered, whether to waive jury trial and whether the client will testify.

(b)   A lawyer's representation of a client, including representation by appointment, does not constitute an endorsement of the client's political, economic, social or moral views or activities.

(c)   A lawyer may limit the scope of the representation if the limitation is reasonable under the circumstances and the client gives informed consent.

(d)   A lawyer shall not counsel a client to engage, or assist a client, in conduct that the lawyer knows is criminal or fraudulent, but a lawyer may discuss the legal consequences of any proposed course of conduct with a client and may counsel or assist a client to make a good faith effort to determine the validity, scope, meaning or application of the law.

COMMENT

Allocation of Authority Between Client and Lawyer

[1] Paragraph (a) confers upon the client the ultimate authority to determine the purposes to be served by legal representation, within the limits imposed by law and the lawyer's professional obligations. The decisions specified in paragraph (a), such as whether to settle a civil matter, must also be made by the client. See Rule 1.4(a)(1) for the lawyer's duty to communicate with the client about such decisions. With respect to the means by which the client's objectives are to be pursued, the lawyer shall consult with the client as required by Rule 1.4(a)(2) and may take such action as is impliedly authorized to carry out the representation.

[2] On occasion, however, a lawyer and a client may disagree about the means to be used to accomplish the client's objectives. Clients normally defer to the special knowledge and skill of their lawyer with respect to the means to be used to accomplish their objectives, particularly with respect to technical, legal and tactical matters. Conversely, lawyers usually defer to the client regarding such questions as the expense to be incurred and concern for third persons who might be adversely affected. Because of the varied nature of the matters about which a lawyer and client might disagree and because the actions in question may implicate the interests of a tribunal or other persons, this Rule does not prescribe how such disagreements are to be resolved. Other law, however, may be applicable and should be consulted by the lawyer. The lawyer should also consult with the client and seek a mutually acceptable resolution of the disagreement. If such efforts are unavailing and the lawyer has a fundamental disagreement with the client, the lawyer may withdraw from the representation. See Rule 1.16(b)(4). Conversely, the client may resolve the disagreement by discharging the lawyer. See Rule 1.16(a)(3).

[3] At the outset of a representation, the client may authorize the lawyer to take specific action on the client's behalf without further consultation. Absent a material change in circumstances and subject to Rule 1.4, a lawyer may rely on such an advance authorization. The client may, however, revoke such authority at any time.

[4] In a case in which the client appears to be suffering diminished capacity, the lawyer's duty to abide by the client's decisions is to be guided by reference to Rule 1.14.

Independence from Client's Views or Activities

[5] Legal representation should not be denied to people who are unable to afford legal services, or whose cause is controversial or the subject of popular disapproval. By the same token, representing a client does not constitute approval of the client's views or activities.

Agreements Limiting Scope of Representation

[6] The scope of services to be provided by a lawyer may be limited by agreement with the client or by the terms under which the lawyer's services are made available to the client.

When a lawyer has been retained by an insurer to represent an insured, for example, the representation may be limited to matters related to the insurance coverage. A limited representation may be appropriate because the client has limited objectives for the representation. In addition, the terms upon which representation is undertaken may exclude specific means that might otherwise be used to accomplish the client's objectives. Such limitations may exclude actions that the client thinks are too costly or that the lawyer regards as repugnant or imprudent.

[7] Although this Rule affords the lawyer and client substantial latitude to limit the representation, the limitation must be reasonable under the circumstances. If, for example, a client's objective is limited to securing general information about the law the client needs in order to handle a common and typically uncomplicated legal problem, the lawyer and client may agree that the lawyer's services will be limited to a brief telephone consultation. Such a limitation, however, would not be reasonable if the time allotted was not sufficient to yield advice upon which the client could rely. Although an agreement for a limited representation does not exempt a lawyer from the duty to provide competent representation, the limitation is a factor to be considered when determining the legal knowledge, skill, thoroughness and preparation reasonably necessary for the representation. See Rule 1.1.

[8] All agreements concerning a lawyer's representation of a client must accord with the Rules of Professional Conduct and other law. See, e.g., Rules 1.1, 1.8 and 5.6.

Criminal, Fraudulent and Prohibited Transactions

[9] Paragraph (d) prohibits a lawyer from knowingly counseling or assisting a client to commit a crime or fraud. This prohibition, however, does not preclude the lawyer from giving an honest opinion about the actual consequences that appear likely to result from a client's conduct. Nor does the fact that a client uses advice in a course of action that is criminal or fraudulent of itself make a lawyer a party to the course of action. There is a critical distinction between presenting an analysis of legal aspects of questionable conduct and recommending the means by which a crime or fraud might be committed with impunity.

[10] When the client's course of action has already begun and is continuing, the lawyer's responsibility is especially delicate. The lawyer is required to avoid assisting the client, for example, by drafting or delivering documents that the lawyer knows are fraudulent or by suggesting how the wrongdoing might be concealed. A lawyer may not continue assisting a client in conduct that the lawyer originally supposed was legally proper but then discovers is criminal or fraudulent. The lawyer must, therefore, withdraw from the representation of the client in the matter. See Rule 1.16(a). In some cases, withdrawal alone might be insufficient. It may be necessary for the lawyer to give notice of the fact of withdrawal and to disaffirm any opinion, document, affirmation or the like. See Rule 4.1.

[11] Where the client is a fiduciary, the lawyer may be charged with special obligations in dealings with a beneficiary.

[12] Paragraph (d) applies whether or not the defrauded party is a party to the transaction. Hence, a lawyer must not participate in a transaction to effectuate criminal or fraudulent avoidance of tax liability. Paragraph (d) does not preclude undertaking a criminal defense incident to a general retainer for legal services to a lawful enterprise. The last clause of paragraph (d) recognizes that determining the validity or interpretation of a statute or regulation may require a course of action involving disobedience of the statute or regulation or of the interpretation placed upon it by governmental authorities.

[13] If a lawyer comes to know or reasonably should know that a client expects assistance not permitted by the Rules of Professional Conduct or other law or if the lawyer

intends to act contrary to the client's instructions, the lawyer must consult with the client regarding the limitations on the lawyer's conduct. See Rule 1.4(a)(5).

CLIENT-LAWYER RELATIONSHIP
RULE 1.4. Communication

(a) A lawyer shall:

(1) promptly inform the client of any decision or circumstance with respect to which the client's informed consent, as defined in Rule 1.0(e), is required by these Rules;

(2) reasonably consult with the client about the means by which the client's objectives are to be accomplished;

(3) keep the client reasonably informed about the status of the matter;

(4) promptly comply with reasonable requests for information; and

(5) consult with the client about any relevant limitation on the lawyer's conduct when the lawyer knows that the client expects assistance not permitted by the Rules of Professional Conduct or other law.

(b) A lawyer shall explain a matter to the extent reasonably necessary to permit the client to make informed decisions regarding the representation.

COMMENT

[1] Reasonable communication between the lawyer and the client is necessary for the client effectively to participate in the representation.

Communicating with Client

[2] If these Rules require that a particular decision about the representation be made by the client, paragraph (a)(1) requires that the lawyer promptly consult with and secure the client's consent prior to taking action unless prior discussions with the client have resolved what action the client wants the lawyer to take. For example, a lawyer who receives from opposing counsel an offer of settlement in a civil controversy or a proffered plea bargain in a criminal case must promptly inform the client of its substance unless the client has previously indicated that the proposal will be acceptable or unacceptable or has authorized the lawyer to accept or to reject the offer. See Rule 1.2(a).

[3] Paragraph (a)(2) requires the lawyer to reasonably consult with the client about the means to be used to accomplish the client's objectives. In some situations — depending on both the importance of the action under consideration and the feasibility of consulting with the client — this duty will require consultation prior to taking action. In other circumstances, such as during a trial when an immediate decision must be made, the exigency of the situation may require the lawyer to act without prior consultation. In such cases the lawyer must nonetheless act reasonably to inform the client of actions the lawyer has taken on the client's behalf. Additionally, paragraph (a)(3) requires that the lawyer keep the client reasonably informed about the status of the matter, such as significant developments affecting the timing or the substance of the representation.

[4] A lawyer's regular communication with clients will minimize the occasions on which a client will need to request information concerning the representation. When a client makes a reasonable request for information, however, paragraph (a)(4) requires prompt compliance with the request, or if a prompt response is not feasible, that the lawyer, or a member of the lawyer's staff, acknowledge receipt of the request and advise the client when a response may be expected. Client telephone calls should be promptly returned or acknowledged.

Explaining Matters

[5] The client should have sufficient information to participate intelligently in decisions concerning the objectives of the representation and the means by which they are to be pursued, to the extent the client is willing and able to do so. Adequacy of communication depends in part on the kind of advice or assistance that is involved. For example, when there is time to explain a proposal made in a negotiation, the lawyer should review all important provisions with the client before proceeding to an agreement. In litigation a lawyer should explain the general strategy and prospects of success and ordinarily should consult the client on tactics that are likely to result in significant expense or to injure or coerce others. On the other hand, a lawyer ordinarily will not be expected to describe trial or negotiation strategy in detail. The guiding principle is that the lawyer should fulfill reasonable client expectations for information consistent with the duty to act in the client's best interests, and the client's overall requirements as to the character of representation. In certain circumstances, such as when a lawyer asks a client to consent to a representation affected by a conflict of interest, the client must give informed consent, as defined in Rule 1.0(e).

[6] Ordinarily, the information to be provided is that appropriate for a client who is a comprehending and responsible adult. However, fully informing the client according to this standard may be impracticable, for example, where the client is a child or suffers from diminished capacity. See Rule 1.14. When the client is an organization or group, it is often impossible or inappropriate to inform every one of its members about its legal affairs; ordinarily, the lawyer should address communications to the appropriate officials of the organization. See Rule 1.13. Where many routine matters are involved, a system of limited or occasional reporting may be arranged with the client.

Withholding Information

[7] In some circumstances, a lawyer may be justified in delaying transmission of information when the client would be likely to react imprudently to an immediate communication. Thus, a lawyer might withhold a psychiatric diagnosis of a client when the examining psychiatrist indicates that disclosure would harm the client. A lawyer may not withhold information to serve the lawyer's own interest or convenience or the interests or convenience of another person. Rules or court orders governing litigation may provide that information supplied to a lawyer may not be disclosed to the client. Rule 3.4(c) directs compliance with such rules or orders.

COUNSELOR

RULE 2.4. Lawyer Serving as a Third-Party Neutral

(a) A lawyer serves as a third-party neutral when the lawyer assists two or more persons who are not clients of the lawyer to reach a resolution of a dispute or other matter that has arisen between them. Service as a third-party neutral may include service as an arbitrator, a mediator or in such other capacity as will enable the lawyer to assist the parties to resolve the matter.

(b) A lawyer serving as a third-party neutral shall inform unrepresented parties that the lawyer is not representing them. When the lawyer knows or reasonably should know that a party does not understand the lawyer's role in the matter, the lawyer shall explain the difference between the lawyer's role as a third-party neutral and a lawyer's role as one who represents a client.

COMMENT

[1] Alternative dispute resolution has become a substantial part of the civil justice system. Aside from representing clients in dispute-resolution processes, lawyers often

serve as third-party neutrals. A third-party neutral is a person, such as a mediator, arbitrator, conciliator or evaluator, who assists the parties, represented or unrepresented, in the resolution of a dispute or in the arrangement of a transaction. Whether a third-party neutral serves primarily as a facilitator, evaluator or decisionmaker depends on the particular process that is either selected by the parties or mandated by a court.

[2] The role of a third-party neutral is not unique to lawyers, although, in some court-connected contexts, only lawyers are allowed to serve in this role or to handle certain types of cases. In performing this role, the lawyer may be subject to court rules or other law that apply either to third-party neutrals generally or to lawyers serving as third-party neutrals. Lawyer-neutrals may also be subject to various codes of ethics, such as the Code of Ethics for Arbitration in Commercial Disputes prepared by a joint committee of the American Bar Association and the American Arbitration Association or the Model Standards of Conduct for Mediators jointly prepared by the American Bar Association, the American Arbitration Association and the Society of Professionals in Dispute Resolution.

[3] Unlike nonlawyers who serve as third-party neutrals, lawyers serving in this role may experience unique problems as a result of differences between the role of a third-party neutral and a lawyer's service as a client representative. The potential for confusion is significant when the parties are unrepresented in the process. Thus, paragraph (b) requires a lawyer-neutral to inform unrepresented parties that the lawyer is not representing them. For some parties, particularly parties who frequently use dispute-resolution processes, this information will be sufficient. For others, particularly those who are using the process for the first time, more information will be required. Where appropriate, the lawyer should inform unrepresented parties of the important differences between the lawyer's role as third-party neutral and a lawyer's role as a client representative, including the inapplicability of the attorney-client evidentiary privilege. The extent of disclosure required under this paragraph will depend on the particular parties involved and the subject matter of the proceeding, as well as the particular features of the dispute-resolution process selected.

[4] A lawyer who serves as a third-party neutral subsequently may be asked to serve as a lawyer representing a client in the same matter. The conflicts of interest that arise for both the individual lawyer and the lawyer's law firm are addressed in Rule 1.12.

[5] Lawyers who represent clients in alternative dispute-resolution processes are governed by the Rules of Professional Conduct. When the dispute-resolution process takes place before a tribunal, as in binding arbitration (see Rule 1.0(m)), the lawyer's duty of candor is governed by Rule 3.3. Otherwise, the lawyer's duty of candor toward both the third-party neutral and other parties is governed by Rule 4.1.

ADVOCATE
RULE 3.3. Candor Toward the Tribunal

(a)   A lawyer shall not knowingly:

(1)   make a false statement of fact or law to a tribunal or fail to correct a false statement of material fact or law previously made to the tribunal by the lawyer;

(2)   fail to disclose to the tribunal legal authority in the controlling jurisdiction known to the lawyer to be directly adverse to the position of the client and not disclosed by opposing counsel; or

(3)   offer evidence that the lawyer knows to be false. If a lawyer, the lawyer's client, or a witness called by the lawyer, has offered material evidence and the lawyer comes to know of its falsity, the lawyer shall take reasonable remedial measures, including, if necessary, disclosure to the tribunal. A lawyer may refuse to offer

evidence, other than the testimony of a defendant in a criminal matter, that the lawyer reasonably believes is false.

(b) A lawyer who represents a client in an adjudicative proceeding and who knows that a person intends to engage, is engaging or has engaged in criminal or fraudulent conduct related to the proceeding shall take reasonable remedial measures, including, if necessary, disclosure to the tribunal.

(c) The duties stated in paragraphs (a) and (b) continue to the conclusion of the proceeding, and apply even if compliance requires disclosure of information otherwise protected by Rule 1.6.

(d) In an ex parte proceeding, a lawyer shall inform the tribunal of all material facts known to the lawyer that will enable the tribunal to make an informed decision, whether or not the facts are adverse.

COMMENT

[1] This Rule governs the conduct of a lawyer who is representing a client in the proceedings of a tribunal. See Rule 1.0(m) for the definition of "tribunal." It also applies when the lawyer is representing a client in an ancillary proceeding conducted pursuant to the tribunal's adjudicative authority, such as a deposition. Thus, for example, paragraph (a)(3) requires a lawyer to take reasonable remedial measures if the lawyer comes to know that a client who is testifying in a deposition has offered evidence that is false.

[2] This Rule sets forth the special duties of lawyers as officers of the court to avoid conduct that undermines the integrity of the adjudicative process. A lawyer acting as an advocate in an adjudicative proceeding has an obligation to present the client's case with persuasive force. Performance of that duty while maintaining confidences of the client, however, is qualified by the advocate's duty of candor to the tribunal. Consequently, although a lawyer in an adversary proceeding is not required to present an impartial exposition of the law or to vouch for the evidence submitted in a cause, the lawyer must not allow the tribunal to be misled by false statements of law or fact or evidence that the lawyer knows to be false.

Representations by a Lawyer

[3] An advocate is responsible for pleadings and other documents prepared for litigation, but is usually not required to have personal knowledge of matters asserted therein, for litigation documents ordinarily present assertions by the client, or by someone on the client's behalf, and not assertions by the lawyer. Compare Rule 3.1. However, an assertion purporting to be on the lawyer's own knowledge, as in an affidavit by the lawyer or in a statement in open court, may properly be made only when the lawyer knows the assertion is true or believes it to be true on the basis of a reasonably diligent inquiry. There are circumstances where failure to make a disclosure is the equivalent of an affirmative misrepresentation. The obligation prescribed in Rule 1.2(d) not to counsel a client to commit or assist the client in committing a fraud applies in litigation. Regarding compliance with Rule 1.2(d), see the Comment to that Rule. See also the Comment to Rule 8.4(b).

Legal Argument

[4] Legal argument based on a knowingly false representation of law constitutes dishonesty toward the tribunal. A lawyer is not required to make a disinterested exposition of the law, but must recognize the existence of pertinent legal authorities. Furthermore, as stated in paragraph (a)(2), an advocate has a duty to disclose directly adverse authority in the controlling jurisdiction that has not been disclosed by the opposing party. The underlying

concept is that legal argument is a discussion seeking to determine the legal premises properly applicable to the case.

Offering Evidence

[5] Paragraph (a)(3) requires that the lawyer refuse to offer evidence that the lawyer knows to be false, regardless of the client's wishes. This duty is premised on the lawyer's obligation as an officer of the court to prevent the trier of fact from being misled by false evidence. A lawyer does not violate this Rule if the lawyer offers the evidence for the purpose of establishing its falsity.

[6] If a lawyer knows that the client intends to testify falsely or wants the lawyer to introduce false evidence, the lawyer should seek to persuade the client that the evidence should not be offered. If the persuasion is ineffective and the lawyer continues to represent the client, the lawyer must refuse to offer the false evidence. If only a portion of a witness's testimony will be false, the lawyer may call the witness to testify but may not elicit or otherwise permit the witness to present the testimony that the lawyer knows is false.

[7] The duties stated in paragraphs (a) and (b) apply to all lawyers, including defense counsel in criminal cases. In some jurisdictions, however, courts have required counsel to present the accused as a witness or to give a narrative statement if the accused so desires, even if counsel knows that the testimony or statement will be false. The obligation of the advocate under the Rules of Professional Conduct is subordinate to such requirements. See also Comment [9].

[8] The prohibition against offering false evidence only applies if the lawyer knows that the evidence is false. A lawyer's reasonable belief that evidence is false does not preclude its presentation to the trier of fact. A lawyer's knowledge that evidence is false, however, can be inferred from the circumstances. See Rule 1.0(f). Thus, although a lawyer should resolve doubts about the veracity of testimony or other evidence in favor of the client, the lawyer cannot ignore an obvious falsehood.

[9] Although paragraph (a)(3) only prohibits a lawyer from offering evidence the lawyer knows to be false, it permits the lawyer to refuse to offer testimony or other proof that the lawyer reasonably believes is false. Offering such proof may reflect adversely on the lawyer's ability to discriminate in the quality of evidence and thus impair the lawyer's effectiveness as an advocate. Because of the special protections historically provided criminal defendants, however, this Rule does not permit a lawyer to refuse to offer the testimony of such a client where the lawyer reasonably believes but does not know that the testimony will be false. Unless the lawyer knows the testimony will be false, the lawyer must honor the client's decision to testify. See also Comment [7].

Remedial Measures

[10] Having offered material evidence in the belief that it was true, a lawyer may subsequently come to know that the evidence is false. Or, a lawyer may be surprised when the lawyer's client, or another witness called by the lawyer, offers testimony the lawyer knows to be false, either during the lawyer's direct examination or in response to cross-examination by the opposing lawyer. In such situations or if the lawyer knows of the falsity of testimony elicited from the client during a deposition, the lawyer must take reasonable remedial measures. In such situations, the advocate's proper course is to remonstrate with the client confidentially, advise the client of the lawyer's duty of candor to the tribunal and seek the client's cooperation with respect to the withdrawal or correction of the false statements or evidence. If that fails, the advocate must take further remedial action. If withdrawal from the representation is not permitted or will not undo the effect of the false evidence, the advocate must make such disclosure to the tribunal as is reasonably necessary to remedy the situation, even if doing so requires the lawyer to reveal information

that otherwise would be protected by Rule 1.6. It is for the tribunal then to determine what should be done — making a statement about the matter to the trier of fact, ordering a mistrial or perhaps nothing.

[11] The disclosure of a client's false testimony can result in grave consequences to the client, including not only a sense of betrayal but also loss of the case and perhaps a prosecution for perjury. But the alternative is that the lawyer cooperate in deceiving the court, thereby subverting the truth-finding process which the adversary system is designed to implement. See Rule 1.2(d). Furthermore, unless it is clearly understood that the lawyer will act upon the duty to disclose the existence of false evidence, the client can simply reject the lawyer's advice to reveal the false evidence and insist that the lawyer keep silent. Thus the client could in effect coerce the lawyer into being a party to fraud on the court.

Preserving Integrity of Adjudicative Process

[12] Lawyers have a special obligation to protect a tribunal against criminal or fraudulent conduct that undermines the integrity of the adjudicative process, such as bribing, intimidating or otherwise unlawfully communicating with a witness, juror, court official or other participant in the proceeding, unlawfully destroying or concealing documents or other evidence or failing to disclose information to the tribunal when required by law to do so. Thus, paragraph (b) requires a lawyer to take reasonable remedial measures, including disclosure if necessary, whenever the lawyer knows that a person, including the lawyer's client, intends to engage, is engaging or has engaged in criminal or fraudulent conduct related to the proceeding.

Duration of Obligation

[13] A practical time limit on the obligation to rectify false evidence or false statements of law and fact has to be established. The conclusion of the proceeding is a reasonably definite point for the termination of the obligation. A proceeding has concluded within the meaning of this Rule when a final judgment in the proceeding has been affirmed on appeal or the time for review has passed.

Ex Parte Proceedings

[14] Ordinarily, an advocate has the limited responsibility of presenting one side of the matters that a tribunal should consider in reaching a decision; the conflicting position is expected to be presented by the opposing party. However, in any ex parte proceeding, such as an application for a temporary restraining order, there is no balance of presentation by opposing advocates. The object of an ex parte proceeding is nevertheless to yield a substantially just result. The judge has an affirmative responsibility to accord the absent party just consideration. The lawyer for the represented party has the correlative duty to make disclosures of material facts known to the lawyer and that the lawyer reasonably believes are necessary to an informed decision.

Withdrawal

[15] Normally, a lawyer's compliance with the duty of candor imposed by this Rule does not require that the lawyer withdraw from the representation of a client whose interests will be or have been adversely affected by the lawyer's disclosure. The lawyer may, however, be required by Rule 1.16(a) to seek permission of the tribunal to withdraw if the lawyer's compliance with this Rule's duty of candor results in such an extreme deterioration of the client-lawyer relationship that the lawyer can no longer competently represent the client. Also see Rule 1.16(b) for the circumstances in which a lawyer will be permitted to seek a tribunal's permission to withdraw. In connection with a request for permission to withdraw that is premised on a client's misconduct, a lawyer may reveal information relating to the representation only to the extent reasonably necessary to comply with this Rule or as otherwise permitted by Rule 1.6.

TRANSACTIONS WITH PERSONS OTHER THAN CLIENTS
RULE 4.1. Truthfulness in Statements to Others
In the course of representing a client a lawyer shall not knowingly:

(a) make a false statement of material fact or law to a third person; or

(b) fail to disclose a material fact to a third person when disclosure is necessary to avoid assisting a criminal or fraudulent act by a client, unless disclosure is prohibited by Rule 1.6.

COMMENT
Misrepresentation
[1] A lawyer is required to be truthful when dealing with others on a client's behalf, but generally has no affirmative duty to inform an opposing party of relevant facts. A misrepresentation can occur if the lawyer incorporates or affirms a statement of another person that the lawyer knows is false. Misrepresentations can also occur by partially true but misleading statements or omissions that are the equivalent of affirmative false statements. For dishonest conduct that does not amount to a false statement or for misrepresentations by a lawyer other than in the course of representing a client, see Rule 8.4.

Statements of Fact
[2] This Rule refers to statements of fact. Whether a particular statement should be regarded as one of fact can depend on the circumstances. Under generally accepted conventions in negotiation, certain types of statements ordinarily are not taken as statements of material fact. Estimates of price or value placed on the subject of a transaction and a party's intentions as to an acceptable settlement of a claim are ordinarily in this category, and so is the existence of an undisclosed principal except where nondisclosure of the principal would constitute fraud. Lawyers should be mindful of their obligations under applicable law to avoid criminal and tortious misrepresentation.

Crime or Fraud by Client
[3] Under Rule 1.2(d), a lawyer is prohibited from counseling or assisting a client in conduct that the lawyer knows is criminal or fraudulent. Paragraph (b) states a specific application of the principle set forth in Rule 1.2(d) and addresses the situation where a client's crime or fraud takes the form of a lie or misrepresentation. Ordinarily, a lawyer can avoid assisting a client's crime or fraud by withdrawing from the representation. Sometimes it may be necessary for the lawyer to give notice of the fact of withdrawal and to disaffirm an opinion, document, affirmation or the like. In extreme cases, substantive law may require a lawyer to disclose information relating to the representation to avoid being deemed to have assisted the client's crime or fraud. If the lawyer can avoid assisting a client's crime or fraud only by disclosing this information, then under paragraph (b) the lawyer is required to do so, unless the disclosure is prohibited by Rule 1.6.

TRANSACTIONS WITH PERSONS OTHER THAN CLIENTS
RULE 4.4. Respect for Rights of Third Persons
(a) In representing a client, a lawyer shall not use means that have no substantial purpose other than to embarrass, delay, or burden a third person, or use methods of obtaining evidence that violate the legal rights of such a person.

(b) A lawyer who receives a document relating to the representation of the lawyer's client and knows or reasonably should know that the document was inadvertently sent shall promptly notify the sender.

COMMENT

[1] Responsibility to a client requires a lawyer to subordinate the interests of others to those of the client, but that responsibility does not imply that a lawyer may disregard the rights of third persons. It is impractical to catalogue all such rights, but they include legal restrictions on methods of obtaining evidence from third persons and unwarranted intrusions into privileged relationships, such as the client-lawyer relationship.

[2] Paragraph (b) recognizes that lawyers sometimes receive documents that were mistakenly sent or produced by opposing parties or their lawyers. If a lawyer knows or reasonably should know that such a document was sent inadvertently, then this Rule requires the lawyer to promptly notify the sender in order to permit that person to take protective measures. Whether the lawyer is required to take additional steps, such as returning the original document, is a matter of law beyond the scope of these Rules, as is the question of whether the privileged status of a document has been waived. Similarly, this Rule does not address the legal duties of a lawyer who receives a document that the lawyer knows or reasonably should know may have been wrongfully obtained by the sending person. For purposes of this Rule, "document" includes e-mail or other electronic modes of transmission subject to being read or put into readable form.

[3] Some lawyers may choose to return a document unread, for example, when the lawyer learns before receiving the document that it was inadvertently sent to the wrong address. Where a lawyer is not required by applicable law to do so, the decision to voluntarily return such a document is a matter of professional judgment ordinarily reserved to the lawyer. See Rules 1.2 and 1.4.

LAW FIRMS AND ASSOCIATIONS

RULE 5.6. Restrictions on Right to Practice

A lawyer shall not participate in offering or making:

(a) a partnership, shareholders, operating, employment, or other similar type of agreement that restricts the right of a lawyer to practice after termination of the relationship, except an agreement concerning benefits upon retirement; or

(b) an agreement in which a restriction on the lawyer's right to practice is part of the settlement of a client controversy.

COMMENT

[1] An agreement restricting the right of lawyers to practice after leaving a firm not only limits their professional autonomy but also limits the freedom of clients to choose a lawyer. Paragraph (a) prohibits such agreements except for restrictions incident to provisions concerning retirement benefits for service with the firm.

[2] Paragraph (b) prohibits a lawyer from agreeing not to represent other persons in connection with settling a claim on behalf of a client.

[3] This Rule does not apply to prohibit restrictions that may be included in the terms of the sale of a law practice pursuant to Rule 1.17.

MAINTAINING THE INTEGRITY OF THE PROFESSION

RULE 8.3. Reporting Professional Misconduct

(a) A lawyer who knows that another lawyer has committed a violation of the Rules of Professional Conduct that raises a substantial question as to that lawyer's honesty, trustworthiness or fitness as a lawyer in other respects, shall inform the appropriate professional authority.

(b) A lawyer who knows that a judge has committed a violation of applicable rules of judicial conduct that raises a substantial question as to the judge's fitness for office shall inform the appropriate authority.

(c) This Rule does not require disclosure of information otherwise protected by Rule 1.6 or information gained by a lawyer or judge while participating in an approved lawyers assistance program.

COMMENT

[1] Self-regulation of the legal profession requires that members of the profession initiate disciplinary investigation when they know of a violation of the Rules of Professional Conduct. Lawyers have a similar obligation with respect to judicial misconduct. An apparently isolated violation may indicate a pattern of misconduct that only a disciplinary investigation can uncover. Reporting a violation is especially important where the victim is unlikely to discover the offense.

[2] A report about misconduct is not required where it would involve violation of Rule 1.6. However, a lawyer should encourage a client to consent to disclosure where prosecution would not substantially prejudice the client's interests.

[3] If a lawyer were obliged to report every violation of the Rules, the failure to report any violation would itself be a professional offense. Such a requirement existed in many jurisdictions but proved to be unenforceable. This Rule limits the reporting obligation to those offenses that a self-regulating profession must vigorously endeavor to prevent. A measure of judgment is, therefore, required in complying with the provisions of this Rule. The term "substantial" refers to the seriousness of the possible offense and not the quantum of evidence of which the lawyer is aware. A report should be made to the bar disciplinary agency unless some other agency, such as a peer review agency, is more appropriate in the circumstances. Similar considerations apply to the reporting of judicial misconduct.

[4] The duty to report professional misconduct does not apply to a lawyer retained to represent a lawyer whose professional conduct is in question. Such a situation is governed by the Rules applicable to the client-lawyer relationship.

[5] Information about a lawyer's or judge's misconduct or fitness may be received by a lawyer in the course of that lawyer's participation in an approved lawyers or judges assistance program. In that circumstance, providing for an exception to the reporting requirements of paragraphs (a) and (b) of this Rule encourages lawyers and judges to seek treatment through such a program. Conversely, without such an exception, lawyers and judges may hesitate to seek assistance from these programs, which may then result in additional harm to their professional careers and additional injury to the welfare of clients and the public. These Rules do not otherwise address the confidentiality of information received by a lawyer or judge participating in an approved lawyers assistance program; such an obligation, however, may be imposed by the rules of the program or other law.

MAINTAINING THE INTEGRITY OF THE PROFESSION
RULE 8.4. Misconduct

It is professional misconduct for a lawyer to:

(a) violate or attempt to violate the Rules of Professional Conduct, knowingly assist or induce another to do so, or do so through the acts of another;

(b) commit a criminal act that reflects adversely on the lawyer's honesty, trustworthiness or fitness as a lawyer in other respects;

(c) engage in conduct involving dishonesty, fraud, deceit or misrepresentation;

(d) **engage in conduct that is prejudicial to the administration of justice;**

(e) **state or imply an ability to influence improperly a government agency or official or to achieve results by means that violate the Rules of Professional Conduct or other law; or**

(f) **knowingly assist a judge or judicial officer in conduct that is a violation of applicable rules of judicial conduct or other law.**

COMMENT

[1] Lawyers are subject to discipline when they violate or attempt to violate the Rules of Professional Conduct, knowingly assist or induce another to do so or do so through the acts of another, as when they request or instruct an agent to do so on the lawyer's behalf. Paragraph (a), however, does not prohibit a lawyer from advising a client concerning action the client is legally entitled to take.

[2] Many kinds of illegal conduct reflect adversely on fitness to practice law, such as offenses involving fraud and the offense of willful failure to file an income tax return. However, some kinds of offenses carry no such implication. Traditionally, the distinction was drawn in terms of offenses involving "moral turpitude." That concept can be construed to include offenses concerning some matters of personal morality, such as adultery and comparable offenses, that have no specific connection to fitness for the practice of law. Although a lawyer is personally answerable to the entire criminal law, a lawyer should be professionally answerable only for offenses that indicate lack of those characteristics relevant to law practice. Offenses involving violence, dishonesty, breach of trust, or serious interference with the administration of justice are in that category. A pattern of repeated offenses, even ones of minor significance when considered separately, can indicate indifference to legal obligation.

[3] A lawyer who, in the course of representing a client, knowingly manifests by words or conduct, bias or prejudice based upon race, sex, religion, national origin, disability, age, sexual orientation or socioeconomic status, violates paragraph (d) when such actions are prejudicial to the administration of justice. Legitimate advocacy respecting the foregoing factors does not violate paragraph (d). A trial judge's finding that peremptory challenges were exercised on a discriminatory basis does not alone establish a violation of this rule.

[4] A lawyer may refuse to comply with an obligation imposed by law upon a good faith belief that no valid obligation exists. The provisions of Rule 1.2(d) concerning a good faith challenge to the validity, scope, meaning or application of the law apply to challenges of legal regulation of the practice of law.

[5] Lawyers holding public office assume legal responsibilities going beyond those of other citizens. A lawyer's abuse of public office can suggest an inability to fulfill the professional role of lawyers. The same is true of abuse of positions of private trust such as trustee, executor, administrator, guardian, agent and officer, director or manager of a corporation or other organization.

Table of Online Resources

http://www.cybersettle.com (ODR)

http://www.news24.com

http://www.squaretrade.com (ODR)

http://www.trafford.com

http://www.uscourts.gov (courts)

http://www.cand.uscourts.gov (courts)

http://www.abanet.org/dispute/webpolicy.html (documents)

http://www.adr.org (organization; provider)

http://www.cbuilding.org (organization; provider)

http://www.cpradr.org (organization; provider)

http://www.cpradr.org/publicpolicyprojects (rules and documents)

http://www.icann.org/udrp (ODR)

http://www.policyconsensus.org (organization; provider)

http://www.businessofgovernment.org/pdfs/Bingham_Report.pdf (documents)

http://www.publicconversations.org/pcp/uploadDocs/CommunityGuide3.0.pdf (document)

http://www.susskind.info/content/contributions/democracy.pdf (document)

http://www.uww-adr.com/2002/pdfs/effectiveadvocacy.pdf (organization; provider)

http://www.odr.info (ODR)

http://arbiter.wipo.int (ODR)

Table of Statutes

Table of Cases

Italic type indicates principal cases.

Collected References

AARON, Marjorie Corman (1996). "ADR Toolbox: The Highwire Art of Evaluation," 14 *Alternatives to High Cost Litig.* 62.

ABEL, Richard L. (1982). "The Contradictions of Informal Justice," in Richard L. Abel ed., 1 *The Politics of Informal Justice: The American Experience.* 2 vols. New York: Academic Press.

ABRAMSON, Harold I. (2004). *Mediation Representation: Advocating in a Problem-Solving Process.* 1-4 South Bend, Ind.: National Institute for Trial Advocacy (NITA).

ACUFF, Frank L. (1997). *How to Negotiate Anything with Anyone Anywhere Around the World.* New York: American Management Association.

ADLER, Jane W., Deborah R. HENSLER & Charles E. NELSON (1983). *Simple Justice: How Litigants Fare in the Pittsburgh Court Arbitration Program.* Santa Monica, Cal.: RAND.

ALFINI, James J. (1991). "Trashing, Bashing, and Hashing It Out. Is This the End of 'Good Mediation'?," 19 *Fla. St. U. L. Rev.* 47.

_____(1989). "Summary Jury Trials in State and Federal Courts: A Comparative Analysis of the Perceptions of Participating Lawyers," 4 *Ohio St. J. on Disp. Resol.* 213.

AMERICAN BAR ASSOCIATION (2002). "Resolution on Mediation and the Unauthorized Practice of Law." Washington, D.C.: ABA, Section of Dispute Resolution, available at *http://www.abanet.org/dispute/resolution2002.pdf.*

ANDERSON, Heather & Ron PI (2005). "Evaluation of Early Mediation Pilot Programs," *http://www.courtinfo.ca.gov/reference/documents/empprept.pdf.*

ANDERSON, Mary B. (1999). *Do No Harm: How Aid Can Support Peace — Or War.* Boulder," Colo.: Lynne Rienner Publishers.

ANGIER, Natalie (2002). "Why We're So Nice: We're Wired to Cooperate," *N.Y. Times,* July 23, p. F1.

ARNOLD, Tom (1995). "20 Common Errors in Mediation Advocacy," 13 *Alternatives to High Cost Litig.* 67.

AUERBACH, Jerold S. (1983). *Justice Without Law?* New York: Oxford University Press.

AUVINE, Brian et al. (1977). *A Manual for Group Facilitators.* Madison, Wis.: Center for Conflict Resolution.

AXELROD, Robert (1984). *The Evolution of Cooperation.* New York: Basic Books.

AYRES, Ian (1995). "Further Evidence of Discrimination in New Car Negotiations and Estimates of Its Cause," 94 *Mich. L. Rev.* 109.

_____(1991). "Fair Driving: Gender and Race Discrimination in Retail Car Negotiations," 104 *Harv. L. Rev.* 817.

BABCOCK, Linda & Sara LASCHEVER (2003). *Women Don't Ask: Negotiation and the Gender Divide.* Princeton: Princeton University Press.

BARTOS, Otomar J. (1978). "Simple Model of Negotiation: A Sociological Point of View," in I. William Zartman, ed., *The Negotiation Process: Theories and Applications*. Beverly Hills, Cal.: Sage Publications.

BASTRESS, Robert M. & Joseph D. HARBAUGH (1990). *Interviewing, Counseling, and Negotiating: Skills for Effective Representation*. Boston: Little, Brown.

BAZERMAN, Max H. & Margaret A. NEALE (1992). *Negotiating Rationally*. New York: Free Press.

BEGLEY, Sharon (2000). "The Stereotype Trap," *Newsweek*, November 6, p. 66.

BENNETT, Mark & Michele S.G. HERMANN (1996). *The Art of Mediation*. Notre Dame, Ind.: NITA.

BERCOVITCH, Jacob (1996). "The Structure and Diversity of Mediation in International Relations," in Jacob Bercovitch & Jeffrey Z. Rubin eds., *Mediation in International Relations: Multiple Approaches to Conflict Management*. New York: St. Martin's Press.

BERCOVITCH, Jacob ed. (1996). *Resolving International Conflicts: The Theory and Practice of Mediation*. Boulder, Colo.: Lynne Rienner Publishers.

BERMAN, Greg & John FEINBLATT (2005). *Good Courts: The Case for Problem Solving Justice*. New York: New Press.

_____ (2001). "Problem-Solving Courts: A Brief Primer," 23 *Law & Poly.* 125.

BERNARD, Phyllis (2003). "Cross-Cultural Mediation Process Skills: Understanding the Cultural Geography for Mediation," Synopsis of Comments, Panel Presentation for the ABA Section on Dispute Resolution International Conference in Washington, D.C.

BERNARD, Phyllis & Bryant GARTH eds. (2002). *Dispute Resolution Ethics: A Comprehensive Guide*. Washington, D.C.: ABA Press.

BERNSTEIN, Lisa (1993). "Understanding the Limits of Court-Connected ADR: A Critique of Federal Court-Annexed Arbitration Programs," 141 *U. Pa. L. Rev.* 2169.

BICKERMAN, John (1996). "Evaluative Mediator Responds," 14 *Alternatives to High Cost Litig.* 70.

BINDER, David A., Paul BERGMAN & Susan C. PRICE (1991). *Lawyers as Counselors: A Client-Centered Approach*. St. Paul: West Group.

BINDER, David A., Paul BERGMAN, Susan C. PRICE & Paul K. TREMBLAY (2004). *Lawyers as Counselors: A Client-Centered Approach* (3d ed.). St. Paul: West Group.

BINGHAM, Lisa B. (2003). "Mediation at Work: Transforming Workplace Conflict at the United States Postal Service." Washington, D.C.: IBM Center for The Business of Government, available at *http://www.businessofgovernment.org/pdfs/Bingham_Report.pdf*.

_____(2002). "Why Suppose? Let's Find Out: A Public Policy Research Program on Dispute Resolution," 2002 *J. Disp. Resol.* 101.

BLEEMER, Russ ed. (2005). *Mediation: Approaches and Insights*. Huntington, N.Y.: Juris Publication.

BORDONE, Robert C. (1998). "Electronic Online Dispute Resolution: A Systems Approach — Potential, Problems, and a Proposal," 3 *Harv. Negot. L. Rev.* 175.

BOWLING, Daniel & David HOFFMAN eds. (2003). *Bringing Peace into the Room*. San Francisco: Jossey-Bass.

BRAZIL, Wayne D. (2000). "Continuing the Conversation About the Current Status and the Future of ADR: A View from the Courts," 2000 *J. Disp. Resol.* 11.

_____(1990). "A Close Look at Three Court-Sponsored ADR Programs: Why They Exist, How They Operate, What They Deliver, and Whether They Threaten Important Values," 1990 *U. Chi. Legal F.* 303.

_____(1988). "Protecting the Confidentiality of Settlement Negotiations," 39 *Hastings L. J.* 955.

_____(1984). "Settling Civil Cases: What Lawyers Want from Judges," *Judges' J.* 14 (Summer).

BREGER, Marshall J. (2000). "Should an Attorney Be Required to Advise a Client of ADR Options?," 13 *Geo. J. Legal Ethics* 427.

BRETT, Jeanne M. (2001). *Negotiating Globally: How to Negotiate Deals, Resolve Disputes, and Make Decisions Across Cultural Boundaries*. San Francisco: Jossey-Bass Publishers.

BRETT, Jeanne M. & Michele GELFAND eds. (2004). *The Handbook of Negotiation and Culture*. Stanford, Cal.: Stanford Business Books.

BROWN, Jennifer Gerarda (2004). "Creativity and Problem-Solving," 87 *Marq. L. Rev.* 697.

_____(1997). "The Role of Hope in Negotiation," 44 *UCLA L. Rev.* 1661.

BRYAN, Penelope E. (1992). "Killing Us Softly: Divorce Mediation and the Politics of Power," 40 *Buff. L. Rev.* 441.

BULDOC, Danielle Sheri (1990). *Mediator Style Perspectives: An Innovative Look at Mediator Behavior* (unpublished master's thesis, Arizona State University).

BURNS, Stacy Lee (2000). *Making Settlement Work: An Examination of the Work of Judicial Mediators.* Aldershot, Eng.: Ashgate.

BURTON, John W. (1987). *Resolving Deep-Rooted Conflict: A Handbook.* Lanham, Md.: University Press of America.

BUSH, Robert A. Baruch (2002). "Substituting Mediation for Arbitration: The Growing Market for Evaluative Mediation, and What It Means for the ADR Field," 3 *Pepp. Disp. Resol. L.J.* 111.

_____(1989-1990). "Mediation and Adjudication, Dispute Resolution and Ideology: An Imaginary Conversation," 3 *J. Contemp. Legal Issues* 1.

BUSH, Robert A. Baruch & Joseph P. FOLGER (1994). *The Promise of Mediation: Responding to Conflict Through Empowerment and Recognition.* San Francisco: Jossey-Bass Publishers.

CAMACHO, Alejandro Esteban (2005). "Mustering the Missing Voices: A Collaborative Model for Fostering Equality, Community Involvement and Adaptive Planning in Land Use Decisions, Installment One," 24 *Stan. Environ. L.J.* 3.

CARNEVALE, Peter J.D., Donald E. CONLON, Kathy A. HANISCH & Karen L. HARRIS (1989). "Experimental Research on the Strategic-Choice Model of Mediation," in Kenneth Kressel & Dean G. Pruitt eds., *Mediation Research: The Process and Effectiveness of Third-Party Intervention.* San Francisco: Jossey-Bass Publishers.

CARR, Frank, with Kim HURTADO, Charles LANCASTER, Charles MARKERT & Paul TUCKER (1999). *Partnering in Construction: A Practical Guide to Project Success.* Chicago: Forum on the Construction Industry, ABA.

CARROLL, Eileen & Kevin MACKIE (2000). *International Mediation: The Art of Business Diplomacy.* The Hague: Kluwer.

CARTER, Jimmy (1982). *Keeping Faith: Memoirs of a President.* Toronto: Bantam Books.

CHAYES, Antonia & Martha MINOW eds. (2003). *Imagine Coexistence: Restoring Humanity After Violent Ethnic Conflict.* San Francisco: Jossey-Bass Publishers.

CIALDINI, Robert B. (1993). *Influence: The Psychology of Persuasion* (rev. ed.). New York: Collins.

CLERMONT, Kevin M. & Stewart J. SCWAB (2004). "How Employment Discrimination Plaintiffs Fare in Federal Court," 1 *J. Empirical Legal Studies* 429.

CLINTON, William J. (2001). Acceptance Speech for the International Advocate for Peace Award, March 21. Benjamin N. Cardozo School of Law, at *http://www.cardozo.yu.edu/cojcr/final_site/ IAP_Award/2001/clintpdf.pdf.*

COBEN, James R. (2004). "Gollum, Meet Sméagol: A Schizophrenic Rumination on Mediator Values Beyond Self-Determination and Neutrality," 5 *Cardozo J. Confl. Res.* 65.

_____(2000). "Mediation's Dirty Little Secret: Straight Talk About Mediator Manipulation and Deception," *J. Alternative Disp. Resol. Emp.* 4 (Winter).

COBEN, James & Peter THOMPSON (2006). "Disputing Irony: A Systematic Look at Litigation About Mediation," 11 *Harv. Negot. L. Rev.* (forthcoming).

COCHRAN, Robert F., Jr. (1990). "Legal Representation and the Next Steps Toward Client Control: Attorney Malpractice for the Failure to Allow the Client to Control Negotiation and Pursue Alternatives to Litigation," 47 *Wash. & Lee L. Rev.* 819.

COFFEE, Jr., John C. (1995). "Class Wars: The Dilemma of the Mass Tort Class Action," 95 *Colum. L. Rev.* 1343.

COGLIANESE, Cary (1997). "Assessing Consensus: The Promise and Performance of Negotiated Rulemaking," 46 *Duke L.J.* 1255.

COHEN, Jonathan R. (2003). "Adversaries? Partners? How About Counterparts? On Metaphors in the Practice and Teaching of Negotiation and Dispute Resolution," 20 *Conflict Resol. Q.* 433.

_____ (2000). "Apology and Organizations: Exploring an Example from Medical Practice," 27 *Fordham Urb. L.J.* 1447.

COLE, Sarah (2005). "Mediation Certification: Has the Time Come?," 11 *Disp. Resol. Mag.* 7.

COLE, SARAH R., Nancy H. ROGERS & Craig A. McEWEN (2001). "Dilemmas Presented by Institutionalization of Mediation," in 1 *Mediation: Law, Policy & Practice* ch. 2 (2d ed.). 3 vols. St. Paul: West Group.

——(2001). "Legal Services by Mediator: Conflict of Interest, Advertising, Joint Practice, and Unauthorized Practice," in 1 *Mediation: Law, Policy & Practice* ch. 10 (2d ed. & Supp. 2002). 3 vols. St. Paul: West Group.

——(2001). "Regulating for Quality, Fairness, Effectiveness, and Access: Mediator Qualifications, Certification, Liability and Immunity, Procedural Requirements, and Other Measures," in 1 *Mediation: Law, Policy & Practice* ch. 11 (2d ed. & Supp. 2002). 3 vols. St. Paul: West Group.

COLEMAN, Peter T. & Morton DEUTSCH (2000). "Some Guidelines for Developing a Creative Approach to Conflict," in Morton Deutsch & Peter T. Coleman eds., *The Handbook of Conflict Resolution: Theory and Practice.* San Francisco: Jossey-Bass Publishers.

CONDLIN, Robert J. (1985). "'Cases on Both Sides': Patterns of Argument in Legal Dispute-Negotiation," 44 *Md. L. Rev.* 65.

CONNOR, Lawrence D. (1996). "How to Combine Facilitation with Evaluation," 14 *Alternatives to High Cost Litig.* 15.

COOLEY, John W. (1997). "Mediation Magic: Its Use and Abuse," 29 *Loy. U. Chi. L.J.* 1.

COSTANTINO, Cathy A. & Christina Sickles MERCHANT (1996). *Designing Conflict Management Systems: A Guide to Creating Productive and Healthy Organizations.* San Francisco: Jossey-Bass Publishers.

COVEY, Stephen R. (1989). *The Seven Habits of Highly Effective People: Restoring the Character Ethic.* New York: Simon and Schuster.

CPR INSTITUTE FOR DISPUTE RESOLUTION (1995). "The ABCs of ADR: A Dispute Resolution Glossary," 13 *Alternatives to High Cost Litig.* 147.

CRAVER, Charles B. & David W. BARNES (1999). "Gender, Risk Taking, and Negotiation Performance," 5 *Mich. J. Gender & L.* 299.

CROCKER, Chester A., Fen Osler HAMPSON & Pamela AALL eds. (2001). *Turbulent Peace: The Challenges of Managing International Conflict.* Washington, D.C.: United States Institute of Peace Press.

——(1999). *Herding Cats: Multiparty Mediation in a Complex World.* Washington, D.C.: United States Institute of Peace Press.

CURRAN, Daniel & James K. SEBENIUS (2003). "The Mediator as Coalition Builder: George Mitchell in Northern Ireland," 8 *Intl. Negot.* 111.

CURRAN, Daniel, James K. SEBENIUS & Michael WATKINS (2004). "Case Analysis: Two Paths to Peace: Contrasting George Mitchell in Northern Ireland with Richard Holbrooke in Bosnia Herzegovina," *Negot. J.* 513.

DANA, Howard H. (2005). "Court-Connected Alternative Dispute Resolution in Maine," 57 *Maine L. Rev.* 349.

DE BONO, Edward (1999). *Six Thinking Hats* (rev. ed.). Boston: Little, Brown.

DEASON, Ellen E. (2005). "Procedural Rules for Complementary Systems of Litigation and Mediation Worldwide," 80 *Notre Dame L. Rev.* 553.

——(2001). "Enforcing Mediated Settlement Agreements: Contract Law Collides with Confidentiality," 35 *U.C. Davis L. Rev.* 33.

DELGADO, Richard, Chris DUNN, Pamela BROWN, Helena LEE & David HUBBERT (1985). "Fairness and Formality: Minimizing the Risk of Prejudice in Alternative Dispute Resolution," 1985 *Wis. L. Rev.* 1359.

DEZALAY, Yves, & Bryant G. GARTH (1996). *Dealing in Virtue: International Commercial Arbitration and the Construction of a Transnational Legal Order.* Chicago: University of Chicago Press.

DICKENS, Charles (1853). *Bleak House* (1956 ed.). Boston: Houghton Mifflin.

DODD, Carley H. (1987). *Dynamics of Intercultural Communication.* New York: McGraw-Hill.

DOERRE, Sharon (2001). "Negotiating Gender and Authority in Northern Syria," 6 *Intl. Negot.* 251.

DONNELL, Susan M. & Jay HALL (1980). "Men and Women as Managers: A Significant Case of No Significant Difference," *Organizational Dynamics* 60 (Spring).

DRYZEK, John S. (2000). *Deliberative Democracy and Beyond: Liberals, Critics, Contestations*. New York: Oxford University Press.

DUBLER, Nancy N. & Carol B. LIEBMAN (2004). *Bioethics Mediation: A Guide to Shaping Shared Solutions*. New York: United Hospital Fund.

EDELMAN, Lauren B., Howard S. ERLANGER & John LANDE (1993). "Internal Dispute Resolution: The Transformation of Civil Rights in the Workplace," 27 *Law & Socy. Rev.* 497.

EDMONDS, David & John EIDINOW (2001). *Wittgenstein's Poker: The Story of a Ten-Minute Argument Between Two Great Philosophers*. New York: Ecco.

EISENBERG, Melvin (1976). "Private Ordering Through Negotiation: Dispute Settlement and Rule-making," 89 *Harv. L. Rev.* 637.

ELSTER, Jon (1995). "Strategic Uses of Argument," in Kenneth J. Arrow et al. eds., *Barriers to Conflict Resolution*. New York: W.W. Norton.

FEERICK, John D. (1997). "Toward Uniform Standards of Conduct for Mediators," 38 *S. Tex. L. Rev.* 455.

FELSTINER, William L.F., Richard L. ABEL & Austin SARAT (1980-1981). "The Emergence and Transformation of Disputes: Naming, Blaming, Claiming . . . ," 15 *Law & Socy. Rev.* 631.

FISHER, Roger, Elizabeth KOPELMAN & Andrea Kupfer SCHNEIDER (1994). *Beyond Machiavelli: Tools for Coping with Conflict*. Cambridge, Mass.: Harvard University Press.

FISHER, Roger & Daniel SHAPIRO (2005). *Beyond Reason: Using Emotions in Negotiations*. New York: Viking-Penguin.

FISHER, Roger, William URY & Bruce PATTON (1991). *Getting to YES: Negotiating Agreement Without Giving In* (2d ed.). Boston: Houghton Mifflin.

FISS, Owen M. (1984). "Against Settlement," 93 *Yale L.J.* 1073.

FOLBERG, J. (2003). "Arbitration Ethics: Is California the Future?," 18 *Ohio St. J. on Dis. Resol.* 343.

FOLGER, Joseph P. & Robert A. Baruch BUSH (1996). "Transformative Mediation and Third-Party Intervention: Ten Hallmarks of a Transformative Approach to Practice," 13 *Mediation Q.* 263.

FOLLETT, Mary Parker (1995). "Constructive Conflict," in Pauline Graham ed., *Mary Parker Follett — Prophet of Management: A Celebration of Writings from the 1920s*. Boston: Harvard Business School Publishing.

FREEMAN, Jody (1997). "Collaborative Governance in the Administrative State," 45 *UCLA L. Rev.* 1.

FREEMAN, Jody & Laura I. LANGBEIN (2000). "Regulatory Negotiation and the Legitimacy Benefit," 9 *N.Y.U. Envtl. L.J.* 60.

FRESHMAN, Clark (1997). "Privatizing Same-Sex 'Marriage' Through Alternative Dispute Resolution: Community-Enhancing Versus Community-Enabling Mediation," 44 *UCLA L. Rev.* 1687.

FRESHMAN, Clark, Adele HAYES & Greg FELDMAN (2002). "The Lawyer-Negotiator as Mood Scientist: What We Know and Don't Know About How Mood Relates to Successful Negotiation," 2002 *J. Disp. Resol.* 1.

FRIEDMAN, Gary (1993). *A Guide to Divorce Mediation*. New York: Workman Publishing.

FRIEDMAN, Gary & Jack HIMMELSTEIN (2005). "The Loop of Understanding." Center for Mediation in Law, available at *http://www.mediationinlaw.org/contact.html*.

_____ (2005). "The Understanding-Based Approach to Mediation." Center for Mediation in Law, available at *http://www.mediationinlaw.org/about.html*.

_____ (2003). Center for Mediation in Law, Memo No. 2, Elements of Mediator-Parties Contract.

FULLER, Lon L. (1971). "Mediation — Its Forms and Functions," 44 *S. Cal. L. Rev.* 305-339.

_____ (1963). "Collective Bargaining and the Arbitrator," 1963 *Wis. L. Rev.* 3.

_____ (1962). "Collective Bargaining and the Arbitrator," in Mark L. Kahn ed., *Collective Bargaining and the Arbitrator's Role: Proceedings of the Fifteenth Annual Meeting, National Academy of Arbitrators*. Washington, D.C.: BNA.

GADLIN, Howard & Elizabeth Walsh PINO (1997). "Neutrality: A Guide for the Organizational Ombudsperson," 13 *Neg. J.* 17.

GALANTER, Marc S. (2004). "The Vanishing Trial: An Examination of Trials and Related Matters in Federal and State Courts." 1 *J. of Empirical Legal Studies* 459.

GALANTER, Marc S. (2003). "The Vanishing Trial: An Examination of Trials and Related Matters in Federal and State Courts." Report to the Symposium on the Vanishing Trial. ABA, Section of Litigation, available at *http://www.abanet.org/litigation/vanishingtrial/vanishingtrial.pdf*.

____(1983). "Reading the Landscape of Disputes: What We Know and Don't Know (and Think We Know) About Our Allegedly Contentious and Litigious Society," 31 *UCLA L. Rev.* 4.

____(1974). "Why the 'Haves' Come out Ahead: Speculations on the Limits of Legal Change," 9 *L. & Socy. Rev.* 95.

GALTON, Eric (2005). "A Meeting of Strangers, Ripple from Peace Lake: Essays for Mediators and Peacemakers", Trafford Publishing, Lakeside Productions, available at *http://www.trafford.com*.

____(2000). "Mediation of Medical Negligence Claims," 28 *Cap. U. L. Rev.* 321.

GALTON, Eric & Tracie McFadden BURNS eds. (1993). *Mediation: A Texas Practice Guide*. Dallas: Texas Lawyer Press.

GANDHI, Mohandas K. (1948). *Autobiography: The Story of My Experiments with Truth*. Trans. Mahadev Desai. Washington, D.C.: Public Affairs Press.

GARDNER, Howard, Mihaly CSIKSZENTMIHALYI & William DAMON (2001). *Good Work: When Excellence and Ethics Meet*. New York: Basic Books.

GAUTHIER, David (1986). *Morals by Agreement*. Oxford, Eng.: Clarendon Press.

GENN, Hazel (1999). *Mediation in Action*. London, U.K.: Calouste Gulbenkian Foundation.

GIBSON, James L. (2004). "Truth, Reconciliation, and the Creation of a Human Rights Culture in South Africa," 38 *Law & Socy. Rev.* 5.

GIFFORD, Donald G. (1985). "A Context-Based Theory of Strategy Selection in Legal Negotiation," 46 *Ohio St. L.J.* 41.

GILSON, Ronald J. & Robert H. MNOOKIN (1994). "Disputing Through Agents: Cooperation and Conflict Between Lawyers in Litigation," 94 *Colum. L. Rev.* 509.

GINSBURG, Tom & Richard H. McADAMS (2004). "Adjudicating in Anarchy: An Expressive Theory of International Dispute Resolution," 45 *Wm. & Mary L. Rev.* 1229.

GOBODO-MADIKIZELA, Pumla (2003). *A Human Being Died That Night: A South African Story of Forgiveness*. Boston: Houghton Mifflin.

GOLANN, Dwight (2004). "How to Borrow a Mediator's Powers," 30 *Litigation* 41 (Spring).

____ (1996). *Mediating Legal Disputes*. Boston: Little, Brown.

GOLANN, Dwight & Eric E. VAN LOON (1999). "Legal Issues in Consensus Building," in Lawrence Susskind, Sarah McKearnan & Jennifer Thomas-Larmer eds., *The Consensus Building Handbook: A Comprehensive Guide to Reaching Agreement*. Thousand Oaks, Cal.: Sage Publications.

GOLDBERG, Stephen B. (1989). "Grievance Mediation: A Successful Alternative to Labor Arbitration," 5 *Negot. J.* 9.

GOLDSTEIN, Joseph & Jay KATZ (1965). *The Family and the Law: Problems for Decision in the Family Law Process*. New York: Free Press.

GONCZ, Kinga & Raymond SHONHOLTZ (2000). "Applying Collaborative Processes in Former Communist Countries." *IAP2* (First Quarter).

GREATBATCH, David & Robert DINGWALL (1989). "Selective Facilitation: Some Preliminary Observations on a Strategy Used by Divorce Mediators," 23 *Law & Socy. Rev.* 613.

GREEN, Eric D. (1986). "A Heretical View of the Mediation Privilege," 2 *Ohio St. J. on Disp. Resol.* 1.

GREEN, Eric D. et al. eds. (1982). "The CPR Legal Program Mini-Trial Handbook," in CPR, *Corporate Dispute Management 1982: A Manual of Innovative Corporate Strategies for the Avoidance and Resolution of Legal Disputes*. New York: M. Bender.

GREEN, Eric D., Jonathan B. MARKS & Ronald L. OLSEN (1978). "Settling Large Case Litigation: An Alternative Approach," 11 *Loy. L.A. L. Rev.* 493.

GREENBERG, Melanie C., John H. BARTON & Margaret E. McGUINNESS eds. (2000). *Words over War: Mediation and Arbitration to Prevent Deadly Conflict*. Lanham, Md.: Rowman & Littlefield Publishers.

GREENHALGH, Leonard (1987). "Relationships in Negotiation," 3 *Negot. J.* 235.

GRILLO, Trina (1991). "The Mediation Alternative: Process Dangers for Women," 100 *Yale L.J.* 1545.

GULLIVER, P.H. (1979). *Disputes and Negotiations: A Cross-Cultural Perspective*. New York: Academic Press.

GUNNING, Isabelle R. (1995). "Diversity Issues in Mediation: Controlling Negative Cultural Myths," 1995 *J. Disp. Resol.* 55.

GUTHRIE, Chris (2003). "Panacea or Pandora's Box?: The Costs of Options in Negotiation," 88 *Iowa L. Rev.* 601.

____(2001). "The Lawyer's Philosophical Map and the Disputant's Perceptual Map: Impediments to Facilitative Mediation and Lawyering," 6 *Harv. Negot. L. Rev.* 145.

HACKETT, Donald & Charles L. MARTIN (1993). *Facilitation Skills for Team Leaders*. Menlo Park, Cal.: Crisp Publications.

HAMPSHIRE, Stuart (2000). *Justice Is Conflict*. Princeton: Princeton University Press.

HARTER, Philip J. (2000). "Assessing the Assessors: The Actual Performance of Negotiated Rule-making," 9 *N.Y.U. Envtl. L.J.* 32.

____(1982). "Negotiating Regulations: A Cure for Malaise," 71 *Geo. L.J.* 1.

HAWKINS, Lee, Jr. (2004). "GM's Finance Arm Is Close to Settling Racial-Bias Lawsuit," *Wall St. J.*, January 30, p. A1.

HAYNES, John M. (1992). "Mediation and Therapy: An Alternative View," 10 *Mediation Q.* 21.

____(1997). *Divorce Mediation: A Practical Guide for Therapists and Counselors*. New York: Jossey-Bass.

HEGLAND, Kenny (1982). "Why Teach Trial Advocacy? An Essay on Never Ask Why," in Jack Himmelstein & Howard Lesnick eds., *Humanistic Education in Law* (Monograph 3: Project for the Study and Application of Humanistic Education in Law). New York: Columbia University School of Law.

HENIKOFF, Jamie & Michael MOFFITT (1997). "Remodeling the Model Standards of Conduct for Mediators," 2 *Harv. Negot. L. Rev.* 87.

HENKIN, Louis (1979). *How Nations Behave: Law and Foreign Policy* (2d ed.). New York: Columbia University Press.

HENSLER, Deborah R. (2002). "Suppose It's Not True: Challenging Mediation Ideology," 2002 *J. Disp. Resol.* 81.

____(2001). "In Search of 'Good' Mediation: Rhetoric, Practice, and Empiricism," in Joseph Sanders & V. Lee Hamilton eds., *Handbook of Justice Research in Law*. New York: Kluwer Academic/Plenum Publishers.

____(1986). "What We Know and Don't Know About Court-Administered Arbitration," 69 *Judicature* 270.

HERRMAN, Margaret ed. (2005). *The Blackwell Handbook of Mediation: Foundations of Effective Negotiations*. New Jersey: Blackwell Publ.

HINDLE, Tim (1998). *Managing Meetings*. London: Dorling Kindersley.

HOFSTADTER, Douglas R. (1985). *Metamagical Themas: Questing for the Essence of Mind and Pattern*. New York: Basic Books.

HOMANS, George Caspar (1974). *Social Behavior: Its Elementary Forms* (rev. ed.). New York: Harcourt, Brace, Jovanovich.

HONEYMAN, Chris (1990). "On Evaluating Mediators," 6 *Negot. J.* 23.

HOWARTH, Joan W. (2000). "Toward the Restorative Constitution: A Restorative Justice Critique of Anti-Gang Public Nuisance Injunctions," 27 *Hastings Const. L.Q.* 717.

HUGHES, Scott H. (2004). "Mediator Immunity: The Misguided and Inequitable Shifting of Risk," 83 *Or. L. Rev.* 107.

____(2001). "The Uniform Mediation Act: To the Spoiled Go the Privileges," 85 *Marq. L. Rev.* 9.

HYMAN, Jonathan M. & Lela P. LOVE (2002). "If Portia Were a Mediator: An Inquiry into Justice in Mediation," 9 *Clinical L. Rev.* 157.

INTERCONTINENTAL HOTEL ADVERTISEMENT in National Law Journal, *Natl. L.J.*, Apr. 10, 2000, at A-8.

IZUMI, Carol L. & Homer C. LA RUE (2003). "Prohibiting 'Good Faith' Reports Under the Uniform Mediation Act: Keeping the Adjudication Camel Out of the Mediation Tent," 2003 *J. Disp. Resol.* 67.

JACOBS, Margaret A. (1997). "Legal Beat: Private Jury Trials: Cheap, Quick, Controversial," *Wall St. J.*, July 7, p. B1.

JANIS, Irving L. (1982). *Groupthink: Psychological Studies of Policy Decisions and Fiascoes* (2d ed.). Boston: Houghton Mifflin.

JONES, Gregory Todd & Douglas YARN (2003). "Evaluative Dispute Resolution Under Uncertainty: An Empirical Look at Bayes' Theorem and the Expected Value of Perfect Information," 2003 *J. Disp. Resol.* 427.

JUSTICE SYSTEM JOURNAL (2005). "Special Issue: Making Dispute Resolution Work," 26(3) Justice Sys. J.

KAHNEMAN, Daniel & Amos TVERSKY (1995). "Conflict Resolution: A Cognitive Perspective," in Kenneth J. Arrow et al. eds., *Barriers to Conflict Resolution*. New York: Norton.

KAKALIK, James S., Terence DUNWORTH, Laural A. HILL, Daniel McCAFFREY, Marian OSHIRO, Nicholas M. PACE & Mary E. VAIANA (1996). *An Evaluation of Mediation and Early Neutral Evaluation Under the Civil Justice Reform Act*. Santa Monica, Cal.: RAND.

KATSH, Ethan & Janet RIFKIN (2001). *Online Dispute Resolution: Resolving Conflicts in Cyberspace*. San Francisco: Jossey-Bass Publishers.

KAYE, Judith S. (1997). "Changing Courts in Changing Times: The Need for a Fresh Look at How Courts Are Run," 48 *Hastings L.J.* 851.

KELLEY, Tom, with Jonathan LITTMAN (2001). *The Art of Innovation: Lessons in Creativity from IDEO, America's Leading Design Firm*. New York: Currency/Doubleday.

KELMAN, Herbert C. (1972). "The Problem Solving Workshop in Conflict Resolution," R.L. Merrit ed., in Communication in International Politics. Beverly Hills, CA.: Sage Publications.

KENTRA, Pamela A. (1997). "Hear No Evil, See No Evil, Speak No Evil: The Intolerable Conflict for Attorney-Mediators Between the Duty to Maintain Mediation Confidentiality and the Duty to Report Fellow Attorney Misconduct," 1997 *BYU L. Rev.* 715.

KICHAVEN, Jeff (2003). "Apology in Mediation: Sorry to Say, It's Much Overrated." International Risk Management Institute, available at *http://www.irmi.com/Expert/Articles/2003/Kichaven09.aspx*.

KIM, Anne S. (1994). Note, "Rent-a-Judges and the Cost of Selling Justice," 44 *Duke L.J.* 166.

KIRTLEY, Alan (1995). "The Mediation Privilege's Transition from Theory to Implementation: Designing a Mediation Privilege Standard to Protect Mediation Participants, the Process and the Public Interest," 1995 *J. Disp. Resol.* 1.

KISSINGER, Henry (1979). *White House Years*. Boston: Little, Brown.

KLONOFF, Robert H. & Edward K.M. BILICH (2000). "Resolution of Class Actions," in *Class Actions and Other Multi-Party Litigation: Cases and Materials* ch. 8. St. Paul: West Group.

KOLB, Deborah M. & Associates eds.(1994). *When Talk Works—Profiles of Mediators*. San Francisco: Jossey-Bass.

KOLB, Deborah M. & Judith WILLIAMS (2003). *Everyday Negotiation: Navigating the Hidden Agendas in Bargaining* (rev. ed.). San Francisco: Jossey-Bass Publishers.

KOROBKIN, Russell (2002). "Aspirations and Settlement," 88 *Cornell L. Rev.* 1.

_____ Russell (2000). "A Positive Theory of Legal Negotiation," 88 *Geo. L.J.* 1789.

KOROBKIN, Russell & Chris GUTHRIE (1994). "Psychological Barriers to Litigation Settlement: An Experimental Approach," 93 *Mich. L. Rev.* 107.

KOROBKIN, Russell, Michael MOFFITT & Nancy WELSH (2004). "The Law of Bargaining," 87 *Marquette L. Rev.* 839.

KOVACH, Kimberlee K. (2001). "New Wine Requires New Wineskins: Transforming Lawyer Ethics for Effective Representation in a Non-Adversarial Approach to Problem Solving: Mediation," 28 *Fordham Urb. L.J.* 935.

_____(1997). "Good Faith in Mediation — Requested, Recommended, or Required? A New Ethic," 38 *S. Tex. L. Rev.* 575.

KOVACH, Kimberlee K. & Lela P. LOVE (1996). " 'Evaluative' Mediation Is an Oxymoron," 14 *Alternatives to High Cost Litig.* 31.

KRESSEL, Kenneth & Dean PRUITT (1989). *Mediation Research: The Process and Effectiveness of Third Party Intervention*. San Francisco: Jossey-Bass Publishers.

KRITEK, Phyllis Beck (1994). *Negotiating at an Uneven Table: A Practical Approach to Working with Difference and Diversity*. San Francisco: Jossey-Bass Publishers.

LaFREE, Gary & Christine RACK (1996). "The Effects of Participants' Ethnicity and Gender on Monetary Outcomes in Mediated and Adjudicated Civil Cases," 30 *Law & Socy. Rev.* 767.

LAMBROS, Thomas D. (1984). "The Summary Jury Trial and Other Alternative Methods of Dispute Resolution: A Report to the Judicial Conference of the United States Committee on the Operation of the Jury System," 103 *F.R.D.* 461.

LANDE, John (2003). "Possibilities for Collaborative Law: Ethics and Practice of Lawyer Disqualification and Process Control in a New Model of Lawyering," 64 *Ohio St. L.J.* 1315.

_____(2002). "Using Dispute System Design Methods to Promote Good-Faith Participation in Court-Connected Mediation Programs," 50 *UCLA L. Rev.* 69.

LANDES, William M. & Richard A. POSNER (1979). "Adjudication as a Private Good," 8 *J. Legal Stud.* 235.

LANDRY, Sherry (1996). "Med-Arb: Mediation with a Bite and an Effective ADR Model," 63 *Def. Couns. J.* 263.

LAO-TZU (1991). *Tao Te Ching*. Trans. Steven Mitchell. New York: Harper & Row.

LAX, David A. & James K. SEBENIUS (1986). *The Manager as Negotiator: Bargaining for Cooperation and Competitive Gain*. New York: Free Press.

LEDERACH, John Paul (2003). "Cultivating Peace: A Practitioner's View of Deadly Conflict and Negotiation," in John Darby & Roger MacGinty eds., *Contemporary Peacemaking: Conflict, Violence and Peace Processes*. New York: Palgrave Macmillan.

_____(1995). *Preparing for Peace: Conflict Transformation Across Cultures*. Syracuse, N.Y.: Syracuse University Press.

LEHMAN, Warren (1979). "The Pursuit of a Client's Interest," 77 *Mich. L. Rev.* 1078.

LERMAN, David (1999). "Restoring Justice," *Tikkun* 13 (September-October).

LEVIN, Murray S. (2001). "The Propriety of Evaluative Mediation: Concerns About the Nature and Quality of an Evaluative Opinion," 16 *Ohio St. J. on Disp. Resol.* 267.

LEVINE, Hephzibah (2005). "Mediating the War of Olives and Pines: Consensus-Based Land-Use Planning in a Multi-Cultural Setting," 21 *Negot. J.* 29.

LEVITT, Matthew A. (1997). "Kilometer 101: Oasis or Mirage? An Analysis of Third-Party Self-Interest in International Mediation," 15 *Mediation Q.* 155.

LEVY, Jerome S. & Robert C. PRATHER (1999) "Fly on the Wall," in *Texas Practice Guide: Alternative Dispute Resolution* App. A.

LEWICKI, Roy J. & Barbara Benedict BUNKER (1995). "Trust in Relationships: A Model of Development and Decline," in Barbara Benedict Bunker, Jeffrey Z. Rubin et al. eds., *Conflict, Cooperation, and Justice: Essays Inspired by the Work of Morton Deutsch*. San Francisco: Jossey-Bass Publishers.

LIEBMAN, Carol B. (2000). "Mediation as Parallel Seminars: Lessons from the Student Takeover of Columbia University's Hamilton Hall," 16 *Negot. J.* 157.

LIPSKY, David B., Ronald L. SEEBER & Richard D. FINCHER (2003). *Emerging Systems for Managing Workplace Conflict: Lessons from American Corporations for Managers and Dispute Resolution Professionals*. San Francisco: Jossey-Bass Publishers.

LOVE, Lela P. (2000). "Images of Justice," 1 *Pepp. Disp. Resol. L.J.* 29.

_____(2000). "Training Mediators to Listen: Deconstructing Dialogue and Constructing Understanding, Agendas, and Agreements," 38 *Fam. & Conciliation Cts. Rev.* 27.

_____(1997). "The Top Ten Reasons Why Mediators Should Not Evaluate," 24 *Fla. St. U. L. Rev.* 937.

_____(1993). "Glen Cove: Mediation Achieves What Litigation Cannot," 20 *Consensus* (MIT-Harvard Public Disputes Program) 1, 1-2 (October).

LOVE, Lela P. & John W. COOLEY (2005). "The Intersection of Evaluation by Mediators and Informed Consent: Warning the Unwary," *Ohio St. J. of Disp. Res.* (forthcoming).

LOVE, Lela P. & Kimberlee K. KOVACH (2000). "ADR: An Eclectic Array of Processes, Rather than One Eclectic Process," 2000 *J. Disp. Resol.* 295.

LOVE, Lela P. & Cheryl B. McDONALD (1997). "A Tale of Two Cities: Day Labor and Conflict Resolution for Communities in Crisis," *Disp. Resol. Mag.* 8 (Fall).

LOVE, Lela P. & Joseph B. STULBERG (2004). "Targets and Techniques to Generate Movement," in *Training Materials* (unpublished).

_____(2003). "Partnerships and Facilitation: Mediators Develop New Skills for Complex Cases," *Disp. Resol. Mag.* (Spring). Washington, D.C.: American Bar Association (Section of Dispute Resolution).

_____(1997). "Understanding Dispute Resolution Processes," in *Michigan Mediator Skill-Building Manual.*

_____(1996). "Practice Guidelines for Co-Mediation: Making Certain That 'Two Heads Are Better than One,'" 13 *Mediation Q.* 179.

LOVENHEIM, Peter & Emily DOSKOW (2004). *Becoming a Mediator: Your Guide to Career Opportunities.* Berkeley, Calif.: Nolo Press.

LUBAN, David (1995). "Settlements and the Erosion of the Public Realm," 83 *Geo. L.J.* 2619.

_____(1987). "Some Greek Trials: Order and Justice in Homer, Hesiod, Aeschylus and Plato," 54 *Tenn. L. Rev.* 279.

LUBMAN, Stanley B. (1997). "Dispute Resolution in China After Deng Xiaoping: 'Mao and Mediation' Revisited," 11 *Colum. J. Asian L.* 229.

LYNCH, William P. (2002). "Problems with Court-Annexed Mandatory Arbitration: Illustrations from the New Mexico Experience," 32 *N.M. L. Rev.* 181.

MACHIAVELLI, Niccolo (1998). *The Prince* (2d ed.). Trans. Harvey C. Mansfield. Chicago: University of Chicago Press.

MALLEY, Robert & Hussein AGHA (2001). "Camp David: The Tragedy of Errors," *N.Y. Rev. Books,* August 9, p. 59.

MARCUS, Mary G., Walter MARCUS, Nancy A. STILWELL & Neville DOHERTY (1999). "To Mediate or Not to Mediate: Financial Outcomes in Mediated Versus Adversarial Divorces," 17 *Mediation Q.* 143.

MATZ, David (1999). "Ignorance and Interests,"4 *Harv. Negot. L. Rev.* 59.

MAULL, John (1996). "ADR in the Federal Courts: Would Uniformity Be Better?," 34 *Duq. L. Rev.* 245.

MAUTE, Judith L. (1991). "Public Values and Private Justice: A Case for Mediator Accountability," 4 *Geo. J. Legal Ethics* 503.

MAZADOORIAN, Harry N. (2004). "To Draft or Not to Draft: The Rights and Wrongs of Drafting and Signing Settlements," *Disp. Resol. Mag.* 31 (Spring).

McADOO, Bobbi, Nancy WELSH & Roselle L. WISSLER (2003). "Institutionalization: What Do Empirical Studies Tell Us About Court Mediation," *Disp. Res. Mag.* 8.

McEWEN, Craig A. (1999). "Toward a Program-Based ADR Research Agenda," 15(4) *Negot. J.* 325.

_____(1998). "Managing Corporate Disputing: Overcoming Barriers to the Effective Use of Mediation for Reducing the Cost and Time of Litigation," 14 *Ohio St. J. on Disp. Resol.* 1.

_____(1996). "Mediation in Context: New Questions for Research," 3:2 *Disp. Resol. Mag.* 16.

McEWEN, Craig A. & Elizabeth PLAPINGER (1997). "RAND Report Points Way to Next Generation of ADR Research," *Disp. Resol. Mag.* 10 (Summer).

McEWEN, Craig A. & Richard J. MAIMAN (1981). "Small Claims Mediation in Maine: An Empirical Assessment," 33 *Me. L. Rev.* 237.

McEWEN, Craig A. & Nancy H. ROGERS (1994). "Bring the Lawyers into Divorce Mediation," *Disp. Resol. Mag.* 8 (Summer).

McGOVERN, Francis E. (1997). "Beyond Efficiency: A Bevy of ADR Justifications (An Unfootnoted Summary)," *Disp. Resol. Mag.* 12 (Summer).

McMUNIGAL, Kevin C. (1990). "The Costs of Settlement: The Impact of Scarcity of Adjudication on Litigating Lawyers," 37 *UCLA L. Rev.* 833.

MEIERHOEFER, Barbara S. (1990). *Court-Annexed Arbitration in Ten District Courts.* Washington, D.C.: Federal Judicial Center.

MELTSNER, Michael & Philip G. SCHRAG (1974). "Negotiation," in *Public Interest Advocacy: Materials for Clinical Legal Education.* Boston: Little, Brown.

MENKEL-MEADOW, Carrie (2004-2005) "The Lawyer's Role(s) in Deliberative Democracy," 5 *Nev. L.J.* 347.

____(2004). "Is the Adversary System Really Dead? Dilemmas of Legal Ethics as Legal Institutions and Roles Evolve," in Jane Holder, Colm O'Cinneide & Michael Freeman eds., *Current Legal Problems*. Oxford, U.K.: Oxford Univ. Press.

____(2004). "Remembrance of Things Past? The Relationship of Past to Future in Pursuing Justice in Mediation," 5 *Cardozo J. Conflict Resol.* 97.

____(2004). "What's Fair in Negotiation? What Is Ethics in Negotiation?," in Carrie Menkel-Meadow & Michael Wheeler eds., *What's Fair: Ethics for Negotiators*. San Francisco: Jossey-Bass.

____(2003). "Conflict Theory," in Karen Christensen & David Levinson eds., 1 *Encyclopedia of Community: From the Village to the Virtual World*. Thousand Oaks, Cal.: Sage Publications.

____(2003). "Correspondences and Contradictions in International and Domestic Conflict Resolution: Lessons from General Theory and Varied Contexts," 2003 *J. Disp. Resol.* 319.

____(2003). "Introduction: From Legal Disputes to Conflict Resolution and Human Problem Solving," in Carrie Menkel-Meadow, *Dispute Processing and Conflict Resolution: Theory, Practice and Policy*. Aldershot, Eng.: Ashgate/Dartmouth.

____(2002). "Ethics Issues in Arbitration and Related Dispute Resolution Processes: What's Happening and What's Not," 56 *U. Miami L. Rev.* 949.

____(2002). "Ethics, Morality and Professional Responsibility in Negotiation," in Phyllis Bernard & Bryant Garth eds., *Dispute Resolution Ethics: A Comprehensive Guide*. Washington, D.C.: ABA Section of Dispute Resolution.

____(2002). "The Lawyer as Consensus Builder: Ethics for a New Practice," 70 *Tenn. L. Rev.* 63.

____(2002). "Practicing 'In the Interests of Justice' in the Twenty-First Century: Pursuing Peace as Justice," 70 *Fordham L. Rev.* 1761.

____(2001). "Aha? Is Creativity Possible in Legal Problem Solving and Teachable in Legal Education?," 6 *Harv. Negot. L. Rev.* 97.

____(2001). "Ethics in ADR: The Many "C's" of Professional Responsibility and Dispute Resolution," 28 *Fordham Urb. L.J.* 979.

____(2000). "Introduction," in Carrie Menkel-Meadow ed., *Mediation: Theory, Policy and Practice*. Aldershot, Eng.: Ashgate Publishing Ltd.

____(2000). "Teaching About Gender and Negotiation: Sex, Truths and Video Tape," 16 *Negot. J.* 357.

____(1999). "Do the 'Haves' Come Out Ahead in Alternative Judicial Systems? Repeat Players in ADR," 15 *Ohio St. J. on Disp. Resol.* 19.

____(1999). "Ethics and Professionalism in Non-Adversarial Lawyering," 27 *Fla. St. U. L. Rev.* 153.

____(1997). "The Silences of the Restatement of the Law Governing Lawyers: Lawyering as Only Adversary Practice," 10 *Geo. J. Legal Ethics* 631.

____(1997). "When Dispute Resolution Begets Disputes of Its Own: Conflicts Among Dispute Professionals," 44 *UCLA L. Rev.* 1871.

____(1996). "Is Mediation the Practice of Law?," 14 *Alternatives to High Cost Litig.* 57.

____(1996). "The Trouble with the Adversary System in a Postmodern, Multicultural World," 38 *Wm. & Mary L. Rev.* 5.

____(1995). "Ethics and the Settlements of Mass Torts: When the Rules Meet the Road," 80 *Cornell L. Rev.* 1159.

____(1995). "The Many Ways of Mediation: The Transformation of Traditions, Ideologies, Paradigms, and Practices," 11 *Negot. J.* 217.

____(1995). "Whose Dispute Is It Anyway?: A Philosophical and Democratic Defense of Settlement (in Some Cases)," 83 *Geo. L.J.* 2663.

____(1993). "Professional Responsibility for Third-Party Neutrals," 1 *Alternatives to the Higher Costs of Litigation* 129.

____(1993). "Public Access to Private Settlements: Conflicting Legal Policies," 11 *Alternatives to High Cost Litig.* 85.

____(1985). "For and Against Settlement: Uses and Abuses of the Mandatory Settlement Conference," 33 *UCLA L. Rev.* 485.

____(1984). "Toward Another View of Legal Negotiation: The Structure of Problem Solving," 31 *UCLA L. Rev.* 754.

MENKEL-MEADOW, Carrie & David BINDER (1983). *The Stages and Phases of Negotiation.* Washington, D.C.: ABA Lawyering Skills Institute.

MENKEL-MEADOW, Carrie, Lela P. LOVE, Andrea Kupfer SCHNEIDER, & Jean R. Sternlight (2005). *Dispute Resolution: Beyond the Adversarial Model.* New York: Aspen Publishers.

MENKEL-MEADOW, Carrie, Andrea Kupfer SCHNEIDER & Lela P. LOVE (2006). *Negotiation: Processes for Problem Solving.* New York: Aspen Publishers.

MIALL, Hugh (1992). *The Peacemakers: Peaceful Settlement of Disputes Since 1945.* New York: St. Martin's Press.

MILNER, Neal (2002). "From the Trenches and the Towers: Illusions and Delusions About Conflict Management—In Africa and Elsewhere," 27 *Law & Soc. Inquiry* 621.

MINOW, Martha (1998). *Between Vengeance and Forgiveness: Facing History After Genocide and Mass Violence.* Boston: Beacon Press.

MITCHELL, George J. (1999). *Making Peace.* New York: Knopf.

MNOOKIN, Robert H. (2003). "Strategic Barriers to Dispute Resolution: A Comparison of Bilateral and Multilateral Negotiations," 159 *J. Institutional & Theoretical Econ.* 199.

_____(2003). "When Not to Negotiate: A Negotiation Imperialist Reflects on Appropriate Limits," 74 *U. Colo. L. Rev.* 1077.

_____(1993). "Why Negotiations Fail: An Exploration of Barriers to the Resolution of Conflict," 8 *Ohio St. J. on Disp. Resol.* 235.

MNOOKIN, Robert H. & Lewis KORNHAUSER (1979). "Bargaining in the Shadow of the Law: The Case of Divorce," 88 *Yale L.J.* 950.

MNOOKIN, Robert H., Scott R. PEPPET & Andrew S. TULUMELLO (2000). *Beyond Winning: Negotiating to Create Value in Deals and Disputes.* Cambridge, Mass.: Belknap Press of Harvard University Press.

MOBERLY, Robert (1994). "Ethical Standards for Court-Appointed Mediators and Florida's Mandatory Mediation Experiment," 21 *Fla. St. U. L. Rev.* 701.

MOFFITT, Michael L. (2005). "Disputes as Opportunities to Create Value," in Michael L. Moffitt and Robert C. Bordone eds., *The Handbook of Dispute Resolution.* San Francisco: Jossey-Bass Publishers.

_____(2005). "Pleadings in the Age of Settlement," 80 *Indiana L.J.* 727.

_____(2005). "Schmediation and the Dimensions of Definition," 10 *Harv. Negot. L. Rev.* 69.

_____(2003). "Suing Mediators," 83 *B.U. L. Rev.* 147.

_____(2003) "Ten Ways to Get Sued: A Guide for Mediators," 8 *Harv. Negot. L. Rev.* 81.

_____(2000). "Will This Case Settle? An Exploration of Mediators' Predictions," 16 *Ohio St. J. on Disp. Resol.* 39.

_____(1997). "Casting Light on the Black Box of Mediation: Should Mediators Make Their Conduct More Transparent?," 13 *Ohio St. J. on Disp. Resol.* 1.

_____(1996). "Loyalty, Confidentiality and Attorney-Mediators: Professional Responsibility in Cross-Profession Practice," 1 *Harv. Negot. L. Rev.* 203.

MOFFITT, Michael L. & Robert C. BORDONE (2005). *The Handbook of Dispute Resolution.* San Francisco: Jossey-Bass.

MOORE, Christopher W. (2004). *The Mediation Process: Practical Strategies for Resolving Conflict* (3d ed.). San Francisco: Jossey-Bass.

MORAWETZ, Nancy (1993). "Bargaining, Class Representation, and Fairness," 54 *Ohio St. L.J.* 1.

MORRILL, Calvin (1995). *The Executive Way: Conflict Management in Corporations.* Chicago: University of Chicago Press.

MORRIS, Michael, Janice NADLER, Terri KURTZBERG & Leigh THOMPSON (2002). "Schmooze or Lose: Social Friction and Lubrication in E-Mail Negotiations," 6 *Group Dynamics* 89.

NADER, Laura & Elisabetta GRANDE (2002). "Current Illusions and Delusions About Conflict Management—In Africa and Elsewhere," 27 *Law & Soc. Inquiry* 573.

NADLER, Janice (2001). "Electronically-Mediated Dispute Resolution and E-Commerce," 17 *Negot. J.* 333.

NALEBUFF, Barry & Ian AYRES (2003). *Why Not? How to Use Everyday Ingenuity to Solve Problems Big and Small.* Boston: Harvard Business School Press.

NELKEN, Melissa L. (1996). "Negotiation and Psychoanalysis: If I'd Wanted to Learn About Feelings, I Wouldn't Have Gone to Law School," 46 *J. Legal Educ.* 420.

NIEMIC, Robert J., Donna STIENSTRA & Randall E. RAVITZ (2001). *Guide to Judicial Management of Cases in ADR.* Washington, D.C.: Federal Judicial Center.

NOESNER, Gary W. & Mike WEBSTER (1997). "Crisis Intervention: Using Active Listening Skills in Negotiations," *FBI L. Enforcement Bull.,* August 1, p. 13.

NOLAN-HALEY, Jacqueline M. (1999). "Informed Consent in Mediation: A Guiding Principle for Truly Educated Decisionmaking," 74 *Notre Dame L. Rev.* 775.

OBERMAN, Susan (2005). "Mediation Theory vs. Practice: What Are We Really Doing? Resolving a Professional Conundrum," 20 *Ohio St. J. on Disp. Resol.* 775.

PEARSON, Jessica & Nancy THOENNES (1989). "Divorce Mediation: Reflections on a Decade of Research," in Kenneth Kressel & Dean G. Pruitt eds., *Mediation Research: The Process and Effectiveness of Third-Party Intervention.* San Francisco: Jossey-Bass Publishers.

PEPPET, Scott R. (2004). "Contract Formation in Imperfect Markets: Should We Use Mediators in Deals?," 19 *Ohio St. J. on Disp. Resol.* 283.

_____(2004). "ADR Ethics," 54(1) *J. Legal Educ.* 72.

_____(2003). "Contractarian Economics and Mediation Ethics: The Case for Customizing Neutrality Through Contingent Fee Mediation," 82 *Tex. L. Rev.* 227.

PETER, James T. (1997). "Med-Arb in International Arbitration," 8 *Am. Rev. Intl. Arb.* 83.

PHILLIPS, Barbara A. (1997). "Mediation: Did We Get It Wrong?," 33 *Willamette L. Rev.* 649.

PLAPINGER, Elizabeth & Donna STIENSTRA, with the assistance of Laurel HOOPER & Melissa PECHERSKI (1996). *ADR and Settlement in the Federal District Courts: A Sourcebook for Judges & Lawyers.* Washington, D.C.: Federal Judicial Center.

PLOUS, Scott (1993). *The Psychology of Judgment and Decision Making.* Philadelphia: Temple University Press.

POSNER, Richard A. (1986). "The Summary Jury Trial and Other Methods of Alternative Dispute Resolution: Some Cautionary Observations," 53 *U. Chi. L. Rev.* 366.

POTTER, Antonia (2005). "We the Women: Why conflict Mediation is Not Just a Job for Men," Center for Humanitarian Dialogue (October).

POWELL, Gary N. (1990). "One More Time: Do Female and Male Managers Differ?," *Acad. Mgmt. Executive* 68 (August)

POU, Charles Jr. (2003). "Embracing Limbo: Thinking About Rethinking Dispute Resolution Ethics," 108 *Penn. St. L. Rev.* 199.

PRICE, Marty (2000). "Personalizing Crime: Mediation Produces Restorative Justice for Victims and Offenders," *Disp. Resol. Mag.* 8 (Fall).

PRUITT, Dean G. (1983). "Achieving Integrative Agreements," in Max H. Bazerman & Roy J. Lewicki eds., *Negotiating in Organizations.* Beverly Hills, Cal.: Sage Publications.

PRUITT, Dean G. & Steven A. LEWIS (1977). "The Psychology of Integrative Bargaining," in Daniel Druckman ed., *Negotiations: Social-Psychological Perspectives.* Beverly Hills, Cal.: Sage Publications.

PUBLIC CONVERSATIONS PROJECT (2003). "Constructive Conversations About Challenging Times: A Guide to Community Dialogue" (version 3.0). Public Conversations Project, at *http://www.publicconversations.org/pcp/uploadDocs/CommunityGuide3.0.pdf.*

PUTNAM, Robert D. (1993). "Diplomacy and Domestic Politics: The Logic of Two-Level Games," in Peter B. Evans, Harold K. Jacobson & Robert D. Putnam eds., *Double-Edged Diplomacy: International Bargaining and Domestic Politics.* Berkeley: Univ. of Cal. Press.

RAIFFA, Howard (1985). "Post-Settlement Settlements," 1 *Negot. J.* 9.

_____(1982). *The Art and Science of Negotiation.* Cambridge, Mass.: Belknap Press of Harvard University Press.

RAIFFA, Howard, John RICHARDSON & David METCALFE (2002). *Negotiation Analysis: The Art and Science of Collaborative Decision Making.* Cambridge, MA: Harvard-Belknap Press.

REIMUND, Mary Ellen (2003). "Mediation in Criminal Justice: A Restorative Approach," *Advoc. (Idaho)* 22 (May).

REYES, Robert M., William C. THOMPSON & Gordon H. BOWER (1980). "Judgmental Biases Resulting from Differing Availabilities of Arguments," 39 *J. Personality & Soc. Psychol.* 2.

RICIGLIANO, Robert (2003). "Networks of Effective Action: Implementing an Integrated Approach to Peacebuilding," 34 *Security Dialogue* 445.

RISKIN, Leonard L. (2003). "The New Old Grid and the New New Grid System," 79 *Notre Dame L. Rev.* 1.

____(1994). "Mediator Orientations, Strategies and Techniques," 12 *Alternatives to High Cost Litig.* 111.

____(1991). "The Represented Client in a Settlement Conference: The Lessons of *G. Heileman Brewing Co. v. Joseph Oat Corp.*," 69 *Wash. U. L.Q.* 1059.

____(1984). "Toward New Standards for the Neutral Lawyer in Mediation," 26 *Ariz. L. Rev.* 329.

____(1982). "Mediation and Lawyers," 43 *Ohio St. L.J.* 29.

RISKIN, Leonard, James WESTBROOK & James LEVIN (1998). *Instructor's Manual to Accompany Dispute Resolution and Lawyers*. St. Paul: West Pub. Co.

ROBBENNOLT, Jennifer K. (2003) "Apologies and Legal Settlement: An Empirical Examination," 102 *Mich. L. Rev.*

ROBINSON, Peter (2003). "Centuries of Contract Law Can't Be All Wrong: Why the UMA's Exception to Mediation Confidentiality in Enforcement Proceedings Should Be Embraced and Broadened," *J. Disp. Resol.* 135.

ROGERS, Catherine A. (2002). "Fit and Function in Legal Ethics: Developing a Code of Conduct for International Arbitration," 23 *Mich. J. Intl. L.* 341.

ROSE, Carol M. (1995). "Bargaining and Gender," 18 *Harv. J.L. & Pub. Poly.* 547.

ROSE, L. Christopher (1999). Note, "Nevada's Court-Annexed Mandatory Arbitration Program: A Solution to Some of the Causes of Dissatisfaction with the Civil Justice System," 36 *Idaho L. Rev.* 171.

ROSENTHAL, Robert & Lenore JACOBSON (1968). *Pygmalion in the Classroom: Teacher Expectation and Pupils' Intellectual Development*. New York: Holt, Rinehart and Winston.

ROSS, Lee (1995). "Reactive Devaluation in Negotiation and Conflict Resolution," in Kenneth J. Arrow et al. eds., *Barriers to Conflict Resolution*. New York: W.W. Norton.

RUBIN, Jeffrey Z. & Frank E.A. SANDER (1991). "Culture, Negotiation, and the Eye of the Beholder," 7 *Negot. J.* 249.

RUBINSON, Robert (2004-2005). "A Theory of Access to Justice," 29 *J. Leg. Prof.* 89.

SALACUSE, Jeswald W. (1998). "Ten Ways That Culture Affects Negotiating Style: Some Survey Results," 14 *Negot. J.* 221.

SANDER, Frank E.A. (1976). "Varieties of Dispute Processing," 70 *F.R.D.* 111.

SANDER, Frank E.A. & Michael L. PRIGOFF (1990). "Professional Responsibility: Should There Be a Duty to Advise of ADR Options?," *A.B.A. J.* 50 (November).

SANDER, Frank E.A., & Jeffrey Z. RUBIN (1988). "The Janus Quality of Negotiation: Dealmaking and Dispute Settlement," 4 *Negot. J.* 109.

SANDER, Frank E.A. & Stephen B. GOLDBERG (1994). "Fitting the Forum to the Fuss: A User-Friendly Guide to Selecting an ADR Procedure," 10 *Negot. J.* 49.

SCANLON, Kathleen M. (2002). *Drafter's Deskbook for Dispute Resolution Clauses*. New York: CPR Institute for Dispute Resolution.

SCARDILLI, Frank J. (1997). "*Sisters of the Precious Blood v. Bristol-Meyers Co.*: A Shareholder-Management Dispute," reprinted in Leonard L. Riskin & James E. Westbrook, *Dispute Resolution and Lawyers* (2d ed.). St. Paul: West Group.

SCHELLING, Thomas C. (1960). *The Strategy of Conflict*. Cambridge, Mass.: Harvard University Press.

SCHNEIDER, Andrea Kupfer (2005). "Public and Private International Dispute Resolution," in Michael L. Moffitt & Robert C. Bordone eds., *The Handbook of Dispute Resolution*. San Francisco: Jossey-Bass Publishers.

____(2002). "Shattering Negotiation Myths: Empirical Evidence on the Effectiveness of Negotiation Style," 7 *Harv. Negot. L. Rev.* 143.

____(2000). "Building a Pedagogy of Problem-Solving: Learning to Choose Among ADR Processes," 5 *Harv. Negot. L. Rev.* 113.

____(1999). "Getting Along: The Evolution of Dispute Resolution Regimes in International Trade Organizations," 20 *Mich. J. Intl. L.* 697.

SCHÖN, Donald A. (1983). *The Reflective Practitioner*. New York: Basic Books.

SCHNEYER, Ted (1991). "Professional Discipline for Law Firms?," 77 *Cornell L. Rev.* 1.

SCHUMACHER, E.F. (1977). *A Guide for the Perplexed.* New York: Harper & Row.

SCHWARZ, Roger (2002). *The Skilled Facilitator: A Comprehensive Resource for Consultants, Facilitators, Managers, Trainers, and Coaches* (2d ed.). San Francisco: Jossey-Bass Publishers.

SEBENIUS, James K. (1996). "Sequencing to Build Coalitions: With Whom Should I Talk First?," in Richard J. Zeckhauser, Ralph L. Keeney & James K. Sebenius eds., *Wise Choices: Decisions, Games, and Negotiations.* Boston: Harvard Business School Press.

SENGER, Jeffrey M. (2004). "Decision Analysis in Negotiation," 87 *Marq. L. Rev.* 723.

SEUL, Jeffrey R. (1999). "How Transformative Is Transformative Mediation?: A Constructive-Developmental Assessment," 15 *Ohio St. J. on Disp. Resol.* 135.

SHAPIRO, Justine & B.Z. GOLDBERG, dirs. and prods. (2001). *Promises* (film). New York: Cowboy Pictures.

SHELL, G. Richard (1999). *Bargaining for Advantage: Negotiation Strategies for Reasonable People.* New York: Viking.

SHERMAN, Edward F. (1993). "Court-Mandated Alternative Dispute Resolution: What Form of Participation Should Be Required?," 46 *SMU L. Rev.* 2079.

SHESTOWSKY, Donna (2004). "Procedural Preferences in Alternative Dispute Resolution: A Closer, Modern Look at an Old Idea," 10 *Pysch., Public Poly. and Law* 211.

SILBEY, Susan S. & Sally E. MERRY (1986). "Mediator Settlement Strategies," 8 *Law & Poly.* 7.

SLAIKEU, Karl A. (1989). "Designing Dispute Resolution Systems in the Health Care Industry," 5 *Negot. J.* 395.

STEMPEL, Jeffrey W. (2000). "The Inevitability of the Eclectic: Liberating ADR from Ideology," 2000 *J. Disp. Resol.* 247.

STERNLIGHT, Jean R. (1999). "Lawyers' Representation of Clients in Mediation: Using Economics and Psychology to Structure Advocacy in a Nonadversarial Setting," 14 *Ohio St. J. on Disp. Resol.* 269.

STIENSTRA, Donna et al. (1997). *A Study of the Five Demonstration Programs Established Under the Civil Justice Reform Act of 1990.* Washington, D.C.: Federal Judicial Center.

STILLINGER, C., M. EPELBAUM, D. KELTNER & L. ROSS (1990). "The 'Reactive Devaluation' Barrier to Conflict Resolution" (unpublished manuscript, Stanford University).

STIPANOWICH, Thomas J. (2004). "ADR and 'the Vanishing Trial': The Growth and Impact of ADR," 1 *J. of Empirical Legal Studies* 843.

STONE, Douglas, Bruce PATTON & Sheila HEEN (1999). *Difficult Conversations: How to Discuss What Matters Most.* New York: Viking

STRAIN, Jason & Elizabeth KEYES (2003). "Accountability in the Aftermath of Rwanda's Genocide," in Jane E. Stromseth ed., *Accountability for Atrocities: National and International Responses.* Ardsley, N.Y.: Transnational Publishers.

STRAUS, David A. (1999). "Managing Meetings to Build Consensus," in Lawrence Susskind, Sarah McKearnan & Jennifer Thomas-Larmer eds., *The Consensus Building Handbook: A Comprehensive Guide to Reaching Agreement.* Thousand Oaks, Cal: Sage Publications.

STULBERG, Joseph B. (1998). "Fairness and Mediation, " 13 *Ohio St. J. Disp. Res.* 909.

_____(2001). *Taking Charge/Managing Conflict.*

_____(1987). *Taking Charge/Managing Conflict.* Lexington, Mass.: Lexington Books.

_____(1981). "The Theory and Practice of Mediation: A Reply to Professor Susskind," 6 *Vt. L. Rev.* 85.

SUNSTEIN, Cass R. (2000). "Deliberative Trouble? Why Groups Go to Extremes," 110 *Yale L.J.* 71.

SUSSKIND, Lawrence (1999). "An Alternative to *Robert's Rules of Order* for Groups, Organizations, and Ad Hoc Assemblies That Want to Operate by Consensus," in Lawrence Susskind, Sarah McKearnan & Jennifer Thomas-Larmer eds., *The Consensus Building Handbook: A Comprehensive Guide to Reaching Agreement.* Thousand Oaks, Cal: Sage Publications.

_____(1981). "Environmental Mediation and the Accountability Problem," 6 *Vt. L. Rev.* 1.

SUSSKIND, Lawrence & Liora ZION (2002). *Strengthening the Democratic Process in the United States: An Examination of Recent Experiments* (unpublished manuscript), available at *http://www.susskind.info/content/contributions/democracy.pdf.*

SUSSKIND, Lawrence & Jeffrey CRUIKSHANK (1987). *Breaking the Impasse,* New York: Basic Books.

SWARD, Ellen E. (2003). "A History of the Civil Trial in the United States," 51 *U. Kan. L. Rev.* 347.

TANNEN, Deborah (1998). *The Argument Culture: Moving from Debate to Dialogue.* New York: Random House.

_____(1990). *You Just Don't Understand: Women and Men in Conversation.* New York: Morrow.

THOMAS, Kenneth (1976). "Conflict and Conflict Management," in Marvin D. Dunnette ed., *Handbook of Industrial and Organizational Psychology.* Chicago: Rand McNally College Publishing.

THOMPSON, Anthony C. (2002). "Courting Disorder: Some Thoughts on Community Courts," 10 *Wash. U. J. L. & Poly.* 63.

THOMPSON, Leigh L. (2005). *The Mind and Heart of the Negotiator* (3d ed.). Upper Saddle River, N.J: Prentice Hall.

THOMPSON, Leigh & Janice NADLER (2002). "Negotiating via Information Technology," 58 *J. Soc. Issues* 109.

TICKELL, Shari & Kate AKESTER (2004). *Restorative Justice: The Way Ahead.* London: Justice.

TONN, Joan C. (2003). *Mary Parker Follett: Creating Democracy, Transforming Management.* New Haven: Yale University Press.

TRANTINA, Terry L. (2001). "How to Design ADR Clauses That Satisfy Clients' Needs and Minimize Litigation Risk," 19 *Alternatives to High Cost Litig.* 137.

UMBREIT, Mark S. (1988). "Mediation of Victim Offender Conflict," 1988 *J. Disp. Resol.* 85.

URY, William (1991). *Getting Past No: Negotiating with Difficult People.* New York: Bantam Books.

URY, William L., Jeanne M. BRETT & Stephen B. GOLDBERG (1988). *Getting Disputes Resolved: Designing Systems to Cut the Costs of Conflict.* San Francisco: Jossey-Bass Publishers.

WALDMAN, Ellen A. (2001). "Credentialing Approaches: The Slow Movement Toward Skills-Based Testing Continues," *Disp. Resol. Mag.* 13 (Fall).

_____(1997). "Identifying the Role of Social Norms in Mediation: A Multiple Model Approach," 48 *Hastings L.J.* 703.

WATSON, Lawrence M., Jr. (2002). *Effective Advocacy in Mediation: A Planning Guide to Prepare for a Civil Trial Mediation.* Upchurch Watson White & Max Mediation Group, available at *http://www.uww-adr.com/2002/pdfs/effectiveadvocacy.pdf.*

WECKSTEIN, Donald (1996). "Mediation Certification: Why and How?," 30 *U.S.F. L. Rev.* 757.

WEISBERG, Robert (2003). "Restorative Justice and the Danger of 'Community,'" 2003 *Utah L. Rev.* 343.

WELSH, Nancy A. (2004). "Remembering the Role of Justice in Resolution: Insights from Procedural and Social Justice Theories," 54 *J. Legal Educ.* 49.

_____(2004). "Stepping Back Through the Looking Glass: Real Conversations with Real Disputants About Institutionalized Mediation and Its Value,"19 *Ohio St. J. on Disp. Resol.* 573.

_____(2001). "Making Deals in Court-Connected Mediation: What's Justice Got to Do with It?," 79 *Wash. U. L.Q.* 787.

_____(2001). "The Thinning Vision of Self-Determination in Court-Connected Mediation: The Inevitable Price of Institutionalization," 6 *Harv. Negot. L. Rev.* 1.

WESTON, Maureen A. (2001). "Checks on Participant Conduct in Compulsory ADR: Reconciling the Tension in the Need for Good-Faith Participation, Autonomy, and Confidentiality," 76 *Ind. L.J.* 591.

WILLIAMS, Gerald R. (1996). "Negotiation as a Healing Process," 1996 *J. Disp. Resol.* 1.

_____(1983). *Legal Negotiation and Settlement.* St. Paul: West Group.

WISSLER, Roselle L. (2005). "Barriers to Attorneys' Discussion and Use of ADR,"19 *Ohio St. J. on Disp. Resol.* 459.

_____(2004). "The Effectiveness of Court-Connected Dispute Resolution in Civil Cases," 22 *Conflict Res. Q.* 55.

_____(2000). "Attorneys' Use of ADR Is Crucial to Their Willingness to Recommend It to Clients," *Disp. Resol. Mag.* 36 (Winter).

_____(1997). "The Effects of Mandatory Mediation: Empirical Research on the Experience of Small Claims and Common Pleas Courts," 33 *Willamette L. Rev.* 565.

ZARTMAN, I. William (2003). "The Timing of Peace Initiatives: Hurting Stalemates & Ripe Moments," in John Darby & Roger MacGinty eds., *Contemporary Peacemaking: Conflict, Violence and Peace Processes.* New York: Palgrave Macmillan.

Index